THE BIOLOGY OF AQUATIC VASCULAR PLANTS

The Biology of
Aquatic Vascular Plants

C. Duncan Sculthorpe

M.A., F.L.S.

Edward Arnold (Publishers) Ltd. London

Printed in Great Britain by
William Clowes & Sons Limited
London, Colchester and Beccles

To my Mother and Father
with gratitude

I saw that one enquiry only gave occasion to another, that book referred to book, that to search was not always to find, and to find was not always to be informed, and that thus to pursue perfection, was, like the first inhabitants of Arcadia, to chace (*sic*) the sun which when they had reached the hill where he seemed to rest, was still beheld at the same distance from them.

SAMUEL JOHNSON

Preface to Dictionary of the English Language
(1755)

A written account is a mere thread, spun artificially into a chain-like form, whereas, in the weft of thought from which it is derived, the elements are interconnected according to a more complex mode.

AGNES ARBER

The Mind and the Eye: a study of the biologist's standpoint
(1954)

Preface

Aquatic vascular plants are only superficially treated in modern textbooks of general botany; if, indeed, they are mentioned at all. They are also somewhat neglected by the more advanced works on plant morphology, physiology and ecology, and even by books on freshwater biology which are often unduly preoccupied with the aquatic fauna and micro-organisms.

In 1920 the Cambridge University Press published Agnes Arber's *Water Plants: a study of aquatic angiosperms*. Although now very much out of date on many topics, this delightful monograph still provides a fascinating, lucid and eminently readable introduction to the structure and life of aquatic flowering plants. It is, in fact, the only book of its type in the English language, and was valuably reprinted in 1963, but without any significant revisions and with only a few additions to the bibliography, mainly of a taxonomic nature.

Numerous specialised treatments of aquatic angiosperms and pteridophytes have been published during the past forty-five years. Some are systematic manuals or check-lists of regional aquatic floras: the others are mainly horticultural handbooks and pamphlets. Almost all of them adopt a floristic approach. There seems to have been no attempt whatsoever to provide a reasonably up-to-date monograph treating all aspects of the comparative biology of freshwater and marine vascular plants. Such is my principal aim in writing this book.

Since 1920 the original literature relating to aquatic vascular plants has become voluminous. There has been much fruitful research on problems of vegetative and reproductive morphology, and limited progress towards a better understanding of phenotypic plasticity and its possible morphogenetic causes. Some aquatic plants have proved highly convenient experimental subjects and have figured prominently in physiological studies of solute absorption, photosynthesis, respiration, growth and photoperiodism. There have been innumerable ecological surveys of aquatic communities, especially in north temperate countries. With the increasing economic importance of hydrobiological projects and the growing menace of water pollution, there has recently come due recognition of the profound influences which aquatic communities may exert on their environment. Investigations into the nature of this dynamic interaction are now in progress.

Although very many questions remain unanswered, these various fields of enquiry have yielded heavy crops of original papers. Data lie scattered throughout journals of agriculture, hydrobiology, medicine, geology and even engineering, in addition to those devoted to pure botany. My subsidiary aim has therefore been to review the research literature as thoroughly as possible and provide a reasonably comprehensive bibliography.

The book is written primarily for undergraduate and graduate students, but I venture to hope it may also provide a useful background text for teachers of biology and for research workers associated with the field of aquatic biology.

The theme of the book is the interaction, in both directions, between the vascular plant body and the aquatic environment, as manifest on the structural, physiological and ecological levels. This theme involves the closest possible relation of function to structure, and a constant implicit comparison with terrestrial vascular plants. The treatment is comparative throughout, with no intended geographical or taxonomic bias in the selection of examples. Frequent emphasis is given to possible trends of biological specialisation, although it must be appreciated that direct evidence of their evolutionary reality is often lacking. Concepts of affinity and ancestry are outlined in the appropriate context of the data on which they are based.

It is unfortunately impossible, in a book of this size, to illustrate all the subjects which merit illustration. In selecting and preparing the various line diagrams, photographs and maps I have therefore concentrated primarily on those topics which are somewhat difficult to comprehend from a written text, are interesting from a comparative point of view, or are least likely to be seen by the reader himself.

I gratefully acknowledge the permission to reproduce published material granted by the following holders of copyright: Macmillan and Co. Ltd., London (for extracts from Seneca's *Quaestiones Naturales*, translated by J. Clarke, with notes by Sir A. Geikie); Heinemann Educational Books Ltd., London (for extracts from Theophrastus' *Enquiry into Plants*, translated by Sir A. Hort); Cambridge University Press (for extracts from *Water Plants: a study of aquatic angiosperms* and *The Mind and the Eye: a study of the biologist's standpoint* by Agnes Arber); Hamish Hamilton Ltd., London, Laurence Pollinger Ltd., London, and Harper and Row, Publishers, Inc., New York (for extracts from *The White Nile* by Alan Moorehead); the Controller of Her Majesty's Stationery Office, London (for Figs. 2.1, 2.2, 2.5, 2.6, 2.7, 2.8, 2.9, 5.12, 5.20, 12.9 and 12.10); the Council of the Royal Society of Edinburgh (for Figs. 12.1 A, 12.2 A, 12.3 A, and 12.4 A); the British Ecological Society (for Fig. 5.14); Blackwell Scientific Publications Ltd., Oxford, and the Editors of *New Phytologist* (for Fig. 11.8 B); the Boyce Thompson Institute for Plant Research, Inc., Yonkers, New York (for Figs. 7.10, 13.5, 14.4, 14.5 and 14.6); Duke University Press, Durham, North Carolina (for Fig. 12.8); the Lake Kariba Co-ordinating Committee, Salisbury, Rhodesia (for Figs. 14.2 and 14.3); Oliver and Boyd Ltd., Edinburgh (for Figs. 2.14, 12.1 B, 12.2 B, 12.3 B, and 12.4 B); the Royal Botanical Society of the Netherlands and the Botanical Museum and Herbarium of the State University of Utrecht (for Fig. 8.2); Messrs. Klinkhardt and Biermann, Brunswick (for Figs. 15.1, 15.2 and 15.3); *Country Life*, London (for Fig. 15.4) and *Amateur Gardening*, London (for Fig. 15.5).

I am very deeply indebted to Mr. D. F. Westlake (Freshwater Biological

Association, Wareham, England) for his stimulating comments on the type-script and invaluable counsel on topics of metabolism and productivity, for permitting me to read several of his papers prior to their publication and drawing my attention to certain Russian, eastern European and other works, and for preparing Fig. 5.11. During the past five years numerous other people have readily given me the benefit of their specialised knowledge, donated copies of their publications, loaned herbarium specimens, sent gifts of living plants, or provided photographs for use as illustrations. For this kind assistance I wish to thank Dr. E. C. S. Little (A.R.C. Weed Research Organisation, Oxford, England), Dr. R. W. Edwards and Mr. M. Owens (Water Pollution Research Laboratory, Stevenage, England), Mr. D. Philcox (Royal Botanic Gardens, Kew, England), Professor Dr. H. C. D. de Wit and Dr. R. A. H. Legro (Agricultural University, Wageningen, Netherlands), Dr. H. D. Schotsman (National Museum of Natural History, Paris), Dr. H. Wild (Herbarium and Botanic Garden, Salisbury, Rhodesia), Mr. J. H. H. Thompson (Lake Kariba Co-ordinating Committee, Salisbury, Rhodesia), Dr. A. A. Obermeyer (Botanical Research Institute, Pretoria, South Africa), Professor A. Johnson (University of Malaya, Kuala Lumpur), Professor H. St. John (Bernice P. Bishop Museum, Honolulu, Hawaii), Dr. A. E. Hitchcock (Boyce Thompson Institute for Plant Research, Yonkers, New York), Dr. T. F. Hall, Jr. (Tennessee Valley Authority, Muscle Shoals, Alabama), Professor W. R. Accorsi (University of São Paulo, Brazil), and the Director and Staff of the Botanic Garden of Rio de Janeiro.

I would like to express very warm thanks to Mr. J. E. Dandy, Keeper of Botany at the British Museum (Natural History), for checking the nomenclature and authorities of all Helobian and certain other taxa, and for advising me on several points of taxonomic procedure. Any errors in the citation of names or authorities will be mine alone.

I am also most grateful to Professor C. W. Wardlaw for permitting me to use the seminar library of his department and facilitating my access to the Science Library of the University of Manchester during the period 1960 to 1964.

I remember well the interest expressed by numerous former colleagues on the staff of Salford Technical College which did much to strengthen my determination when the spirit ebbed. I would particularly thank Mr. B. A. Fox for his encouragement, Mr. F. Neuer for his linguistic assistance, and Mr. W. Wood for his enthusiastic technical help.

Finally, it gives me immense pleasure to record my appreciation of the sterling guidance of Dr. A. P. Hughes (A.R.C. Unit of Flower Crop Physiology, University of Reading), who read and criticised the entire typescript and made innumerable suggestions for its improvement, and the great assistance rendered by my publishers, who have very patiently fostered the project since its initiation.

C. D. S.

London
November, 1966

1*

Explanatory Notes

REFERENCES TO PUBLICATIONS

Throughout the text references to original papers, books and other publications are indicated by the name of the author(s), or just the senior author followed by '*et al.*' for works by three or more persons, and the date of publication. Multiple citations are in chronological, not alphabetical, order. Full details of all cited works will be found in the bibliography.

NOMENCLATURE OF ORGANISMS

An effort has been made to bring the nomenclature of plants and other organisms as far up to date as possible. Organisms are referred to by their current scientific names, and specific epithets are spelled throughout the text with a small initial letter. The names used by particular authors are of course retained in the titles of works in the bibliography, even if these names are invalid or superfluous. To conserve space, the appropriate authority for each scientific name is not included in the text or in the legends to illustrations, but is given in the index of organisms.

ILLUSTRATIONS

The letters I, J and Q are omitted from the alphabetical sequence used to key the parts of composite line diagrams. The linear magnification or reduction of each figure from natural size is given in the appropriate legend. The projection on which each sketch map of plant distribution is based is noted in the legend, so that allowance may be made for any inherent areal distortion.

UNITS OF MEASUREMENT

The many different units appearing in the original literature have been standardised on the metric system as far as possible, and, with very few exceptions, are expressed and abbreviated according to the recommendations of the British Standards Institution (BS 1991, 1954). Readers may find the following conversion factors useful:

Length:

$$1 \text{ m} = 39\cdot370 \text{ inches} = 3\cdot281 \text{ feet}$$
$$1 \text{ km} = 0\cdot621 \text{ miles}$$
$$1 \ \mu = 0\cdot001 \text{ mm}$$
$$1 \text{ m}\mu = 10^{-6} \text{ mm} = 10 \text{ Å}$$

Area:

   1 m^2 = 10·764 square feet = 1·196 square yards
   1 km^2 = 0·386 square miles
      1 ha = 0·01 km^2 = 2·471 acres

Volume:

   1 m^3 = 35·315 cubic feet

Flow:

   1 m^3/min = 0·589 cubic feet/s (cusec)

Capacity:

   1 l. = 0·220 gallons

Weight:

   1 kg = 2·205 pounds
   1 m.t. = 1000 kg = 0·984 British (long) tons = 1·103 United States (short) tons = 10 metric centners, metric quintals or Doppel-zentners

Weight per unit Area:

   1 m.t./ha = 100 g/m^2
   1 kg/ha = 0·892 pounds/acre

Pressure:

   1 kg/cm^2 = 14·21 pounds/square inch

Light intensity:

   1 lux = 0·093 foot-candle

DESIGNATION OF CHEMICAL COMPOUNDS

   To avoid overburdening the text, certain organic herbicides, growth substances, metabolic inhibitors and chelators are designated by abbreviations or by common or trade names. A list of these is given below, in alphabetical order.

Designation	*Chemical name*
Amitrole	3-amino-1,2,4-triazole
Atrazine	2-chloro-4-ethylamino-6-isopropylamino-*s*-triazine
2,4-D	2,4-dichlorophenoxyacetic acid
Dalapon (DCPA)	2,2-dichloropropionic acid
2,4-DB	4-(2,4-dichlorophenoxy)butyric acid
2,6-DBN	2,6-dichlorobenzonitrile
Dicryl	*N*-(3,4-dichlorophenyl)methacrylamide
Diquat	1,1'-ethylene-2,2'-dipyridylium dibromide
Diuron	3-(3,4-dichlorophenyl)-1,1-dimethylurea
DNBP	4,6-dinitro-*o-sec*-butylphenol
2,4-DP	2-(2,4-dichlorophenoxy)propionic acid
EDTA	ethylenediamine-tetra-acetic acid
Endothal	3,6-endoxohexahydrophthalic acid

Designation	Chemical name
Fenac	2,3,6-trichlorophenylacetic acid
IAA	indol-3-ylacetic acid
IAN	indol-3-ylacetonitrile
IBA	indol-3-ylbutyric acid
IPA	indol-3-ylpropionic acid
Karsil	N-(3,4-dichlorophenyl)-2-methylpentanamide
Kuron (2,4,5-TP)	2-(2,4,5-trichlorophenoxy)propionic acid
MCPA	2-methyl-4-chlorophenoxyacetic acid
MCPP	2-(2-methyl-4-chlorophenoxy)propionic acid
MIA	monoiodoacetamide
Monuron (CMU)	3-(4-chlorophenyl)-1,1-dimethylurea
NAA	naphthylacetic acid
PAA	phenylacetic acid
Paraquat	1,1′-dimethyl-4,4′-bipyridylium di(methyl sulphate)
PCP	pentachlorophenol
Phygon-XL	2,3-dichloronaphthoquinone
POA	phenoxyacetic acid
Propazine	2-chloro-4,6-bis(isopropylamino)-s-triazine
Simazine	2-chloro-4,6-bis(ethylamino)-s-triazine
Solan	N-(3-chloro-4-methylphenyl)-2-methylpentanamide
2,4,5-T	2,4,5-trichlorophenoxyacetic acid
TCA	trichloroacetic acid
TCBA	2,3,6-trichlorobenzoic acid
TDE (DDD)	1,1-dichloro-2,2-di(4-chlorophenyl)ethane
TIBA	2,3,5-triiodobenzoic acid

Coumarin, kinetin, zeatin, and gibberellic acid are not abbreviated.

Radioactive isotopes are denoted by the appropriate chemical symbol pre-indexed by the atomic weight of the particular isotope, e.g., ^{14}C.

Contents

The Salient Features of
Aquatic Vascular Plants

For there are some plants which cannot live except in wet; and again these are distinguished from one another by their fondness for different kinds of wetness; so that some grow in marshes, others in lakes, others in rivers, others even in the sea. . . . Some are water plants to the extent of being submerged, while some project a little from the water; of some again the roots and a small part of the stem are under the water, but the rest of the body is altogether above it.

THEOPHRASTUS (370-c. 285 B.C.) *Enquiry into Plants*

Vascular plants have conquered the land. Inheriting from remote marine ancestors a multicellular body with unlimited apical growth and a dimorphic life-cycle with a dominant sporophyte generation, they gradually enlarged and adapted their organs to endure the mechanical and physiological rigours of terrestrial life and they ultimately developed the seed habit. They escaped from aquatic environments and the most successful no longer need water as a medium for fertilisation. This great evolutionary advance must have begun long before the mid-Palaeozoic era, for heterospory, primitive seeds and remarkable elaboration of structure were already manifest in the arborescent pteridophytes, seed-ferns and early coniferophytes of the Devonian, Carboniferous and Permian swamps. Some trends of specialisation led only to extinction, but the long main line of evolution culminated in the spread of contemporary angiosperms over much of the land surface, replacing gymnosperms as the dominant vegetation and invading even parched and arid habitats.

Yet, despite the flourishing conquest of the land, some few pteridophytes and angiosperms, most of them herbs, have ventured back into fresh waters, and even further, into the sea. Here they live and reproduce in a partly or wholly submerged state. The size of this specialised minority is difficult to assess, and of course varies according to how loosely an aquatic vascular plant is defined, but even the most liberal estimate is unlikely to exceed 1 per cent of angiosperms and 2 per cent of pteridophytes. Many still possess relics of their terrestrial heritage, such as a very thin cuticle, functionless stomata and poorly lignified xylem tracheary elements. Although, in a sense, returning to their ancestral environment, the aquatic angiosperms have not reverted to fertilisation by motile ciliated sperms. They have inevitably carried with them the advanced reproductive methods of their terrestrial relatives, which now seem little more than an anachronistic impediment. From whatever depth at which they grow, most species still strive to raise their flowers above the surface of the water for pollination by insects or by wind. In only very few highly specialised plants is the pollen shed below the surface and carried to the stigmas by water currents. Even in these select species the ovules are still enclosed and the non-motile male gametes are still conveyed by a pollen tube, so that fertilisation is accomplished below water in just the same way as in terrestrial angiosperms.

Aquatic vascular plants have successfully colonised standing and flowing, fresh, brackish and saline waters in all climatic zones. Although most are rooted, some species have abandoned any attachment to the substrate and float freely in the water, whilst a few are occasionally epiphytic. The sea-grass, *Phyllospadix*, is sometimes found on seaweeds along the coasts of Japan and Pacific North America, and the Asiatic podostemad, *Cladopus nymani*, can grow as an epiphyte on bamboo shoots (Ostenfeld, 1927b; van Steenis, 1949d). A few aquatic species of *Utricularia* live in the small pools of water in the leaf rosettes of certain tropical bromeliads, which are themselves epiphytic (Lloyd, 1942). Some aquatic angiosperms are notably tolerant of environmental extremes. In Burma, *Najas graminea* grows in hot springs in which the average temperature is about 35°C, whilst a variety of *Najas tenuifolia* has been found in sulphide-rich water at 60°C in the volcanic lake of Mt. Kelud in central Java (de Wilde, 1962). *Eleocharis sellowiana* thrives in a similar crater lake, the Laguna de Alegria in El Salvador, where sulphurous fumaroles and springs on the shore bring the pH of the water down as low as 2·0 (Fassett and Armitage, 1961).

Although few in number, aquatic vascular plants hold extraordinary botanical interest. They comprise a perplexing assemblage of growth habits and are often astonishingly plastic in somatic organisation, so that their wide phenotypic variation creates acute problems for the taxonomist. Compared with land plants, their vegetative body exhibits numerous structural modifications. Some of these may have adaptive significance. In certain aquatic angiosperms vegetative reduction is so extreme that orthodox morphological distinctions, as of stem, root and leaf, may no longer be easily drawn. During the reproductive phase of many species, profound reduction and specialisation are again evident, often accompanying the transition from aerial to submerged flowers, from ento- or anemophily to genuine hydrophily, and from a freshwater to a marine existence. There are also tendencies towards the replacement of allogamy by autogamy and of sexual reproduction by vegetative propagation. The natural affinities of most families of aquatic vascular plants are obscure and have long evoked immense speculation and controversy. Some, such as the Isoetaceae, the aquatic ferns and the Nymphaeaceae, may well be isolated refugees, relict and perhaps neotenous descendants of primitive stocks which, on land, proved ill-adapted and long ago became extinct. Other aquatic groups show striking resemblances to certain living terrestrial families and are probably of more recent origin. It certainly appears that the aquatic habit has been acquired by many unrelated angiosperms and at many different times during the history of this group.

Although the former nutritional and medicinal importance of most aquatic vascular plants has gradually waned, many species are still of great economic significance, in relation to wild-life conservation, navigation, inland fisheries, irrigation schemes and other hydrobiological concerns. Their impact on these various human activities develops through their interaction with the environment, their biotic relationships to other aquatic organisms, and their frequent creation of embarrassing weed infestations.

THE VARIABILITY OF THE AQUATIC HABIT, AND THE CONCEPT OF 'VASCULAR HYDROPHYTES'

Aquatic vascular plants may be described by several convenient technical terms, such as 'aquatic tracheophytes' or 'aquatic cormophytes'. In contemporary literature, ecologists often favour the use of 'aquatic macrophytes' but this term has no precise taxonomic meaning. Essentially, it refers to the larger aquatic plants, as distinct from the microscopic planktonic and benthic plants, and therefore includes aquatic mosses, liverworts and larger algae as well as vascular plants. The only term used widely in this book is 'vascular hydrophytes'.

It is difficult to suggest a definition of vascular hydrophytes that is universally acceptable yet not utterly artificial. The difficulty arises mainly because aquatic habitats cannot be sharply distinguished from terrestrial ones. In most climates there is a seasonal fluctuation of the water table. Habitats with standing water for most of the year may dry out completely in the summer whilst normally terrestrial soils may be flooded during a rainy season. At no time is there an abrupt change from land to water, but rather a gradual transition from dry through waterlogged to submerged soils. The reversion of vascular plants to aquatic life has involved colonisation of all these transitional habitats as well as the water itself, and some of the marginal sites that are periodically flooded have come to possess their own distinctive plant associations (Noirfalise and Sougnez, 1961).

In his classification of life forms, Raunkiaer (1934) considered hydrophytes as plants which have vegetative parts submerged or floating at the water surface, but not emerging into the air, and which survive unfavourable seasons as submerged buds attached to the parent plant or lying free on the substrate. This concept excludes many plants, such as *Glyceria*, *Phragmites*, *Schoenoplectus* and *Typha*, which have submerged lower parts but essentially aerial leaves (Fig. 1.1), and also annuals, such as most species of *Najas*, *Euryale*, *Hydrothrix*, *Subularia* and *Trapa*, which survive as seeds. Some species of *Nymphaea* and *Potamogeton*, which produce reduced land forms if the habitat dries out, may also be regarded as hemicryptophytes in Raunkiaer's system, whilst *Zannichellia palustris* and plants that survive an exceptional drought as seeds behave as therophytes, and *Scirpus grossus* and similar species that pass the tropical dry season as subterranean tubers or rhizomes could be deemed geophytes.

Environmental circumstances may substantially modify the duration of the life cycle. *Montia fontana* and species of *Callitriche* have annual terrestrial, and both biennial and perennial aquatic forms (Royer, 1881; Schenck, 1885;

FIG. 1.1. A, *Sparganium emersum*, an emergent hydrophyte with aerial leaves and inflorescences and submerged rhizomes and roots. Around the leaf bases are colonies of the free-floating *Lemna gibba*, whilst in the centre rear are the leaves of another emergent species, *Alisma plantago-aquatica*; B, Floating-leaved *Nymphaea* with the aerial leaves of the emergent *Nelumbo nucifera* in the background at left and right.

Walters, 1953; de Jongh and Hegnauer, 1963). Some species of *Ranunculus* subg. *Batrachium*, e.g. *R. aquatilis, R. peltatus* and *R. tripartitus*, behave as annuals if the habitat dries out in the summer but perennate readily if water remains (Cook, 1963). In the tropics, certain species of *Monochoria* and *Tenagocharis*, which are perennial in permanently aquatic habitats, flower precociously and behave as annuals when they are growing in ricefields, which are inundated for only 3 to 4 months and then drained for the paddy to ripen (Backer, 1951f; van Steenis, 1954, 1957).

In his modification of Raunkiaer's concept, Iversen (1936) still regarded as aquatic only those plants with submerged or floating vegetative parts, but he did include the types that can produce dwarfed land forms as well as those that perennate under water. For some reason, he found it necessary to use the term *limnophytes*, not hydrophytes, a practice followed also by Poplawskaja (1948). This is an unfortunate term because of its literal suggestion of freshwater plants as distinct from brackish-water or marine types, although both authors used it to embrace all these. Iversen further introduced the term *amphiphytes* to cover plants which normally possess aerial and aquatic leaves but which can develop water forms. The distinction between amphiphyte and limnophyte is inevitably vague and there are many borderline examples, such as the batrachian *Ranunculi* and many species of *Callitriche*, which do not fall clearly into either category. The habitually submerged tropical Podostemaceae, moreover, cannot produce land forms, yet flower only when the water recedes at the onset of the dry season and the vegetative organs begin to die.

Den Hartog and Segal (1964) took account of the Podostemaceae in defining hydrophytes as 'plants which are able to achieve their generative cycle when all vegetative parts are submerged or are supported by the water (floating leaves), or which occur normally submerged but are induced to reproduce sexually when their vegetative parts are dying due to emersion'. Completion of the life cycle would be a valuable criterion if rigidly interpreted to mean the formation of submerged reproductive organs and achievement of both pollination and fertilisation under water; for this is the ultimate adaptation to aquatic life. But den Hartog and Segal made no such distinction. It is therefore difficult to see any biological significance in their exclusion of plants with partly aerial foliage from consideration as hydrophytes. Floating leaves are as much adapted to aerial as to aquatic life, as Iversen (1936) in fact admitted. The erect leaves of such plants as *Butomus* and *Phragmites* may be essentially terrestrial in general form and anatomy but their basal parts (rhizomes, tubers, stolons, roots etc.) inhabit the same aquatic and frequently oxygenless environment as those of wholly submerged plants and they exhibit comparable morphological reactions. Similarly, there is little reason to attempt to separate freely floating plants with usually aerial foliage (e.g. *Eichhornia crassipes*) or leaves that may be erect or lie flat on the surface according to growth conditions (e.g. *Pistia stratiotes, Salvinia* spp.) from those whose organs habitually rest on the surface (e.g. most spp. of *Lemna*) or are partly submerged and partly aerial (e.g. *Stratiotes aloides*).

The definitions proposed by several American botanists are much wider and more realistic. Weaver and Clements (1938), for example, regarded herbaceous vascular hydrophytes as plants growing 'in water, in soil covered with water, or in soil that is usually saturated'. Muenscher (1944) restricted this slightly to 'those species which normally stand in water and must grow for at least a part of their life cycle in water, either completely submersed or emersed'. Similarly, Reid's (1961) concept of hydrophytes as plants 'whose seeds germinate in either the water phase or the substrate of a body of water, and which must spend part of their cycle in water' embraces an assortment of aerial-leaved plants as well as submerged, floating-leaved and free-floating types. Fassett's (1957) working definition was equally comprehensive.

Many woody and herbaceous plants, which are considered typically terrestrial, tolerate periods of partial or total immersion, often developing structural modifications comparable in kind and sometimes in degree with those of a naturally submerged plant. Certain polymorphic plants such as *Ipomoea carnea*, *Polygonum amphibium*, and some species of *Callitriche* and *Elatine* exhibit quite different phenotypes in water, wet muddy soil and drier sandy soil (Massart, 1902; Fassett, 1939a, 1951; Turesson, 1961; Mohanty and Mishra, 1963). In monsoon climates the number of normally emergent or terrestrial plants that produce distinctive submerged foliage throughout the rainy season is legionary. In view of their morphological responses, these plants may usefully be claimed as hydrophytes, whether they reproduce during immersion or not.

The concept of a hydrophyte adopted here is essentially that of the American botanists. The choice of examples is frankly acknowledged as subjective, the aim being to examine as many aspects of interaction between the vascular plant body and the aquatic environment as possible. The different forms of hydrophyte may then be seen in a realistic perspective, not as artificially isolated and somewhat anomalous types, but as examples of different stages in the morphological, ecological, and, in a sense, evolutionary continuum extending between mesophytic vegetation on moist terrestrial soils and hydrophilous plants permanently submerged in deep waters. Acceptance of the limitations of space and personal experience, however, necessitates the exclusion of certain plants from this book. Of the many plants of saline and brackish-water habitats only the submerged species will be considered, as these are probably closely related to freshwater forms. The highly specialised mangrove forests of estuaries and other tidal waters in the tropics, and the plant communities of salt-marshes generally, will be excluded. Even so circumscribed, the field covered is still extremely wide: the examples cited in later chapters are drawn from all climatic zones and include not only vascular plants living habitually in water but also some species of semi-aquatic and terrestrial habitats subject to seasonal inundation.

CLASSIFICATION OF VASCULAR HYDROPHYTES ACCORDING TO LIFE FORMS
AND GROWTH FORMS

From the foregoing account of the difficulties attending rigid definition of vascular hydrophytes, it should immediately be appreciated that the bewildering diversity of habit and plasticity of organisation sorely frustrate any attempt to construct a precise biological classification of this heterogeneous group. Undeterred by the profuse natural variation, many authors have devised systems based on criteria of life form and growth form. In her elaboration of the original scheme proposed by Schenck (1885), Arber (1920) recognised two primary groups of aquatic angiosperms, *rooted* and *non-rooted*, which she subdivided according to the type of foliage and inflorescence produced, and the position of these organs with respect to water level, in an effort to portray the various degrees of commitment to aquatic life. She freely admitted that the lines of demarcation between several classes were blurred by transitional types.

Penfound's (1952a) scheme, following in outline that of Hess and Hall (1945), split hydrophytes into *wet-land types*—in soils saturated with water, and *aquatic types*—in soils covered with water for most of the growing season. He recognised three reasonably discrete forms of aquatic—*emergent, floating* and *submerged*, but proceeded to subdivide these on the basis of highly arbitrary criteria of vegetative structure. In consequence, the classes were far from mutually exclusive, and whilst the scheme accommodated the American species cited, it could not be universally applied without considerable modification. In his study of the hydrophytes of the Danube valley in Czechoslovakia, Hejný (1957, 1960) simply recognised three groups: *euhydatophytes*—with vegetative organs submerged and inflorescences submerged or aerial; *hydatoaerophytes*—with a partly submerged and partly floating vegetative body (i.e. floating-leaved) and aerial inflorescences; and *tenagophytes*—amphibious plants occurring in habitats with marked fluctuation of water level. Poplawskaja (1948) discriminated between submerged plants which produce submerged hydrophilous flowers and those which produce aerial flowers, but her scheme otherwise resembled that of Hejný.

On the basis of their attachment to the substrate, Luther (1949) classified hydrophytes (including aquatic cryptogams as well as angiosperms) into: *haptophytes*—plants which are attached to, but do not penetrate, the substrate (e.g. many algae, lichens and bryophytes, and the Podostemaceae amongst the angiosperms); *rhizophytes*—whose basal parts actually penetrate the substrate; and *planophytes*—freely floating plants with submerged or surface-floating assimilatory organs. This third group included microscopic *planktophytes* (phytoplankton) and macroscopic *pleustophytes* (larger floating algae, liverworts, ferns and angiosperms). Luther further divided the pleustophytes into three groups according to the level at which they float, a differentiation that cannot be sharply sustained because such plants as *Lemna* spp., *Ceratophyllum* spp., *Stratiotes aloides* and aquatic *Utricularia* spp. rise and fall through the water according to the season and their stage of development.

Den Hartog and Segal (1964) elaborated a scheme of growth forms to supplement Luther's divisions of rhizophytes and pleustophytes. Considering only European plants, they distinguished eleven basic types of growth habit, each named according to the principal example: e.g. rhizophytes possessing a short stem and rosette of stiff leaves, with or without stolons (e.g. *Isoetes lacustris, Littorella uniflora*) were distinguished as *Isoetids*; rhizophytes with long stems,

entire submerged leaves, no floating leaves, and aerial or submerged reproductive organs (e.g. species of *Elodea, Najas, Zannichellia*) as *Elodeids*, etc.

The more detailed the analysis becomes, the greater is the need to qualify
the definitions with acknowledgement of transitional examples. Many of the
polymorphic and amphibious plants, such as *Hippuris vulgaris, Polygonum
amphibium* and species of *Callitriche* (see also Fig. 1.2) may belong to more than
one life-form class or basic growth type. Numerous submerged rhizophytes,

FIG. 1.2. Two amphibious hydrophytes: A, *Hydrocotyle vulgaris* extending from below
water (at centre left) to above the water table (at right); B, Trailing shoots of *Myriophyllum brasiliense* emerging above the water.

e.g. species of *Cabomba, Elodea, Hottonia, Myriophyllum, Najas* and *Ranunculus*, commonly become fragmented, the detached shoots forming tangled masses and behaving as pleustophytes. Conversely, freely floating species of *Ceratophyllum, Eichhornia, Pistia* and *Utricularia* sometimes anchor themselves in the substrate and then appear to be rhizophytes.

The plastic behaviour of these hydrophytes shows how hopeless it is to try to set absolute limits to habit classes, whatever criteria are used. The uninitiated may be forgiven for enquiring whether such biological classifications have any valuable purpose at all, for this is often obscured by the profusion of quasi-precise definitions, accompanied by qualifications and footnotes, and unwieldy terminology. Clearly, however, it is desirable to create some element of order amidst the chaotic natural abundance of species, if only to facilitate methodical description and comparison. Classification of hydrophytes by life forms and growth forms has notable value for ecologists. Most aquatic plant communities cannot be satisfactorily distinguished by their floristic composition alone, since many species have extremely wide geographical and ecological distributions. However, a single growth form, or a particular combination of growth forms, often dominates each community and so may be used alone, or together with floristic composition, as a diagnostic character.

Whilst a biological classification can have tangible value, its elaboration has several intrinsic dangers. Not the least of these is the tendency to impose preconceived limits on inherently variable phenomena and then to attribute fundamental biological significance to the categories, discontinuities and patterns, unmindful of their possibly complete artificiality. It should also be appreciated that schemes of life forms or growth forms resemble all other linear biological classifications in accentuating examples of parallel evolution and placing in close association organisms that may be utterly unrelated.

It is not proposed to devise here an elaborate new scheme or to add further new terms to the already confused vocabulary of the subject. All that will be hazarded is a simple recognition of the principal life and growth forms, similar to that adopted by Tansley (1949), Spence (1964) and other British ecologists. The sole aim of the scheme is to provide a working basis for the treatment of various topics in subsequent chapters.

TABLE 1.1. The life forms of vascular hydrophytes

A. Hydrophytes attached to the substrate

(1) EMERGENT HYDROPHYTES:

Occur on exposed or submerged soils, from where the water table is 50 cm or more beneath the soil surface to where the soil is covered by 150 cm or more of water; mainly rhizomatous or cormous perennials; in heterophyllous species submerged and/or floating leaves precede the mature aerial leaves; many species may exist as (usually sterile) submerged forms; all produce aerial reproductive organs.

e.g., *Butomus, Eleocharis, Glyceria, Ludwigia, Phragmites, Saururus, Schoenoplectus, Typha, Zizania.*

(2) FLOATING-LEAVED HYDROPHYTES:

Occur on submerged soils in water depths of about 0·25 to 3·5 m; some species may exist as reduced land forms: in heterophyllous species submerged leaves precede or accompany the floating leaves; many species produce aerial leaves in crowded habitats; reproductive organs floating or aerial.

(*i*) Rhizomatous or cormous types, with floating leaves on long flexible petioles.

e.g., *Aponogeton distachyos, Nymphaea, Nuphar.*

(*ii*) Stoloniferous types, with trailing stems ascending through the water and producing floating leaves on relatively short petioles.

e.g., *Brasenia, Luronium, Nymphoides, Potamogeton natans.*

(3) SUBMERGED HYDROPHYTES:

Occur on submerged soils at all water depths to about 10 to 11 m; foliage entirely submerged; leaves often filiform, ribbon-shaped, broad and *Ulva*-like, fenestrated or finely divided; a few species may produce land forms; reproductive organs aerial, floating or submerged.

(*i*) Caulescent types, with or without a rhizome, the long flexuous leafy stems rooting from the nodes.

e.g., *Elodea, Hydrilla, Lagarosiphon, Najas, Potamogeton pectinatus.*

(*ii*) Rosette types, with radical leaves arising from a condensed, often tuberous rootstock or a rhizome; often stoloniferous.

e.g., *Aponogeton fenestralis, Cryptocoryne affinis, Isoetes, Littorella, Sagittaria subulata, Vallisneria.*

(*iii*) Thalloid types, with the plant body reduced to a more or less cylindrical or flattened, creeping or floating, polymorphic thallus, often bearing erect or trailing secondary branches.

e.g., the Podostemaceae, such as *Hydrobryum, Podostemum, Terniola, Tristicha, Zeylanidium.*

B. Free-floating hydrophytes

Occur mainly in sheltered sites on standing and slow-flowing waters; all are typically unattached, but some species with extensive root systems may become anchored in shallow water; numerous species may produce land forms when stranded on marginal wet soil; very diverse in form and habit, ranging from large stoloniferous plants, with rosettes of aerial and/or floating leaves and well-developed submerged roots (e.g., *Ceratopteris cornuta, Eichhornia crassipes, Hydrocharis, Limnobium, Pistia, Trapa*), to minute surface-floating or submerged plants, with a reduced assimilatory thallus having few or no roots (e.g., *Lemna, Wolffia*); reproductive organs floating or aerial, very rarely submerged (e.g., *Ceratophyllum, Salvinia*); numerous submerged taxa rise to the surface to flower, and may sink to the substrate to perennate (e.g., *Lemna trisulca, Stratiotes*, aquatic species of *Utricularia*).

THE ZONATION OF AQUATIC VEGETATION

Perhaps the most familiar feature of natural aquatic vegetation is the zonation of life forms that may often be discerned parallel to the shore in lakes, large swamps, ponds, canals and slow-flowing rivers which are not grossly polluted or otherwise disturbed by man. In the typical sequence, totally submerged communities in deeper water give way nearer the shore to a zone of floating-leaved plants, which are spatially succeeded by emergent reed-swamp communities occupying the marginal zone from a water depth of about

FIG. 1.3. Colonies of floating-leaved *Nymphaea alba* on an ornamental lake; the shore fringed by emergent hydrophytes.

FIG. 1.4. A sheltered bay on Esthwaite Water in the English Lake District, showing a marginal reedswamp of *Phragmites communis* (at right) and a zone of floating-leaved *Nuphar lutea* (arrowed) extending to deeper water exposed to slight wave action (at left).

1 m to wet soil on the shore (Figs. 1.3, 1.4). In many habitats submerged associations will also be found in shallow water, and stands of emergent species may occur well offshore on spits or banks of accumulated silt in apparently deep water. One life form, not uncommonly the floating-leaved, may be quite absent, whilst in suitably sheltered places free-floating plants may also be present in any of the three main zones.

It is not unusual for different life forms to coexist, one community creating a habitat favourable for another. Reed-swamps, for example, may have open fringes invaded by other hydrophytes which enjoy the shelter from wind and waves. Tansley (1949) described the very open reed-swamp of the Ant broads in East Anglia where floating *Lemna* spp. and *Hydrocharis morsus-ranae* and floating-leaved species of *Nuphar*, *Nymphaea* or *Potamogeton* penetrate between the foliage of the dominant emergent *Schoenoplectus lacustris*. Shortly after its appearance in Norfolk, the free-floating fern *Azolla filiculoides* formed an association with *Typha angustifolia* in the open reed-swamp of several broads (Marsh, 1914). *Lemna minor* is a similar prevalent species of *Typha* reed-swamp in Wisconsin lakes (Curtis, 1959). Submerged plants may extend as an under-layer into either the floating-leaved or reed-swamp zone and may themselves be rooted amidst a carpet of algae or mosses. Plants which float below the surface, e.g. *Ceratophyllum*, *Lemna trisulca*, *Stratiotes* and *Utricularia*, some-times become thoroughly tangled amongst rooted communities giving an apparently uniform mixture of vegetation.

Although communities of different life forms may coexist in these various ways, they retain their essential integrity and can generally occur independently elsewhere, in contrast to the layers of numerous terrestrial communities, which are usually interdependent parts of a larger vegetation unit. Indeed, certain mature aquatic communities actually inhibit the establishment of layered vegetation by their very closed structure. There is a notable tendency for many common dominant species of all life forms to give rise, largely through vigorous vegetative reproduction, to more or less pure stands, which are not easily invaded by competitors. Mature reed-swamps of this type very effectively resist infiltration by submerged and free-floating plants, especially the larger rosette species, and by other emergent hydrophytes. Dense canopies of the floating leaves of *Nuphar* and *Nymphaea* and thick mats of stoloniferous free-floating plants, such as *Pistia* and *Eichhornia crassipes*, severely curtail the penetration of light and entry of oxygen through the surface, thereby inhibiting the growth of vascular plants and phytoplankton in the water beneath.

The ecological zonation of life forms has been described most thoroughly in Europe and North America, but is essentially similar in comparable habitats elsewhere. Detailed surveys of the specific composition of zones and com-munities will be found in a multitude of ecological papers, of which the more comprehensive may usefully be cited here. Butcher (1927, 1933) and Butcher *et al.* (1930, 1931, 1937) studied the flora of several clean and polluted English rivers; Reid (1892), Walker (1905), Godwin (1923) and Griffiths (1932, 1936) described the composition and dispersal of several English pond and marsh floras; West (1905, 1910), Matthews (1914) and Spence (1964) made very extensive surveys of the vegetation of Scottish lakes; Pearsall's (1917, 1918a, b, 1920, 1921b) pioneer research, supplemented by that of Misra (1938), afforded data on the floristic composition and succession of hydrophyte communities, and on the environmental factors influencing their distribution, in Esthwaite and other waters in the English Lake District. Tansley (1949) summarised the earlier English studies and added data collected from the broads of East Anglia and from several rivers. A survey of the floras of Welsh lakes, initiated by the National Museum of Wales, is being made at the present time (Seddon, 1963, 1964).

The pioneer floristic study in continental Europe was that of Magnin (1893) on the vegetation of the Jura lakes. More recent analytical surveys of the floras of standing and running, freshwater, brackish and saline habitats have been conducted by Lohammar (1938), du Rietz (1939), Olsen (1950), Lundh (1951), af Rantzien (1951a), Kaáret (1953), Forsberg (1959, 1960, 1964) and Gillner (1960) in Sweden; Cederkreutz (1947), Luther (1949, 1951) and Niemi (1962) in southern Finland; Kornaś (1959) and Kornaś et al. (1960) in the Bay of Gdańsk in Poland; Gehu (1960), Doignon (1963) and Rastetter (1963) in France; van Langendonck (1935) and Noirfalise and Sougnez (1961) in Belgium; van Goor (1921), van Donselaar (1961), Beeftink (1962) and den Hartog (1963) in the Netherlands; Christiansen (1934), Sauer (1937), Siedel (1955, 1956, 1959), Neuhäusl (1959) and Müller and Görs (1960) in Germany; Hejný (1957, 1960), Soó (1957), Simon (1960), Kopecký (1961, 1965), Kárpáti (1963), Somsak (1963), Straškraba (1963) and Kopecký and Hejný (1965) in the Danube valley and delta and other eastern European sites; and Lipin and Lipina (1950), Shcherbakov (1950), Ekzertsev (1958, 1963), Ekzertsev and Ekzertseva (1963), Minkina (1962), Zhadin and Gerd (1963) in Russia. Accounts of the vascular plant communities of the Balkan Lake Ohrid and the Siberian Lake Baikal will be found in the major works by Stanković (1960) and Kozhov (1963). Braun-Blanquet and Tüxen (1943), Löhmeyer (1962) and den Hartog and Segal (1964) put forward systematic ecological classifications for the hydrophyte communities of central and north-west Europe.

Notable data pertaining to the flora of Egyptian waters may be found in Zaki (1960) and in the extensive limnological study by Elster and Vollenweider (1961). The vegetation of Japanese lakes, reservoirs and swamps has been described by, *inter alia*, Nakano (1911), Hogetsu (1941, 1953), Jimbô et al. (1955), Yamaguti (1955) and Kamuro (1957).

The early American work on aquatic plant communities was purely descriptive: attention was not focussed on the dynamic successional aspects until about 1935. Studies of the flora of numerous Wisconsin lakes have been published by Rickett (1921, 1924), Denniston (1922), Fassett (1930), Wilson (1935, 1937, 1939, 1941), Juday (1942), Juday et al. (1943), Potzger and van Engel (1942), Swindale and Curtis (1957) and Curtis (1959). Wylie (1920), Jones (1925) and Sigler (1948) made floristic surveys of waters in Iowa; Brown (1911) in North Carolina; Veatch (1933) in Michigan; Penfound et al. (1945) in North Alabama, de Gruchy (1938) and Penfound (1953b) in Oklahoma; Moyle (1945) and Moyle and Hotchkiss (1945) in Minnesota; Johnson

(1941) in north-west Colorado; Reed (1930) and Harris and Silvey (1940) in Texas; Davis (1937) in Tennessee; Wohlschlag (1950) in Indiana; Hevly (1961) in Arizona; and Stookey *et al.* (1964) in Illinois. Penfound (1949, 1952b), Penfound and Hathaway (1938) and Penfound and Schneidau (1945) made extensive studies of the vegetation of lakes and marshes in Louisiana in relation to wild-life resources and land reclamation, whilst Mason (1957) reviewed the marsh floras of California. Various submerged marine communities in the coastal waters of Bermuda, Florida, Texas and Puerto Rico have been analysed by Bernatowicz (1952), Burkholder *et al.* (1959), Odum *et al.* (1959), Phillips (1960), Odum (1963) and Conover (1964).

In two of the oldest papers on hydrophyte communities, Pieters (1894, 1902) described the plants of L. St. Clair, near Detroit, and of L. Erie, whilst more recently van Oosten (1957) considered the flora of the Great Lakes generally, along with their fauna. Valuable data on the plants of waters in the St. Lawrence system may be found in Louis-Marie's (1931) *Flore-manuel de la province de Québec* and in Pageau's (1959) study of the Lac Saint-Louis.

The apparent bias of these references is due only in part to the greater accessibility of the literature of north temperate countries. With the exception of a few studies of infestations of aquatic weeds, there is a very real dearth of comprehensive ecological data on the hydrophyte communities of most parts of the tropics and south temperate zone.

SYSTEMATIC DISTRIBUTION OF VASCULAR HYDROPHYTES

Since many vascular hydrophytes belong to lesser-known families, it may be useful to give here a brief introductory review of their systematic distribution, salient biological features and possible affinities. Bailey (1949, 1951, 1953), Eames (1953, 1961), Puri (1962, 1965), Davis and Heywood (1963) and others have pertinently emphasised the severe limitations of phylogenetic concepts as applied to larger taxa of vascular plants, and have very eloquently pleaded for unbiassed analysis and cautious interpretation of the maximum possible number of characters ('summations of evidence') in studying the relationships and classification of such groups. So far as hydrophytes are concerned, much might be gained by admitting, at the outset, that the natural affinities and ancestry of many families are profoundly enigmatic. Botanists are still seriously ignorant, or deeply divided in their interpretation, of many aspects of the morphology, cytogenetics and geological history of aquatic taxa. In this present state of inadequate knowledge, phylogenetic speculation is sometimes provocative and may inspire the pursuit of some hitherto untrodden path of inquiry, but all too often it seems no more than wild intellectual diversion, flourishing precociously on the very lack of factual data and unequivocal evidence. No tangible purpose would be served here by a detailed exposition of the many involved and controversial arguments put forward in the effort to trace the phylogeny of hydrophyte families. Only the more plausible and stimulating ideas will be mentioned. Some of these will be considered further in later chapters.

The families deemed to consist more or less exclusively of hydrophytes are listed in Table 1.2, together with their constituent genera, notes on their life form, mode of spore production or pollination, and distribution, and references to taxonomic or other relevant publications.

Perhaps the most striking features apparent in the table are the small total number and small individual size of the families, despite the broad concept of a vascular hydrophyte. Of the thirty-three families, thirty have fewer than ten genera, seventeen are monogeneric and three are monotypic (Hippuridaceae, Scheuchzeriaceae, Lilaeaceae). The number of species probably exceeds 100 in only two families (Podostemaceae and Haloragaceae). It is impossible to give precise estimates of species in most families because of differences of taxonomic opinion and lack of adequate data for confused genera. It is conceivable that the species content of families rich in tropical or south temperate taxa is underestimated. This possibility is accentuated by the recent description of new species of *Cabomba*, *Echinodorus* and *Salvinia* in the American tropics (Fassett, 1953, 1955; de la Sota, 1962), of *Elodea* in both North and South America (St. John, 1962b, 1963, 1964, 1965), of *Lagarosiphon* in South Africa (Obermeyer, 1964), of *Aponogeton* in Ceylon and Malaysia (de Wit, 1958b; van Bruggen, 1962), and of *Callitriche* in Australasia (Mason, 1959). On the other hand, thorough taxonomic revisions are sorely needed in several poorly understood groups and might substantially reduce the numbers of species recognised at present.

Of the families of aquatic pteridophytes, the Isoetaceae is a natural entity quite distinct from all the truly terrestrial living members of the Lycopodinae. The other four families all belong to the Filicinae, but only the Ceratopteridaceae are remotely fern-like in appearance. The Marsileaceae, Azollaceae and Salviniaceae, which have often been thrust together into the convenient but grossly unnatural order Hydropteridales, have lost all outward resemblance to other ferns as a result of extreme vegetative reduction and specialisation. Their obscure origin and advanced heterosporous habit have aroused profuse interest and speculation (p. 266). All five families occur only in fresh waters but are reasonably widely distributed, although the Ceratopteridaceae are absent from temperate regions and the Azollaceae and Salviniaceae, both predominantly tropical, are somewhat restricted by their free-floating habit.

It is conspicuous that none of the aquatic dicotyledonous families includes any marine representatives. Hydrophily is attained only in the Ceratophyllaceae and a few species of the Callitrichaceae. These plants appear to be slightly more tolerant of salinity than most freshwater species and sometimes extend a short way into brackish water. The origins of both these small families, especially the Ceratophyllaceae, are notoriously enigmatic (pp. 312-13). The Nymphaeaceae is a very heterogeneous family and there have been several recent attempts to segregate certain of its genera (notably *Cabomba* and *Brasenia*, *Euryale* and *Victoria*, and *Nelumbo*) as various distinct families or even orders. All eight genera exhibit both primitive and advanced structural characters and are possibly derived from ancient Ranalian stocks (p. 275).

2

TABLE I.2 Synopsis of families of aquatic vascular plants

Family	No. of: Genera	Species	Genera	Life form*	Spore production (Pteridophytes) or pollination (Angiosperms)	Geographical and habitat range	Important publications on, or relevant to, classification and phylogeny of whole or part of family
A. Pteridophytes							
1. ISOETACEAE	2	c. 60	*Isoetes* *Stylites*	E, S	Heterosporous	Cosmopolitan (but mainly at high altitudes in tropics) Some spp. terrestrial for at least part of year; all aquatic spp. in fresh water	Pfeiffer, 1922; Weber, 1922; Grenda, 1926; Manton, 1950; Arnstutz, 1957; Ninan, 1958; Alston, 1959b; Rauh & Falk, 1959; Löve, 1962; Pant & Srivastava, 1962, 1965; Reed, 1962; Jermy, 1964; Kubitzki & Borchert, 1964
2. CERATOPTERIDACEAE (Parkeriaceae)	1	c. 6	*Ceratopteris*	E, S, Ff	Homosporous	Pan-tropical and sub-tropical Fresh water	Benedict, 1909; Holttum, 1949; Stokey, 1951; Ninan, 1956; DeVol, 1957; Pal, 1959; Javalgekar, 1960; Johnson, 1961; Pal & Pal, 1962, 1963
3. MARSILEACEAE	3	c. 70	*Marsilea* *Pilularia* *Regnellidium*	E, S, Ff	Heterosporous	Cosmopolitan Some spp. semi-terrestrial; all aquatic spp. in fresh water	Campbell, 1904; Bower, 1926; Stason, 1926; Christensen, 1938; Johnson & Chrysler, 1938; Chrysler & Johnson, 1939; Holttum, 1949; Dittmer et al., 1954; Hyde & Wade, 1954; Reed, 1954, 1962; Bonnet, 1958; Alston, 1959a; Pichi-Sermolli, 1959; Meeuse, 1961; Crabbe, 1964
4. AZOLLACEAE	1	c. 6	*Azolla*	Ff	Heterosporous	Tropical and warm temperate Fresh water	Bower, 1928; Christensen, 1938; Herzog, 1938; Svenson, 1944; Holttum, 1949; Demalsy, 1953; Dittmer et al., 1954; Hyde & Wade, 1954; Reed, 1954, 1962; Bonnet, 1958; Alston, 1959a; Pichi-Sermolli, 1959; di Fulvio, 1961; Meeuse, 1961; Lawalrée, 1964
5. SALVINIACEAE	1	c. 12	*Salvinia*	Ff	Heterosporous	Tropical and warm temperate Fresh water	Bower, 1928; Herzog, 1935, 1938; Christensen, 1938; Holttum, 1949; Mahabalé, 1954; Reed, 1954; Bonnet, 1955, 1958; Alston, 1959a; Pichi-Sermolli, 1959; Meeuse, 1961; de la Sota, 1962, 1963, 1964; Lawalrée, 1964

B. Dicotyledons†

Family	genera	spp.	Genera		Pollination	Distribution	References
6. NYMPHAEACEAE (*sensu lato*)	8	*c.* 60	*Nymphaea*, *Barclaya*, *Brasenia*, *Cabomba*, *Euryale*, *Nelumbo*, *Nuphar*, *Victoria*	Fl, E, S	Entomophilous; few autogamous	Cosmopolitan Fresh water	Caspary, 1888; Conard, 1905; Schuster, 1907; Miller & Standley, 1912; Small, 1931; Pring, 1934; Fassett, 1953; Li, 1955; Beal, 1956; Moseley, 1958, 1961, 1965; Wood, 1959; van Leeuwen, 1963; Khanna, 1964; Meyer, 1964; Tutin, 1964; Ramji & Padmanabhan, 1965
7. CERATOPHYLLACEAE	1	*c.* 6	*Ceratophyllum*	S, Ff	Hydrophilous	Cosmopolitan Fresh water	Engler, 1888; Jones, 1931; Muenscher, 1940; van Steenis, 1949a; Wood, 1959; Webb, 1964
8. ELATINACEAE	2	*c.* 30	*Elatine*, *Bergia*	E, S	? Entomophilous; many perhaps autogamous	Cosmopolitan (but *Elatine* mainly temperate, *Bergia* mainly tropical) Fresh water	Fernald, 1917, 1941; Fassett, 1939a; Gauthier & Raymond, 1949; Backer, 1951a
9. TRAPACEAE (Hydrocaryaceae)	1	4	*Trapa*	Ff	Entomophilous	Palaeotropical and warm temperate Eurasian Fresh water	Gams, 1927; Just, 1946; Vasil'ev, 1947; van Steenis, 1949b; Miki, 1952; Janković, 1955, 1956; Ram, 1956; Nakano, 1964
10. HALORAGACEAE (*sensu stricto*)	6	*c.* 100	*Haloragis*, *Laurembergia*, *Loudonia*, *Meziella*, *Myriophyllum*, *Proserpinaca*	E, S	Anemophilous	Cosmopolitan (but especially south temperate) Some spp. semi-terrestrial; all aquatic spp. in fresh water	Schindler, 1905; Fernald, 1919, 1924; Pearsall, 1933; Fernald & Griscom, 1935; Tuyama, 1940; Patten, 1954; Löve, 1961
11. HIPPURIDACEAE	1	1	*Hippuris*	E, S	Anemophilous	North temperate and cool South American Fresh water	Schindler, 1904; Polunin, 1959; McCully & Dale, 1961b
12. CALLITRICHACEAE	1	*c.* 25	*Callitriche*	E, Fl, S	Anemophilous; some hydrophilous	Cosmopolitan Some spp. semi-terrestrial; all aquatic spp. in fresh water	Hegelmaier, 1864, 1867; Jörgensen, 1923, 1925; Pax & Hoffmann, 1931; Pearsall, 1934; Fassett, 1951; Soueges, 1952; Schotsman, 1954, 1958, 1961a, b, c, 1962; Jones, 1955c; David, 1958; Mason, 1959; Moar, 1960; Savidge, 1960
13. MENYANTHACEAE	5	*c.* 35	*Menyanthes*, *Fauria*, *Liparophyllum*, *Nymphoides*, *Villarsia*	E, Fl	Entomophilous	Cosmopolitan Fresh water	Lindsey, 1938

TABLE 1.2—contd.

Family	No. of: Genera	No. of: Species	Life form*	Genera	Spore production (Pteridophytes) or pollination (Angiosperms)	Geographical and habitat range	Important publications on, or relevant to, classification and phylogeny of whole or part of family
14. PODOSTEMACEAE (Podostemonaceae)	c. 25	c. 120	S	Podostemum Dicraea Griffithella Indotristicha Mniopsis Mourera Tristicha Terniola Willisia, etc.	Entomophilous, anemophilous or autogamous	Tropical (rarely sub-tropical) Flowing (often torrential) fresh water	Warming, 1881, 1882, 1888, 1891; Willis, 1902, 1914, 1915, 1926; Went, 1910, 1912, 1926; Chodat & Vischer, 1917; Imamura, 1929; Engler, 1930; Fassett, 1939b; van Steenis, 1949d; van Royen, 1951, 1953, 1959a, b
15. HYDROSTACHYACEAE	1	c. 10	S	Hydrostachys	?	Tropical & subtropical African Fresh water	Schloss, 1913

C. Monocotyledons †

Family	No. of: Genera	No. of: Species	Life form*	Genera	Spore production (Pteridophytes) or pollination (Angiosperms)	Geographical and habitat range	Important publications on, or relevant to, classification and phylogeny of whole or part of family
16. BUTOMACEAE	5	c. 10	E, Fl	Butomus Hydrocleys Limnocharis Ostenia Tenagocharis	Entomophilous; some probably autogamous	Temperate & tropical (except Africa south of equator) Fresh water	Buchenau, 1903; Johri, 1936b, 1938a, b; Core, 1941; Pichon, 1946; Roper, 1952; Rao, 1953; van Steenis, 1954; van Oosstroom & Reichgelt, 1964a
17. HYDROCHARITACEAE	14	c. 90	S, Ff	Hydrocharis Blyxa Egeria Elodea Enhalus Halophila Hydrilla Lagarosiphon Limnobium Nechamandra Ottelia Stratiotes Thalassia Vallisneria	Entomophilous, anemophilous, hydro-anemophilous or hydrophilous	Cosmopolitan (mainly in warm regions)—some genera Old, others New World Fresh & salt water	Ostenfeld, 1927a; Wager, 1928; Marie-Victorin, 1931, 1943; Dandy, 1934, 1935; Miki, 1934; Ernst-Schwarzenbach, 1945, 1951, 1953, 1956; den Hartog, 1957b, 1959; Lakshmanan, 1961, 1963a, b, 1965a; St. John, 1961, 1962a, b, 1963, 1964, 1965; Obermeyer, 1964; van Oosstroom & Reichgelt, 1964a
18. ALISMACEAE (Alismataceae)	12	c. 70	E, Fl, S	Alisma Baldellia Burnatia Caldesia Damasonium Echinodorus Limnophyton Luronium Machaerocarpus Ranalisma Sagittaria Wiesneria	Entomophilous; ? few anemophilous or autogamous	Cosmopolitan (but especially north temperate) Fresh water	Buchenau, 1903; Small, 1909; Samuelsson, 1932; Johri, 1935a, b, c, 1936a; Maheshwari & Singh, 1943; Fernald, 1946; Pichon, 1946; Tournay & Lawalrée, 1949; Baldwin & Speese, 1955; Bogin, 1955; Fassett, 1955; den Hartog, 1957a; Lousley, 1957a; Carter, 1960; Pogan, 1961, 1963a, b; Stant, 1964; van Oosstroom & Reichgelt, 1964a

Family	Genera	Species	Genera		Pollination	Distribution	References
19. SCHEUCHZERIACEAE	1	1	*Scheuchzeria*	E	Anemophilous	Cold north temperate Fresh water	Buchenau, 1903; Britton, 1909; Uhl, 1947; Sledge, 1949; van Ooststroom & Reichgelt, 1964a; Tallis & Birks, 1965
20. JUNCAGINACEAE	4	c. 15	*Cycnogeton Maundia Tetroncium Triglochin*	E	Anemophilous	North & south temperate (few in American tropics) Fresh & brackish water	Buchenau, 1903; Britton, 1909; Uhl, 1947; Löve & Löve, 1958b; Löve & Leith, 1961; Hara, 1962; van Ooststroom & Reichgelt, 1964a
21. LILAEACEAE (Heterostylaceae)	1	1	*Lilaea*	E	Anemophilous	Pacific North & South American Fresh (alkaline) water	Taylor, 1909; Uhl, 1947; Agarwal, 1952; Singh, 1965d
22. POSIDONIACEAE	1	2	*Posidonia*	S	Hydrophilous	Mediterranean, S.W. Asiatic & Australasian coasts Salt water	Ostenfeld, 1927b
23. APONOGETONACEAE	1	c. 30	*Aponogeton*	Fl, S	Entomophilous or autogamous	Palaeotropical & southern African Fresh water	Krause & Engler, 1906; Camus, 1923; Jumelle, 1936; van Steenis, 1948; Troupin, 1953; deWit, 1958a, b; van Bruggen, 1962; Singh, 1965c; Bosser & Raynal, 1966; Obermeyer, 1966a; Podlech, 1966
24. ZOSTERACEAE	2	c. 12	*Zostera Phyllospadix*	S	Hydrophilous	Temperate coasts (except South American & West African) Salt water	Taylor, 1909; Ostenfeld, 1927b; Miki, 1933; Tutin, 1936, 1942; van Ooststroom & Reichgelt, 1964b
25. POTAMOGETONACEAE	2	c. 90	*Potamogeton Groenlandia*	Fl, S	Anemophilous; few hydro-anemophilous	Cosmopolitan Fresh (rarely brackish) water	Fryer et al, 1898–1915; Ascherson & Graebner, 1907; Chrysler, 1907; Taylor, 1909; Hagström, 1916; Ostenfeld, 1927b; Fernald, 1932; Dandy, 1937; Miki, 1937; Dandy & Taylor, 1938–42; Ogden, 1943, 1953; Uhl, 1947; Stern, 1961; Clason, 1964; Singh, 1964, 1965a; Sattler, 1965
26. RUPPIACEAE	1	3	*Ruppia*	S	Hydrophilous	Temperate & subtropical Brackish & salt water	Chrysler, 1907; Ascherson & Graebner, 1907; Taylor, 1909; McCann, 1945; Uhl, 1947; Reese, 1962; Singh, 1964, 1965a; van Ooststroom & Reichgelt, 1964b
27. ZANNICHELLIACEAE	6	c. 25	*Zannichellia Althenia Amphibolis Cymodocea Halodule Syringodium*	S	Hydrophilous	Cosmopolitan (but marine genera mainly tropical) Brackish & salt (rarely fresh) water	Ascherson & Graebner, 1907; Chrysler, 1907; Taylor, 1909; Ostenfeld, 1927b; Miki, 1934; Uhl, 1947; den Hartog, 1964a; Singh, 1964, 1965a; van Ooststroom & Reichgelt, 1964b
28. NAIADACEAE	1	c. 35	*Najas*	S	Hydrophilous	Cosmopolitan Fresh (rarely brackish) water	Rendle, 1899, 1900, 1901; Chrysler, 1907; Taylor, 1909; Clausen, 1936; Miki, 1937; Chase, 1947; af Rantzien, 1952; de Wilde, 1961, 1962, 1964; Singh, 1965b; Fore & Mohlenbrock, 1966

TABLE I.2—contd.

Family	No. of: Genera	Species	Genera	Life form*	Spore production (Pteridophytes) or pollination (Angiosperms)	Geographical and habitat range	Important publications on, or relevant to, classification and phylogeny of whole or part of family
29. MAYACACEAE	1	c. 10	Mayaca	E, S	Entomophilous	Tropical American & West African Fresh water	Pilger, 1930; Smith, 1937; van Bruggen, 1958
30. PONTEDERIACEAE	7	c. 30	Pontederia Eichhornia Heteranthera Hydrothrix Monochoria Reussia Scholleropsis	E, S, Ff	Entomophilous (few probably autogamous)	Pan-tropical & temperate American Fresh water	Solms-Laubach, 1883; Schwartz, 1927, 1928, 1930; Alexander, 1937; Backer, 1951f; Castellanos, 1958; Singh, 1962
31. LEMNACEAE	4	c. 28	Lemna Spirodela Wolffia Wolffiella	Ff	? Unspecialised	Cosmopolitan Fresh water	Kurz, 1867a, b; Hegelmaier, 1868, 1896; Engler, 1889; Thompson, 1896, 1898; Rostowzew, 1905; Saeger, 1929; Bravo, 1930; Hicks, 1937; Brooks, 1940; Lawalrée, 1945, 1952; Maheshwari, 1954, 1956a, b, 1958, 1959; Hillman, 1961c; Maheshwari & Kapil, 1963a, b, 1964; van Ooststroom & Reichgelt, 1964c; Daubs, 1965; Alston, 1966
32. SPARGANIACEAE	1	c. 15	Sparganium	E, Fl	Anemophilous	North temperate and Australasian Fresh water	Graebner, 1900; Rydberg, 1903; Fernald, 1922; Backer, 1951c; Grontved, 1954; Cook, 1961a, b; van Ooststroom & Reichgelt, 1964c
33. TYPHACEAE	1	c. 10	Typha	E	Anemophilous	Cosmopolitan Fresh water	Graebner, 1900; Roscoe, 1927; Hotchkiss & Dozier, 1949; Backer, 1951d; Grontved, 1954; van Ooststroom & Reichgelt, 1964c

* Life forms are indicated as follows: E, emergent; Fl, floating-leaved; Ff, free-floating; S, submerged.

† The order in which the families of angiosperms are arranged in the table corresponds with the relative positions they occupy in the phylogenetic system of classification proposed by Hutchinson (1959). The precise circumscription of some families, however, differs from that of Hutchinson. Amongst numerous groups of aquatic vascular plants, family limits are still immensely difficult to set, often because of disagreement or lack of data about quite fundamental morphological problems. Consequently, the composition of certain families (e.g. Nymphaeaceae and Potamogetonaceae) is very largely a matter of opinion. In circumscribing the families of both pteridophytes and angiosperms in the above table and throughout the text, an attempt has been made to minimise confusion and to achieve a balanced recognition of the many current views on morphological and phylogenetic relationships. These guiding principles have resulted in a narrow view of numerous families, e.g. Salviniaceae, Azollaceae, Zosteraceae, Potamogetonaceae, Posidoniaceae, Ruppiaceae, Trapaceae and Hippuridaceae, but a wide view of certain others, e.g. Nymphaeaceae and Zannichelliaceae, where segregation of genera is not considered justified because of inadequate morphological understanding. Even so, readers should appreciate that this treatment is open to criticism and revision.

The tropical Podostemaceae are unique amongst extant vascular plants in their ability to colonise rocky substrates in torrential waters, their astonishing reduction and diversity, and their frequent discrete endemism. Accompanying vegetative specialisation is a trend towards increasing zygomorphy of the flowers. This trend involves the loss of entomophily, rather than increased adaptation to it, and seems to benefit the plant in no way at all. Some highly zygomorphic species appear to have become autogamous, perhaps as a result of the difficulty of achieving cross-pollination. The origin of the Podostemaceae is obscured by the very strange morphology of all its members. However, there are good grounds for believing that the family is old and possibly related to the terrestrial Rosalian families, Saxifragaceae or Crassulaceae (p. 285). The Hydrostachyaceae, comprising perhaps ten or more submerged dioecious species in Africa, especially Natal, shows some resemblances to the Podostemaceae but is poorly known and much in need of detailed study.

The relationships of the remaining dicotyledonous families are also far from clear. The aerial-flowering, entomophilous Menyanthaceae was formerly included within the terrestrial Gentianaceae but was shown by Lindsey (1938) to be quite distinct in numerous features of floral and vegetative anatomy. The genus *Trapa*, which also has aerial entomophilous flowers, is now accepted by most botanists as a discrete monogeneric family, the Trapaceae (sometimes known by the later superfluous name, Hydrocaryaceae). It differs from the largely terrestrial Onagraceae, to which it was formerly assigned, in gross morphological and anatomical characters and in numerous embryological features, such as its eight-nucleate embryo sac, lack of endosperm, and extremely unequal cotyledons (Just, 1946; Ram, 1956; Maheshwari, 1964). The notion that the Trapaceae may not even be closely related to the Onagraceae has been firmly supported by Eames (1953), on the basis of anatomical distinctions, and by Miki (1952), who considered that its affinities lay rather with the Lythraceae.

The Haloragaceae *sensu stricto* (i.e. without the gigantic *Gunnera*) shows considerable floral reduction associated with anemophily. The unusual south temperate bias is principally caused by the largest genus, *Haloragis*, which has many Australasian species: *Myriophyllum*, the second largest genus, is more or less cosmopolitan in range. At various times, derivation of the Haloragaceae from the Onagraceae has been postulated, but this relationship is decidedly tenuous and must have involved tremendous evolutionary modifications. The monotypic *Hippuris* (Hippuridaceae) is a most perplexing plant. It has certain similarities to the Haloragaceae but differs markedly in its sympodial growth, leaf structure, hermaphroditism and extreme floral reduction.

The monocotyledonous families include many of the most widespread and familiar hydrophytes of all life forms. The Alismaceae, Butomaceae and Hydrocharitaceae are grouped by many botanists as the order Alismatales, and the Scheuchzeriaceae, Juncaginaceae, Lilaeaceae, Posidoniaceae, Aponogetonaceae, Zosteraceae, Potamogetonaceae, Ruppiaceae, Zannichelliaceae and Najadaceae as the order Najadales. For many years, following Engler (1879), all these families were lumped together in the rather unnatural order Helobiales, because of their apparently stronger affinities with each other than with remaining monocotyledons. This practice still lingers on in the frequent description of these families as 'Helobian'.

The Alismaceae and Butomaceae both consist largely of entomophilous emergents of freshwater habitats and are very widespread, with a preponderance of temperate species. The Hydrocharitaceae, in contrast, occur primarily in warmer regions and are mostly submerged. Numerous genera are monotypic, e.g. *Enhalus*, *Stratiotes*, or have only very few species, e.g. *Hydrocharis*, *Limnobium*, *Thalassia*. Of the freshwater genera, only two (*Ottelia* and *Vallisneria*) occur in both the neo- and palaeotropics. *Egeria*, *Elodea*, and *Limnobium* are American: all the rest occur in the Old World. The marine genera (*Enhalus*, *Halophila* and *Thalassia*) occur along the tropical coasts of the Indian and Pacific Oceans and the Caribbean, with the greatest density of species in Indo-Malaysian waters (den Hartog, 1957b). Within this family, a rough but interesting parallel may be discerned between three biological trends: from hermaphroditism to unisexuality and dioecism, from ento- or anemophily through hydro-anemophily to true hydrophily, and from freshwater to marine life. In floral morphology, embryological development and vegetative anatomy, the Alismaceae, Butomaceae and Hydrocharitaceae all exhibit both primitive and advanced features and are probably of relatively ancient origin (pp. 278–80, 310–11).

The least specialised families of the Najadales are predominantly temperate (Scheuchzeriaceae, Juncaginaceae, Lilaeaceae) or palaeotropical (Aponogetonaceae), whereas the largest (Potamogetonaceae) and possibly most specialised (Najadaceae) are more or less truly cosmopolitan within their edaphic limits. The various families may be arranged in morphological series displaying trends of floral reduction, pollination behaviour and habitat range comparable with those shown by genera of the Hydrocharitaceae. The Posidoniaceae, Zosteraceae and Zannichelliaceae include all the remaining marine angiosperms. However, hydrophily is attained not only in these sea-grasses but also in several taxa that inhabit fresh and brackish waters, the Najadaceae, Ruppiaceae, *Zannichellia*, and *Althenia*. A few species of *Potamogeton*, e.g. *P. filiformis* and *P. pectinatus*, resemble *Elodea* of the Hydrocharitaceae in their transitional mode of pollination, the microspores floating to the stigmas on the water surface. The relationships within the Najadales are obscure and debatable, but it is highly probable that such families as the Zosteraceae, Zannichelliaceae and especially the Najadaceae, are not primitively simple, as Campbell (1897) and Rendle (1901, 1930) thought, but are in fact highly advanced, due to extreme reduction and specialisation (p. 301).

In the Lemnaceae, most botanists still recognise two additional genera, *Spirodela* and *Wolffiella*, although there are certain grounds for including these in, respectively, *Lemna* and *Wolffia*. These ubiquitous free-floating plants include the smallest known angiosperms, and are remarkable for the profound reduction of their vegetative body to a flat or globose thallus, with a few simple roots or no roots at all. The inflorescence is also greatly modified. The

Lemnaceae have close affinities with and may be derived from the Araceae, especially the free-floating *Pistia* (p. 290).

The monoecious Sparganiaceae and Typhaceae each comprise just a single genus of anemophilous, emergent or rarely floating-leaved hydrophytes. The two families appear to be closely allied in leaf anatomy and pollen morphology as well as gross floral organisation (Erdtman, 1952; Metcalfe, 1963). They may have been derived by reduction and specialisation from terrestrial ancestors which also yielded the contemporary Liliaceae (Hutchinson, 1959). The Mayacaceae and Pontederiaceae are interesting but poorly understood families of essentially tropical distribution. Both appear to be entomophilous, and some members of the Pontederiaceae show a trend towards zygomorphy and heterostyly. Their origins are very obscure. The Mayacaceae may have affinities with the Commelinaceae, a tropical and subtropical family of terrestrial succulent herbs (including the familiar *Tradescantia*). The Pontederiaceae is also close to the latter family in some features, but in others it appears related to the Liliaceae (Hutchinson, 1959).

Many more hydrophytes, too numerous to list fully, are found scattered throughout otherwise terrestrial families of pteridophytes, monocotyledons and dicotyledons. In some families whole genera are more or less aquatic; e.g., *Acorus, Anubias, Cryptocoryne, Lagenandra* (Araceae), *Schoenoplectus* (Cyperaceae), *Glyceria, Phragmites* (Gramineae), *Jussiaea, Ludwigia* (Onagraceae), *Bacopa* (Scrophulariaceae), and *Littorella* (Plantaginaceae). Or only certain species of a genus may be hydrophytes; e.g. some species of *Equisetum* (Equisetaceae), *Crinum* (Amaryllidaceae), *Abolboda* and *Xyris* (Xyridaceae), *Eriocaulon* (Eriocaulaceae), *Juncus* (Juncaceae), *Carex, Cyperus, Eleocharis, Rhynchospora* (Cyperaceae), *Echinochloa, Ischaemum, Leersia, Paspalidium, Phalaris* (Gramineae), *Cardamine, Rorippa* (Cruciferae), *Aeschynomene* (Papilionaceae), *Mimosa* (Mimosaceae), *Ammannia, Lythrum, Rotala* (Lythraceae), *Polygonum* (Polygonaceae), *Alternanthera* (Amaranthaceae), *Asteracantha, Cardanthera, Hygrophila, Justicia, Nomaphila* (Acanthaceae), *Lobelia* (Lobeliaceae), *Mentha* (Labiatae), *Bidens* and *Cotula* (Compositae). In certain families there are aquatic monotypes, e.g. *Calla, Orontium, Peltandra, Pistia* (Araceae), *Philydrum* (Philydraceae), *Vossia* and *Zizania* (Gramineae), *Subularia* (Cruciferae), *Didiplis* and *Decodon* (Lythraceae).

The vast majority of these widely scattered hydrophytes are emergent, but some are heterophyllous and can produce land or water forms, e.g. species of *Armoracia* (Cruciferae), *Limnophila* (Scrophulariaceae), *Oenanthe* (Umbelliferae) and *Ranunculus* (Ranunculaceae). A few are surface-floaters, e.g. *Phyllanthus fluitans* (Euphorbiaceae), *Pistia* (Araceae) and *Trapella* (Pedaliaceae), or live entirely submerged, either rooted or floating freely at some depth, e.g. *Hottonia* (Primulaceae), *Aldrovanda* (Droseraceae) and aquatic species of *Utricularia* (Lentibulariaceae).

Whatever their vegetative modifications, however, all these hydrophytes clearly resemble the terrestrial members of their respective families in floral structure. All have aerial ento- or anemophilous flowers. The total absence of hydrophily, restriction to freshwater habitats, preponderance of emergent life forms, and isolation amidst strongly terrestrial taxa inculcate the firm belief that the aquatic habit is of much more recent origin in these families than in such groups as the Alismatales, Najadales, Nymphaeaceae and Podostemaceae. Very few members of the largest and most advanced monocotyledonous families, Cyperaceae, Gramineae and Orchidaceae, venture into the water and there is an equally conspicuous paucity of hydrophytes amongst the advanced gamopetalous dicotyledons. This evoked from Arber (1919b, 1920) the notion that the highly evolved angiosperms, with marked terrestrial adaptations in both their vegetative and reproductive organs, probably lack the plasticity of the early aquatic pioneers derived from more primitive stocks, and are therefore unable to revert easily to life in the increasingly competitive aquatic environment.

The Salient Features of the
Aquatic Environment

Descriptive ecological surveys are inevitably restricted in both time and scope. They often yield only tantalising static glimpses of the complex dynamic relationships between communities and their environment. The causal effects of environmental factors, the patterns of biotic interactions and the temporal successions of different communities are rarely fully demonstrable, although they may often be inferred on good circumstantial grounds. Reviews of the ecology of a group of organisms frequently concentrate on either the distribution and life-biology of selected species or on the systematic composition of selected communities or habitats. The first approach tends to omit or obscure any coherent picture of natural community structure whilst the second often degenerates into a tedious floristic catalogue. Despite the dearth of ecological data for many parts of the tropics and south temperate zone, to try to review the immense variety of hydrophyte communities without severe over-simplification would require vastly more space than is available here. It would also necessitate a reconciliation of the bewildering terminologies and classifications of Scandinavian and other continental ecologists with those of English and American workers, itself a Herculean task.

Since this book is not concerned solely with the ecology of hydrophytes, a preferable approach seems to be to assess the probable significance of salient features of the aquatic environment to plant and community life and distribution, thereby sketching a background to the treatments of vegetative and reproductive structure and physiology in subsequent chapters. Yet even this approach has its shortcomings. The intricate pattern of environment–community interaction is notoriously difficult to analyse, and the various physiographic, climatic, edaphic and biotic factors tend to be somewhat arbitrarily delineated. Environmental factors themselves interact, and no single one may be deduced as fundamental in controlling plant growth and distribution. Furthermore, as will be discussed in Chapter 12, the flora and fauna themselves may modify the nature of some aquatic habitats so profoundly that one must concur in Westlake's (1959a) acknowledgement that: '. . . the environment is almost as much a product of the community as the community is of the environment.'

For amplification of this limited treatment, readers should consult the classic reference works, notably Volume 1 of Hutchinson's *Treatise on Limnology* (1957); *Grundriss der Limnologie* by Ruttner (1962), also available in an English translation (1963); Welch's *Limnology* (1952) and *Limnological Methods* (1948); Volumes 1 and 2 of Gessner's *Hydrobotanik* (1955, 1959); *Freshwater Biology* by Ward and Whipple (1959); and the recent survey *Limnology in North America*, edited by Frey (1963), which reviewed research pursued in Canada, Greenland, Mexico, the U.S.A., Central America and the West Indies, and is an excellent means of tracing further information. Eminently readable, introductory accounts of the nature and ecology of fresh, estuarine and littoral sea-water are provided by Carpenter (1928), Morgan (1930), Yonge (1949), Macan and Worthington (1951), Coker (1954), Harvey (1957), Hynes (1960), Reid (1961), Needham and Needham (1962), Macan (1963) and Lewis (1964).

THE VARIETY OF AQUATIC HABITATS

Bodies of water inhabited by vascular plants may be arbitrarily divided into four main types:

(a) Standing fresh waters: lakes, reservoirs, ponds, inundated paddy fields, mine-workings, swamps, and also canals and ditches where the current is negligible.
(b) Flowing fresh waters: springs, streams, rivers, bayous and irrigation channels.
(c) Brackish waters: estuaries, lagoons, inland seas, and lakes on salt deposits and in arid regions.
(d) Saline coastal waters: ocean shores, sheltered bays, reefs and quiet creeks.

Within each type innumerable variations are created by local geology, climate and human interference. No given water-body may be considered ecologically as a single entity, except perhaps in terms of water chemistry; each is rather a great complex of changing microhabitats supporting many different communities.

With the exception of man-made and maintained lakes and reservoirs, standing waters are geologically transitory features of the earth's surface. In the course of time their basins are filled up by sediment carried in from the catchment area and eroded from the shoreline, and by dead organisms and products of their decay. Around the margins, in shallower water, the growth of rooted vegetation accelerates sedimentation and consequent modification of the substrate. Some waters change more rapidly than others: the visible stage of development is not necessarily an accurate indication of age.

The conditions of life in a lake are closely related to its origin and the geology of its surroundings. Tectonic lakes, exemplified by Loch Ness and the lakes of the East African Rift Valley, were created by longitudinal faulting of the earth's crust and hence are generally long, narrow and relatively deep, mainly with rocky shorelines. Some natural lakes are volcanic in origin: the crater of an extinct volcano may fill with water, as in L. Nkugute in Uganda, or basaltic lava may flow from fissures in the earth's surface, solidify and later subside, leaving a shallow depression, as in L. Neagh in Ireland. Many lakes in the north temperate zone originated through glacial activity. At higher altitudes on harder rocks, glaciers often gouged deep clefts which, when the climate ameliorated and the ice retreated, became rocky lake basins dammed by moraines deposited at the forefront of the original glacier. Many lakes in the palaeogenic Highlands of Scotland and in north-west England were so formed. The retreat and disintegration of ice sheets over plateaus and lowlands on softer rocks, and the discharge of fluvio-glacial drift-material from existing valleys left behind scattered masses of melting ice isolated by mixed boulders, stones and clay. In the cavities, or kettle-holes, left by this melting outwash there developed relatively shallow lakes, extensive areas of which may be seen in Wisconsin, U.S.A., and on the plains around the Baltic Sea. Lochs Leven, Lindores and Watten are less spectacular Scottish examples. The remaining principal lake types are the sinks developing by solution on surface limestone, as near Durness in the extreme north of Scotland and in parts of Florida, U.S.A., and the brackish or saline lakes developing on natural salt deposits, as in the English Midlands, and especially where evaporation greatly exceeds precipitation, as in Utah and the Dakotas, U.S.A.

Tectonic, volcanic and glacial rock-basin lakes usually start with little sediment, and erosion of their shoreline yields mainly large rock fragments, gravels and coarse sands. Inwashed sediment, derived from the (usually) desolate, infertile, hard-rock catchment area, is mainly organic and deficient in basic silt. As a result of their exposure and turbulence, poor nutrient status and largely inhospitable substrates, such lakes tend to be sparsely colonised and biologically 'primitive'. In contrast, shallower and more sheltered lakes on soft sedimentary rocks or glacial drift usually start with, and continue to receive, a rich supply of fine inorganic silts and clays, and so tend to become densely colonised and very productive, especially if the catchment area includes fertile agricultural soils.

Man has created many aquatic habitats. Disused mine-workings, stone-quarries and gravel- and clay-pits soon fill with water and become colonised by hydrophytes. The needs of agriculture, communication, industry and domestic life have resulted in an immense range of standing and flowing waters, from farm-ponds, canal networks and irrigation systems to artificial reservoirs and lakes as vast as Kariba, which has a surface area of about 450 000 hectares (1750 square miles).

A river differs from standing water not only in having a continuous current but also in draining a greater variety of rocks and in encountering geological irregularities and artificial obstacles which progressively modify its course and chemical composition, introducing a multitude of local peculiarities. As a result of this individual behaviour, any naive textbook classification of a river into, for example, torrential upper, swift middle, and sluggish lowland courses is valueless. Similarly, classifications based upon fish populations (Carpenter, 1928; Huet, 1954; Illies, 1955) or plant communities (Butcher, 1933) are too restricted in scope to be of general ecological application. It is the very local factors of the microhabitat which are significant to both flora and fauna (Percival and Whitehead, 1929; Ricker, 1937; Berg, 1948).

Rivers, like lakes, evolve as time passes: swift-flowing reaches become shorter, slow-flowing ones longer, and the forging of the current creates new habitats, such as oxbow lakes. The flood plain flanking the lowermost reaches is greatly enriched by the deposition of silt and organic debris. Most of the largest flood plains occur in the warmer regions of the world, for example Egypt, India, Pakistan, Nigeria and the southern U.S.A., where the Nile, Ganges, Brahmaputra, Niger and Mississippi may overflow for great distances, creating permanently inundated expanses, areas flooded only after heavy rains, and permanently marshy areas. Similar lakes and swamps may also develop far inland where the terrain is suitably flat or where subsidence occurs, as in the 'Sudd' region of the White Nile in the Sudan, the Lukanga swamp of Zambia, and the Okovango river system in Botswana. In north temperate countries many smaller flood plains have been obliterated by rigid control of the rivers and reclamation of the fertile alluvial soil.

Estuarine and coastal waters differ from freshwater habitats in the complex influences of salinity, fluctuation of water level and sometimes severe wave action. Many estuaries have been drastically modified by constant dredging, which alters the substrate and counteracts the deposition of silt, and by industrial activity in associated ports.

For more than a century, natural fresh and salt waters in densely populated and heavily industrialised regions, especially in western Europe and North America, have become increasingly polluted. In large and deep bodies of water, where the biological equilibrium is reasonably stable and the changes induced by living organisms are small and slow, the impact of sudden pollution is relatively slight. In very shallow lakes and almost all flowing waters, plants and animals occupy a more significant volume of the habitat and pollution here produces gross ecological imbalance. Pollution by sewage and other domestic products, poisonous industrial effluents, pesticides and radioactive wastes has been steadily increasing and must now be treated as an integral feature of the aquatic environment. So far, it has been treated principally, indeed too often exclusively, as a physiochemical phenomenon. Its biological, and particularly botanical, consequences have been much neglected.

LIGHT TRANSMISSION UNDER WATER, AND THE DOWNWARD
PENETRATION OF ROOTED VEGETATION

The influence of intensity and spectral composition of light on the distribution of aquatic vegetation has been discussed by Shirley (1935, 1945) and Gessner (1955). Rooted plants may colonise suitable substrates down to a depth where the light intensity is only 1 to 4 per cent of the average intensity at the surface of the water. Pearsall and Ullyott (1933) drew attention to the practical difficulties of determining this depth limit especially when the flora is scanty. The cover distribution of plants in clean and shallow waters may often be conveniently recorded by aerial photography (e.g. D.S.I.R., 1959; Edwards

FIG. 2.1. Photographing the cover of hydrophytes in the shallow English R. Ivel by means of an automatic camera suspended from a balloon. (From D.S.I.R., 1959, by courtesy of the Controller of Her Majesty's Stationery Office, London.)

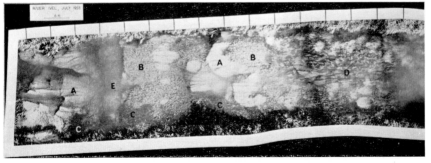

FIG. 2.2. An example of a mosaic photograph obtained by the device shown in Fig. 2.1. The hydrophyte cover is almost complete and comprises: A, *Callitriche* spp.; B, *Berula erecta*; C, *Ranunculus pseudofluitans*; D, *Hippuris vulgaris*; E is a strip from which the plants had been cropped. 1cm $\simeq$ 2.6 m. (From D.S.I.R., 1959, by courtesy of the Controller of Her Majesty's Stationery Office, London.)

and Brown, 1960; and Figs. 2.1, 2.2), but the depth distribution can be accurately determined only by a long and tedious series of soundings.

The actual depth at which the limiting intensity is reached, and the quality of light penetrating to any given depth, vary from site to site, according to (a) the colour of the water, which may become yellow or brown due to dissolved organic matter derived from the substrate, the catchment area, or polluting wastes; (b) the concentration of suspended organic and inorganic particles, brought in by affluents and pollutants and varying with turbulence and flow; and (c) the concentration of phyto- and zooplankton, which may fluctuate seasonally. Several specific examples will illustrate the interplay of these three factors. In Wisconsin, Rickett (1921, 1924), Juday (1934), Wilson (1935, 1937, 1941) and Potzger and van Engel (1942) recorded lower limits of rooted vegetation varying from 2·3 to 3 m in Sweeney L. and Little John L., both highly coloured, to 5 m in Weber L., containing much organic matter, 7 m in Muskellunge L., a fairly clear poor-water lake, and 10 m in Green L., a rich and productive, yet clear-water lake. Denniston (1922) noted a limit of 5 m in L. Mendota at a time of abundant phytoplankton, but Rickett (1921) found rooted plants down to 6·5 m in certain sites in the same lake.

In northern England Pearsall (1918a, 1920) observed limits of 2·75 m in Bassenthwaite, a peat-stained lake; 4 m in Esthwaite, a rich-water lake turbid with phytoplankton; 6·5 m in Windermere, also rich and productive; 7·7 m in Wastwater and 10 m in Ennerdale, both clear unproductive lakes. The limit in Windermere was later found by Pearsall and Hewitt (1933) to have risen to 4·3 m, and the penetration of blue light (510 to 400 mμ) to have substantially decreased. A subsequent study of seasonal changes in the lake by Pearsall and Ullyott (1934) revealed that during the early growth and maximal activity of rooted hydrophytes the light intensity at the lower limit of 4·3 m was only 1·5 to 2·5 per cent of full surface daylight, whereas at other times it was 4 to 6 per cent. The minimal light intensities coincided with a diatom climax in mid-June and a dense bloom of blue-green algae in early August (Fig. 2.3). In his survey of Scottish lochs, Spence (1964) found the greatest colonised depths in clear calcareous waters, shallower limits in poor to fairly rich brown waters, and the least colonised depths in rich waters possessing abundant plankton.

Submerged bryophytes sometimes extend to greater depths than rooted angiosperms. West (1910) recorded dense beds of *Fontinalis* to 12·2 m in the clear L. Baile in Scotland, whilst Fassett (1930) and Juday (1934) observed a thick carpet of *Drepanocladus* and *Fontinalis* at 18 to 20 m in the exceptionally transparent Crystal L. in Wisconsin. Charophytes may penetrate deeper still: *Nitella* has been found down to 27 m in the volcanic L. Towada in northern Japan (Jimbô et al., 1955).

With few exceptions, however, the limited penetration of light confines the rooted vascular plants of lakes to the uppermost 10 m or less, the so-called photic zone.

In rivers and streams, the light climate resembles that in oceans and lakes in being greatly influenced by the general decrease in irradiance with increasing depth and by the selective attenuation of certain wavelengths by the water and dissolved solutes. It may also be compared with the woodland light climate in the importance of shading effects, here exerted by marginal vegetation and by floating and submerged hydrophytes themselves. In addition to these features, the light climate in flowing waters has a unique variability as a result of changes in turbidity (Westlake, 1966a). In various British, European and American rivers, the percentage of the surface light intensity which penetrated to a depth

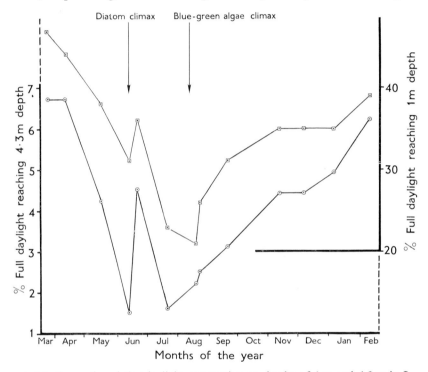

FIG. 2.3. Seasonal variation in light penetration to depths of 1 m and 4·3 m in L. Windermere in 1932–33. (From data of Pearsall and Ullyott, 1934.)

of 1 m was noted by Westlake to vary from 40 to 50 per cent to as little as 1 to 15 per cent on different occasions. In a turbid sewage effluent the light was sometimes virtually extinguished at 1 m depth and never exceeded about 25 per cent of the surface intensity, whilst in the R. Nile only a 1×10^{-2} to 1×10^{-7} fraction of the surface intensity reached 1 m.

In rivers turbid with algal blooms, the wavelengths most rapidly attenuated are those maximally absorbed by the photosynthetic pigments. The water itself absorbs wavelengths mainly in the infrared and ultraviolet bands of the spectrum, whilst organic solutes cause a rather rapid attenuation of the blue, violet and ultraviolet. In the absence of phytoplankton, transmission of red and green wavelengths is least altered, although covers of vascular hydrophytes themselves absorb much red and blue light, and so greatly increase the proportion of yellow-green in the light penetrating to lower depths (Westlake, 1964, 1966a.)

Turbidity may also be created by suspended silt or waste solids from mines, quarries, coal-washeries, biscuit factories, meat- and egg-processing plants, and sewage effluents. Suspended solids absorb light fairly uniformly in all bands of the spectrum. In badly polluted rivers the overall extinction of light is often rapid. Owens and Edwards (1964) found at one site in the R. Tame in the English Midlands, where the concentration of suspended solids was 220 ppm, only a 1×10^{-6} fraction of the surface light intensity reached a depth of 1 m. The resulting opacity of the water may completely inhibit photosynthesis and the settling particles may smother the vegetation. Surber (1953) reported the complete elimination of all submerged plants from part of the Menominee R. in Michigan by suspended ochre particles washed in from mines upstream.

DIRECT INFLUENCES OF TEMPERATURE

Fluctuations of temperature in aquatic habitats are generally much less violent than in the aerial environment and seem to have little influence on the distribution of many hydrophytes. Even so, they are probably significant for the hour-to-hour metabolism of any species and may exert an important indirect influence in some standing waters through their interaction with oxygen concentration and nutrient supply. Although the temperature at different depths in temperate lakes varies little in winter, there develops in spring and early summer, as a result of surface heating, a demarcation of an upper warm layer, the epilimnion, and a lower colder layer, the hypolimnion (Fig. 2.10). The epilimnion is thoroughly mixed and its depth progressively increased by currents and eddies set up by winds and by the entry of warm water from inflowing rivers. The hypolimnion is less disturbed, although oscillation of the water over the irregular lake-bed may create some turbulence and mixing. Between the epi- and hypolimnions, the zone of sharpest change in temperature per unit depth, known as the thermocline, becomes increasingly well-defined as the summer proceeds. In late summer and autumn heat is lost from the surface water and the epilimnion cools; gales eventually mix the layers of water, restoring the slight winter gradient of temperature from surface to bottom. Permanent thermal stratification is often found in deep standing waters in the tropics, as in L. Tanganyika and numerous Indonesian lakes (Ruttner, 1962). In the African crater lake, Nkugute, Beadle (1963) found that the hypolimnion, extending from 15 m deep to the bottom, at 58 m, was quite uncirculated. In many stratified lakes, whether in tropical or temperate regions, the photic zone and epilimnion roughly coincide. Even where the photic zone includes part or all of the thermocline the overall temperature range from the surface to uncolonised depth is not great. It is extremely unlikely that temperature influences the distribution of aquatic vegetation in any given site.

Seasonal and daily variations of temperature in flowing waters are greatest in summer and/or at lower altitudes, where the air temperatures fluctuate more and where there is an influx of surface run-off water affected by local weather conditions. At any one point, however, turbulence tends to minimise fluctuations of temperature and may reduce the diurnal amplitude, from the early morning minimum to the afternoon maximum, to as little as 1°C. Diurnal fluctuations may be irregular if the weather is unsettled, and even in reaches where the current velocity and turbulence are appreciable the daily range in summer months may be 6 to 10°C or even more (Macan, 1958; Crisp *et al.*, *in litt.*). Wide variations occur in shallow sluggish reaches where surface heating is marked or where water is withdrawn to cool industrial machinery and the condensers of electricity generating stations and then discharged back into the river. In such sites the temperature may reach its maximum in the evening and the diurnal range may be 8°C or more (Alexander *et al.*, 1935; D.S.I.R., 1959).

Surface heating is greatest in stagnant ponds, canals and swamps. The consequent temperature stratification is often greater in turbid than in clear ponds of similar size and morphology (Butler, 1963). The average temperature in a large pond is generally close to the average air temperature and tends to vary in the same direction, although a divergence may sometimes occur, as when bright sunshine heats the water but an accompanying cold wind lowers the air temperature (Macan and Maudsley, 1966). The mean temperatures in static waters of small area and depth may be well above those of lakes and rivers in the same region (Fig. 2.4), and as a result the plant communities generally reach their population climax earlier in the year.

The greater uniformity of the temperature regime in aquatic, as compared with aerial, habitats is perhaps partly responsible for the vast geographical range of numerous hydrophytes of all life forms. Some, such as *Ceratophyllum demersum*, *Lemna minor* and *Phragmites communis*, are more or less cosmopolitan. Others range less widely but exhibit notable latitudinal extension: the New World *Sagittaria montevidensis*, for example, is distributed in both north and south temperate zones and in tropical latitudes, whilst *S. latifolia*, a temperate North American species, extends south to tropical sites (Bogin, 1955). That temperature does not fundamentally control the distribution of many species is also suggested by the extent of their altitudinal range. Magnin (1893) found over 20 species ranged from 200 to 1000 m in the Jura mountains. *Menyanthes trifoliata* ascends to 1000 m in the British Isles (Warburg, 1962), whilst species of *Callitriche*, *Lemna* and *Myriophyllum* were recorded to above 2400 m near Chimborazo in Ecuador (Spruce, 1908). In India, *Pistia stratiotes* ascends from sea level to about 1000 m; *Indotristicha ramosissima* to 1200 m; *Aeschynomene indica*, *Dicraea stylosa* and *Zeylanidium olivaceum* to at least 1500 m: *Potamogeton nodosus*, common throughout the plains of India and South Andamans, reaches 2700 m in the Sikkim Himalayas (Subramanyam, 1962). In Malaysia, *Ceratophyllum demersum*, *Monochoria vaginalis* and *Typha angustifolia* extend from the lowlands up to 1500 to 1700 m (van Steenis, 1949a; Backer, 1951d, f).

Not all hydrophytes, however, display such extensive ranges of temperature tolerance. Some species penetrate the tropics only at high altitudes, where average temperatures are lower and resemble more closely those prevailing in the temperate areas of their distribution. The North American ranges of *Brasenia schreberi, Nymphaea odorata* and *Proserpinaca palustris*, for example, reach their southernmost limits in the volcanic lakes of El Salvador. Although well within the tropics (latitude 13 to 14°N) these lakes are situated above 1000 m and have an average November surface temperature of only 18°C. Here, too, the South American *Eleocharis sellowiana* reaches its northernmost station (Fassett and Armitage, 1961, in Cole, 1963). Essentially a cool north

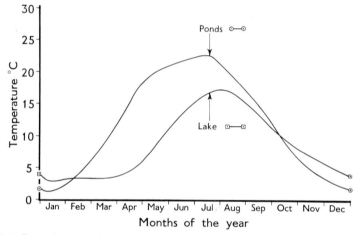

FIG. 2.4. Generalised graph showing disparity in average temperature of surface waters between a typical temperate lake and ponds in the same area. (Based on data of Pearsall, 1920.)

temperate plant, *Sparganium emersum* extends southward to Australasia but its occurrences in the intervening tropics of central Sumatra and New Guinea are principally at altitudes of 1500 to 2400 m (Backer, 1951c). *Callitriche platycarpa*, another north temperate taxon, has similarly been recorded from mountain sites between 2700 and 3225 m in New Guinea (Backer, 1951e). Several tropical and subtropical species have been successfully introduced to cool temperate localities but only where the climate is exceptionally mild or where the water is artificially warmed by the effluents from factories, as in certain British stations for *Egeria densa, Najas graminea* and *Vallisneria spiralis*. Further indication of the importance of temperature for some hydrophytes is given by the post-glacial migrations of several European species and by the confinement in the British Isles of certain Mediterranean plants to those parts of south and west England, Ireland and Scotland that have a mild oceanic climate.

The marine angiosperms, inhabiting coastal waters from about the high-water mark to a depth of 10 to 15 m, also seem to be influenced by temperature.

Three genera—*Phyllospadix, Posidonia* and *Zostera*—occur mainly in temperate seas whilst *Amphibolis, Cymodocea, Enhalus, Halodule, Halophila, Syringodium* and *Thalassia* are subtropical and tropical genera found especially in the Indian and Pacific Oceans. Setchell's (1920) study of their distribution paints a clear picture of precise latitudinal restriction. Classifying the sea into five latitudinal zones, he found that eighteen of the thirty-four species he considered were confined to his tropical zone (mean maximum temperature above 25°C), four to the subtropical zone (20 to 25°C) and four to the temperate zone (15 to 20°C). Only *Zostera marina* ventured into the two colder boreal zones. Six species extended through two of the warmer zones and one species (*Halophila ovalis*) was distributed, in parts of its range, through subtropical and temperate as well as tropical zones. Miki (1934) extended this study and confirmed Setchell's conclusions, finding that all three of the marine Hydrocharitaceae (*Enhalus, Halophila* and *Thalassia*) are indeed megathermic, occurring principally where minimum temperatures do not fall below 20°C. The northernmost stations of *Enhalus acoroides* and *Thalassia hemprichii*, for example, appear to be correlated with February water isotherms of 23 and 21°C respectively. Miki also found that *Halophila ovalis*, in its temperate extensions to Japan and Tasmania, reaches waters with a February isotherm of only 10°C but is sterile in these cold sites and reproduces sexually only in the tropics.

DISSOLVED SUBSTANCES (OTHER THAN GASES) OF BIOLOGICAL
SIGNIFICANCE

Inorganic nutrients. There is no reason to doubt that vascular hydrophytes require the same macro- and micronutrients that are essential for the healthy growth of terrestrial green plants. Rooted emergents probably obtain these exclusively from the substrate whereas submerged and floating-leaved plants may absorb ions from both the substrate and the water. Free-floating species must obtain all their nutrients from the water: Pearsall (1921a) found this life form abundant only in waters rich in electrolytes, especially calcium, magnesium, nitrate and silicate. The ions of major metabolic significance in fresh water are potassium, calcium, magnesium, iron, ammonium, nitrate, sulphate, chloride, phosphate and bicarbonate.

The ionic content of standing waters usually reflects the geology and fertility of the catchment area (Rodhe, 1949). A higher total concentration and greater variety of ions occur in lakes in cultivated drainage basins in softer calcareous rocks than in those on older hard rocks at high altitudes. Pearsall (1921a) remarked upon the paucity of nitrates and calcium and low total ion concentration in the soft water of the Cumbrian lakes, situated in hard Ordovician and Silurian slates and grits. In contrast, the lakes of southern Wisconsin, draining chalk and limestone, are rich in calcium, magnesium and bicarbonate and their water is hard and alkaline (Wilson, 1939). Total hardness or alkalinity (dissolved carbonate and bicarbonate, expressed as ppm $CaCO_3$) is often used as an arbitrary basis for classifying waters into nutrient types (e.g. Zimmermann, in Curtis, 1959). Spence (1964) observed that of the Scottish lakes he surveyed

40 per cent had 1 to 15 ppm CaCO$_3$, a class he regarded as nutrient-poor, 40 per cent had 16 to 60 ppm and were considered moderately rich, whilst only 20 per cent had more than 60 ppm and could be deemed rich water.

Receiving tributaries from a wider area, and often themselves traversing several geological formations, rivers may ultimately have a more heterogeneous ionic content. Locally, however, the composition of the water is still clearly related to the surface geology. Kemp (1963) found in Natal that streams from sandstone and granite have marked similarities but differ from those draining Beaufort and Ecca rocks in having higher proportions of sodium and chloride, as do waters from Dwyka rock, although these have a lower proportion of silica. Streams draining chalk formations, e.g. the R. Chess, R. Ivel and R. Test in southern England (Owens and Edwards, 1962), usually have high total hardness, 100 to 300 ppm CaCO$_3$ or more, and are typically nutrient-rich.

No useful purpose would be served by enumerating here representative analyses of natural and artificial waters, as are given by Suckling (1944) and many of the ecological papers cited in this and other chapters, for the specific concentrations and relative proportions of ions in any one habitat are in fact extremely variable. Local, seasonal and annual variations render single samples taken at a particular place and time quite inadequate to indicate the ionic composition of a river or lake. The causes of these variations include precipitation and evaporation, the activities of plankton and rooted hydrophytes themselves, processes occurring in bottom deposits, and pollution. The concentrations of potassium, nitrate, chloride, phosphate and sulphate, for example, are supplemented by precipitation. Gorham (1958) revealed a significant correlation between the prevailing south-west winds and high concentrations of chloride in rain water falling in the English Lake District; and remarked in a later paper (Gorham, 1961) on the similarity of the total concentration and proportions of the various ions in rain water over Newfoundland and in the water of lakes in Nova Scotia. The chloride concentration in freshwater lakes generally has been found by Holden (1961) to vary with the distance of the lake from the coast.

All planktonic algae absorb nitrates and phosphates for protein synthesis: diatoms also absorb silicates from which to build their skeleton. Increasing plankton populations may use dissolved nutrients faster than they are replenished from the catchment area, until the short supply of one ion becomes limiting, as does silicate for *Asterionella* in L. Windermere (Lund, 1950). Pearsall (1930) observed that in nine English lakes the minimal concentrations of iron, silicate, phosphate phosphorus and nitrate nitrogen were reached in summer after the phytoplankton climax. Where the plankton flora is varied there may be selective exhaustion of different ions as different species wax and wane.

Nitrates may also be extracted from rivers (D.S.I.R., 1963, 1964), reservoirs (Houghton, 1963), and presumably lakes, and either converted to ammonia or nitrogen by denitrification processes occurring under substantially anaerobic conditions in the bottom muds, or assimilated in protein synthesis by benthic micro-organisms. Owens and Edwards (1963) observed the extraction of about 1 g nitrate nitrogen/m² day at 20°C from the overlying water by a river mud covered with an algal bloom.

The wide variation in ionic composition experienced by most waters has been invoked to explain, at least in part, the fact that many hydrophytes seem to lack strong preferences for particular types of water and cannot be simply classified as calcifuge or calcicole. Pearsall (1920), and later Tansley (1949), concluded that in the English Lakes variations in water chemistry do not influence the distribution of rooted vascular plants unless they are correlated with variations in the nature of the substrate. However, Spence (1964) emphasised that by comparison with the Scottish lochs he examined, the English Lakes display far less variation in ionic composition and nutrient status (in terms of hardness) and may therefore be regarded as a single, more nearly homogeneous, water regime. It is also pertinent to note that the apparent wide tolerance of most hydrophytes has been assessed by gross and rather ill-defined criteria, such as total hardness. Judged by finer criteria the distributions of given species or life forms might become more meaningful. In their study of submerged communities in several Wisconsin lakes, Swindale and Curtis (1957) found positive correlations between, on the one hand, certain prominent species of large stature or rosette habit and, on the other hand, respectively higher or lower conductivities, pH, and concentrations of calcium, magnesium, nitrate, marl and organic matter. Similarly, Forsberg and Forsberg (1961) established a relationship between the distribution of *Najas marina* in European fresh-water habitats and their conductivity. Spence (1964) observed that the Scottish lochs colonised by *Subularia aquatica* are typically poor in electrolytes whereas those colonised by *Potamogeton praelongus* are typically rich, and that a *Lobelia dortmanna-Juncus bulbosus* var. *fluitans* association characterises waters of far lower alkalinity than those in which a *Potamogeton filiformis-Chara* association typically occurs. He concluded that, at least in Scotland, it is the general water chemistry of a lake that controls whether or not a given species can grow in it. However, the possibility should not be overlooked that interacting biotic factors may create misleading plant-water relationships. *Isoetes lacustris* and *I. setacea*, for example, are often regarded as habitués of nutrient-poor oligotrophic waters. Yet they have been recorded at a few eutrophic sites in Wales and Sweden. Seddon (1965) suggested that these two species are gener-ally absent from eutrophic waters as a result of their inferior competitive powers and they thrive in such sites only where coarse substrates and turbu-lence inhibit colonisation by reed-swamp and caulescent submerged plants.

Soluble Organic Substances. It has been known for over 40 years that un-polluted fresh and saline waters contain appreciable concentrations of dissolved (or colloidal) organic matter. In some lakes the total amount may considerably exceed that of particulate organic matter, and Fogg (1959) emphasised that although the average total concentration (about 5 ppm) is small compared with that of dissolved mineral substances, the concentration of organic carbon in some poorly productive lakes may be equal to the concentration of carbon as carbon dioxide and bicarbonate ions. In lake or sea water more than one hundred times as much nitrogen may occur in dissolved organic form as in nitrates and ammonium ions.

The nature of all these dissolved or colloidal organic compounds is not yet known. One of the earliest studies revealed the presence of free amino acids such as cystine, histidine, tryptophane and tyrosine in the Wisconsin lake, Mendota (Peterson *et al.*, 1925); these and other amino acids, organic acids, sugars, purines and polypeptides have subsequently been detected in many waters. Auxin-like compounds and vitamins such as biotin, cobalamin, niacin and thiamin have been found in concentrations as low as one part per thousand million in the sea and in ponds and lakes.

The concentration of dissolved organic matter in a particular lake is remarkably constant, scarcely varying with either time or depth. Little is known of the source of identified compounds. Fractions may be derived from both drainage of surrounding land and *in situ* decomposition of aquatic organisms. From their investigations of over 500 Wisconsin lakes, Birge and Juday (1927, 1934) concluded that the plankton is the principal source. Numerous planktonic and benthic algae, belonging to different taxonomic groups, are now known to release extracellular organic compounds. Various ectocrines (antibiotic- and hormone-type compounds having potent effects on the growth, behaviour or reproduction of similar or different organisms) may be actively secreted by the algal cells, whilst polysaccharides may be leached out of their mucilaginous sheaths. Sugars, amino acids and perhaps other organic molecules probably escape by diffusion through the leaky cell membranes (Watt, 1966).

The significance of dissolved organic matter to hydrophytes may be direct, through its influence on metabolism and growth, as well as indirect, through richly coloured substances modifying light transmission below the surface. Perhaps the greatest importance of certain amino acids, organic acids and polypeptides lies in their ability to form chelate complexes with manganese, zinc, copper, iron and phosphate, thereby providing an accessible reservoir of these ions whilst simultaneously preventing their becoming toxic or being precipitated (Fogg and Westlake, 1955; Shapiro, 1957, 1958).

Soluble Pollutants. The critical toxic components of industrial effluents include heavy metals, detergents, aromatic solvents, acids, alkalis and salts. Their toxicity generally increases with rise in temperature or fall in dissolved oxygen content, and may be variously influenced by the pH and ionic composition of the water. Copper, lead, iron and zinc occur in many industrial wastes and may also be leached into natural waters from mines. Chromates and cyanides reach aquatic habitats in effluents from electroplating and engineering factories; chlorine from the bleaching involved in paper and textile manufacture; ammonia, thiocyanates, mono- and dihydric phenols in the spent still-liquor from gas works. Synthetic detergents used in industry and ship-cleaning are common in many inland and estuarine waters, where they often create billowing masses of foam. Acidic, alkaline and greasy wastes issue from many sources, such as the tanning, meat-processing and woollen industries. Sewage, the most complex pollutant even after purification, carries ammonia, copper, zinc, cyanide, phenols, detergents, and much organic matter rich in nitrogen and carbon (D.S.I.R., 1958–1964).

Although minimised by dilution in large bodies of water, the effects of these effluents in rivers, canals and shallow waters generally are penetrating and drastic, though they are in time dissipated by dilution, oxidation and precipitation, and adsorption on the substrate (Hynes, 1959).

The toxicity of most poisons to specific hydrophytes under different environmental conditions has yet to be thoroughly investigated, but chlorine, chromates, cyanides, heavy metals, phenols and aromatic solvents are probably toxic to all, even in low concentrations. Certain solvents are in fact employed in America to eradicate aquatic plants from irrigation systems. Mixtures of poisons are often far more toxic than their constituents, through either mutual enhancement of their physiological action, or formation of ultratoxic compounds, such as the cyanogen chloride produced in mixtures containing chlorine and thiocyanates (Hynes, 1960).

In one of the first comprehensive studies of a pollution problem, Carpenter (1926) examined the biological changes in certain Welsh trout and salmon rivers that were recovering from contamination by lead (and zinc) derived from disused mines. Although some cryptogams and invertebrates became re-established in mildly polluted reaches, it was only when intermittent pollution had quite ceased, after several years even, that *Callitriche*, batrachian *Ranunculi* and other angiosperms reappeared, together with molluscs and fishes. In contrast, the susceptibility of vascular hydrophytes to copper appears to be lower than that of fishes, many invertebrates and algae. In the R. Dove, in water polluted with the relatively low concentration of 0·12 ppm copper, Pentelow and Butcher (1938) found that whereas the algal flora was sparse and unusual and only two species of animal were present, the higher plants were abundant and unaffected. Heavy metals deposited near roots and rhizomes may be responsible for the yellowing of the foliage of emergents, e.g. *Glyceria maxima*, seen in habitats polluted by sewage (Hynes, 1960).

Some hydrophytes are susceptible to low concentrations of anionic detergents, of which about 4 to 6 ppm are commonly present in most purified sewage effluents (Southgate, 1957). Teepol (an alkyl sulphate) and several alkyl benzene sulphonates are lethal to *Apium, Callitriche, Groenlandia* and *Ranunculus* species at concentrations of 2 to 6 ppm, whereas the non-ionic Lissapol has no deleterious effect, even at 20 ppm (Ministry of Housing, 1956; Roberts, 1959).

Pollution by radioactive wastes creates the terrible hazard of accumulation by living tissues and subsequent release of high concentrations when the organisms die. Preliminary surveys of samples of *Apium nodiflorum, Callitriche* sp., *Elodea canadensis, Glyceria* sp., *Rorippa nasturtium-aquaticum* and other hydrophytes collected from rivers in south-east England in 1957 showed levels of total β-activity from 10 to 1000 counts/min g ash (D.S.I.R., 1958). Further sampling of a well-colonised stretch of the R. Lee in 1958 revealed a significant correlation between the levels of total $\beta\gamma$-activity in river water and in a species of *Ranunculus*. The concentration factor (activity per g material divided by activity per ml water) was calculated as 200 (on a wet weight basis), 2000 (on dry weight) and 6000 (on ash). The bulk of the total activity was attributable to isotopes of ruthenium, zirconium and rare earths presumed to have reached the river as fall-out in rain (D.S.I.R., 1959).

Hydrophytes absorb radioactive isotopes from dilute solutions at rapid rates until the internal concentration greatly exceeds the external; further slow uptake accompanies the increase in organic matter during growth. Concentration factors may sometimes be excessively high and are perhaps consistently higher than for the corresponding stable isotopes.

The concentration factors for the uptake of ^{89}Sr by excised terminal leaflets of *Rorippa nasturtium-aquaticum* are lower in hard water than in soft, probably

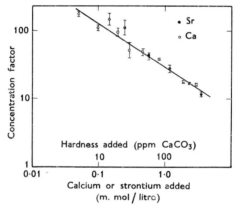

FIG. 2.5. Effect of calcium or strontium carrier on concentration of ^{89}Sr by excised terminal leaflets of *Rorippa nasturtium-aquaticum*. (Initial total hardness: 20 ppm as $CaCO_3$; period of contact: 7 days; temperature: 21°C; limits indicate standard error of five replicates.) (From D.S.I.R., 1959, by courtesy of the Controller of Her Majesty's Stationery Office, London.)

because stable Ca and Sr, in equivalent amounts, have similar inhibitory effects on the uptake of ^{89}Sr, the concentration factor decreasing with increasing Ca or Sr concentration or hardness (as calcium carbonate) (D.S.I.R., 1959; Fig. 2.5). When transferred to a dilution of the original contaminated hard or soft water, uptake of ^{89}Sr by excised leaflets continues, but at a reduced rate. Some of the active strontium is released from leaflets transferred to uncontaminated water of similar chemical composition, the release being most marked in the first 24 h after transfer and greater from killed than living leaflets. The length of exposure to contaminated water has no influence upon the percentage of activity subsequently released in clean water. Uptake of ^{89}Sr by rooted specimens in flowing water during a 5-week experimental period is similar, in its initial rapidity and later diminution, and in the magnitude of the concentration factors, to that of excised leaflets in short-term experiments (4 to 14 days). The retarding effect of increasing hardness upon the uptake of ^{89}Sr has also been demonstrated with *Elodea canadensis, Myriophyllum spicatum* and *Ranunculus pseudofluitans* in flowing water (D.S.I.R., 1960; Fig. 2.6). Bachmann (1961) has studied the uptake of radioactive heavy metals by aquatic plants.

Radioactive waste may also be absorbed by mud deposits. [89]Sr taken up by mud is rapidly released if the mud is agitated in clean water, and slowly leached if the mud remains static. The similar, almost complete uptake of [144]Ce and ^{137}Cs may or may not be reversible. Both phenomena could be deleterious: reversible absorption may clean polluted waters for a limited time but will

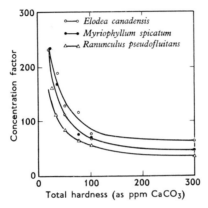

FIG. 2.6. Effect of hardness of water on concentration of ^{89}Sr by intact submerged hydrophytes in flowing water during a 7-day growth period. (From D.S.I.R., 1960, by courtesy of the Controller of Her Majesty's Stationery Office, London.)

re-contaminate them when floods or animals disturb the substrate, whilst irreversible absorption will culminate in an extremely active substrate (D.S.I.R., 1959).

SALINITY

Salinity exerts a critical, and probably complex, influence on the distribution of vegetation in estuaries, offshore waters, coastal lagoons and exceptional inland habitats. However, it is extremely difficult to define salinity as an environmental factor. Any change in the salinity of a habitat must also involve changes in the electroconductivity, hydrogen-ion concentration, density, osmotic pressure, and relative proportions of other ions besides sodium and chloride (Carl, 1937; Conover, 1964). Until more is known of the relative significance of each of these to specific plants, the distribution of communities in brackish and saline waters cannot be fully understood.

At present it is possible to discern, in an essentially qualitative manner, only gross variations in the tolerance of salinity exhibited by different hydrophytes, although even the available data are sometimes contradictory. *Eichhornia crassipes*, for example, was found by Penfound and Earle (1948) to be intolerant of more than faintly brackish water, specimens showing epinasty and chlorosis and quickly dying; yet it has also been reported (C.C.T.A./C.S.A., 1957) to grow freely in estuaries and brackish lagoons and to survive for even several days in sea water. Most freshwater plants, however, appear very susceptible to increasing salinity and so penetrate only a very short way into brackish water. In an estuary in southern Finland, Luther (1951) found that *Hippuris vulgaris* extended from freshwater reaches to a salinity of 5 parts per thousand, *Butomus umbellatus* to 4 parts per thousand, *Elodea canadensis, Lemna* spp., *Nuphar lutea* and *Sagittaria sagittifolia* to 3 parts per thousand, and *Hydrocharis morsus-ranae, Potamogeton natans* and *Sparganium emersum* to only 2 parts per thousand. Luther further observed that in Finland certain freshwater plants, e.g. *Myriophyllum spicatum, Najas marina, Utricularia neglecta, Callitriche hermaphroditica, Potamogeton filiformis* and *P. pectinatus,* are found almost exclusively in brackish water. Whilst at high salinities these species grow in both calm and turbulent waters, at low salinities they conspicuously prefer the turbulent sites. On the assumption that the main photosynthetic carbon source for these submerged plants is bicarbonate (see p. 115), Steemann Nielsen (1954) suggested that in Finland it is only in brackish waters that the pH is sufficiently high for there to be an adequate concentration of bicarbonate ions. He further argued that at low salinities the bicarbonate concentration will be low, and hence turbulence becomes important in renewing the supply and steepening the diffusion gradient into the plant.

Normally, very few plants are habitual colonists of brackish water. In the north temperate zone the most conspicuous members of the species-poor communities of brackish habitats are probably species of *Najas* (*N. marina, N. muenscheri*), *Ruppia* (*R. spiralis, R. maritima*), *Scirpus* (*S. maritimus*), and *Zannichellia* (*Z. palustris*).

At the saline extreme of the habitat-spectrum are found the submerged marine angiosperms, e.g. *Enhalus, Halophila, Thalassia* and *Zostera*, which penetrate no nearer to fresh water than about 3·5 to 5 parts per thousand (den Hartog, 1957b). Some species that reproduce by seed regularly, e.g. *Halodule wrightii* in Texas lagoons, seem able to invade hypersaline environments, tolerating salinities of more than 60 parts per thousand (Conover, 1964).

Brackish and saline habitats may occur inland where human activity, surface geology or climate creates bodies of water containing high concentrations of dissolved salts. Rivers and streams in oil-drilling areas, for example, may become heavily polluted with brine, and in consequence their fauna and flora are substantially modified (Clemens and Finnell, 1957). Inland salt lakes usually possess but few species of plants, perhaps largely because of the problem of invasion of habitats that are well-isolated from the sea coast, whence potential colonists might be expected to originate. The flora of such lakes, as of blocked brackish waters in coastal areas, is influenced primarily by the instability and fluctuation of the salt content, which may, at its maximum, far exceed that of the sea. The nature of the principal salt—whether sodium chloride, sodium sulphate or magnesium sulphate—does not appear to be of major significance.

Tolerant freshwater species, typically *Myriophyllum spicatum, Potamogeton filiformis, P. pectinatus, P. pusillus,* and *Zannichellia palustris,* dominate the flora of the shallow brackish lakes on surface salt deposits in the English Midlands (Hynes, 1960). Numerous shallow lakes on the prairies of Minnesota and the Dakotas exemplify the type of standing water created on salt-rich Cretaceous strata in arid regions where evaporation exceeds precipitation. They have a very high solute concentration, a pH of 8·4 to 9·0, and are especially rich in sulphates (more than 150 ppm): calcium and magnesium are the main cations. *Najas marina, Ruppia maritima* and other estuarine species figure prominently in their flora (Moyle, 1945). The flora of four unusual volcanic lakes in El Salvador, which are notable for their high chloride, sulphate, phosphorus and sodium contents, is dominated by *Najas marina, Potamogeton pectinatus* and *Ruppia maritima* (Fassett and Armitage, 1961). These same plants also thrive in certain solution lakes at an altitude of over 1000 m to the east of the Pecos R. in New Mexico: here the water has a total solute concentration of more than 25 000 ppm and is rich in both sulphate and chloride, with sodium as the dominant cation (Cole, 1963). In another North American saline lake which is remarkable for its high boron content (850 ppm) the flora is again dominated by the tolerant *Ruppia maritima* (Wetzel, 1964).

The floristic changes accompanying enclosure and reclamation of coastal waters provide further examples of the influence of salinity. During reclamation of the Zuider Zee, for example, the decrease in concentration of sodium and chloride has been accompanied by an increase in calcium and bicarbonate, brought in by freshwater affluents, but magnesium and sulphate have remained constant. These changes in ionic proportions have greatly influenced the composition of the plankton, whilst the high salt content retained by the substrate has apparently hindered colonisation by freshwater vascular plants, although *Potamogeton pectinatus* has managed to establish submerged meadows extending widely from the mouth of the R. Yssel (Turrill, 1963). Where fresh waters flow into the sea through salt marshes, it is sometimes possible to discern natural transitions from marine communities (e.g. of *Zostera*) through halophytic communities (dominated by such plants as *Salicornia*) or associations of salt-tolerant plants (such as *Blysmus compressus, Phragmites communis* and *Scirpus maritimus*) to freshwater communities (Chapman, 1964).

OXYGEN AND OTHER GASES IN THE WATER AND THE SUBSTRATE

Although dissolved air may be markedly richer in oxygen than atmospheric air, the total volume of air that can be held in aqueous solution is very small, and under normal conditions the amount of oxygen dissolved in a unit volume of fresh or salt water does not exceed, and is usually considerably less than, 5 per cent of that present in an equivalent volume of the atmosphere. Moreover, the rate of diffusion of oxygen in water is several thousand times less than its rate of diffusion in air. Oxygen concentration is therefore a much more critical factor in the aquatic than in the aerial environment. Low oxygen supplies or even anoxia may confront both planktonic and benthic organisms at certain times. In the temperate zones, dissolved oxygen is most plentiful in winter, when temperatures are usually low, flow rates and turbulence high, and organisms inactive, and most scarce during the summer, when temperatures are higher and living populations reach their greatest density. In both standing and flowing waters, especially when plants are abundant, the dissolved oxygen concentration may rise from an early morning minimum to an afternoon maximum and then fall steadily during the night when photosynthesis has ceased and the plants exert a net respiratory oxygen demand. Conspicuous diurnal rhythms of this classical type are not always apparent: in polluted

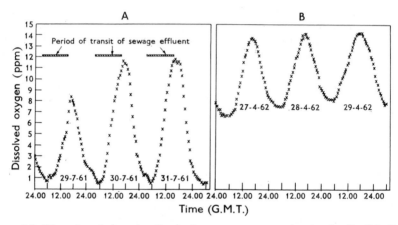

FIG. 2.7. Diurnal variations in dissolved oxygen concentration in the English R. Lark about 3·2 km below the point of discharge of sewage lagoons. A, sewage lagoons in operation; B, 3 months after the discharge had ceased, by which time much of the deposited organic matter had been scoured from the reach by high winter flows. (From D.S.I.R., 1963, by courtesy of the Controller of Her Majesty's Stationery Office, London.)

habitats the daily amplitude may be very narrow or the oxygen concentration may fluctuate irregularly. An influx of spent gas liquor, for example, disrupts the natural rhythm of oxygen concentration and may reduce the diurnal amplitude to as little as 2 to 4 ppm (D.S.I.R., 1959). Gross organic pollution usually has drastic biological consequences, as it severely depletes the oxygen supply: the daily minimum may fall to 1 ppm or even less (Fig. 2.7).

Changes in the dissolved oxygen concentration of a given volume of water which receives no tributaries or surface run-off water are caused by three processes: (a) interchange of oxygen between the water and the atmosphere; (b) consumption of oxygen by direct chemical oxidations and by aerobically respiring bacteria, plants and animals in the water and the substrate; (c) production of oxygen by the photosynthesis of plants in the water and on the surface of the substrate. By continuous exchange of molecular oxygen through the air–water interface, a dynamic equilibrium may be attained at which the water is saturated with oxygen. The actual saturation concentration depends upon the partial pressure of oxygen in the air, the concentration of other substances in the water, and the temperature. At $0°C$ and normal atmospheric pressure the 100 per cent saturation concentration is about 14 to 15 parts of oxygen per million of fresh clean water: this value decreases with increase in temperature, reaching zero at $100°C$. Many natural waters commonly have a saturation deficit: the average oxygen content in the surface water of over 500 lakes in north-east Wisconsin, for example, was found by Juday and Birge (1932) to be only 82 per cent of saturation. Such waters tend to absorb oxygen from the atmosphere, a process generally termed reaeration (or reoxygenation).

Dissolution of the oxygen liberated from plant communities during active photosynthesis may theoretically produce up to five times the oxygen concentration that could be dissolved from air at a given temperature: values up to about 200 per cent saturation are known to be attained in natural habitats. This phenomenon of supersaturation, also created by a rise in temperature, is usually local and transitory, and it results in a net loss of oxygen to the atmosphere. Oxygen exchange rates, under constant conditions of temperature and turbulence, are proportional to the degree of undersaturation (i.e. the saturation deficit) or supersaturation. They are also dependent on the area of the interface, are almost directly related to current velocities, and are also related to water depth; the rate being lower, the greater the depth.

Practical determination of the rate of reaeration, i.e. the mass of oxygen passing through the air–water interface in unit time, is fraught with difficulties, so that results obtained by different methods may conflict. Gasometric methods measure changes in the composition, volume or pressure of the air enclosed by a tent or box over a given area of water of known oxygen deficit. Although this is often the only practicable technique for large rivers, lakes, estuaries and the sea, the constraint to which the water surface is subjected by the enclosure may lead to erroneous results (Gameson *et al.*, 1955). Other techniques, used for smaller rivers and streams, estimate the rate of change of dissolved oxygen content between two stations before and during the passage of a volume of water which has been partly or completely deoxygenated by physical methods or by the controlled addition of a suitable reducing agent, e.g. sodium sulphite and a cobalt catalyst. To eliminate photosynthetic oxygen production the experiments must be performed at night (Gameson *et al.*, 1955; Gameson and Truesdale, 1959; Edwards *et al.*, 1961). An alternative method, utilising the changes in oxygen content created naturally by photosynthesis upstream, measures the oxygen changes occurring during a 24-h period as the water flows through a reach darkened by an opaque plastic sheet suspended above the surface. This technique, however, is applicable only to small productive rivers with a conspicuous diurnal oxygen rhythm, and probably gives erroneous results if used in windy weather, as a result of the shelter given by the plastic sheet (D.S.I.R., 1962; Edwards, 1962). All the techniques also require estimation of the consumption of oxygen by dissolved and suspended matter, mud deposits and plants, and correction of these estimates for variations in temperature and oxygen concentration (Edwards *et al.*, 1961). Employing data obtained in America by Churchill *et al.* (1962) and in England by Gameson *et al.* (1955)

and themselves, Owens *et al.* (1964) derived an empirical equation which may be used to predict reasonably accurately the rates of reaeration to be expected in rivers from their mean velocities (in the range 3·05 to 152·5 cm/s) and mean depths (in the range 0·12 to 3·36 m) (see also Ministry of Technology, 1965).

Agitation of the water surface, accelerating gaseous exchange, is of course significantly greater in even a calmly flowing river than in a standing pond; but it is further increased wherever flowing water encounters rapids, waterfalls or weirs. The precise effect of these obstacles depends largely on whether the water is supersaturated with, or deficient in, oxygen when it meets them. If it is supersaturated, oxygen will be rapidly lost to the air; if it has a deficit, oxygen will be added to the water as it falls (Fig. 2.8). The magnitude of the loss or gain is affected primarily by the velocity of the river and the height and manner in which the water falls (D.S.I.R., 1958, 1959). Gameson (1957) and Barrett *et al.* (1960) showed that the oxygen gain by reaeration can be significantly greater at weirs than through the surface of the flowing river, but Owens and Edwards (1963) emphasised that the beneficial effect of weirs might be offset by the reduction in velocity and consequent accumulation of oxygen-consuming mud deposits in the reach immediately upstream of the obstacle.

Polluting substances generally reduce rates of reaeration (Downing *et al.*, 1957). Thick oil films on the water surface may completely prevent oxygen uptake (Hynes, 1960). Anionic detergents of the alkyl aryl sulphonate type persist in rivers for long periods and in certain circumstances retard reaeration (D.S.I.R., 1955). Gameson *et al.* (1955) emphasised that they exert their most deleterious effect at fairly low rates of oxygen uptake. They have little or no effect when reaeration rates are very high, as in swift turbulent reaches, or very low, as in stagnant water (Southgate, 1957).

An appreciable oxygen demand may be exerted in the water other than by macroscopic plants and animals. In habitats that are clean or polluted by organic effluents this biochemical oxygen demand is essentially bacterial: the demands of purely chemical reactions and planktonic algae (except during heavy blooms) are relatively small. Direct chemical oxidation of the simple reducing agents in many industrial wastes, e.g. ferrous salts and sulphides from mines and the sulphites in wood-pulp liquors (Hynes, 1959), is usually rapid and the oxygen demand therefore immediate. Microbial conversions of these compounds, e.g. oxidation of ferrous bicarbonate and sulphate to ferric hydroxide by iron bacteria, and of sulphides to sulphur and sulphates by some sulphur bacteria, are similarly quite rapid. Bacterial breakdown of sewage, first of the organic carbonaceous constituents, and then of the liberated ammonia, amines and sulphides, is slower, even though the necessary organisms are usually present in the effluent before it reaches the river. According to Phelps (1944), sewage takes only about 70 per cent of its total oxygen demand in 5 days, about 90 per cent by 10 days, and 99 per cent by 20 days. Breakdown of some organic substances, e.g. wood pulp, which is a poor microbial food, or phenols, which initially sterilise the effluent, is even slower. The overall oxygen demand of slowly oxidised effluents therefore extends well downstream in flowing waters, affecting organisms some distance from the point of entry. The discharge of sewage or other organic pollutants into shallow lakes which are already bio-logically productive causes extreme depletion of dissolved oxygen, as Bonomi (1964) recently found in L. Varese in Italy.

Through photosynthetic oxygen production dense populations of planktonic algae may effectively supply much of the oxygen consumed in lake and river waters, at least during daylight hours. Although phytoplankton had negligible effects on the oxygen balance of the rivers Ivel and Lark during recent investi-gations (Edwards and Owens, 1962; Owens and Edwards, 1963), it was significant as an oxygenator in the Avon, Great Ouse and six other English rivers (Owens and Edwards, 1964). Evidence that algal oxygen produ:tion is very significant, perhaps even exceeding reaeration from the atmosphere on

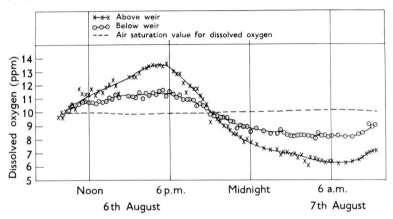

FIG. 2.8. Variations in dissolved oxygen concentration in the English R. Ivel above and below a weir about 2·1 m high, on two days in August, 1958. (From D.S.I.R., 1959, by courtesy of the Controller of Her Majesty's Stationery Office, London.)

summer days, also comes from the studies of Knöpp (1960) in the R. Rhine, and Winberg and Sivko (1962) in the R. Svisloch. It is likely that in many nutrient-rich lakes, where blooms are more common and extensive than in flowing waters, phytoplankton may be seasonally even more signifi-cant.

A large proportion of the total oxygen consumption in a habitat may be accounted for by the substrate, especially if the water is polluted and the mud predominantly organic and densely populated with bacteria and invertebrates (Westlake, 1959b; Edwards and Rolley, 1965; Fig. 2.9). In rivers, downstream of sources of organic pollution, where current velocities are sufficiently low, suspended solids settle as a silt-like organic sludge. Of the few mud-dwelling animals able to survive in such grossly polluted water, containing only very little oxygen, the tubificids (e.g. *Limnodrilus* and *Tubifex*) are amongst the most conspicuous, often colonising the sludge in tremendous numbers, averaging up to $1·7 \times 10^6/m^2$ (Meschkat, 1937). If the water is better oxygenated the tubificids are often joined by naid worms (e.g. *Nais*) and chironomid larvae

3

(e.g. *Chironomus* and *Procladius*) which, like the tubificids, enjoy the abundance of organic and bacterial food and can tolerate reasonably high concentrations of ammonia and hydrogen sulphide. Further downstream the chironomids dominate and then give way, as the oxygen supply improves and the suspended-solids concentration falls, to algal blooms and a fauna often dominated by *Asellus aquaticus*, *Sialis lutaria* and certain leeches and molluscs (Richardson, 1929; Pentelow *et al.*, 1938). Both *Asellus* and the chironomids

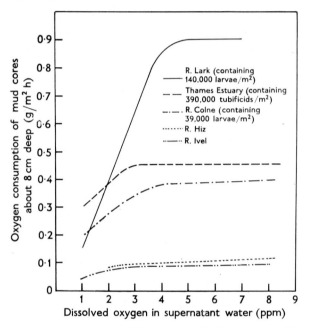

FIG. 2.9. Oxygen consumption of mud from various English rivers at different oxygen concentrations and standard temperature (20°C). (From D.S.I.R., 1963, by courtesy of the Controller of Her Majesty's Stationery Office, London.)

may reach high population densities, up to $1 \cdot 0$ to $1 \cdot 4 \times 10^5/\text{m}^2$ or more (Thienemann, 1954; D.S.I.R., 1963).

In their study of the oxygen balance of the unpolluted R. Ivel in southern England, Edwards and Owens (1962) estimated that the respiration of mud deposits amounted to about 3 to 4 g oxygen/m² day in late spring and summer, a value corresponding to about 30 per cent of the total oxygen demand of the habitat. Using a polarographic respirometer developed by Knowles *et al.* (1962), Owens and Edwards (1963) found that the average oxygen consumption of mud cores from the R. Lark polluted by a sewage effluent was as high as 0·95 g/m² h at 20°C, of which rate about 30 per cent was probably due to the populations of *Chironomus riparius* (*C. thummi*) larvae, estimated at $1 \cdot 4 \times 10^5/\text{m}^2$ (Fig. 2.9). Some 12 months later, when pollution had ceased and much of the sludge had been scoured, the oxygen demand of the mud had fallen to

0·14 g/m² h at 20°C. Owens and Edwards estimated that even if the biochemical oxygen demand of the water were 1·25 ppm/h, mud deposits could account for about 20 per cent of the total oxygen consumption in a river 3 m deep and for more than 50 per cent in one less than 0·75 m deep.

Although the oxygen consumption of organic sludges and bacterial suspensions appears to be independent of the dissolved oxygen concentration when this exceeds 1 ppm, there is good evidence that the oxygen consumption of natural muds does vary with the oxygen content of the supernatant water, especially when extensive algal blooms cover the mud surface (D.S.I.R., 1963). Results obtained by Edwards and Rolley (1965) from their study of mud cores from the rivers Gade, Hiz, Ivel and Lark suggest that, except when the mud has a high density of chironomids, this relationship may be expressed by the equation: $R = aC^b$, where R is the rate of oxygen uptake of the mud, C is the oxygen content of the overlying water, within the range 2 to 10 ppm, and a and b are constants. A similar empirically derived relation holds for the oxygen consumption of submerged aquatic plants (p. 129).

In a recent 12-month survey the oxygen consumption of two river muds was found to be minimal in winter and maximal during a spring diatom bloom when one of the muds, from the R. Ivel, bore an algal population of $2·6 \times 10^6$ cells/cm²; subsidiary peaks of oxygen uptake in August and September were also probably due to algal growth (D.S.I.R., 1964). Although Baity (1938), studying sewage sludges 0·1 to 4 cm deep, and Fair *et al.* (1941), with sludges 1 to 10 cm deep, found that oxygen consumption increased with depth, Edwards and Rolley (1965) found no significant changes in oxygen uptake in deposits ranging from 2 to 17 cm deep.

Edwards and Rolley (1965) found that the oxygen consumption of numerous river muds was not directly correlated with the number of bacteria they possessed, as Hayes and MacAulay (1959) had observed, or with their dehydrogenase activity or organic carbon content: nor was it directly proportional to the biomass or number of chironomid larvae present. Observed disparities between the oxygen demand of muds containing tubificids and the higher demand of the extracted tubificid population suggest that the mud might not be wholly aerobic throughout the depth inhabited by the worms and hence that their respiration may be partly anaerobic (Edwards, 1962). Certain other invertebrates also exert abnormally high respiratory demands when extracted from their natural substrates (Eriksen, 1963). In contrast, the addition of up to about 40 000 *Chironomus* larvae/m² to river muds usually causes much greater increases in the oxygen consumption of the mud than would be expected from the respiratory demands of the larvae. These discrepancies are almost certainly due to indirect effects of the larvae on the structure and overall oxygen demand of the mud (D.S.I.R., 1963, 1964).

In the absence of invertebrates from the surface layers, the mud receives its oxygen by diffusion from the water. Larvae of *Chironomus* and related genera, however, maintain a continuous circulation of water through the tubes they build around themselves and so, in satisfying their own respiratory needs, they indirectly enrich the supply of dissolved oxygen in the surface mud. The introduction of *Chironomus riparius* larvae to settled organic sludge causes the extension of higher oxidation potentials to greater depths. Devoid of larvae, such deposits are usually anaerobic and intensely black below about 3 cm depth. When about 12 500 larvae/m² are present, the light brown oxidised surface layer penetrates much deeper and its boundary with the black anaerobic mud is no longer clear: with 50 000 larvae/m² these effects are even more marked (Edwards, 1958). The depth of the oxidised surface layer of river muds also appears to be directly proportional to the population density of tubificids, up to about 50 000/m² (Schumacher, 1963). Further evidence of the importance of macro-invertebrates in increasing interchange between substrate and water has recently come from studies of the movement of tracer lithium, which is not readily adsorbed onto mud particles, from the overlying water into the interstitial liquid of various river muds containing populations of up to about 100 000 chironomid larvae or tubificids/m². The proportion of lithium present in the mud at depths of 4 cm, at the end of the 6-h experimental period, is significantly greater with high than with low population densities (D.S.I.R., 1964; Edwards and Rolley, 1965).

There is also evidence that dense invertebrate populations transfer large amounts of mud from one depth to another through feeding and defaecation. Chironomid larvae, at a density of about 20 000/m², have been shown to increase the thickness of a mud zone (labelled by glass particles containing radioactive scandium) initially inserted at a depth of 5 cm: being primarily surface feeders, however, they do not raise particles to the surface. In contrast, a similar population of tubificids, which feed below and defaecate on or near the surface like earthworms, transfers about 100 times as much material from lower layers to the top of the mud (Westlake, 1959a; Edwards, 1962). By increasing the turnover of particles, and reducing heterogeneity, and by irrigating and deepening the oxidised surface layer, macro-invertebrates must increase the volume of mud within which oxidative decomposition can occur and must accelerate such oxidation.

If current velocities become sufficiently high, as after heavy rainfall, settled deposits may be rapidly scoured, causing a sudden re-suspension of particles and heavy depletion of dissolved oxygen. It was recently shown that erosion of the top 0·5 cm of cores of R. Gade mud about 16 cm deep, raising the suspended-solids concentration in the overlying water from 20 to about 4250 ppm, increased the rate of oxygen consumption about six-fold, from 0·2 to 1·2 g oxygen/m² h (D.S.I.R., 1964; Edwards and Rolley, 1965). This deleterious effect may be somewhat alleviated by the higher reaeration rates and greater dilution of pollutants during high flows. Other recent studies suggest that in building their tubes, chironomid larvae, in populations of 5000/m² or more, stabilise organic muds and so reduce the likelihood of scouring (Edwards, 1962). This beneficial effect is not shown by tubificids to any comparable extent and is of course lost when the larvae eventually pupate and emerge. Conditions in a polluted reach may thus improve during the winter if the mud is consolidated by extensive quiescent populations of chironomids. In spring, however, the stability of the mud is seriously impaired when rising temperatures induce mass emergence of the flies, and gas, evolved in anaerobic decomposition at lower depths, accumulates in the tube layer, lifting large masses of surface sludge into the water, with consequent sudden increases in suspended solids and oxygen demand (Edwards, 1957).

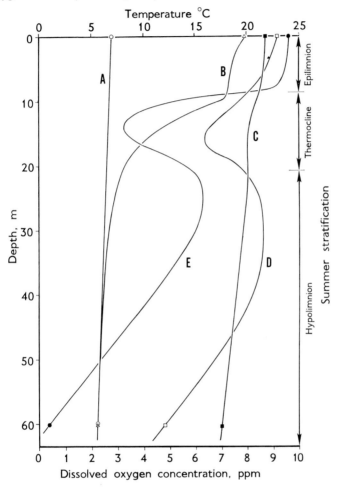

FIG. 2.10. Generalised graph showing interrelated variations of temperature and dissolved oxygen concentration with depth in temperate lakes. A, winter temperature B, summer temperature, showing thermal stratification; C, D, and E, show the changes in oxygen content which might accompany the development of thermal stratification from winter C to summer D and E in a typical nutrient-rich lake, or the increasing productivity of a given lake over a number of years, from a poorly productive state C to a highly productive state E. Extreme metalimnetic falls in oxygen content, such as that shown by curve E, could be principally caused by certain planktonic organisms, such as *Diaptomus*, which reach a maximum population density in this depth range and do not migrate to any significant extent (see, for example, Shapiro, 1960).

Thermal stratification in lakes is accompanied by chemical stratification (of the concentrations of dissolved nutrients and oxygen) and changes in the nature of the muds (Mortimer, 1941, 1942; Hayes and Phillips, 1958; Hayes *et al.*, 1958). Dissolved nutrients in the hypolimnion are scarcely used since the deficiency of light prevents the growth of phytoplankton or rooted plants. The decay of organisms sinking from the more productive epilimnion depletes the dissolved oxygen of the hypolimnion which cannot be replenished whilst stratification persists. The more densely populated and productive the epilimnion, and the more well-defined and steep the thermocline, the more pronounced is the stagnation of the hypolimnion (Fig. 2.10). In nutrient-rich (eutrophic) lakes the dissolved oxygen concentration falls with increasing depth and may reach zero in the hypolimnion, the bottom mud typically becoming anoxic and blackened throughout its depth. The development of such reducing muds, which may occur within the photic zone in shallow rich-water lakes if these are protected from wind and hence stratified (Ruttner, 1963), enriches the nutrient supply of the water. In aerobic conditions many ions become bound in colloidal complexes with ferric iron in the surface mud but in the absence of oxygen the reduction of the iron to the ferrous state breaks the complexes and the nutrient ions are released into the water. In lakes deficient in electrolytes and of low alkalinity, or in the absence of seasonal stratification, the dissolved oxygen concentration shows negligible change with depth (Fig. 2.10), the water does not stagnate and the muds are typically brown and oxidised at the surface, although they are, like river muds, usually devoid of oxygen below a few centimetres' depth.

In both standing and flowing fresh waters and in brackish and saline habitats carbon dioxide is generally in abundant supply, either as the free dissolved gas or as bicarbonate ions, in both the bottom mud and the overlying water. In lakes during the spring and summer, as a result of algal photosynthesis near the surface and organic decomposition in the hypolimnion, the upper waters may have a significantly lower carbon dioxide content and higher pH than waters nearer the bottom (Juday *et al.*, 1935). Toxic gases may accumulate in substrates and water deficient in oxygen, as in the deeper hypolimnion of stratified lakes, e.g. L. Tanganyika, where hydrogen sulphide is abundant (Beadle, 1963), and L. Kivu, which has a high methane content (Burke, 1963; Tazieff, 1963). Through anaerobic decomposition in rich organic muds well within the photic zone, carbon dioxide, hydrogen sulphide, methane and ammonia may also be present in and above substrates colonised by vascular plants in polluted rivers, natural swamps and productive eutrophic lakes (Misra, 1938). Hydrogen sulphide is generated abundantly from black sulphide muds in rivers which have a naturally low pH or are polluted by acidic industrial wastes (Doudoroff and Katz, 1950).

FACTORS INFLUENCING THE DISTRIBUTION OF COMMUNITIES,
SPECIES AND GROWTH FORMS: SUBSTRATE, TURBULENCE AND LIGHT

Assuming that the dissolved nutrient regime is suitable and that oxygen is not deficient for long periods in either the water or substrate, colonisation by rooted hydrophytes may occur down to depths where light intensity becomes the limiting factor. The distribution of particular growth forms, communities or species within the photic zone of a given water-body, as distinct from the occurrence and overall depth penetration of any rooted vegetation, appears to be governed primarily by turbulence, the nature of the substrate, and light intensity and quality. These several factors interact and all vary with increasing depth of water.

The principal influence of the substrate upon the distribution of rooted vegetation is due to its physical texture rather than its chemical composition. The physical properties of submerged soils are the composite product of the nature of the bedrock, erosion by turbulence and currents, elutriation of the eroded material, deposition of inwashed inorganic and organic sediments, and the activities of the flora and fauna themselves. Except in the rare instances where they are more or less vertical, lake shores, whatever their physical composition, are gradually and continually eroded. Erosion of a rocky shore is slow and irregular, the weathering of softer parts leaving projecting harder ridges: erosion of littoral sand, clay or peat is rapid and thorough. The boulders and stones of mixed glacial drift material may resist wave action and remain *in situ*, providing an extremely coarse substrate in the shallowest marginal water. Eroded material is moved to deeper water and sorted by elutriation. Gravel and coarse sands may only be carried a very short distance but fine sands, silts and clays are carried further; the largest particles being dropped first at the least depth, the finest last at the greatest depth. Erosion and elutriation thus create graded substrates in which there is an overall decrease in particle size with increasing depth of water. The substrate may form a smooth gentle slope with a gradual change in texture, but if wave action and elutriation are extreme, a submerged terrace may be formed (Fig. 2.11).

In thermally stratified lakes the degree of turbulence, and hence the depth to which wave action penetrates, is proportional to the depth and area of the lake basin, whilst in shallow unstratified standing waters it depends principally upon the area (Mortimer, 1942; Ruttner, 1963). Large deep lakes are thus more likely to display extreme elutriation and continuous terrace formation than are small shallow ones, whilst within a given lake coarser substrates are generally found at the top of exposed shores than at the top of sheltered shores. It is important to realise that the causal significance of turbulence does not rest solely with its effect upon substrate texture. Hydrophytes vary considerably in their ability to withstand the forces of wind and waves but very few (mainly submerged rosettes and strong rhizomatous species) can thrive in the complete absence of shelter. Hence in a given body of standing water, whether a particular marginal area is colonised or not will depend to a large extent on whether it is protected from, or exposed to, strong turbulence, i.e. on the physiographic aspect of the shoreline. If eroded material is swept away from an exposed shoreline and elutriated at an acute angle, an underwater bank or spit is built up and the water between this spit and the shore is sometimes sufficiently sheltered to permit some submerged plant growth. Similar spits are often formed by affluents pouring suspended sediments on the lake floor.

Since there is some reason to believe that submerged and floating-leaved hydrophytes, like emergents, can and do absorb dissolved nutrients through their roots, certain chemical features of the substrate may be significant within one given body of water. If, for example, excessive consumption by phytoplankton and/or the persistence of an oxidised zone at the surface of the substrate should seasonally reduce the supply of an ion in the water to a limiting level, a hydrophyte might still be able to obtain enough of that ion by contact

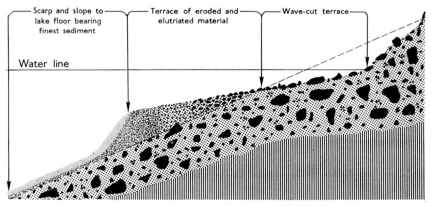

FIG. 2.11. Diagram showing terrace formation as a result of erosion of a lake shore composed of mixed glacial drift material. The bedrock is indicated by vertical hatching and the original shoreline by a broken line. (After Pearsall, 1917.)

exchange between soil particles and root surface. The proportion in a given substrate of inorganic colloids, with their adsorbed ion reserves, could then be important.

Little is known of the precise influence of changes in light intensity and quality under water on the distribution of life forms and species. Some plants of particular habit may tolerate, or even prefer, sustained low intensities and/or deficiencies in certain wavelengths. Changes in intensity and quality occurring as light passes down through aquatic vegetation itself may exert a crucial effect on the development and structure of layered communities, as well as on the photosynthetic efficiency and productivity of the vegetation (pp. 117, 447).

Emergent and floating-leaved hydrophytes seem unable to colonise the bare rocks, boulders, stones and gravel associated with maximum turbulence, but they may sometimes form stands on spits of finer soil in apparently deep water some way out from an inhospitable shoreline. Generally, however, these two life forms are absent from exposed sites where turbulence is strong and/or coarse substrates predominate. In large lakes reed-swamp may be completely lacking or limited to sheltered bays and fans of detritus dropped at the mouths of affluents (Fig. 2.12). The smaller and less exposed the lake, the greater is the extent of reed-swamp, and the more likely that floating-leaved vegetation,

FIG. 2.12. Reed-swamp in Esthwaite Water in the English Lake District, July 1964.
A, reed-swamp (arrowed) around the head of the lake and over the delta of the Black
Beck (which enters from the centre right of the photograph); B, pioneer reed-swamp
fringing a fairly open bay at the foot of the lake; C, mature reed-swamp (arrowed)
extending right round another more sheltered bay at the foot of the lake, and here
accompanied by a floating-leaved community.

3*

which is generally still less tolerant of wind and waves, will also be present. In Scotland, in L. Ness (area 5650 ha, mean depth 132 m) Spence (1964) noted only two areas of reed-swamp, in a sheltered bay and the delta of the R. Urquhart, whilst in L. Lurgainn, another relatively large rock-basin lake (area 327 ha, mean depth 18·6 m) with rocky and stony shores, the only three sites of reed-swamp were all in sandy inlets. In fine contrast, Kilconquhar and Black L., Fife, two shallow kettle-hole lakes with less than 1 per cent of the area of L. Ness, both possessed almost uninterrupted reed-swamp along their shores, accompanied by areas of floating-leaved vegetation.

Coarse substrates in lakes are usually devoid also of submerged vascular plants, except when finer sediments trapped between the fragments provide a rooting medium colonisable by certain rosette plants, often of stoloniferous habit (Fig. 2.13). Such pioneers, exemplified by *Littorella*, *Lobelia* and *Isoetes*, are conspicuous in the typically sparse flora of submerged sands, although these unstable substrates, too, are often devoid of higher plants. The highest population densities and most varied submerged floras occur on fine inorganic silts and clays and organic muds, especially in deeper, less turbulent water: see, for example, Pearsall's (1917, 1918a, 1920) accounts of the deep-water communities of Esthwaite and other English lakes. The observations of Spence (1964) in several Scottish lochs also demonstrate this trend. In L. Kinardochy, for example, total plant cover on the soil surface was found to increase with decreasing particle size and increasing depth, from less than 20 per cent cover on rocks and coarse sand in depths to 40 cm, to more than 60 per cent cover on fine sandy muds below 120 cm depth. In L. Tarff, again, plant cover increased as soils became finer, reaching more than 80 per cent at 120 cm depth, then decreased in deeper water as the proportion of sand in the substrate rose once more (Fig. 2.14). To permit thorough colonisation, substrates must not only be of suitable fine texture: they must also be stable. Forsberg (1964) drew attention to the incapacity of *Myriophyllum spicatum*, *Ranunculus circinatus* and other aquatic angiosperms to root securely in the soft but shifting soil of L. Tåkern in Sweden.

Interspecific differences in the range of water depth inhabited were also revealed by Spence's (1964) survey. Amongst emergents, for example, *Carex rostrata* and *Equisetum fluviatile* both dominated certain communities on deep muds but whereas the former reached water depths of up to 60 cm only, the latter penetrated to a depth of 150 cm. On exposed sandy substrates an *E. fluviatile* community was commonly present in the depth range 40 to 150 cm whereas in shallower water, of 8 to 55 cm depth, *Eleocharis palustris* was the typical reed-swamp dominant.

Complete transects of the colonised shores of given lakes again revealed variation in plant distribution with substrate, turbulence and water depth. In the shallowest water of one shore of L. Maberry exposed to prevailing winds, Spence (1964) found only sparse *Littorella-Lobelia* (less than 5 per cent cover) on a sloping terrace of coarse sand. From 30 cm to 150 cm depth there was a steep scarp of barren boulders beyond which the bottom muds bore up to 80 per cent cover dominated by *Isoetes*. On the opposite, more sheltered shore, the gently sloping, sandy and muddy soil showed a sequence, from shallow to deep water, of emergent *Eleocharis* (75 per cent cover), submerged *Lobelia* (35 per cent), floating-leaved *Potamogeton natans* (50 per cent), and submerged *Isoetes* (85 per cent), giving way to the alga *Nitella* at about 200 cm depth. On the west shore of L. Corby there was a typical zonation of growth forms: an emergent *Phragmites communis* stand ended at an uncolonised peat

FIG. 2.13. Esthwaite Water, July 1964. A, view from part of the windward shore, showing coarse, wave-swept substrate devoid of reed-swamp or floating-leaved plants; B, another part of the same shore, showing sparse growth of emergent sedges (centre foreground) in quieter water sheltered by the stony spit; C, view down through the water at the edge of the sedge stand in B, showing coarse stony substrate with rosettes of *Littorella* colonising the interstitial sediment.

scarp, at the bottom of which, at about 40 cm depth, was sloping soft black mud bearing a floating-leaved community of *Nuphar lutea* with an under-layer of numerous submerged plants. In deeper water, beyond about 110 cm, the soft organic mud was densely colonised by a submerged linear-leaved community dominated by *Callitriche hermaphroditica* and *Potamogeton obtusifolius*.

Spence noted that in Scottish lochs generally, submerged broad-leaved plants predominated only in water more than 150 cm deep, and suggested that

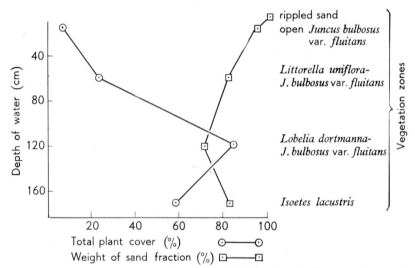

FIG. 2.14. Effect of substrate on degree of colonisation in a shallow open bay on the south shore of L. Tarff, Scotland. (Redrawn from Spence, 1964, by courtesy of the author, the editor and Oliver and Boyd, Edinburgh.)

for this life form fine muds, diminished turbulence and low light intensity are all significant. In contrast, the typical occurrence of submerged rosette plants throughout a wide range of depth is perhaps a reflection of their ability to withstand reasonable turbulence and to grow on a variety of substrates. Spence very properly pointed out that since turbulence, light and the texture of the substrate all vary with depth, as vegetation does, no one of these factors can normally be singled out as the prime controller of the distribution of communities, growth forms or species.

In flowing waters erosion and elutriation are repeated many times between the source and the sea. Turbulence and current velocity are of greater significance for plant colonisation than in lakes (Gessner, 1950; Bournaud, 1963). Despite the fact that rivers are generally much shallower than lakes, varying light intensity and quality may still influence plant distribution especially where suspended solids or algae are abundant.

In torrential and very swift-flowing reaches, the inhospitable substrate of bare rock, unstable boulders, stones or heavy shingle restricts the flora mainly to algae, lichens and bryophytes. Vascular plants, unable to root securely and withstand the extreme turbulence, are generally absent, at least in the temperate zones, although in the tropics certain thalloid, cushion- and rosette-shaped members of the remarkable family Podostemaceae are outstandingly successful in these severe habitats. With decrease in current velocity and erosion, angiosperm communities eventually become established. In Britain, for example, one of the first of these, on fine shingle in fairly fast-flowing water, usually comprises submerged dissected-leaved species of batrachian *Ranunculi* and *Myriophyllum*, sometimes accompanied by the heterophyllous *Berula erecta* and linear-leaved *Callitriche* species. Broad-leaved submerged plants are absent, presumably because of their vulnerability to turbulence and requirement for finer rooting media. Batrachian *Ranunculi* also predominate on sand although submerged linear-leaved *Potamogeton* species are often abundant and may replace them. If the current is less swift and some silt is dropped, a few emergent and heterophyllous species, notably *Hippuris vulgaris*, *Sagittaria sagittifolia* and *Sparganium* spp., may also be present, whilst in sluggish reaches with abundantly silted muddy bottoms these are commonly joined or replaced by other emergents, such as *Glyceria* spp., *Phragmites communis*, *Schoenoplectus lacustris*, *Typha* spp., sedges or rushes. The submerged flora is here typically dominated by *Callitriche* spp., *Ceratophyllum demersum*, *Elodea canadensis*, *Potamogeton* spp. (broad- as well as linear-leaved), and *Myriophyllum* may again be abundant. In the less turbulent marginal water, sheltered by the banks or by emergent stands, floating-leaved communities of *Nuphar*, *Nymphaea*, *Nymphoides* or *Potamogeton* spp. may also become established.

Pollution by effluents carrying suspended solids may drastically modify the nature of the substrate and hence change the sequence of vegetation and floristic composition of the communities. Jones (1949) suggested that the absence of rooted vegetation from one Welsh river, the Rheidol, may be partly due to its inability to colonise the unstable shifting layer of inwashed lead-mine debris that covers the substrate. Unless organic pollution is relatively mild, recolonisation by vascular plants is generally delayed until conditions have markedly improved. When suspended solids from sewage and other wastes settle and become consolidated on an originally sandy or gravelly bed, dissected-leaved communities of *Myriophyllum* and batrachian *Ranunculi* are replaced by a flora of silt-loving species, such as *Elodea canadensis*, *Potamogeton pectinatus*, *P. natans* and *Glyceria maxima*, all of which enjoy the enhanced nutrient supply and may, though not invariably, show very vigorous growth. The most resilient of these plants appears to be *Potamogeton pectinatus* which frequently penetrates further upstream than others and may reach the most heavily polluted zone. Unlike the foliage of most hydrophytes its linear leaves are kept free of settling particles by even the slightest current and are not colonised by such filamentous sewage-bacteria and -fungi as *Sphaerotilus* and *Leptomitus*. *Ceratophyllum*, batrachian *Ranunculi* and *Myriophyllum* usually return when most of the suspended solids have been dropped, whilst *Nuphar*, *Nymphaea*, most species of *Potamogeton* and other hydrophytes are typically still less tolerant and recolonise only clean reaches (Butcher, 1933; Hawkes, 1957; Hynes, 1959, 1960).

A Link with Land Plants:
The Structure and Physiology of
Emergent Foliage

The aerial stems and leaves of emergent hydrophytes show very close resemblances, in both form and anatomy, to those of related land plants. Living in essentially the same environment they display structural features similarly related to the mechanical and physiological problems of an aerial existence. Resistance to the bending strains imposed upon erect stems and vertical leaves and to the tearing effect of wind on dorsiventral leaves is afforded, as in herbaceous land plants, by the development and disposition of collenchyma, sclerenchyma and lignified vascular elements. The danger of excessive loss of water is an inevitable consequence of the efficiency of the leaf as a photosynthetic organ and although emergent foliage, standing above a free water surface, is often surrounded by air of high relative humidity, it transpires at substantial rates.

Although emergent organs show no gross differences from terrestrial shoots they do exhibit local reactions to the aquatic environment. The young foliage is necessarily submerged during its early development and whilst it may not then be subject to loss of water by transpiration it is often surrounded by a medium deficient in oxygen, which it must somehow tolerate for a limited period. It is perhaps also in response to this scarcity of oxygen that many emergent organs, near and just below the water level, develop masses of a secondary air-storage tissue, aerenchyma. The lenticel tissue of some land plants becomes similarly hypertrophied if their stems are temporarily submerged. Many emergent hydrophytes and land plants endure immersion for considerable periods of time, either in the laboratory or in natural habitats when the water table is suddenly raised, as by monsoon rains and floods. New leaves and stems produced under water often differ in structure from the typical aerial organs but the differences are of degree rather than kind. The thickness and hairiness of the leaf, frequency of stomata and extent of cuticle are often reduced, the shape of the leaf is altered, and the volume of spongy mesophyll increased. These slight changes, reminiscent of those discernible in many land plants grown in dense shade, form a transition to the more profound modifications of entirely submerged hydrophytes.

STRUCTURE OF EMERGENT LEAVES

Most emergent monocotyledons, e.g. species of *Butomus*, *Typha*, *Acorus* and *Phragmites*, are rhizomatous and produce erect, more or less linear leaves: those of *Butomus umbellatus* provide an example of anatomical organisation. Triangular in transverse section, each leaf has a sheathing channelled base. The cuticularised epidermal cells are elongated parallel to the long axis of the leaf and their outer and radial walls are thickened with cellulose. Chloroplasts are absent from the epidermal cells but occur in the guard cells of the stomata, which are distributed on all surfaces of the leaf. As in most erect leaves the mesophyll is not differentiated into palisade and spongy tissues: with the exception of three or four layers of compact cells beneath the epidermis it is composed of large air spaces traversed at intervals by diaphragms. The walls separating these lacunae are composed of single rows of parenchymatous cells. The distribution of the closed collateral vascular bundles which run longitudinally through the leaf is similar to that displayed by many monocotyledon stems and is related to the resistance to bending strains. The bundles are smaller but more numerous in the compact subepidermal tissue; in the lacunate mesophyll they are few and notably well-developed, and each is embedded in a parenchymatous sheath at the junction of the walls of the air chambers. The xylem is composed mainly of annular-, spiral-, and reticulate-thickened tracheids, and parenchyma cells; the protoxylem is usually represented in the larger bundles by a conspicuous lacuna. Sieve tubes, companion cells and parenchyma are present in the phloem, and sclerenchyma fibres form a supporting column external and internal to young bundles, and a complete sheath around the older ones. (Hasman and Inanç, 1957).

The flat upright leaves of *Zizania aquatica* exemplify a similar anatomical organisation which is encountered, with slight specific differences, in most emergent grasses. The leaf is strengthened by sclerenchyma cells and by siliceous epidermal hairs along its margins. Both upper and lower epidermes are cuticularised, hairy, and possess stomata. Four very large air spaces run along the leaf in the mesophyll in the region of the midvein. Through the transverse diaphragms, composed of several tiers of stellate cells, which interrupt these lacunae, there pass small transverse vascular bundles which link the midvein to the innermost of the lateral veins on each side (Weir and Dale, 1960).

The leaves of some emergent monocotyledons are differentiated into a stalk and a blade which shows a dorsiventral anatomy similar to that of most dicotyledons. There is convincing evidence that this type of leaf is in some species a phyllode, homologous with only the petiole and sheathing base of a dicotyledonous leaf, a theory first proposed by de Candolle (1827). Arber's (1918) investigations leave no doubt that the 'pseudo-lamina' of leaves of members of the Alismaceae and Pontederiaceae represents a flattened and elaborated tip of a phyllode-like leaf. Arber revealed the existence of inverted vascular bundles in several hydrophytes in the Pontederiaceae, an anatomical feature consistent with the derivation of the pseudo-lamina by horizontal compression of the distal part of the petiole, in which the vascular strands are normally arranged in an arc or a ring (Fig. 3.1; see also Fig. 3.4). In *Pontederia cordata* she observed that the majority of the bundles were inversely placed, whilst some, including the median vein, were normally orientated; a few were obliquely orientated. Species of *Heteranthera* exemplify conceivable stages in the elaboration of the pseudo-lamina (Fig. 3.2). Arber also found phyllodic anatomy in the leaves of

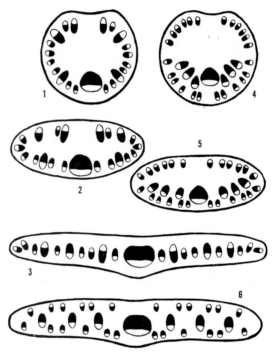

FIG. 3.1. Diagrams illustrating the hypothetical derivation of a pseudo-lamina from an ancestral petiole, with accompanying changes in the orientation of the vascular strands, as seen in transverse section. Xylem of each vascular strand in solid black. 1, 2, 3, yielding a pseudo-lamina with just one series of mixed bundles, some normally, some inversely and some obliquely orientated. 4, 5, 6, yielding a pseudo-lamina with three series of bundles, the midrib and principal lateral bundles normally orientated, the upper series of small bundles inversely orientated, and the lower series normally orientated.

some members of the Alismaceae such as *Sagittaria sagittifolia* where the lateral veins of the emergent blade possess both normal and inverted bundles. In *S. montevidensis* the principal veins and a series of small bundles near the lower surface are all normally orientated, but small bundles in a series near the upper surface are inverted.

Most emergent dicotyledons produce erect leafy stems, a habit shown by species of *Alternanthera, Bacopa, Decodon, Didiplis, Hygrophila, Ludwigia, Lythrum, Micranthemum, Menyanthes, Neptunia* and *Rotala*. The close anatomical resemblances between these aerial leaves and those of typical terrestrial dicotyledons are exemplified by *Hygrophila polysperma* and *Menyanthes trifoliata*. The ternate leaf of the latter species possesses stomata on both surfaces; chloroplasts occur in the guard cells but not the ordinary epidermal cells. The mesophyll shows a marked differentiation into upper palisade and lower spongy layers. The petiole possesses a ring of widely spaced vascular

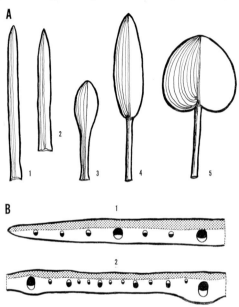

FIG. 3.2. Leaf form and venation (A) and anatomy in transverse section (B) of species of *Heteranthera*. A, venation shown in only half of the leaf: 1, *H. graminea*, 2, *H. zosteraefolia* (submerged leaf), 3, *H. zosteraefolia* (floating leaf), 4, *H. limosa*, 5, *H. reniformis* (all ×0·75); B, palisade mesophyll stippled; xylem of vascular bundles in solid black: 1, *H. zosteraefolia*, 2, *H. reniformis* (both ×25). (B, after Arber, 1918, 1922a).

bundles as seen in transverse section. The lacunate cortex is the only feature which is notably correlated with the subaquatic habit of the plant (Metcalfe and Chalk, 1950). The ovate-oblong sessile leaf of *Hygrophila polysperma* bears marginal spines, and has trichomes and stomata on both surfaces. The cuticularised epidermal cells have thick outer walls, are irregular in outline, and lack chloroplasts. The upper palisade layer is usually one cell thick, the spongy layer from two to three cells thick. The vascular strands possess spiral-thickened vessels and some of the mesophyll cells contain the cystoliths typical of related terrestrial members of the same family, the Acanthaceae (Reams, 1953).

PHYSIOLOGICAL ASPECTS OF EMERGENT FOLIAGE

As noted earlier, the main physiological problem confronting young organs arising from rhizomes and rootstocks buried in the substrate is the risk of oxygen deficiency in the water through which they must grow into the air above. Erect leaves or leafy stems are normally submerged until they reach a length of from 5 to 30 cm, even longer if the water table is unusually high. It might be expected that during their initial growth these organs must be capable of respiring anaerobically. Laing (1940b) showed that young leaves of *Typha latifolia* can sustain anaerobiosis for a limited time, sufficient under natural conditions for them to emerge from the water, and it is likely that other species have a similar capacity.

Once the foliage has emerged, gaseous exchange between the atmosphere and the internal tissues presumably begins; oxygen required for respiration and carbon dioxide for photosynthesis are readily available. A high proportion of the mesophyll in many emergent leaves is occupied by lacunae which may increase in size during growth. In *Sparganium erectum*, for example, schizogenous cavities develop very early in the mesophyll, forming zones of arm parenchyma. These cells later die, thus creating larger lysigenous lacunae (Cook, 1962a). This extensive system of air spaces, together with the intercellular spaces of the palisade mesophyll, facilitates gaseous exchange between the photosynthetic cells and the atmosphere. Samantarai (1938) and Laing (1940c) showed that of all the vegetative organs in various species of *Typha*, *Pontederia, Peltandra, Scirpus* and *Sparganium*, the leaves possessed the highest oxygen concentration, which varied from 19·6 to 10·0 per cent. Evolution of oxygen during photosynthesis produced a gradient of concentration extending down through the internal atmosphere of the petioles and leaf bases to the underground organs. Similar gradients of oxygen concentration have been demonstrated in *Cladium mariscus* (Conway, 1937), *Menyanthes trifoliata* (Coult and Vallance, 1951, 1958), *Equisetum fluviatile* (Barber, 1961) and *Spartina alterniflora* (Teal and Kanwisher, 1966). The aerial foliage is probably the main source of oxygen for the organs buried in the substrate (pp. 157-61).

Whilst they may be able to secure adequate oxygen and carbon dioxide, emergent leaves, in common with other aerial organs, must at the same time lose water by transpiration. Cuticularisation of the epidermis restricts the escape of water vapour largely to the stomata but despite the frequently high relative humidity above the water, especially in sheltered habitats, emergent leaves transpire freely, as was first shown by Bokorny (1890) using *Myriophyllum brasiliense*. Otis (1914) demonstrated that the rate of evaporation from a water surface occupied by emergent hydrophytes is up to three times greater than the rate from a free water surface of equivalent area under similar conditions. The rate is greatly influenced by the area of exposed foliage, the height of the plants above water and the density of the community, and it also varies with the external conditions and the species of plant. Otis found that the rate of transpiration of *Pontederia cordata, Typha latifolia, Acorus calamus*, and *Scirpus validus* was particularly high, that of *Zizania aquatica* and *Sagittaria latifolia* consistently lower. As in many land plants, transpiration losses incurred during the night were small relative to those in the daytime. Gessner (1945) confirmed that loss of water by transpiration is compensated in *Alisma, Hippuris* and

Sagittaria entirely by water pulled upwards as a result of the diffusion pressure deficit in the aerial foliage, i.e. a transpiration current as in herbaceous land plants.

Many emergents also display guttation, water being exuded from hydathodes at the enlarged terminations of veins around the margins of the leaves. In addition to its normal hydathodes *Hygrophila polysperma* also has on both the

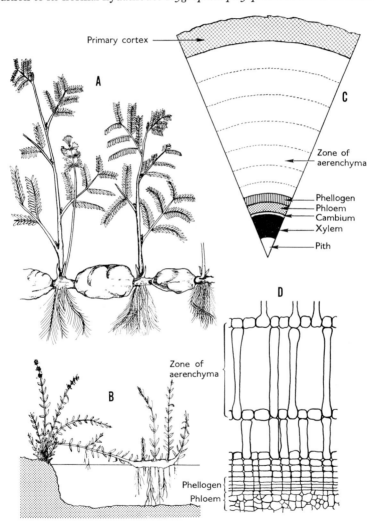

FIG. 3.3. Habit sketches of *Neptunia oleracea* (A, ×0·2) and *Decodon verticillatus* (B, ×0·03), showing spongy aerenchymatous stems. C, diagrammatic T.S. of a sector of the stem of *Ludwigia peruviana* (×12); D, drawing of part of a T.S. of the stem of *L. peruviana*, showing the origin of the aerenchyma from a deep-seated phellogen (×60). (C and D, after Schenck, 1889.)

upper and lower epidermis of its leaf multicellular trichomes which secrete water (Reams, 1953).

The aerenchyma which some emergent organs develop at or below water level may arise from either a vascular cambium, or, more commonly, a lateral phellogen. Examples of the former type occur in leguminous genera such as *Aeschynomene*: the bulk of the stem of *A. aspera*, an Indian emergent, consists of spongy air-filled tissue which is in fact secondary xylem (Moeller, 1879); a similar aerenchyma swells the submerged parts of the stems of the Venezuelan *A. hispidula* (Ernst, 1872) and of *Herminiera elaphroxylon* (Kotschy, 1858), a constituent of the Nile sudd. The absence of pit-membranes from these xylem elements (Goebel, 1891–1893) suggests that gases may diffuse freely within the tissue.

Schenck (1889) found aerenchyma produced by a phellogen to be common in the semi-aquatic members of the Onagraceae, Lythraceae, Leguminosae and Euphorbiaceae. In some species of *Jussiaea* and *Ludwigia* (Onagraceae) it arises from a pericyclic phellogen. In *L. peruviana*, for example, the phellogen initials produce, by periclinal divisions, layers of small compact cells; subsequently, at intervals around the circumference of each layer some cells elongate rapidly in a radial direction, thus pushing outwards the layers external to them and creating air chambers running parallel to the axis (Fig. 3.3: C, D). In several lythraceous genera, notably *Lythrum, Decodon, Ammannia* and *Peplis*, the cork normally formed by the deep-seated phellogen (which arises between the sieve tube zone and phloem fibres) is replaced or accompanied under water by aerenchyma (Graham, 1964). A similar tissue arising from a cortical phellogen is exhibited by *Sesbania aculeata, S. marginata, Lotus pedunculatus* (Papilionaceae) and *Neptunia oleracea* and *Mimosa pigra* (Mimosaceae), on whose submerged stems it may occur as a uniform sheath or as bladder-like swellings about the nodes (Metcalfe and Chalk, 1950; and see Fig. 3.3: A). Aerenchymatous cells differ from cork in having unsuberised cellulose walls and a cytoplasmic lining. These and other observations of the replacement of cork by aerenchyma and the hypertrophy of lenticel tissue in the submerged parts of emergent stems support the idea that aerenchyma is the response of a quite normal phellogen to some factor of the aquatic medium. Arber (1920) regarded the question of the function of aerenchyma as unimportant; in her view, any useful purpose served by the tissue is quite fortuitous. However, since the organs possessing aerenchyma often lack an extensive primary lacunar system, this secondary tissue may be valuable in storing oxygen. It may also aid buoyancy in *Decodon verticillatus*, whose stems are weak and remain erect only for a time, soon bending over. Where they touch the water aerenchyma develops, and adventitious roots are produced which anchor this floating region of the axis: the shoot apex meanwhile resume its erect growth (Fig. 3.3: B). A curious feature noticed by Schrenk (1889) seems to deny any possible respiratory function of the tissue in this species: in older stems the aerenchyma is sometimes sealed off from both the water and the internal tissues by suberised cells.

EFFECTS OF SUBMERGENCE UPON EMERGENT SPECIES

Numerous terrestrial plants, in either the seedling or mature stages of growth, are known to be able to live for considerable periods completely or partly submerged. Examples recorded from natural habitats include the seedlings of

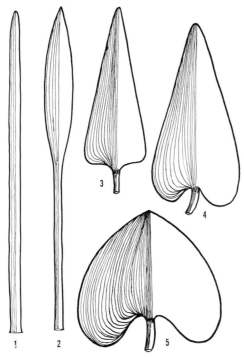

FIG. 3.4. Leaf form and venation in *Pontederia cordata* (venation shown in only half of the leaf). 1, Submerged leaf of f. *taenia* (× 1); 2, emergent blade and about one-third of the petiole of f. *taenia* (× 2); 3, emergent blade of f. *angustifolia* (× 0·2); 4, emergent blade of f. *cordata* (× 0·3); 5, emergent blade of f. *latifolia* (× 0·2).

Aesculus hippocastanum (Arber, 1920), and mature specimens of *Achillea ptarmica*, *Trifolium resupinatum*, *Cirsium dissectum*, and even the parasitic *Cuscuta* spp. (Glück, 1911; Compton, 1916); *Solanum dulcamara* often grows with the root system and lower internodes submerged. Aquatic forms are more frequent amongst the floras of temperate and tropical marshes, swamps and bogs, where seasonal inundations are common. Species of *Alisma*, *Bacopa*, *Butomus*, *Campanula*, *Cardamine*, *Crinum*, *Cryptocoryne*, *Didiplis*, *Echinodorus*, *Elatine*, *Gratiola*, *Heteranthera*, *Hygrophila*, *Juncus*, *Ludwigia*, *Menyanthes*, *Nomaphila*, *Polygonum*, *Pontederia*, *Ranunculus*, *Rorippa*, *Rotala* and *Sium* can grow entirely submerged even in deep water, although they are then usually sterile. The relative ease with which some take to the water has led to their common use as ornamental plants in aquaria (pp. 513-14).

The extent of the morphological differences induced by submergence varies considerably; in some species the emergent and aquatic forms differ only in the degree of lignification whilst in others they are so distinct as to have achieved separate taxonomic recognition. The leaves of submerged forms are often relatively elongated, a difference which is most conspicuous when the aerial shape is ovate, elliptic or rounded. *Pontederia cordata*, for example,

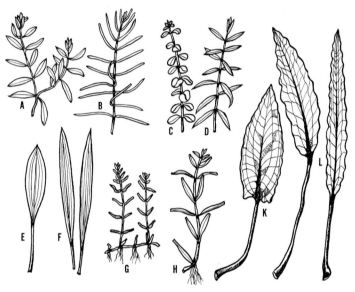

FIG. 3.5. Leaf form in emergent (A, C, E, G, K) and submerged (B, D, F, H, L) specimens of various hydrophytes. A, B, *Didiplis diandra* (× 0·75); C, D, *Rotala rotundifolia* (× 0·3); E, F, *Echinodorus grisebachii* (× 0·25); G, H, *Elatine triandra* (× 0·6); K, L, *Cryptocoryne wendtii* (× 0·4).

normally has a more or less heart-shaped leaf blade but submerged specimens, forma *taenia* (Fassett, 1957), have ribbon-like leaves with little or no differentiation of a blade (Fig. 3.4). In *Rotala indica* and *R. rotundifolia* the emergent leaves are rounded, the submerged ones slender and lanceolate. Relatively narrower and longer leaves are also found in submerged specimens of *Cryptocoryne beckettii, C. ciliata, C. thwaitesii, C. wendtii, Didiplis diandra, Echinodorus brevipedicellatus, E. grisebachii, E. tenellus, Ludwigia arcuata, L. repens* and *L. palustris* (Petch, 1928; Fassett, 1957; Figs. 3.5 and 3.6). Similar quantitative changes are induced in aquatic forms of species whose leaves are normally linear. *Butomus umbellatus*, in deep water, forms very long limp leaves, whilst in the aquatic forms of *Limosella aquatica* and *Hydrocotyle vulgaris*, the petiole is often elongated to as much as ten times its emergent length. Growing in water of about 10 cm depth *Sparganium erectum* attains a height of 50 to 80 cm but reaches 200 cm in deep water (Cook, 1962a). In *Elatine triandra* the maximum length of the internodes is 5 mm and of the leaves 6 mm in terrestrial

FIG. 3.6. Silhouettes of representative leaves from a young specimen of *Echinodorus brevipedicellatus*: A, growing as an emergent; B, after 6 weeks' submergence in about 30 cm of water (all ×0·4).

forms, whereas in shallow water forms, the corresponding values are 8·5 mm and 6·5 mm, and in deep water forms, 14 mm and 13 mm (Fassett, 1957). Two extreme variations of *Alisma gramineum* — one of which has emergent linear leaves 7 to 35 cm long and sometimes expanded distally into a small blade, and the other has submerged ribbon leaves up to 60 cm long—have been distinguished by Tournay and Lawalrée (1949) as forma *arcuatum* and forma *gramineum* respectively although Glück (1905, 1911) showed that, as in other plants of this type, the extreme and intermediate forms are dependent on the water level and have no taxonomic significance. Only two stations for this species are known in Britain and it is remarkable that in one of them, near Droitwich in Worcestershire, the extreme emergent form occurs, whilst the submerged form is present in the other at Surfleet in Lincolnshire (Lousley, 1957a).

In contrast, a few species such as *Gratiola aurea* become dwarfed under water: the leaves of submerged specimens of *Campanula aparinoides, Cryptocoryne lutea, C. petchii*, and *C. walkeri* are also notably smaller than those of emergent specimens (Petch, 1928; Fassett, 1957). The habit of growth may be altered as in *Bacopa monnieri* and *Ludwigia lacustris*, both of which have prostrate creeping stems, rooting profusely at the nodes, when exposed, but erect sparsely rooting stems under water.

Emergent hydrophytes growing under water show also anatomical reactions to the aquatic environment. Numerous marginal plants such as *Hydrocotyle vulgaris, Lysimachia vulgaris*, and *Mentha aquatica* are normally hairy (Yapp, 1912), as are the tropical *Nomaphila stricta* and *Hygrophila lacustris*: the foliage produced under water, however, is quite glabrous. The leaves of submerged specimens are usually thinner and limper; the amount of chlorophyll often seems decreased, but non-photosynthetic pigments, especially anthocyanins and anthoxanthins, often appear in the foliage. *Bacopa myriophylloides, Cardamine lyrata, Cryptocoryne thwaitesii* and *C. wendtii, Didiplis diandra, Echinodorus tenellus* and species of *Hygrophila* and *Nomaphila* are much paler under water whilst the submerged foliage of *Bacopa caroliniana, Cryptocoryne beckettii, C. lutea, C. petchii*, and *Rotala indica* is frequently suffused with reddish and brownish purple.

The palisade mesophyll is often reduced and the spongy tissue correspondingly increased in amount so that the volume occupied by intercellular air spaces is proportionately higher. Chloroplasts may be developed in the epidermis and the stomatal distribution is often altered. The lower epidermis of the hairy leaves of the xeromorphic form of *Polygonum amphibium*, for example, shows a much higher stomatal frequency than the upper epidermis, but in the glabrous leathery leaves of the floating form the stomata are restricted to the upper epidermis (Massart, 1902; Turesson, 1961). Mohanty and Mishra (1963) found that the xeromorphic form of the Indian shrub *Ipomoea carnea* possesses about four times the leaf area and three to five times the absolute stomatal number of the aquatic form. Associated also with the transition from a xeromorphic to an aquatic habit is a decreased distribution of stomata per unit area on the lower surface of the leaves. In *Lythrum salicaria*, however, the stomatal frequency is similar in both aerial and submerged leaves (Bodmer, 1928).

Similar anatomical changes occur in the stem. Costantin (1884) remarked upon the diminution of the xylem and reduced lignification of the phloem fibres in species of *Ricinus* and *Lupinus*, and also noticed an increase in stem diameter and volume of air spaces, and a decrease in the fibrous and conducting elements of *Rorippa amphibia*, *Mentha aquatica* and *Veronica anagallis-aquatica* grown under water. Schenck (1884) also recorded an elaboration of the air spaces and parenchymatous tissue and a reduction of mechanical and vascular elements in submerged shoots of *Cardamine pratensis*. Cortical lacunae develop in many land plants immersed by flood waters (Kramer, 1951).

The effects of the aquatic medium upon typically emergent or terrestrial plants thus appear to be quantitative rather than qualitative, involving changes in the shape and size of leaves and the degree of development of various tissues. These alterations, discernible also in shaded land plants, which often bear thin leaves lacking a sharp differentiation of the mesophyll and possessing chloroplasts in their epidermis, generally become more conspicuous the deeper the water in which the plant is immersed and reflect two of the main problems confronting plants in water—the diminished light intensity and reduced oxygen supply. The reduction of the lignified tissues may be correlated with the presence of excess water in the environment. Guppy (1906) and later Arber (1920) considered the angiosperms to have been endowed from very early in their evolution with different degrees of genetic adaptability and vegetative plasticity which were manifest in varying capacities for the adoption of an aquatic existence: thus the habitats occupied by extant species have been determined by these capacities. It is generally true that plants living naturally in swamps, marshes, and similar habitats take to submerged life much more readily than do most land plants. These amphibious plants thus provide, in both a structural and an ecological sense, a gradual transition between truly terrestrial and truly aquatic floras.

4

Life in Two Environments:
The Structure and Physiology
of Floating Leaves

Floating leaves exhibit the utmost conservatism of form and structure. Their uniformity throughout groups of quite unrelated hydrophytes affords an excellent demonstration of parallel evolution in a very restricted and sharply defined habitat, the actual surface of the water. Here, the greatest stability and most effective resistance to the tearing and immersing action of wind, waves, and rain would be achieved by a strong, leathery, peltate leaf, circular in shape, with an entire margin, water-repellent upper surface, and long pliable petiole. Few floating leaves attain this mechanical ideal but a definite trend towards it is discernible in numerous species, notably some members of the Nymphaeaceae. Even the ideal form, however, has mechanical deficiencies, and floating-leaved hydrophytes are generally unable to withstand severe winds and turbulent waters, and so colonise only sheltered habitats with still or slow-flowing water.

Floating leaves are unique in being exposed to both air and water at the same time. The expansion of the lamina in the horizontal plane is reflected in the dorsiventral anatomical organisation. Carbon dioxide and oxygen are absorbed principally through the stomata present in the upper epidermis. Despite the conspicuous cuticle and wax bloom, transpiration is often appreciable. The mesophyll is usually differentiated into an upper photosynthetic palisade tissue and an extensive lacunate tissue, bounded by the lower epidermis in which stomata do sporadically occur in some species, probably as relict ancestral features. Localised masses of spongy tissue aid buoyancy, and further support and resistance to tearing may be given by the skeleton of vascular strands, by collenchyma cells, or rarely sclerenchyma fibres, associated with the veins, and by sclerotic cells scattered through the mesophyll.

FORM AND STABILITY

Floating leaves may be arranged in a morphological series (Figs. 4.1 and 4.2) culminating in a more or less circular peltate form, to which the greatest physical advantages accrue (Hiern, 1872). A simple linear-lanceolate blade, narrowing gradually into the petiole and possessing a sharply pointed apex, is shown by *Baldellia ranunculoides* and some forms of *Potamogeton nodosus*; *Potamogeton spirillus* has a rather broader leaf with a blunt apex. An ovate

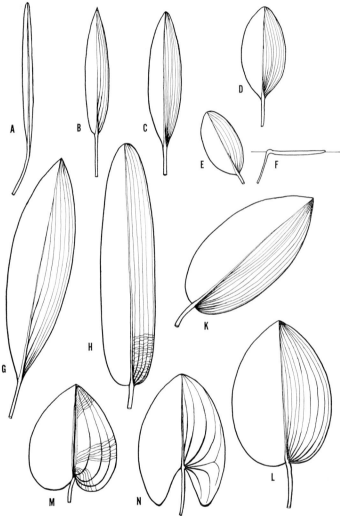

FIG. 4.1. Form and venation of floating laminae. A, *Aponogeton junceus* ssp. *rehmannii* ($\times 0.5$); B, *Potamogeton nodosus* ($\times 0.4$); C, *P. spirillus* ($\times 2$); D, *P. vaseyi* ($\times 2$); E, F, *Luronium natans* ($\times 1$); G, *Potamogeton thunbergii* ($\times 0.6$); H, *Aponogeton desertorum* ($\times 0.5$); K, *Potamogeton natans* ($\times 0.6$); L, *P. pulcher* ($\times 1$); M, *Hydrocleys nymphoides* ($\times 0.6$); N, *Sagittaria guayanensis* ($\times 0.8$). (All except F are views of the abaxial surface; F is a lateral view with the water-line indicated. Venation is shown in only half of the leaf in each example.)

or elliptic blade, rounded and obtuse at the apex, is seen in *Luronium natans*, *Potamogeton vaseyi* and *P. coloratus*, whilst *Potamogeton thunbergii* and *P. nodosus* commonly have oblong-elliptic leaves which are rounded or cuneate at the base. Floating leaves in the genus *Aponogeton* are of relatively uniform shape, varying from elliptic to oblong, as in *A. distachyos* and *A. desertorum*, to

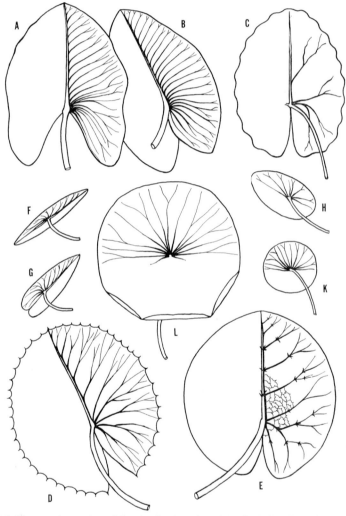

FIG. 4.2. Form and venation of floating laminae (continued). A, *Nuphar advena* (× 0·2); B, *N. fraternum* (× 0·2); C, *Nymphoides peltata* (× 0·5); D, *Nymphaea nouchali* (× 0·2); E, *Euryale ferox* (× 0·04); F, *Cabomba piauhyensis* (× 1); G, *C. caroliniana* (× 1); H, *C. australis* (× 1); K, *C. aquatica* (× 1); L, *Brasenia schreberi* (× 0·2). (All except L are views of the abaxial surface; L shows the adaxial surface. Venation is shown in only half of the leaf in each example.)

elongate-oblong, as in *A. subconjugatus,* always with a more or less rounded base and apex. The petiole of these various lanceolate to oblong leaves has a rather abrupt joint at its summit which permits the blade to lie flat on the surface.

The trend towards a circular form involves, firstly, the further expansion of the blade, and secondly, the extension of its basal lobes, as a result of which the attachment of the petiole approaches more nearly to the centre. In *Potamogeton natans* and *P. polygonifolius* the leaf is frequently elliptic in outline, but rounded to subcordate at its base; in mature specimens of *P. pulcher* a more pronounced ovate shape is apparent. Further expansion is shown by *Hydrocleys nymphoides* where the ovate to suborbicular lamina has a slightly cordate base, and by *Sagittaria guayanensis* where the base is deeply cordate. In waterlilies of the genus *Nuphar* the blade is broadly elliptic or oblong with a deep notch, at the summit of which the petiole is attached, and prominent, rather pointed, basal lobes. These are usually from one-quarter to one-third of the length of the leaf, as in *N. lutea,* and may diverge at an angle of 45 to 80°, as in *N. advena.* The laminae of *Euryale* and *Nymphaea* (related closely to *Nuphar*) and of *Nymphoides* (of the quite unrelated Menyanthaceae) achieve an orbicular shape with a deep basal sinus reaching to the more or less central insertion of the petiole. Truly peltate leaves are found only in the less well-known genera of the Nymphaeaceae: their shape varies from lanceolate or elliptic, to oval and roughly circular, and they range in width from about 2 mm in *Cabomba piauhyensis* and 1 cm in *C. aquatica,* to 10 cm in *Brasenia schreberi,* 0·5 to 1 m or more in the lotuses, *Nelumbo lutea* and *N. nucifera,* and up to 2 m in the gigantic South American lily, *Victoria amazonica.* The approximately central attachment of the petiole in these broadly oval to circular leaves is the most efficient for mechanical stability.

RESISTANCE TO WETTING AND TEARING

As wind sweeps over the surface of exposed water it tends to lift the edges of a floating lamina and tear it away from its attachment to the petiole. Waves and surface currents exert a similar influence and also tend to immerse the leaf. Any structure lying flat on the surface receives considerable support from the water beneath, but whilst this may be beneficial in calm conditions it is disadvantageous during falls of rain or hail. Assailed relentlessly over its whole surface, a floating leaf is unable to adjust itself, and so receives a more severe battering from rain than does an aerial leaf, which is not supported from below and can to a certain extent alter its position. It is therefore imperative that floating leaves should be able to withstand the horizontal tearing strains imposed by wind and waves and the more or less vertical impact of rain which tends to submerge them. The moderate success which they achieve in resisting these forces is due partly to features of their shape, their texture, and the structure of their upper surface.

It is clear that a dissected or fenestrated leaf, having a greater number of weak points than an entire leaf, would be more easily torn, and, despite its smaller surface area which would tend to accumulate much less falling water, more quickly submerged. In fact, no floating leaves are conspicuously sub-divided: all are more or less entire in outline. Only a few species deviate from

FIG. 4.3. A, leaves of *Nymphaea capensis* with toothed margins. B, a cultivated hybrid *Nymphaea* just after a shower of rain, showing residual water repelled as small drops by the waxy cuticle.

the truly entire, smooth margin shown by the laminae of the vast majority. The orbicular leaves of *Nymphoides peltata* and sometimes *Nymphaea caerulea*, for example, have sinuate margins, whilst those of *Nymphaea nouchali* and *N. capensis* have toothed edges (Figs. 4.2 and 4.3).

A second feature of leaf form is exhibited by only a few species, such as the huge *Victoria amazonica*, *V. cruziana*, and also the smaller *Nymphaea odorata* var. *gigantea*. The edge of the leaf is turned up around its whole circumference forming a vertical rim some 2 to 20 cm high (Fig. 4.4). Whilst this may improve resistance to lateral tearing and may prevent immersion by all but severe waves, it must inevitably favour the accumulation of water falling on the leaf.

Much of the strength of floating leaves results from their leathery texture. Some are notably more coriaceous than others. The laminae of the larger and more successful forms, such as *Nymphaea*, *Victoria*, *Brasenia*, *Euryale*, *Nuphar lutea* and *Nuphar advena*, *Potamogeton natans*, *Potamogeton nodosus*, and *Potomogeton epihydrus* are extremely tough and leathery by comparison with the thinner, smaller and more easily torn leaves of *Nymphoides*, *Aponogeton*, and *Sagittaria*: those of *Potamogeton alpinus* and *Potamogeton polygonifolius* are intermediate in texture. Additional support is given by the principal veins, especially in orbicular and peltate laminae where they form a skeleton of ribs radiating through the mesophyll from the summit of the petiole. In the lanceolate, elliptic and oblong leaves of some species of *Potamogeton* and *Aponogeton*, and of *Baldellia ranunculoides* and *Luronium natans* the venation displays the parallel or parallel-reticulate pattern typical of monocotyledons, but in those which approach or achieve the peltate form it becomes increasingly radial, regardless of whether the species are monocotyledons or dicotyledons. In most types, mechanical tissue is associated with each principal vein. Collenchyma occurs in the younger and smaller leaves; a few sclerenchyma fibres may appear in the older ones. The tissue may form a column running above and below, or a complete sheath around, each vascular bundle, and is sometimes excessively developed on the underside, so that the vein protrudes from the lower surface of the leaf. The tissue is also well developed at the junction of the veins with the petiole where the tearing strains are severe.

The most elegant example of mechanical reinforcement may be seen on the spiny lower surface of the immense peltate leaves of *Victoria amazonica* (Fig. 4.4). Numerous stout ribs radiate from the insertion of the lamina on the petiole to the upturned margin: these are braced at intervals by smaller tangential ribs, thus forming a circular grid on which the upper tissues of the leaf appear to be laid. Near the centre of the leaf the ribs may be as much as 8 cm deep, but towards the perimeter they become shallower and less spiny. Each rib is a downward-projecting ridge of mesophyll containing several vascular strands and many lacunae. Although sclerenchyma is lacking (it is, indeed, absent from all members of the Nymphaeaceae), the system of ribs gives the leaf considerable strength and stability. This was charmingly demonstrated by Joseph Paxton, who raised the first specimen of *V. amazonica* to flower in cultivation. In Fitch and Hooker (1851) he related that when his plant was approaching maturity,

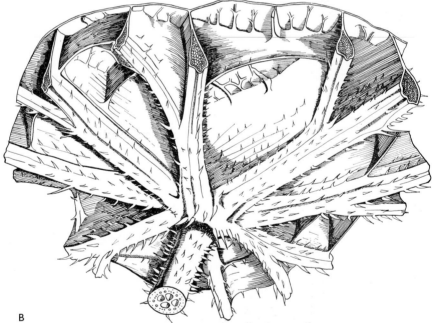

B

FIG. 4.4. The giant South American waterlily, *Victoria amazonica*. A, a cultivated specimen at the Royal Botanic Garden, Kew, England, showing the enormous leaves with upturned margins. (Covering the remaining water surface is a dense population of the free-floating *Pistia stratiotes*); B, sketch of the architecture of the underside of the leaf at the summit of the petiole, showing the stout spiny ribs and transverse partitions ($\times 0.3$). (After Fitch and Smith, 1851.)

'. . . the leaves being four feet eight inches [1·42 m] in diameter, and exhibiting every appearance of possessing great strength from the deep thick ribs, which form the foundation of the blade, I was desirous of ascertaining the weight which they would bear, and, accordingly, placed my youngest daughter, eight years of age, weighing forty-two pounds, upon one of the leaves; a copper-lid, weighing fifteen pounds, being the readiest thing that presented itself, was first placed upon it, in order to equalise the pressure, making together fifty-seven pounds [25·86 kg]. This weight the leaf bore extremely well, as did several others upon which the experiment was tried.' It was, in fact, from the architectural principles embodied in the supporting system of these leaves that Paxton subsequently evolved his designs for a new tropical glasshouse to accommodate the growing plant and for that apotheosis of the Victorian conservatory, the monumental iron and glass palace (the Crystal Palace) that housed the 1851 Exhibition in London's Hyde Park.

In small floating leaves of elliptic, oblong or ovate shape, support and buoyancy are principally endowed by the air-filled lacunae which are sometimes hypertrophied in the region of the midrib, especially where this merges into the petiole, e.g. in *Hydrocleys nymphoides*.

The upper surface of most floating leaves is glabrous and excessive wetting is prevented by the wax bloom of the cuticle (Fig. 4.3). *Zizania aquatica*, however, exhibits a structural modification for water repellancy. The upper epidermal cells occur in longitudinal files which are composed partly of short cells and stomata but mainly of long cells which bear protruding hairs. The outer walls of all the cells, including the hairs, are locally thickened, forming blisters which are more than twice as tall as they are wide. The pockets of air trapped between these hairs effectively prevent the epidermis from being wetted (Weir and Dale, 1960). This type of anatomical device occurs also in certain free-floating plants (pp. 187, 197) and is strongly reminiscent of the plastron, a dense pile of water-repellent hairs covering the cuticle around each spiracle in certain aquatic insects.

ACCOMMODATION OF THE PETIOLE

The expansion of the laminae in only one plane, on the surface of the water, creates vigorous competition for space in a floating-leaved community. Exposure of the maximum leaf area to incident light is only possible if the maturing laminae are borne away to some distance by their petioles, leaving the water surface above the rhizome or rootstock clear for the expansion of young leaves pushing up through the water (Fig. 4.5). Most species achieve this habit through the great length and pliability of their petioles, but growth is often so luxuriant that a colony covers every available piece of water surface and the leaves inevitably overlap to a considerable extent.

The length of the petioles is partly correlated with the habit of growth. In most species the axis from which the leaves develop is a rhizome growing on the surface of, or buried in, the substrate. Elongation of the petioles bears the laminae up to the surface, a vertical distance of as much as 2 m. The actual

4

length of the petioles frequently exceeds this because they do not grow vertically but at an angle which increases as the leaves mature. The horizontal spread of the foliage from one rhizome is therefore considerable: the leaves of a single specimen of *Victoria amazonica*, which is rather unusual in that its petioles do not elongate to a great extent, quickly cover an area of as much as 36 to 40 m².

FIG. 4.5. A, young specimen of *Nuphar lutea*, showing well-spread laminae; B, mature specimen of *Nymphaea* × Midnight, showing a leaf mosaic with a certain amount of overlap.

In *Brasenia schreberi* and many species of *Potamogeton* and *Nymphoides* the rhizome forms lateral branches which develop into ascending elongated stems, which trail through the water for 3 m or more in some species. The petioles, which arise obliquely from these stems, thus tend to be shorter than when they grow directly from a rhizome, but they are similarly longer than is

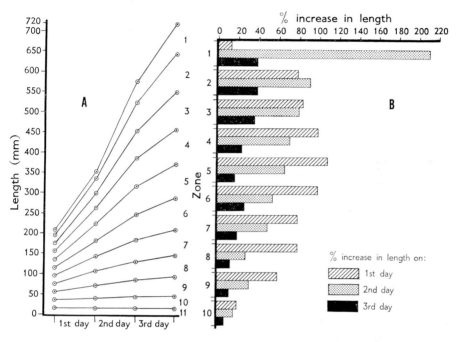

FIG. 4.6. Accommodation of the petiole of *Nymphoides peltata*. A, graph showing the elongation of a petiole over a period of 3 days. (The petiole was initially 215 mm in length, marked out into 11 zones, 10 of 20 mm length and 1 of 15 mm); B, bar diagram showing the percentage increase in length in zones 1 to 10 in each of the 3 days. (From data of Funke, 1937.)

strictly necessary for the laminae to reach the surface. The extra length of the petioles in all forms not only allows exposure of the photosynthetic tissues to light, but also permits the laminae to respond freely to wind and water movement whilst still retaining a floating position. Laminae whose positions were rigidly determined by inflexible petioles would soon be submerged by water movement or sudden increases in depth.

The accommodation of mature petioles to an increased depth of water was demonstrated by Funke (1937), using *Nymphoides peltata* and *Sagittaria sagittifolia*. The petioles of mature specimens transplanted to deep water recommenced growth until their laminae again reached the surface. The rate of growth was found to be as much as 17 mm/h and was effected by both division and extension of cells. In the petiole of *Nymphoides* the greatest elongation occurred initially in the middle zones, but later in the upper part nearest to the laminae (Fig. 4.6). Funke induced abnormal elongation of the petioles of *Nymphoides*, *Sagittaria*, and five species of *Nymphaea*, by growing the plants in solutions containing 1 ppm IAA, IPA, IBA, or NAA, which promoted immense cell expansion. Solutions containing an auxin concentration of 3 or 7·5 ppm inhibited longitudinal growth in the petiole, which showed marked twisting accompanied by hyponastic curvature of the laminae (Funke, 1938, 1939). Thus the petioles of at least some floating-leaved hydrophytes retain a capacity for renewed growth, which is perhaps regulated partly by auxins. Germ (1951) and Gessner and Weinfurter (1952) described geotropic growth curvatures of *Nymphaea* petioles.

A physiological aspect of petiolar accommodation which has not received much experimental attention is the nature of the stimulus which arrests growth so that the lamina is in fact brought, or restored, just to the surface of the water and not protruded into the air. It seems certain that neither the increasing light intensity nor the decreasing pressure of the overlying water, as the petioles near the surface, are directly responsible (Arber, 1920). There is some indication that the higher oxygen concentration of the atmosphere may be an influence. Karsten (1888) inverted tubes of oxygen-free air over leaves of *Marsilea*, *Ranunculus sceleratus* and the free-floating *Hydrocharis* as they neared the surface, and found that elongation of the petioles continued, the laminae becoming aerial instead of floating. A similar suggestive demonstration was made by Funke (1938) using *Nymphoides peltata* and *Sagittaria sagittifolia* grown in two types of aquaria, one with a layer of paraffin oil covering the water, the other with constant artificial aeration. In the latter type, in the presence of excess oxygen in the water, the growth of existing petioles and the formation of new ones were both markedly reduced. Gessner (1959) suggested that the normal elongation of *Nymphaea* petioles might be due to reduced carbon dioxide tension in the aquatic medium, and considered that Karsten's (1888) experimental findings could be so interpreted. However, recent experiments on shoot elongation in a species of *Callitriche* (p. 244) suggest that neither oxygen nor carbon dioxide tension is the significant factor, but that petiole or stem growth is arrested at the surface when the leaves begin to lose water by transpiration. The continued petiolar elongation and production of aerial leaves by some species of *Nuphar* and *Nymphaea* in crowded shallow habitats (Fig. 4.7) may be due to lack of light or space on the surface or to suppression of transpiration amidst the clustered foliage.

EARLY DEVELOPMENT OF FLOATING LEAVES

The inception of floating leaves occurs at the apex of either a horizontal rhizome or rootstock or an ascending elongated stem. The former type is of special interest since the rhizome is the primary permanent axis of the plant and serves as a perennating organ. The rhizomes of species of *Nuphar* and *Nymphaea* have large apices which are readily accessible and therefore of use in the experimental study of the origin of leaves and flowers (Wardlaw, 1952a, b; 1956). Cutter (1957a) found that in *Nuphar lutea* and *Nymphaea alba*, where the leaf and flower primordia are spirally arranged around the apex, there is a

FIG. 4.7. A, crowded specimens of *Nymphaea* spp. with partly aerial foliage; B, *Nuphar advena* growing in only about 20 cm of water and producing mainly aerial foliage. (See also Fig. 15.6.)

progressive accummulation of young unexpanded leaves and flowers because the rate of inception exceeds the rate of seasonal expansion. She concluded that the leaves probably do not develop until 3 or 4 years after their inception. Whereas in ferns an isolated lateral primordium of the shoot apex develops into a bud, Cutter (1958) found that in *Nuphar* a primordium isolated from the apex by tangential cuts always developed into a normal dorsiventral leaf. It is thus apparent that in these rhizomatous species the fate of a primordium as a potential leaf is determined very early even though its subsequent development may take several years.

   In all species the very young leaves are of course submerged and whilst this circumstance eliminates the dangers of transpiration, other problems, notably the shortage of oxygen near the substrate, the pressure of the overlying water and the development of a high osmotic pressure in the cells, must arise. It appears that floating leaves can tolerate a low concentration or complete lack of oxygen during their early submerged life. Young leaves of *Nuphar advena* can respire anaerobically for several days, producing detectable amounts of alcohol in an oxygen concentration of 3 per cent and less, without suffering a setback to their rate of growth (Laing, 1940b). The ability of young foliage to withstand a certain range of water pressures may influence the ecological distribution of the species. Laing (1941) observed that growth of *Nuphar advena* was not completely inhibited by a pressure of water equivalent to 3 m depth but that development of the young leaves was significantly better when the pressure was equivalent to not more than 1·3 to 1·9 m. The cells of the actively growing young leaves of all species are sites of high metabolic activity: synthesising sugars and receiving osmotically active solutes translocated from the storage cells of the rhizome or shoot axis, they will possess a high osmotic pressure and a high diffusion pressure deficit. Inflation of the young tissues by the osmotic intake of water may thus be a serious risk until the epidermis becomes fully cuticularised. It has been suggested (Goebel, 1891–1893; Schilling, 1894) that the conspicuous mucilaginous sheath on many young floating leaves may restrict the inward passage of water. When the organs become prominently cuticular-ised early in development, as in *Potamogeton natans* and *Nelumbo nucifera*, there is little or no mucilage. On the young and more delicate leaves of *Nymphoides peltata*, and most members of the Nymphaeaceae, a coat of mucilage is present which also persistently invests the submerged parts of the mature organs. The secretion from the ephemeral glandular hairs of *Brasenia schreberi* is remarkably copious: in this species the mucilage coat may exceed in thickness the diameter of the petiole or young lamina itself (Schrenk, 1888).

ANATOMICAL AND PHYSIOLOGICAL ASPECTS OF MATURE LEAVES

   The dorsiventral anatomy of mature floating laminae is remarkably uniform in both monocotyledons and dicotyledons, as may be illustrated by *Potamogeton* and *Nymphaea* (Figs. 4.8 and 4.9). In the laminae of both genera the upper part of the mesophyll is occupied by a well-differentiated, richly-chloroplasted, palisade tissue which is homogeneous except for large air spaces beneath the stomata in the upper epidermis. The cells of the spongy mesophyll are more regularly arranged than in terrestrial leaves, forming columns between the lower epidermis and the lower surface of the palisade layer, the columns extending through the leaf as a polygonal network, the meshes of which are very large air chambers.

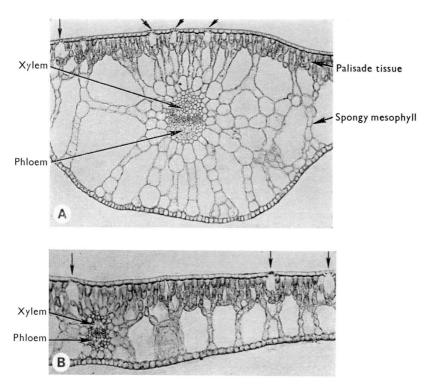

FIG. 4.8. Photomicrographs of T.S. floating leaf of *Potamogeton* sp. A, midrib region; B, part of the lamina (both × 100). Note the restriction of stomata (arrowed) to the upper epidermis, the aggregation of chloroplasts along the inner horizontal walls of the upper epidermal cells, the differentiation of the mesophyll, and the conspicuous lacunae.

Some support may be given to the palisade and spongy tissues of the leaves of such plants as *Euryale*, *Nuphar*, *Nymphaea*, *Nymphoides* and *Victoria* by scattered sclerenchymatous idioblasts (sclereids), which may be present also in the petioles, underground organs, floral parts and fruits (Conard, 1905; Foster, 1956). These specialised cells are generally absent from young organs: they appear later in ontogeny as the tissues increase in volume. Each idioblast differentiates from a young parenchyma cell, the walls of which become heavily lignified and may ultimately bear secreted crystals of calcium oxalate. During differentiation the shape of the cell is often greatly elaborated. Some of the

idioblasts in the leaves of *Nymphaea* and *Nymphoides*, for example, are columnar with branched ends, their long axes being orientated at 90° to the epidermis
—i.e. parallel to the long axes of the palisade cells. Others achieve a stellate or
much branched form and project into the lacunae of the spongy tissue. Small,
rounded, extremely thickened idioblasts are also occasionally seen, but are
generally more common in the fruits and seeds. The total frequency of idioblasts varies with the species, as well as with the age and type of organ. Mature
floating leaves with a high frequency are remarkably tough: in one such species,

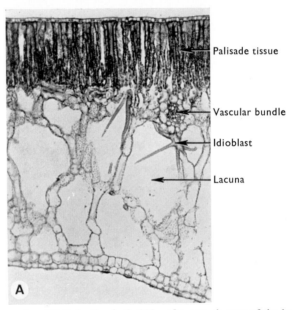

FIG. 4.9. Photomicrographs of T.S. floating leaf of *Nymphaea* sp. A, part of the lamina
(× 200). (B and C on facing page; D on p. 88.)

Nymphaea stellata, the basal region of the leaf may have more than 3900 idioblasts per cm^2 (Gaudet, 1960; Malaviya, 1962, 1963).

The mesophyll of floating leaves gains further mechanical strength from the
turgor of its cells and from the vascular bundles and their sheaths. The
vascular elements are often quite strongly developed especially in the midrib
and principal lateral veins: phloem is usually better differentiated than xylem,
the protoxylem often being represented only by a lacuna. In the majority of
floating leaves—those of members of the Alismaceae, Butomaceae, Potamogetonaceae and Nymphaeaceae—vessels are lacking and the conducting elements of the xylem comprise only annular- and spiral-thickened tracheids
(Cheadle, 1942). Vessels do occur in the floating leaves of some grasses such as
Zizania (Weir and Dale, 1960), but they are few in number and poorly lignified.

Both the upper and lower epidermes of floating laminae are cuticularised, the former much more strongly in coriaceous types, and often contain scattered chloroplasts in all their cells, although in *Zizania aquatica* chloroplasts occur

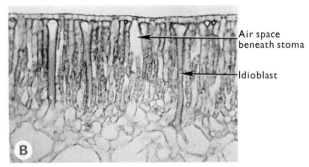

FIG. 4.9. Photomicrographs of T.S. floating leaf of *Nymphaea* sp. B, part of the palisade tissue (× 280).

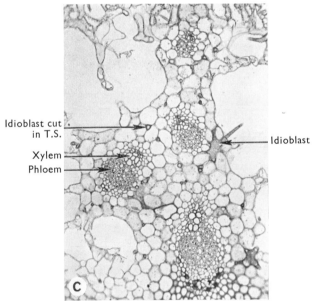

FIG. 4.9. Photomicrographs of T.S. floating leaf of *Nymphaea* sp. C, central region of the midrib (× 200).

only in the guard cells. Anthocyanins are commonly present in the lower, and sometimes in the upper, epidermis of floating leaves, especially those of *Nymphoides* and *Nymphaea* (Wheldale, 1916). Stomatal distribution varies in different species. The more common pattern is the restriction of stomata

4*

entirely to the upper epidermis, as in *Brasenia, Nelumbo, Nymphaea, Nymphoides* and some species of *Potamogeton* and *Callitriche*. These stomata are developed at a very early stage, whilst the leaf is still in the bud (Costantin, 1886), but presumably function only when the upper epidermis is exposed to the atmosphere. Should the stomata open whilst the leaf is still submerged, the internal tissues are protected from the risk of waterlogging by the tight rolling

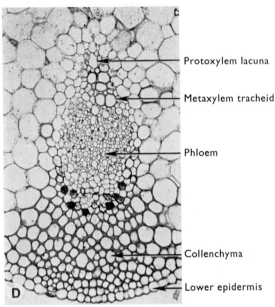

FIG. 4.9. Photomicrographs of T.S. floating leaf of *Nymphaea* sp. D, lower part of the midrib (× 300). Note the mesophyll differentiation, idioblasts, somewhat reduced xylem, well-developed phloem, and collenchyma beneath the lowermost vascular strand of the midrib.

of the lamina, the coat of mucilage secreted by glandular hairs, and the protrusion of the cuticular ridges of the guard cells which probably prevents occlusion of the stomatal aperture (Haberlandt, 1914). This last feature is also advantageous when the lamina has unrolled on the surface and the epidermis is exposed to rain. In the course of the normal stomatal rhythm the aperture is closed by the interlocking of these ridges. The average stomatal frequency varies in different parts of the mature leaf, amongst individuals, between species, and in different conditions. In *Nymphaea alba*, for example, stomata do not occur in the region of the attachment of the petiole: elsewhere on the lamina, frequencies varying from 150 to 460 per mm^2 have been recorded, the lower frequencies occurring, surprisingly, under intense illumination (Roshardt, 1915, 1922).

The lower epidermis of some floating leaves sometimes possesses stomata. Shinobu (1952) found a mean stomatal frequency of 3 per mm^2 in the lower epidermis of *Potamogeton fryeri* and 4 per mm^2 in that of *P. gramineus* as compared with frequencies in the upper epidermis of 136 and 174 per mm^2 respectively. He also observed differences in the occurrence of stomata in the lower epidermis according to the habitat: in *Potamogeton distinctus* the frequency on a form growing in shallow water was 3·6 per mm^2 but on a deep water form only 0·75 per mm^2. Since the leaves were floating in both habitats and the stomatal frequency on the upper epidermis did not differ significantly in the two forms, these data are not easily interpreted. However, in all the species examined, the stomata in the lower epidermis resembled those in the upper in development, structure, and orientation parallel to the veins. Shinobu considered such stomata as functionless and regarded them as relict ancestral features.

In the lower epidermis of the leaves of *Nymphaea* and several other genera are small groups of cells which stain deeply with certain dyes. These cell-groups, termed hydropoten by Mayr (1915), have been thought by numerous authors to be sites at which ions are absorbed from the water into the mesophyll. Recently, Lüttge (1964) showed that when a sulphate solution, labelled with ^{35}S, is applied for two hours to the lower surface of the leaf of *Nymphaea* × *marliacea*, from 2·5 to 3·7 times more sulphate ions are absorbed by the hydropoten than by the surrounding epidermal cells. The absorbed ions are translocated to the veins of the mesophyll. Treatment with the respiratory inhibitor, sodium azide, greatly reduces absorption through the hydropoten, which suggests that an active mechanism may be involved here, as in root absorption.

The organisation of the lamina is thus related to the dual nature of its environment. Although the structure of the mesophyll and presence of stomata in the upper epidermis facilitate the absorption of oxygen and carbon dioxide they are also unfortunately well-suited, as in land plants, to the loss of water vapour. Transpiration from floating-leaved hydrophytes is appreciable though not as great per unit area as from emergent species because the transpiring surface is largely restricted to the horizontal plane. Otis (1914) showed the rate of transpiration of *Nymphaea odorata* to be slightly less than the rate of evaporation from a free water surface of equivalent area, whereas that of several emergent species was up to three times as great. As in land plants the stomata provide the main route of water loss, at least in moving air. The ratio of the rates of stomatal to cuticular transpiration in *Nuphar lutea* has been recorded as 9·9:1 in wind but only 3·2:1 in still air (Renner, 1910).

Gessner (1945) observed that leaves of *Nuphar*, *Nymphaea* and *Nelumbo* rapidly dry out if they are cut and their petioles are placed in water, and he suggested that normal water losses from the foliage are compensated not by suction, but by root pressure. Yet the water lost through the cuticle and stomata of the upper surface as the leaves dried out must have been drawn from the lower tissues of the lamina, and ultimately the upper part of the petiole, through the mesophyll and parenchymatous ground tissue. In intact foliage, such water movement, caused by normal evaporative losses, could surely pull a normal transpiration current upwards from the rooted organs. It is difficult to understand why root pressure should be invoked as the motive force. The rapidity with which the cut leaves dried in Gessner's experiments may have been partly due to accidental introduction of air-locks into the very weak-walled xylem elements before the petioles were immersed, and to the fact that since the laminae were not actually floated, the thinly cuticularised lower surface probably lost water as freely as the upper surface, even though it has few or no stomata.

That water may also be lost by guttation is strongly suggested by the presence of hydathodes on the lower surface and margins of floating leaves of *Nymphaea*, *Nymphoides* and some other genera (Schrenk, 1888; Metcalfe and Chalk, 1950). Direct demonstration of exudation through these pores is well-nigh impossible when the leaves are normally in contact with free water, and so the possibility remains that the hydathodes are functionless relict structures, like the sporadic stomata in the lower epidermis. This possibility is enhanced by the anomalous potential hydathodes of *Hydrocleys nymphoides*, where, at the leaf apex, the cuticle persistently covers the epithem and vein-ending, and a pore never develops (Sauvageau, 1893).

LAND FORMS

Three features—the possession of strong leathery laminae, the formation of aerial leaves in crowded colonies, and the occurrence of plants in littoral habitats where they are liable to be stranded by falls in water level—all suggest that floating-leaved hydrophytes could produce emergent land forms with reasonable facility. Naturally-occurring or experimentally-induced land forms have been recorded for several species, including *Nuphar pumila* (Mer, 1882), *Nymphaea alba* (Bachman, 1896), *Nymphoides peltata* (Schenck, 1885), *Potamogeton coloratus*, *P. natans*, *P. gramineus*, *P. × fluitans* and *P. × zizii* (Fryer, 1887; West, 1905). These all show similar changes of habit, developing as a close rosette of smaller foliage with abbreviated inter-nodes and very short petioles often more or less buried in the soil. The margins of the laminae are frequently inrolled over the upper surface, a feature perhaps analogous to the rolling of the leaves of some xeromorphic plants and tending to protect the stomata from air movement and reduce the rate of transpiration. The proximity of the rosette to the soil has a similar effect. However, a reduced frequency of stomata probably provides the greatest transpiration check: stomata are infrequent on or even absent from aerial leaves of *Nuphar lutea* (Grüss, 1927). Such land forms are capable of living for some time out of water, those of *Nymphaea alba* existing for a whole summer and those of *Potamogeton gramineus* for several seasons, perennating underground.

LIMITATIONS OF FLOATING-LEAVED PLANTS

Despite their adaptive modifications of vegetative structure floating-leaved hydrophytes are an ecologically restricted group. The trend towards a mechanic-ally efficient peltate leaf, the cuticularisation and coriaceous texture of the lamina, and the growth capacity and flexibility of the petioles may be interpreted as structural features well suited to the environment. Yet the problems of life in the narrow confines of the water surface are severe and somewhat unpredictable. Strong winds, fast currents, heavy rain and flood-waters quickly create havoc amongst floating-leaved communities. The degree of adaptation and corresponding resilience of the plant body differ from species to species. Those whose leaves are borne on long herbaceous floating stems and whose laminae least approach an orbicular or peltate form are probably most susceptible. The giant *Victoria amazonica* has very heavy and ill-shaped petioles which have little capacity for elongation, and it is consequently restricted to much shallower water than many smaller lilies: Spruce (1908) observed it in the Amazon region in water less than 1 m deep. In view of this edaphic restriction it is perhaps surprising that the species has survived at all. Even amongst species of similar form and size, less tangible differences of resilience occur: *Nuphar lutea* appears to tolerate more water movement than *Nymphaea alba* and is therefore the more common in English lowland rivers (Heslop-Harrison, 1955c) whilst neither species appears able to withstand as much wave action as the related hybrid *Nuphar × spennerana* and *Nymphaea alba* ssp. *occidentalis* both of which inhabit barren and exposed lakes at higher altitudes (Pearsall, 1920). Common observation leaves no doubt that the apparently adaptive structures do not wholly solve the problems confronting them and the risks of tearing and immersion are ever present. Floating-leaved plants generally are unable to colonise littoral habitats exposed to prevailing winds, where the water is rough. Within the narrow ecological niche provided by stationary or very slow-flowing water about 0·5 to 3·5 m deep over a stable silted substrate, this life form achieves qualified success.

Life in the Water: The Structure and Physiology of Submerged Organs

Submerged hydrophytes form a reasonably discrete and homogeneous biological group since the vegetative organs of the vast majority of species remain under water at all times and display similar morphological and anatomical modifications, some of which may validly be interpreted as reactions to the aquatic environment. A few species are exceptional, either because they may show different life forms in different habitats or because they are intermediate in habit between typical, rooted, submerged plants and other life forms. Species of *Ceratopteris*, for example, live as free-floating or emergent plants equally successfully as when they are rooted under water. The rootless *Ceratophyllum* can be treated as a free-floating plant, like *Aldrovanda vesiculosa* and many species of *Utricularia*, which also lack roots and grow at some depth beneath the surface, but it differs from these in its submerged flowers and genuine hydrophily and is therefore more thoroughly committed to a submerged existence. The Podostemaceae are also exceptional amongst submerged hydrophytes by virtue of their highly specialised and reduced vegetative structure in which stem, root and leaf have lost their distinct identities.

Certain physiological problems confronting terrestrial vascular plants are minimised or even eliminated in the aquatic environment. The support given to submerged organs by the water itself, together with the buoyancy endowed by their air-filled lacunate tissues, alleviates the need for mechanical strength and rigidity, and submerged hydrophytes generally do not possess a dominant erect axis. Their stems, petioles and leaves contain little or no lignin even in the vascular tissues: sclerenchyma and collenchyma are often absent. Paradoxically, these mechanical tissues do occur in some of the most highly modified species. The outer cortex of the stem of *Ceratophyllum demersum*, for example, is collenchymatous, whilst the cortical vascular strands of the thallus of *Mourera aspera*, one of the Podostemaceae, are sheathed in collenchyma, which is later converted to sclerenchyma (Went, 1924). Conspicuous lignified fibres occur also in the leaves of most submerged marine angiosperms, where their pattern of development is sometimes so specific as to afford a reliable criterion of identification (Duchartre, 1872; Sauvageau, 1890, 1891).

The extremely thin cuticle of submerged organs, and the thinness of leaves and presence of chloroplasts in their epidermis, are sometimes regarded as adaptations to an aquatic life. It is probably more accurate to treat them as reactions to the absence of excessive irradiance. As a result of the restricted and differential penetration of light into water, the conditions of illumination for most submerged hydrophytes approximate those for many land plants living in shaded habitats. It is significant that numerous terrestrial shade plants similarly possess thin leaves with epidermal chloroplasts and diminished cuticle. It is probably quite fortuitous that these structural modifications are valuable in solving certain severe problems created by an aquatic environment.

The difficulty of obtaining adequate oxygen, which is often scarce, is mitigated to some extent by the permeability of the thin cuticle and epidermis: dissolved gases can pass in or out through the whole surface of the plant. Mineral nutrients may also be absorbed through at least certain areas of the epidermis, although the principal route of ion uptake for all but the most highly reduced species may still be the roots, as in land plants. There is evidence that bicarbonate ions are available to submerged plants as an additional carbon source in photosynthesis.

The slow rate of diffusion in aqueous solution retards the escape of oxygen produced in photosynthesis and the consequent accumulation of gas within the tissues is partly responsible for the origin of the extensive lacunae typically present in submerged organs. Transport and storage of oxygen within these lacunae greatly facilitate the respiration of the living tissues, at least during the hours of daylight: at night, when photosynthesis has ceased, there may sometimes be a shortage of oxygen in the organ.

The absorption of substances through the cuticle, the reduction of the vascular system, and the virtual lack of lignification in the xylem have led many writers to the dogmatic statement that no transport of water and ions through the xylem occurs in submerged plants. Other authors have concluded, largely from physiological experiments performed between 1860 and 1920, that a sustained flow, analogous to the transpiration current of land plants, does in fact occur. Critical analysis of the evidence, together with the results of more recent experiments, suggests that neither view is completely acceptable (Wilson, 1947; Gessner, 1956).

THE FOLIAGE OF SUBMERGED SPECIES

The Form of the Shoot System. Most submerged hydrophytes display one of two main habits of growth: an abbreviated axis producing a rosette of radical leaves, or an elongated flexuous stem which is clothed with leaves and rooted, sometimes only sparsely, from its nodes. As in land plants, the difference between these two habits is attributable to a difference in apical organisation. If the shoot apex is relatively flat and broad, the stem is much reduced, the internodes are condensed, and the leaves arise in a radical cluster, as in *Aponogeton, Isoetes* or *Vallisneria*. The stem may be an erect herbaceous rootstock, a corm-like or tuberous organ, or a woody or herbaceous rhizome. If the apical meristem is long and narrow, with the leaf primordia low down on its flanks, as in *Elodea* and *Hippuris* (Stant, 1954; Wardlaw, 1956 and see Fig. 5.13), the stem is elongated and each internode well-developed. The shoot apex of *Elodea canadensis*, for example, is devoid of leaf initials for at least 100 μ: the internodes are initiated by longitudinal growth and division of cells from the base of the leaf insertion discs (Dale, 1957a).

In the few genera which have been thoroughly studied, the zonation of the apical meristem resembles that of related terrestrial herbs (see Clowes, 1961; Esau, 1953, 1965). The tunica is often two-layered, the corpus somewhat variable but usually composed of the corpus initials, the inner layers of the peripheral meristem and the central rib meristem. *Hippuris* is unusual in having four, five or six layers of cells in the tunica (Jentsch, 1960). Application of adenine labelled with ^{14}C to *Cabomba*, *Elodea* and *Vallisneria* has shown that DNA is synthesised in the nuclei of all the apical cells (Clowes, 1959), which suggests that the central distal part of the apical meristem is not quiescent, as maintained by many French morphologists (see Buvat, 1955). In *Cymodocea*, *Elodea*, *Hippuris*, *Posidonia* and *Ruppia* the mode of origin of leaves resembles that found typically in many dicotyledons. Each leaf primordium is initiated by mainly periclinal divisions of the second layer of the apex, together with anticlinical divisions of the surface cells. In *Ceratophyllum* the internal cells of each primordium are derived from a strand of cells radiating from the corpus (Herrig, 1915; Jones, 1931; Foster, 1936).

The leaves of caulescent submerged hydrophytes may be alternate, e.g. *Potamogeton*; paired and opposite, e.g. most species of *Cabomba*; or whorled, e.g. *Hippuris* and most species of *Elodea* and *Myriophyllum*. *M. hetero-phyllum* is a notable exception in its genus in having a pseudo-whorled arrangement: the leaves are really inserted alternately, but several condensed internodes occur between two successive long internodes, the leaves consequently appearing to form a whorl (England and Tolbert, 1964).

In some plants with whorled leaves the number of leaves per whorl on a mature shoot is more or less definite, e.g. usually four in *Myriophyllum spicatum*, but on juvenile shoots it often varies according to the size of the apex. A young shoot of *Myriophyllum verticillatum* commonly has whorls of four leaves whereas older shoots have whorls of five. In a shoot of *Elodea canadensis* the basal nodes, which were formed when the apex was young and small, bear only two leaves whereas the distal nodes, formed later when the apex has enlarged, bear whorls of three. The shoot apex of *Egeria densa* is even bigger and four leaves usually occur at each node (Dale, 1957b). In other species the number is variable even in mature shoots. McCully and Dale (1961a) studied *Hippuris vulgaris* and could not find a single shoot on which the number of leaves per whorl was constant from the apex to the lowest node: it was found to vary from two to sixteen. Variation between whorls was ascribed to differences in the size of the leaf insertion discs: the larger the circumference of each disc, the greater the number of leaves in the whorl. In *Ceratophyllum demersum*, Pearl (1907) revealed a relatively high degree of correlation between the number of leaves per whorl and the position of the whorl on the axis. The mean number per whorl was found to be highest, and the absolute number least variable, on the main stems: the maximum variation in leaf number was found on the secondary lateral stems. Variations in leaf arrangement in both *Hippuris vulgaris* and *Ceratophyllum demersum* have also been studied by Loiseau and Grangeon (1963).

As a result of the buoyancy conferred by their internal air spaces, and the support they receive from the surrounding water, elongated flexuous stems are relieved of the burden of holding the foliage erect, the so-called 'column requirement' which terrestrial stems must meet (Bower, 1930, 1947). Consequently, this type of submerged plant shows little evidence of a dominant shoot axis: growth is sympodial rather than monopodial. The stems attain great lengths and generally branch very freely, the older parts dying as the apices forge ahead.

In some submerged hydrophytes the lateral shoots arise in a specific pattern, and branching may be further suppressed by apical dominance. In at least some of the submerged Hydrocharitaceae, as in the free-floating members of the same family (p. 188), axillary buds do not occur in the axil of every leaf. In *Enhalus*, *Halophila* and *Ottelia*, for example, they are present in the axil of every second leaf, whilst in *Vallisneria* there may be from two to four leaves between successive leaves with axillary buds (Bugnon and Joffrin, 1962; Cutter, 1964). Apical dominance is especially marked in *Egeria densa*, in which lateral buds diverge from the axis at every twelfth node: even in a detached piece of stem bearing but two buds, often only the distal one will grow into a shoot, the proximal one remaining dormant (King, 1943). The development of axillary buds in *Elodea* was shown by Homès and van Schoor (1937), using an agar block technique, to be directly or indirectly inhibited by auxin formed at the stem apex. It is, however, interesting to note that Allsopp (1956b) presented evidence that auxin does not directly inhibit the growth of lateral shoots. He cultured the rhizomatous fern, *Marsilea drummondii*, in media supplemented with either IAA or IAN, and found that the lateral buds of excised nodes, decapitated plants and intact plants grew out quite normally in all tested concentrations of the two auxins. The results of recent experiments by Fleury (1966) suggest that apical dominance in *M. drummondii* is controlled by antagonistic hormonal and nutritional factors, the interactions of which establish correlations of growth between the apical bud, lateral buds, leaves and roots.

Various natural and synthetic auxins have been found to promote internodal growth when applied to solutions in which submerged plants are cultured. Soltys *et al.* (1938) described the responses of species of *Elodea* to dilutions of IAA and *l*-histidine compounds, and King (1943) reported the promotion of axial elongation in *Egeria densa* by treatment with IAA, IBA, IPA and other compounds. Inanç (1960) compared the influences of IAA, PAA and POA on the growth of shoots of *Elodea canadensis* and *Najas minor* cultured for twelve months in filtered pond water after 21 days' exposure to the auxin solutions. Optimal elongation in both species was promoted by a 10^{-5} M concentration (approximately 15 ppm) of each of the compounds. All the tested concentrations (10^{-4} to 10^{-10} M: approx. 150 to 0·00015 ppm) of each compound were growth-promoting in *Najas* but 10^{-4} M PAA and POA inhibited growth in *Elodea* (Fig. 5.1). The promotion of growth was enhanced by artificial aeration of the cultures. Whilst these results generally resemble those obtained for many terrestrial plants they differ in one qualitative respect: in neither species was there any enhanced development of the inner cortex, endodermis or phloem parenchyma.

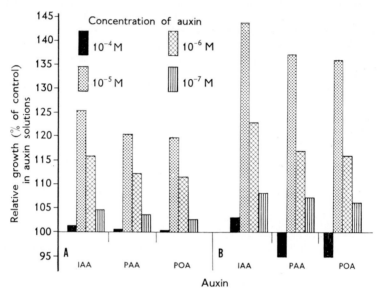

FIG. 5.1. Relative growth in length of stem cells of *Najas minor* (A) and *Elodea canadensis* (B) in various concentrations of each of the auxins, IAA, PAA and POA. (Exposure time: 10 days, with continuous aeration of the solutions; temperature: 25°C; each bar of the histogram represents the mean of 40 measurements.) (From data of Inanç, 1960.)

The Form of Entire Leaves. Three main types of leaf occur in submerged hydrophytes—entire, fenestrated and dissected. The entire form is the most common and may be found amongst both monocotyledons and dicotyledons, in all types of habitat, in all climatic zones. Fenestrated leaves are produced by only a few tropical monocotyledons of the genus *Aponogeton* which grow on the island of Madagascar. Dissected leaves occur widely in numerous dicotyledonous genera throughout tropical, subtropical and temperate regions, and like the fenestrated type they are produced in stagnant as well as slow- or swift-flowing fresh waters.

Entire submerged leaves are frequently thin and more or less translucent: their shape varies from awl-like and linear to ovate and sagittate. The great majority are conspicuously elongated, especially in rosette species, and have a filiform, setaceous or ribbon-like appearance (Fig. 5.2). *Potamogeton pectinatus*, *P. trichoides* and *P. filiformis*, and several species of *Ruppia* and *Zannichellia* exhibit filiform or setaceous leaves. Ribbon leaves occur in numerous species of *Potamogeton*, *Sagittaria* and *Vallisneria*, and in most marine angiosperms, whilst small linear or linear-lanceolate cauline leaves are exemplified by *Egeria*, *Elodea*, *Hippuris*, *Hydrilla*, *Lagarosiphon*, *Najas*, *Nechamandra* and some species of *Callitriche* (Fig. 5.3). A few rosette species, such as *Isoetes* spp.,

FIG. 5.2. Submerged foliage of: A, *Isoetes malinverniana* (×0·3); B, *Potamogeton pectinatus* (×0·3). (C and D on p. 98.)

Littorella uniflora, *Limosella subulata*, and *Subularia aquatica*, are notable amongst vascular plants in retaining the primordial awl-like leaf form: as the young leaves differentiate they undergo remarkably little modification, other than elongation, and at maturity are still more or less subulate.

The morphological identity of the solid, petiole-like, subulate leaves with the flat, ribbon-like types has been demonstrated in those monocotyledons belonging to Helobian families (Arber, 1921, 1924, 1925b). The ribbon leaf of *Sagittaria sagittifolia* is clearly equivalent to the subulate leaf of *S. subulata* and *S. graminea* var. *teres*: both types have a sheathing base and an upper limb, which is either more or less radial and petiole-like in its anatomy, or uniformly flattened and traversed longitudinally by one or more series of vascular strands, some of which are normally, but others inversely, orientated. Representatives of the two types are also found in the marine *Cymodocea* and *Syringodium*, where *S. isoetifolium* has the petiolar, radial form of leaf, and *C. nodosa* the ribbon form, *S. filiforme* being intermediate in structure. There is very little doubt that the ribbon and other leaf types in such monocotyledonous genera as

FIG. 5.2. Submerged foliage of: C, *Vallisneria spiralis* f. *tortifolia* (× 0·3); D, *Sagittaria graminea* var. *teres* (× 0·5).

Enhalus, Potamogeton, Sagittaria, Syringodium, Vallisneria etc. are in fact phyllodes, homologous with the petiole alone of a typical dicotyledonous leaf.

Species of *Potamogeton* show transitional stages in the connation of paired stipules and their adnation to the leaf to form a sheathing base (Monoyer, 1926).

FIG. 5.3. Submerged foliage of: A, *Elodea ernstiae* (×0·5); B, *Egeria densa* (×0·3). (C and D on p. 100.)

Although the linear or linear-lanceolate, cauline leaves of *Egeria, Elodea* and *Lagarosiphon* are typically quite small, the filiform and ribbon leaves of other genera often attain astonishing lengths, relative to their widths. Those of numerous species of *Potamogeton, Ruppia* and *Zannichellia* may be up to 20 cm

FIG. 5.3. Submerged foliage of: C, *Lagarosiphon major* (× 0·25); D, *Groe nlandia densa* (× 0·3).

long yet less than 1 mm wide. Ito (1899a) noted that the leaves of *Enhalus acoroides* measured at least 60 cm long by only 1 to 1·5 cm wide. The similar ribbon leaves of *Vallisneria gigantea* often reach a length of 1 to 1·25 m, whilst just over 2 m has been recorded in *Sagittaria sagittifolia* (Arber, 1920). In several species the dimensions of ribbon leaves vary in different habitats according to the depth and movement of the water. The exceedingly plastic North American species, *Sagittaria subulata*, comprises at least three relatively distinguishable phases: the widespread var. *subulata* occurs as either a dwarfed tidal plant or a more elongated freshwater form; var. *gracillima*, with even longer, narrower leaves is found in some eastern states, whilst in slow Floridan streams there occurs a third phase, var. *kurziana*, whose greatly elongated leaves are said to reach lengths of up to 15 m (Bogin, 1955; Adams and Godfrey, 1961). *Isoetes lacustris* also shows a wide range of stature. The commonest form in English lakes is about 10 cm tall, but in several Welsh localities the awl-like leaves are typically longer, and in the Irish Lough Bray the species reaches a height of 30 to 50 cm. In Lough Camelaun, also in Ireland, a fourth habitat type, with stout leaves 20 to 27 cm tall, has been recorded (Marshall, 1911). In this species, stature is at least partly under genetical control and not solely induced by environmental conditions, since the disparity of size between the various races is maintained in laboratory cultures (Manton, 1950).

From the ribbon-like form a series may be traced, through either cauline or radical leaves involving a shortening and broadening of the leaf, culminating in a flat membranous structure (Fig. 5.4). *Potamogeton crispus* and *P. octandrus*, for example, have broadly lanceolate leaves whilst an oblong shape is achieved in *P. lucens* and *P. praelongus*. Amongst rosette species narrowly lanceolate

FIG. 5.4. Submerged foliage of: A, *Potamogeton crispus* (× 0·3); B, *Cryptocoryne aponogeti-folia* (× 0·3); C, *Nuphar sagittifolium* (× 0·4).

leaves occur in *Cryptocoryne aponogetifolia* and *C. affinis*, broadly lanceolate ones in *Halophila ovalis* and *Ottelia alismoides*. In *Cryptocoryne griffithii*, *C. longicauda* and *C. scurrilis* the leaves are ovate with a cordate base whilst *Nuphar sagittifolium* possesses very thin translucent laminae, of sagittate shape. Many of these broad leaves typically display either undulate margins, as in *Echinodorus intermedius*, *Nuphar sagittifolium* or *Potamogeton crispus*, or bullate surfaces, as in *Cryptocoryne aponogetifolia*, *C. longicauda* and *C. nurii*, which have sometimes been vaguely described as adaptations to life in flowing water. There is, however, no definite correlation between either feature and the existence of a current in their natural habitats. Most of the species have been found at one time or another in natural standing water, and the undulate or bullate character is still displayed by mature foliage cultivated in pools or aquaria.

The shape of entire submerged leaves may have physiological significance. All the various types, but especially the ribbon-like and broad thin forms, have a high ratio of surface area to volume, which presumably increases their efficiency in absorbing adequate supplies of dissolved carbon dioxide, oxygen and mineral nutrients. This structural feature is probably a response to the diminished light intensity, rather than the aquatic nature of the environment, but its facilitation of gaseous exchange and salt absorption is likely to have been of selective advantage in the evolution of submerged floras.

The entire form of leaf could be mechanically advantageous in slow-flowing water: of the various shapes, the linear ribbon probably evades tearing more effectively than the broad membranous type, its great length and pliability allowing it to trail with the current. Although some leaves of *Elodea* and *Potamogeton*, for example, have fine longitudinal fibrous strands, entire leaves generally have no significant strengthening tissue and depend for their support entirely on their internal turgor and the greater density of the water. Their consequent vulnerability prohibits such species from successfully colonising torrential or swift-flowing waters or the wave-swept littoral zones of lakes. The marine angiosperms are exceptional in having through their leaves longitudinal strands of well-lignified sclerenchyma fibres, in a subepidermal position or as a sheath round the veins (Fig. 5.10). The development and eventual distribution of these fibres differs quite markedly in different species (Duchartre, 1872; Sauvageau, 1890, 1891). Whilst this skeletal system therefore cannot be treated as a straightforward adaptive response to the conditions of the environment it is undoubtedly of some mechanical value. Interspecific differences in the ability to withstand waves have been noted in several genera, *Zostera marina*, for example, being said to tolerate more wave action than *Z. angustifolia* (Tutin, 1936), and are perhaps due to differences in the pattern of the fibres. Yet even those species with the most heavily strengthened foliage are unable to withstand the incessant pounding by waves, and are torn to shreds by spring-tides and cast upon the shore in masses.

Leaf Form in *Aponogeton*. The submerged foliage of members of the tropical genus *Aponogeton* offers an interesting spectrum of leaf form (Figs. 5.5 and 5.6). A narrowly lanceolate entire lamina is typical of species of northern Australia and New Guinea, such as *A. elongatus* and *A. loriae*, the Malayan *A. stachyosporus*, and the Sinhalese *A. crispus* and *A. rigidifolius*, the margin varying from slightly undulate to tightly crinkled (de Wit, 1958a, b; van Bruggen, 1962). The leaves of *A. undulatus* are very similar but often thinner and more translucent, a feature evident also in a fourth species from Southern

Asia, *A. natans*, whose submerged laminae are more oblong-lanceolate and only slightly waved.

Four remarkable species endemic to the island of Madagascar complete the series. The leaves of *A. ulvaceus* resemble those of *A. natans* in being broadly lanceolate to oblong but differ in their thin, membranous, translucent texture,

FIG. 5.5. Leaf form in *Aponogeton* spp.: A, *A. loriae* (× 0·2); B, *A. stachyosporus* (× 0·2); C, *A. crispus* (× 0·1). (D, E and F on p. 104.)

and in being furled and spirally twisted. Riede (1921) observed that the furling and twisting are caused by the marginal regions of the leaf growing at much faster rates than the median regions: so great is the disparity between the rates that the length along one margin may be as much as three times the length along the midrib. In *A. bernieranus* small areas of the interstitial tissue of the lamina are lacking at maturity (Krause and Engler, 1906) whilst in *A. fenestralis* and *A. henckelianus* the oblong lamina is thoroughly perforated, consisting almost entirely of a lace-like skeleton of veins. The youngest leaves of these species are quite imperforate, but in successively older leaves the fenestration becomes more conspicuous (Serguéeff, 1907; and see Fig. 5.6). Serguéeff found that during the development of the leaf of *A. fenestralis* each

FIG. 5.5. Leaf form in *Aponogeton* spp.: D, *A. undulatus* (× 0·2); E, *A. ulvaceus* (part of two mature leaves) (× 0·3); F, *A. ulvaceus* (young plant) (× 0·3).

potential 'window' becomes delimited by the suberisation of a rectangle of mesophyll cells. The cells so isolated die leaving a perforation surrounded by a corky lining. The holes in the leaves of the terrestrial *Monstera deliciosa* form in the same way.

Great speculation has been devoted to the possible function of fenestration. Of the many ingenious suggestions, most of them neither confirmed nor disproved, the reduction of resistance to flowing water is perhaps the least far-fetched. Goebel's (1891–1893) hypothesis that the perforations might compensate for a lack of internal air spaces was undermined by Serguéeff's finding that lacunae do in fact occur in the mesophyll of the young leaf. It is doubtful whether the surface area/volume ratio and efficiency of assimilation are really

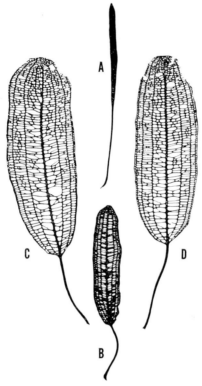

FIG. 5.6. Leaf form in *Aponogeton fenestralis*: A, young imperforate leaf; B, later-formed, partly fenestrated leaf; C, D, mature, fully fenestrated leaves (all × 0·4).

significantly higher than in the membranous entire leaves of other species, and it must also be remembered that much of the photosynthetic tissue is lost as the perforations develop. A fenestrated leaf certainly offers less hindrance to a current and its tough texture, which is belied by the lace-like appearance, efficiently resists tearing. *A. fenestralis* has in fact been collected from torrential waters although it also grows with no modifications of structure in slow-flowing and even stagnant conditions.

Dissected Leaves. Subdivision of the leaf, analogous to fenestration, occurs amongst submerged dicotyledonous hydrophytes (Figs. 5.7 and 5.8). Here the venation pattern, lacking the marginal framework of an *Aponogeton*

lamina, lends itself to dissection and the leaf becomes split into many free
segments radiating from the petiole. In *Hottonia palustris* and *H. inflata*, for
example, each of the whorled leaves is once or twice pinnate, the segments

FIG. 5.7. Dissected submerged foliage: A, *Hottonia palustris* (× 0·5); B, *Cabomba australis*
(× 0·4); C, *Myriophyllum verticillatum* (× 0·4); D, *Ceratophyllum demersum* (× 0·4).

being linear and dorsiventrally flattened. The opposite or whorled leaves of species of *Cabomba* are divided into three to seven parts at the summit of the petiole, each part being di- or trichotomously dissected into radiating segments which give the leaf the overall shape of a fan (Fassett, 1953). The segments of *C. caroliniana* are somewhat flattened, and have spatulate tips, whereas those of *C. aquatica, C. australis* and *C. warmingii* are finer and less markedly dorsiventral.

FIG. 5.7. Dissected submerged foliage: E, *Limnophila indica* (×0·3); F, *Ceratopteris thalictroides* (×0·3).

Division of the leaves into linear or filiform segments, which are rather sparsely forked and minutely denticulate, is seen in species of *Ceratophyllum*, such as *C. demersum* and *C. echinatum*. These resemble the long fine capillary segments of *Myriophyllum* and *Ranunculus* subg. *Batrachium* in being radially

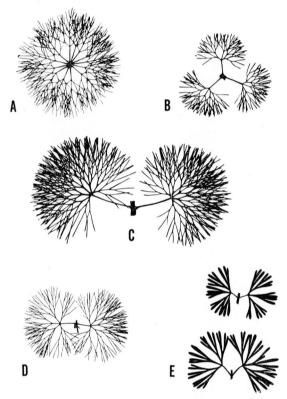

FIG. 5.8. Silhouettes of dissected submerged leaves (whorled in A and B, paired in C, D and E): A, *Limnophila indica*; B, *Cabomba warmingii*; C, *Cabomba caroliniana*; D, *C. aquatica*; E, *C. caroliniana* var. *paucipartita* (all ×0·5).

symmetrical. Leafy shoots of *Ceratophyllum* sometimes possess basal lateral branches whose leaves are extremely finely divided into whitish thread-like segments. It is claimed that these so-called 'rhizoid-shoots' penetrate the substrate and may aid absorption and anchorage in this rootless plant (Glück, 1906). The leaves of *Myriophyllum spicatum*, *M. alterniflorum*, *M. verticillatum*, *M. hippuroides* and *M. verrucosum* are usually in whorls of three to six and are simply pinnate, with from five to forty segments. The spirally arranged, often sessile leaves of batrachian *Ranunculi*, such as *R. circinatus*, *R. rionii*, *R. trichophyllus* and *R. sphaerospermus*, are from twice to several times trifid, the capillary segments diverging or lying in one plane and sometimes reaching a considerable length, for example up to 30 cm in some races of *R. fluitans* (Cook, 1963).

As in entire leaves, quantitative variation is apparent in dissected leaves, which show differences in the degree of subdivision and length and thickness of the segments in different conditions. The segments of *Myriophyllum* are very slender on specimens in standing pools but may be much shorter and firmer in flowing water (Schenck, 1885). In very shallow water or habitats where no water stands for part of the year, the segments of batrachian *Ranunculi* are frequently shorter, thicker and more rigid (Clapham, 1962). Species of *Ceratophyllum* and *Hottonia* are similarly variable. The pteridophyte *Ceratopteris thalictroides*, which is sometimes rooted and is one of the few rosette plants with dissected foliage, has leaves which vary from just pinnatifid to three- or even four-times pinnate (Pal and Pal, 1962). Varieties of *Cabomba caroliniana* are known in which the number and size of the segments of the leaves differ from the type species, which has 80 to 150 terminal segments, each 0·4 to 1·0 mm wide. The horticultural variety *multipartita* has a greater number of more delicate segments whilst var. *paucipartita* has fewer, each 1·0 to 1·8 mm wide (van Ramshorst and Florschütz, 1956).

Dissected leaves undoubtedly have a higher surface area/volume ratio than most entire aerial leaves, but the common assumption that they are also more efficient than entire submerged leaves in obtaining dissolved gases and mineral salts is possibly erroneous. It has been calculated that the cylindrical segments of the leaves of *Myriophyllum spicatum* are in fact two to three times wider, and those of *Ceratophyllum demersum* five to six times wider, than the diameter necessary to give them as high a surface area/volume ratio as that of the flat membranous leaf of some species of *Potamogeton* (Uspenskij, 1913). Nor is the dissection of the leaf a direct reaction to flowing water, since it occurs in many species of stagnant habitats. However, it is probable that dissected leaves, like the ribbon and fenestrated types, offer little mechanical resistance to the current, their segments trailing freely in the water. This structural feature may thereby have contributed to the ability of such species to colonise streams and slow-flowing rivers as well as standing water.

The Anomalous Thallus of the Podostemaceae. There is surely no stranger and more provocative family of angiosperms than the Podostemaceae. By virtue of their profoundly modified form and lack of truly recognisable stems and roots they stand aloof from almost all other vascular plants. The vegetative body is reduced to a creeping or floating thallus (Fig. 5.9) which in some species closely resembles certain freshwater and marine algae and in others is strongly reminiscent of bryophytes or lichens (Warming, 1881, 1882, 1888, 1891; Went, 1910, 1912, 1926). The family is distributed throughout the tropics, with one genus (*Podostemum*) extending into the American subtropics, but all species inhabit an almost uniform environment. They grow on naked weathered rocks, at depths of up to 75 to 100 cm, in running water at temperatures of 14 to 27°C (Willis, 1914). The only variable factor is really the velocity

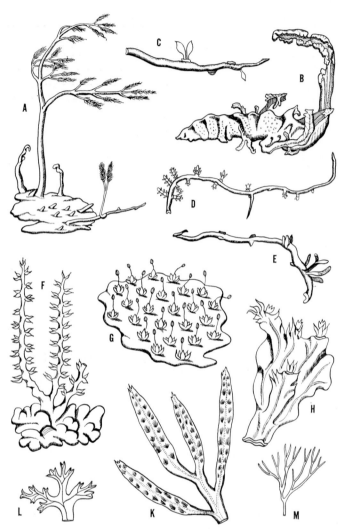

FIG. 5.9. Vegetative morphology of the Podostemaceae: A, *Wettsteiniola accorsii*, creeping flattened thallus with one erect leafy shoot, two young shoots, and developing stolons, one bearing a young shoot (×0·8); B, *Mourera aspera*, creeping branching thallus with several erect shoots (×0·8); C, *M. aspera*, stolon bearing buds (×1·6); D, *Tristicha trifaria*, stolon with developing buds (×1·2); E, *Mniopsis weddelliana*, creeping root with paired leafy buds (×1·4); F, *Dicraea dichotoma*, attached thallus and free-floating branches bearing secondary shoots (×0·2); G, *Zeylanidium johnsonii*, attached thallus bearing erect flowering shoots (×0·8); H, *Griffithella hookeriana*, attached thallus bearing marginal secondary shoots (×2·5); K, *Oenone multibranchiata*, upper surface of thallus bearing 'gill tufts' (×1·5); L, *Podostemum ceratophyllum* f. *chondroides*, ultimate segments of the thallus (×2·5), M, *P. ceratophyllum* f. *abrotanoides*, ultimate segments of the thallus (×2·5). (A to E, after Accorsii, 1944, 1951; F to H, after Subramanyam, 1962; K, after Matthiesen, 1908; L and M, after Fassett, 1957.)

of the current, which is torrential in some habitats in hill streams but quite sluggish in numerous lowland rivers.

Despite the overwhelming similarity of habitat conditions, the organs of the family are bewilderingly polymorphic. The thallus is probably basically a rhizome-like, horizontal, photosynthetic root: the presence of a root cap (although this is usually abnormal in structure and sometimes collenchymatous) supports this interpretation. Typically, e.g. in *Indotristicha ramosissima, Mniopsis saldanhana, M. weddelliana, Podostemum* spp., and *Tristicha trifaria,* the root is filamentous and hemicylindrical, the ventral surface being flat, the dorsal slightly convex. It creeps over the rocks to which it adheres by hairs or by exogenous projections known as haptera, which secrete a cement from their discoid tips. From the thallus there arise endogenous secondary shoots which float freely in the water and bear simple, subulate, linear or flattened leaves. The branches of these shoots differ from true lateral shoots in not arising from axillary buds (Willis, 1902; Engler, 1930; Accorsi, 1944, 1946). The leaves may be arranged in two ranks, as in *Griffithella,* three ranks, as in *Indotristicha,* or four ranks, as in *Willisia,* and they may be imbricate or sparse. In the least specialised taxa the erect shoots often vary widely in form: *Podostemum,* for example, is represented in eastern North America by one highly variable species *P. ceratophyllum,* of which f. *abrotanoides* is the most lax and slender, and f. *chondroides* the most rigid and coarse extreme (Fassett, 1939b).

Increasing dorsiventrality characterises the more specialised endemic genera of all continents. The flattening of the root thallus is manifest in a multitude of different habits. In *Dicraea dichotoma,* for example, the thallus is narrow and ribbon-like, and is usually proximally attached but distally free-floating, whilst in *D. stylosa* it is broad, freely branched, often floating and very similar in appearance to *Fucus* and other seaweeds. In other genera, such as *Farmeria, Griffithella, Hydrobryopsis,* and *Zeylanidium,* the thallus is usually closely attached to the substrate by haptera or elongated ventral epidermal cells and is highly polymorphic, varying from thin and ribbon-like, e.g. *Zeylanidium lichenoides* and *Farmeria indica,* to fleshy and crustaceous, e.g. *Z. olivaceum* and *Willisia selaginoides,* or broad and fucoid, e.g. *Griffithella hookeriana.* The progressive elaboration of the root thallus in these advanced genera is accompanied by the gradual reduction of the secondary leaf-bearing shoots, whose photosynthetic function is largely assumed by the tissues of the dorsiventral thallus. The leafy shoots of *Griffithella, Willisia* and *Zeylanidium,* for example, appear as tiny moss-like tufts emerging from the surface and margins of the thallus.

The flattened frondose thalli of *Terniola* and *Castelnavia* have been considered to arise by the fusion of flattened, dorsiventral, secondary shoots (Willis, 1902), but they could equally be interpreted as the ultimate stage in the morphological series involving progressive elaboration of the assimilatory root and reduction of the leafy shoots. On the older parts of the stellate or suborbicular thallus of *Terniola zeylanica,* for example, the simple entire leaves are arranged in closely-packed dwarf rosettes but on the younger parts no vestige of an erect shoot is present and the leaves occur solitarily on the surface

5

and edge of the thallus. Firm anchorage to the rocks is accomplished in *Terniola* by hairs, not haptera.

The family displays a wide range of size, as well as form. The shoots of lax specimens of *Podostemum ceratophyllum*, for example, may reach lengths of 80 cm (Fassett, 1957) whilst the broad alga-like thallus of *Dicraea stylosa* attains just over half this length, about 45 cm (Subramanyam, 1962). At the other extreme are such species as *Rhyncholacis minima* which reaches a maximum length of only 2 cm, its spatulate leaf segments measuring not more than 1 to 2 mm long by 0·2 mm wide (van Royen, 1959b).

The astonishing polymorphism of the Podostemaceae may be attributed to the lack of a rigid skeletal framework and to the potential meristematic capacity of almost all the cells of the thallus. The resemblance of many thalloid types to far-distant cryptogams is not easily interpreted. Whether or not the different habits of growth or the structure of the individual organs have any adaptive significance is also an awkward problem. Willis (1902, 1914, 1915) considered it improbable that any of the various types of thalli is specially adapted to life in either violent torrents or slow-flowing shallows, since species without profound modifications also occur widely in both, and achieve as great success in colonisation as do the more complex forms. Emphasising that the dorsiventrality of organisation is in no way advantageous, Willis concluded that of all the features of vegetative structure the only one which might have adaptive value is the development of haptera or clinging hairs.

CARBON ASSIMILATION IN SUBMERGED ORGANS

The Structure of the Photosynthetic Tissues. Two major problems confronting a photosynthetic organ under water are the absorption of a suitable dissolved carbon source and the reception of necessary intensities of appropriate wavelengths of light. Rates of diffusion of gases in solution are generally two to three orders of magnitude slower than in air, and the achievement of a high ratio of surface area to volume is probably of even greater importance for a submerged organ than for most aerial leaves and stems. The restricted and differential penetration of light into water creates a habitat very similar to that of densely shaded land plants and seems to have evoked similar anatomical responses. The structural modifications of submerged leaves, stems and some petioles related to their efficiency as organs of photosynthesis are their thinness, reduced cuticularisation and increased distribution of chloroplasts.

The high surface area/volume ratio of typically thin, ribbon-like, fenestrated or dissected leaves and the thalloid assimilating roots of the Podostemaceae facilitates both the penetration of light and diffusion of dissolved gases to the innermost tissues. The disadvantage accruing from the relatively higher volume of cylindrical stems and petioles is compensated by the more extensive cortical system of intercellular spaces, through which diffusion may freely occur. Absorption is also facilitated by the permeability of the unthickened cellulose walls of the epidermal, mesophyll, and cortical cells, and by the enormous specific area of these walls abutting on the intercellular spaces. A cuticle is often stated to be absent from submerged organs but a definite, albeit thin, layer has been observed on the epidermis of the leaves and stems of several species, e.g. *Elodea canadensis, Groenlandia densa, Hottonia palustris* and *Myriophyllum spicatum* (de Lamarlière, 1906; Hasman and Inanç, 1957), and may have escaped notice on others as a result of its extreme reduction. Even when it does occur it probably offers little, if any, resistance to diffusing substances.

Most entire and dissected submerged leaves have a homogeneous mesophyll, the lack of differentiation of palisade and spongy layers being related to the variable position of the organ with respect to incident light. In contrast, the flattened thalli of some genera of Podostemaceae, which are firmly attached to the substrate, possess a well-marked, upper palisade tissue. In many thin, translucent, entire leaves and centric, filiform leaflets the mesophyll is very much reduced: in the broad leaves of *Potamogeton lucens* and the lanceolate ones of *P. crispus* it comprises only a single layer of cells, whilst in aquatic species of *Elatine* even this layer is absent from the distal part of the leaf. In *Elodea canadensis* and *Najas graminea* the mesophyll is totally lacking and the two epidermal layers are contiguous throughout the leaf on either side of the single vein (Bailey, 1884; Schenck, 1886; Metcalfe and Chalk, 1950; Fig. 5.10).

As in herbaceous land plants, chloroplasts generally occur throughout the mesophyll of leaves and the outer cortex of many stems and petioles. The circulation of cytoplasm and of chloroplasts within mesophyll cells, which is often clearly visible in *Elodea* leaves, may be maintained by energy derived from photo- or oxidative phosphorylation. Tageeva and Kazantsev (1962) noted that in healthy leaf cells of *Elodea canadensis* the velocity of chloroplast movement usually differs from that of cytoplasmic streaming, and it also varies according to the season. Chloroplast movement is greatly reduced if the leaves are detached from the stem, and may be arrested in intact leaves if the illumination is very intense. If the leaves of *Egeria densa* are detached and kept in tap water in the dark for about five days, the chloroplasts become senescent. They appear small and yellow, and the lamellar ultra-structure of both the stroma and the grana becomes degraded (Ikeda and Ueda, 1964).

A feature prevalent in submerged leaves, stems, and some petioles, but occurring in land plants only in some dicotyledons living in deep shade, is the additional presence of chloroplasts in the epidermis (Fig. 5.10). There are some exceptions, such as *Callitriche* (Schenck, 1886) and *Zizania* (Weir and Dale, 1960), but in general, concomitant with the progressive reduction of the mesophyll, there is an increase in the abundance of epidermal chloroplasts. In species of *Ceratophyllum, Myriophyllum, Potamogeton* and marine angiosperms, such as *Cymodocea, Posidonia* and *Zostera*, the epidermis is richer in chloroplasts than any other tissue (Sauvageau, 1890, 1891; Schenck, 1886; Solereder, 1913). In these organs the mesophyll or cortex serves mainly for the storage of starch and oils and the epidermis becomes the principal site of photosynthesis. Abundant chloroplasts also occur in the epidermis of the flattened root thalli of the Podostemaceae (Warming, 1888, 1891; Went, 1912, 1926).

In the most highly modified submerged hydrophytes the epidermis lacks stomata and forms a truly continuous covering layer (Fig. 5.10). Stomata are unknown in the submerged organs of *Egeria, Elodea, Enhalus, Halophila, Thalassia, Vallisneria,* and other genera of the Hydrocharitaceae (Solereder, 1913), in the Podostemaceae (Chodat and Vischer, 1917; Went, 1926; Metcalfe and Chalk, 1950), in *Althenia, Cymodocea, Phyllospadix, Posidonia* and *Zostera*

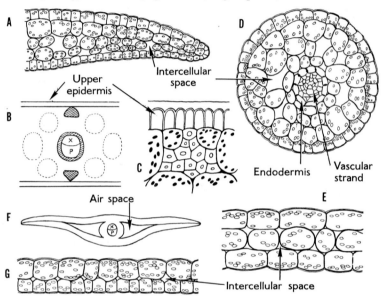

FIG. 5.10. Anatomy of submerged leaves, as seen in T.S.: A, part of lamina of *Callitriche obtusangula* (× 80); B, midrib of *Cymodocea nodosa* (diagrammatic; lacunae shown by broken lines; fibres shaded; xylem X; phloem P) (× 80); C, part of subepidermal region of *Cymodocea nodosa* (chloroplasts of the mesophyll cells in solid black) (× 400); D, complete leaf segment of *Myriophyllum spicatum* (× 100); E, part of lamina of *Potamogeton pusillus* (× 250); F, complete leaf of *Najas graminea* (diagrammatic; xylem X; phloem P) (× 50); G, part of lamina of *Elodea canadensis* (× 200). Note the frequency of epidermal chloroplasts, absence of stomata, poorly differentiated mesophyll, abundance of intercellular spaces, subepidermal fibres (in B and C), and reduction to two epidermal layers (in F and G). (B and C, after Sauvageau, 1891.)

(Sauvageau, 1890, 1891), in *Ceratophyllum* (Solereder, 1908), and in permanently submerged leaves of *Isoetes* (Goebel, 1891–1893; Foster and Gifford, 1959) and *Zizania* (Weir and Dale, 1960). Shinobu (1952) confirmed the absence of stomata from the submerged leaves of the majority of species of *Potamogeton* such as *P. pusillus* and *P. crispus*, but did find them in *P. perfoliatus*. Occasional stomata have also been found in *Potamogeton lucens* (Sauvageau, 1891), *Lobelia dortmanna* (Armand, 1912), *Pontederia cordata* (Costantin, 1885a, b), species of *Callitriche* (Pax and Hoffmann, 1931), and of *Myriophyllum* and *Proserpinaca* (Metcalfe and Chalk, 1950). These sporadic stomata are of course functionless. Occlusion of the stomatal aperture and penetration of water to the internal tissues is prevented by a persistent roof of cuticle, the interlocking of the cuticular ridges of the guard cells, or the cessation of development at an early stage (Porsch, 1905).

Carbon Sources for Submerged Hydrophytes. The notion that submerged plants may use as a carbon source not only free carbon dioxide but also bicarbonate ions has provoked argument ever since it was first expressed by Angelstein (1911). Tréboux (1903) had previously found that dilute acids accelerated the rate of photosynthesis in certain species. From experiments with *Elodea* and *Callitriche*, Wilmott (1921) claimed that this acceleration of the rate was due to the acid releasing carbon dioxide from local deposits of calcium carbonate on the surface of plants in chalky water, and that the effect was not shown by the same plants in soft water. He also calculated that a bicarbonate solution gave a rate of photosynthesis similar to that which would be expected in the carbon dioxide concentration likely to arise by spontaneous decomposition of the bicarbonate. These conclusions led him to challenge Angelstein's view that submerged plants are able to assimilate bicarbonate ions.

Now all these early experiments may be criticised for their use of the bubble-counting technique for estimating the rate of photosynthesis. This technique, which still survives as the notorious '*Elodea* experiment' of elementary textbooks, is inherently unsuitable for its alleged purpose. Bubbles are only evolved when the internal gas pressure reaches a certain value and even then their composition may vary enormously in a single species, under apparently similar conditions, and over a very short time. The rate of bubbling is thus a highly inaccurate estimate of the rate of photosynthesis, even if corrections are made for the varying oxygen concentration of the bubbles.

Whilst investigating the directed transfer of ions through submerged leaves, Arens (1936a) found that bicarbonate was actually absorbed. Steemann Nielsen (1944, 1946, 1947) studied the influence of the concentrations of carbon dioxide, bicarbonate and carbonate ions on the photosynthesis of various aquatic angiosperms and the aquatic moss, *Fontinalis*. He demonstrated that both free carbon dioxide and bicarbonate ions could be directly assimilated by *Myriophyllum spicatum* and the other angiosperms whereas *Fontinalis* used only carbon dioxide. Carbonate ions were not available to either type. Photosynthesis in *M. spicatum* was found to be independent of the hydrogen ion concentration in the range pH 4 to 10, and also independent of the ionic composition of the water if free carbon dioxide was the carbon source. With bicarbonate ions as the source, however, the photosynthetic intensity was very dependent on the absolute concentration of both cations and anions.

Results similar to Steemann Nielsen's were obtained by Ruttner (1948) who found that whereas *Fontinalis antipyretica* uses free carbon dioxide at a more or less constant rate but ceases to photosynthesise when the supply is exhausted, *Elodea canadensis* is able to continue, using bicarbonate ions as the carbon source. In a later paper (1953) he classified autotrophic green plants into two groups according to their carbon source: (a) land plants and aquatic mosses—able to use only free carbon dioxide; (b) aquatic seed plants and algae—able to use both free carbon dioxide and bicarbonate ions. It might be thought that the essential difference between these groups could be the possession of the enzyme carbonic anhydrase by only group (b) but Steemann Nielsen and Christiansen (1949) showed that some plants of both groups in fact possess it.

Despite the evidence, doubts of the ability to use bicarbonate ions have been expressed by some physiologists. Rabinowitch (1945) was somewhat unsure of the reliability of Arens' experiments and apparently unaware of Steemann Nielsen's early work, and he rather hesitantly supported the view that bicarbonate could not be used. In the second volume of his treatise (1951), however, he accepted the evidence for assimilation of bicarbonate. Briggs (1959) suggested that in some systems where bicarbonate ions are absorbed, carbon dioxide is still the actual reactant, and the effect of the bicarbonate ions is merely to increase the concentration of carbon dioxide at the sites of consumption, i.e. the chloroplasts.

The present state of knowledge of carbon sources is thus highly unsatisfactory. Previous experimental results conflict, interpretations differ, and numerous perplexing questions remain unanswered. Why, for instance, should *Fontinalis* differ so strikingly from the submerged angiosperms which have been studied? No-one seems to have investigated the behaviour of other aquatic mosses, such as *Drepanocladus* or *Hypnum* spp. Nor has there been any critical study of submerged angiosperms other than such habitual experimental subjects as *Elodea* and *Myriophyllum*. It would be unwise to attempt to generalise from the data so far obtained. Further research is clearly needed to discover whether other species differ in their behaviour, and whether the nature of the carbon source for any given species varies with other experimental conditions or according to which stage of photosynthesis is limiting.

Although the question of whether the bicarbonate, once inside the photosynthesising cells, is assimilated directly, or converted to carbon dioxide which is then fixed, is unresolved, bicarbonate absorption may have adaptive significance. The photosynthesis of a plant able to use bicarbonate ions would not be inhibited if the pH of the medium rose too high for free carbon dioxide to be present, i.e. above pH 9. This could be of considerable advantage to those hydrophytes inhabiting alkaline hard waters where bicarbonate is the principal form of available carbon in the existing range of hydrogen ion concentrations. The capacity could also aid continued assimilation in water initially of low pH value, should free carbon dioxide be depleted by absorption into actively photosynthesising plants (see p. 451).

Variations in the Rate of Photosynthesis. The principal factors influencing the net rate of photosynthesis, other than the concentration of a suitable carbon source, are the intensity of solar radiation, the depth and colour of water and the velocity of the current (Gessner, 1938, 1955, 1959; Hogetsu, 1939; Meyer, 1939; Burr, 1941; Rabinowitch, 1945, 1951; Verduin, 1952; Hammann, 1957; D.S.I.R., 1963; Westlake, 1964, 1966a, b, in press). Kostychev and Soldatenkow (1926) showed the attainment of a maximal rate in the middle of the day followed by a consistent decrease in the afternoon. With an improved technique, expressing the rate of apparent photosynthesis in terms of oxygen evolved per unit time, Gessner (1938) also demonstrated a close correlation between the daily variation in the photosynthesis of aquatic plants and the daily variation in the intensity of solar radiation. Meyer (1939) developed an apparatus based on that used by Blackman and Smith (1911) and James (1928), which enabled the photosynthetic rate to be determined at hourly intervals without manipulating the plant material during the experiment. He used apical shoots of *Ceratophyllum demersum* and confirmed Gessner's correlation of the diurnal rhythm with the curve of solar radiation, the rate of apparent photosynthesis rising rapidly in the morning to a peak between 10 a.m. and 12 noon, and afterwards steadily declining. Similar relationships between the photosynthetic rates of whole communities in fresh and salt waters and the daily variations in solar radiation have been described by Odum (1957b), Odum and Wilson (1962) and Edwards and Owens (1962). The correlation between photosynthesis and solar radiation is not always close: Meyer (1939) and others have noted that not uncommonly the rate of photosynthesis is conspicuously depressed during the afternoon, so that the diurnal curve is somewhat skewed.

In view of the gradual extinction of light with increasing depth of water, maximal rates of photosynthesis might be expected to occur immediately below the surface. However, some published data suggest that photosynthesis may be slightly suppressed near the surface (Ruttner, 1926). Using shoot apices of *Ceratophyllum* and *Elodea*, Schomer (1934) found that maximal photosynthesis did occur at the surface on dull days but at some depth on bright days. With increasing depth the rate of photosynthesis decreased, the decline being more rapid in water stained with dissolved organic matter, until the compensation point (rate of photosynthesis $\equiv$ rate of respiration) was reached, at 10 to 15 m in a clear lake but only 1 to 2 m in a highly coloured one. More recently, Felföldy (1960) found that the maximal rate of photosynthesis of *Potamogeton perfoliatus* in L. Balaton was attained at a depth of 2 m on a day when the light intensity at the surface was about $1\cdot1$ g cal/cm^2 min.

In contrast, Manning *et al.* (1938), Meyer and Armitage (1941) and Meyer *et al.* (1943) found no real evidence of suppression of photosynthesis near the surface. In their experiments the rate of apparent photosynthesis of species of *Ceratophyllum*, *Elodea*, *Heteranthera*, *Najas*, *Potamogeton* and *Vallisneria* increased with increasing illumination up to the surface intensities, which varied from $0\cdot3$ to about $1\cdot1$ g cal/cm^2 min.

It has been suggested that the relatively high light intensities at the surface may have some deleterious effect on photosynthetic organs and so reduce their efficiency. Arnold (1931) observed a gradual diminution in the rate of photosynthesis (measured by the bubble-counting technique) in strong illumination under otherwise allegedly constant environmental conditions. Gessner's (1938) more reliable experiments showed clearly that very high light intensities (80 000 to 135 000 lux) do not of themselves retard photosynthesis. In densely colonised natural habitats competition for light is often severe, and it is very probable that most submerged communities, especially those that produce a floating canopy of foliage which heavily shades the lower organs, attain the greatest rates of photosynthesis per unit biomass near the surface (see Westlake, 1964, 1966a, b).

Most of the early experiments on the photosynthesis of submerged hydrophytes were performed with the plants immersed in more or less static water, often enclosed within small bottles. It is likely that significantly higher

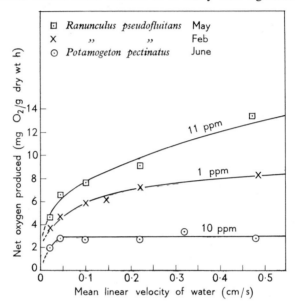

FIG. 5.11. Effect of water movement on the rate of photosynthesis of *Potamogeton pectinatus* and *Ranunculus pseudofluitans*. (Mean concentration of dissolved oxygen shown against each curve.) (Drawn by D. F. Westlake, Freshwater Biological Association, Wareham, England.)

rates of photosynthesis may be attained in flowing water. In static water, especially when the plant is further protected by an enclosing vessel, depletion of carbon dioxide and bicarbonate ions and accumulation of oxygen are likely to occur in the water immediately surrounding the foliage, particularly in plants with densely arranged leaves, such as *Egeria*, *Elodea* and *Lagarosiphon*.

Westlake (in press) studied the effects of low velocity currents on the photosynthesis of apical shoots of *Ranunculus pseudofluitans* and *Potamogeton pectinatus* at 15°C under total irradiance of up to 0·174 g cal/cm² min (slightly over 30 000 lux), an intensity which considerably exceeds the usual light saturation values for plants in static water. He used laminar flows of mean velocities from 0·02 to 0·5 cm/s, which may occur naturally within stands of submerged plants, although in the open water of many streams the flows are turbulent and much faster, of the order of 20 cm/s. The rate of photosynthesis of both species (Fig. 5.11) was found to increase rapidly with increase in flow from static conditions to low velocities. The specimens of *P. pectinatus* appeared to be of low photosynthetic capacity and reached a maximum rate at a current velocity of 0·05 cm/s. Photosynthesis of *R. pseudofluitans* increased further in faster flows, although the rate of increase was less at the higher velocities, beyond about 0·2 cm/s. At a velocity of 0·5 cm/s, the net photosynthetic rates of this species were from three to six times greater than those attained in static conditions: the maximum gross rate recorded was 15·5 mg oxygen evolved/g dry weight h. There was some indication that in water of low oxygen concentration the net rate of photosynthesis is increased as a result of a slight reduction in the rate of respiration. The Q_{10} for the photosynthesis of light-saturated plants in water fairly poor in free carbon dioxide was found to be about 1·4, a value which suggests that the process is diffusion-limited. Westlake's observations are congruous with the hypothesis that photosynthesis is primarily limited by the rate of supply of the carbon source to the surface of the leaves, and that an increase in current velocity accelerates this supply by reducing the thickness of the layer of almost stagnant water close to each leaf, across which metabolites move at not much more than the rate of molecular diffusion. This concept is applicable also to the supply of respiratory oxygen and nutrient ions (see pp. 129-31, 134).

Seasonal variations in the maximal photosynthetic rates attained by several submerged hydrophytes have been observed by Westlake and by other workers (D.S.I.R., 1963): these variations appear to be closely correlated with variations in chlorophyll content (Fig. 5.12).

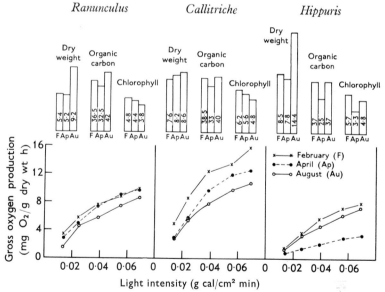

FIG. 5.12. Seasonal variations in gross photosynthesis, dry weight (as percentage wet weight), organic carbon content (as percentage dry weight), and chlorophyll content (optical density at 663 mμ of a 90 per cent acetone extract per unit dry weight) of *Callitriche obtusangula*, *Hippuris vulgaris* and *Ranunculus pseudofluitans*. (From D.S.I.R., 1963, by courtesy of the Controller of Her Majesty's Stationery Office, London.)

5*

Life in the water

The Evolution of Oxygen and the Origin of the Lacunar System. It has long been known that the system of air-filled lacunae which characterises most submerged stems, petioles and leaves appears very early in development: a network of lacunae is already manifest within 1 mm of the stem apex in both *Elodea* and *Myriophyllum* (Dévaux, 1889; and see Fig. 5.13). The schizogenous origin of these lacunae, involving the enlargement of chinks between the young cells and the subsequent division of the cells surrounding the air spaces, has been followed in *Hippuris vulgaris* (Barratt, 1916), *Egeria densa* (Hulbary, 1944), and *Elodea canadensis* (Dale, 1957a), but the possible causal factors have received little study. In *E. canadensis*, Dale (1957b) found that shoot apices of plants grown under strong illumination with good carbon dioxide supply, and hence having a high photosynthetic rate, all have vertical chinks reaching up to the apical initials. Similar extensive chinks were found in shoots growing in bright light in unshaded natural habitats, but specimens grown in the laboratory in either dim illumination or moist air lacked them. Dale concluded that the influence of light on the origin of schizogenous lacunae is indirect, through the production of oxygen in photosynthesis.

As a result of its slow rate of diffusion in aqueous solution, oxygen produced by photosynthesising cells cannot escape rapidly into the surrounding water and it therefore tends to come out of solution and accumulate in the inter-cellular spaces. Dale (1957b) showed directly that the increase in pressure in these spaces distends them and creates a progressively more extensive system of lacunae further back from the apical regions. This explanation of the origin of the lacunae was in fact postulated over seventy years ago, by Goebel (1891–1893).

During periods of active photosynthesis the gas pressure steadily builds up: Angelstein (1911) recorded an excess pressure of 0·2 atm in *Egeria densa*. The leaves, stems and petioles become further distended until the internal pressure overcomes the surface tension of water at small holes and tears in the epidermis, through which bubbles of gas are then extruded. Neither the gas in the inner-most lacunae nor that lost in bubbles is pure oxygen: as early as 1837 Dutrochet remarked upon its extremely variable composition. Cloëz (1863) reported that the bubbles evolved during active photosynthesis contained a mixture of oxygen and nitrogen; later, small concentrations of carbon dioxide were also revealed. Kniep's (1915) analysis of bubbles produced by *Cabomba caroliniana*, *Elodea canadensis* and a batrachian *Ranunculus* revealed the following composition: 30·0 to 54·4 per cent O_2, 46·6 to 72·1 per cent N_2 and 0·6 to 3·3 per cent CO_2, whilst data of Macdonald (in Prime, 1952) show ranges of 13 to 45 per cent O_2, 54 to 81 per cent N_2 and 1 to 6 per cent CO_2 for *Elodea*. Bubbles released by *Ranunculus pseudofluitans* in Westlake's (in press) recent experiments contained only 7 to 18 per cent O_2 and only traces of CO_2; the residue was assumed to be N_2. Recent analyses indicate that when the bubbles reach the surface of the water their oxygen content is often slightly higher than that of the water (Ministry of Technology, 1965). If the rate of photosynthesis is

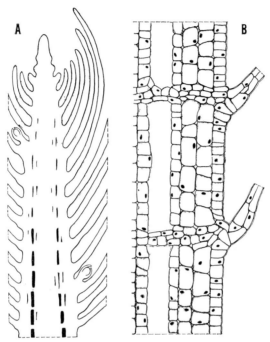

FIG. 5.13. *Elodea canadensis*: A, diagrammatic L.S. of the terminal 3 mm of the shoot apex (with the progressive elongation of the lower internodes reduced) showing the general form of the apex and the appearance of conspicuous intercellular chinks (shown in solid black) in the potential cortical region ($\times 30$); B, L.S. of the 20th and 21st nodes showing cortical lacunae extending the length of an internode and traversed by persistent compact tissue at the nodes (nuclei in solid black) ($\times 90$).

high and bubbling is sustained, the evolved gas becomes progressively richer in oxygen, the concentration reaching 90 per cent on rare occasions (van Tieghem, 1866).

The rate of bubbling under standard conditions of temperature and flow generally increases with increase in light intensity. For some species, e.g. *Hippuris vulgaris*, the rate also appears to rise with increase in the degree of supersaturation of the water, but for others, e.g. *Berula erecta*, it does not. As a result of their different rates of photosynthesis under standard conditions, different species may exhibit different bubbling rates. In very low light intensities, *Hippuris vulgaris*, for example, produces bubbles whereas *Berula erecta* does not. When these two species lose bubbles at a comparable rate,

B. erecta loses a greater proportion of oxygen as a result of its lower net rate of photosynthesis (D.S.I.R., 1963; Ministry of Technology, 1965). Although the streaming of bubbles from submerged organs is often very conspicuous during bright warm days it probably represents only a very small proportion of the total photosynthetic oxygen output. Most of the oxygen diffuses into the water or is retained within the plant. The proportion which escapes to the atmosphere as bubbles has been estimated, on the unrealistic assumption that the bubbles are pure oxygen, to be less than 1 per cent of the

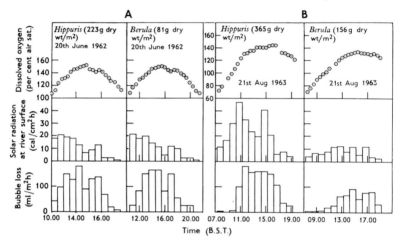

FIG. 5.14. Loss of gas bubbles (bottom graphs) from standing crops of *Berula erecta* and *Hippuris vulgaris* in the R. Ivel in 1962 (A) and 1963 (B), in relation to light intensity at the surface (middle graphs) and dissolved oxygen concentration in the overlying water (top graphs). (From Edwards and Owens, 1965; by courtesy of the authors, the British Ecological Society, and Blackwell Scientific Publications Ltd., Oxford.)

total daily production of a submerged *Sagittaria* community in a subtropical river (Odum, 1957b). Measurements have recently been made of the bubble loss from communities of *Berula erecta* and *Hippuris vulgaris* in the R. Ivel in England (Fig. 5.14). These show that the rate of evolution of gas increases with increasing intensity of solar radiation at the water surface and with increasing supersaturation of the water. In June 1962 the bubble loss was found to represent about 6·5 per cent of the total daily oxygen production. In August 1963 the corresponding loss was only about 4 per cent although the crop of plants was greater and the light intensities and oxygen concentrations similar to those in 1962. This difference in gas losses provides a further indication that average rates of photosynthesis probably vary during the summer months, perhaps rising steadily from the beginning and falling steadily towards the end of the growing season in temperate habitats (Edwards and Owens, 1965; Ministry of Technology, 1965).

Although in such obligate submerged plants as *Elodea* the appearance of lacunae may be attributed to an environmental factor—the retarding effect of the water on the outward diffusion of photosynthetic oxygen—it is probable that amphibious ancestral stocks already possessed the capacity to develop a lacunar system. Numerous morphologists, such as Costantin (1884), Goebel (1891–1893), Gin (1909) and Glück (1905, 1911, 1924), have emphasised that many contemporary amphibious plants have in their aerial organs definite lacunae which become even more conspicuous if the plant is submerged. The ability to develop lacunae is probably genetically endowed and in submerged hydrophytes the apparent reaction to the aquatic environment may well be no more than the full realisation of this potential.

The Extent of the Lacunar System. Schizogenous lacunae develop most extensively in the cortex of stems, the ground tissue of petioles, and the mesophyll of all but the most reduced leaves. The number and size of the lacunae vary somewhat with the age and nature of the organ. Most commonly the outer cortex of the stem or peripheral ground tissue of the petiole comprises compactly arranged, parenchymatous or collenchymatous cells, and a similar zone of parenchyma, some two to five cells wide, surrounds the central stele of the stem or each of the vascular strands of the petiole or leaf. It is thus in the middle cortex of the stem, and the intermediate ground tissue of the petiole and leaf, that the longitudinal lacunae chiefly occur (Figs. 5.15 and 5.16).

The number of lacunae seen in transverse section is sometimes specific: in *Isoetes lacustris* there are four, and in *Lobelia dortmanna* and *Littorella uniflora* usually two, running the length of the leaf. In larger organs the number is more variable. The lacunae may be arranged in a ring, as in the stems of *Ceratophyllum* and *Myriophyllum*, or several rings, as in the stem of *Hippuris*, or in a reticulate pattern, as in the petiole of *Nuphar*. The radial plates of parenchyma which separate the spaces are frequently but one cell thick: in some petioles they are two to several cells thick.

The exact pattern of the lacunae sometimes varies in a characteristic way between different species of a genus, and is therefore of some value as a criterion of identification. Conard (1905) described very fully the patterns of the lacunae in petioles of different species of *Nymphaea*. In one group of species, four large spaces occur near the centre of the petiole, whilst in a second group there are two extremely large lacunae at the centre and two lesser ones at each end of these. In both types the principal lacunae are accompanied by many small spaces arranged in a less definite way.

Scattered throughout the parenchymatous lacunate tissue, which often stores starch, oil, or tannins, there are more specialised cells in some genera. Mucilage-secreting glands project into the air spaces in the petioles of *Brasenia* (Schrenk, 1888), as do cells bearing clustered crystals of calcium oxalate in the petioles of *Nelumbo* (Solereder, 1908) and the stems and leaves of *Myriophyllum* (Hasman and Inanç, 1957). Sclerenchymatous idioblasts, often of bizarre shape (Fig. 5.17), are quite common in the walls of the lacunae in the petioles of *Euryale*, *Nuphar*, *Nymphaea*, *Nymphoides* and *Victoria* (Metcalfe and Chalk, 1950; Gaudet, 1960; Malaviya, 1962, 1963).

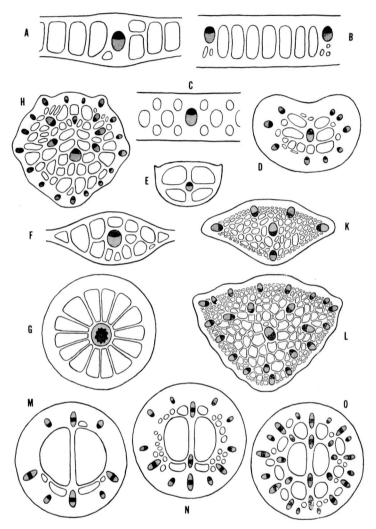

FIG. 5.15. Diagrams of the distribution of lacunae and vascular strands in submerged organs, as seen in T.S. (phloem, shaded; xylem, solid black): A, *Sagittaria sagittifolia*, part of ribbon leaf (×30); B, *Zostera marina*, part of ribbon leaf (×30); C, *Cymodocea nodosa*, midrib region of ribbon leaf (×30); D, *Syringodium isoetifolium*, subulate leaf (×25); E, *Isoetes lacustris*, subulate leaf (×8); F, *Potamogeton* sp., midrib region of ribbon leaf (×30); G, *Myriophyllum spicatum*, stem (×20); H, *Sagittaria sagittifolia*, petiole of emergent leaf (×5); K, *Nuphar pumila*, petiole of floating leaf (×12); L, *N. lutea*, petiole of floating leaf (×4); M, *Nymphaea mexicana*, petiole of floating leaf (×10); N, *N. odorata*, petiole of floating leaf (×6); O, *N. tuberosa*, petiole of floating leaf (×5). (B to D, after Sauvageau, 1891; M to O, after Conard, 1905.)

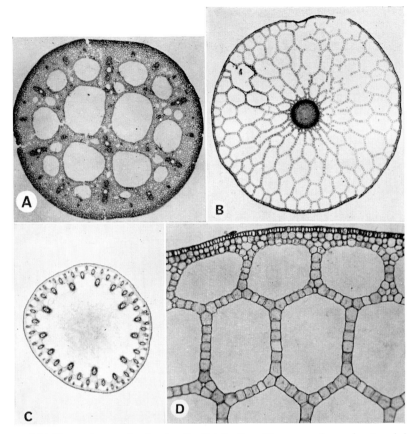

FIG. 5.16. Photomicrographs showing the distribution of lacunae and vascular strands in various submerged organs, as seen in T.S.: A, *Nymphaea alba*, petiole, ventral surface uppermost (× 6·5); B, *Hippuris vulgaris*, stem (× 6); C, *Juncus bulbosus*, stem (× 10); D, *Hippuris vulgaris*, part of outer cortex of stem (× 30). (E, F and notes on p. 126.)

Occurrence of Diaphragms. The fragility of the lacunate tissue, and the danger of waterlogging through wounds, are counteracted partly by the radial plates which separate the lacunae and oppose strains exerted at right angles to the long axis, and partly by the water-tight transverse diaphragms which interrupt the lacunae at intervals (Duval Jouve, 1872; le Blanc, 1912; Snow, 1914, 1920; Sifton, 1945). The diaphragms vary in both form and occurrence. In the petioles of *Nuphar* and *Brasenia* the lacunae are at first continuous but at certain points, groups of cells in the walls later swell into the cavity, branch freely, and divide rapidly to form an occluding spongy mass of loosely arranged cells (Fig. 5.18). Each very delicate diaphragm of *Victoria amazonica* consists of a single layer of cells united by lateral outgrowths of their walls (de Bruyne, 1922). In *Hippuris*, *Pontederia*, *Potamogeton*, *Sagittaria* and several other

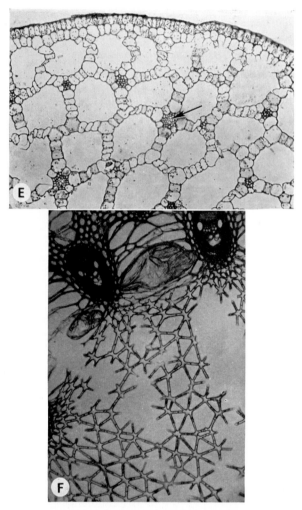

FIG. 5.16. Photomicrographs showing the distribution of lacunae and vascular strands in various submerged organs, as seen in T.S.: E, *Potamogeton natans*, part of outer cortex of stem (×50); F, *Juncus bulbosus*, part of pith of stem (×80). Note the very large lacunae in A; the great number of regularly arranged lacunae in B (some with walls broken in the preparation of the section); the small peripheral lacunae and large hollow pith in C; the stellate parenchyma F which partly occupies the pith cavity in C; the roughly hexagonal shape of the lacunae in D; and the uniseriate lamellae in D and E. Note also the scattered vascular bundles in A, which is a dicotyledon; the peripheral rings of bundles in C, which is a monocotyledon; the root-like central vascular cylinder in B, which is a stem; and the cortical vascular bundles (one arrowed) in E.

genera each diaphragm is one, or occasionally two to three, cells thick, and consists early in development of very thin-walled cells with small spaces at their angles. These cells later draw apart, often at points along their contact faces as well as at the angles, so that the diaphragm becomes multiperforate. In *Hippuris*, the walls become thickened at the angles and the spaces enlarge so excessively that the cells of the mature diaphragm are stellate (Arber, 1920; see also Figs. 5.18 and 5.19).

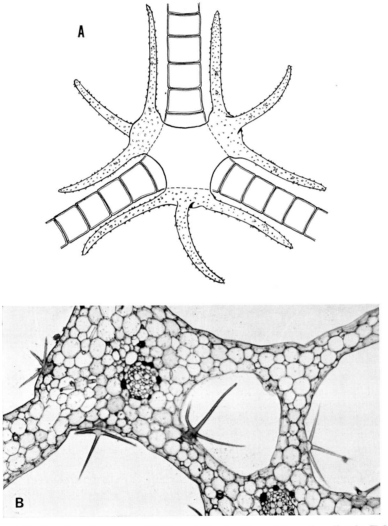

FIG. 5.17. A, sclerenchymatous idioblast at the junction of three lamellae in T.S. lacunae of the petiole of *Nuphar lutea* (× 300); B, photomicrograph of T.S. lacunae of the petiole of *Nymphaea alba*, showing several sclerenchymatous idioblasts (× 150).

Diaphragms are most commonly found at the nodes of submerged stems and scattered throughout petioles. They are especially characteristic of the Nymphaeaceae and aquatic monocotyledons, but are inexplicably lacking in some organs, such as the petiole of *Nymphaea* (Metcalfe and Chalk, 1950), and are relatively infrequent in submerged leaves.

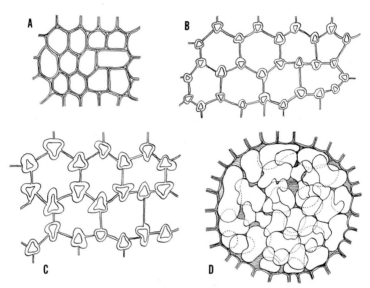

FIG. 5.18. A, B, C, drawings showing the development of the nodal diaphragm tissue in the stem of *Hippuris vulgaris*, as seen in T.S. ($\times 240$) (after Arber, 1920). D, semi-diagrammatic T.S. of a diaphragm of spongy tissue occluding a lacuna in the petiole of *Nuphar lutea* (intercellular passages shaded) ($\times 100$).

The Importance of Internal and External Oxygen Supplies for Respiration. In view of the frequent scarcity and slow rate of diffusion of oxygen in water, it is possible that submerged organs are sometimes embarrassed by the respiratory oxygen demand of their living tissues. During periods of illumination much of the oxygen produced in photosynthesis is probably retained within the lacunar system, through which it diffuses from the leaves down through the petioles and stems to the underground organs, where it is least plentiful. The rate of downward diffusion is governed principally by the steepness of the concentration gradient and the frictional resistance of the diaphragms, and is probably, on average, about 4 per cent of the rate of diffusion in air (Coult, 1964). It is likely that since most submerged organs have a low tissue/air space volume ratio their respiratory demand will be adequately met during daylight hours.

When photosynthesis stops, the internal oxygen supply will steadily fall and may become more or less exhausted at some time during the night, especially if prevailing temperatures and respiration rates are high. Thereafter, the tissues will be dependent on oxygen diffusing into the plant from the surrounding water. Recent experimental research strongly suggests that the respiration of submerged hydrophytes in the dark is limited by the rate at which oxygen diffuses from the medium to the living cells. With decreasing concentration of dissolved oxygen, there is a logarithmic decrease in the rate of respiration of many freshwater species, and a proportionate decrease in the rate of respiration

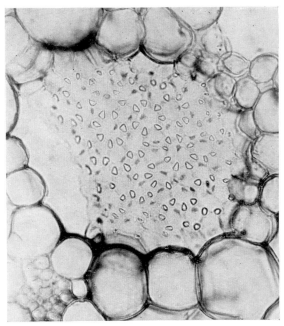

FIG. 5.19. Photomicrograph of T.S. lacuna in the cortex of the stem of *Potamogeton natans*, showing a multiperforate diaphragm (×350).

of *Posidonia* (and perhaps other marine angicsperms), as of marine algae (Pannier, 1957, 1958; Gessner and Pannier, 1958; Gessner, 1959; Owens and Maris, 1964; see also Kutyurin et al., 1964). The respiration rates of numerous freshwater species have been found to be dependent on the oxygen concentration of the surrounding water up to at least 17 ppm (Fig. 5.20), a value which is equivalent to about 200 per cent saturation at temperatures of 15 to 20°C. In some species oxygen consumption continues to increase with increases in the external oxygen concentration up to about 400 per cent. Using *Callitriche obtusangula*, *Berula erecta*, *Hippuris vulgaris* and *Ranunculus pseudofluitans* in darkness at constant temperatures of 10°, 15° and 20°C, Owens and Maris (1964) found that the relation between oxygen consumption of the plant and oxygen content of the water could be described as: $R = aC^b$; where R is the rate of respiration per unit dry weight per hour, *C* is the dissolved oxygen concentration, and *a* and *b* are constants. They emphasised the similarity between this relationship and an equation which describes systems where simultaneous diffusion and chemical reaction occur. They also found that rates

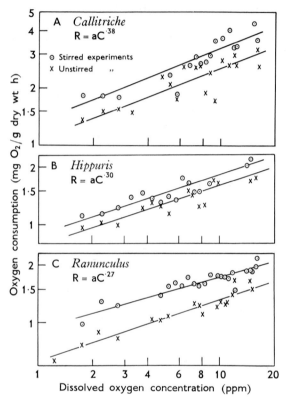

FIG. 5.20. Effect of dissolved oxygen concentration on the rates of respiration of excised shoots of *Callitriche obtusangula, Hippuris vulgaris,* and *Ranunculus pseudofluitans* at 20°C. (From D.S.I.R., 1962, by courtesy of the Controller of Her Majesty's Stationery Office, London.)

of oxygen consumption are generally higher if the water surrounding the plant is agitated, presumably because this steepens the concentration gradient through the plant surface. Respiration rates are also raised by increases in temperature: Owens and Maris calculated Q_{10} values of 1·32 to 3·48, and noted that the acceleration of the rate of respiration, as of other physiological reactions, diminishes as higher temperatures are reached.

In his experiments with *Ranunculus pseudofluitans* in flowing water, Westlake (in press) found the same relationship between oxygen consumption and dissolved oxygen concentration as described by Owens and Maris (1964). He recorded consumption rates of similar magnitude (i.e. from 0·4 to 2·8 mg oxygen/g dry weight h at 20°C) to the rates previously reported for this and other temperate submerged species. He further observed that the rise in respiration rate caused by an increase in the velocity of the current (from 0·2 to 0·9 mm/s) was greatest when the dissolved oxygen concentration was low; when the latter was high the rise was only small. These results are consistent with the notion that when the diffusion gradient into the plant is not steep, i.e. when the oxygen content of the water is low, an increase in current velocity reduces the thickness of the layer of almost stagnant water immediately outside each leaf and so accelerates the transfer of oxygen through this rate-limiting zone.

It therefore seems likely that during the night in natural habitats the dissolved oxygen concentration is the most critical factor influencing the respiration of submerged hydrophytes. At low oxygen concentrations the presence or absence of a turbulent or laminar flow may also be very significant.

The Lack of Lacunae in the Podostemaceae. Frequent attention has been directed to the remarkable absence of lacunae from the thalli of the Podostemaceae and its possible relation to the rapid current and high aeration of the water in which they live. Willis (1902) noted that when some species are, by chance, isolated in stagnant rocky pools they soon die, but it must also be recognised that not all members of the family live in torrential water: Willis himself (1914) recorded *Podostemum subulatus* and *Farmeria metzgerioides* in a habitat near Peradeniya in Ceylon where the current was only about 0·8 km/h. Lacunae may have been absent from ancestral stocks, and the family could consequently have been restricted to well-aerated water throughout its evolution. It is also possible that the ancestral stocks had lacunae, but that the ability to develop them has subsequently been lost, through their being superfluous in habitats where gaseous exchange is greatly facilitated by a swift current and saturation of the water with oxygen. In support of this second hypothesis it may be mentioned that lacunae do occur in some few species of *Wettsteiniola* and *Rhyncholacis*, perhaps as relict ancestral features, and, secondly, that the floating thalli of some species of *Mourera* and *Oenone*, which lack lacunae, bear clusters of delicate filamentous emergences (Fig. 5.9, K) which have been interpreted as structures facilitating gaseous exchange (Matthiesen, 1908; Steude, 1935). However, it must be admitted that any attempt to assess the validity of either hypothesis is sorely hindered by our ignorance of the ancestors of the family. The recent studies by Pannier (1960) indicate that the Podostemaceae resemble other freshwater plants in the dependence of their respiration rates on the oxygen concentration of the surrounding water, up to values of more than 200 per cent saturation.

ABSORPTION OF IONS BY SUBMERGED LEAVES

Permeability of the Epidermis. Although the thin cuticle and epidermis of submerged organs presumably allow the free passage of dissolved oxygen and carbon dioxide, there is evidence that not all epidermal cells are equally permeable to dissolved salts. Mayr (1915) observed that in strictly submerged species of *Aponogeton, Ceratophyllum, Myriophyllum, Potamogeton,* batrachian *Ranunculus, Sagittaria* and other genera only certain groups of epidermal cells, stainable *in vivo* with various dyes, were easily permeable to salts. These localised groups, termed hydropoten, were not found in the epidermis of normally aerial organs growing temporarily under water. Similarly, Lyr and Streitberg (1955) and van Ramshorst (1957a) found that typically emergent species of *Cryptocoryne,* such as *C. beckettii, C. nevillii* and *C. lutea,* lacked hydropoten whereas the more or less strictly submerged *C. affinis, C. griffithii* and *C. longicauda* possessed them.

The Uptake of Cations. From a line of research initiated rather more than 30 years ago, it has become clear that the entry of certain cations into submerged leaves may be linked to the photosynthetic utilisation of bicarbonate. Arens (1930, 1933) applied solutions of bicarbonates, notably calcium bicarbonate, to the abaxial surface of illuminated *Potamogeton* leaves, and found that nearly all the ions disappeared from these solutions, an equivalent amount of cations appearing, however, in the medium adjacent to the adaxial surface. Whereas the pH on the abaxial side remained constant, that on the adaxial side rose sharply. No ion movement occurred in darkness or when salts other than bicarbonates were used. Arens concluded that in the light, cations enter the abaxial epidermis along with equivalent bicarbonate ions and subsequently leave the adaxial side with either hydroxyl or carbonate ions. Gessner's (1937) observation that bicarbonate ions also entered the adaxial surface of leaves of *Potamogeton perfoliatus* is not as neatly explained. Several years later, Steemann Nielsen (1944, 1946, 1947), using *Potamogeton lucens,* fully confirmed Arens' observations but at the same time also confirmed the adaxial uptake of bicarbonate. He subsequently (1951) reconciled the two phenomena by suggesting that the electrical charge of the bicarbonate absorbed through both surfaces is neutralised by the simultaneous uptake of equivalent cations; the bicarbonate is assimilated within the leaf and the hydroxyl ions which are then formed are excreted with equivalent cations through only the adaxial surface.

The specific sites of calcium and potassium uptake in the epidermis were located by Arens (1936a, b) in *Elodea* leaves, and it was shown that neither immature cells nor cells situated above or below a vein absorb cations. In subsequent experiments (Arens, 1938a, b) the excretion of calcium and potassium was located by examining illuminated *Elodea* leaves in bicarbonate solutions containing also manganous ions, as an indicator of hydroxyl ions, with which in the presence of oxygen they form a brown precipitate; excretion was found to occur at the same sites as uptake but on the adaxial surface only. Arens (1938b) also discussed his findings in relation to Mayr's hydropoten.

Steemann Nielsen (1951) suggested that once cations have entered the leaf surface they probably diffuse passively through the cytoplasm, rather than the vacuoles, cell walls or intercellular spaces (see p. 136). Mazia (1938) showed that calcium ions are probably insoluble in the vacuolar fluid, since in *Elodea* leaves the entry of calcium into the vacuoles, facilitated by slight plasmolysis, is accompanied by the precipitation in them of calcium oxalate.

The subject of the uptake and transport of cations has been reviewed by Lowenhaupt (1956) who suggested that the following processes might be involved. An energy-rich coupling agent, synthesised at the chloroplasts, migrates to the plasmalemma of the epidermal cells (either adaxial or abaxial). This agent binds cations at the outer surface of the membrane, becomes re-orientated to the inner surface and releases the cation into the cytoplasm. Bicarbonate ions are similarly bound and diffuse to the chloroplasts: the cations diffuse through the leaf and are pumped out, together with hydroxyl ions, in a manner similar to that of their entry. Lowenhaupt showed that in *Potamogeton crispus* it is the release of cations from the plasmalemma which is the process dependent upon light and also upon oxygen. Although the hypothetical reaction sequence is light-dependent, Lowenhaupt's further observation that *Potamogeton* leaves will take up extra calcium ions in the dark, following exposure to light in the absence of calcium, suggests that the coupling agent can be stored by the cells and used later when cations are available.

Winter (1961) has recently shown that rubidium absorbed by *Vallisneria* leaves could be separated into three fractions, similar to those isolated by Epstein and Leggett (1954) in studying the uptake of strontium by excised barley roots. One fraction can be washed out of the material by deionised water; a second fraction, believed to be located in the cell walls, can be removed by cation exchange, whilst the third fraction is irremovable and presumably represents those cations which have been transferred through the plasmalemma into the cytoplasm. The transfer of rubidium ions from the second to the third fraction was found to be inhibited by MIA and to be strongly influenced by temperature, both of which facts suggest that the process is somehow linked to respiration.

Submerged marine angiosperms live in a medium in which the concentration of non-essential sodium far exceeds that of essential cations such as calcium, potassium and magnesium. Even so, the essential cations seem to be preferentially absorbed: it is possible that the uptake of potassium, for example, may be brought about by the excretion of sodium. The ratio of potassium to sodium in *Zostera marina* is 1·15 whereas in sea-water it is only 0·04. The angiosperms do not, however, seem to be as efficient in this respect as certain marine algae, for in *Ulva lactuca* (Chlorophyta) the corresponding ratio is 10·45 and in *Rhodymenia palmata* (Rhodophyta) it is 78·00 (Sutcliffe, 1962).

Marl Encrustation. The carbonate deposits, known collectively as marl, which commonly encrust the submerged parts of hydrophytes in alkaline calcareous waters have been variously attributed to the metabolic activities of bacteria and epiphytic algae. They are probably caused, at least in entirely submerged plants, largely by the absorption and transfer of bicarbonate ions through the leaves. Unused bicarbonate ions probably migrate to the adaxial surface of the leaves and there react with hydroxyl ions, producing carbonate which is precipitated. Absorption of dissolved carbon dioxide from water containing a high concentration of calcium bicarbonate would have the same result. In several hard-water lakes of southern Michigan, Wetzel (1960) found that amongst floating-leaved and emergent plants such as *Nymphaea*, *Scirpus* and *Pontederia*, which absorb atmospheric carbon dioxide, the marl deposits on the submerged organs were highly variable and proportional to the extent of the epiphytes present. Amongst submerged species of *Najas*, *Myriophyllum* and *Potamogeton*, however, the deposits were conspicuously heavier and their extent was correlated with the form of the species and the ability to absorb bicarbonate ions.

The Uptake of Anions (other than Bicarbonate). In general, the absorption of anions by such plants as *Elodea* appears to be independent of the external ion concentration down to about 3 μM. In certain conditions there may be competition between bicarbonate and other anions. If at an alkaline pH the concentration of other anions is relatively low, bicarbonates are preferentially absorbed but in solutions lacking bicarbonate, nitrate, for example, is absorbed freely regardless of the pH (Olsen, 1953). There is no evidence to suggest that anions other than bicarbonate are transported from one side of submerged leaves to the other. Lowenhaupt (1956) showed that phosphate could be absorbed through either surface, but neither it nor iodide showed directed transfer.

Other than bicarbonate, the principal anions absorbed by submerged vascular plants are probably sulphate, phosphate, chloride and nitrate. There is evidence that ammonium cations may be absorbed as an alternative nitrogen source, at least by some species such as *Callitriche intermedia* (Schwoerbel and Tillmanns, 1964a, b). This ability could be advantageous in habitats polluted with sewage effluents.

Jeschke and Simonis (1965) recently found that the uptake of phosphate, labelled with ^{32}P, and sulphate, labelled with ^{35}S, by leaves of *Egeria densa* was dependent on the external concentration in the range 10^{-8} to 5×10^{-3} M. In the middle of this concentration range, the uptake of both anions was promoted by light. Most of the phosphate absorbed was found to be in the inorganic, rather than the organic, form within the cells, especially at low temperatures, low pH or high external phosphate concentration. From their various experiments Jeschke and Simonis concluded that over the whole range of external concentrations the absorption of both ions involves an active process, with expenditure of free energy. They suggested that the net rate of uptake is limited at low external concentrations by the rate of diffusion through the static aqueous medium immediately surrounding the leaves; at intermediate concentrations, by the process of active uptake; and at high concentrations, by the rate of diffusive influx into the leaves.

Most of the present knowledge of anion uptake concerns the absorption and transport of chloride, and is the outcome of extensive research conducted by Arisz and his colleagues at Gröningen. They used excised segments of the leaves of *Vallisneria spiralis* measuring 7·5 cm by about 4 mm, of which the terminal 2·5 cm was applied to a medium containing sodium or potassium chloride. The subsequent absorption and translocation of chloride ions was then studied under different conditions, the leaf segments being divided into three zones, each 2·5 cm long, and analysed at the end of each experiment.

Chloride may be accumulated in the cell vacuoles in any part of the leaf exposed to light. If the zone in contact with the test solution is illuminated and the rest of the leaf is in darkness, all the chloride taken up is accumulated in the contact zone. Conversely, darkening of the contact zone with the rest of the leaf in light promotes transport of the chloride into the illuminated zones. The chloride content of the leaf segment as a whole remains constant throughout, no ions being lost to the bathing medium, as would be expected if they were translocated through the freely permeable cell walls. The accumulation of chloride in all zones of the leaf is inhibited by applying potassium cyanide, at a concentration of 3×10^{-4} M, to the contact zone: this suggests that the ions do not diffuse passively through the walls but are moved from cell to cell via the cytoplasm. 10^{-4} M 2,4-dinitrophenol inhibits accumulation where it is applied but does not interfere with transport to other zones or accumulation there. The conclusion drawn from these observations (Arisz, 1953, 1954) is that three distinct processes must be involved:

(a) Absorption into the cytoplasm: sensitive to cyanide; apparently dependent on respiration.
(b) Translocation through the cytoplasm.
(c) Secretion from the cytoplasm into the vacuole: sensitive to dinitrophenol; apparently dependent on respiration.

To explain the transport over a distance of 7·5 cm with no leakage to the external medium, Arisz invoked the concept of a 'symplasm'—a continuous system composed of the cytoplasm of all the parenchyma cells linked by plasmodesmata passing through their walls.

The effect of light upon uptake and absorption also occurs in the absence of carbon dioxide. Light generally promotes uptake and therefore increases transport in the symplasm. If the leaves are pre-exposed to light and then exposed to chloride ions in darkness, the rate of uptake is greatly increased (Arisz and Sol, 1956; Sol, 1958). These observations resemble Lowenhaupt's (1956) on calcium uptake by *Potamogeton*, and could similarly be explained by postulating that the binding of the ion involves a coupling agent synthesised at some stage in photosynthesis, perhaps during photolysis or phosphorylation. Sucrose administered to either the absorbing zone or the free part of the leaf in the dark promotes the secretion of chloride into the vacuoles in the region of application, perhaps by acting as a source of respiratory energy for the transfer of the ions across the tonoplast (Arisz and Sol, 1956; Sol, 1958).

Arisz (1963, 1964) recently reviewed the experimental work on *Vallisneria* in the context of current theories of the mechanism of electrolyte absorption. He pointed out that the peripheral plasma membrane in the leaves of *Vallisneria* is not permeable to electrolytes and further emphasised that during chloride uptake there appears to be no measurable efflux of chloride ions from the leaves. He suggested that ion pairs are taken up by a process requiring the expenditure of free energy potentials, and argued that active uptake does not involve simultaneous influx and efflux (i.e. ion exchange) between the tissue and the external medium, as suggested by Briggs *et al.* (1961).

In earlier experiments, Arisz (1958) compared the effects of several metabolic inhibitors on part of the leaf of *Vallisneria* where absorption and accumulation of chloride both occur, with their effects on an adjoining part where only accumulation occurs. He found that arsenate and uranyl ions inhibit uptake into the cytoplasm whereas azide prevents accumulation in the vacuoles. Transport from zone to zone, being unaffected by any inhibitor, appears not to be related to any active metabolic process, which suggests the somewhat surprising conclusion reached also by Steemann Nielsen (1951) for cation movement: namely, that the ions diffuse quite passively through the cytoplasm. Arisz (1964) further remarked that the chloride ions (and also monovalent cations and dipolar ions, such as asparagine) maintain their specific properties and reactivity during transport, and therefore considered it unlikely that they are bound to carriers. Transport in *Vallisneria* leaves is not polar: it may occur in any direction, dependent on a concentration gradient.

At the present time, it is far from easy to reconcile these data, and the conclusions drawn from them, with the recent experimental and theoretical work on the uptake and transport of solutes in the tissues of land plants. It should first be noted that the free space through which ions may move in the tissues of most vascular land plants is probably the cell walls and intercellular spaces, in which diffusion appears to be much faster than through the cytoplasm (Sutcliffe, 1962; Jennings, 1963). Ions lost from the cytoplasm and vacuole diffuse in the wall water, from which they may be taken up by any adjacent cell, thus affording a convenient route for passive transport through a parenchymatous tissue. Xylem transport, accelerated by transpiration, is much faster still. Arisz and the other European physiologists whose work has been briefly surveyed in the foregoing pages generally consider that in aquatic plants the plasmodesmatal connections (i.e. a symplasm) play a much more important role in internal transport, because ions lost from the cytoplasm and vacuole are likely to be washed out of the intercellular spaces and cell walls, which are in diffusive aqueous continuity with the external medium. From their experimental work it would seem that *Elodea* and *Potamogeton* provide possible examples of transport through a symplasm. Arisz's studies with metabolic inhibitors appears to suggest symplasm or xylem transport in *Vallisneria*. On the other hand, Winter's findings on rubidium uptake by the same plant are congruous with the conventional notion of a tripartite system, comprising free space, ion exchange space (possibly the cell walls) and non-free space (the cytoplasm). As Sutcliffe (1962) properly pointed out, further experiments are needed to justify the notion of symplasm transport and resolve this technically very difficult problem.

As yet there is no definite correlation between the physiological concept of a symplasm and the ultra-structure of *Vallisneria* cells. In the related species *Elodea canadensis,* the cortical parenchyma (which is not markedly dissimilar in structure from the *Vallisneria* mesophyll) shows perforations in the cellulose framework of its walls from a very early stage of development. Visible under the polarising microscope, these pit-fields are traversed by plasmodesmata and occur only on those parts of the walls which are in contact with neighbouring cells (Wilson, 1957). Observations from terrestrial plants suggest that the endoplasmic reticulum is continuous between cells, its protein membranes being in constant movement through the plasmodesmata. Sutcliffe (1962) considered that the binding and release of ions may be a general property of cytoplasmic protein associated with these membranes. In this context, it is worth noting that the initiation of protoplasmic streaming by light in the mesophyll cells of *Vallisneria spiralis* is inhibited by pre-treatment for 1 h in 0·001 M solutions of several potassium, calcium and rubidium salts (Jager, 1958). These salts are thought to modify the properties of the contractile proteins in the cytoplasm. Dehydration of the cytoplasm, brought about by plasmolysis with sucrose, might be expected to have a similar effect, and it has been found to cause a marked decrease in the uptake of chloride by *Vallisneria* leaves (Arisz and Schreuder, 1956; Sol, 1958).

VASCULAR ANATOMY AND PHYSIOLOGY OF SUBMERGED ORGANS

Reduction of the Vascular System, with Special Reference to the Xylem. The outstanding modifications of the vascular system in submerged organs are the reduction in the number and the degree of lignification of the xylem conducting elements, and, in stems, the condensation of most or all of the vascular strands into a central cylinder. In only very few stems, such as those of *Ranunculus trichophyllus* (Arber, 1920) and *R. fluitans* (Wilson, 1947), and in the petioles of floating-leaved and emergent hydrophytes do the vascular bundles retain their individual identity (Figs. 5.15 and 5.16). In *Nymphoides peltata*, for example, the widely spaced bundles of the petiole are typically arranged in an arc, the median bundle being considerably larger than the laterals. The petioles of *Pontederia* and *Sagittaria* similarly possess arcs or rings of spaced bundles. Both the arrangement and orientation of the bundles vary amongst the Nymphaeaceae: in the petioles of *Barclaya* and *Nuphar* only simple bundles occur, whilst *Euryale*, *Victoria* and *Nymphaea* also possess some double bundles (Figs. 5.15 and 5.21), and *Nelumbo* has a mixture of normally and inversely orientated bundles (Metcalfe and Chalk, 1950). The arrangement also varies in different species of the same genus, e.g. *Nymphaea* (Conard, 1905).

Although the bundles remain separate, their structure is somewhat reduced. They lack true vessels in many genera, the conducting elements being long annular- or spiral-thickened tracheids, some or all of which eventually disorganise, leaving a xylem lacuna and phloem strand in each bundle. Cambium is absent from the mature bundles of both the aquatic monocotyledons and the Nymphaeaceae, but ephemeral cambial activity has been discerned in the very young petioles of *Potamogeton natans* and *Sagittaria sagittifolia* (Arber, 1922b).

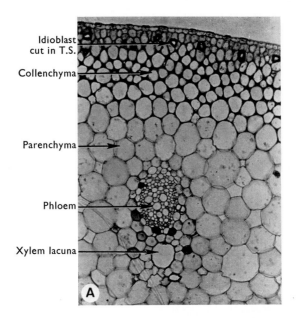

Idioblast cut in T.S.

Collenchyma

Parenchyma

Phloem

Xylem lacuna

A

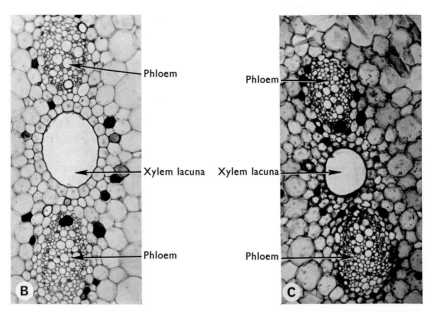

Phloem

Xylem lacuna

Phloem

B

Phloem

Xylem lacuna

Phloem

C

FIG. 5.21. Photomicrographs of T.S. petiole of *Nymphaea alba*: A, outer cortex, showing single vascular bundle and subepidermal collenchyma and idioblasts; B and C, two double vascular bundles (all × 100). Note in each the relatively well developed phloem and the xylem lacuna, that in B having an especially conspicuous lining epithelium.

In the vast majority of elongated submerged stems, the vascular strands are condensed into a central cylinder strongly reminiscent of the stelar core of roots. Schenck (1886) advanced the thesis that this feature is not caused merely by the vascular reduction but has adaptive mechanical significance. Submerged stems, especially in flowing water, resemble roots in being subject to pulling strains, which are best resisted by a rope-like core. In support of this interpreta-

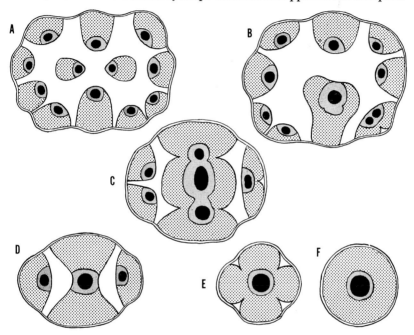

FIG. 5.22. Diagrammatic T.S. stele of the stem of *Potamogeton* spp. to illustrate reduction and fusion of the vascular bundles (phloem zone, stippled; xylem lacuna, solid black; xylem parenchyma, shaded; conjunctive tissue clear): A, *P. pulcher*; B, *P. natans*; C, *P. crispus*; D, *P. lucens*; E, *P. pusillus*; F, *P. pectinatus*. Intermediate stages in the fusion of bundles are visible in B and C. (After Schenck, 1886; Sauvageau, 1894; Raunkiaer, 1903; and Chrysler, 1907.)

tion Schenck directed attention to the fact that the aerial stems of saprophytes and parasites are subject to bending, not pulling, strains; and their vascular tissues, although reduced like those of aquatics, remain organised in their more peripheral ancestral position.

Sanio (1865) was the first to realise that the reduced axial strand of numerous species of *Potamogeton, Ceratophyllum and Hippuris* is the surviving remnant of a whole system of vascular bundles. A series may be traced in the genus *Potamogeton* illustrating conceivable stages in the fusion and reduction of the bundles (Schenck, 1886; Sauvageau, 1894; Raunkiaer, 1903; Chrysler, 1907; and Figs. 5.22, 5.23 and 5.24). In the stems of floating-leaved species, such as *P. pulcher* and *P. natans*, the stele contains several groups of more or less distinct leaf traces and cauline bundles. The bundles are condensed into three groups in both *P. crispus* and *P. lucens* but in the latter there is considerably more reduction of the xylem and phloem regions. In the linear-leaved submerged species, such as *P. pusillus*, the xylem groups of all the individual bundles have become fused into a single axial passage but the areas of phloem remain separate, whilst in *P. pectinatus* there is a more or less homogeneous zone of phloem surrounding the axial lacuna. Some species of *Potamogeton* also possess minute vascular strands running longitudinally through the paren-

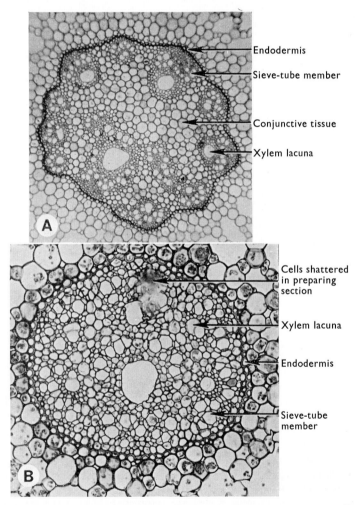

FIG. 5.23. Photomicrographs of T.S. stele of the stem of *Potamogeton natans* (A, compare with Fig. 5.22 B) and *P. crispus* (B, compare with Fig. 5.22 C) (A, ×90; B, ×120). Note the conspicuous endodermis, sieve-tube members and xylem lacunae.

chyma at the junctions of the walls of the lacunae (Figs. 5.16 E, and 5.25). These cortical bundles are linked to the stele by transverse strands running through the nodal diaphragms. The genus *Potamogeton* as a whole lacks vessels, and the annular- or spiral-thickened tracheids usually become disorganised leaving only a xylem lacuna (Cheadle, 1942).

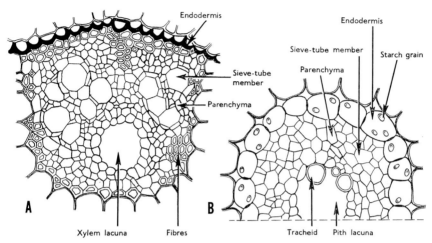

A   B

Xylem lacuna   Fibres   Tracheid   Pith lacuna

Endodermis   Endodermis

Sieve-tube member   Starch grain

Sieve-tube member   Parenchyma

Parenchyma

FIG. 5.24. A, T.S. fusion bundle from the stele of the stem of *Potamogeton natans*, showing two phloem groups (their distinctness emphasised by the group of fibres intruding from the endodermis) and a single xylem lacuna; thickened walls of the endodermal cells in solid black (× 300). B, T.S. half of stele of the stem of *Callitriche obtusangula*, showing reduced xylem elements surrounded by a cylinder of phloem; the endodermal cells contain starch grains and have very weak Casparian bands on their radial walls (× 400).

Incomplete fusion into a central stele is seen in the dicotyledon, *Peplis portula* (Gin, 1909). A zone of separate external phloem groups surrounds the complete ring of xylem, which possesses true vessels. Internal to this is another zone of phloem, typical of related terrestrial members of the Lythraceae, and an axial pith.

Hippuris vulgaris (Fig. 5.26) shows a complete cylinder of xylem, possessing true vessels with spiral or reticulate thickening, surrounded by a narrow zone of phloem. The centre of older stems is a 'pseudopith'—actually xylem paren-chyma, as was pointed out by Sanio (1865) who observed ephemeral thickened elements in the centre of the apex of the shoot. These appear above the entry of the first leaf traces, and further from the apex become thinner-walled and eventually disappear, so that the centre of the xylem in the mature stem is occupied only by homogeneous 'pith-like' parenchyma. Using serial micro-tome sections, Arber (1920) fully confirmed Sanio's observations: at the level of entry of the first leaf traces she found twenty-one differentiated cauline elements, most of which disappeared by the time the stele reached 0·2 mm in diameter, although a few persisted, fusing with either the xylem ring or the leaf traces passing down from the second node. Development of the incipient vascular system above the level of the first leaf primordia, as in *Hippuris* and also *Elodea*, is very unusual in the megaphyllous spermatophytes and ferns, although it is also found in the microphyllous cryptogams (Wetmore, 1943; Allsopp, 1964).

The xylem is more reduced in species of *Myriophyllum*, e.g. *M. spicatum*, but the general vascular structure closely resembles that of *Hippuris*, and according to Vöchting (1872), similarly includes ephemeral cauline elements in the

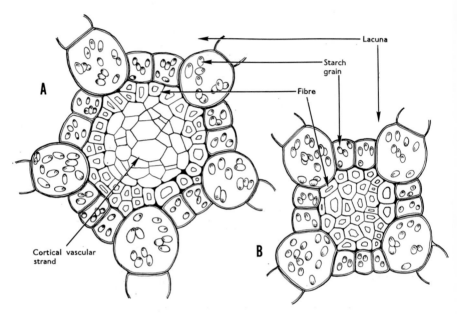

FIG. 5.25. T.S. cortical bundles in an old stem of *Potamogeton natans*: A, vascular bundle with fibre sheath; B, fibre bundle (both × 450).

embryonic pseudopith. In *M. heterophyllum* the conducting elements of the xylem differentiate in the fourth or fifth internode, those of the phloem at about the seventh or eighth node (England and Tolbert, 1964). It is interesting to note that amongst the extant terrestrial relatives of *Myriophyllum* there are species of *Haloragis* with a typical cambial ring and cylinder of secondary xylem, and species of *Gunnera* with a large number of variously orientated steles (Metcalfe and Chalk, 1950).

The vascular structure in *Callitriche* and *Ceratophyllum* is highly reduced. *Callitriche* has a weak axial stele with a few scattered xylem elements surrounded by phloem. The central pith contains at most two or three cells in transverse section and is resorbed early in the development of submerged species (Pax and Hoffman, 1931; Schenck, 1886; and see Fig. 5.24). The mature stele of *Ceratophyllum* has an axial lacuna created by the resorption of a small group of

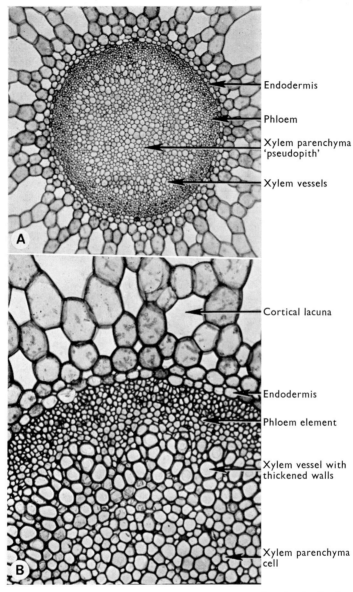

FIG. 5.26. Photomicrographs of T.S. stele of the stem of *Hippuris vulgaris*: A, the complete stele (× 50); B, small sector in a radial plane (× 150). Note the concentric arrangement of the vascular tissues, the relatively narrow zone of phloem, the thickened xylem tracheary elements, and the pseudopith of xylem parenchyma.

procambial cells (Sanio, 1865). This is bordered by vertically-elongated, non-lignified, starch-containing cells, which represent the xylem and are surrounded by two rings of sieve tubes and companion cells interspersed with parenchyma. True vessels and tracheids are completely absent (Solereder, 1908).

In many submerged monocotyledonous stems, including *Potamogeton* species, the apical structure is quite normal and the extreme reduction of the mature vascular cylinder is caused by the potential elements failing to undergo complete differentiation. In the apex of *Egeria densa*, for example, the inter-phase cells are of similar shape and size to those of other undifferentiated tissues: the number of faces ranges from 9 to 21, about 85 per cent of cells being in the 12- to 16-hedron range; 95 per cent of the faces are four-, five- or six-sided (Matzke and Duffy, 1955, 1956). Cells destined to differentiate as xylem become vacuolated at the seventh leaf whorl from the apex in *Elodea canadensis*: scalariform thickenings appear in a few cells but these soon disintegrate, as do the other xylem cells, leaving an axial lacuna. Differentiation of the surrounding phloem is also weak, and begins rather later, at about the twentieth leaf whorl (Dale, 1957a). In mature stems a few annular- to spiral-thickened tracheids occur in the nodes but the internodes are quite devoid of thickened elements.

Egeria, Najas, Ruppia, Zannichellia and the marine angiosperms all resemble *Elodea* in lacking true vessels and in being almost totally devoid of any vascular elements with even annular thickenings (Cheadle, 1942). Sporadic annular- or spiral-thickened tracheids have been recorded in the nodes of *Althenia* (Prillieux, 1864), and *Najas, Ruppia* and *Zannichellia* (Chrysler, 1907).

Despite its virtual lack of lignification *Egeria densa* contains flavonoid compounds (in the form of anthocyanins) and tyrosine, from which the phenolic C_6-C_3 precursors of lignins could be synthesised. If supplied with a precursor, such as eugenol in the presence of peroxide, it will form appreciable lignin. Siegel (1962) suggested that under natural conditions there is competition between metabolic pathways in the regions of differentiation, the potential precursors being converted to other products more rapidly than they can be transformed into lignins.

The Podostemaceae also lack true vessels, although annular- and spiral-thickened elements, probably tracheids, occur sporadically in some genera, e.g. *Mourera*. The degree of reduction of the vascular system as a whole varies widely amongst both root- and shoot-thalli. In the filamentous assimilatory roots of such species as *Mniopsis saldanhana* there is a central vascular system possessing two xylem groups with a few thickened elements. According to Engler (1930), the xylem is sometimes absent. The floating thalli of *Mourera aspera* have both a central cylinder and numerous cortical bundles. The several vascular bundles of the central cylinder lack sieve tubes and their thickened xylem elements soon collapse, leaving lacunae. The xylem is represented in the mature thallus by parenchyma groups in a ground tissue which consists, paradoxically, of narrow lignified cells with pitted walls. The cortical bundles rarely develop lacunae, retaining their weakly thickened xylem elements even in mature regions (Steude, 1935). The entire vascular system of *Hydrobryum japonicum* is reduced to a network of elongated thin-walled cells (Imamura,

1929). A highly modified form of secondary growth by tangential cell divisions has been recorded from the basal part of the thallus of *Weddellina squamulosa* (Matthiesen, 1908).

The trend of reduction is evident also in the vascular system of submerged leaves, especially the setaceous and filiform types and the radial segments of dissected leaves, in which there is usually but a single vein. In the segments of *Ceratophyllum* and *Myriophyllum*, and the leaves of most submerged monocotyledons, such as *Elodea*, *Thalassia*, *Vallisneria* and *Zostera*, the vascular strands are vessel-less and either devoid also of tracheids, the xylem being represented by a small lacuna, or with just a few more or less ephemeral elements bearing annular thickenings (Solereder, 1908, 1913, Cheadle, 1942; Hasman and Inanç, 1957). The 'leaves' of the Podostemaceae recall those of bryophytes in having a very feeble midrib composed of thin-walled, slightly elongated cells (Goebel, 1891–1893).

Transport of Water and Ions through Xylem Elements. There is a curious notion, prevalent in numerous botanical textbooks which accord merely a superficial treatment to hydrophytes, that submerged plants absorb water and ions exclusively through the epidermis of their leaves and stems, their roots serving only for anchorage and their vascular system, by virtue of its reduction, being utterly functionless. Arber (1920) very properly criticised the naive and somewhat teleological nature of this generalisation. She argued that the functional efficiency of xylem conducting elements is not proportional to their degree of lignification, if, as seems reasonable to assume, water and dissolved salts move principally through their cavities, not their walls. She suggested that in uninjured submerged organs, air locks are unlikely to be important and that non-lignified conducting elements or xylem lacunae could be as efficient a pathway for transport as the heavily lignified vessels and tracheids of trees. Much impressed by the physiological experiments of Sauvageau, Hochreutiner, von Minden and Thoday and Sykes, Arber declared her support for the view that a current of water, and presumably dissolved salts, definitely flows through the shoots of submerged plants.

Lacking an evaporating surface, submerged hydrophytes clearly cannot possess a transpiration current of the type occurring in terrestrial plants. However, this does not negate the possibility that transport of water and ions through the xylem elements still occurs. The flow might be motivated by exudation pressures exerted in either the root or the shoot, or in both. It must be acknowledged that Arber herself inclined to this view, using the word 'transpiration' only on the grounds that Burgerstein's (1904) more appropriate term 'guttation' was too clumsy to be admitted to the English language (see footnote on p. 266 of Arber, 1920).

Critical reappraisal of the experimental techniques and data of earlier workers raises severe doubts of the existence of an appreciable, sustained flow through submerged stems (Wilson, 1947; Gessner, 1956). The first intimation that a flow might exist came from Unger's (1862) gravimetric estimation of the transfer of water from one vessel to another by submerged shoots threaded through a connecting U-tube. In a period of 8 days, 0·8 g water was so transferred by *Ranunculus fluitans* and 1·6 g by *Potamogeton crispus*: rootless shoots of the latter apparently transferred no water. Sauvageau's (1891) experiments, in which a cut shoot was sealed into a modified potometer, showed slight uptake of water by several submerged monocotyledons, although Weinrowsky (1899) considered this could have been caused by the slight hydrostatic pressure to which the shoot was subjected in the apparatus. By a modification of the technique used for land plants, Hochreutiner (1896) arranged shoots of *Potamogeton pectinatus* and other species with their bases in dilute eosin solution and their upper parts in water, and *vice versa*. Subsequent sections of the shoots revealed the movement of the dye solution through the xylem lacunae in a morphologically upward direction only, but the rates observed were slow—not more than a few cm per day. Snell (1908) obtained similar results with *Elodea* and *Potamogeton*, but Thoday and Sykes' (1909) experiments with cut shoots of *Potamogeton lucens* revealed astonishing rates of eosin movement—from 5·7 to 9·5 cm/min. Thut's (1932) apparatus, based on that of Unger (1862), has been criticised by Wilson (1947) because of its great size and consequent insensitivity for recording small changes in weight. From his gravimetric estimates of the rate of water movement through *Egeria densa* and *Myriophyllum spicatum*, and volumetric estimates of the rate of exudation from rooted stumps of these, *Ranunculus circinatus* and other species, Thut concluded that any current in submerged stems is due to root pressure.

Wilson (1947) discussed very thoroughly the extreme practical difficulties involved in studying and recording the movement of small volumes of water through submerged hydrophytes and went to great pains to perfect an apparatus which would provide reliable measurements of the genuine uptake of water by a cut shoot. Water is in fact expelled from a submerged shoot by a flow of gas through the intercellular spaces (such a flow could arise from the production of oxygen in photosynthesis), and Wilson pertinently emphasised that this expulsion would have been recorded in earlier experiments as water uptake. The rates of uptake which Wilson observed in cut shoots of *Ranunculus fluitans* were of similar magnitude (1 to 10 mm^3/h) to the rates of expulsion caused by a gas-flow, and were of similar short duration, lasting for only 10 to 15 h. Shoots prepared 10 to 15 h before the actual experiment showed negligible rates of uptake. From the variability and transient nature of the process of uptake, Wilson concluded that any flow of water that occurs is better treated as an indication of the adjustment of the water balance of the tissues than as a sustained current comparable with that of land plants.

The recent experiments of Höhn and Ax (1961) provide more convincing evidence of a continuous current. The apical leafy parts of *Nomaphila stricta* were found to exude water during daylight and to absorb it during the night, whilst the basal rooted parts absorbed water at all times. A diurnal rhythm was evident in both the rate of absorption and the rate of exudation. Maximal absorption by the rooted parts occurred at about the same time as maximal exudation by the apical leafy parts. The upward movement of water was enhanced by an increased concentration of carbon dioxide, and this feature, together with the observed influence of light, suggests that photosynthesis is somehow involved. Whether the influence of the process is osmotic, through the accumulation of sugars, or mechanical, through the displacement of water by a gas-flow generated by the evolution of oxygen, is not clear.

Höhn and Ax also found that rooted stumps of *Nomaphila stricta* continued to absorb water, although at a lower rate than before decapitation, and, more surprisingly, that cut leafy shoots retained the ability to exude water for at least a day. These observations suggest that root pressure is primarily responsible for the movement of water through the plant, but may perhaps be supplemented by exudation pressures exerted in the shoot.

In attempting to interpret these data in the context of the previous experimental work, which fails to establish the existence of a sustained water flow, it must be remembered that although submerged specimens were used in Höhn and Ax's experiments *Nomaphila stricta* is in fact not an obligate submerged plant, but rather an emergent which can grow immersed for quite long periods. Like related species of *Nomaphila* and *Hygrophila* it presumably possesses functional stomata and hydathodes and with its relatively well developed vascular tissues it is not directly comparable with the somewhat reduced, truly submerged hydrophytes.

It is obvious that the experimental data on the water relations of submerged hydrophytes do not lend themselves to generalisation. A sustained flow of water through the intact rooted shoots of obligate submerged species has still not been satisfactorily demonstrated; nor has the possibility that it does exist been completely nullified. If it does occur it must be motivated by root pressure and/or exudation pressure in the shoot. Observations that the osmotic pressure in the roots of some submerged plants, including *Elodea*, may be as much as 4 atm higher than in the leaves, are consistent with the possible existence of root pressure (Hannig, 1912; Snell, 1912). The conspicuous presence of an endodermis in the shoot as well as the root of many submerged plants, and the knowledge that in land plants this layer probably regulates the transfer of water and ions into the stele (Priestley and North, 1922; Scott and Priestley, 1928) support the idea that exudation pressures might develop also in the stem. A well-developed endodermis occurs in both shoots with a central vascular cylinder, such as *Hippuris vulgaris* (Barratt, 1916), and shoots with discrete vascular bundles, such as *Ranunculus fluitans* (Wilson, 1947). In the latter species the endodermis forms a continuous sheath around each bundle throughout the shoot, extending to within 2 mm of the tips of the leaf segments.

Although not yet fully understood in land plants, exudation pressure seems to involve both osmosis and active metabolic processes. A higher osmotic concentration in the xylem than in the cortical tissues or the medium could result in the movement of water into the conducting elements and the development there of a positive pressure. For this osmotic movement to be sustained for any length of time, the osmotic differential must be maintained, i.e. the solute concentration in the xylem elements must be kept higher than in the surrounding cells; this might be accomplished by active accumulation of ions, a process which requires respiratory energy. In this context it is interesting to note that Wilson (1947) found that in 0·2 per cent aqueous sodium bicarbonate the initial rate of uptake of shoots of *Ranunculus fluitans* was from ten to fifteen times greater than the rate in tap water. The observed inhibition of this solute stimulus by very low concentrations of cyanide suggests that respiration is somehow involved in the process of uptake. The precise significance of these data is not clear, and until further experiments are performed, any statements on the relation between exudation pressure and the transient water uptake of submerged shoots can only be speculative (see also pp. 174–75).

An important fact militating against the possibility of a flow caused even by exudation pressures is the absence from many submerged hydrophytes of any adequate structures through which the current could pass out of the plant. Earlier workers such as Sauvageau (1891) presumed that the water which they found to be taken up was expelled through the hydathodes occurring on sub-merged leaves. To demonstrate exudation through these pores directly is not easy. Von Minden (1899) and Weinrowsky (1899) claimed that drops of water persistently reappeared at the tips of the leaves of *Callitriche hermaphroditica*, *Littorella uniflora*, *Potamogeton crispus* and several other species when these were exposed just above the water level in a saturated atmosphere. However, von Minden (1899) and others have also shown that in many species, the hydathodes quickly become visibly blocked by brownish deposits amongst the epithem cells. Applying an artificial root pressure of 1 atm to cut shoots of *Ranunculus fluitans* in eosin solution, Wilson (1947) found that exudation occurred through the hydathodes on only the very youngest, still-growing leaves of each shoot, and concluded that the pores must become functionally blocked even earlier than is evident from the appearance of the brownish deposits. In some plants water could perhaps be exuded through secondary apical openings which arise through the resorption of groups of stomata, as in *Callitriche hermaphroditica* (Borodin, 1870), or the death of the apical cells, as in *Groenlandia densa* (Sauvageau, 1891). But it must also be pointed out that there are numerous plants, such as *Cymodocea* and *Posidonia*, which possess neither hydathodes nor apical openings.

The only conclusion that may safely be drawn from the conflicting experi-mental data is that whilst a transpiration current of the type occurring in aerial organs clearly cannot exist in submerged plants, a transient flow of water and dissolved salts might occur, motivated either by exudation pressure in the root or shoot or by a gas-flow generated during periods of active photosynthesis.

The Structure and Function of Phloem. In most submerged organs the phloem is relatively better developed than the xylem: it does not undergo quite such extreme modification. In numerous aquatic monocotyledons the phloem appears to be highly specialised in having sieve-tube members with transverse, rather than oblique, end walls (Cheadle and Whitford, 1941; Esau *et al.*, 1953). Mehta and Spanner (1962, 1963) and Mehta (1964) recently found that the ultra-structure of the sieve tubes and sieve plates in the petiole of the dicoty-ledonous *Nymphoides peltata* closely resembles that of the sieve elements in many terrestrial herbs and favours the electro-osmotic theory rather than the pressure-flow theory of phloem transport. Quantitative studies of transport in this species are now being made with radioactive tracers, such as [137]Cs (Spanner and Prebble, 1962). Arisz (1958) presented evidence to suggest that chloride ions, as well as organic molecules, might be transported in the sieve tubes of *Vallisneria spiralis*.

LAND FORMS OF SUBMERGED HYDROPHYTES

Submerged hydrophytes are very similar to many terrestrial herbs in their average water content and in certain epidermal characters. Water contents ranging from 86 to 95 per cent of the fresh weight have been recorded for healthy non-calcareous material of species of *Callitriche, Ceratophyllum, Elodea, Hippuris, Littorella, Myriophyllum, Najas, Potamogeton, Ranunculus* and *Vallisneria* (Rickett, 1921; Westlake, 1965a). These values are not unusually high, as is sometimes suggested: they are closely comparable to the water contents of numerous herbaceous land plants. The proportion of water in the fresh weight of the woodland annual, *Impatiens parviflora*, for example, varies in different vegetative organs from 86 to 96·5 per cent, the lower values within this range occurring in the leaves and the higher values in larger shaded plants (Evans and Hughes, 1961).

The common statement that submerged plants are quite glabrous needs considerable qualification. Uni- or multicellular hairs are quite frequent on the vegetative organs of, for example, *Hippuris, Myriophyllum, Proserpinaca*, the batrachian *Ranunculi* and some of the Podostemaceae (Solereder, 1908; Steude, 1935; Metcalfe and Chalk, 1950; Cook, 1963). Anthocyanins, oil droplets and other inclusions are commonly present in the epidermal cells of *Cabomba, Myriophyllum, Potamogeton*, and the Podostemaceae (Lister, 1903; Wheldale, 1916; Arber, 1920; Metcalfe and Chalk, 1950). Mucilage-secreting glandular hairs are abundant on the submerged organs of many of the Nymphaeaceae, whilst each leaf segment of *Ceratophyllum* has an apical multiseriate gland which secretes oil (Schrenk, 1888; Conard, 1905; Jones, 1931). Many members of the Helobian families possess mucilage-secreting scales in the axils of their leaves: these squamulae intravaginales lack vascular tissue and develop, in such genera as *Sagittaria*, from the abaxial surface of the succeeding leaf (Arber, 1923, 1925a).

In view of their not abnormally high water content, epidermal hairs, and surface secretions of oil or mucilage, it is not perhaps surprising that some submerged hydrophytes can withstand exposure to air for short periods of up to a few hours. The capacity to develop persistent land forms, however, is much more limited, presumably because most submerged plants have only a thin cuticle, lack strengthening tissues, depend largely on turgor for support, and so cannot withstand excessive transpiration.

The structural changes occurring in the development of land forms are essentially the converse of those discernible when emergent species are immersed for long periods. The land form of *Myriophyllum spicatum*, for example, produces a dense turf of dwarf much-branched stems rooting profusely from the nodes. The leaves are smaller, broader, thicker and fewer in number than those on submerged stems (Schenck, 1885). The similarly shorter and thicker leaves of *M. alterniflorum* show a dorsiventral organisation, in contrast to the radial symmetry of the submerged leaves, and the xylem elements are more strongly developed in the terrestrial stems. The epidermal cells of the leaf have the sinuous outline typical of an aerial dicotyledon leaf instead of the regular outline they possess under water: the epidermis is poor in chloroplasts but possesses stomata (Arber, 1920). Abbreviated internodes and thicker leaves are also evident in the land form of *M. verrucosum*. The profusely rooted stems attain heights of only about 10 cm whereas submerged they reach 60 cm or even 1 m. Under water the leaves are in whorls of three but on the land form they are paired and opposite, sometimes alternate, and have fewer, shorter and broader segments (Brenan and Chapple, 1949).

Land forms of normally submerged species of *Callitriche* and *Ranunculus* subg. *Batrachium* have also been described (Hegelmaier, 1864; Askenasy, 1870; Schenck, 1886). In these the modifications are again primarily quantitative: a shortening of the internodes, a reduction in the size of the leaves, and a decrease in the frequency of the epidermal chloroplasts.

The danger of excessive transpiration amongst land forms may be alleviated by one or more of several features. The dense crowding of the foliage close to the soil probably minimises the effect of wind on the transpiration rate. The very free development of adventitious roots may permit more efficient absorption of water. The thicker cuticle probably diminishes evaporation through the epidermis and restricts loss of water largely to the stomata.

Plants such as *Egeria*, *Elodea*, *Najas*, the fragile linear-leaved species of *Potamogeton*, and some of the marine angiosperms, generally survive for only short periods out of water, even in a saturated atmosphere. The exceptional survival of some of the Podostemaceae is attributable to the accumulation of siliceous bodies in the peripheral tissues and epidermal hairs of the thallus (Goebel, 1891–1893). Species such as *Podostemum subulatus*, which lack the silica, undergo severe shrinkage out of water (Metcalfe and Chalk, 1950). The strengthening effect of the siliceous bodies is probably quite fortuitous but is certainly of some value to plants inhabiting shallow tropical rivers which are liable to sudden falls in water level. Its value is, however, limited and although the thalli are able to exist for a few days if they are stranded, they cannot survive the whole dry season. It is therefore apparent that concomitant with their reduction and specialisation, the most highly modified submerged hydrophytes have irrevocably lost the vegetative plasticity necessary to produce land forms, and they are consequently utterly committed to an aquatic existence.

6

Life in the Substrate:
The Structure and Physiology of
Underground Organs

In their principal functions of anchorage and absorption the underground organs of hydrophytes resemble those of terrestrial plants. Yet the soft substrate to which the vast majority of rooted hydrophytes are restricted is far less suitable a medium for growth than are most soils on land. Its frequent instability, resulting from silting and erosion, creates severe mechanical problems. To gain a permanent anchorage in loose gravel, shifting sand or deep silt plants must have a ramifying system of vigorous rhizomes or fibrous adventitious roots which will bind and stabilise the particles. Hydrophytes with delicate attentuated shoots rooting only sparsely from the nodes are confined largely to deeper or quieter water where erosion is less severe and the substrate more consolidated. The poor aeration of the substrate, and the accumulation there and in the overlying water of carbon dioxide, methane and sulphides pose physiological problems for both roots and underground stems, whose metabolically active growing points are often at or just below soil level. These organs must somehow endure a deficiency of oxygen whilst simultaneously absorbing nutrients and synthesising new protoplasmic constituents, processes which are, at least in part, dependent upon energy yielded by aerobic respiration.

The rooted organs of hydrophytes are frequently said to show a pronounced reduction of form and structure, but this generalisation is quite unjustified. It is true that amongst the somewhat weakly developed adventitious roots of numerous submerged species, a trend of vascular reduction roughly parallel to that in their leaves and stems may be discerned, but it is equally true that many other hydrophytes have exceedingly well-developed systems of rhizomes and roots which show few anatomical modifications when compared with those of related land plants.

THE MORPHOLOGY AND EXTENT OF UNDERGROUND ORGANS

The foliage of most emergent and some floating-leaved plants arises from a stout basal stem, which may be an elongated, branching or condensed rhizome,

6*

or an abbreviated, herbaceous or woody rootstock, growing at the surface of the soil or buried at some depth. These organs are anchored by fibrous adventitious roots which appear early in development, replacing the transitory primary root, and subsequently form an extensive and richly ramified system. Development of the underground organs of emergent reeds and bulrushes is so great that in mature plants the weight of the rhizomes and roots often equals, and may far exceed, that of the aerial foliage.

The extent, mode of growth, and vigour of the rooted organs vary widely and no one habit appears more successful than any other in performing the essential function of anchorage. *Nymphaea* (Fig. 6.1), *Nuphar, Peltandra, Phragmites* and *Pontederia*, for example, have stout spongy rhizomes, which may be relatively slow-growing with a persistent apical rosette of crowded foliage, as in *Nymphaea alba*, or extensively creeping with abundant lateral branches, as in *Phragmites communis*. The tough and sometimes woody rhizomes of *Acorus* (Fig. 6.1), *Cyperus, Scirpus* and *Typha* also branch freely and may cover vast areas in each growing season. The average annual increase in length of the rhizomes of *Glyceria maxima, Phragmites communis* and *Typha latifolia* is of the order of 100 cm; in contrast, the stout and very woody rhizomes of *Schoenoplectus lacustris* grow at only about one-tenth of this rate, of the order of 10 cm/year (Westlake, *in litt.*). All these types develop many adventitious roots, which may be long, thick and unbranched, or slender and freely branched to several degrees, the laterals attaining lengths of up to 20 to 30 cm. In *Phragmites communis* both types of root occur, the short and freely branched ones growing in the water whilst the long, stout and sparsely branched ones penetrate the substrate (Pallis, 1916).

The roots of most of these emergent and floating-leaved plants develop profuse hairs. The prospective hair-producing cells are sometimes distinguishable very early in the development of the root: Bloch (1943) recognised them in *Phalaris* by their anthocyanin, which is much deeper in colour than that of the other epidermal cells. In the Nymphaeaceae, as in many monocotyledons, the hairs arise from specialised epidermal cells (Metcalfe and Chalk, 1950). Exceptional anchor-like development of the root caps, as in *Brasenia*, also helps the plant to maintain a secure hold in muddy substrates.

The underground parts (rhizomes, roots, and bases of the aerial shoots) often represent a significant proportion of the biomass (Pallis, 1916; Ivlev, 1945; Blackman and Black, 1959). They have been found to account for more than 30 per cent of the fresh weight biomass in *Butomus umbellatus* and *Carex riparia*; about 40 per cent in *Alisma plantago-aquatica*; 45 to 60 per cent in *Typha angustifolia* and *T. latifolia*; 51 to 67 per cent in *Glyceria maxima*; 45 to 90 per cent in *Schoenoplectus lacustris*; and up to about 80 per cent in *Equisetum fluviatile* and *Phragmites communis* (Aario, 1933; Hejný, 1960; Westlake, 1965a). Such estimates may vary according to the season and state of growth and the sampling technique. The bases of the aerial shoots (stubble) are sometimes not included in the estimates, yet they may be significant. In *Glyceria maxima*, the stubble cut at the soil surface is 2 to 4 per cent of the fresh weight biomass during the growing season, whilst in *Typha angustifolia*

FIG. 6.1. The underground organs of some representative hydrophytes: A, young specimen of *Nymphaea odorata* with rhizome bearing leaf scars and many stout adventitious
roots ($\times$ 0·2); B, *Cryptocoryne aponogetifolia*, showing abbreviated slender rhizome with
an extensive fibrous root system ($\times$ 0·5); C, exposed branching rhizome of *Acorus
gramineus* bearing leaf scars ($\times$ 0·3); D, undersurface of the apical part of the rhizome
of *A. gramineus*, showing stout adventitious roots emerging from the sheathing leaf
bases ($\times$ 0·8); E, corm-like rootstock of *Aponogeton ulvaceus* bearing adventitious roots
(many of the dead leaf- and root-bases have been removed) ($\times$ 0·5); F, entire young
specimen of *Lobelia dortmanna*, showing the profuse unbranched roots with spirally
twisted extremities ($\times$ 0·4).

the stubble cut at a height of 25 cm or more above the soil is over 20 per cent of the biomass (Westlake, 1965a). In *Phragmites communis* and *Glyceria maxima*, the root/shoot ratio varies in different sites (Hurlimann, 1951; Westlake, 1966c). Spence (1964) demonstrated a positive correlation between the height of the flowering shoot of *P. communis* in Scottish habitats and the mean temperature of the warmest month, and further showed that within a particular temperature regime plant height is correlated with the percentage total nitrogen and the percentage metal-ion saturation of the soil. Spence also found that the height of *Equisetum fluviatile* above water level is proportional to the depth of water in which the plants are growing.

The submerged marine angiosperms, such as *Cymodocea*, *Halophila* and *Zostera*, which withstand pounding waves and fluctuation of water level, possess creeping rhizomes anchored beneath each leaf base by thick clusters of long filiform roots which branch freely and are clothed with abundant root hairs at their extremities. The rhizome itself is usually strengthened with bundles of sclerenchyma fibres running longitudinally through the inner or outer cortex. The roots may also possess mechanical tissue: collenchyma occurs in *Cymodocea* and *Zostera*, sclerenchyma in *Posidonia* (Sauvageau, 1889b). It has been estimated that the underground organs of *Thalassia testudinum* represent 75 to 90 per cent of the biomass (Burkholder et al., 1959).

Amongst the smaller emergent and submerged hydrophytes the vulnerability of the individual rhizomes, which are often slender and even filiform, seems to be compensated by their extensive branching and by the matted systems of fibrous roots originating from the nodes. These features are clearly shown by many species of *Anubias*, *Cryptocoryne*, *Eleocharis*, *Marsilea*, *Myriophyllum*, *Pilularia* and *Potamogeton*. Growth of the rhizome is usually sympodial: in *Hippuris vulgaris*, for example, the apical bud forms an erect leafy stem and the horizontal rhizome is maintained by tremendous elongation of the lowest internode of a lateral bud; adventitious roots develop at all nodes where lateral buds appear (McCully and Dale, 1961a). In *Myriophyllum verticillatum*, *Zannichellia palustris* and many species of *Potamogeton* the spiral tendril-like coiling of the adventitious roots probably aids anchorage.

The radical leaves in numerous rosette hydrophytes spring from more or less erect and abbreviated rootstocks at, or just below, soil level. The internodes of this type of stem are very condensed and the position of the shoot apex changes little from year to year. The form of the rootstock varies from slender and soft, as in *Littorella* and *Vallisneria*, to bulbous and succulent, as in *Alisma*, *Echinodorus* and *Sagittaria*, or hard and corm-like, as in *Aponogeton* and *Isoetes* (Figs. 6.1 and 6.6). The rootstock is anchored by adventitious roots from the leaf bases in most types, although in *Isoetes* they grow from the sides of two or three vertical furrows lower down the corm. Many rosette hydrophytes spread horizontally by runners or stolons which root at their nodes, a habit shown well by *Littorella uniflora* and *Lobelia dortmanna*, which form extensive swards stabilising rough and loose inorganic and peaty substrates. These species show two other morphological features which aid anchorage—a tortuous manner of root growth and a high root/shoot ratio (Fig. 6.1): in *Littorella uniflora*, for example, the underground parts account for 46 to 55 per cent of the biomass (Westlake, 1965a).

A few hydrophytes possess both a rootstock and rhizomes. The foliage of *Sparganium erectum*, for example, arises from a woody cormous rootstock which is monopodial in growth and dies after producing an inflorescence in its second or third year. Each spring, axillary buds on the corm develop into slender monopodial rhizomes which produce erect leaves at their nodes (Cook, 1962a). The underground organs of *S. erectum* represent from 30 to about 65 per cent of the fresh weight biomass (Aario, 1933; Hejný, 1960).

Submerged and amphibious plants with long flexuous stems develop adventitious roots to a variable extent. *Callitriche, Heteranthera* and *Limnophila*, for example, produce them freely from the older lower nodes. Dimorphic roots, comparable with those of *Phragmites communis*, are exhibited by *Heteranthera zosteraefolia* (Hildebrand, 1885). In another example, *Bergia capensis*, the plumose water-roots lack hairs but frequently possess chloroplasts and may supplement the leaves as assimilatory organs, whilst the stout white roots which penetrate the soil bear very few laterals but are almost completely covered by hairs (D'Almeida, 1942). Batrachian *Ranunculi* living in flowing water anchor themselves in scantily silted gravel and shingle by means of profuse nodal clusters of fine ramifying roots.

In contrast, species of *Egeria, Elodea, Lagarosiphon, Najas* and *Nechamandra* form few, slender, unbranched roots and these arise from only certain nodes. This dearth is due, in *Egeria* at least, to developmental causes, many of the root primordia remaining dormant within the cortical tissues of the axis. In *E. densa* four dormant root primordia are associated with each lateral bud, i.e. at every twelfth node, two being situated in the primary shoot axis—one on each side of the lateral bud, and two in the base of this bud. These primordia may still remain dormant in shoots as much as 1 m long and normally develop only when that part of the axis containing them is detached (King, 1943). In plants grown from excised bud nodes, King observed that although the two primary roots emerged the secondary primordia in the lateral axis were usually still dormant after even 20 days. All four roots, and occasionally a fifth, could be induced to develop by treatment with the auxins IPA, IBA, IAA or NAA, in that order of effectiveness. It seems probable that under natural conditions the marked apical dominance which is manifest in the prolonged dormancy of the lateral buds also retards the development of roots. In *Elodea canadensis* the roots account for only about 2·6 per cent of the biomass (Borutskii, 1950). Roots probably represent less than 10 per cent of the biomass in most submerged freshwater species (Westlake, 1965a).

Recent studies by Kadej (1966) have revealed that the organisation of the apical meristem of roots of aquatic monocotyledons belonging to Helobian families may change several times during the growth of the root. The differences between the successive patterns of organisation appear to be of similar nature and magnitude to those which have hitherto been used by morphologists to classify basic types of apical root meristem. Kadej observed especially marked changes in *Elodea canadensis* and *Egeria densa*, in which, respectively, four and as many as six different patterns could be distinguished.

The influence of natural and synthetic auxins on the initiation and elongation of the root in species of *Egeria*, *Elodea* and *Najas* has been studied by Soltys *et al.* (1938), King (1943) and Inanç (1960), their results being quantitatively similar to those obtained for the roots of many terrestrial herbs. King found that at a concentration of 1 ppm, IAA, IBA and IPA were increasingly effective in promoting root growth in *Egeria densa* over a period of 16 days. IAA, PAA

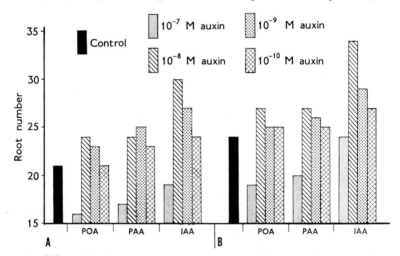

FIG. 6.2. Effects of various concentrations of each of the three auxins, IAA, PAA and POA, on the root number of *Elodea canadensis* in non-aerated (A) and continuously aerated cultures (B). (Exposure time: 21 days; temperature: 25°C; each bar of the histogram represents the mean of 40 measurements.) (From data of Inanç, 1960.)

and POA were observed by Inanç to promote the elongation of roots of *Elodea canadensis* and *Najas minor* when used in concentrations of 10^{-8} to 10^{-10} M (approx. 0·015 to 0·00015 ppm), the effect being enhanced by artificial aeration of the cultures. A concentration of 10^{-8} M proved to be optimal in promoting both root initiation (Fig. 6.2) and root elongation. IAA generally exerted a greater effect than PAA or POA. Inanç also noted that in contrast to many land plants exposed to auxin solutions, neither of the two species she used showed any histological response in either vascular or ground tissues.

Contrary to popular impression, the roots of most submerged hydrophytes (including sparsely rooted plants such as *Elodea*) do develop abundant hairs, at least when they penetrate the substrate (Pond, 1905; Pearsall, 1918a; Arber, 1920). The failure to produce hairs in the water appears to be related to the heavy cuticularisation of the epidermis, which was remarked upon by Arber (1920). Cormack (1937) showed that in darkness, either in soil or in water, or in the presence of light—if the formation of chlorophyll in the tissues is prevented by treatment with ethylene—the roots of *Elodea* have only a thin cuticle and develop abundant hairs. Dale (1951) similarly found that hairs are produced freely in darkness, or in light in the presence of a high carbon dioxide tension which prevents the oxidation of the unsaturated fatty acids occurring as a weak film on the epidermis. It is likely that under natural conditions there is insufficient oxygen in the substrate (or in the root tissues in the absence of photosynthesis) to bring about the formation of a true cuticle, with the result that the epidermal walls remain unhardened and the potential root hairs can develop copiously once the root enters the soil (Cormack, 1949, 1962).

AERATION AND RESPIRATION IN UNDERGROUND ORGANS

The Internal Atmosphere of Rhizomes and Roots. The stout rhizomes and roots of many emergent and floating-leaved plants possess an extensive system of air-filled cortical lacunae which is often more or less continuous with that of the stems, petioles and leaves. The normal intercellular spaces may also account for a considerable proportion of the total volume of the parenchymatous ground tissue, especially where this consists of loose, rounded or stellate cells, as in *Sparganium erectum* (Cook, 1962a). The proportion of lacunae varies according to the species and the size and age of the organ. A slender filiform root with a high surface area/volume ratio, such as that of *Vallisneria spiralis*, has relatively few spaces whereas in the bulky rhizomes of *Nuphar*, *Nymphaea* or *Peltandra* lacunae occupy a much greater proportion of the total volume. Air spaces occupy up to 60 per cent of the total volume of the roots of *Cladium mariscus* (Conway, 1937, 1942) and well over 60 per cent of the total volume of the rhizomes of *Menyanthes trifoliata* (Coult, 1964; and see Fig. 6.3). Very young roots and the apices of rhizomes consist mainly of compact tissue and so have a relatively limited internal atmosphere.

Whilst organs deprived of light generally have lysigenous lacunae, some roots and rhizomes possess the schizogenous spaces more typical of illuminated photosynthetic organs. In the rhizomes of the Nymphaeaceae and Marsileaceae (Fig. 6.8), for example, the lacunae are schizogenous (Sifton, 1945; Allsopp, 1952). The small schizogenous spaces of the young roots of *Callitriche* and *Myriophyllum* are later enlarged by breakdown of the septa between them to give partly lysigenous cavities in the mature roots (Schenck, 1886). Lysigenous spaces also occur in the roots of *Zizania aquatica* (Stover, 1928) and *Sagittaria* (Severin, 1932; and see Fig. 6.4). In the latter, the spaces are created by local splitting of the middle lamellae of the cortical cells which later break down, leaving only very thin partitions between the subepidermal zone and the few layers of cortical cells which persistently surround the stele.

Species possessing both water- and ground-roots provide an interesting demonstration of the relation between the habit of the root and the extent of its internal atmosphere. In the water-root of *Bergia capensis*, for example, there is a subepidermal zone of parenchyma, some three or more cells wide, internal to which is the lacunate part of the cortex: the air spaces are separated by radial plates of rounded or oval cells containing chloroplasts. In the stout ground-root, however, the stele is equally narrow but the cortex is very much wider and, with the exception of two subepidermal layers of parenchyma cells, is composed entirely of lacunae: the cells of the septa bounding the lacunae are radially elongated and have no chloroplasts (D'Almeida, 1942).

Some hydrophytes lack a system of lacunae in either their rhizomes or their roots, or both. *Pontederia cordata*, for example, has a spongy rhizome but its

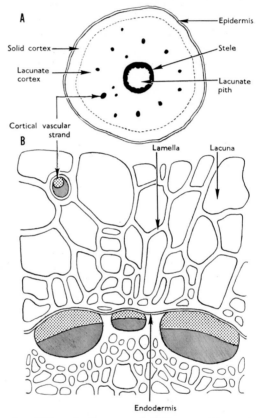

FIG. 6.3. *Menyanthes trifoliata*: A, diagrammatic T.S. young rhizome (× 6); B, diagrammatic T.S. sector of the inner cortex, stele and pith of a young rhizome to show the distribution of lacunae (phloem of vascular bundles stippled; xylem shaded) (× 60).

roots are almost devoid of lacunae, whilst both the rhizomes and the roots of *Acorus*, *Scirpus* and *Typha* are relatively firm in texture and have few large air spaces. The stout hard rootstocks of *Aponogeton* and *Isoetes* similarly lack lacunae although their roots possess them (Figs. 6.6 and 6.7).

The Importance of the Internal Atmosphere as a Source of Oxygen for Respiration. At the depths inhabited by underground stems and roots, submerged soils are generally quite devoid of oxygen. Even in the overlying water the oxygen concentration may frequently fall to 0·4 per cent or less, by volume, if dense vegetation is present. Although the oxygen concentration is high in most emergent, floating and even submerged leaves during active photosynthesis, it is probably low at most times in rhizomes and water- and ground-roots (Samantarai, 1938). Laing (1940c) determined the concentrations of oxygen and carbon dioxide in the internal atmosphere of the rhizomes of *Nuphar advena*, *Peltandra virginica*, *Scirpus validus*, *Pontederia cordata* and *Sparganium eurycarpum* at different times of the day and year. The oxygen concentration in *Nuphar advena* varied in winter from 14·8 per cent down to 2·2 per cent, and on a sunny June day from 7 per cent in mid-afternoon to as low as 0·6 per cent during the night. In winter there was a corresponding accumulation of carbon dioxide from 5·2 per cent to as much as 18·1 per cent. Similar, but less wide, ranges of oxygen and carbon dioxide content were observed in the rhizomes of the other species. In all species the oxygen concentration at any given time was considerably lower than that in the aerial or submerged parts of the leaves. Similar oxygen gradients from the aerial to the underground parts have been demonstrated in *Cladium mariscus* (Conway, 1937), *Menyanthes trifoliatia* (Coult and Vallance, 1951, 1958), *Equisetum fluviatile* (Barber, 1961) and the tidal marsh plant, *Spartina alterniflora* (Teal and Kanwisher, 1966). The oxygen concentration in the rhizomes and roots of these various species has been found to be as low as 2 or 3 per cent.

The existence of linear gradients of oxygen concentration supports the hypothesis that underground organs derive their oxygen supply from the aerial or floating foliage, the gas diffusing through the lacunar system and normal intercellular spaces. The rate of transport of oxygen will be influenced primarily by the steepness of the concentration gradient (i.e. by the relative rates of net photosynthetic oxygen production in the foliage and of respiratory oxygen consumption in the underground organs) and by the resistance to diffusion offered by the diaphragms of the lacunae (Fig. 6.4). Although in the rhizome of *Menyanthes trifoliata*, for example, the cortical lacunae may reach a length of 1·5 cm since diaphragms are relatively infrequent, the small proportion of pore space in each diaphragm creates a severe barrier to diffusion. Occupying only about 0·6 per cent of the area of each diaphragm, the tiny pores offer great frictional resistance, sufficient to reduce the velocity of diffusion of oxygen through the lacunar system to about 4 per cent of that in air (Coult, 1964). More rapid flow of oxygen is possible in the rhizomes of *Iris pseudacorus* and *Equisetum fluviatile*, although in the latter species transport is slowed down by diaphragms at each node of the aerial stem. The velocity of diffusion is further reduced during summer and autumn as the pores of the diaphragms become occluded by the thickening of the bordering cell walls (Barber, 1961).

Conway (1937) and Laing (1940c) emphasised the influence of an additional factor, the compact structure of the basal zone of young leaves. This region of undifferentiated tissue is devoid of lacunae, has only small intercellular spaces, and so offers great resistance to gas flow. Most of the oxygen reaching underground organs is derived from mature foliage which has ceased to grow: young leaves contribute little to the supply even though they may be producing oxygen actively by photosynthesis.

Epigeal rhizomes, such as those of *Nuphar lutea* and *Menyanthes trifoliata*, may obtain some oxygen from photosynthesis in the superficial, chloroplast-containing cells of their own upper surface. This source is not likely to be rich, however, because of the very low light intensities prevailing below a dense canopy of floating or aerial leaves.

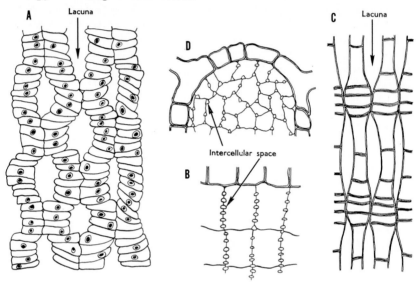

FIG. 6.4. A, T.L.S. middle cortex of a young root of *Stratiotes aloides* to illustrate the schizogenous origin of the lacunae (× 300) (after Arber, 1914); B, T.S. part of cortex of a young root of *Sagittaria sagittifolia*, showing intercellular spaces created by break-down of the middle lamella of the radial walls (× 350) (after Severin, 1932); C, L.S. part of cortex of an older root of *S. sagittifolia*, showing lacunae created by the elongation of only certain cells (× 280) (after Severin, 1932); D, T.S. lacuna of the root of *Nymphaea elegans*, showing multiperforate diaphragm (× 300) (after Conard, 1905).

In view of the low tissue/total volume ratio of spongy rhizomes, it seems probable that, despite the problems confronting gas transport through the lacunar system, sufficient oxygen will usually be available to cope with the respiratory demand, even in the apices and distal extremities of the organ. Williams and Barber (1961) suggested that even the normal system of inter-cellular spaces would probably permit the diffusion of adequate oxygen to the lower organs of the plant. Even so, it is still likely that spongy rhizomes and especially rhizomes lacking extensive lacunae are embarrassed by oxygen deficiency under certain conditions, notably during the hours of darkness when the aerial organs also exert a significant respiratory demand, in warmer water where oxygen consumption is generally accelerated, and in densely populated habitats where the photosynthetic efficiency of the aerial organs may be appreciably reduced by shading. All these conditions may be expected to prevail during the height of the growing season.

So far, only the underground stems have been considered. The likelihood of oxygen deficiency is much greater at the end of the concentration gradient, i.e. in the roots, especially if these derive their oxygen from the stele of the rhizome, as in *Menyanthes trifoliata*. Coult (1964) pointed out that in this species the stelar oxygen supply is maintained by diffusion from the cortical lacunae and intercellular spaces. The velocity of this transport is primarily controlled by the resistance of the endodermis, through which layer the oxygen may pass only by diffusion in aqueous solution, which is several orders of magnitude slower than diffusion in air or in the cortical or stelar lacunae. Movement of oxygen into the roots, which are the organs most likely to need it, is probably the slowest part of the whole process of internal transport downwards from the aerial foliage. In some species, however, anatomical barriers are infrequent and the gas-flow is consequently more rapid. *Spartina alterniflora* has an almost continuous internal atmosphere from the leaves to the root tips. The cellular plates which traverse the lacunae are several centimetres apart and offer no significant resistance to the movement of gases. Within a given plant, oxygen and carbon dioxide diffuse at similar rates, which would not be so if transport was impeded anywhere by an aqueous (cellular) barrier through which oxygen would diffuse thirty to forty times slower than carbon dioxide because of its correspondingly lower solubility (Teal and Kanwisher, 1966).

Optimal growth of the roots of most hydrophytes that have been studied occurs when the external oxygen concentration is high (10 to 20 per cent) and never when it is very low, development usually being inhibited in a medium of nitrogen (Weaver and Himmel, 1930; Dean, 1933; Laing, 1941). Buttery *et al.* (1965) suggested that root apices may die in the low oxygen tensions prevailing in many natural muds.

The Capacity to Withstand Anaerobic Conditions. There is evidence that the roots of several emergent hydrophytes do normally receive adequate oxygen and that they use some of this to oxidise the surrounding anaerobic medium. *Menyanthes trifoliata* and *Eriophorum angustifolium*, for example, both release oxygen from their root tips into an anaerobic environment. Armstrong (1964) recently showed that the rate of oxygen diffusion from the roots of *M. trifoliata* is significantly greater than that from the roots of *E. angustifolium*, and suggested that the former species might therefore be expected to tolerate a stronger reducing medium: redox potentials measured in sample habitats of the two species supported this conclusion. The roots of *Oryza sativa* and *Spartina alterniflora* have also been found to release oxygen to surrounding reducing muds, presumably whenever the internal supply exceeds the respiratory demand (van Raalte, 1943; Teal and Kanwisher, 1966).

Should oxygen be scarce within the plant, however, it would clearly be advantageous if the underground organs possessed some metabolic device to secure the maximum available oxygen, or if they were able to respire anaerobically for limited periods and tolerate the consequent organic by-products. Using a modified Pettenkofer apparatus, Laing (1940a) investigated the respiration of fresh rhizomes of species of *Acorus, Asclepias, Nuphar, Nymphaea, Peltandra, Pontederia, Sagittaria, Scirpus, Sparganium* and *Typha* in water through which air or nitrogen was bubbled, in moist air or moist nitrogen, and in various mixtures of oxygen and nitrogen. The rhizomes of all the plants were found to be able to respire anaerobically, producing ethanol at a rate inversely proportional to the oxygen concentration in 3 per cent and less of oxygen. Freshly dug rhizomes of *Nuphar advena* were also found to contain ethanol. Remarkably prolonged endurance of anaerobic conditions was shown by the rhizomes of both *Pontederia cordata* and *Typha latifolia*, the former even developing new shoots in pure nitrogen.

In a later paper, Laing (1941) showed that the presence or absence of oxygen in the lacunae had no influence on the excellent rate of growth shown by the rhizome of *Nuphar advena* when its apex was surrounded by nitrogen. In contrast, the presence of air around the apex apparently inhibited its growth, even if the rest of the rhizome was surrounded by nitrogen. These phenomena suggest that not only are the rhizomes able to sustain limited anaerobiosis but also that their growing points become so acclimatised to a deficiency of oxygen that development is actually impeded by a good oxygen supply. The optimal oxygen concentration for shoot production was found by Laing to be only about 4·5 per cent for *Typha latifolia* and less than 1·5 per cent for *Nuphar advena* and *Peltandra virginica*.

Other species may tolerate periods of anaerobiosis. The rhizome of *Equisetum fluviatile* can exist for moderate periods in a medium of nitrogen or in low oxygen tensions. In this species lactic acid is accumulated, not ethanol (Barber, 1961). In *Iris pseudacorus*, the formation of ethanol has been shown to account for over 75 per cent of the carbohydrate respired in the rhizome during 7 days of complete anaerobiosis. Only negligible amounts of lactic, succinic and malic acids are detectable: appreciable shikimic acid may be present, but this compound does not accumulate and so must presumably be further metabolised. The rhizome of *I. pseudacorus* will withstand anaerobiosis for as much as a month without any apparent harmful effects. In oxygen tensions as low as 1·5 per cent very little ethanol is produced and respiration is still primarily aerobic, probably because the tissues of the rhizome possess the cytochrome-c oxidase system, which has a notably high oxygen affinity (Henshaw *et al.*, 1961, 1962; Boulter *et al.*, 1963). Coult (1964) noted the existence of a compensation mechanism in the underground organs of *Menyanthes trifoliata*, whereby the rate of oxygen consumption decreases if carbon dioxide accumulates in the tissues.

The Development of Air-Roots. From the lower nodes of *Ludwigia peruviana, Ludwigia adscendens* (Fig. 6.5), *Sesbania aculeata* and several other emergent hydrophytes, there arise modified adventitious roots which grow erect and may eventually protrude above the water. In transverse section the minute stele of each root is seen to be surrounded by an immensely wide zone of aerenchyma, which is produced by a phellogen as in the stems of the same plants (Schenck, 1889). These 'air-roots' are usually interpreted as short circuits to the atmosphere, permitting greater and speedier transport of oxygen to the submerged and underground organs than would be possible if supplies depended entirely on diffusion from the aerial foliage through long trailing stems. Such roots may

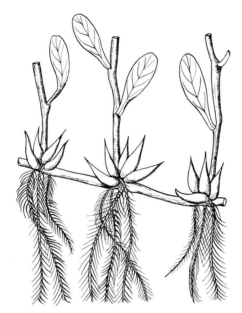

FIG. 6.5. *Ludwigia adscendens*: habit drawing to show inflated 'air-roots' arising at the nodes of the floating stem ($\times 0.6$).

be compared with the pneumatophores which are developed by *Zea* and the swamp cypress, *Taxodium*, in inundated habitats, and which are typical of woody mangroves such as *Bruguiera*, *Ceriops* and *Rhizophora* (Emould, 1921; Mullan, 1932, 1933). In these organs, however, the air spaces are usually provided by an extensive primary lacunate cortex rather than hypertrophied secondary aerenchyma.

THE MECHANICAL IMPORTANCE OF THE LACUNAR SYSTEM

In their lucid and interesting essay, Williams and Barber (1961) doubted that the prime value of the lacunar system in hydrophytes is to ensure adequate transport and storage of oxygen. Whilst acknowledging the frequently anaerobic nature of the aquatic environment and the origin of respiratory oxygen in the aerial foliage, they emphasised that gas-flow through the lacunae is substantially retarded by diaphragms, and that, in any event, the ordinary intercellular spaces would allow sufficient oxygen to diffuse downwards to satisfy the normal respiratory needs of submerged and underground organs. They suggested, very convincingly, that the extensive lacunate parenchyma of the hydrophyte axis is really of great mechanical significance.

It is important to appreciate that the friction between roots or underground stems and particles of the substrate which is vital for successful anchorage is very much reduced in submerged gravels, sands and muds, as compared with terrestrial soils. The roots must also be able to withstand bending stresses, which are more prevalent in water or aqueous soils than the compression stresses to which terrestrial roots are often subject. It may therefore be argued that to gain a satisfactory anchorage a hydrophyte requires a relatively more extensive system of underground organs fitted to resist bending stresses transmitted from the foliage. Continued subdivision of the root system into a vast number of filiform ultimate elements probably does not fully meet this need (although it is, in fact, displayed by numerous hydrophytes, as noted earlier) because of the reduced surface area of the elements and their consequently impaired frictional efficiency. Nor, however, will the requirement be met by the terrestrial type of system comprising stout solid roots, for although this may be frictionally efficient it will probably have too high a respiratory oxygen demand to be satisfied in an oxygen-deficient environment.

Arguing along these lines, Williams and Barber (1961) suggested that the honeycomb structure of lacunate parenchyma may be regarded as the best functional compromise since it meets both the mechanical and the physiological requirements. In an organ of any diameter it offers the maximum possible strength using the minimum possible volume of tissue. The greater the number of intersections between the walls (septa) of the lacunae, the greater is the resistance to bending stresses. Perforations in the walls (mainly the pores of the diaphragms) create mechanical weaknesses and are probably distributed with the minimum frequency consistent with adequate diffusion of gases. In addition to minimising the respiratory oxygen demand, the high air space/tissue volume ratio increases the organ's buoyancy and reinforces its strength through inflation with gases.

It is probable that some plants of all life forms fall short of their mechanical and physiological requirements. Their submerged stems and petioles and underground rhizomes and roots may be more solid in construction and hence have a higher oxygen demand than is physiologically desirable. Species with particularly extensive systems of lacunate parenchyma may thus have an adaptive advantage in habitats which are markedly anaerobic or have unstable muddy substrates (pp. 428-29).

ASPECTS OF THE VASCULAR ANATOMY OF RHIZOMES AND ROOTS

Vascular Organisation in Aquatic Pteridophytes. The comparative anatomy of the vascular system in the underground organs of rooted aquatic pteridophytes reveals several features of interest. The peculiar corm-like rootstock of *Isoetes* (Fig. 6.6) has been variously interpreted, as a stem, a stock,

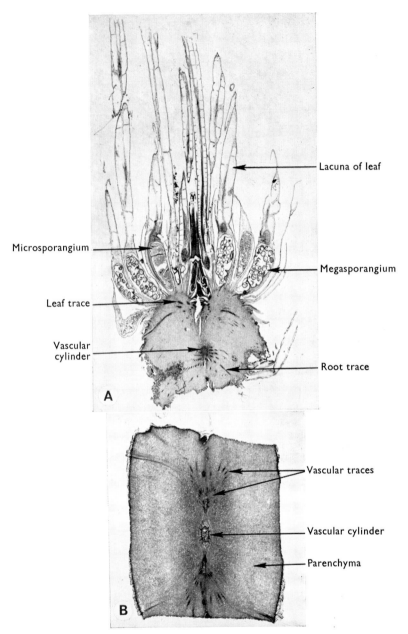

FIG. 6.6. Structure of the 'corm' of *Isoetes*: A, V.S. base of plant, in plane at right angles to basal groove of corm (×4); B, T.S. corm, in plane through axial part of stele (×7.) (C, D and E on p. 166.)

a vertical rhizome, or a condensed stem and rhizophore (Scott and Hill, 1900; Stokey, 1909; Lang, 1915; West and Takeda, 1915; Osborn, 1922; Stewart, 1947). Its vascular organisation supports the notion that it is a combined stem and rhizophore. The upper part of the axis contains a central vertical vascular core which is produced by the shoot apex and which gives off traces to the leaves. Continuous with this 'stem stele', in the lower part of the axis, is a bi-,

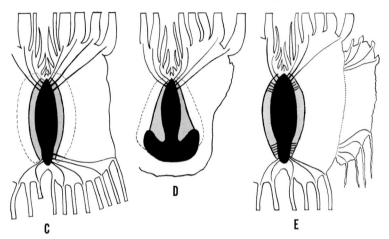

FIG. 6.6. Structure of the 'corm' of *Isoetes*: C, generalised diagram of V.S. young corm, in plane at right angles to basal groove, showing origin of leaf and root traces from axial (upper) and rhizomorphic (lower) parts of stele; D, generalised diagram of V.S. young corm, in plane of basal groove, showing spade-like form of biradiate rhizomorphic stele; E, generalised diagram of V.S. older corm early in new season's growth, in plane at right angles to basal groove, showing leaf and root traces of previous year's corm severed near the cambium and dead secondary storage cortex displaced outward by the new secondary cortex. (In C, D and E the primary vascular cylinder is solid black; the prismatic layer is shaded and bounded by the cambium, shown as a solid line. In C and D the broken line denotes the boundary between secondary parenchyma, to the inside, and primary cortex, to the outside. In E the dotted line denotes the boundary between the old and the new secondary parenchyma.)

tri-, or tetraradiate stele from which the root traces arise. The arms of this 'rhizomorphic stele' curve slightly upwards, giving it a spade- or anchor-shaped outline in a lateral view.

In young plants the entire vascular system of the axis is protostelic, comprising a central xylem core surrounded by a zone of phloem: the xylem possesses short spiral- and reticulate-thickened tracheids interspersed with parenchyma. This primary development, in no way unusual, is followed by a most remarkable form of secondary growth in which a cambium arises just external to the phloem. Each year this meristem produces a layer of secondary parenchymatous cortex to the outside, and, to the inside, a complex secondary tissue containing sieve cells, tracheary elements (which are sometimes only sparsely thickened) and much parenchyma. This tissue cannot be simply categorised as secondary phloem, xylem or parenchyma. It is perhaps best described by the term 'prismatic tissue' which avoids morphological commitment (Bhambie, 1962).

The roots of *Isoetes* develop endogenously and may last for more than one season or be sloughed off at the end of the year after an abscission layer is formed at the surface of the rootstock (Osborn, 1922). Like the shoot apex, each root apex has several meristematic initials. These sometimes split into two equal groups which function independently, creating the typical dichotomy of the root. The vascular system of each mature root is a simple monarch protostele surrounded by an endodermis bearing Casparian bands on its radial walls. The xylem and phloem are collateral, and the stele is attached, on the side of the xylem, to the lining of the large cortical cavity. In transverse section the root therefore shows marked asymmetry (Fig. 6.7). The similar excentric location of the stele in fossil stigmarian-type rootlets is often cited in support of the view that *Isoetes* has affinities with the Lepidodendrales, a group of lycopods which arose in the Devonian and became extinct in the Permian (Stewart, 1947). Such an ancestry is also suggested by the peculiar axial organisation of *Isoetes*. The morphology of the stele, with its differentiation into an upper cylindrical portion and a lower lobed portion, is strongly reminiscent of the habit of the fossil *Pleuromeia*, which, in turn, could be regarded as a miniature derivative of the arborescent Carboniferous lycopods (Andrews, 1961; see also pp. 257-58).

The rhizome of *Marsilea* (Fig. 6.8) appears fairly specialised in its solenostelic vascular system, although the presence of both internal and external phloem and endodermis and the exarch development of the protoxylem are perhaps relatively primitive features (Smith, 1938). However, this genus is certainly highly advanced in having true xylem vessels with perforate end plates in its roots (White, 1963). The vascular organisation of the monotypic *Regnellidium*, an endemic Brazilian relative, is very similar to that of *Marsilea* (Johnson and Chrysler, 1938).

The rhizome of young specimens of *Ceratopteris thalictroides* has a protostele but in older plants this is replaced by a much-dissected dictyostele, each meristele of which has an endodermis and pericycle derived from a common cortical mother-cell layer. The larger irregularly arranged meristeles are hadrocentric, not bicollateral as Ford (1902) stated, whilst most of the smaller ones are collateral (Pal and Pal, 1962).

Polystely in the Nymphaeaceae. Arber (1920) noted that amongst both terrestrial and aquatic angiosperms polystelic anatomy, which does not confer great mechanical strength, occurs mainly in soft spongy rhizomes, which are supported by the soil and not subject to bending strains. The Nymphaeaceae show interesting examples of polystely (Gwynne-Vaughan, 1897). *Victoria amazonica* shows the most complex arrangement: each stele in its very thick rhizome possesses a ring of about twenty vascular strands. In some species of *Nymphaea*, e.g. *N. mexicana*, the bundles are grouped in four or five distinct steles, each surrounded by an endodermis, whilst *Cabomba* shows a reduced form of polystely, each of the two steles comprising but two bundles. Only in

Nelumbo, probably the most advanced genus, is there a central cylinder of bundles enclosed in a general endodermis.

The Trend of Vascular Reduction in the Roots of Aquatic Angiosperms.

The roots of aquatic angiosperms resemble those of terrestrial plants in the central location of the stele, an arrangement which best resists pulling strains. The structure of the vascular tissues themselves, especially in some entirely

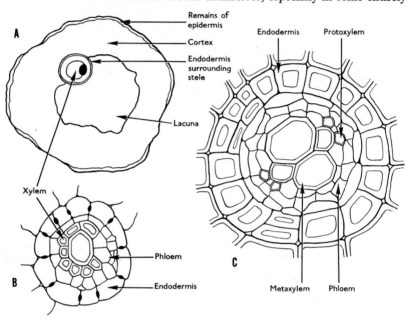

FIG. 6.7. A, diagrammatic T.S. root of *Isoetes lacustris* (phloem indicated in solid black) ($\times 50$); B, T.S. stele of the root of *I. lacustris* (Casparian bands in solid black) ($\times 160$); C, T.S. stele of the root of *Marsilea quadrifolia* ($\times 200$).

submerged species, may however be modified along lines similar to those discernible in the stems and leaves. The roots of emergent species generally show the least vascular reduction. The polyarch stele of *Butomus umbellatus,* for example, is a typical monocotyledonous type (Hasman and Inanç, 1957). The ground tissue of the stele is fibrous and has a large, central, schizogenous canal. The xylem is composed mainly of undifferentiated tracheids, but vessels with either scalariform or simple perforation plates occur in the later metaxylem (Cheadle, 1942). The phloem comprises relatively well-developed sieve tubes and companion cells and the stele is surrounded by the monocotyledonous type of endodermis with thickened transverse, radial and inner tangential walls. The root of *Acorus calamus* (Fig. 6.9) is similar but has fewer xylem groups and the vessels have only scalariform perforation plates. In *Alisma, Damasonium, Limnophyton, Hydrocleys, Pontederia, Echinodorus, Sagittaria, Scheuchzeria,*

Wiesneria and some species of *Sparganium* (as in *Acorus* and *Butomus*) the roots are the only organs in which the xylem possesses vessels as well as tracheids. *Butomus, Hydrocleys* and *Sagittaria* are the more advanced genera in that their vessels have simple perforation plates, which are more or less horizontal, whereas the others usually have scalariform, obliquely-set perforation plates.

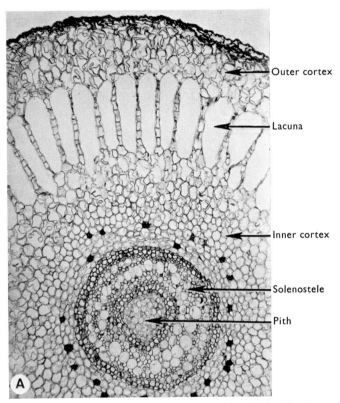

FIG. 6.8. Photomicrographs of T.S. rhizome of a submerged sp. of *Marsilea*: A, sector of rhizome showing cortical lacunae and central vascular cylinder (× 80). (B on p. 170.)

The larger roots of the various genera of the Alismaceae and Butomaceae commonly show slight lignification of the xylem tracheary elements. In *Typha latifolia, T. angustifolia* and *Sparganium androcladum*, vessels occur not only in the roots but also throughout the shoot system (Cheadle, 1942; Stant, 1964).

Progressive reduction is visible in the roots of some submerged monocotyledons (Sauvageau, 1889a, b; and see Fig. 6.10). In the pentarch root of *Potamogeton natans* the walls of the xylem elements, which include some vessels, are appreciably thickened, whilst in *Groenlandia densa* they are quite thin. The five protoxylem strands of *Potamogeton pectinatus* are absent at maturity and the stele has merely an axial, spirally thickened vessel. The roots of *Elodea*,

Najas, Ruppia, Vallisneria, Zannichellia and *Zostera* are further reduced: they lack vessels and none of their few tracheids shows even annular thickening. The stele of *Zannichellia palustris* resembles that of *Potamogeton pectinatus* but the axial element is quite unthickened; in *Najas* there are sometimes two tracheids but in *Vallisneria* only a single central lacuna. Generally, the phloem is less profoundly modified and so appears relatively well-developed, although

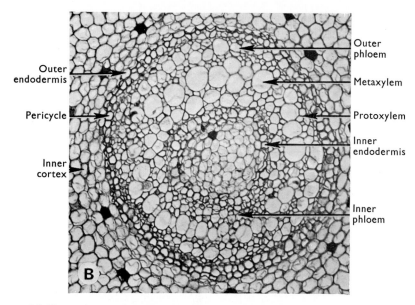

FIG. 6.8. Photomicrographs of T.S. rhizome of a submerged sp. of *Marsilea*: B, vascular cylinder (× 120). This plant does not have a sclerenchymatous inner cortex and pith as do certain emergent species of the genus.

in *Vallisneria* it comprises only three sieve tubes, each with a companion cell, as seen in transverse section.

The roots of aquatic dicotyledons similarly display several degrees of vascular reduction. In the genus *Nymphaea* the stele commonly has six, seven or eight xylem groups and thus appears transitional in structure between typical dicotyledonous and polyarch monocotyledonous types: a few species have four, five or nine xylem groups (Conard, 1905). The protoxylem is exarch. As in other genera of the Nymphaeaceae, vessels are lacking, the conducting elements of the xylem comprising only weakly thickened tracheids. The tetrarch stele of *Myriophyllum spicatum* also has xylem and phloem strands arranged on alternate radii and embedded in parenchymatous ground tissue. The few xylem elements are mainly tracheids, although one or two weakly developed vessels are also present, but the sieve tubes and companion cells of the phloem are well-differentiated (Hasman and Inanç, 1957). The central vascular cylinder is greatly reduced in the aquatic species of *Bergia* and *Elatine* (Metcalfe and Chalk, 1950). In *Callitriche stagnalis* (Fig. 6.10) the stele possesses only two protoxylem tracheids separated by a solitary metaxylem element: the phloem is also reduced to two groups, each with a single sieve tube and one or two companion

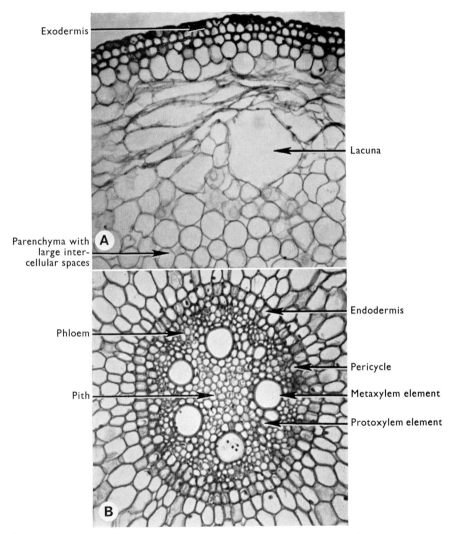

FIG. 6.9. Photomicrographs of T.S. root of *Acorus calamus*: A, part of outer cortex showing thickened exodermis and appearance of lacunae as a result of tangential stretching and collapse of cells; B, central stele showing five conspicuous metaxylem elements (both × 200).

cells, on radii alternating with the protoxylem. This species represents one of the most extreme modifications amongst the submerged dicotyledons.

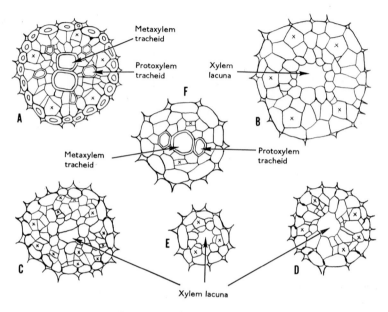

FIG. 6.10. T.S. stele and endodermis of the root of several hydrophytes to show vascular reduction (sieve-tube members denoted by an X): A, *Potamogeton natans* (×400); B, *P. pectinatus* (×600); C, *Najas marina* (×500); D, *N. minor* (×500); E, *Vallisneria spiralis* (×320); F, *Callitriche stagnalis* (×450). (After Schenck, 1886, and Sauvageau, 1889a, b.)

ABSORPTION OF WATER AND DISSOLVED NUTRIENTS

There is no doubt that for emergent hydrophytes the substrate is the prime source, and the root system the major site of absorption, of water and dissolved nutrients. Both water and salts presumably reach the foliage, as in land plants, by upward translocation in the xylem (and perhaps also the phloem at certain times of the year) and by lateral translocation from the vascular system to the ground tissues.

Whether or not submerged and floating-leaved plants similarly obtain water and ions mainly or wholly from the substrate has long been a topic of controversy, largely because of the chronic lack of direct experimental evidence for salt absorption by the roots of these life forms. Some authors have perpetuated all too readily the notion that water and ions are absorbed exclusively or predominantly through the epidermis of the foliage and that the root system serves only for anchorage. Den Hartog and Segal (1964), for example, considered that 'water plants [by which they meant just submerged and floating-leaved types] . . . are almost completely dependent on the aquatic medium for their metabolism. They obtain their mineral salts, their oxygen and their carbon dioxide direct from the water. The bottom is a substrate for attachment and is only for a limited number of species a second source of mineral requirements'. These authors further remarked: 'The bond between the water plants and the bottom . . . is loose and in a number of cases is even absent, because the nutritive salts are obtained from the water itself.' Yet den Hartog and Segal, in common with previous authors holding similar views, offered no critical evidence whatsoever to support their conviction.

The idea that uptake of water and dissolved salts from the substrate by the roots of hydrophytes does not occur, or is of only minor significance, seems to have developed, at least in part, from the experimental demonstrations of the relatively free movement of ions between the leaves or shoots of such plants as *Elodea*, *Nymphaea*, *Potamogeton* and *Vallisneria* and surrounding aqueous solutions of electrolytes. It should be appreciated, however, that whilst unquestionably valid in themselves these experiments do not indicate that the roots of the plants are unable to absorb. The notion of wholly or mainly foliar absorption is also partly based upon too superficial an examination of certain morphological features, which are often alleged (quite inappropriately) to be 'typical' of submerged and floating-leaved plants: such features include (a) rudimentary nature of the root system, (b) lack or sparsity of root hairs, and (c) vascular reduction. It has been emphasised earlier that far from being rudimentary the root system of many species is remarkably well-developed and represents a considerable proportion of the plant biomass. It has also been pointed out that root hairs are commonly present, at least when the roots penetrate the soil, and may be conspicuously abundant. Moreover, dearth or absence of root hairs, in any event, are not *per se* indications of the inability of the roots to absorb. Reduction in the extent of the xylem and in the degree of lignification of its vessels or tracheids, together with the dubious existence of a sustained current through the xylem, are not germane to the discussion, since the uptake of water and ions by roots are not directly related to these characters.

In this context, one other anatomical feature of aquatic roots merits recognition. With few exceptions, such as some species of *Callitriche* and *Nymphaea*, the stele of the root is surrounded by a very conspicuous endodermis (Figs. 6.7, 6.9, B, and 6.10). The cells of this layer, as in terrestrial vascular plants, may bear Casparian bands, e.g. in *Myriophyllum spicatum*, or have heavily thickened transverse, radial and inner tangential walls, e.g. in *Potamogeton natans*. The frequent presence and fine development of the endodermis in aquatic roots in all manner of habitats contrast strongly with the trend towards structural reduction in the stele and cannot be dismissed as mere relict ancestral features. In view of the probable importance of the endodermis in regulating lateral movement of water and ions in terrestrial roots, it is difficult to reconcile the prominence of the endodermis in aquatic roots with the notion that absorption and transport do not occur.

Yet whilst the much-painted picture of the hydrophyte's root system as insignificant in extent and low in level of differentiation is quite distorted and totally inadequate as a basis for negating the possibility of solute absorption, it must be admitted that there is little experimental evidence that the process does occur to any significant extent. The existing circumstantial data are meagre and equivocal. Snell (1908), for example, observed much more vigorous growth in specimens of *Elodea* and *Potamogeton* rooted in mud than in those kept in the same vessel but anchored away from the mud. The average increase in length of the shoots of *Elodea* in one experiment was 4·4 cm in unattached specimens but 9·85 cm in plants rooted in mud. From such experiments Snell concluded that the roots absorb the major supply of both water and inorganic nutrients. Pond (1905) studied the absorption of water by the roots of *Ranunculus trichophyllus* and found that 5 ml were taken up in each of two 24-h periods by a root 14 cm long. He also experimented with *Elodea*, *Vallisneria* and other submerged plants and ascribed the poor growth and accumulation of starch in non-rooted specimens to a deficiency of potassium, phosphorus, and possibly other macronutrients, and a consequent inhibition of protein synthesis.

Later, Brown (1913) found that the difference between rooted and unattached plants of these submerged genera could be eliminated by passing carbon dioxide through the water for a few hours each day, and concluded that the superior growth of rooted plants in previous experiments and in natural habitats might be due to the greater absorption of dissolved carbon dioxide, which is often more abundant in muddy substrates than in the water.

Several aspects of all these early experiments are open to criticism and precise significance cannot be attached to the essentially qualitative data which they yielded.

More recently, Thut (1932) obtained volumetric estimates of the rate of exudation from rooted stumps of several submerged hydrophytes and concluded that root pressure, resulting from the uptake of water and ions, was genuinely exerted in his experimental plants. More convincing data were obtained by Höhn and Ax (1961) who demonstrated a diurnal rhythm in the rate of water absorption by intact plants and rooted stumps of *Nomaphila stricta*, which, although essentially an emergent hydrophyte, was submerged in these experiments.

Perhaps the most significant findings are those of Frank and Hodgson (1964), who devised an elegant and reliable method of partitioning the aqueous experimental medium surrounding an intact plant, so facilitating the study of the uptake of dissolved compounds by particular isolated organs and their subsequent translocation elsewhere in the plant body. These workers investigated the absorption, during periods of 24 h and 96 h, of the herbicide fenac, labelled with ^{14}C in the -COOH group, by different parts of specimens of *Potamogeton pectinatus* raised from perennating tubers. Auto-radiographs of plants whose foliage had been exposed to the fenac solution revealed the presence of high activity in the leaves, thus confirming the capacity for foliar absorption. But the similarly high activity found in the roots and rhizomes of plants whose roots had been exposed to the radioactive herbicide provides strong evidence that the roots of even so reduced a submerged species as

P. pectinatus are perfectly able to absorb to a comparable extent. Furthermore, limited acropetal translocation was found to occur, with some accumulation of the herbicide in nodal regions. The observed reduction in this translocation in plants from which the tubers were removed prior to exposure to the fenac is congruous with the notion that exudation pressure developed in the tuber (which is likely to be rich in osmotically active substances) might aid upward transport through the shoot system. It would be interesting to apply Frank and Hodgson's technique to the possible absorption of labelled nutrients (rather than herbicides or auxins) by this and other submerged hydrophytes.

Despite the inconclusive nature of the evidence, a few authors, notably Arber (1920), Titcomb (1924), Veatch (1933) and Skene (1947), have firmly emphasised the reality of the absorbing function of aquatic roots and have censured the view that would regard the uptake of water and ions as mainly or wholly foliar. Pearsall (1917, 1918a, 1920) and Misra (1938) were both greatly impressed by the apparent relationships between the distribution of certain hydrophytes in the English Lakes and certain chemical properties of the sub-strates, such as their contents of bases, potassium, nitrate, ammonium ions, or organic matter. Matthews (1914), Rickett (1921, 1924), Veatch (1933), Wilson (1937, 1939, 1941) and Tansley (1949), *inter alia*, described similar ecological relationships from other sites, and, like Pearsall and Misra, inter-preted them to imply that the plants do depend to a considerable extent on nutrients absorbed from the substrate.

In his study of Scottish lakes, which provide a relatively wide spectrum of habitats, Spence (1964) was unable to discern such intimate plant-soil associa-tions. Any connections between features of soil chemistry and the distribution of dominant species, life forms or growth forms seemed, at best, to be very tenuous. Even so, Spence acknowledged that in certain circumstances within a particular water regime, as when ions become depleted in the water, absorption of the required nutrients by exchange between the soil colloids and the roots could attain critical importance. He also suggested that even under normal conditions of nutrient availability, whereas anions may be absorbed equally readily via either the foliage or the roots, cations, which are frequently less soluble, may be absorbed principally from the substrate by the roots.

Since the roots of hydrophytes are evidently able to live and grow in very low oxygen tensions, the respiratory energy requirement for solute absorption need not present a physiological problem. As long as adequate oxygen diffuses through the internal atmosphere to their tips, the roots will presumably be capable of absorbing and accumulating ions from even completely anaerobic substrates. If nutrients are readily available, it is possible that for some sub-merged and floating-leaved plants absorption from the water through the shoot epidermis could be a faster route of supply to the metabolic centres in the mesophyll than transport along the substrate–root–stem–leaf–mesophyll pathway.

7

The Free-Floating Habit

The diversity of habit and morphology amongst free-floating hydrophytes is remarkable. This life form is encountered throughout both Old and New Worlds, from the cold temperate regions to the tropics, and in all manner of freshwater habitats, from the immense lakes and rivers of Africa and Asia to the minute pools of water in the leaf axils and rosettes of tropical bromeliads. Several floating plants, such as *Lemna*, *Pistia* and *Salvinia*, are amongst the most widely distributed of all hydrophytes, and achieve notoriety and economic importance through their phenomenal spread and their creation of obstacles on navigable waterways, irrigation channels and hydro-electric reservoirs.

In the most elaborate version of the life form the foliage develops as a rosette, comprising aerial or surface-floating leaves, a condensed crown-like stem and pendulous submerged roots, as exemplified by the monocotyledon *Eichhornia crassipes*, the dicotyledon *Trapa natans*, and the pteridophyte *Ceratopteris cornuta*. In each of these groups of vascular plants it is possible to trace a trend of structural reduction from the rosette habit. In the pterido-phytes, for example, this trend is manifest in the specialised morphology of *Azolla* and *Salvinia*, both surface-floaters and not in the least fern-like in appearance, *Salvinia* being entirely rootless. Extreme modification may also be seen in the monocotyledonous Lemnaceae, which consist of leaf-like or more or less globose thalli wherein stem and leaf have lost their separate identity. Species of *Wolffia* are rootless and include the smallest known angiosperms. The monotypic *Aldrovanda vesiculosa* and the genus *Utricularia*, which has over 200 species (some of them terrestrial or epiphytic), provide examples of the trend of reduction amongst the dicotyledons. Both genera are rootless. Furthermore, in *Utricularia* stem and leaf are no longer distinguishable, and the morphological nature of the vegetative organs is obscured by their astonish-ing plasticity.

Aldrovanda vesiculosa, *Stratiotes*, aquatic *Utricularia* species, and some species of *Lemna*, *Wolffiella* and *Wolffia* are submerged during vegetative growth, floating at a greater or lesser depth, and, like *Ceratophyllum*, they are therefore transitional in habit between typical submerged hydrophytes and typical surface-floaters. However, they are not so thoroughly committed to an aquatic life as *Ceratophyllum*, for they still produce aerial flowers.

Lacking contact with the substrate, free-floating hydrophytes are generally restricted to sheltered habitats, but this does not necessarily preclude them from colonising flowing waters. Most of the rosette species are stoloniferous and form dense matted communities which are equally successful on slow-flowing rivers as on lakes and stagnant pools. The tendency in the genus *Utricularia* to form anchoring organs culminates in the ability of one or two species to cling to waterworn rocks in swift-flowing streams, thus affording a parallel with the habit of the Podostemaceae.

Free-floating hydrophytes must perforce absorb all their mineral nutrients from the water and most species are therefore confined to habitats rich in dissolved salts (Pearsall, 1921a). In many countries such waters are incidentally calcareous, having a low ratio of potassium and sodium to calcium and magnesium, being rich in carbonate, nitrate and silica, and having a characteristic diatom plankton. Some natural waters are not calcareous but rather of the 'alkali' type, with a high $K + Na/Ca + Mg$ ratio, relatively little nitrate and carbonate, and an essentially desmid plankton. In some localities, this type of water is barren and devoid of almost any vascular plants, but in others, e.g. L. Victoria, the total concentration of dissolved salts is sufficiently high to support a flora of free-floating as well as rooted hydrophytes. Many species of *Utricularia* are exceptional amongst free-floating plants in being able to colonise fen and bog waters in which the pH value, calcium, magnesium and nitrate concentrations may be very low.

FORM AND FUNCTION IN ROSETTE SPECIES

The Habit of the Plant. The leaves of the least modified free-floating hydrophytes are produced in rosettes from the apices of abbreviated vertical stems: from the base of each rosette hangs a cluster of adventitious roots which occasionally penetrate the substrate in shallow water. The position of the leaves varies according to the species and the environmental conditions. The foliage of *Eichhornia crassipes* (Fig. 7.1), for example, is truly aerial, but the angle between the leaves and the water surface varies from about 15 to 45° around the periphery of the rosette and in open water, to 75 to 90° in the centre of the rosette and in densely crowded conditions (Penfound and Earle, 1948). The leaves of *Pistia stratiotes* (Fig. 7.2), *Hydrocharis morsus-ranae* (Fig. 7.3), *Limnobium spongia* and *L. stoloniferum* lie flat on the water in young plants, or in diffuse light in uncrowded habitats, but they frequently rise into the air in mature rosettes or in dense communities. The senescent peripheral leaves of the rosettes of all species gradually become submerged and decay under water.

Most rosette species are perennials and are free-floating throughout growth, with the exception of the initial stages of seedling development. The peculiar temperate plant, *Stratiotes aloides* (Fig. 7.4), is usually submerged during the autumn and winter but rises gradually to the surface in the late spring, the rosette remaining floating throughout much of the summer whilst the aerial flowers are produced and seeds are set. Some species of *Ceratopteris*, e.g. *C. cornuta* (Fig. 7.5), are typically free-floating whereas others, e.g. *C. pteridoides* and *C. thalictroides*, may also be found as rooted submerged plants, which are generally sterile unless the water is shallow, when aerial fertile leaves may be

FIG. 7.1. *Eichhornia crassipes*: A, aerial view of young free-floating rosette with reclining leaves and petioles swollen into buoyant 'floats' ($\times 0.2$); B, side view of dense population of mature plants with tall floatless leaves having sharply angled petioles, the proximal part horizontal and the distal part erect ($\times 0.1$); C, aerial view of mature plant with two daughter rosettes (black arrows) arising close from the parent rootstock, and a third developing rosette being borne away towards the bottom of the photograph on a stout stolon (white arrow). Note also the plumose roots, appearing dark as a result of their purple anthocyanin ($\times 0.2$). (See also views of foliage in Figs. 7.10, 12.5, 13.4 and 13.5.)

produced. Both *Ceratopteris* and the three or four species of *Trapa* differ from the other rosette plants in being annuals.

As in many other hydrophytes, the foliage shows immense variation in size and form in different habitats. When floating in shallow, poorly oxygenated water or when stranded on muddy shores, *Eichhornia crassipes* has rather small leaves, which may only reach a length of about 8 cm with blades about 30 mm broad and 20 mm long: on plants in well-aerated, especially flowing, water, the leaves may attain a length of 125 cm, the blades being conspicuously longer

FIG. 7.2. *Pistia stratiotes*: A, aerial view of part of a population showing mature rosettes reproducing by stolons (two arrowed) and surrounded by young plants with smaller rounded leaves (× 0·25); B, side view of rosette with erect leaves, showing prominent ribs along the undersurface and a very young daughter rosette arising on a short stolon (arrowed) from the parent rootstock (× 0·4); C, aerial view of three young rosettes showing rounded to obovate leaves with velvety pile of hairs on their upper surface (× 1).

than they are wide, about 150 mm by 130 mm. The sessile leaves of *Pistia stratiotes* are broadly obovate to cuneate in shape, reaching 13 cm in length and 5 cm in width, the apex being smoothly rounded in horizontal young leaves but markedly truncate in the crisped, erect, mature foliage. The rosettes of species of *Ceratopteris* vary in diameter from about 5 to 60 cm or more: the older leaves are floating or more or less submerged, the more recently formed usually partly aerial. They vary widely in shape, from elliptical and tapering, with incised margins, to broadly trifoliate, pinnatifid, and even twice- or thrice-divided in mature rosettes.

FIG. 7.3. Aerial view of two young specimens of *Hydrocharis morsus-ranae* (× 0·6).

A trend towards the mechanically ideal form of floating leaf is discernible in other genera. In *Trapa natans* (Figs. 7.6 and 7.7), for example, the lamina is deltoid or rhombic, toothed towards the apex, 1·5 to 7 cm wide and 1·5 to 4·5 cm long (Janković, 1955, 1956; Wild, 1961). The leaf blades of *Limnobium* are rounded to heart-shaped, whilst in *Hydrocharis* a reniform to orbicular outline is reached. The petioles of these plants, like those of rooted floating-leaved hydrophytes, are very variable in length and show accommodation to water depth. By growing a specimen of *Hydrocharis morsus-ranae* in very deep water and then transferring it to shallow water where the shoot apex was only just submerged, Frank (1872) obtained successive leaves with petiole lengths of 11 cm and only 1·5 cm. Arber (1920) stated that in this species the petiole may be any length from 1 to 14 cm but the normal range is about 6 to 8 cm. It is doubtful if any mechanical advantage accrues from a wide range of petiolar accommodation, because the leaf blades of free-floating species, unlike those of rooted genera such as *Nymphaea*, are not exposed to the risk of sudden immersion by an increase in water depth. The whole rosette responds to water movement and provided that its tissues are buoyant and its roots uninjured it will maintain a stable position on the surface. The variability of the length of the petioles may be beneficial in facilitating exposure of the maximum area of photosynthetic surface to incident light. Older leaf-blades are borne away from the shoot apex as their petioles elongate, thus clearing the water surface above

FIG. 7.4. Aerial view of rosettes of *Stratiotes aloides* which have risen to the surface of a pool. (*Nymphaea* leaves at top and left, and *Potamogeton pectinatus* in the water.)

young developing leaves. This effect is manifest in relatively uncrowded habitats when *Trapa*, *Hydrocharis* and other plants form very conspicuous leaf mosaics (Fig. 7.6). Of course, the leaves overlap to an increasing extent as competition between plants becomes more severe.

The foliage of *Stratiotes aloides* differs markedly from all other free-floating plants. The sessile, linear, tapering leaves arise from the condensed vertical stem in a spreading rosette: each leaf is 15 to 50 cm long, stout and rigid, and possesses a spinous-serrate margin, so that the habit of the plant is very reminiscent of an aloe (Fig. 7.4). The renowned cycle of rising and sinking was thought by Nolté (1825) to occur twice each year, but later observers generally agree that the rosette rises only once, just before the flowering phase is reached, and sinks during the late summer or autumn. Even this single cycle is not always perfect—in some habitats the submerged state, less commonly the floating, may be prolonged. The mechanism of the movement has aroused endless speculation but has never been satisfactorily explained. *Stratiotes* usually frequents rather calcareous waters (Davie, 1913), and Montesantos (1913) claimed that calcium carbonate is deposited on mature leaves when the plant is floating: when the specific gravity of the foliage exceeds that of the water, the rosette sinks. Young leaves formed in spring are said to be devoid of a carbonate deposit and it is suggested that as the number of these increases, and the old foliage decays, the specific gravity of the plant eventually falls below that of the water, and the plant gradually rises again. Arber (1920) and

FIG. 7.5. Aerial view of two specimens of *Ceratopteris cornuta*, with gemmiparous plantlets developing on the leaf margins ($\times 0.5$).

others have cited in support of this intriguing explanation Pringsheim's (1888) microscopical observations of the deposition of carbonate crystals on algal filaments and bryophyte leaves immersed in water containing both dissolved carbon dioxide and calcium carbonate. Similar deposition of carbonate has been observed on numerous submerged vascular plants in calcareous waters (pp. 133, 432). Since *Stratiotes* still rises and sinks if it is cultivated in neutral or slightly acidic non-calcareous water, Montesantos' theory does not provide a completely satisfactory explanation of the movement. It is likely that changes in the overall air space/tissue volume ratio of the plant are also significant. Younger leaves photosynthesise more actively and their lacunae and inter-cellular spaces are probably more distended than those of older leaves. The overall air space/tissue volume ratio, and hence the buoyancy of the plant, may be expected to increase during active growth in the spring and to decrease as the foliage becomes senescent in the autumn. Other floating plants which do not sink even in calcareous waters must have a high enough proportion of air space to maintain buoyancy at all times.

The Leaves as Organs of Photosynthesis and Transpiration. The erect aerial leaves of *Eichhornia crassipes* resemble those of numerous emergent monocotyledons in isobilateral organisation. Several layers of palisade cells, containing abundant chloroplasts, extend throughout the leaf under the epidermis of both surfaces, whilst between these two palisade zones is a central lacunate mesophyll, the air spaces of which are traversed at intervals by diaphragms. The epidermis resembles that of many land plants in lacking chloroplasts. Around the periphery of the rosette, the leaf-blades are often inclined

FIG. 7.6. Aerial view of two rosettes of *Trapa natans*, showing developing leaf mosaic and some petioles with median 'floats' (× 0·3).

rather than vertical, and correlated with this the development of the palisade tissue is sometimes greater towards the upper epidermis (Weber, 1950; Hasman and Inanç, 1957).

Similar marked differentiation of palisade and lacunate mesophyll is evident also in the truly floating leaves of *Hydrocharis*, *Limnobium* and *Trapa*, but here the organisation resembles that of the floating leaves of such genera as *Nymphaea* and *Potamogeton*. Dorsiventrality is conspicuous: the palisade tissue is developed in only the upper half of the leaf. The upper epidermis has sculptured outer walls, a rather thick cuticle and few chloroplasts, whereas the cells of the lower epidermis, in contact with the water, are thin-walled and often rich in chloroplasts, and they bear only a relatively thin cuticle. Between the palisade layer and the lower epidermis is a polygonal meshwork of vertical plates of parenchymatous cells, forming a lacunate tissue in which the proportion of air space to cell is very high.

The leaves of species of *Ceratopteris*, e.g. *C. thalictroides*, usually have an undifferentiated mesophyll with conspicuous intercellular spaces. On both the upper and the lower surfaces the epidermis is cuticularised and richly chloroplasted (Pal and Pal, 1962).

7*

The stomatal distribution is correlated, in some genera at least, with the habit of the leaf. The aerial leaves of *Eichhornia* have stomata on both surfaces, the frequency being about 120 per mm² on the blade, 20 per mm² on the transition region at the base of the blade and only 1 per mm² on the petiole, which may therefore undergo only limited photosynthesis despite the many chloroplasts in its superficial cells. The stomata have a quite normal rhythm, opening about 5 a.m., obtaining full aperture from about 10 a.m. to 1 p.m., and closing by 5 p.m. Although the size and form of the leaf may change in

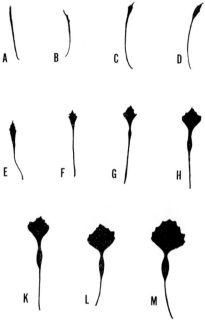

FIG. 7.7. Silhouettes of successive leaves from a seedling of *Trapa natans*. A to G, submerged; H to M, floating; inflation of the petiole first visible in G (all × 0·4).

different environmental conditions, the mean stomatal frequencies, the inter-stomatal distance, and the size of the guard cells and stomatal aperture all remain more or less constant (Penfound and Earle, 1948). In the floating leaves of *Hydrocharis*, *Limnobium*, *Trapa* and *Trapella* the stomata are generally restricted to the upper epidermis (Oliver, 1888; Solereder, 1913; Glück, 1940; Metcalfe and Chalk, 1950; Jankovič, 1955, 1956), although they have been found sporadically on the lower epidermis in *Hydrocharis* (Goebel, 1891–1893). The guard cells usually have protruding cuticular ridges which reduce the risk of water entering the leaf. It is probably by juxtaposition of these ridges, rather than of the cell walls themselves, that the aperture is closed (Haberlandt, 1914). Stomata may occur on both surfaces, or on just the upper surface, of the leaves of *Ceratopteris* (Pal and Pal, 1962).

Montesantos (1913) showed that in *Stratiotes* the stomatal distribution is related to the plant's age, not to its environment. Stomata do not occur on juvenile leaves, but they develop and increase in frequency on successively older leaves. Mature rosettes therefore possess leaves both with and without stomata, regardless of whether they are floating or submerged.

Although direct measurements of the process are lacking, transpiration from the foliage of free-floating rosettes is likely to occur through the stomata, and to a lesser extent through the cuticle, at rates up to six times greater than the rate of evaporation from a free water surface of similar area. The leaves of *Pistia stratiotes* also display guttation, drops of water being exuded through apical hydathodes which resemble those of land plants in having beneath the pore a small cavity and an epithem of thin-walled lobed cells, into which the tracheids of the vein-ending open (von Minden, 1899). Hydathodes also occur at vein-endings in the indentations of the leaf margins in *Trapella sinensis* (Oliver, 1888).

The Buoyancy of the Foliage. In all free-floating rosettes, buoyancy is endowed by the high proportion of air (often 70 per cent or more, by volume) in the foliage. Most of the air space is contributed by the lacunate mesophyll but the extent to which this is developed varies in different plants and different environments. In *Ceratopteris*, *Hydrocharis* and *Limnobium* this tissue is uniformly well-developed throughout the blade with the result that the leaves have a fleshy texture (Fig. 7.8). On older leaves, particularly spongy areas are often found near the base of the midrib, where the mechanical strains are greatest.

In other genera, the lacunate tissue develops so excessively that bladder-like swellings, known as 'floats', are formed. Each leaf of *Pistia*, like that of *Ceratopteris*, is very succulent throughout, but the underside often shows a conspicuous ovoid swelling, several centimetres long, which Ito (1899b) found was composed of spongy parenchyma. In species of *Trapa* the middle of the petiole is often inflated (Figs. 7.6 and 7.7), and buoyancy is further increased by a swelling of the upper part of the stem, which is rather more elongated than that of other rosette species. In *T. natans* this upper part of the stem has a lacunate pith and four or five rings of air spaces in its cortex whereas the pith is compact and there are only two rings of cortical lacunae in the lower stem (Costantin, 1884). Perhaps the most excessive development of lacunate ground tissue occurs in *Eichhornia crassipes* (Figs. 7.1 and 7.10); in some specimens almost the whole petiole is swollen into a bulbous spongy float, which has a volume/fresh weight ratio of over 7 cm^3/g in contrast to about 1·3 cm^3/g for the other vegetative organs (Penfound and Earle, 1948).

The relation of these floats in *Eichhornia*, *Pistia* and *Trapa* to the buoyancy requirement is shown by the fact that in specimens stranded on mud they do not develop, the petioles or bases of the blades remaining slender and elongated. Yet, adaptive though they may be, floats are rarely formed in natural habitats. *Eichhornia crassipes*, for example, fails to develop them in light intensities lower than about 5380 lux, at high temperatures, in crowded conditions,

or when partly rooted in shallow water. Hence although the leaves formed at
the start of the season, when light is unrestricted and space is not at a premium,
may have swollen petioles, mainly float-less foliage is produced in established
communities as competition for space increases and the thickening canopy of
leaf-blades reduces the light intensity. Such buoyancy as a float-less rosette
possesses is due to the quite normal proportion of lacunate tissue. In a dense
community much support is given by the pressure of the surrounding foliage.

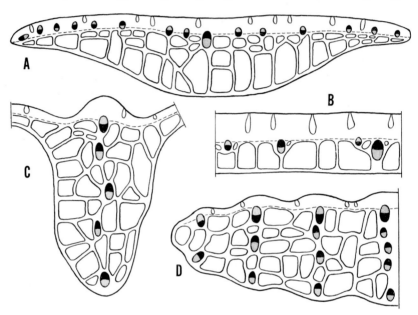

FIG. 7.8. Diagrammatic T.S. leaf of certain free-floating species to show orientation of
the vascular bundles and distribution of lacunae in the spongy mesophyll and beneath
stomata in the palisade mesophyll. (Lower limit of the palisade mesophyll indicated by
a broken line; phloem of the vascular bundles shaded; xylem solid black): A, *Limnobium
stoloniferum*, blade ($\times 4$); B, *Hydrocharis morsus-ranae*, part of blade ($\times 7$); C, *Pistia
stratiotes*, rib of blade ($\times 4$); D, *P. stratiotes*, base of blade ($\times 4$).

The Rigidity of the Leaves. Most floating plants possess little, if any, lignified
tissue and the foliage is kept rigid by the balloon-like inflation of its lacunate
tissues and the collective turgor of its living cells. The succulent foliage of
Ceratopteris, for example, is more or less devoid of lignified elements and
depends for its support entirely on hydrostatic forces (Siegel, 1962). The leaves
of other genera, such as *Hydrocharis*, *Limnobium* and *Pistia*, whose vascular
tissue is similarly reduced, may possess ribs of slightly thickened, non-lignified
cells running longitudinally above and below each vein but their resistance to
strain is very weak and turgor is again largely responsible for support. In the
aerial leaf of *Eichhornia*, angular collenchyma along the margins of the blade
offers some resistance to tearing. The action of wind against the flat 'sail-like'
blade can disperse the buoyant rosettes for several kilometres.

In general, then, the succulent foliage of free-floating plants is mechanically deficient. Excessive transpiration soon brings about loss of turgor and the susceptible flaccid leaves are quickly scorched by a hot sun.

Water Repellancy. Free-floating hydrophytes are of course exposed to falling rain, and any structural modification which repels water is beneficial, especially to tropical species which might otherwise be rapidly submerged by a heavy monsoon storm. Yet remarkably few rosette species have any such modifications. One notable example is *Pistia stratiotes*, whose leaves are densely clothed on both surfaces with short depressed hairs, which give the foliage a velvety appearance (Ito, 1899b; and see Fig. 7.2). Air is trapped between these hairs, and any water falling on the inclined leaf is speedily repelled and the epidermis never wetted. The air layer effectively prevents the plant becoming submerged for unless forcibly held under water the rosette immediately returns to its floating position. In all the other genera the upper and lower surfaces of the leaves are quite glabrous and falling rain is repelled by the smooth waxy cuticle. *Trapa* does possess long uniseriate hairs but these are restricted to the lower surface of the lamina.

Vascular Anatomy of the Leaves. The vascular tissues of the leaves are generally feebly developed: in most genera the protoxylem is represented by a lacuna. Such conducting elements as are present are weakly differentiated tracheids with spiral or annular thickening. Each vascular strand is usually sheathed in parenchyma, although in the aerial leaf of *Eichhornia* the innermost cells of this sheath are collenchymatous (Weber, 1950; Hasman and Inanç, 1957).

Perhaps the most interesting feature of the vascular anatomy of the leaves of *Hydrocharis, Limnobium, Stratiotes* and *Eichhornia* is the occurrence of inversely orientated bundles (Fig. 7.8). In *Eichhornia* these are very numerous near the margin of the leaf-blade: some of the larger lateral veins consist of a pair of bundles, one of which is normally and the other inversely orientated, whilst others comprise only a single normal bundle (Arber, 1918, 1922a). The inverted bundles of the other three genera, all of which belong to the family Hydrocharitaceae, were observed by Solereder (1913) but it was Arber (1918, 1920) who emphasised their significance. She concluded that the leaf-blades of these genera resemble those of other members of the Hydrocharitaceae, Pontederiaceae and Alismaceae in being pseudo-laminae derived by the dorsiventral compression and lateral expansion of the distal part of an ancestral petiole.

Formation of Stolons. The tropical *Eichhornia crassipes* and *Pistia stratiotes* and the temperate *Hydrocharis, Limnobium* and *Stratiotes* are all stoloniferous herbs. During active vegetative growth, the short erect stem produces numerous lateral stolons which travel for some distance beneath the water surface and produce terminal buds which develop into rosettes identical to the parent (Figs. 7.1, 7.2; 10.10, 10.11). Stolon formation is then repeated by each daughter rosette, often at such a rapid rate that a vast area of water becomes colonised by a tangled mass of progeny derived from only a few pioneer individuals.

In the free-floating members of the Hydrocharitaceae the pattern of stolon formation is unusual, since a lateral shoot primordium does not occur in the axil of every leaf. Two shoot buds, the second arising laterally on the first, are present in the axil of every second leaf in *Hydrocharis* and *Limnobium*, whilst in *Stratiotes* there may be from three to ten leaves (often an odd number) between successive leaves subtending axillary buds (Cutter, 1963, 1964). Slight controversy has been evident around the question of whether each bud in *Hydrocharis* is a true axillary structure or is produced by a dichotomy of the apical meristem of the shoot (Bugnon and Joffrin, 1963; Loiseau and Nougarède, 1963). Considering the underlying physiological organisation to be more important, Cutter (1963, 1964) did not attempt to give a rigid morphological interpretation of the nature of the bud. She found that the first of each pair of buds is formed in the apical meristem directly after the primordium of its subtending leaf. Before leaf inception starts on it, the first bud meristem gives rise, laterally, to the second bud primordium.

Normally, only certain buds develop into stolons, and this behaviour is repeated in successive daughter rosettes. Cutter (1963) modified this pattern of organogenesis by growing plants in nutrient solutions supplemented with either kinetin or gibberellic acid, or both. The mean total number of stolons produced successively by a plant after 40 days in a solution containing either 1 mg kinetin/l. or 10 mg gibberellic acid/l. was about four times greater than that of control plants. The number in a solution containing both 1 mg kinetin and 10 mg gibberellic acid/l. was about ten times greater than that of control plants. Cutter suggested that kinetin may counteract apical dominance, so allowing the elongation of more lateral buds than would normally develop into stolons. She also found that in the presence of gibberellic acid the phyllotactic spiral of leaves is altered but the pattern of bud inception is evidently changed in a comparable way, for each pair of buds still occurs in the axil of every second leaf in the spiral. This suggests a definite morphogenetic correlation between the initiation of each bud primordium and that of its subtending leaf. In the presence of kinetin the leaf arrangement is unchanged but fewer buds develop on each axis. Cutter suggested this may be caused by a limiting supply of some other unknown substance required for the inception of buds.

Form and Function of the Root System. Whereas some submerged hydrophytes form relatively few roots, which produce absorptive hairs only on entering the substrate, all free-floating rosette plants have supremely well-developed adventitious roots which produce vast numbers of both lateral roots and epidermal hairs irrespective of whether they are free in the water or buried in the substrate (Fig. 7.9). The root system of *Eichhornia crassipes* represents from 20 to 50 per cent of the plant's biomass, according to the season and habitat (Penfound and Earle, 1948; Westlake, 1965a). The ability of the various genera to develop profuse root hairs in the water, when plants such as

FIG. 7.9. Root systems of various free-floating rosette species (all seen in side view): A, *Eichhornia crassipes* (× 0·25); B, two roots of *E. crassipes*, showing conspicuous dark caps on both main roots and laterals (× 0·8); C, *Pistia stratiotes* (× 0·3); D, *Trapa natans*, ascending submerged stem with clustered short branched roots and longer unbranched roots beginning to grow downward (at right) (× 0·3). (E and F on p. 190.)

Elodea cannot because of oxidation of the fatty cuticle, is an anomaly which might repay investigation.

Eichhornia crassipes and *Pistia stratiotes* provide perhaps the best examples of root systems: both have dense clusters of principal adventitious roots clothed with rows of laterals. Both lateral and main roots often bear conspicuous caps. Other genera have either a rather shallow system of quite freely branched roots, as in *Ceratopteris*, or rapid-growing, long, unbranched roots with hairs over most of their length, as in *Hydrocharis* and *Stratiotes*. Lengths of 100 cm and rates of growth as high as 5 cm/day have been recorded for the roots of *Stratiotes* (Arber, 1914). The root hairs of *Hydrocharis* and *Limnobium* have long been known as excellent material for showing protoplasmic streaming and plasmolysis (D'Arcy Thompson, 1915). The branched adventitious roots of *Trapa* develop in pairs on either side of the leaf scars at the lower nodes of

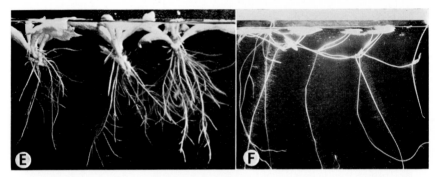

FIG. 7.9. Root systems of various free-floating rosette species (all seen in side view): E, *Ceratopteris cornuta*, young adventitious roots with many hairs ($\times 0.3$); F, *Hydrocharis morsus-ranae*, stolon with long unbranched roots from its nodes; each root with many long hairs ($\times 0.25$).

the floating stem. Their feathery structure, possession of chlorophyll, and development after the leaves have abscissed, have misled many authors to the conclusion that they are submerged dissected leaves with filiform segments. It is worth noting that in the earliest description of *Trapa natans*, Theophrastus (370–c. 285 B.C.) commented upon the peculiar hair-like appearance of these roots and shrewdly concluded that they 'are neither leaves nor stalk'. Mature specimens bear, in addition to the branched green roots, unbranched whitish roots from the lowermost nodes. These are comparable to the ground roots of *Bergia capensis* and *Heteranthera zosteraefolia* and in shallow water they may enter the muddy substrate and anchor the plant.

Relieved of the function of anchorage, the roots of free-floating plants are at least partly responsible for the equivalent function of preserving the stability of the rosette. Destruction of some or all of the roots of *Stratiotes* or *Eichhornia*, for example, disturbs the equilibrium of the plant and the foliage becomes partly or wholly submerged. The roots of most genera, like those of many land plants when illuminated, develop chlorophyll in plastids in their epidermal and outer cortical cells. Although the roots are presumably therefore capable of photosynthesis, the magnitude of their contribution to the net assimilation of the plant is unknown, but is likely to be very small.

There have been no critical studies of the uptake of specific ions by particular rosette species but the ecological restriction of the life form to waters with a high concentration of dissolved salts emphasises the importance of the root system to the mineral absorption of the plant. Many simple growth experiments in the laboratory provide corroboration. Haigh (1936) noted the superior growth of specimens of *Eichhornia crassipes* in shallow water (only

FIG. 7.10. Comparative growth of adult *Eichhornia crassipes* after 2 months in tap water only (left) and in tap water to which composted soil had been added at the rate of 100–150 g (air-dry weight)/l. (right). (From Hitchcock *et al.*, 1949, by courtesy of the Boyce Thompson Institute for Plant Research, Yonkers, New York.)

15 cm deep) once their roots had penetrated the mud, where the supply of nutrients was even richer than in the water. Experimenting with the same species, Hitchcock *et al.* (1949) found that once the first floating leaves had been formed optimum development was shown by plants in water to which had been added 100 to 150 g composted soil/l. (Fig. 7.10).

The Anatomy of the Roots. Several anatomical features of the roots of rosette species are correlated with the problems of the aquatic environment. Like all respiring submerged organs, the roots must obtain an adequate supply of dissolved oxygen. Some undoubtedly reaches the internal tissues by diffusion in solution along a concentration gradient through the epidermis, but this supply may well be supplemented, as in other floating-leaved and emergent hydrophytes, by oxygen diffusing from the sites of photosynthesis in the foliage. The roots certainly possess a system of cortical lacunae through which diffusion could occur and in which the oxygen could be temporarily stored.

In *Eichhornia crassipes* the cortex of the root is divisible into three zones. Immediately below the epidermis is a layer of compact parenchymatous tissue, three to four cells wide, whose cells are fairly thick-walled and resemble the epidermal cells in containing anthocyanin. Surrounding the stele is another zone of parenchyma, five or six cells wide, but here the cells are rounded and arranged in very regular radial rows so that the intercellular spaces are large and very numerous. Between these two zones is the lacunate tissue composed of radial plates of delicate thin-walled cells, the air spaces between the plates being long and narrow (Hasman and Inanç, 1957). Arber (1914) studied the development of the lacunae in the root of *Stratiotes*. In this plant the inner cortex is composed initially of radial plates of cells which undergo rapid mitotic divisions, mainly in a transverse plane. As a result of this, the plates elongate at a rate faster than the root as a whole, and so are forced into a sinuous form, spaces appearing between them (Fig. 6.4). Lacunae are also present in other genera: in the somewhat reduced root of *Ceratopteris*, for example, the cortex has a ring of six air spaces (Ford, 1902).

The roots of *Eichhornia*, *Hydrocharis*, *Pistia*, and also the more reduced *Lemna*, are unusual amongst angiosperms in having limited meristematic activity at the apex and a discrete epidermis, which divides in the anticlinal plane only, and therefore extends as an independent layer right round the outside of the apical meristem. The lateral roots are visible very early in the development of the main root. The outer tissues of each lateral are derived from the endodermis of the parent root, the inner tissues from the pericycle. Meristematic activity ceases at the poles of the cortex and stele, forming a wide quiescent centre, before the lateral emerges from the parent root. Soon after emergence, cell division is completely arrested and all later growth of the lateral is due to elongation (Schade and von Guttenberg, 1951; Clowes, 1961).

The vascular anatomy shows the reduction prevalent in other submerged organs. The stele of *Eichhornia* is polyarch: each xylem strand has an inner protoxylem lacuna, and two outer groups of two or three spiral- or annular-thickened tracheids. The phloem groups are on alternate radii to the xylem and contain sieve tubes, companion cells and parenchyma. An endodermis is present but weakly differentiated. True vessels are absent from *Eichhornia* and all the other genera except *Trapa*, but even this plant shows reduction, its lateral roots each containing but one feeble strand of xylem and phloem (Metcalfe and Chalk, 1950). In the root of *Ceratopteris*, unlike the rhizome or leaf, the pericycle and endodermis, each six cells in perimeter, do not arise from a common mother-cell layer (Pal and Pal, 1962). In transverse section, the vascular tissues are seen to consist of just four protoxylem, two metaxylem and four phloem elements.

REDUCTION IN *AZOLLA* AND *SALVINIA*

Azolla and *Salvinia* are considerably more specialised than *Ceratopteris*. The extreme reduction, accompanying increased adaptation to a free-floating habit, has almost obliterated their morphological affinities with other pterido-phytes. The vegetative structure of both genera is more strongly reminiscent of certain liverworts, a resemblance which misled many early botanists. In his pioneer natural classification, Adanson (1763), for example, actually placed

Salvinia amongst the hepatics. Smith (1938) has also remarked upon the similarity between *Azolla* and several foliose liverworts belonging to the Jungermanniales.

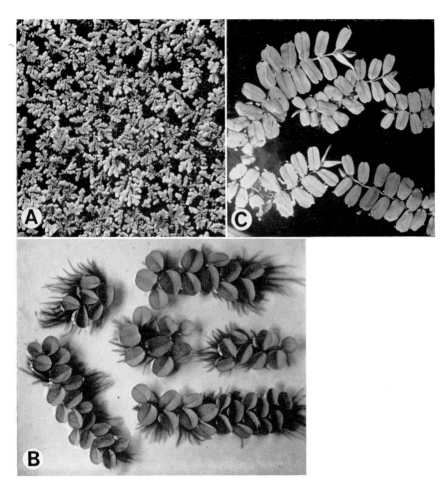

FIG. 7.11. Aerial views of several specimens of: A, *Azolla filiculoides*; B, *Salvinia auriculata*; C, *S. oblongifolia* (all × 0·25).

Both genera are relatively young amongst pteridophytes. *Salvinia* is probably the older of the two, appearing as far back in the fossil record as the Eocene and becoming quite common during the middle Tertiary: Tertiary records of *Azolla* are also known but less frequent (Seward, 1910; Florin, 1940; Arnold, 1947). At the present time both are widely distributed in tropical, subtropical and warm temperate regions.

Both plants are small and have fragile horizontally-floating stems bearing either both roots and leaves, in *Azolla*, or just two types of leaves, in *Salvinia* (Figs. 7.11, 7.12).

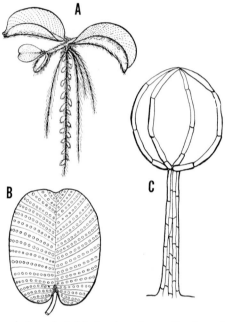

FIG. 7.12. *Salvinia auriculata*: A, habit drawing of part of a plant, showing apical bud, folded aerial leaves, and dissected submerged leaf bearing sporocarps (×0·6); B, diagram of venation and arrangement of water-repellent hairs on the upper surface of the leaf; C, side view of a single water-repellent hair (×30).

The Morphology of *Azolla***,** The stem of *Azolla* is pinnately branched and bears small, clasping, imbricate leaves arranged alternately in two ranks. Each leaf is divided into two parts. The upper, green, floating lobe has a much reduced palisade tissue between the epidermal layers and a small basal cavity on its adaxial surface. This upper lobe is the photosynthetic part of the leaf whereas the lower lobe, which is submerged and almost colourless, is thought to absorb water and dissolved nutrients, thus compensating for the somewhat feeble development of the adventitious roots which occur only sparsely at intervals along the underside of the stem (Eames, 1936; Demalsy, 1953). From an early stage in its differentiation the cavity in each dorsal lobe contains filaments of a symbiotic blue-green alga, *Anabaena azollae*, which reproduce there and are able to fix atmospheric nitrogen (Oes, 1913; Nickell, 1958; Kawamatu, 1965a, b; Johnson *et al.*, 1966).

The anatomy of both stem and root is greatly reduced (Eames, 1936; Demalsy, 1953). Beneath the epidermis of the stem is a thin-walled parenchymatous cortex, some five to eight cells wide, the innermost layer of which originates from the same mother-cell as the endodermis and pericycle. When seen in transverse section, the central cylinder contains about twelve phloem and six xylem elements and its organisation appears to be protostelic (Fig. 7.13). This simple stelar plan may well be a secondary character; the surviving, profoundly modified remnant of a more complex ancestral structure.

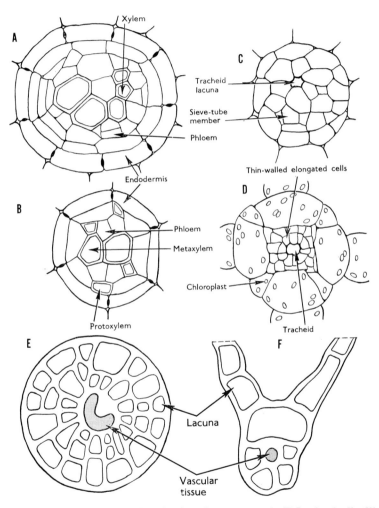

FIG. 7.13. Anatomy of reduced free-floating plants, as seen in T.S.: A, *Azolla filiculoides*, stele of stem ($\times$ 650); B, *A. filiculoides*, stele of root ($\times$ 750); C, *Lemna trisulca*, vascular bundle of thallus ($\times$ 500); D, *Utricularia minor*, vascular bundle and inner mesophyll of leaf segment ($\times$ 600); E, *Salvinia oblongifolia*, stem (diagrammatic) ($\times$ 25); F, *S. rotundifolia*, midrib of aerial leaf (diagrammatic) ($\times$ 12).

The apical cell of each root is tetrahedral but does not divide on its distal face, several separate initials being responsible for the production of the tissues of the root cap (Clowes, 1961). This sack-shaped cap surrounds the mature root for some considerable distance, and at least in *A. imbricata*, is composed of two layers, each one cell in thickness. The cells of the inner layer are normally rounded at first but as the root grows in length they become flattened and membranous (Kawamatu, 1962, 1963). The root hairs, which are formed in transverse zones from the epidermal cells still within the cap, are first extended when the root has reached about half its mature length (Leavitt, 1902). Beneath the many-celled epidermis of the root of *A. filiculoides* is an outer cortical layer, nine cells in perimeter, and an inner cortical layer, six cells in perimeter. This cortex has six irregular intercellular spaces. The endodermis and pericycle are each six cells in perimeter whilst the stele, seen in transverse section, closely resembles that of *Ceratopteris* with its four phloem elements, four tiny protoxylem cells and two larger metaxylem elements (Smith, 1938) (Fig. 7.13).

Azolla owes its buoyancy primarily to the minute epidermal hairs on the upper surface of the dorsal lobes of the leaves. The fine structure of the hairs differs according to the species: the hairs of *A. filiculoides*, for example, are unicellular whereas those of *A. caroliniana* are bicellular. In all species, as in *Pistia stratiotes*, the layer of air trapped by the hairs keeps the surface of the leaves dry and prevents the plant being immersed by rain.

The Morphology of *Salvinia*. Compared with *Azolla*, *Salvinia* shows further modification in its complete lack of roots. The slender horizontal stem bears paired floating leaves which differ in shape from species to species (Herzog, 1935; Bonnet, 1955; de la Sota, 1962, 1963, 1964): in *S. oblongifolia*, for example, they are narrowly oblong, in *S. auriculata* broadly elliptic and in *S. rotundifolia* rounded to orbicular (Fig. 7.11). In all species the apex of the leaf is deeply notched. From each node hangs a long finely-dissected submerged leaf which absorbs water and ions, under the influence of the transpiration pull exerted from the floating leaves, and thus performs the function of the absent roots. The simple epidermal hairs near the midrib on the lower surface of the floating leaves are also thought by numerous authors to be absorptive, although there is no direct evidence. Of the three buds present at each node, one can produce a dissected leaf, another a pair of floating leaves, whilst the third normally remains dormant. Primary lateral stems resemble the main stems in breaking very easily; any part of a stem bearing one or more buds is capable of growing into an independent plant. In crowded conditions stems rarely branch beyond the first degree: it is only in open undisturbed water that secondary laterals appear on the primary lateral shoots (Williams, 1956).

The exact habit of the foliage varies considerably in different communities. In *Salvinia auriculata*, for example, three phases of growth have been distinguished (Hattingh, unpubl.). The primary juvenile phase is generally to be found where sufficient space is available, especially near the shoreline where old mature plants have lain the previous season. The primary floating leaves are more or less rounded and quite small, about 10 mm in diameter, and they lie flat on the surface of the water. Within a few weeks the plants usually exhibit the secondary phase, in which the floating leaves are partly folded into a keel-shape; their average length is 23 mm and average width 28 mm. In the acute competition of the height of the growing season the tertiary phase is reached. Then the terminal buds form compact, almost vertical, acutely folded leaves which are much broader than they are long, measuring about 23 to 25 mm long and up to 38 mm wide. The transformation from primary to tertiary stages is influenced by the climatic conditions and the quietness of the water: it may take as little as 2 to 3 weeks in a suitable habitat. The overall length of each submerged leaf also varies: records of maximum length in *S. auriculata* range from about 5 cm (Wild, 1961) to 20 cm (Hattingh, unpubl.).

Laboratory experiments suggest that temperature and light intensity interact in influencing the growth of *Salvinia* leaves. Templeton (in Blackman, 1956) showed that if the temperature is raised from 25 to 30°C the leaves of *S. natans* are smaller in area, regardless of the light intensity. At the lower temperature of 20°C, however, an increase in area occurs in light of intensity 3230 lux but a decrease in light of intensity 6460 lux. The number of leaves is increased by a rise in temperature, but an increase in light intensity has a similar effect only at 25 and 30°C, not at 20°C.

Species of *Salvinia* vary in the vascular organisation of the horizontal stem. In *S. auriculata*, for example, the vascular cylinder is solenostelic throughout both the nodes and the internodes. *S. cucullata* has an amphiphloic siphono-stele at the nodes but a monostele in the internodes. *S. natans* exhibits similar nodal siphonosteles but is protostelic in its internodes. Mahabalé (1954) chose to arrange these three species in a series advancing from protostelic to soleno-stelic organisation, and concluded that *Salvinia* is more specialised than *Azolla*, in which the vascular cylinder is always a protostele. However, the series might equally be traced in the reverse direction as a reduction trend culminating in an apparently simple protostele, as in *S. natans* or *Azolla*.

Salvinia resembles *Ceratopteris* in its virtual lack of lignification in either the vascular or the ground tissues, and so depends largely on turgor for its mechanical support (Siegel, 1962; and see Fig. 7.13). The buoyancy require-ment is met by a structural adaptation similar to that of *Azolla* and *Pistia*, and comparable in effect to the cuticular plastron used in the respiration of some aquatic insects, i.e. a layer of air-trapping, water-repellent hairs on the upper surface of the floating leaves. The multicellular hairs occur in close parallel rows and reach their maximal development in the tertiary growth phase. In some species, such as *S. hastata*, they are quite simple and unbranched, but in *S. auriculata* their form is more specialised (Fig. 7.12). In this species, each hair comprises a stalk-like basal part and an upper lantern-like arrangement of three or four arms which unite at their apices. Air is trapped both within these looped arms and between the basal parts of the hairs. Drops of water are unable to penetrate between the hairs and so are speedily repelled. The more or less erect position of a mature leaf also facilitates repellancy, the water draining off via the midrib which forms a channel between the inclined halves of the leaf.

REDUCTION IN THE LEMNACEAE

The Form of the Plant. Structural reduction amongst the free-floating monocotyledons belonging to the Lemnaceae is even more drastic than in

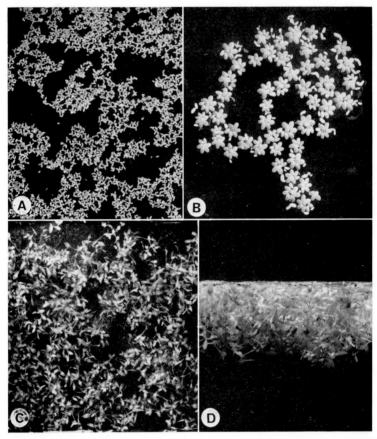

FIG. 7.14. Aerial views of colonies of: A, *Lemna minor* (× 0·2); B, *Spirodela polyrhiza*, with a few thalli of *L. minor* (× 0·4); C, *L. trisulca* (× 0·3); D, side view of colony of *L. trisulca* (× 0·4).

Salvinia or *Azolla*. None of the four genera possesses distinct stems and leaves. The plant body is reduced to a very small thallus which is flattened and leaf-like in *Spirodela* and *Lemna*, rectangular or falcate in *Wolffiella*, and ovoid or globose in *Wolffia*. The position of the thallus relative to the surface of the water varies with the species. All species of *Spirodela* and all except one of *Lemna* actually float on the surface but *L. trisulca* is submerged except when flowering. In numerous species of *Wolffiella* and *Wolffia* part of the thallus floats at the surface whilst the rest is submerged. The thallus of *Spirodela* has from two to twelve or more simple pendulous roots but that of *Lemna* has only one. *Wolffia* and *Wolffiella* are quite devoid of roots (Daubs, 1965).

The form and dimensions of the thallus vary quite widely in *Spirodela* and in *Lemna* (Figs. 7.14 and 7.15). *S. polyrhiza* is one of the largest: its flat, ovate to orbicular thalli reach a length of up to 10 mm. From each thallus hang several roots which may attain a length of 3 cm and have conspicuous root-caps. *L. minor* is smaller, reaching a diameter of only 1·5 to 4·0 mm, and each of its obovate or suborbicular thalli is slightly convex on both surfaces and has only one root, which may however reach a length of 10 cm. As each root enters senescence it loses its cap, becomes wrinkled and turns up at the end. Most species occur naturally as colonies of three or more thalli. Daughter thalli arise from one of two marginal pockets on opposite sides of the basal nodal region of each thallus: in some species, e.g. *S. polyrhiza* and *L. perpusilla*, only the pocket on the right-hand, more convex side of the thallus produces vegetative buds, the one on the left-hand side producing an inflorescence (Jacobs, 1947; Maheshwari and Kapil, 1963a). The colonies of species floating on the water surface are easily broken up by wind, rain and surface-dwelling animals, and often consist of only two generations of thalli, but in *L. trisulca*, which is more protected under water, thalli of several generations often remain attached (Schenck, 1885). In this species the mature thallus is translucent, acute at the apex, and tapers abruptly at the base into a short stalk. As in *L. minor*, each thallus has but one root.

Wolffiella and *Wolffia* include the smallest known angiosperms (Fig. 7.15). *Wolffiella floridana* has cylindrical or strap-shaped thalli which are 6 to 8 mm long and occur solitarily or in coherent stellate masses just under the surface (Fassett, 1957). Most species of *Wolffia*, however, are minute, ovoid, ellipsoid, or nearly globose plants, rarely exceeding 1·5 mm in length and producing daughter thalli from a basal pocket (Lawalrée, 1943). *W. arrhiza* and *W. columbiana* are both ovoid to ellipsoid whilst *W. papulifera* and *W. punctata* have flattened upper surfaces, the former with a central pointed mound, the latter with a slightly upturned apex. When first discovered by Weddell (1849), *W. brasiliensis*, which is usually less than 1 mm in diameter, was growing in the company of the magnificent foliage of *Victoria amazonica*, one of whose leaves would occupy enough surface for probably several millions of the diminutive thalli.

The morphological nature of the reduced thallus of the Lemnaceae has been variously interpreted. Hegelmaier (1868)* considered the thallus to be a modified photosynthetic stem, whilst Goebel (1891–1893) regarded it as a leaf, capable of forming daughter thalli from a meristem presumed to occur in its base. A later modified interpretation (Goebel, 1921) held that the distal part of each thallus represents a cotyledon, the proximal part a hypocotyl. Brooks (1940) argued that the thallus is a sympodial branch bearing a prophyll, a leaf and a bract and terminating in an inflorescence, all the components showing reduction and fusion. Brooks interpreted the left-hand flowering pocket in

---

* In a later work on the family, Hegelmaier (1896) changed his opinion and agreed with the views of van Horen (1869) and Engler (1877).

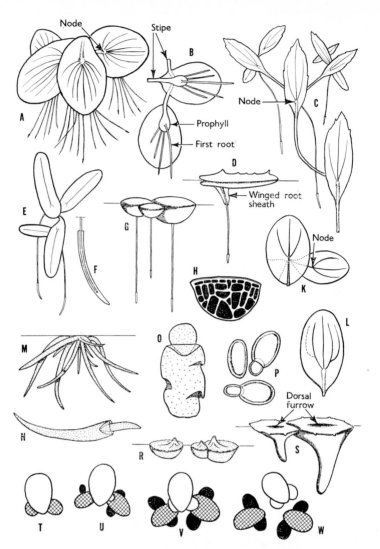

FIG. 7.15. Vegetative morphology of the Lemnaceae: A, *Spirodela polyrhiza*, aerial view (× 2·5); B, *S. polyrhiza*, ventral view of two thalli showing connecting stipes and prophyll penetrated by first root (× 2); C, *Lemna trisulca*, aerial view (× 2·5); D, *L. perpusilla*, lateral view of thallus showing dorsal papillae (largest at node and apex) and winged root sheath (× 10); E, *L. valdiviana*, aerial view (× 4); F, *L. valdiviana*, curved root tip and cap (× 12); G, *L. gibba*, lateral view (× 2·5); H, *L. gibba*, diagrammatic L.S. gibbous thallus showing distribution of lacunae (black) (× 4); K, *L. trinervis*, aerial view with daughter emerging from one of the two lateral pouches (denoted by broken lines) (× 4); L, *L. minor*, aerial view (occasional fifth vein shown as broken line) (× 4·5); M, *Wolffiella floridana*, lateral view (× 2); N, *W. floridana*, single falcate thallus with daughter emerging from basal pouch (× 4); O, *W. welwitschii*, aerial view with daughter emerging from basal pouch (× 3); P, *Wolffia arrhiza*, aerial view (× 10); R, *W. papulifera*, obliquely lateral view (× 8); S, *W. microscopica*, obliquely lateral view (× 20); T, U, V, W, diagrammatic representation of growth of colony of *Lemna minor* on successive days at 25°C under continuous illumination (1st generation daughter thalli cross-hatched, 2nd generation black). (Stippling in M, N, O and R indicates the distribution of pigmented epidermal cells.) (B, E, F, K, M, N, O and R, after Daubs, 1965; S, after Maheshwari, 1954; T, U, V and W, after White, 1940.)

S. polyrhiza as being derived from the bract and the axis, and the right-hand vegetative pocket from the prophyll and the basal part of the thallus axis. After studying the same species, Jacobs (1947) concluded that the plant body is derived from a rosette in which the original vertical axis has become reduced to three much condensed nodes. Perhaps the most widely accepted notion is that originally invoked by van Horen (1869): the proximal part of each thallus is of axial origin, the distal part of foliar origin. This concept of a combined stem and leaf is supported by Engler's (1877) critical comparison of the Lemnaceae with *Pistia* and other members of the Araceae, and by the fact that a vegetative bud of *Pistia* arises in a lateral pocket which is derived partly from the leaf sheath and partly from axial tissue and is therefore comparable with the vegetative pocket of *Lemna* and *Spirodela*. The distal foliar part of the thallus, beyond the marginal pockets, may perhaps be phyllodial in nature, like the limb of the leaf of *Pistia* (Arber, 1919c). The further modifications and homologies of the various parts of the thallus of *Wolffia* and *Wolffiella*, in which the vegetative pocket is basal and the flowering pocket dorsal, have yet to be fully explained.

Anatomical Features. The profound reduction of size and form is accompanied by great simplification of anatomical structure. The thalli are only a few cells thick with large intercellular air spaces; both the upper and lower epidermis, and the parenchymatous tissue between, are rich in chloroplasts. The upper epidermis of such surface-floating species as *L. minor*, *L. perpusilla* and *S. polyrhiza* is highly cuticularised and hence not easily wetted, and it usually possesses stomata, but these are absent from the submerged *L. trisulca*. Stomata occur only on the basal exposed part of the thallus of *Wolffiella*. As in *Lemna*, they are typically found on the upper surface of the floating thalli of *Wolffia*, their frequency varying with the species; *W. microscopica*, for example, has many whereas the larger *W. columbiana* has only one to six. Lacunae are common throughout the family and endow great buoyancy. They are usually most conspicuous in the lower region beneath the poorly differentiated palisade tissue. In most species they are roughly uniform in size and occur throughout the full width of the thallus. In some species they are small above and larger below (e.g. *Wolffia arrhiza*) or are restricted in occurrence, either to the central zone of the thallus (e.g. *L. minima* and *L. trisulca*) or to its basal part (e.g. *Wolffiella lingulata*) (Daubs, 1965). Especially large lacunae occur in *L. gibba*, where the lower part of the thallus is greatly swollen into a convex form by a mass of spongy tissue. Flowing water and high average daily temperatures (about 21°C) are said to favour the development of this spongy tissue (van Horen, 1869; Guppy, 1894). It may be presumed that the smallness and flatness of the thalli of *Spirodela* and *Lemna*, and their consequent high surface area/volume ratio, allow adequate diffusion of carbon dioxide and oxygen to the innermost cells, but it is doubtful if supplies of gases are so easily obtained by the more nearly globose thalli of most species of *Wolffia*.

Calcium oxalate crystals are accumulated by many species. They are deposited as raphides or druses in large parenchymatous cells in the thallus or in the root cortex and epidermis, and are notably abundant in species of *Spirodela* and in *Lemna minor*, *L. perpusilla* and *L. trisulca*. Anthocyanins are often present in one or both epidermal layers throughout the genus *Spirodela* and in *Lemna gibba*, *L. minor*, *L. disperma* and *L. obscura*. In species of *Spirodela* and *Wolffiella* and in *Wolffia punctata*, *W. brasiliensis* and *W. papulifera* both upper and lower epidermes are punctate with cells containing a brown pigment (Daubs, 1965).

Many of the smaller species of the Lemnaceae are extremely difficult to distinguish and the classification of all genera has been inevitably confused for some time. In recent years, chromatographic analysis of extracts of plant material has been used in attempts to resolve similar systematic problems in various terrestrial genera (Alston and Turner, 1963). The technique is far from infallible because environmental factors can modify both the quantity and the nature of the compounds present in an individual of given genotype. Nevertheless, major and consistent differences in the chromatograms obtained from plant extracts could be used as reliable and valid taxonomic characters. There is a distinct possibility that this biochemical approach might be of value in classifying the Lemnaceae. McClure and Alston (1964) studied the patterns of phenolic and other substances occurring in *S. oligorhiza* and *S. polyrhiza* grown under a wide range of rigidly controlled aseptic conditions. The two species are normally distinguished by the slightly greater size, number of roots and number of veins in *S. polyrhiza*. The chromatographic patterns of the two were found to differ in over fifteen major constituents, fewer compounds being common to both plants. Slight quantitative variation was observed, but the essential patterns remained constant in different conditions and thus allowed rapid definitive identification of the species. A comprehensive survey (Alston, 1966) of twenty-one species of the family showed an unexpected diversity of specific patterns of flavonoid compounds and also revealed striking differences between genera. Flavones and glycoflavones are quite common in *Spirodela* and *Lemna*, markedly less common in *Wolffia* and apparently absent from *Wolffiella*. Both *Wolffia* and *Wolffiella* lack anthocyanins. In contrast, flavonols are common in some species of these two genera but are less common in *Spirodela* and quite absent from *Lemna*.

There is no vascular tissue whatsoever in the thallus of *Wolffia* and *Wolffiella*. In *Spirodela* and *Lemna* a principal vascular bundle passes from a point roughly in the centre of the thallus, known as the node or centrum, towards the proximal end of the thallus, but does not quite reach it. In the larger species, at the node, several smaller bundles diverge from the principal one into the distal part of the thallus (Fig. 7.15). Thus the arrangement of the bundles gives the thallus the appearance of an excentrically peltate structure.

The total number of bundles in the distal part of the thallus is about nine in large species such as *S. polyrhiza* (although it is sometimes twelve or more in exceptional specimens), three in *L. perpusilla* and *L. trisulca*, and only one in *L. minima* and *L. valdiviana*. There is evidence that this restricted vascularisation is due to a substance, present in the thallus but as yet unidentified, which inhibits differentiation. In *L. minor*, which usually has four veins with occasionally a fifth, it has been shown (Wangermann and Lacey, 1953; Sargent, 1956) that branching of the veins is greatly increased if TIBA is added to the solution in which the plant is growing. The optimal effect is produced if the TIBA is present at an early primordial stage and in a concentration of about 30 mg/l. The addition of IAA or NAA alone to cultures of four-veined thalli induces the fifth vein but when either is added together with TIBA the response of the plants to the latter is modified. The increased vascularisation induced by the TIBA is reduced by 5 to 35 mg IAA/l. but increased by 35 to 50 mg IAA/l. Concentrations of NAA below 0·001 mg/l. or from 0·1 to 5 mg/l. retard the TIBA effect but in the intermediate range, 0·001 to 0·1 mg/l. they enhance it.

A substance chromatographically identical with IAA has been isolated from extracts of thalli and its growth-promoting activity is not affected by TIBA. Analysis of the extracts also revealed an unidentified growth inhibitor which is apparently reduced in amount by TIBA treatment. It is concluded that TIBA, and other halogenated benzoic acids having a similar effect, do not act as antiauxins but inactivate some naturally occurring inhibitor of the vascular system. In the presence of TIBA the meristem of the thallus forms a greater proportion of procambial cells. The differentiation of these is stimulated by a suitable concentration of a growth promoter and hence the ultimate vascularisation is further enhanced by the addition of auxins, such as IAA or NAA (Sargent, 1956; Sargent and Wangermann, 1959).

The vascular tissues are extremely reduced and devoid of lignification in all species. Each bundle typically shows a simple dorsiventrality, the xylem being towards the upper surface and the phloem towards the lower: an endodermis is not distinguishable. In transverse section, a vascular bundle in *L. trisulca*, for example, comprises a minute xylem lacuna and a single sieve tube with two companion cells, these remnants of the conducting system being sheathed by small parenchymatous cells which are slightly elongated in the long axis of the thallus (Schenck, 1886; and see Fig. 7.13). In larger species such as *S. polyrhiza* the file of xylem tracheids does not disorganise to form a lacuna at quite so early a stage, and the elements may be seen to retain weak annular or rarely spiral thickening (Hegelmaier, 1868; Cheadle, 1942). Vessels are absent from all members of the Lemnaceae.

It will be recalled that the sparse roots are simple, unbranched and capillary in form. Their anatomy provides further evidence of extreme reduction. Beneath the epidermis in *S. polyrhiza* and *S. oligorhiza* there is a narrow zone of parenchymatous cells which are slightly elongated parallel to the long axis of the root, and, like the epidermal cells, often contain chloroplasts. This cortical zone also contains small lacunae. In the centre, surrounded by a cylinder of small elongated cells, is a much reduced stele similar in structure to a vascular bundle in the thallus. The roots of such species as *L. gibba*, *L. minor* and *L. trisulca* are devoid of vascular tissue (Hegelmaier, 1868; Schenck, 1886).

Although they often possess a conspicuous cap and basal sheath, roots of *Spirodela* and *Lemna* are generally devoid of hairs. Surface-floating species probably absorb nutrients through both the root and the lower surface of the thallus (White, 1937b, Gorham, 1941). Ions probably enter through the whole epidermis in the submerged *L. trisulca*. This species is well known to be difficult to obtain free of contamination by algae. Landolt (1957) suggested that the algae might be involved in a loose symbiotic association, providing carbon compounds which are absorbed by the *Lemna*, and that if the algae are absent an external carbohydrate source is perhaps necessary for active growth of the *Lemna*.

The Influence of External Factors on the Growth of *Lemna*. As a result of its small size and the ease with which it may be cultured in inorganic nutrient solutions, *Lemna* is eminently suitable for laboratory experiments. Since about 1920 it has been extensively used in research into certain physiological aspects of growth under controlled conditions. Consequently there has accumulated a vast body of data on the influence and interaction of external factors, such as light intensity, temperature and nutrient supply, on the growth, respiration and ageing of both individual thalli and whole colonies (e.g. Bottomley, 1917, 1920; Mendiola, 1919; Saeger, 1925, 1930, 1933; Ashby *et al.*, 1928; Hicks, 1930, 1932b; Clark and Roller, 1931; Steinberg, 1941, 1946; Ashby and Wangermann, 1949; Gorham, 1950; Pirson and Seidel, 1950; Wangermann and Ashby, 1950; Zurzycki, 1951; Landolt, 1957; Hillman, 1961c; Weislo, 1963; Bornkamm, 1965a, b; Cope *et al.*, 1965).

Both light intensity and temperature influence the rate of multiplication and rate of growth of the thallus of *Lemna minor*. Ashby *et al.* (1928), Ashby (1929a, b) and Ashby and Oxley (1935) studied the changes in the relative rate of increase in the number of thalli, together with variations in the area and weight per thallus, in a wide range of controlled light intensities and temperatures. The increase in thallus number is generally exponential, i.e. the logarithm of thallus number plotted against time gives a straight line graph, the slope of this being a measure of the rate of increase. Robertson-Cuninghame's data (in Blackman, 1956) suggest that temperature and light intensity interact in controlling the rate of increase in thallus area but not the ratio of area to weight. At each of several light intensities the rate of growth in area is increased by a rise in temperature from 20° to 25°C but a rise from 25° to 30°C has no effect. The ratio of thallus area to weight, however, increases with any rise in temperature but decreases with rise in light intensity. According to Blackman (1956), calculations based on the data of Ashby and Oxley (1935) reveal similar effects.

Interaction between nitrogen and light intensity in relation to respiration, growth and assimilation in *Lemna minor* has been investigated by White and Templeman (1937) and White (1937a). The rate of respiration per unit area or per unit dry weight is reduced by nitrogen starvation, probably through the retarded synthesis of protein and consequent low level of enzyme activity. Increase in light intensity from 3230 to 12 920 lux is accompanied by a rise in respiration rate per unit area, probably as a result of the rise in carbohydrate level accruing from the increased rate of photosynthesis per unit area. On a dry weight basis, however, the respiration rate apparently falls, an effect which

White and Templeman (1937) attributed to a higher proportion of the sugar formed at the higher light intensity being converted to structural and reserve polysaccharides such as cellulose and starch.

The influence of variations in the supply of nitrate upon the acceleration of the rate of increase in number of thalli under rising light intensities was found by White (1937a) to be slight. When the nitrate supply is poor and the light intensity high, the consumption of protein in the formation of new protoplasm leads to internal nitrogen starvation, manifest in smaller thalli poor in chlorophyll. When the nitrate supply is good and the light intensity low, however, relatively less nitrogen is consumed, since the poor illumination retards the rate of growth, and hence symptoms of nitrate excess appear.

White (1939) also observed a similar interaction between potassium supply and light intensity. The harmful effect of a poor potassium supply is enhanced by a rise in light intensity because this increases the rate of growth and therefore reduces the relative concentration of potassium in the thallus. The similarly harmful effect of an excess of potassium is exaggerated by falling light intensity since this retards the growth rate and thus increases the relative concentration of potassium in the thallus.

It is apparent from these studies that optimal growth occurs only when there is a suitable balance between light intensity and the concentration of nitrate, and of potassium. If this growth rate is to be maintained, an increase or decrease of one factor must be paralleled by an increase or decrease of the other interacting factor.

Yoshimura (1952) compared nitrate and ammonium ions as nitrogen sources for *S. polyrhiza* and *L. valdiviana* during an experimental period of 1 h, partly in light and partly in the dark. It was concluded that higher light intensities stimulate the rate of photosynthesis and hence increase the internal oxygen concentration. This favours the absorption of ammonium ions but retards the reduction of nitrate to nitrite and ammonia and hence retards the uptake of nitrate ions.

The development of the root in *Lemna minor*, and perhaps other species, is correlated with the carbohydrate/protein ratio of the thallus (White, 1937b). Carbohydrate is consumed by both the root and thallus meristems, the supply to the root diffusing from the sites of photosynthesis. The steepness of the diffusion gradient to the root meristem is increased by higher light intensities which lead to an excess of carbohydrate in the thallus. With a constant carbohydrate level, a rise in nitrate supply stimulates the rate of growth of the thallus and the rate of consumption of carbohydrate there, and so leads to a reduction in the carbohydrate diffusing to the root. A decrease in light intensity with a constant nitrate supply has the same effect. White (1937b) pointed out that a longer root, formed when the carbohydrate/protein ratio exceeds unity, should increase the absorption of nitrate whilst a short root, formed when the ratio is less than unity, should absorb less nitrate; the internal balance of the plant could thus be automatically adjusted. In a later paper, White (1938) also described an interaction between potassium supply and light intensity (presumably via carbohydrate content) in relation to root length. A fall in either potassium supply or light intensity is accompanied by a decrease in root length. This effect is less marked if both factors are reduced but is enhanced if one is reduced and the other kept constant. Manganese deficiency also retards root growth, and induces chlorosis of the thallus, in *S. polyrhiza* (Yoshimura, 1941).

Gorham (1941) studied the response of *L. minor* to several growth-promoting substances added to the culture solution. IAA, IBA and NAA each stimulated an increase in both the rate of multiplication and the total area of the thalli. The optimal response was induced by concentrations varying between 0·01 and 0·05 ppm. Vitamin B_1 elicited no response, probably because *L. minor*, like *S. polyrhiza* and *L. valdiviana*, is itself able to synthesise this substance (together with vitamins A and C), and is therefore independent of an external source, at least during normal autotrophic nutrition in illuminated cultures (Yoshimura, 1943a). Hillman (1960b) and Loos (1962) described certain growth-promoting effects of kinetin on *Wolffia columbiana* and of gibberellic acid on *Lemna minor*.

The actual mode of uptake of growth substances by *L. minor* has been the subject of recent research by Blackman *et al.* (1959) and Blackman and Sargent (1959), using phenoxyacetic acids, labelled with ^{14}C in the $-COOH$ group, and TIBA, labelled with ^{131}I in the 2-position. At constant temperature (25°C) and light intensity (3230 lux) the initial rate of uptake of both 2,4-D and TIBA is rapid and depends upon the concentration of growth substance in the culture solution. Within a short time (1 to 2 h), the rate of uptake falls to zero and in the subsequent 22 h there is a loss of substance from the plants back to the solution. The fact that the rate of uptake is profoundly influenced by the pH of the solution, whereas the rate of egress is not, suggests that the substances are taken up in the molecular form. The net rate of uptake is clearly determined by the nature of the processes controlling the rates of entry and egress. Dalapon, labelled with ^{36}Cl, is absorbed largely in the ionic form by both roots and thalli. The initial net rate of uptake is high and apparently dependent on physiochemical processes: later, the rate falls to a lower steadier level and uptake then seems to be mediated by active metabolic processes involving thiol groups. This herbicidal compound is accumulated to different levels, according to the species of plant and the temperature, and inhibits root growth by blocking mitosis in the apex at the prophase stage (Prasad and Blackman, 1964, 1965a, b).

Interesting observations have recently been made on the interaction of flashing light, continuous red and far-red light of low intensity, and certain growth substances on the rate of growth of *L. minor*. The growth rate per unit of light increases greatly with diminution in the duration of each light flash below 1 min, and is maximal when flashes of 0·01 s are alternated with dark periods of 0·03 s. Under a regime of alternating flashes and dark periods of equal duration, supplementary continuous illumination with far-red light decreases the rate of photosynthesis whereas red light increases it. When, under a similar regime, the culture medium is supplemented with 0·645 ppm kinetin the growth rate is accelerated, but the addition of 25 ppm IAA inhibits the rate of photosynthesis, an effect which is enhanced if the frequency of light flashes is increased. Whereas only the older thalli accumulate starch reserves under continuous illumination, young thalli accumulate them too in flashing light. These phenomena are consistent with the notion that higher photosynthetic efficiencies are attained on exposure to short intense flashes of light separated by longer dark periods (Dickson and Chua, 1963; Chua and Dickson, 1964).

Under certain conditions the rate of increase of the number of thalli in colonies of *Lemna* may not be exactly exponential: cycles of growth have been reported by several workers. Dickson (1938a, b) considered that such cycles are caused by the periodic removal of thalli from cultures for sampling purposes, but White (1940) demonstrated a genuine rhythm in the dry weight and number of thalli in a colony of *L. minor* deprived of potassium. This rhythmic cycle was attributed to a sudden temporary increase in the production of daughter thalli consequent upon transferring a colony with an above-normal potassium supply to a nutrient medium lacking potassium. White suggested that the cycle was maintained by the translocation of the residual potassium in the plants through successive generations of first-formed daughter thalli. Gorham (1941) found some indication of a seasonal variation in the rate of multiplication of the thalli of *L. minor*, irrespective of environmental factors. From cultures of *L. minor* under continuous illumination, Pirson and Göllner (1953) and Bornkamm (1966) obtained evidence of a seasonal growth rhythm influenced by temperature: the rate of production of dry matter, the protein content and the protein/carbohydrate ratio all reached a maximum in summer and a minimum in winter. In *L. trisulca*, assimilation by the daughter thalli of organic nutrients synthesised in the mother thallus slightly depresses the growth rate of the limb of the latter. Scarcity of these nutrients increases the intensity of dominance between different daughter thalli, whereas the addition of soluble sugars, kinetin or gibberellic acid to the culture medium reduces it (Guern, 1963a, b; 1965).

Given a suitable temperature and intensity of light and an adequate supply of mineral nutrients, the thalli of *L. minor* live for up to 5 to 6 weeks, and each gives rise to only a limited number of daughter thalli which varies between different clones of the species. The gradual reduction in area in successive generations of thalli formed by a particular mother thallus is due to a decrease in the number, not the size, of the cells (Ashby *et al.*, 1949). The rate at which *L. minor* ages is quite independent of the concentration of growth-promoting substances in the thallus (Wangermann and Lacey, 1953), but does seem to be related to the concentration of the nitrogen source and to the rate of respiration. Minimal rates of ageing, and hence long life, are associated with low rates of respiration, which occur when the supply of a nitrogen source is low (less than 0·1 ppm N), whereas high respiration rates, which occur at intermediate concentrations of the nitrogen source (about 0·25 ppm N), result in maximal rates of ageing and a short life (Wangermann and Lacey, 1955).

Greenwood and Nelder (1964) recently examined the possibility that, over long periods, *Lemna* might develop an adaptation to the presence of drugs in

8

the medium similar to that shown by some micro-organisms. They grew a strain of *L. minor* for periods of up to 190 days in nutrient solutions supplemented with non-lethal amounts of certain drugs, such as sodium azide, sodium nitrite, proflavine and propamidine isethionate. However, they were unable to detect any acceleration of the growth rate with time: instead, there was some indication that enhanced sensitivity to each drug resulted from prolonged immersion in the supplemented media.

REDUCTION IN *ALDROVANDA* AND *UTRICULARIA*

Structural reduction in *Aldrovanda* and *Utricularia* is in some features almost as far-reaching as that shown by *Azolla*, *Salvinia*, and the Lemnaceae; in other features it is even more drastic. Both these dicotyledonous genera belong to otherwise terrestrial families: *Aldrovanda* to the Droseraceae, and *Utricularia* to the quite unrelated Lentibulariaceae. Some species of *Utricularia* are in fact land plants, living independently or as epiphytes, mainly in the tropics. Of the aquatic species some are distributed widely throughout the north temperate zone, some are tropical and extend into the southern hemisphere, whilst others form distinct groups peculiar to parts of the New World or to Australia (Barnhart, 1916; Lloyd, 1942). The monotypic *Aldrovanda*, in contrast, is a far-ranging Old World plant, occurring eastwards from southern France to Japan and southwards to Australia, India and northern Botswana (Lloyd, 1942).

Both genera are notable for their carnivorous habit which has aroused the curiosity of botanists ever since the plants were first described. However, there is no reason to believe that carnivory is specifically associated with adaptation to an aquatic life, although it is undoubtedly of incidental value, especially in habitats deficient in nitrates or ammonium ions. The fact that all the terrestrial relatives of these plants, in both the Droseraceae and Lentibulariaceae, are also carnivorous suggests that the habit was possessed by ancestral stocks prior to the evolution of the aquatic types.

Aldrovanda vesiculosa and *Utricularia* are rootless, even as seedlings. Although free-floating, the majority of the species are submerged, like *Lemna trisulca*. A few species of *Utricularia* in shallow water become anchored in the substrate by means of modified branches of the axis. This tendency towards anchorage culminates in two remarkable tropical species which thrive in swift-flowing streams. Both the South American *U. neottioides* and the African *U. rigida* cling to the rocky substrate by numerous coralloid fleshy stems, from which arise the normal leafy branches (von Luetzelburg, 1910).

The Habit of *Aldrovanda*. The slender, sparsely branched axis of *Aldrovanda vesiculosa* is usually 10 to 15 cm long and bears whorls of eight leaves which closely resemble those of *Dionaea muscipula*, the related Venus' fly trap of the Atlantic States of America, although they are rather smaller, each attaining a length of only 0·8 to 1·0 cm (Fig. 7.18). The wedge-shaped, winged petiole of each leaf is armed at its distal end with four to six, stiff, serrate bristles.

The lamina measures about 6 mm long by 4 mm wide, and its two lobes, inclined at about 45 to 50° to each other, bear several types of trichome (Caspary, 1859, 1862; Goebel, 1891–1893). On their outer surface, as on the rest of the plant, there are squat, two-armed, mucilage-secreting trichomes, whilst on the marginal zone of their inner surface there are stellate, four-armed trichomes, which also secrete mucilage. Between this zone and the midrib each lobe is thicker and bears on its inner surface digestive and absorptive bun-shaped glands and long, narrow, sensitive trichomes.

When the sensitive hairs are stimulated by a passing animal the two halves of the lamina fold together, as in *Dionaea,* and thus imprison the prey (de Lassus, 1861; Cohn, 1875). The initially rapid closure is followed, if the stimulus is strong enough, by further slow closure, until most of the two lobes are firmly appressed. It has been shown (Ashida, 1934) that the first rapid movement is due to the sudden loss of turgor in the inner epidermis of the thick inner zone of the lobes, whilst the subsequent slower movement is caused by actual growth of the outer epidermis. Growth of the inner epidermal cells, once they have regained turgor, later restores the lobes to their open position. There is little doubt that the captured prey is gradually broken down by secretions from the digestive glands and the soluble products are eventually absorbed (Lloyd, 1942).

The Habit of Aquatic Species of *Utricularia.* The vegetative body of the aquatic species of *Utricularia* (Figs. 7.16, 7.17 and 7.18) comprises an elongated, fragile, branched axis bearing numerous delicate 'leaves', which are deeply dissected into filiform or slightly flattened segments, some of which bear the small, hollow, bladder-like traps (Treviranus, 1848; Goebel, 1891–1893). Each trap is usually stalked, and, in different species, is spherical, ovoid or pear-shaped, varying in size from 0·3 to 5·0 mm long. The aperture at the narrow end is closed by a valve-like door which is attached to the wall of the trap along its dorsal semicircular margin; its free edge rests firmly on the thick collar or threshold of the aperture. This collar allows the door to open only inwards. The edge of the aperture bears branched antennae and bristles which create a funnel leading to the door. The surface of the trap, and of the rest of the plant, bears scattered spherical mucilage glands. The outer surface of the door bears four stiff bristles, which act as triggers, and long- and short-stalked glands, which secrete mucilage and also sugar, which may lure prey.

The short-stalked cruciform glands on the inside wall of the trap extract water from the fluid contents, and since the door is water-tight the diminution in volume creates a tension within the trap, manifest in the increasing concavity of its side walls. If a passing animal touches the trigger-bristles the door is opened slightly, thus releasing the tension. The walls immediately expand to their natural convex position and with the sudden inrush of water the prey is forcibly engulfed. With the closure of the door, the animal is imprisoned. As no digestive enzyme has been found to be secreted in the traps, and as the cruciform glands seem to be absorptive rather than secretory, it is held by some authorities that the prey, which are usually crustaceans, aquatic larvae or fish fry, are slowly asphyxiated within the traps and then undergo bacterial decay, the soluble products being absorbed. Other writers consider that the benzoic acid found in the traps by von Luetzelburg (1910) inhibits bacterial decay and that digestion is wrought by secretions from the trap itself.

It is not possible here to describe the variety and full complexity of the structure and mechanism of the traps in different species. Readers desiring further information should consult Cohn (1875), Brocher (1911), Ekambaram (1916), Withycombe (1923), Skutch (1928) and the stimulating classic accounts

FIG. 7.16. A, Aerial view of specimens of *Utricularia gibba* (× 1); B, Side view of single axis of *U. vulgaris* showing finely dissected leaves (× 0·8).

by Darwin (1875) and Lloyd (1942). These last two, together with the papers by Ashida (1934, 1935, 1937), provide fuller details of *Aldrovanda.*

Culture of the Plant. It is of some interest to know whether the carnivorous habit of these two dicotyledonous genera is in fact obligatory. Although Schenck was alleged by Cramer, in a lecture delivered in 1877, to have cultured

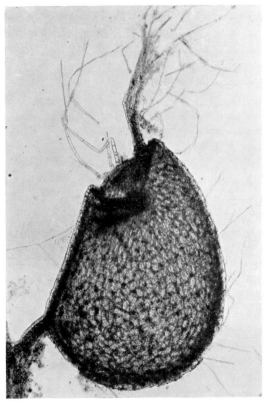

FIG. 7.17. Photomicrograph of a single trap of *Utricularia vulgaris,* showing general form, trigger-bristles, and aperture at narrow end (compare with Fig. 7.18 B) (×20).

Aldrovanda in an inorganic medium for as long as 2 years (Lloyd, 1942), Ashida (1934, 1935) was unable to grow it for even a week in any solution of mineral salts, unless these were supplemented with organic remains of other hydrophytes, such as *Typha,* amongst which it grew in nature. The experience of several workers suggests that *Utricularia* may differ from *Aldrovanda* in being able to grow vegetatively in the absence of organic matter and the microfauna which it supports. Pringsheim and Pringsheim (1962), for example, showed that specimens of *Utricularia gibba,* freed of all contaminants, may be grown in an inorganic medium containing potassium nitrate, calcium sulphate, ammonium phosphate and magnesium sulphate, to which is added a trace element solution supplying boron, cobalt, copper, iron, manganese, molybdenum, zinc and EDTA. At 20 to 26°C, pH 7·1 to 7·3, with artificial light for

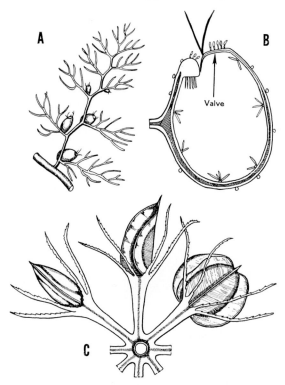

FIG. 7.18. A, *Utricularia vulgaris*: single leaf bearing traps (×2); B, *U. flexuosa*: diagrammatic L.S. trap, showing two-layered wall, internal and external glands, trigger bristles and valve (×20) (after Goebel, 1891–1893), C, *Aldrovanda vesiculosa*: three leaves of a whorl, showing bristles and various positions of the bilobed lamina: closed at left, partly open in centre, fully open at right (×2·5).

12 h/day, good vegetative growth is achieved. However, inflorescences are produced only if a mixture of meat extract and peptone is added aseptically to the basic medium.

Morphological Diversity in the Aquatic Species of *Utricularia.* Of more immediate concern is the bewildering plasticity of vegetative organisation, which creates vexed problems for both the taxonomist and the morphologist (Arber, 1920; Bouby, 1961; Taylor, 1961, 1964). In certain species of *Utricularia*, e.g. the north temperate *U. vulgaris* and *U. neglecta*, the body of the plant is more or less uniformly modified, all the lax cylindrical stems being of similar structure, each bearing two lateral rows of alternate, pinnately divided, green 'leaves' which carry numerous traps. The segments of the leaves are somewhat flattened and denticulate, with minute solitary or clustered bristles on the teeth. The main stem occasionally possesses a third row of rudiments, each of which develops into an erect, slender, whitish stem with very long internodes and two lateral rows of reduced mussel-shaped leaves which bear stomata. These curious stems, which do not arise in leaf axils, were first observed by Buchenau (1865) and were later called 'tendrils' by Pringsheim (1869) and 'air-shoots' by Goebel (1891–1893) who concluded from the protrusion of their tips into the air that they facilitate the oxygen supply to the submerged parts. Glück (1906) questioned their efficacy in this respect and considered them to be reduced inflorescences. He also showed them to be capable of forming ordinary vegetative shoots by apical growth. *U. vulgaris* and *U. neglecta* also show another type of modified branch, the so-called 'rhizoid', several of which usually appear from the base of the inflorescence axis (Buchenau, 1865). These are rather more rigid than the normal shoots and bear reduced leaves divided into claw-like groups of curved segments, which possess a great number of mucilage glands. Like the air-shoots, these rhizoids lack traps. Their function has been vaguely thought to be anchorage, but Glück (1906) pointed out that if this is so, they are remarkably ineffective. It is possible that, like the inflated whorled branches in the corresponding position in *U. inflata* var. *minor* and *U. stellaris*, they may help to keep the aerial inflorescence erect (Treviranus, 1848).

In the pan-tropical *U. gibba* and several related species, such as the African *U. cymbantha*, which is one of the smallest of the genus, the stems are very slender and filiform, the internodes very long, and the leaves only once or twice divided. Air-shoots are absent from this group of species but rhizoids are present, and are more numerous and better developed than in the *U. vulgaris* type (Lloyd, 1942).

U. oligosperma and its co-species, all large plants of South and Central America extending north to peninsular Florida, are notable for the marked dimorphism of their leaves. One type of leaf, generally lacking traps, is divided into many, long, spindle-shaped segments, whilst the other type is sparsely divided and bears numerous traps. The two types occur on distinct branches so that the body as a whole shows a clear differentiation into dense tufts of assimilatory leaves and groups of specialised trap-bearing leaves (Rossbach, 1939).

A different dimorphism is exhibited by the north temperate species *U. intermedia*, *U. minor* and *U. bremii*, in which one type of stem, responsible for assimilation, bears palmately divided green leaves lacking or having only occasional traps, whilst a second type bears extremely reduced colourless leaves with many traps. This latter type, distinguished as an 'earth-shoot', is usually buried in the substrate (although it may emerge from it) and effectively anchors the plant (Glück, 1913). Arber (1920) drew a functional parallel between the earth-shoot and the rhizoid-shoot of *Ceratophyllum*. Whether either organ in fact aids the absorption of nutrients is questionable.

The tendency towards anchorage is accentuated in the North American *U. resupinata* and the Australian *U. biloba* where nearly all the main stems are buried in the substrate; the leafy branches, or the leaves alone, projecting into the water. The erect leaves resemble those of terrestrial species more closely than those of other aquatic members of the genus, for they are simply divided into a few terete lobes which are usually trap-less. A further peculiarity is that in *U. biloba* a leaf lobe can develop into a stem. In both species traps are borne mainly on erect secondary stems (Goebel, 1891–1893; Lloyd, 1942).

A unique pattern of organisation is found in *U. purpurea* and several other species occurring only in the New World (Barnhart, 1916). The stems bear whorls of four to seven branches, each of which in turn produces irregularly spaced whorls of two to four or five branches of the third degree. Leaves of the type occurring in other members of the genus seem to be absent. The terminal part of each branch of the third or fourth order narrows into a filiform stalk which often bears a trap.

The morphology of the two species formerly segregated as *Biovularia* is somewhat reminiscent of *U. purpurea* because of the absence of leaves. However, both *U. olivacea* and *U. minima* are very delicate plants with the traps borne on simple, undivided stalks, which usually arise from the stem singly, or rarely in pairs (Lloyd, 1942).

One other aquatic *Utricularia* deserves mention. *U. tubulata* is the only aquatic member of a large group of Australasian species related by their trap structure: according to Lloyd (1942), it has never been collected since it was first found in 1875 growing in certain mountain swamps in Queensland. Its morphology is unusual. Each whorl on the long stem comprises four, linear, flattened leaves alternating with four, long-stalked traps: both the leaves and the stalks of the traps are basally united to form a sheath around the node.

Several much-cited species of *Utricularia* are transitional in habit between the truly aquatic and the obligate terrestrial or epiphytic types. Both *U. nelumbifolia* and *U. humboldtii* have been described growing in the water which collects in the axils of the leaves of certain members of the Bromeliaceae, such as *Brocchinia* and *Tillandsia*, whose foliage is clustered in large rosettes. *U. nelumbifolia* was found by Gardner (1846) in such a habitat on *Tillandsia* growing at an altitude of over 1600 m in the Organ Mountains of Brazil. It apparently produces, from the base of its inflorescence, numerous runners which reach into the water-filled rosettes of other neighbouring *Tillandsias* and there give rise to daughter plants. *U. humboldtii* was similarly found by Im Thurn and Oliver (1887), on the Roraima expedition of 1884, growing in the axils of *Brocchinia micrantha* on the Kaieteur Savannah of Guyana. In these strange associations the aquatic and epiphytic habits are combined: *U. humboldtii* also grows quite independently on swampy substrates.

This brief review of the principal patterns of vegetative organisation and habit is sufficient to indicate the amazing plasticity of the body of *Utricularia*. Apparent leaves often produce stolons which, in turn, may give rise to further leaves, or to traps, rhizoid-like branches or even inflorescences. Interpretation of the various organs is made more difficult by the frequent occurrence of transitional types of shoots: numerous so-called dimorphic species would indeed be described more accurately as polymorphic. In any descriptive account of *Utricularia* the terms stem and leaf are customarily used for convenience. Whether or not these organs are homologous with those of typical dicotyledons, and if they are not, how they may be acceptably interpreted, are moot points around which endless discussion has revolved. A consideration of the form, anatomy and development of the vegetative body and a reappraisal of the many inconclusive arguments put forward by earlier workers led Arber (1920) to the opinion that '. . . the attempt to fit so elusive a genus into the Procrustean bed of rigid morphology, is doomed to failure.'

It is generally agreed that the orthodox distinction of stem and leaf is transcended throughout the genus. However, the possible homologies of the stems, leaf-like organs, and traps of the aquatic species are controversial, and it is therefore impossible to assess the modifications associated with the aquatic, as distinct from the carnivorous, habit. Comparison of the aquatic with the terrestrial species sheds little light upon this problem for the latter are equally perplexing in their morphology. The tropical *U. subulata*, for example, has delicate filiform stems bearing very small, undivided, spatulate or ligulate leaves: traps occur on the stems and on the surface and margins of the leaves (Lloyd, 1942). The leaf-like organs of the epiphytic *U. jamesoniana* are of two types—elliptical and trap-less, and linear with marginal stalked traps (Skene, 1947). The rosette of foliage of the Australian *U. hookeri* and related species grows from a corm-like vertical axis and comprises three types of organ, identical in origin: anchoring, root-like stems; stalked traps; and linear, leaf-like organs (Goebel, 1898–1901). Another group of Australian species, exemplified by *U. dichotoma*, exhibit an additional type of stem, which is very much elongated and acts as a runner.

The position of the trap in such aquatic species as *U. vulgaris* suggests that each trap may represent a modified segment of a leaf (Goebel, 1891–1893), but its derivation in those terrestrial species where the traps occur individually on stalks from the stems, or in *U. purpurea* where they develop at the tips of stem-like branches, is much less clear. Anatomical and morphogenetic studies of trap development (e.g., Kurz, 1960; Abel and von Denffer, 1962) may ultimately help to resolve these difficulties of interpretation.

It may briefly be noted that the entire vegetative body of *Utricularia* has been variously interpreted as a dissected leaf, a modified root system, a wholly axial structure, or as a structure derived from both stem and leaves. Origin from a root system is highly unlikely, and the apical growth and development of whorled branches weigh heavily against origin from a leaf (Goebel, 1891). Compton's (1909) suggestion that the runners are caulome structures and the leaves are modified photosynthetic stems, i.e. phylloclades, has much to recommend it, at least so far as the terrestrial species with narrow leaves bearing marginal traps and the aquatic species of the *U. purpurea* type are concerned. The extreme plasticity and abnormal behaviour of many species militate against all the theories so far proposed. The problem of the morphological nature of the organs of *Utricularia* is thus still unresolved, and is likely

8*

to remain so for some considerable time. It is evident, however, that *Utricularia* represents the climax of evolutionary specialisation within the Lentibulariaceae. This conclusion is also supported by the comparative embryology of the family (Kausik, 1938; Khan, 1954).

Anatomical Features of *Aldrovanda* **and** *Utricularia.* Reaction to the aquatic environment is more easily discernible in the anatomy of *Aldrovanda* and *Utricularia,* both of which show several features familiar in submerged plants. Vascular reduction is evident in the leaves and stems of all species. The stem of *U. vulgaris,* for example, has a more or less central vascular cylinder surrounded by an endodermis (van Tieghem, 1868; Schenck, 1886). The few tracheids are weakly developed and surrounded by small groups of phloem elements. Although the general organisation of the stem is radial, the stele is slightly dorsiventral as a result of the presence in its upper part of fibrous ground tissue. The cortex of the stem is lacunate.

The leaf segments of most of the aquatic species of *Utricularia* are radially symmetrical. Schenck (1886) found that in *U. minor,* as in some of the highly reduced submerged monocotyledons, the epidermis is better developed and richer in chloroplasts than any other part of the leaf. The mesophyll contains four longitudinally-running lacunae and a single, minute, axial, vascular strand which comprises elongated thin-walled cells surrounding a central annular-thickened tracheid (Fig. 7.13). The midrib of *Aldrovanda vesiculosa* similarly carries but a single annular xylem element, although the phloem is relatively well-developed. In the thin marginal zone of the lamina, the upper and lower epidermes are contiguous but in the thicker zone near the midrib they are separated by a single layer of large thin-walled cells, which are elongated transverse to the long axis of the leaf. The cortex of the petiole contains numerous lacunae separated by partitions only one cell thick (Fenner, 1904).

LAND FORMS OF FREE-FLOATING PLANTS

It might be expected that the least modified free-floating plants, like rooted floating-leaved genera such as *Nymphaea,* would be capable of producing land forms. Since they normally possess aerial leaves, or produce them in crowded conditions, the change of habit from free-floating to terrestrial requires no profound modifications of structure. *Eichhornia crassipes* and *Pistia stratiotes* were noted earlier as capable of accomplishing the transition, specimens stranded on mud differing only in their somewhat dwarfed growth and lack of buoyant 'floats'. Most species of *Ceratopteris* similarly form close rosettes and survive quite well when they are rooted in waterlogged soil. Land forms have also been induced, and on rare occasions found in natural habitats, in species of *Trapa, Hydrocharis morsus-ranae* (Glück, 1906) and *Trapella sinensis* (Oliver, 1889).

Although the more reduced, surface-floating plants show increased adaptation to their habit they have not entirely lost the ability to produce land forms. Despite a high water content, e.g. 95·8 per cent in *Lemna minor* (Rickett, 1921), and a largely unprotected epidermis, species of *Lemna* and *Spirodela* living normally on the surface film are able to survive for a time if they become stranded. Guppy (1894) induced land forms of *L. minor* and *S. polyrhiza* on wet mud, and both grew actively, freely budding off daughter thalli, for more than a year.

With the assumption of a submerged habit, however, the facility with which land forms may arise is markedly reduced. *Lemna trisulca, Aldrovanda vesiculosa* and most of the aquatic species of *Utricularia* are unable to survive for more than a very short time on wet soil. In the rare land forms of a few species, such as *U. intermedia* and *U. minor* (Glück, 1906; von Luetzelburg, 1910), the foliage possesses stomata and develops as a short dense turf close to the substrate, thus resembling the land forms of other dissected-leaved hydrophytes such as *Myriophyllum*.

8

Vegetative Polymorphism and the Problem of Heterophylly

As early as the mid-sixteenth century the remarkable heterophylly of many common aquatic plants had caught the eye of European herbalists and botanical illustrators. A woodcut in Otto van Brunfels' *Herbarum vivae eicones*, published in 1530, depicted both the short-petioled, flaccid, submerged leaves and the more familiar, long-petioled, floating leaves of the Eurasian yellow waterlily *Nuphar lutea*. Henry Lyte's *Niewe Herball* of 1578, a translation of R. Dodoens' *Histoire des Plantes* (1557), carried a lively and observant account of the submerged capillary leaves and variously-lobed aerial or floating laminae of a batrachian *Ranunculus*, and some 45 years later Gaspard Bauhin gave the first prose description of a heterophyllous waterlily, actually *Nymphaea alba*, in his *Pinax Theatri Botanici* (1623). Early in the eighteenth century, the arrowhead *Sagittaria sagittifolia*, with its contrasting ribbon-shaped submerged phyllodes and sagittate emergent pseudo-laminae, was illustrated under the name *S. aquatica foliis variis* by Loeselius in his *Flora Prussia* (1703), and Scheuchzerus commented in 1719 upon the tendency of *Schoenoplectus lacustris* to produce floating as well as sparse aerial leaves. During the last 130 years or so, the heterophylly of these and many other hydrophytes has attracted sporadic attention and sorely taxed the minds and expertise of all who have tried to investigate and interpret it.

Heterophylly is not peculiar to hydrophytes. It also occurs in many terrestrial vascular plants, both woody and herbaceous. Heterophylly has been attributed in different aquatic and terrestrial species to internal causes, such as the age, genotype or nutrient status of the plant, and to the influence of environmental factors, notably the photoperiod, temperature or moisture conditions.

Arber's (1919a, 1920) general accounts of heterophylly are lucidly written, rich in examples, and still very pertinent, despite subsequent experimental findings. Reviews of certain aspects of the phenomenon have been written recently by Bauer (1952), Streitberg (1954), Sinnott (1960), Wangermann (1961), Davis and Heywood (1963), Allsopp (1955, 1965a, b) and Bradshaw (1965).

TERMINOLOGY AND DESCRIPTION OF HETEROPHYLLY

In current botanical usage, the term heterophylly embraces several related phenomena, which are all manifestations of foliar plasticity. These phenomena cannot be precisely defined, because of their intrinsically variable nature.

In its strictest sense, heterophylly means the presence on a single individual of two or more distinct types of leaf. These may differ markedly in shape, yet have similar gross anatomical organisation (e.g. the variously shaped submerged leaves of some species of *Cabomba, Ceratophyllum* and *Potamogeton*) or they may differ in habit and anatomy, yet be of comparable shape (e.g. the aerial and floating leaves of some species of *Nymphaea, Sparganium* and *Zizania*). In extreme examples of heterophylly, the leaf types differ in all three aspects— habit, shape and anatomy, and a full-grown plant may bear submerged, floating and aerial leaves. The change from one leaf type to another may be abrupt and easily recognised, or more gradual, with sequential intermediate forms.

Although one leaf form may be typically submerged and another floating or aerial, confusion is easily created if this apparent relation between form and habit is regarded as absolute and if the manner of growth and fluctuation of water level are not taken into account. In *Callitriche intermedia*, for example, the ascending shoot bears linear submerged leaves and obovate floating leaves (Fig. 8.1: A, B). Jones (1955a, c) pointed out that since the apical rosette remains on the surface provided that the water level does not rise, the elongation of the upper internodes causes the submergence of successive, older, obovate leaves. If the apex is submerged by a rise in water level it forms linear leaves above the formerly floating obovate leaves until it again reaches the surface (Fig. 8.1: C, D, E).

The heterophylly of some aquatic (and terrestrial) plants is often described as the foliar manifestation of heteroblastic development, i.e. an ontogenetic sequence in which early-formed 'juvenile' leaves are markedly different from later-formed 'adult' ones (Goebel, 1898–1901). What constitutes 'markedly different' cannot be rigidly defined: it varies with the morphological feature that is studied. Differences of outline shape, for example, may be immediately clear—as between the dissected fan-shaped laminae and the entire linear ones in *Cabomba piauhyensis*—but significant differences of stomatal frequency or size of epidermal cells may become evident only after a statistical survey. Whatever criterion is used, the greater the number of intermediate types the less abrupt and obvious are the transitions between them, and the more difficult it becomes to categorise the sequence as heteroblastic rather than homoblastic, in which there is just a very gradual elaboration of size and structure during ontogeny. It should be appreciated that the homoblastic and heteroblastic types of development are clearly separable only when they are treated as theoretical extremes. In practice, no really sharp distinction can be drawn.

In some hydrophytes a heteroblastic sequence is manifest regardless of the environment. The first-formed leaves of *Sagittaria sagittifolia*, for example, are invariably the normally submerged type, irrespective of whether the plant is in water or on land, and the later-formed ones are the floating or aerial type usually associated with the flowering phase. It should be realised, however, that there is no *a priori* reason to assume that the ribbon-shaped or dissected submerged leaves of all other heterophyllous hydrophytes are juvenile, or their laminate floating or aerial leaves necessarily adult. Nor is there any reason to

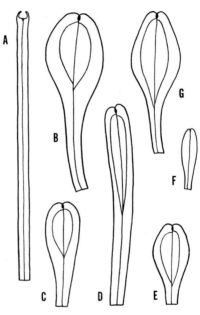

FIG. 8.1. Form and principal venation of the leaves of *Callitriche* spp. *C. intermedia*: A, extreme linear leaf from a submerged shoot in flowing water; B, extreme obovate leaf from a floating rosette in still water; C, leaf in a floating rosette; D, leaf formed after immersion of the floating rosette; E, leaf formed when apical rosette reached the surface of the water again. *C. obtusangula*: F, leaf from a submerged axillary shoot; G, leaf from a floating rosette. (A, B, ×3; C, D, E, ×3·2; F, G, ×2·4) (after Jones, 1955c).

invest the terms juvenile and adult with a quasi-fundamental importance. Although individual leaves, growing by diffuse meristems, have a determinate structure and life cycle (like most animals), the axial growth of vascular plants, maintained by terminal and lateral meristems, is essentially indeterminate. Consequently, it is not easy to recognise mutually exclusive juvenile and adult regions in vegetative shoots. It is sometimes stated or implied that adultness refers to the attainment of reproductive maturity. This criterion may be meaningful when animals are considered, but is still vague if applied to plants, which do not have persistent sex organs and may, as in numerous hydrophytes, be shy-flowering and primarily vegetative in mode of reproduction.

In its widest sense, the term heterophylly is applied to the capacity of many amphibious plants for developing contrasting vegetative forms in different microhabitats. All the leaves on a given individual may be identical in form, but the species as a whole comprises a spectrum of distinct vegetative variants, from permanently emergent 'land forms' to 'water forms' permanently submerged at considerable depths. Such polymorphism is exhibited by *Polygonum amphibium* (Massart, 1902; Turesson, 1961) and by certain species of *Callitriche*, *Elatine* and *Peplis* (Fassett, 1939a, 1951, 1957). Numerous plants which in normal conditions are heterophyllous (in the strict sense) can produce distinct but individually homophyllous forms in experimental environments or in unusual conditions in natural habitats. *Callitriche intermedia* and *C. obtusangula* are normally heterophyllous (Figs. 8.1 and 8.2) but they produce entirely broad-leaved land forms on marginal mud or entirely linear-leaved water forms submerged in deep flowing water (Jones, 1955c; David, 1958). *Sagittaria sagittifolia* in deep running water may form only very long ribbon-shaped submerged leaves, a state commonly described as f. *vallisneriifolia*. If re-immersed, land forms may again become truly heterophyllous, as also may water forms exposed to the air if the water recedes.

THE TAXONOMIC SIGNIFICANCE OF HETEROPHYLLY

Through the inability or omission of many botanists to distinguish experimentally between phenotypic and genotypic variation, and through their readiness to award vegetative variants of a species separate taxonomic recognition (as varieties, subspecies or even distinct species), the nomenclature and relationships within several hydrophyte groups have become notoriously chaotic. In this context, Schotsman (1954) spoke of the 'somewhat shady reputation' of the Callitrichaceae, and Cook (in Allen, 1963) called *Ranunculus* subg. *Batrachium* 'a morass of man-made confusion'.

Fassett (1951) described the bewildering polymorphism of many species of *Callitriche* (he illustrated no fewer than ten quite distinct individuals of *C. heterophylla*) and drew attention to the occasionally very close morphological similarities of ecological forms which really belong to different species. Schotsman (1961b) found little morphological difference between four karyotypes of *C. obtusangula* or between six of *C. stagnalis* in European populations. Savidge (1960) attributed the past confusion amongst European taxa largely to the existence of three closely related species (*C. polymorpha*, *C. platycarpa* and *C. stagnalis*), which he showed to be genuinely distinct by biometric studies of floral and other characters. All these workers have endorsed Pearsall's (1934) warning of the unreliability of identifications based wholly or primarily on leaf characters and the necessity for a classification based on fruit structure. Even this is seriously hampered by the frequent sterility of the water forms of normally ento- or anemophilous taxa.

Classification primarily by flower and fruit structure is similarly required in the batrachian *Ranunculi* because of the extreme phenotypic variation, complicated by genetically determined heterophylly in certain strains of some species.

Variants of some taxa, notably *R. aquatilis* and *R. peltatus*, are so distinct that they have been described in the past as quite separate species, e.g. *R. bauhinii*, *R. elongatus* and *R. truncatus* (Cook, 1962b, 1963; Clapham, 1962; Davis and Heywood, 1963).

Other genera of infamous taxonomic repute include *Potamogeton*, in which leaf form and anatomy may vary widely with age, water depth, current speed, nutrient supply, light intensity and perhaps other factors (Dandy, 1937;

FIG. 8.2. *Callitriche obtusangula*: aerial view of the water form in autumn, showing a summer rosette with rhomboid leaves (arrowed) and all other branches with linear winter leaves (×0·5). (From Schotsman, 1954, by courtesy of the author, the Royal Botanical Society of the Netherlands, and the Botanical Museum and Herbarium of the State University of Utrecht.)

Dandy and Taylor, 1938–1942; Clapham, 1962); *Sagittaria*, some species of which are remarkably constant in vegetative structure, others immensely plastic (Bogin, 1955); *Echinodorus*, in which only flower- and fruit-structure are of general taxonomic reliability, although Fassett (1955), following Micheli's original treatment of the genus, made interesting and valuable use of a microscopic leaf character—the form of pellucid markings visible in transmitted light; *Cryptocoryne*, a tropical Asiatic genus of which many species appear quite different when submerged from when partly or wholly emergent (de Wit, 1958a, b); and also *Hippuris*, *Elatine* and *Montia*. After an exhaustive study of the morphological plasticity of *Hippuris*, McCully and Dale (1961a, b) supported the recommendation of Polunin (1959) that *H. maritima*, *H. montana* and *H. tetraphylla*, distinguished by American botanists on the basis of leaf shape and number of leaves per whorl, should be considered as phenotypic variants of the sole, generally accepted taxon, *H. vulgaris*. Fassett (1939a) found that individuals of different species of *Elatine* cultivated in similar environmental conditions exhibited much closer resemblances than individuals of any single species grown in different conditions, e.g. fully submerged or stranded on mud. He therefore rejected vegetative organs and plant habit in favour of seed structure as a basis for classification. Walters (1953), de Jongh and Hegnauer (1963), and Moore (1963) have all emphasised that the limits of the phenotypic plasticity of the cosmopolitan amphibious *Montia fontana* have yet to be adequately determined.

SOME FURTHER EXAMPLES OF HETEROPHYLLY AMONGST HYDROPHYTES

In certain hydrophytes, notably the Nymphaeaceae, heterophylly is confined to the seedling stages, or to the earliest phase of growth from the perennating rhizome or tuber. The first leaf of the submerged seedling of *Brasenia schreberi*, for example, is usually subulate, the second linear-oblong with the short petiole attached to its lower end; the next four to seven leaves show a progressive broadening of the lamina, through an excentrically peltate condition, to the centrally peltate form of the floating leaves (Wood, 1959). The submerged seedling stages are somewhat similar in *Nymphaea* and *Nuphar*, in both of which a few short-petioled, translucent, sinuate, submerged leaves may be formed when the rhizome resumes growth each year (Fig. 8.3). These leaves are generally devoid of stomata and soon succeeded by the typical floating leaves (Costantin, 1886; Arber, 1920). In *Nelumbo* there is an abrupt change from the erect seedling to the horizontal 'juvenile' shoot: the first two leaves usually have floating excentrically peltate laminae whereas all the subsequent ones are emergent and centrally peltate (Wang, 1956).

In *Victoria*, too, the seedling displays an interesting morphological sequence from the acicular, bladeless, first leaf. The second leaf has a lanceolate blade, often with two hastate basal lobes and superficially resembling the typical

FIG. 8.3. Side views of young specimens of *Nuphar pumila* (A) and *Nymphoides aquatica* (B) with short-petioled, semi-translucent, juvenile, submerged leaves. The first floating leaf may be seen arising from the rootstock in the centre of B (both × 0·5).

leaves of *Barclaya longifolia*. In the third leaf the lamina is relatively wider, assuming a deltoid-hastate outline, the two auricles being basally fused to give an adaxial pouch near the attachment to the petiole. Further progressive fusion of the auricles is apparent in later leaves, which therefore tend more and more towards the mature orbicular peltate form, and are usually floating from the fourth one onwards. During its ontogeny, each mature leaf roughly recapitulates the morphological stages manifest in successive leaves of the seedling (Gwynne-Vaughan, 1897). In *Cabomba caroliniana* the first two or three pairs of leaves are lanceolate and devoid of laminae: they are succeeded by numerous leaves which have reduced laminae and are transitional to the typical paired submerged leaves whose laminae are finely dissected (Raciborski, 1894).

In *Ceratophyllum demersum*, the first few leaves of the seedling, as in *Cabomba*, are much simpler than the later typical foliage. The first node of the plumule bears two simple linear leaves decussately opposite to the cotyledons: the second node usually has three such linear leaves. From the third node onwards the leaves are forked or further divided, thus approaching the mature type, and borne in whorls of four or more (Schleiden, 1838). In the North American *C. echinatum*, however, forked or compound leaves are already present at the first node (Muenscher, 1940).

Leaf variation is confined to the seedling phase of a few *Callitriche* species: the later-formed foliage is not notably polymorphic even in widely different habitats. *C. stagnalis* first produces narrowly elliptical single-veined leaves which eventually give way to large, ovate, multiveined leaves reaching 2·5 cm long and 1 cm wide whilst the shoot is still submerged. The later uppermost leaves are usually smaller (about 10 mm by 7 mm) and form a floating rosette: they are strongly ovate to almost circular, and have at least five veins. This mature leaf form is not significantly altered by either prolonged immersion or complete emergence (Jones, 1955a, c, 1956).

Numerous aquatic monocotyledons similarly display a leaf sequence that may be interpreted as heteroblastic development. In the Pontederiaceae, certain emergents (e.g. *Pontederia cordata*) and floating species (e.g. *Eichhornia crassipes*) have submerged seedling stages showing a transition from the linear or spatulate first-formed leaves to the mature pseudo-laminate ones (Fig.13.5). The earliest leaves of *Ottelia* (Hydrocharitaceae) are typically linear to narrowly lanceolate and usually submerged: later ones show a successive broadening into a stalked ovate pseudo-lamina, and may be submerged, floating or aerial in habit. The Eurasian *Sagittaria sagittifolia* (Figs. 8.4 and 8.5) and the American *S. cuneata*, *S. intermedia* and *S. montevidensis* all typically form submerged, linear to narrowly lanceolate phyllodes; then stalked, oblong, ovate or cordate, floating leaves; and eventually stalked, sagittate, emergent leaves (Bogin, 1955). Arber (1920) noted that the leaves intermediate between the youngest ribbon forms and mature sagittate types display successive stages in the lateral expansion of the distal zone of the phyllode to give a wide pseudo-lamina, with accompanying outward curvature and apical separation of the veins. Two other widespread American taxa, *S. latifolia* and *S. rigida*, also have submerged linear leaves and emergent foliage but generally lack floating leaves. The emergent leaves of *S. rigida* possess linear to elliptical blades whilst those of *S. latifolia* show bewildering variations in different habitats and may be of any form from linear to ovate or sagittate (Bogin, 1955).

Broadly comparable maturity sequences may also be seen in *Luronium*, and some species of *Alisma, Aponogeton* and *Echinodorus*. The early-formed leaves

FIG. 8.4. *Sagittaria sagittifolia*: mature specimens bearing variously shaped floating leaves (lower half of photograph) and sagittate aerial leaves (upper half) (× 0·05).

of *Luronium natans* are generally submerged and reduced to linear, translucent, flattened petioles like those of *Sagittaria*: later, from either the rootstock or the ascending floating stems, long- or short-stalked leaves are formed, with lanceolate, elliptic or ovate, floating blades (Fig. 8.6). *Alisma plantago-aquatica* and *A. lanceolatum* are typically emergent in habit, with long-stalked, lanceolate to ovate leaves, rounded or sub-cordate at the base, but the first leaves formed each season, or in the developing seedling, often comprise no more than a hemicylindrical petiole, of which the distal part may or may not be flattened into a small, sometimes floating pseudo-lamina. The mature, lanceolate to ovate, floating leaves of *Aponogeton natans* are generally preceded by a variable number of submerged, linear to lanceolate, translucent, *Ulva*-like leaves with furled margins (Fig. 8.7). *Echinodorus nymphaeifolius* may be compared with several species of *Sagittaria* and *Alisma* in having thin, flaccid, ribbon-shaped, submerged leaves followed by long-petioled, emergent ones which are ovate

in shape and deeply cordate at their base. *E. berteroi* exhibits a more complete
leaf series: a shortening and widening of the blade and an increase in petiole
length accompany the transition from submerged to floating and ultimately
emergent forms (Fassett, 1955; and see Fig. 8.8).

The heterophyllous species and natural hybrids of *Potamogeton* typically
exhibit translucent, membranous, submerged leaves of linear to lanceolate-
elliptical shape, and much broader, coriaceous, floating leaf-blades which are

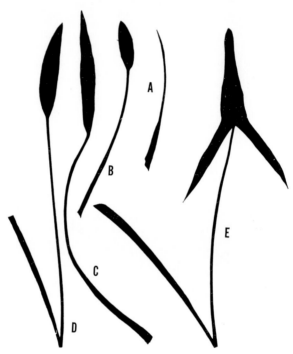

FIG. 8.5. *Sagittaria sagittifolia*: silhouettes of representative leaves from a specimen of
a cultivated strain which was grown in fairly shallow water, about 15 cm deep:
A, submerged leaf; B, C and D, floating leaves; E, aerial leaf (all ×0·4).

elliptical to oblong or strongly ovate (Figs. 8.9 and 8.10). Amongst the many
north temperate examples are *P. alpinus*, *P. amplifolius*, *P. capillaceus*, *P.
coloratus*, *P. epihydrus*, *P. gramineus*, *P. natans*, *P. nodosus*, *P. oakesianus*,
P. polygonifolius, *P. pulcher*, *P. spirillus*, *P. vaseyi*, *P. × nitens* and *P. × zizii*. In
some but not necessarily all of these taxa the leaf variation may be interpreted
as heteroblastic development. *P. perfoliatus* is distinct in being conspicuously
heterophyllous whilst exclusively submerged. Its sessile amplexicaul leaves
range in shape from narrowly lanceolate to ovate or orbicular, and are immensely variable in size.

There are many aquatic dicotyledons of caulescent habit which change the
character of their leaves when the shoot apex reaches the water surface and

emerges into the aerial environment. For as long as the shoot remains immersed the leaves are pinnatifid or much dissected into filiform, linear or spatulate segments, which are devoid of stomata and may vary in form in different habitats, often being much longer and more flexuous in deep, shaded, or placid water than in shallow, exposed, or flowing water. The floating or aerial leaves are often strikingly different in appearance: they may still be divided but with

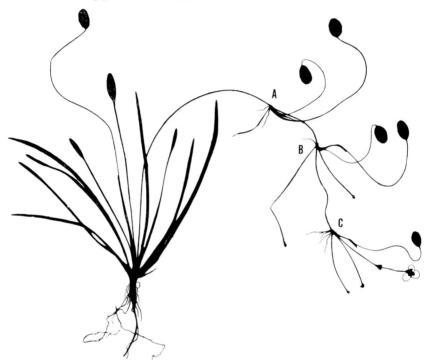

FIG. 8.6. *Luronium natans*: silhouette of submerged parent plant (at left) and an ascending stem bearing at each of the nodes A, B and C a rosette of floating leaves and flowers; parent itself shows transitions to floating leaves (×0·5).

smaller stouter segments, or they may be entire, with lobed, crenate, dentate or serrate margins. In some species they are conspicuously hairy, in contrast to the sparsely hairy or glabrous submerged leaves. Leaves of transitional form may be submerged, floating or aerial (Shull, 1905; MacDougal, 1914; Schaeppi, 1935; Streitberg, 1954).

Examples of this type of heterophylly may be seen in certain species of *Apium*—as *A. inundatum*; *Armoracia*—*A. aquatica*; *Cabomba*—*C. aquatica, C. australis, C. caroliniana*; *Hydrotriche*—*H. hottoniiflora*; *Limnophila*—*L. heterophylla, L. indica, L. sessiliflora* (Figs. 8.11, 8.12); *Megalodonta*—*M. beckii*; *Myriophyllum*—*M. brasiliense, M. heterophyllum, M. scabratum* (Figs. 8.12, 8.13); *Oenanthe*—*Oe. aquatica, Oe. fluviatilis*; *Proserpinaca*—

P. palustris; certain batrachian *Ranunculi* (Fig. 8.14); *Rorippa—R. amphibia*; *Sium—S. latifolium*; and *Synnema—S. triflorum* (Fig. 8.15). The floating leaves of *Cabomba* spp. and aerial leaves of *Megalodonta beckii* are not formed in many habitats and hence mature plants often appear homophyllous (Fassett, 1953, 1957). The leaves of *Sium latifolium, Oenanthe aquatica, Oe. fistulosa* and *Oe. fluviatilis* are all pinnately divided one or more times into paired sessile segments. On heterophyllous individuals in fairly shallow water, the first submerged leaves each season are often once-pinnate, with deeply incised

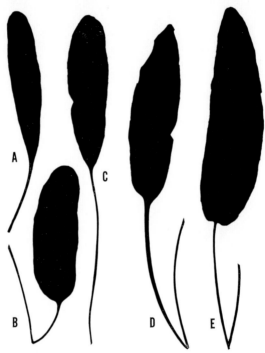

FIG. 8.7. *Aponogeton natans*: silhouettes of successive leaves: A to E submerged. (F, G and notes on facing page.)

segments; or twice- or thrice-pinnate, with capillary segments. Later, aerial leaves appear which may again be compound-pinnate, but with wider lanceolate segments which are deeply lobed or toothed: these may be succeeded by once- or twice-pinnate leaves, with ovate serrate segments. In other circumstances, e.g. totally immersed in deeper water or entirely emergent on damp soil, specimens may bear just one of these various leaf types (Shull, 1905; Arber, 1920; Tutin, 1962).

The heterophylly of some species involves an alteration of venation and other anatomical features with only relatively minor changes in gross shape. Although typically emergent, *Ranunculus flammula, R. lingua* and *R. sceleratus*, for example, can grow in considerable depths of water, producing submerged and floating or aerial leaves. The floating leaves may have a marked preponderance of stomata on their upper epidermis, whilst the submerged leaves, although not finely divided like those of the heterophyllous batrachian *Ranunculi*, are usually flaccid, relatively narrower and thinner, and possess few or no stomata (West, 1910; Glück, 1911; Arber, 1920). In *Hippuris vulgaris* the

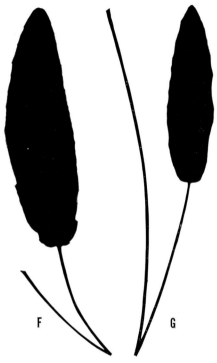

FIG. 8.7. *Aponogeton natans*: silhouettes of successive leaves: F, submerged; G, floating. The overall change in shape is less conspicuous than in many heterophyllous species but there are significant anatomical differences. The submerged leaves are thin, translucent, furled, and usually devoid of stomata, while the floating leaves are thicker, opaque, flat, more markedly dorsiventral in anatomy, and have stomata in the upper heavily cuticularised epidermis (all × 0·4).

lowest leaf-whorl subtending the rhizome has two or three reduced 'rhizome leaves', about 0·5 to 1·5 mm long and 1 to 2 mm wide. Under water, the ascending stems bear close whorls of long, flaccid, stomata-less leaves, 1·5 to 7 cm long and 0·75 to 3 mm wide, whilst above the surface they have relatively longer internodes and whorls of shorter rigid leaves, 0·4 to 3·5 cm long by 1 to 3 mm wide, bearing stomata (Costantin, 1886; McCully and Dale, 1961a). All the leaves of *Zizania aquatica* are linear to narrowly lanceolate. Under water, they are thin and lack stomata, whilst those that float on the surface have an unwettable, hairy, upper epidermis containing stomata, and those in the air are stiff, erect, and have stomata on both surfaces (Weir and Dale, 1960).

INTERNAL AND EXTERNAL FACTORS INFLUENCING HETEROPHYLLY

As many of the heterophyllous species mentioned in preceding pages have not yet received critical experimental study, it would be misleading to attempt a generalised explanation of the control of heterophylly in aquatic plants. Even

FIG. 8.8. *Echinodorus berteroi*: A, two specimens with juvenile ribbon leaves (× 0·4); B, one of the specimens in A, re-potted and grown on in the same water depth (30 cm), showing a transition through lanceolate to cordate leaves. Later cordate leaves are floating or aerial (× 0·25).

the limited investigations so far made are sufficient to show that no one mechanism is likely to operate in all instances, and that the underlying morphogenetic phenomena involve far more than a simple direct effect of a single factor in the internal or external environments of the plant. It is often extremely difficult to disentangle the several factors involved and separate sharply their causal effects. Full investigations of many more species, with finer analysis and experi-

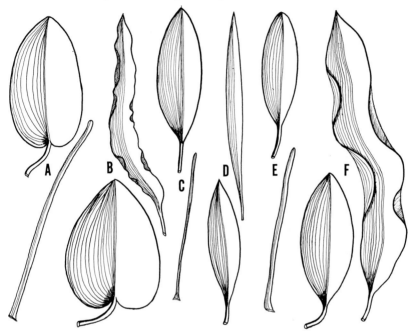

FIG. 8.9. Heterophylly in *Potamogeton* spp.: showing, for each of six species, a typical submerged leaf (linear to lanceolate) and a typical floating leaf-blade (elliptic to ovate); venation is indicated on only half of each leaf. A, *P. natans* (×0·6); B, *P. pulcher* (×0·75); C, *P. vaseyi* (×2·5); D, *P. gramineus* (×1); E, *P. spirillus* (×2); F, *P. amplifolius* (×0·5).

mental control of the environment, may eventually permit a more comprehensive elucidation of heterophylly. The following pages are devoted to a short review of present knowledge in the belief that, however incomplete, it holds considerable botanical interest, and in the hope that its very deficiencies and conflicts will stimulate further study.

Many workers have offered experimental evidence to support the interpretation of the heterophylly of some species as an ontogenetic sequence of the heteroblastic type. The crucial features of this evidence are: (a) the juvenile (usually submerged) leaf form is the first to appear whatever the environment; (b) the adult (usually floating or aerial) leaf form normally arises whilst the shoot apex is still wholly submerged; and (c) the adult leaves may sometimes themselves remain under water. These points preclude the possibility that the change in foliar characters might be wrought by a change from aquatic to aerial in the medium around the shoot meristem.

In numerous species of *Alisma, Aponogeton, Echinodorus, Luronium, Sagittaria* and the Nymphaeaceae, the submerged and floating or aerial leaves are distinguishable in the bud stage. The juvenile state persists in *Alisma plantago-aquatica, A. gramineum, Potamogeton natans, Sagittaria sagittifolia*

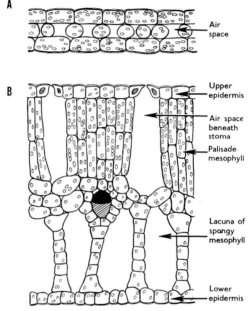

FIG. 8.10. *Potamogeton nodosus*: T.S. parts of submerged ribbon leaf (A) and floating leaf-blade (B), showing contrasting anatomy. Note reduction of submerged leaf to three cell layers with abundant epidermal chloroplasts: floating leaf with stomata in the upper epidermis, few epidermal chloroplasts, and well differentiated mesophyll; xylem of vascular bundle in solid black, phloem shaded (A, × 240; B, × 180) (after Streitberg, 1954).

and *Sparganium erectum* when the plant is immersed in deep or swift-flowing water, or grown in low intensities of white light, or in red or green light. In normal intensities of white light or generally in blue, the adult floating and/or aerial leaves subsequently develop (Goebel, 1880, 1891–1893, 1895, 1896; Glück, 1905, 1924; Funke, 1931). In these species and in *Eichhornia azurea* and *Hydrocleys nymphoides*, reversion to the juvenile ribbon-leaved state may be induced by immersing mature aerial-leaved individuals in deep or heavily-shaded water, or by drastically pruning their foliage or roots and transferring them to distilled water or barren substrates (Costantin, 1886; Wächter, 1897; Esenbeck, 1914). Goebel (1898, 1908), Vischer (1915), Troll (1937) and others have concluded that heteroblastic development is profoundly influenced by the nutritional status of the plant, conditions of poor nutrition created by depletion of carbohydrate and other reserves, weak light, removal of leaves etc. inducing the production of juvenile foliage.

FIG. 8.11. A, B, C, *Limnophila sessiliflora*: A, submerged shoots ($\times 0.4$); B, aerial shoots ($\times 0.4$); C, submerged foliage with axillary shoots bearing less-dissected leaves ($\times 0.3$). D, *Cabomba caroliniana*: shoot apex just below water surface showing dissected submerged leaves and first entire floating leaves about to expand from apical bud ($\times 0.6$).

Allsopp (1951–1955) and Edwards and Allsopp (1956) found that in sporelings of the amphibious pteridophyte, *Marsilea drummondii*, the heteroblastic sequence from the subulate first leaf through spatulate and bifid intermediate types to the quadrifid or quadrifoliate adult form could be affected by the composition of the aseptic culture media. Carbohydrate or nitrate starvation induces reversion to juvenile foliage and reduction from the solenostelic to the protostelic condition. As in certain heteroblastic land plants (see Wardlaw, 1965), lower sugar concentrations favour the juvenile, and higher sugar concentrations the adult, leaf forms. The absence of a nitrogen source from the medium prevents sporelings reaching the adult vegetative state. Whereas in a medium containing 1 per cent glucose the leaves produced are the quadrifid type devoid of stomata in the lower epidermis, as in natural water

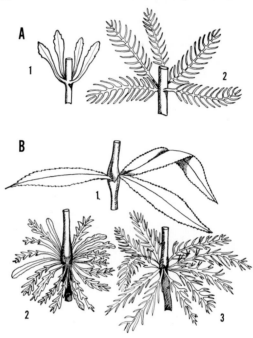

FIG. 8.12. A, *Myriophyllum spathulatum*: (1) aerial leaves, (2) submerged leaves; B, *Limnophila aquatica*: (1) aerial leaves, (2) transitional leaves, (3) submerged leaves (A, ×0·8; B, ×0·6).

forms of the species, raising the glucose concentration to 5 per cent produces, within the aqueous medium, the shorter-stalked quadrifoliate leaves with stomata in both epidermes, as typically found in natural land forms. This land type of leaf is also induced by high light intensities. Allsopp suggested that the structural differentiation distinctive of natural land or water forms is perhaps mediated through the carbohydrate balance of the plant. Factors retarding photosynthesis, or accelerating growth and consequent depletion of carbo-hydrate in growing tissues, result in the attainment of a lower level of differen-tiation. Modification of leaf segmentation is quite separable from changes in general morphology and anatomical differentiation. The first true leaf of sporelings in high sugar concentrations is invariably of the juvenile spatulate form yet highly differentiated in structure, whilst a later leaf of sporelings in low sugar concentrations frequently exhibits the adult quadrifid form yet may have only a low degree of anatomical differentiation.

The principal conclusion reached by Allsopp (1954a, 1963, 1964, 1965a) is that heteroblastic manifestations in *Marsilea* and other sporelings and seedlings are correlated with the progressive enlargement of the shoot apex, the degree of which is determined by protein synthesis there, which, in turn, depends upon the nutritional status, especially the carbohydrate and nitrate availability,

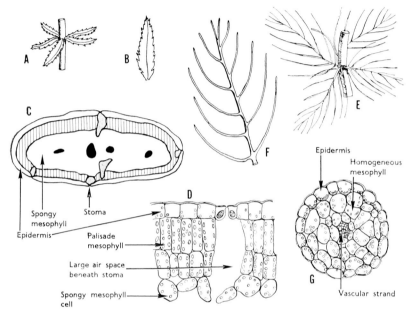

FIG. 8.13. Heterophylly in *Myriophyllum heterophyllum*: A, whorl of aerial leaves (× 0·8); B, single aerial leaf (× 1·5); C, diagrammatic T.S. aerial leaf (palisade mesophyll, vertical hatching; large air spaces, shaded; vascular tissue, solid black) (× 20); D, sector of upper part of T.S. aerial leaf (× 90); E, whorl of submerged leaves (× 0·8); F, single submerged leaf (× 1·5); G, T.S. segment of submerged leaf (× 150).

of the whole plant. Further evidence of the importance of protein synthesis was obtained recently by White (1966). He found that if thiouracil, an inhibitor of protein synthesis, is added to the culture medium, the rate of leaf formation by young sporelings of *Marsilea drummondii* and *M. vestita* is retarded and the leaves develop features typical of land forms. Water forms with adult leaves are converted to land forms in the presence of thiouracil. When similarly treated, land forms with adult leaves are less modified: their leaves appear to revert to the juvenile spatulate, bifid or trifid type yet retain the venation of the adult quadrifid type. White suggested that the rate of protein synthesis and consequent rate of growth may be more significant than slight changes in apical volume in the determination of land or water forms.

Allsopp's concept, unlike the earlier hypotheses proposed by Goebel and Troll, satisfactorily explains the fact that the first leaves of a lateral shoot (i.e. those formed whilst the apex of the axillary bud is still small) are often the juvenile type, even though the rest of the plant has adult leaves. This pheno-menon may be seen in numerous hydrophytes, e.g. *Limnophila* (Fig. 8.11),

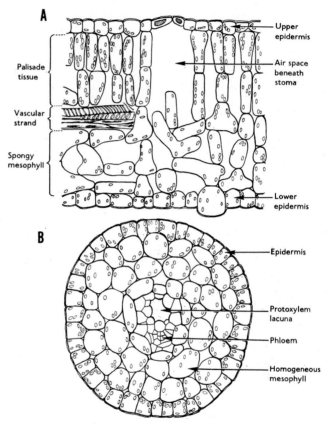

FIG. 8.14. T.S. leaves of a batrachian *Ranunculus* sp.: A, part of laminate floating leaf ($\times 120$); B, complete segment of capillary submerged leaf ($\times 250$).

Synnema (Fig. 8.16), *Cabomba* (Fig. 8.17), and in certain conifers and terrestrial angiosperms (see Ashby, 1948a, b; Sinnott, 1960).

In other experiments with *Marsilea*, Allsopp (1956a, 1959, 1962) investigated the effects of various growth substances. He suggested that the retarding effect of IAN, at a concentration of 10 ppm, on the heteroblastic leaf sequence, and its suppression of anatomical features typical of land forms, are indirect consequences of its great promotion of internodal elongation, which presum-ably drains the nutrient supply at the shoot apex. In a 2 per cent glucose medium the presence of gibberellic acid increases the rate of heteroblastic development, judged by the degree of leaf segmentation, but does not further accelerate the normally increased rate found in media containing 4 per cent glucose. At a concentration of 10 ppm, gibberellic acid exerts a powerful effect on the differentiation of land and water forms. It inhibits the development of features distinctive of land forms in sporelings grown in a high glucose concentration, which normally induces such features, and moreover, it transforms

FIG. 8.15. Heterophylly in *Synnema triflorum*: A, submerged shoot; B, two aerial shoots (both × 0·4).

land types, already developed in high glucose concentration, into water forms. These effects parallel those of IAN, high temperature or low sugar concentration, and in view of the apparently multiple and obscure influences of gibberellic acid on growth, flower induction and other morphogenetic phenomena, they cannot be simply explained. Allsopp rejected the notion invoked by some other workers, that gibberellic acid acts as a specific juvenility hormone.

In recent papers, Gaudet (1964a, b; 1965b) argued that in *Marsilea vestita* the numerous morphological differences between adult leaf forms could not be referred to changes in the size or cell division pattern of the shoot apex, because the primordia of aerial and submerged leaves show very close similarities until comparatively late in their development. The land form of leaf is notable for its heavily cuticularised epidermes with many stomata, whereas

the water-leaf epidermes have few stomata and are but lightly cuticularised: a
floating leaf has an upper epidermis of the land type and a lower epidermis of
the water type. Gaudet ascribed these anatomical distinctions, and also the
different venation patterns, to differences in the activity of the marginal meristem of the leaf. The typical venation of the land leaf appears to be due to the
more sustained life of this meristem than in the water leaf. The activity of the
marginal meristem seems to be inhibited by etiolation (Gaudet, 1965a).
Etiolated leaves resemble land leaves formed in the presence of light in having

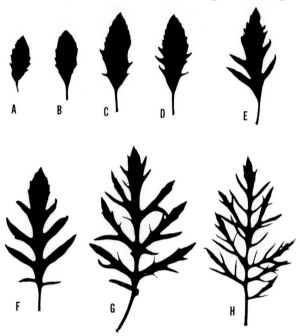

FIG. 8.16. Silhouettes of a series of leaves (A to H) produced on a submerged axillary
shoot of *Synnema triflorum*, showing transition from early, almost entire form to later,
much-divided form (all ×0·4).

long petioles and many stomata but differ in their venation pattern and in the
fact that their leaflets fail to expand. Darkness appears to induce some morphogenetic change which permits conversion of water forms into land forms. The
youngest uncoiled leaves of an etiolated submerged plant develop into land
leaves on subsequent exposure to light.

There are several other hydrophytes in which the shoot apex appears to
be of constant size during the formation of different leaf types. Furthermore,
the leaf primordia may be quite indistinguishable up to a certain stage in their
ontogeny. These taxa are principally species whose heterophylly appears to be
a response to emergence or submergence, e.g. *Callitriche intermedia, Hippuris
vulgaris* and *Ludwigia arcuata* (Fig. 8.18), although the distinct submerged and

aerial leaves of, for example, *Myriophyllum heterophyllum* and *Proserpinaca palustris*, have often been regarded in the past as forming a heteroblastic sequence.

According to McCallum (1902), primordia of *Proserpinaca palustris* can still change into either aerial or submerged leaves when they are as long as 3 to 4 mm. Burns (1904) stated that such primordia comprise a midrib and lateral lobes. Under water, the lobes merely grow into long filaments producing

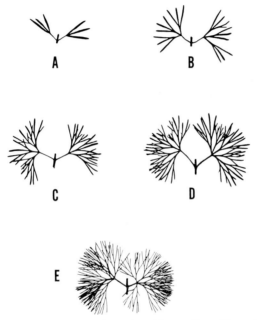

FIG. 8.17. Silhouettes of five successive pairs of leaves (A to E) produced on a submerged axillary shoot of *Cabomba australis*, showing increasing subdivision of the three primary segments of each leaf (all × 0·5).

the dissected aquatic leaf, whereas if the apex is above the surface laminar tissue becomes intercalated between the lobes and midrib, yielding the aerial leaf form. Askenasy (1870) found that young floating and submerged leaves of *Ranunculus aquatilis* are similarly indistinguishable up to a point when the presumptive submerged leaf ceases to change shape, its segments just increasing in size. Leaf primordia of *Callitriche intermedia* are identical as far back from the apex as the fourth pair, and there is no disparity of size or structure between the apical domes of linear-leaved and ovate-leaved shoots (Jones, 1955a, b, c, 1956). But whereas young linear leaves lie more or less parallel to the stem, young ovate leaves stand out at an angle of about 90°. Prompted by the remarks of Pearsall and Hanby (1926) on the relationship between the angle of vein-branching, the hydrostatic pressure in lateral veins and the extent of lobing of palmate leaves in the terrestrial *Aesculus* and *Vitis*, Jones suggested that in

9

C. intermedia the angle between the apical leaves and the axis may influence the form of the leaves.

In the transition from ovate to linear foliage occurring when floating apices of *Callitriche intermedia* are submerged, the intermediate leaves have attenuated bases and rounded tips, and the multiveined condition typical of ovate leaves persists into leaves of linear form. Conversely, the transitional leaves appearing

FIG. 8.18. Heterophylly as a response to submergence in *Ludwigia arcuata*: A, two aerial cuttings with narrowly lanceolate leaves (× 0·7); B, same two cuttings after submergence, showing change to longer linear leaves (× 0·5).

when a submerged linear-leaved apex reaches the surface are distally attenuated and broader at their base, but the numerous veins develop as soon as an ovate form is discernible: the one-veined state typical of linear leaves does not persist (Fig. 8.1). It is clear that primordial development may be modified at a late stage and that leaf form and venation are separately determined. The eventual structure of transitional leaves partly depends on the history of the primordium and is explicable only if leaf development is assumed to be basipetal. Cell enlargement begins earlier in linear than in ovate leaves, and follows a distinctly different path, yielding elongated rather than isodiametric cells. Cell division must also be important, since cell size does not alter significantly up to the stage where an ovate or linear shape is already evident (Jones, 1956). As determinants of leaf shape, cell division and cell enlargement cannot be sharply separated because division is not restrained by vacuolation and may proceed at a similar rate afterwards (Brown, 1956).

The leaf variation of *Myriophyllum heterophyllum* (Fig. 8.13), as of the foregoing species, cannot be attributed to changes in the structure of the shoot apex. Although its corpus is slightly variable, the apex shows no significant structural changes throughout the production of the different leaf types: submerged dissected leaves lacking stomata, transitional leaves with sporadic stomata, and aerial entire leaves which are amphistomatic (England and Tolbert, 1964). The same may be true of *M. brasiliense* and *M. scabratum*, which have a comparable apical organisation (Jentsch, 1960). Again, in *Ranunculus flabellaris*, a heterophyllous species outside subgenus *Batrachium*, there is no variation in the size or organisation of either submerged or terrestrial apices throughout the formation of the diverse leaf types. The leaf primordia, too, are similar up to the point where they have branched to give the three principal segments of the future leaf. Along these segments secondary lobes then appear in acropetal sequence, faster in a submerged than an aerial apex, and cell division is suppressed in the alternating regions, which ultimately become the sinuses of the leaf. The submerged, dissected type of leaf is produced as result of continued cell division in the elongating lobes and its inhibition along their margins. As in *Callitriche intermedia*, if the growing apex is put into the converse environment, transitional leaves are formed from primordia that have already been initated (Bostrack and Millington, 1962).

Hippuris vulgaris, in contrast, does show variation of apical structure. Submerged apices are larger than aerial apices and of a different shape: four, five and six layers have been reported in the tunica (Jentsch, 1960). But the leaf primordia, each of which originates by periclinal divisions of seven cells in the second cell-layer, are quite indistinguishable until they reach a length of 50 μ. During the growth of each primordium, leaf shape appears to be determined early; lateral vein, mesophyll and stoma development rather later; and the form of the epidermal cells later still. Transitional leaf forms afford a gradual sequence, not abrupt as in *Marsilea* and certain batrachian *Ranunculi* (McCully and Dale, 1961a, b).

It is apparent, then, that in certain hydrophytes foliar variation cannot be equated with heteroblastic development, and differences of shape or size in the shoot apex or early primordia cannot be invoked to explain it. The variation seems to be created by modification of the patterns of cell division and/or cell enlargement in the later stages of primordial growth. However, there still loom the questions: What are the environmental stimuli and how do they exert this morphological effect?

For some species, variations in salt supply, light intensity, photoperiod or temperature seem to be critical. The nutritional importance of calcium is well known: if this element is deficient, cell walls collapse, cytoplasm is affected and meristems tend to degenerate, these effects resulting in a spectacular distortion of vegetative organs, starting at the youngest leaves and root and stem apices. Through its role in the synthesis of structural components the calcium supply powerfully influences the growth rate of foliar primordia. In addition, calcium may affect the uptake of certain other ions from the medium. Pearsall and Hanby (1925) presented evidence that the heterophylly of *Potamogeton perfoliatus*, and the similar but less extreme leaf variation of *P. praelongus*, are due, at least in part, to variations in the potassium/calcium ratio in the substrate, especially if calcium is in short supply. In the presence of a large excess of potassium, the upper epidermal cells are longer and the palisade cells are of larger diameter, whilst broader leaves with more numerous cells are associated with an excess of calcium.

Changes in leaf shape in response to photoperiod have been reported in numerous terrestrial and aquatic plants, for example *Ipomoea nil* and *Proserpinaca palustris* (Ashby, 1950; Davis, 1956; Sinnott, 1960). In addition to photoperiod, temperature is important in *Ranunculus flabellaris*. Grown terrestrially at 28°C, this species bears the expanded laminate leaves typical of land specimens, but at 16°C the leaves are dissected and comparable to those of submerged forms. Conversely, submerged shoots grown at 16°C have the normal dissected foliage, but at 28°C produce expanded leaves tending towards the characteristic land form. The deeply dissected submerged leaves appearing naturally in spring may be attributed, at least partly, to the effects of short days and low temperatures on the distribution and frequency of cell divisions in the primordia, and the expanded aerial leaves of summer to the effects of long days and higher temperatures. Seasonal rise and fall in day-length and temperature are probably responsible for the production, in either water or air, of forms intermediate between these extremes (Bostrack and Millington, 1962). A temperature effect comparable with that in *R. flabellaris* has also been described in *Oenanthe*: Combes (1947) found that low temperatures induced the production of the deeply incised, compound-pinnate type of submerged leaf.

Preliminary studies similarly suggest that in certain heterophyllous batrachian *Ranunculi*, e.g. *R. baudotii*, *R. lobbii*, *R. ololeucos*, *R. peltatus* and *R. tripartitus*, the form of the leaves produced by a normally submerged plant is under the primary control of photoperiod and temperature. Both the dissected submerged type of leaf and the laminate floating type are initiated under water. In these species leaf morphogenesis evidently proceeds along one of two sharply delimited pathways, for the change from one leaf type to the other is very abrupt; sequential intermediate types do not occur. The strict pattern of behaviour may, however, be upset by abnormal circumstances. If the shoot apex is experimentally raised out of the water it strangely produces dissected leaves of the aerial type, not laminate leaves (Cook, 1963). The stimulus of photoperiod may also influence specimens under terrestrial conditions. When grown fully emergent in a warm mist, *R. aquatilis* produces in long summer days leaves that resemble those of the typical land form, but in short winter days its leaves resemble the typical submerged form (Davis and Heywood, 1963).

Certain experimental and natural phenomena suggest that the aquatic or aerial nature of the medium may itself affect leaf variation. These phenomena are not fully explicable at present: further analysis is needed to discover whether they are really due to the actual water content of the medium or to other factors which may simultaneously change with the transition between water and air. Bostrack and Millington (1962) were unable to induce, by low temperature treatment alone, the most extremely dissected forms of submerged leaves occurring naturally in *Ranunculus flabellaris* at certain times of the year. That the water relations between the environment and the shoot apex or leaf primordia are significant is also suggested by the relative ease with which aquatic leaf types may be induced on land forms of *Hippuris vulgaris*, *Limnophila heterophylla*, *Myriophyllum brasiliense*, *Proserpinaca palustris*, *Ranunculus baudotii* and several other species grown in an atmosphere of high humidity (Burns, 1904; Goebel, 1908; Woltereck, 1928; Gessner, 1940; McCully and Dale 1961b). Yet this may not be a simple effect; other factors may interact. Growing *Hippuris vulgaris* under a continuous mist, McCully and Dale found that whereas in a light intensity of 5380 lux mainly aquatic leaves appear, in 10 760 lux many shoots develop the broad aerial form of leaf. They found no evidence, however, to support the idea that the change from submerged to aerial leaves might be correlated with the higher oxygen tension of the aerial compared to the aquatic medium.

Experimental induction of aerial leaves under water is more difficult to accomplish. Using *Myriophyllum brasiliense*, Goebel (1908) and Woltereck (1928) succeeded only with shoots in which aerial leaf primordia had already been initiated during exposure above the surface. As mentioned earlier, Allsopp (1955) induced land forms of *Marsilea drummondii* in aqueous media of high osmotic (glucose) concentration. Similarly, McCallum (1902) induced aerial leaves on submerged-leaved shoots of *Proserpinaca palustris* immersed in a nutrient solution of osmotic concentration just lower than that causing plasmolysis. Comparable results have been obtained with submerged-leaved shoots of *Callitriche intermedia* and *Hippuris vulgaris* in diluted sea water of high osmotic concentration (Jones, 1955b; McCully and Dale, 1961b). Although these induced leaves in *C. intermedia* approach the typical, ovate, floating, leaf form and have numerous stomata, they are smaller, possess only a single vein and curiously undergo much more expansion in some cells than in others.

These experimental phenomena seem to indicate that aquatic leaf types are initiated in the presence of excess water and aerial leaf types in conditions where water is in shorter supply and tends to be lost. Media of high osmotic concentration, favouring a diminution of cell turgor, are perhaps comparable physiologically with the normal aerial environment, into which water is lost by transpiration. In contrast, either in an atmosphere of high humidity or under water, the great reduction or complete inhibition of transpiration will, together with the higher osmotic concentration within the plant (at least in freshwater species), favour maximum turgidity. With reference to *Callitriche intermedia*, Jones (1955b) suggested that cell turgor pressure might influence leaf form through its effect on the production and control of auxin. Whether or not auxin is a mediator, it is pertinent to note that whilst the concept of osmotic and turgor relations permits a reasonably acceptable explanation of immersion and emersion effects

in those species in which cell *enlargement* is principally involved in the development of different leaf types, it is less convincing where, as in *Ranunculus
flabellaris*, modification of cell *division* patterns is mainly responsible. Nor will
it suffice to explain the natural occurrence, during summer months in northern
latitudes, of aerial-type leaves on submerged shoots of *Hippuris vulgaris*
(Costantin, 1886) and *Proserpinaca palustris* (Burns, 1904), for there is no
reason to suppose that the water at that season in any way approaches experimental media of high osmotic concentration. This natural phenomenon is
perhaps attributable to a photoperiodic-temperature effect as in *Oenanthe*
and the *Ranunculus* species discussed.

Transpiration losses and turgor relations certainly seem to influence internodal elongation in at least one plant with submerged stems and floating apical
rosettes. McComb (1965) found that floating shoots of *Callitriche stagnalis*
grow rapidly if transpiration is prevented by smearing their leaves with Vaseline.
Shoots grown in air of high relative humidity were seen to reach almost twice
the length of shoots grown in dry air over a similar 5-day period. Treatment of
floating rosettes with gibberellic acid has the same result as the suppression of
transpiration: internodal elongation is stimulated and the treated shoots come
to resemble those normally formed under water by submerged apices. McComb
suggested that the normal elongation of submerged shoots is probably due to a
relatively high internal gibberellin content associated with the inhibition of
transpiration: when the apex reaches the surface, transpiration begins and the
rate of gibberellin synthesis falls, reducing internodal elongation and so causing
the formation of a floating rosette. Although the nature of the hypothetical link
between transpiration or turgor relations and gibberellin synthesis is quite
obscure, it is interesting to note that McComb's findings are congruous with
Allsopp's observations on the effects of gibberellic acid on land forms of
Marsilea.

THE ADAPTIVE AND EVOLUTIONARY SIGNIFICANCE OF HETEROPHYLLY

In his *Philosophie Zoologique*, Lamarck (1809) regarded the leaf variation of
the batrachian *Ranunculi* as induced by the environment. Numerous later
botanists, subscribing to the Lamarckian view that direct modification of the
phenotype could be important in evolution, have likewise interpreted the submerged leaves of heterophyllous hydrophytes as an adaptive response to an
aquatic medium, and the emergent leaves as a similar response to an aerial
medium. It is now clear, however, that this simple notion cannot be applied to
all examples of heterophylly. It is true that in some plants leaf variation appears
to be influenced by environmental factors, but these stimuli may not necessarily
be associated with the aquatic or aerial nature of the medium: the critical
factor may be temperature or photoperiod rather than water supply. In other
plants comparable phenotypic differences may be manifest irrespective of
external factors: the leaf types may be distinguishable at the earliest primordial
stage, and may be determined by the nutritional status of the shoot meristem
or the genetic constitution of the individual.

The survey of foliar plasticity in the preceding pages of this chapter has given weight to Arber's (1920) remark: '. . . for the old conception of heterophylly as *induced* by aquatic life, we should substitute the idea that such a difference between the juvenile and mature forms of leaf as would render the juvenile leaf well suited to life in water, has been in many cases one of the necessary preliminaries to the migration from land to water, and that the aquatic Angiosperms thus include, by a process of sifting, those plants whose terrestrial ancestors were endowed with a strong tendency towards heterophylly.' Heslop-Harrison (1953b) expressed a similar view in slightly broader terms: 'The great phenotypic plasticity of aquatic or amphibious flowering-plants (and also of certain ferns occupying similar habitats) is possibly connected with the fact that these habitats have been adopted *secondarily* by plants already adapted to a terrestrial habitat.'

There is perhaps a further important dimension to the understanding of heterophylly in aquatic vascular plants. Some of the species which have been discussed appear to have a set sequence of leaf types, from submerged to floating and/or emergent, and do not alter very much, if at all, as a result of changes in environmental conditions. The sequence is usually ontogenetic, the juvenile submerged leaves appearing first, in or out of water, and the adult aerial leaves appearing later, often just prior to flowering. Although the sterile juvenile state may sometimes be prolonged by immersion in very deep water or under low light intensities, mature plants when reimmersed do not readily revert to juvenile foliage without harsh experimental conditioning. These heteroblastic plants thus have an innate but strictly limited phenotypic variability, which is an integral feature of their ontogeny and is not significantly influenced by the environment. Such species may, in consequence, have only a limited ecological amplitude. Yet they could be highly successful colonists, forming extensive stands which reproduce efficiently within a confined range of habitats. Most of them seem to be particularly suited to shallower marginal waters. Here, their ribbon-leaved juvenile phase is probably able to compete with obligate submerged plants and may have a selective advantage over the seedlings of non-heterophyllous emergents, whilst their adult phase will be able to photosynthesise, flower and achieve pollination in the aerial environment. Species of this type might be described (with hindsight) as being preadapted to their ecological niche.

Although it may be ecologically restricting, heteroblastic development could conceivably have great evolutionary potential, via neoteny. This phenomenon, in the broadest sense (see de Beer, 1958), involves the retardation of somatic development relative to reproductive development, with the result that reproductive maturity is attained whilst the body is still in a juvenile vegetative state. Plants with a heteroblastic mode of development could give rise, by neoteny, to a whole new line of specialised forms able to reproduce sexually in a vegetative state equivalent to the ancestor's juvenile phase. It is interesting to speculate on the possibly neotenous origin of certain hydrophytes which, as flowering adults, strikingly resemble the seedling or juvenile phases of closely related species. The dwarfed eastern Asiatic *Sagittaria pygmaea*, which flowers whilst bearing only submerged ribbon leaves, may perhaps be a neotenous descendant of the heterophyllous Asiatic *S. trifolia*. Davis and Heywood (1963) commented on the resemblance of vegetative structure between flowering adults of the submerged or floating *Sparganium minimum* and seedling stages of the emergent *S. erectum*. The Lemnaceae and *Pistia* afford a further example (p. 290). The possible significance of neoteny in angiosperm evolution has been explored very fully by Takhtajan (1959a, b), who effectively developed Arber's (1920) theme in suggesting that the aquatic flowering plants generally may have evolved by neoteny from heteroblastic terrestrial ancestors.

In contrast to the species with a more or less fixed ontogenetic variation, other heterophyllous hydrophytes seem to have the ability to respond freely to environmental changes. Amongst the batrachian *Ranunculi* there appear to be marked differences in the extent of foliar plasticity, both between species and between populations of a species. These differences are permanent, and hence must be genotypically determined. They may have some adaptive significance. Cook (1964a) observed that certain species, e.g. the heterophyllous *R. baudotii*, are suited to an aquatic existence; and others, e.g. the laminate-leaved *R. hederaceus*, to emergent or terrestrial life. He found that the fertile F_1 hybrid of *R. baudotii* and *R. hederaceus* is morphologically intermediate between its parents and does not thrive either in water or on exposed soils. When selfed, however, it yields an F_2 of groups of individuals which are mostly dissimilar from either parent: many of these appear suited to aquatic or terrestrial habitats which are not normally colonised by either *R. baudotii* or *R. hederaceus*. The phenotypic variations of the heterophyllous species are genuinely plastic responses, not sequential phases of ontogeny. Even so, they are somewhat limited. The change of leaf form probably involves an abrupt switch from one sharply defined morphogenetic pathway to another in response to day-length and temperature, a stimulus which is not directly related to the aquatic or aerial nature of the environment. Bradshaw (1965) suggested that control of the mechanism by an indirect, rather than a direct, stimulus may be advantageous, especially in moving water where the shoot apices trail and oscillate in the current and the stimulus of the water surface is unlikely to be clear-cut. Such a mode of control could be disadvantageous, however, because of the inability of the plants to respond appropriately to sudden drastic changes in water level. The heterophyllous species belonging to subg. *Batrachium* are probably best-suited to marginal habitats with shallow water: they are not notably successful in deep or fast-flowing water or on exposed wet soils.

Finally, there are those heterophyllous hydrophytes in which phenotypic changes may be stimulated by the degree of submergence or emergence, with or without the interaction of photoperiod and temperature as indirect stimuli. Their leaf morphogenesis is evidently less rigidly directed: between the typical submerged and floating or aerial forms numerous sequential intermediates may be produced. These species often display an astonishing degree of plasticity and seem able to exist in a variety of terrestrial, emergent, floating, shallow-water and deep-water states. As a result of their free and appropriate responses

to changes in water depth they may well have a much wider ecological amplitude than other heterophyllous hydrophytes.

NEOMORPHOSIS IN AQUATIC PLANTS

It may be of some interest, in the general context of vegetati\e plasticity, to
mention briefly the unusual morphogenetic phenomena observed recently by
Miettinen and Waris (1958) and Waris (1959, 1962). Seedlings of *Oenanthe
aquatica* were cultured in aseptic nutrient media supplemented with sucrose
and glycine or arginine. After 3 to 4 months of normal growth, they entered a
long period of morbidity, at the end of which embryonic nodules were spon-
taneously constricted from the tips of their lateral roots. These nodules grew
vigorously, exhibiting a completely new pattern of development, and reached
a level of differentiation comparable to cotyledon-stage seedlings, but with
rather poor roots. At all developmental stages multiplication occurred through
the detachment of further nodules from colourless epidermal outgrowths of
the narrow or broad green leaves.

The morphological effects induced by the amino acids were so profound that
these new individuals, or neomorphs, which reached a length of a few centimetres, no longer manifested the specific or generic characters and were scarcely
recognisable even as belonging to the family Umbelliferae. They also differed
from the normal plants in being apparently adapted to submerged growth and
in containing significantly greater amounts of free amino acids. Transfer to
normal media, lacking glycine or arginine but containing sucrose, promoted
growth, notably in the roots, and after some 4 months certain plants began to
form normal leaves. Ribose added to the basic medium accelerated the transition to normal growth but inhibited increase in size.

In a medium supplemented with leucine instead of glycine, seedlings of *Oe.
lachenalii* produced on their *shoot* apices embryonic nodules which developed
into neomorphs rather different in structure from those of *Oe. aquatica*. These
seemed to have lost the ability to form roots, had undergone some increase in
chromosome number, and showed no transition to normal growth after transfer
to leucine-free media.

Waris discussed the phenomenon of neomorphosis, which he also induced in
carrot seedlings, in relation to the much less profound morphological effects of
amino acids described by previous workers in such plants as the pea and tobacco.
He concluded that various vegetative organs are differently influenced by
amino acids, the meristems being exceptionally plastic, and he surmised that
differentiation in plants may depend upon physiological antagonism and
equilibria between intermediary metabolites, especially sugars and amino
acids, at particular cell organelles, such as the nucleus, ribosomes, mitochondria
and plastids.

9*

Sexual Reproduction and
Natural Affinities

It is in their reproductive phase that vascular hydrophytes betray their terrestrial ancestry with the greatest clarity. Whereas their vegetative organs show discrete and even profound modifications of form and anatomy in reaction to the aquatic environment, the reproductive organs are remarkably similar to those of related land plants in both general organisation and microscopic structure. The contrast is perhaps most vivid in certain specialised free-floating angiosperms: the submerged vegetative body of *Utricularia* is rootless and so drastically modified that stems and leaves are not easily distinguished, yet the flowers are aerial, entomophilous and clearly similar to those of *Pinguicula* and other members of the Lentibulariaceae.

The prime interest of the reproductive phase of all the aquatic ferns except *Ceratopteris* lies in their heterospory, a habit of rich evolutionary potential. Otherwise, their reproductive organisation exhibits many parallels with that of the higher leptosporangiate land ferns.

The flowers of the overwhelming majority of aquatic angiosperms are adapted to aerial life, with either insects or wind as pollinating agents. Modifications directly related to the aquatic habit affect not the flowers themselves but their associated peduncles, leaves or lateral shoots, which may assist the elevation and equilibrium of the flowers above the water. The genera of various aerial-flowering families may be arranged in morphological series exhibiting trends of structural modification and pollination similar to those discernible amongst terrestrial angiosperms: reduction and specialisation of floral parts, substitution of anemophily for entomophily, abandonment of cross- for self-pollination in either chasmogamous or cleistogamous flowers.

The ultimate adaptation to aquatic life is the formation of wholly submerged hydrophilous flowers. Conceivable stages in the transition to this advanced habit may be seen in families of the Najadales, genera of the Hydrocharitaceae and species of the unigeneric Callitrichaceae. It is possible to trace a series from entomophily and anemophily through hydro-anemophily, in which the stigmas are raised to the surface and the floating male flowers or floating pollen carried to them by wind, water currents or surface tension, to truly submerged pollination, in which the liberated drifting microspores are individually filiform or adherent in long chains and become entangled amidst the typically filiform, feathery or peltate stigmas. Transitions from emergent and floating-leaved to submerged habit, from hermaphroditism to dioecism, from radially symmetrical (actinomorphic) flowers to highly reduced, bilaterally symmetrical (zygomorphic) flowers, and from freshwater to brackish-water and marine existences run more or less parallel to the trend in mode of pollination. True hydrophily is found only in *Althenia, Ceratophyllum, Najas, Ruppia, Zannichellia*, ten marine genera and several species of *Callitriche*. The probable affinities of these few specialised plants support the belief that hydrophily and marine life are both recently acquired habits and that the former is a prerequisite for the latter. It must be appreciated, however, that the arrangement of geologically modern taxa in morphological series has no valid phylogenetic significance. It increases comprehension of similarities and distinctions between discrete types of floral structure and pollination behaviour and illustrates conceivable courses of specialisation. But the sequences do not imply direct descent of the advanced reduced taxa from the less specialised or even necessarily from a common ancestral stock.

I INITIATION OF REPRODUCTIVE GROWTH

THE INFLUENCE OF EXTERNAL FACTORS, ESPECIALLY DAY-LENGTH

For many years botanists believed that the transition from vegetative to reproductive growth occurred in response to changes in the nutrition of the plant. Grainger (1947) applied this concept to the summer-flowering habit of most temperate submerged angiosperms, suggesting that only in summer, when days are relatively long, is there sufficient net accumulation of carbohydrate to provide for the development of flowers. Now there is evidence that in some hydrophytes the initiation of the reproductive phase may depend upon nutrition. *Utricularia gibba*, for example, cultured aseptically, flowers only if the basal inorganic medium adequate for vegetative growth is supplemented with organic nitrogenous matter, such as sterilised dead *Daphnia* or a mixture of peptone and beef extract (Pringsheim and Pringsheim, 1962; Harder, 1963). The carnivory of the plant may thus be indispensable in natural habitats for the fulfilment of its life cycle. In *Marsilea*, the formation of sporocarps is favoured by strong illumination (presumably encouraging higher rates of photosynthesis). In fairly low light intensities sporocarps develop on adding 5 per cent sucrose to the culture medium (Allsopp, 1951).

For some hydrophytes, however, as for many land plants, the decisive factors stimulating reproductive growth may be the photoperiodic rhythm and/or temperature. Intensity of illumination may influence the subsequent development of reproductive primordia, higher intensities favouring higher rates of photosynthesis and permitting the maturation of a greater number of reproductive organs. The summer-blooming temperate hydrophytes may be long-day plants, whilst the relatively few spring-flowering species, such as *Hottonia palustris* and several batrachian *Ranunculi*, could be short-day plants. The response of tropical hydrophytes might be expected to be short-day or day-length-indifferent.

There is little evidence yet to support or refute these suggestions: the physiology of reproduction has been studied in very few hydrophytes and the sparse data do not permit generalisations. The north temperate emergents, *Phalaris arundinacea* and *Rorippa nasturtium-aquaticum*, are known to be long-day plants in which the photoperiodic response is independent of temperature (Spector, 1956; Bleasdale, 1964). A photoperiodic response may also be involved in the apparently exceptional carnivorous *Utricularia*. The flowering of *U. gibba* in a supplemented medium observed by Pringsheim and Pringsheim (1962) occurred in artificial light given for 12 h each day. Harder (1963) subsequently obtained maximal flowering under an 11 h photoperiod: application of gibberellin failed to promote flowering, an effect noted also with several short-day land plants. Flowering of the tropical and subtropical *Eichhornia crassipes* seems to be influenced by temperature rather than day-length. Hitchcock *et al.* (1949) found that flowers appeared provided the minimum night temperature did not fall below 21°C: if it fell to 16°C plants would not flower, whatever the daily period of illumination.

The study of many tropical hydrophytes is handicapped by their notorious reluctance to flower in cultivation. Many members of taxonomically confused genera such as *Anubias*, *Aponogeton*, *Cryptocoryne*, *Echinodorus* and *Lagenandra*, imported into Europe as aquarium plants, prove difficult to cultivate and often remain unidentified until the rare occasions on which they bloom. Specimens of one aroid, for example, grown by European aquarists for several years, had been thought by some authorities to belong to *Lagenandra* until an inflorescence appeared in an aquarium and enabled the material to be identified as *Cryptocoryne versteegii* (van Ramshorst, 1957b). After much experiment, Legro (1955) devised a technique for cultivating amphibious species of *Cryptocoryne* as emergents, and simulating the fluctuations of temperature and humidity they probably experience in natural habitats in India, Ceylon and south-east Asia. In this way he induced the Sinhalese *Cryptocoryne nevillii*, for example, to bloom. Initially, flowering appeared to be induced by the simulated dry season but later experiments (Legro and de Wit, 1956) revealed that rigorous drying-off is unnecessary and that *C. nevillii* is in fact a short-day plant flowering only in a photoperiod of less than 12 h: two other tropical species, *C. beckettii* and *C. willisii*, proved to be daylength-indifferent.

Rarity of flowering, together with profound morphological reduction, has also created an acute taxonomic problem in the Lemnaceae. However, these plants are eminently suitable for laboratory studies of the physiology of flowering because of (a) the ease and rapidity with which large clones may be cultured aseptically on nutrient media under stringently controlled conditions, and (b) the fact that floral and vegetative primordia may be distinguished easily without elaborate dissection, especially in *Wolffia* where they develop at different sites on the thallus. Flowering *in vitro* has been achieved and intensively studied in two species of *Lemna* (reviewed by Hillman, 1961b, c, 1962b; see also Matreyev, 1963) and one of *Wolffia* (Maheshwari and Chauhan, 1963). In these species the transition from vegetative to reproductive growth involves complex and sensitive photoperiodic responses.

Kandeler (1955) found that *Lemna gibba* (strain Gl) would flower in long or continuous photoperiods of daylight-fluorescent illumination if the medium had been aged, by the growth of cultures in it for several weeks, but would not flower in any photoperiod if the medium was frequently changed. The critical day-length at about 30°C was 12 to 14 h. Hillman (1958, 1959a, b, 1961a) confirmed this behaviour in *L. gibba* (strain G3), and also discovered a conditional short-day response in *L. perpusilla* (strain 6746). This species flowered whatever the photoperiod when grown on a simple Hoagland-type culture medium at 25 to 27°C, but its sensitivity to long photoperiods was inhibited when EDTA (or other chelators) was added to the medium, for it then responded as a typical short-day plant, flowering maximally in a photoperiod of 10 h. Addition of EDTA to fresh media enabled *L. gibba* to flower as a long-day plant, i.e. it imitated the 'aged medium effect'. Hillman suggested that aged media may contain natural chelators.

Recently, greater purification of the medium has been shown to have the same effect as high concentrations of chelators, i.e. *L. gibba* becomes a long-day, *L. perpusilla* a short-day plant. Low concentrations of cupric ions (2 μM/l.) added to purified media reverse the effect, so that *L. perpusilla* again becomes daylength-indifferent whilst *L. gibba* will not flower in any photoperiod (Hillman, 1962a). It is probable that chelators added to fresh media, or naturally present in aged cultures, form stable complexes with metallic ions such as copper, which evidently contaminate all but the highly purified media, and thus prevent them interfering with the photoperiodic sensitivity of the plants. Hillman suggested that copper may block the reversible phytochrome pigment system, assuming this to be involved in *Lemna*, creating a condition normally existing only in short-days so that *L. gibba* no longer flowers but *L. perpusilla* will flower, irrespective of the actual photoperiod. He also suggested that copper may accomplish this physiological effect by interfering with iron metabolism. Evidence that iron is involved in the photoperiodic mechanism (perhaps in the actual phytochrome system) had previously come from the demonstration that the short-day response of *L. perpusilla* on a well-chelated medium is inhibited by a deficiency of iron not low enough to affect vegetative growth (Hillman, 1961d).

The early studies of Kandeler and Hillman showed that *L. gibba* and *L. perpusilla* afford interesting examples of opposite photoperiodic behaviour within a single genus and also that *L. perpusilla* is one of the select group of short-day plants sensitive to just one photoperiodic cycle. Further evidence of the complexity of the responses and their probable mediation by the phytochrome system has come from the effects of interrupting the dark period and of applying different qualities of light. Flowering of *L. perpusilla* in short days is abolished by exposure to red light (540 to 695 mμ) in the dark period (Hillman,

1958, 1959a). The inhibitory effect of red light is maximal 9 h after the start of the dark period (Purves, 1961). This time-dependent sensitivity is somewhat similar to that of *Xanthium*, the cocklebur (see Salisbury, 1963). The fact that the red-light inhibition in *L. perpusilla* is not reversed (as it is in numerous short-day plants) by subsequent exposure to far-red light (695 to 800 mμ) is strongly reminiscent of the behaviour of the short-day Japanese morning glory, *Ipomoea nil* (see Nakayama, 1958), as also is the remarkable inhibition of flowering by far-red light, especially early in the dark period, which *is* reversible by subsequent exposure to red (Purves, 1961). Purves considered it unlikely that two pigments are involved and suggested that both the reversible far-red inhibition and the irreversible red inhibition involve the phytochrome system. Just how these complex effects might be mediated is not yet known.

Exposure to far-red light early in a non-inductive long dark period promotes flowering in some long-day plants, e.g. the dill, *Anethum*, and the henbane, *Hyoscyamus*. Kandeler (1956) found that *Lemna gibba* flowered rapidly on fresh media if the light source was relatively rich in far-red wavelengths and that exposure to far-red at any time up to about the middle of a non-inductive long dark period promoted flowering, but did not ascertain whether this promotion was reversed by subsequent exposure to red light.

In recent experiments Oda (1962) was unable to confirm Hillman's report that the photoperiodic response of *Lemna perpusilla* 6746 is affected by the presence of EDTA in Hoagland-type media. In Oda's cultures the strain behaved as a typical short-day plant under white fluorescent light even in the absence of EDTA, but showed a conditional response in other light qualities. In red or green light a short-day response was shown, but in blue or far-red light the plant was daylength-indifferent: in no case was the response modified by adding EDTA to the medium. In a later paper, Esahi and Oda (1964) described certain effects of light intensity and of external sucrose concentration.

Further doubts about the effects of EDTA were raised by Umemura *et al.* (1963) who found that *L. gibba* G3 behaved as a long-day plant regardless of the presence or absence of EDTA in the medium. Similarly, Kandeler (1962) reported that the induction of flowers in *L. gibba* G1 under short-day conditions by the addition of EDTA or by exposure to white light rich in far-red wavelengths did not occur invariably: in some experiments the stimulatory effect was quite absent. In a subsequent paper, Kandeler (1964) acknowledged that the results of his earlier experiments appeared to have been greatly influenced by the atmospheric carbon dioxide concentration which had not been controlled. It therefore seems possible that the conflicting results obtained by other workers may be due to unsuspected variations in carbon dioxide concentration or some other environmental factor.

Wolffia microscopica behaves in culture as a short-day plant, requiring at least one cycle with a minimal dark period of 12 to 14 h. EDTA added to the medium promotes flowering irrespective of the photoperiod, whilst addition of the recently isolated zeatin initiates flowering under a long-day regime, a profound effect unique amongst kinins (Maheshwari and Chauhan, 1963; Maheshwari and Venkataraman, 1966).

Little is known of the significance of micronutrients (other than copper or iron) or growth promoters in the flowering of *Lemna* and other hydrophytes. Flowering of *Spirodela polyrhiza* is apparently promoted by molybdenum deficiency (Yoshimura, 1943b). Application of gibberellins in concentrations promoting vegetative growth actually inhibit the initiation of flowers in short-day or daylength-indifferent *L. perpusilla*, an effect that is not fully understood (Hillman, 1960a).

Photoperiodic responses are probably involved in the initiation of the reproductive phase in some aquatic pteridophytes. *Salvinia natans*, for example, appears to be a short-day plant (Nakayama, 1952). In nature, sporo-- carps appear in photoperiods of 13 h or less: they may be induced experimentally under a short-day regime of 7 h light/17 h dark, two cycles being sufficient to induce sporocarps in 80 per cent of specimens, seven cycles eliciting a 100 per cent response. Nakayama demonstrated that the photoperiodic stimulus is perceived by the floating leaves: it must be transmitted in some form to the growing points of the submerged leaves, which is where the sporocarps are actually initiated. Shibata (1958, 1959, 1961) obtained evidence that a balance of certain organic acids may influence sporocarp formation.

REPRODUCTIVE MATURITY AND PRECOCIOUS FLOWERING

There is evidence that in certain hydrophytes, as in some terrestrial angio-sperms, the ability to reproduce is related to the age of the plant, a minimal vegetative or juvenile period elapsing before flowers ever appear. However, this relationship is variable and is not yet comprehensible in the context of the effect of ecological factors. The tropical *Nymphaea lotus*, *N. rubra* and *N. stellata*, for example, flower within 12 to 16 weeks of germination whereas in the temperate *N. alba* and *Nuphar lutea* about 3 years elapse before flowers are first produced (Heslop-Harrison, 1955a, b; Cutter, 1957a). Is this dis-parity a simple reflection of the slower growth rate in cool temperate waters or are specific differences of physiological organisation also involved? In some genera displaying heteroblastic development, e.g. *Sagittaria*, flowers are typically associated with adult emergent foliage. It would be valuable to discover whether flowering is under photoperiodic control in these species and if so whether the juvenile foliage is sensitive to photoperiodic induction. It is conceivable that the submerged leaves are sensitive but that either the light filtering through to them does not contain adequate inductive wave-lengths or the appropriate photoperiodic regime only occurs later in the growing season so that in natural habitats flowers always appear when emergent foliage has developed.

In some taxa, however, juvenile specimens do reproduce. Both *Alisma gramineum* and *Nuphar lutea*, for example, can flower when they possess only submerged foliage (Arber, 1920). Van Steenis (1957) drew attention to several particularly interesting tropical hydrophytes which grow in ricefields during the three to four months when the crop is inundated. If they are to survive, these species must reproduce before the fields are drained: they therefore flower precociously whilst still in a juvenile vegetative state, and consequently they differ in appearance, sometimes to such an extent that they have been described as distinct taxa. *Elattosis apetala*, which Gagnepain described from Tonkin (Indo-China) as a new monotype in the Butomaceae, has proved to be a dwarfed specimen of the palaeotropical *Tenagocharis latifolia* collected after anthesis, and similar to the juvenile flowering forms of this species reported from India and Africa (van Steenis, 1954). Plants described as *Monochoria linearis*, *M. pauciflora* and *M. plantaginea* were recently recognised as precociously flowering narrow-leaved specimens of *M. vaginalis*, whilst *M. australasica* appears to be a submerged or juvenile form of *M. cyanea* (Backer, 1951f). Similarly, the African *Limnophyton parviflorum* and the Indo-Chinese *Caldesia sagittarioides* are juvenile flowering forms of the palaeotropical *L. obtusifolium* (den Hartog, 1957a). Cleistogamous flowers are frequently produced by ribbon-leaved dwarf specimens of *Ottelia ovalifolia* (Ernst-Schwarzenbach, 1956). The induction of precocious flowering and modification of growth habit by ecological and climatic factors are thus of great physiological and taxonomic interest.

THE ORIGIN OF FLORAL PRIMORDIA

Morphological aspects of the transition to reproductive growth in hydrophytes have received even less attention than physiological topics. In most hydrophytes, as in angiosperms generally, inflorescences or flowers are usually axillary or rarely terminal, in which case the vegetative growth of the axis is resumed by the development of one or more lateral buds. The aerial flowering nodes of the axis of many submerged plants often have reduced scale-like leaves and are more or less discretely separated from the submerged sterile nodes by a few nodes with intermediate-type leaves. Emergent or land forms of such plants usually show no such differentiation of fertile and sterile parts, axillary flowers being formed at even the lowermost nodes of the plant, as in *Myriophyllum brasiliense* and *M. verrucosum*.

In several geophytic genera of the Nymphaeaceae, however, the flowers are not axillary and are not produced from detached meristems: they arise on the apical meristem itself. In *Nuphar* and *Nymphaea* they occur in leaf sites in the genetic spiral, the exact sequence of leaves and flowers varying between species. Sometimes vegetative buds occupy prospective flower sites, which suggests that the physiological requirements for bud inception are not grossly different from those for flower formation (Cutter, 1957a, b; 1959; Chassat, 1962). Flowers and leaves are formed in separate spirals at the rhizome apex in *Euryale* and *Victoria*. Occasionally a flower is missing from its prospective site but the general organisation of the apex is not disrupted. Later-formed flowers still arise in their normal morphological position, to the anodic side of the axil of an older leaf, indicating that the site of origin of any given flower is more intimately associated with the leaves than with previous flowers (Cutter, 1961). Wang (1956) noted that in *Nelumbo nucifera*, the flower bud appears to the dorsal side of the leaf base, not in the axil. It is remarkable that in these genera the apical meristem produces both leaves and flowers and also continues its own indeterminate growth. Its complex and perhaps unique physiology must involve a specific and finely balanced oscillation between the conditions inducing flowers and those inducing leaves (or buds), in order to create the regular temporal and spatial sequence of these organs (Dormer and Cutter, 1959; Cutter, 1961, 1965).

In most aquatic angiosperms the flowers probably mature and expand in one single season but in some rhizomatous species floral primordia may remain dormant for a period. Grainger (1947) suggested that in *Nuphar lutea*, for example, this dormant phase extends from the summer of inception to the following spring but Cutter (1957a) has shown that in both *N. lutea* and *Nymphaea alba* it may be as long as three or four years.

II CERTAIN ASPECTS OF THE REPRODUCTION OF AQUATIC PTERIDOPHYTES

The following remarks concern the unique character of the reproduction of the several aquatic genera and their resemblances to, and differences from, other pteridophytes. Complete descriptive accounts of the minutiae of their reproductive cycles are readily accessible in such standard texts as Eames (1936), Smith (1938), and Foster and Gifford (1959), and in the original literature.

The spore-producing organs of *Ceratopteris, Marsilea, Pilularia* and *Regnellidium* are aerial, developing only when the plants are emergent or floating on the surface, whereas in *Salvinia* and many species of *Isoetes* they are formed under water. The free-floating *Azolla* resembles the former group for its spore-containing organs appear in the axil of the dorsal aerial leaf-lobe.

THE ISOETACEAE

In its heterospory and possession of solitary sporangia on the adaxial surface of its sporophylls, *Isoetes* resembles both the living *Selaginella*, and its fossil relatives, and also the fossil Pleuromeiaceae. It differs from all these, however, in not having its sporophylls aggregated into discrete strobili. Each leaf is a potential sporophyll. In any one season, the first-formed leaves are usually sterile: within these are, successively, leaves with megasporangia, leaves with microsporangia, and the innermost youngest leaves whose sporangia usually abort. This arrangement, with the megasporophylls below (i.e. outside) the microsporophylls, is comparable with that of *Selaginella*, if allowance is made for the fact that in *Isoetes*, because of the condensation of the axis, the leaves are all crowded in a rosette at the shoot apex (Smith, 1900; and see Figs. 6.6, 9.1).

The huge sporangia of *Isoetes* are basically the eusporangiate type, arising from several initials and having a several-layered wall. When mature, they differ from those of all other living lycopods, but resemble those of the Pleuromeiaceae, in having incomplete partitions (trabeculae) derived from plates and columns of potential sporogenous cells that remain sterile. The functional significance of these trabeculae, which are more numerous in megasporangia, is not understood: they may perhaps aid mechanical support or increase the surface area of the nutritive tapetum (Smith, 1900; Eames, 1936). During megasporogenesis in some species, the meiotic division is abnormal and involves no reduction in chromosome complement: each mother cell divides to form two diploid nucleate megaspores and two abortive enucleate ones (Pant and Srivastava, 1965).

Desiccation can play no part in the dehiscence of the sporangia of submerged species. The spores are liberated by the eventual decay of the sporophyll. In a few species with buried axes, the sporophylls absciss the following spring by a swelling of mucilaginous cells at their base, and as they rise to the surface of the water the sporangia rupture (Osborn, 1922). The spores are probably dispersed for short distances by waves, currents and disturbances of the substrate. Although mega- and microsporangia are of similar size, the megaspores are very much larger than the microspores and their cytoplasm is rich in food reserves.

The dioecious gametophytes of *Isoetes* may develop within a few days of liberation of the spores, or after a longer delay. In mode of development they resemble those of *Selaginella* in being essentially endosporic, but in structure they are more reduced and specialised. Unique amongst vascular cryptogams, the male gametophyte produces only four antherozoids, and these are multiflagellate, in contrast to the 128 or 256 biflagellate antherozoids of *Selaginella* (Liebig, 1931). The female gametophyte resembles that of *Selaginella* in its robust cellular structure, but its free surface, which is exposed late in development after fracture of the ridge of the megaspore wall, bears fewer archegonia (LaMotte, 1933). Since fertilisation is probably achieved only when antherozoids are liberated close to a megaspore, there may be considerable wastage of gametophytes. The embryogeny of *Isoetes* is broadly comparable with that of *Selaginella*, except for the conspicuous absence of a suspensor (Liebig, 1931; LaMotte, 1933).

The many aquatic and few terrestrial species of *Isoetes* constitute a morphologically uniform and apparently natural genus, which seems to have a basic chromosome complement of $n = 11$. Some species may be high polyploids, e.g. *I. lacustris*, which has $n = 54$ to 56; some may be aneuploids, e.g. *I. hystrix*, which has $n = 10$ (Manton, 1950; Pichi-Sermolli, 1959). Certain recently studied Indian species form a series of diploids, triploids, tetraploids and hexaploids (Pant and Srivastava, 1965). Until quite recently, *Isoetes* appeared to be the only living genus of the family Isoetaceae. Just over 10 years ago, however, a new genus was described, and named *Stylites*. This comprises two species, *S. andicola* and *S. gemmifera* (regarded as conspecific by some writers), which were found living on the margins of lakes at an altitude of about 4750 m in the Andes of central Peru (Amstutz, 1957; Rauh and Falk, 1959). In view of the marked resemblances of leaf and root structure between these plants and *Isoetes triquetra*, a species which also lives in the South American High Andes, Kubitzki and Borchert (1964) recently wondered whether *Stylites* ought to be maintained as a distinct genus or included in *Isoetes*. There are, however, several structural differences which justify the generic segregation. *Stylites* differs from *Isoetes* in the morphology of its megaspores, and even more conspicuously, in gross habit. The shoot axis of *Isoetes* is normally un-branched (in rare exceptions the apex may dichotomise and form two rosettes of leaves, but even then the 'corm' does not become fully divided), whereas in *Stylites* the axis regularly dichotomises at least three times and a leaf rosette arises from the apex of each branch. A further morphololological distinction is that in *Stylites* roots develop from only one side of each portion of the branching axis (Rauh and Falk, 1959).

The Isoetaceae stands distinct and remote from all other living lycopods. With even the Selaginellaceae, it has only two important features in common: heterospory, a habit which has certainly developed numerous times in unrelated vascular plants, and the presence of a ligule on the adaxial surface of the leaf base, a character which, on its own, is hardly adequate to indicate close natural affinity. The differences between the two families are numerous and striking: in the root system, sporangia, gametophytes and antherozoids, the Isoetaceae is clearly distinct and more specialised than the Selaginellaceae.

The phylogenetic affinities of *Isoetes* and *Stylites* probably lie rather with the heterosporous fossil lycopods of the Pleuromeiaceae and, more remotely, the Lepidodendrales (Mägdefrau, 1931; Eames, 1936; Smith, 1938; Alston, 1959b; Andrews, 1961). Conspicuous resemblances between these various groups may be seen in such morphological features as the form and proportions of the leaves, the presence of a ligule, the trabeculate solitary sporangia which are usually adaxially positioned on the sporophyll, the production of more than four megaspores in each megasporangium, the differentiation of the lower part of the axis as a permanent root-bearing structure (the rhizophore), and the arrangement of the roots and their stigmarian-type anatomy (with a small, excentric, monarch stele). There are, however, important differences in the structure of the rhizophore and the gross habit of the plant. These differences suggest that the various genera ought not to be regarded as forming a con-tinuous evolutionary sequence, and indicate that the Pleuromeiaceae is probably closer to the Isoetaceae than to the Lepidodendrales. The lepidodendrid rhizophore comprised four, very long, root-bearing branches which radiated horizontally from the base of the aerial trunk. Each branch was often remotely dichotomised, and it increased in girth by secondary vascular growth and periderm formation. The rhizophore of the Pleuromeiaceae, although still massive, was very different in form: its four arms were very short, unbranched, and upwardly curved. Such fossil rhizophores are probably entirely stelar in nature, any soft cortical tissues being lost during preservation. If the outer parenchymatous tissues are removed from the 'corm' of *Isoetes*, the lower radiate portion of the stele looks quite remarkably similar to the rhizophore of the Pleuromeiaceae.

Pleuromeia lived during Triassic time, and there is some evidence to support the belief that it inhabited the margins of pools in salt marshes or deserts. It grew to about 2 m in height and might be regarded as a very small descendant of

the enormous arborescent lepidodendrids of the Carboniferous. The unbranched form of its stem suggests that its ancestors probably had a habit
resembling *Sigillaria* rather than *Lepidodendron* or *Bothrodendron*, in both of
which the aerial trunk was freely branched. *Nathorstiana*, a second member of
the Pleuromeiaceae, was a lower Cretaceous plant and markedly smaller than
Pleuromeia, with an unbranched erect stem only a few centimetres tall. It
therefore provides a connecting link between *Pleuromeia* and the living *Isoetes*
and *Stylites*, in which the shoot axis and rhizophore are so reduced and tele-
scoped that they are no longer externally distinguishable: the axial differentiation survives only in the form of the stele.

The sequence: Lepidodendrales (*Sigillaria*-type)→*Pleuromeia*→*Nathorstiana*→*Stylites*→*Isoetes* is a plausible, though incomplete, morphological
series. Direct descent along this line is highly unlikely. There is clearly a very
great gap between the lepidodendrids and *Pleuromeia*: such a line of evolution
must have involved profound reduction and modification of both stem and
rhizophore. The later links in the sequence are also unlikely to have been
direct, for discoveries of fossil material suggest that the Isoetaceae had already
attained its present morphological organisation by the middle of the Mesozoic
era, i.e. about the time that the Pleuromeiaceae flourished (Andrews, 1961).
The sequence of genera merely suggests, in terms of known plants, certain
possible types of organisation through which evolutionary specialisation culminating in the contemporary Isoetaceae might have proceeded. Accepted as
such a morphological series, rather than as a direct phylogeny, it supports the
general notion that *Isoetes* and *Stylites* are probably relict dwarfed herbs of
perennial rosette habit, derived by neotenic reduction from ancient arborescent
lepidodendrids.

THE CERATOPTERIDACEAE

The homosporous *Ceratopteris* is the least specialised of the aquatic ferns.
Although it exhibits a conspicuous differentiation of fertile and sterile leaves,
its sporangia are not grouped in sori: they merely lie scattered and remote in
rows on the abaxial surface of the finely-divided aerial sporophylls, and are
more or less covered by the revolute margin of the leaf segment; there are no
protective indusia (Fig. 9.2). Sporangial development is the strictly leptosporangiate type characteristic of higher terrestrial ferns. In some species an
almost complete annulus is present in the mature sporangium, but in others it
is entirely absent. Wind disperses the spores. The independent gametophyte
bears both antheridia and archegonia. It is exosporic in development and
occasionally lacks an apical cell, e.g. in *C. thalictroides* (Pal and Pal, 1963). The
marginal antheridia do not protrude beyond the prothallial tissue as they do
in most leptosporangiate ferns.

Species of *Ceratopteris* probably form a polyploid series with a basic haploid
chromosome complement of $n = 40$ (Pal, 1959; Pal and Pal, 1962, 1963). The
diploid complement of the much-studied *C. thalictroides* has recently been
shown to be $2n = 80$. Earlier estimates of a haploid number between 76 and 78,

as obtained by Ninan (1956), Javalgekar (1960) and others, were probably derived from tetraploid specimens (Pal and Pal, 1963). Whatever the cytogenetic relationships of the various species ultimately prove to be, the genus as a whole undoubtedly has very close morphological affinities, in both sporophytic and gametophytic phases, with the higher leptosporangiate ferns of the Polypodiaceae *sensu lato* or Adiantaceae, to which families it has actually been transferred by some authorities (Christensen, 1938; Holttum, 1949; Stokey, 1951).

THE HETEROSPOROUS AQUATIC FERNS

The five remaining aquatic genera differ strikingly from other leptosporangiate ferns in being heterosporous and producing their spores in a very specialised organ, the sporocarp. *Marsilea, Regnellidium* and *Pilularia* seem to be closely related and are usually grouped together as the family Marsileaceae. They produce at the base of their petioles hard, globose or ovoid-oblong, short-stalked sporocarps, which are borne solitarily, as in *Pilularia, Regnellidium* and most species of *Marsilea* (Fig. 9.2), or in groups of two to twelve or more, as in a few species of *Marsilea*, e.g. *M. quadrifolia* and *M. polycarpa*. Sori develop on the inner surface of each half of the sporocarp. Each sorus is the gradate type (sometimes tending towards the mixed type) as in the more specialised land ferns, and is covered by a pouch-like indusium which at its free end adjoins the sporocarp wall (Fig. 9.1).

The bilaterally symmetrical sporocarp is now generally agreed to be of laminar origin but the possible manner of its derivation has long been a topic of lively controversy. Johnson (1933) interpreted the sporocarp to have been derived from a complete leaf, chiefly because of its similar apical growth. But its vascularisation, comprising a single main vein originating from one end of the stele of the petiole and giving off, alternately to right and left, dichotomously branching lateral veins, strongly suggests it originated from one or more basal segments (pinnae) of a leaf. On this hypothesis its formation could have been due to apposition of a pair of pinnae (Büsgen, 1890; Johnson and Chrysler, 1938); to the adaxial infolding of a single pinna (Campbell, 1905; Bower, 1926) or to the infolding of a compound basal pinna with several bilobed pinnules bearing sporangia on the inner margins of the lobes. This last notion, advanced by Puri and Garg (1953), gives the most satisfactory explanation of the exact location of the sori in relation to the vascular bundles of the sporocarp.

Since other ferns lacking sporocarps are homosporous (except for *Platyzoma*, a dioecious member of the Polypodiaceae with incipient heterospory: see Tyron, 1964), it has often been suggested that the sporocarp arose during or after (but not before) the evolution of heterospory, but there is no pertinent evidence. There is, of course, no *a priori* reason to regard the sporocarp as uniquely associated with the heterosporous habit. The association of the two characters may be quite coincidental. The sporocarp might well have been developed as a resistant organ adapted to survival in habitats where there is a seasonal alternation of short wet periods and long droughts (Eames, 1936). In this context, it is salutary to remember that the sporocarp of *Azolla* and *Salvinia*, though functionally comparable, has a quite different morphological origin from that of the Marsileaceae.

The great resistance and stony nature of the sporocarp of the Marsileaceae may be attributed to the heavy thickening of the walls of the columnar and

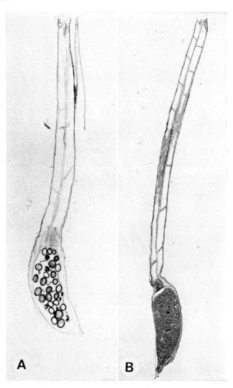

FIG. 9.1. Reproductive structures in aquatic pteridophytes: A, B, photomicrographs of L.S. sporophylls of *Isoetes* sp. bearing a megasporangium (A) or a microsporangium (B) (both ×5). (C and D on facing page, E on p. 262.)

hour-glass cells of the hypodermis (Fig. 9.2). These cells bear a very striking resemblance to the thickened cells in the mature testa of many angiosperm seeds (Corner, 1964). Sporocarps probably do not open for 2 to 3 years, or perhaps longer, until the stony wall has decayed. The spores apparently retain their viability for 20 to 30 years (Smith, 1938). Further development occurs in an aqueous medium. The sporocarp of *Regnellidium* splits into two valves, that of *Pilularia* into four or more valves: in both genera the sporangia are extruded in a gelatinous mass formed from the tissues in which the sori were formerly embedded. In *Marsilea*, the germination of the sporocarp is a more complex process. A ring of gelatinous tissue, extending round the inside of the sporocarp wall in the dorsiventral plane, imbibes water rapidly, swells enormously and forces apart the two halves of the sporocarp along the ventral margin and the apex. Within 10 to 20 min, the ring pushes out, pulling the sori with it: it soon breaks on the ventral side and continues to expand as a cylindrical worm-like

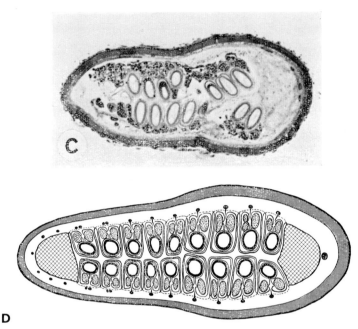

FIG. 9.1. Reproductive structures in aquatic pteridophytes: C, photomicrograph of L.S. sporocarp of *Marsilea* sp. (in plane at right angles to dorsiventral plane), showing mega- and microsporangia (× 12); D, diagrammatic L.S. sporocarp of *Marsilea* sp. (in same plane as C), showing two rows of sori; each sorus covered by an indusium and containing one of a vertical row of megasporangia (with a thick-walled megaspore) and one of each of two vertical rows of microsporangia (stippled); the line of abscission bounding the receptacle of each sorus indicated by a broken line; gelatinous ring of the sporocarp wall is cross-hatched; vascular strands are solid black; outer thickened part of sporocarp wall is shaded (see also Fig. 9.2).

structure bearing the two alternating rows of sori (Fig. 9.2). This structure may persist for a few days, the spores being liberated by rupture of each sorus. The indusia and sporangial walls yield a gelatinous matrix in which the discharged spores remain embedded.

The spores germinate immediately they are liberated, and the endosporic gametophytes develop in a very short time: in *Marsilea vestita*, for example, functional gametes are produced within 6 to 22 hours of spore germination (Smith, 1938; Atkinson, 1943). Each male gametophyte produces sixteen antherozoids which are multiflagellate, like those of *Isoetes*, and liberated by

rupture of the microspore wall (Sharp, 1914). The bulk of the female gametophyte consists of non-cellular cytoplasm laden with starch grains and other
food reserves: only at the apical nodule is a cellular tissue formed. Here a
solitary simple archegonium is differentiated which splits the megaspore wall
as it grows and ultimately protrudes slightly into the surrounding gelatinous
sheath (Campbell, 1892; and see Fig. 9.2). Antherozoids swarm through this
sheath towards the archegonium, many apparently dying on the way. If
fertilisation is not achieved, the gametophyte continues to grow for a while
but no further archegonia are differentiated. Embryonic development begins

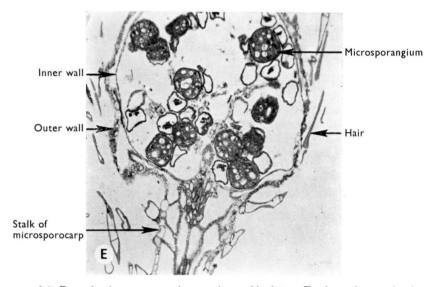

FIG. 9.1. Reproductive structures in aquatic pteridophytes: E, photomicrograph of
L.S. part of microsporocarp of *Salvinia* sp. (× 60) (see also Fig. 9.2).

a few hours after fertilisation and closely resembles that of terrestrial leptosporangiate ferns, especially the Polypodiaceae. Within about 4 days, the first
leaf of the new sporophyte is usually clearly visible. This rapid development,
as that of the gametophytes, may be an adaptation to life in habitats with only a
short favourable wet season (Eames, 1936).

Pilularia and *Regnellidium* closely resemble *Marsilea* in most vegetative and
reproductive structures: in one or two important features, however, they appear
somewhat more advanced by virtue of further reduction. In leaf structure, for
example, *Marsilea* seems the least specialised in having four segments per
mature leaf, whereas in *Regnellidium* only two segments remain, and in *Pilularia* none, photosynthesis here being performed by the subulate or filiform
petiole. Trends of reduction may also be seen in the sporocarps (Goebel, 1882;
Meunier, 1888; Johnson, 1933; Eames, 1936; Chrysler and Johnson, 1939).
The number of sori per sporocarp is similarly large in *Marsilea* and *Regnel-*

lidium: it is reduced to four in all but one species of *Pilularia*, and to two in *P. minuta*. In all three genera, both mega- and microsporangia occur within each sorus, and only a solitary megaspore matures within each megasporangium. The number of sporangia in each sorus is reduced from several in *Marsilea* to three (one mega- and two microsporangia) in *Pilularia minuta*.

Although *Azolla* and *Salvinia* superficially resemble the Marsileaceae in being heterosporous and having sporocarps they differ in many morphological features and almost certainly evolved along distinct lines (Eames, 1936; Takhtajan, 1953; Pichi-Sermolli, 1959; Zimmermann, 1959). Their sporocarps are more specialised in being strictly monosporangiate at maturity. In *Azolla* two to four sporocarps are formed in the axil of the dorsal lobe of the oldest leaf on a lateral shoot (Pfeiffer, 1907; Demalsy, 1953). Each sporocarp first comes to possess a single megasporangium. If this develops further, producing a single functional megaspore, the microsporangial initials on its stalk abort, but if its contents degenerate, microsporangia continue to be initiated on its stalk in basipetalous succession and develop to maturity, each yielding sixty-four microspores. The sporocarps of *Salvinia* occur in rows or sympodial clusters on segments of the submerged leaves, and each contains only one type of sporangium from the very start of development. Unlike those of *Azolla*, both types of sporocarp are similar in size and external form. In each row or cluster, the first few sporocarps each contain up to about twenty-five megasporangia, which are borne solitarily on short stalks or in groups on branched stalks, according to the species. In each sporangium thirty-two megaspores are formed but only one reaches functional maturity. The later-formed sporocarps contain many microsporangia on branched stalks, and as in *Azolla* sixty-four microspores develop in each sporangium (Arnoldi, 1910; Kundt, 1910; Yasui, 1911; Zawidski, 1912).

From a comparative point of view, both genera thus appear advanced in producing distinct mega- and microsporocarps and forming only one functional megaspore in each megasporangium. *Azolla* could be regarded as the less specialised of the two in its initial bisporangiate phase of sporocarp development, but as the more specialised in reduction of its megasporangia to one per sporocarp.

In both genera the sporocarp wall clearly differs from that of the Marsileaceae in being a modified indusium. It grows up from a ridge of cells encircling the base of each potential cluster of sporangia and soon extends beyond as a cup-like sheath. Its free margins eventually meet, obliterating the apical pore and it thus encloses the sporangia. It comprises just two layers of cells, often separated by large air spaces in *Salvinia*, in which genus the outer layer usually bears many fine hairs (Fig. 9.2).

During later development the periplasmodium derived from the tapetal cells, and from degenerating megaspores if these are present, undergoes very important changes. In the megasporangium of *Salvinia* it forms a vacuolated but hardened coat, the perispore, around the surviving functional megaspore. In the microsporangium it also becomes vacuolated and later hardens into an alveolar 'massula' in which the microspores are embedded. Mature sporocarps

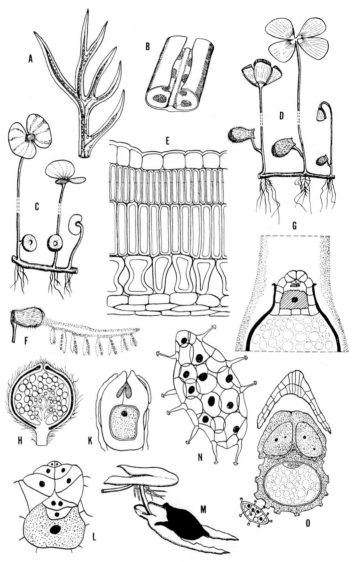

FIG. 9.2. Reproductive structures in aquatic ferns: A, B, *Ceratopteris thalictroides*: A, underside of several segments of fertile leaf (× 0·6); B, enlarged view of part of A, showing revolute margins and scattered sporangia (× 5). C, *Regnellidium diphyllum*, habit sketch showing paired leaflets and rounded sporocarps (× 0·25); D, E, F, G, *Marsilea vestita*: D, habit sketch showing quadrifoliate leaves and bean-shaped sporocarps (× 1·5); E, T.S. part of mature sporocarp wall, showing epidermis, two layers of thickened columnar cells, one layer of thickened 'hour-glass' cells with large inter-cellular spaces, and flattened thin-walled cells beneath (× 240); F, germinating sporo-carp with gelatinous structure bearing sori (× 1·5); G, diagrammatic L.S. anterior

sink from the parent plant to the substrate and when they have decayed the spores are liberated, rising to the surface enclosed in their perispore or massula. Development of the endosporic gametophytes occurs at the surface. The microspores germinate within the massula, which is still enclosed in the microsporangium. As they develop, the male prothalli protrude through the massula and sporangial wall. Two antheridia differentiate in each prothallus, and each yields four antherozoids. The female gametophyte, when mature, protrudes through the perispore and sporangium wall and develops two backward-projecting wings which are thought to stabilise the structure in a plane most favourable for subsequent embryonic development. Several deeply-sunken archegonia differentiate along the exposed surface of the gametophyte. If fertilisation is not achieved, further archegonia appear lateral to the first group (Arnoldi, 1910; Lasser, 1924).

According to Mahabalé (1954) there is evidence amongst various species of *Salvinia* of a certain correlation between massular structure, fertility of spores, chromosome complement and geographical distribution. *Salvinia natans*, for example, appears relatively unspecialised in its 'solid' massulae (i.e. with few vacuoles), fully fertile spores, low haploid complement ($n = 4$, 8, 15 or 24), and wide geographical range extending into warm temperate regions. In inter-glacial time it probably had an even wider distribution (p. 403). In contrast, species such as *S. auriculata*, *S. cucullata* and *S. oblongifolia* could be regarded as more advanced in their highly vacuolated massulae, sterile micro- or megaspores, and restricted tropical ranges. *S. auriculata* has a higher haploid complement than *S. natans*: $n = 15$, 24 or 32. *S. cucullata* appears to have $n = 12$ and may be a largely sterile triploid. Mahabalé also regarded *S. natans* as the most primitive type in vascular organisation, but the evidence for this view is far from unequivocal (see p. 197). The broad concept of affinities within the genus, as expressed by Mahabalé, is interesting, but further data, especially for the several poorly known species, are needed for substantiation.

---

nodule of germinated megaspore, showing archegonium with egg (shaded), neck canal cell and ventral canal cell, vacuolated female gametophyte cytoplasm and ruptured megaspore wall; all surrounded by gelatinous sheath ($\times 100$); H, *Salvinia auriculata*, diagrammatic L.S. microsporocarp showing two-layered (indusial) wall with epidermal hairs, and microsporangia on branched stalks ($\times 6$); K, L, M, *S. natans*: K, Diagrammatic V.S. uninucleate megaspore (stippled) surrounded by hard perispore, which is indented at apex forming a cavity (shaded) looking similar to the pollen chamber of a gymnosperm ovule; all surrounded by parts of megasporangium wall ($\times 125$); L, diagrammatic V.S. mature archegonium with short neck, binucleate neck canal cell, ventral canal cell and egg (stippled) ($\times 300$); M, lateral view of young sporophyte (with first leaf, stem and rhizoids) arising from female gametophyte which protrudes from the megaspore (black) and has two backward-projecting wings, or 'stabilisers' ($\times 5$); N, O, *Azolla filiculoides*: N, microsporangial massula containing microspores (black) and bearing barbed glochidia ($\times 280$). O, Megaspore (showing early development of female gametophyte) within alveolar massula, accompanied by two other megasporangial massulae and apical part of sporocarp wall (at top), and a microsporangial massula (at bottom left) ($\times 80$). (G, after Campbell, 1892; K, after Arnoldi, 1910; L, after Yasui, 1911; M, after Lasser, 1924; O, after Smith, 1938.)

The mature microspores of *Azolla* are scattered in alveolar massulae, which in certain species, e.g. *A. caroliniana* and *A. filiculoides*, develop barbed hairs, known as glochidia (Fig. 9.2). These facilitate entanglement with megasporic massulae under water, thereby increasing the likelihood of subsequent fertilisation. The solitary mature megaspore is also embedded in a large alveolar massula, to which there adheres a group of smaller massulae containing abortive megaspores, and also the ruptured apical parts of the sporocarp and megasporangial walls. These accessory structures are often described as floats or swimming apparatus, but, in fact, they do not endow buoyancy. Ripe megasporic massulae apparently often sink when liberated. Gametophyte development is endosporic and generally similar to that in *Salvinia*, except that the female prothallus does not become photosynthetic. The male prothallus produces eight antherozoids. As in *Salvinia*, a second crop of archegonia appears if none of the first are fertilised (Campbell, 1893; Belajeff, 1898; Hannig, 1911).

The embryogeny of *Azolla*, generally similar to that of other leptosporangiate ferns, is notable for the retarded development of the root, which is probably an embryonic symptom of the morphological reduction associated with the floating aquatic habit. Smith (1938) disdained this argument 'because other hydrophytic ferns, as *Marsilea*, have a rapid development of the primary root' and offered instead a spurious physiological explanation. He omitted to mention that *Marsilea* and its relatives are essentially amphibious plants which typically develop good root systems, whereas *Azolla* and *Salvinia*, which should be compared with other free-floating plants, both exhibit profound vegetative reduction. At maturity, *Azolla*, like *Lemna*, has rather poorly developed roots whilst *Salvinia*, like *Aldrovanda* and *Utricularia*, is quite rootless.

It should be apparent from the foregoing account that *Azolla* and *Salvinia* cannot be considered to have any affinities with the Marsileaceae. The differences between the two groups are many and profound: the only diagnostic common feature is the heterosporous habit, which has clearly arisen many times amongst vascular plants and is not acceptable as a sole criterion of relationship. Recent taxonomic treatment of these ferns has varied. *Azolla* and *Salvinia* are preferably segregated in distinct families, for there are significant differences between them in both gross morphology and finer reproductive structure. The group comprising the Salviniaceae and Azollaceae on the one hand, and the Marsileaceae on the other, have both been assigned the status of order (Salviniales; Marsileales), sub-class (Salviniidae; Marsileidae) or even class (Salviniata; Marsileata) (Eames, 1936; Christensen, 1938; Smith, 1938; Reed, 1954; Bonnet, 1958; Pichi-Sermolli, 1959; Meeuse, 1961).

The phylogenetic affinities of the Marsileaceae and Salviniaceae are obscure. Bower (1926) and Takhtajan (1953) suggested that the Marsileaceae may be derived from the terrestrial Schizaeaceae. Pichi-Sermolli (1959) considered this affinity to be remote but did acknowledge a possible origin from a schizaeoid ancestral stock. In view of the soral structure of the Marsileaceae, Smith (1938) argued that the affinities of the group lie not with the Schizaeaceae, in which the sporangia develop simultaneously, but with higher leptosporangiate ferns having a gradate sorus and involucroid indusium. Smith also disputed Bower's (1928) derivation of *Azolla* and *Salvinia* from filmy ferns such as the Hymeno-phyllaceae on the grounds of important differences in sporangial development. Perhaps the most stimulating speculation is that of Meeuse (1961). He was much impressed by resemblances of leaf form and venation between *Marsilea* and the fossil Caytoniales and by the similarity of the sporocarp of the Marsileaceae to the basal, stalked, bisexual, sporangium-bearing organs of the Glossop-teridales (see Plumstead, 1956, and Thomas, 1958). He also drew attention to resemblances between the leaf segments, sporocarps and megaspores of *Azolla* and *Salvinia* and the corresponding organs of extinct seed-ferns such as *Neuropteris*, *Pecopteris* and *Saarotheca*. Whilst recognising that superficial similarities may sometimes be misleading, Meeuse felt strongly inclined to believe that the Marsileaceae, *Azolla* and *Salvinia* might represent 'living fossils'—relict descendants of glossopterid or pteridospermous stocks which, on land, were superceded long ago by higher seed plants which no longer required an aquatic environment for fertilisation.

III FLORAL MORPHOLOGY AND POLLINATION IN AQUATIC ANGIOSPERMS

THE PROBLEM OF THE ELEVATION OF AERIAL FLOWERS

The formation of aerial flowers by all floating-leaved and most submerged angiosperms must involve severe mechanical problems. For the flowers to be raised well above the water to facilitate display and cross-pollination and to avoid submergence by waves, the peduncle must be able to withstand both the bending strains from wind sweeping across the surface and the pulling strains exerted by currents, especially in flowing water. In caulescent species the main support is probably provided by the ascending vegetative stems: the peduncles themselves are quite short, arising from the uppermost nodes of the axis. The peduncle of rosette species, however, is a long solitary organ arising from the level of the substrate and dependent on its own strength. Yet numerous hydrophytes manage to produce flowers from remarkable depths. *Lobelia dortmanna* has been seen to flower above the surface from a depth of about 2 m, *Potamogeton berchtoldii* from 2·5 m and *Hippuris vulgaris* from 3 m (West, 1905, 1910; Grainger, 1947).

The aerial flowers themselves display no adaptive features but their associated vegetative organs do sometimes exhibit modifications of habit or anatomy that may help to maintain their elevation and equilibrium. Several species of *Nymphoides* and *Potamogeton*, for example, have a terminal in-florescence or cluster of flowers supported by a raft of floating foliage (Goebel, 1891–1893; and see Fig. 9.3). In the essentially submerged *Heteranthera zosteraefolia* the leaf next to the inflorescence often has an expanded floating lamina, whilst the flower of several species of *Cabomba* is supported by one or more alternate floating leaves of elliptic or orbicular form, contrasting sharply with the opposite or whorled dissected leaves under water (Fassett, 1953). In certain batrachian *Ranunculi*, e.g. *R. baudotii* and *R. peltatus*, the capillary submerged leaves are often replaced at the base of the flower by lobed, reniform, floating laminae. *Hottonia palustris* exemplifies those submerged plants in which the equilibrium of the flower is maintained by an aggregation of the uppermost foliage: the symmetrical whorl of lateral shoots at the base of the flowering stem resists strains exerted from any direction (Prankerd, 1911).

FIG. 9.3. *Nymphoides peltata*: apical clusters of aerial flowers supported by platform of floating leaves (note also the fruiting peduncles which have curved down into the water in left foreground) (× 0·25).

The disposition of mechanical and vascular tissues in the floral axis often resembles that of terrestrial herbaceous dicotyledon stems, and probably endows greater resistance to bending strains. In the peduncle of *Nymphoides peltata*, for example, the lacunate cortex is rather narrower and the vascular bundles more widely spaced and peripheral than in the submerged stems. The inflorescence axis of *Potamogeton natans* and *P. nodosus* shows a dicotyledon-like arrangement of collateral bundles in marked contrast to the condensed central cylinder of the rhizome and vegetative stems (Chrysler, 1907; Singh, 1965a). The aerial peduncle of *Ottelia alismoides* possesses numerous steles, each surrounded by a distinct endodermis and pericycle (Majumdar, 1938). Even the flowering stems of the reduced Hydrostachyaceae, obscure African relatives of the Podostemaceae, have a ring of isolated vascular strands, some-times accompanied by cortical and medullary bundles (Solereder, 1908; Schloss, 1913). In the North American ally of *Hottonia palustris*, *H. inflata*, the aerial flowering stems are swollen and buoyant, due to the presence of much air-filled lacunate tissue (Fig. 9.4).

The flowers of the waterlilies and their relatives may be well-elevated, as in *Brasenia, Nuphar* and several tropical species of *Nymphaea,* or surface-floating, as in most temperate species of *Nymphaea* (Conard, 1905; Small, 1931; Wood, 1959; and see Fig. 9.8). In both types the sturdy peduncle itself provides the principal support for the flower. Its honeycomb construction probably repre-

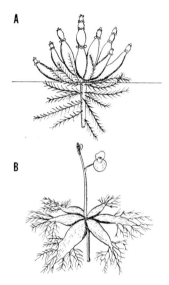

FIG. 9.4. A, *Hottonia inflata*: floating inflorescence with inflated peduncles (flowers and leaves shown diagrammatically) (× 0·15); B, *Utricularia inflata* var. *minor*: whorl of floats at the base of the inflorescence (× 0·6).

sents the most efficient compromise between the various types of organisation best suited to resisting bending and pulling strains and to providing adequate aeration within a large essentially submerged organ (Fig. 9.5). The central group of large lacunae is surrounded by one or more rings of smaller lacunae, the precise arrangement varying between species (Conard, 1905). There is a peripheral subepidermal zone of compact parenchyma, and sometimes collenchyma. The scattered vascular bundles form longitudinal ribs, smallest and most numerous in the peripheral tissue, largest in the tissue between the air canals. The surface-floating type of flower appears balanced and stable but must be subject to the same risks of submergence that confront floating laminae. The accommodating length of the peduncles, the cup-like shape of the flower and the large waxy sepals probably help to resist immersion by waves and sudden increases in water level. Even so, floating flowers of waterlilies and other genera, such as *Luronium,* are extremely vulnerable after anthesis and are often drenched by rain.

The aerial flowers of *Eichhornia crassipes, Hydrocharis, Limnobium, Stratiotes* and *Trapa* owe their stability to the buoyancy and equilibrium of the whole free-floating rosette. The minute inflorescences of surface-floating species of the Lemnaceae, however, borne on the margins or upper surface of the thalli, are very liable to immersion even in relatively quiet stagnant habitats. Of the submerged free-floating hydrophytes, *Lemna trisulca* is comparable in behaviour to *Stratiotes*, for it produces its inflorescences in fertile thalli which float on, not beneath, the surface: the plant in effect rises to the surface to bloom.

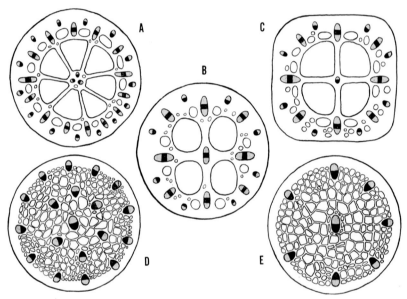

FIG. 9.5. Diagrammatic T.S. of various peduncles of *Nymphaea* and *Nuphar* to show distribution of lacunae and vascular bundles (phloem, shaded; xylem, solid black): A, *Nymphaea caerulea* (×6); B, *N. odorata* (×7); C, *N. tetragona* (×8); D, *Nuphar lutea* (×3); E, *N. pumila* (×5). (A after Conard, 1905.)

In numerous aquatic species of *Utricularia* the inflorescence is supported at its base by a whorl of submerged vegetative axes: in a few taxa, such as *U. inflata, U. stellaris* and occasionally *U. flexuosa*, these lateral shoots are inflated to form buoyant floats (Fig. 9.4). In transverse section, each float of *U. flexuosa*, for example, shows a central ring of vascular strands which all lack cambium and have reduced conducting elements, as in the other vegetative organs: in some strands the xylem and phloem become dissociated. The great bulk of the organ, between the epidermis and the two cell-layers surrounding the vascular strands, consists of a ring of air-filled cortical lacunae separated by radial partitions, one cell in thickness. These lacunae persist, reduced in size, into the ultimate capillary branches of the float (Deva, 1953).

FLORAL MORPHOLOGY AND POLLINATION IN AERIAL-FLOWERING PLANTS

To place the submerged hydrophilous angiosperms in true perspective it is important to appreciate that most aquatic angiosperms resemble terrestrial flowering plants not only in the gross features of floral morphology and pollination but also in exhibiting similar trends of floral specialisation and reduction. Entomophily, associated with conspicuous, nectar-secreting, scented, sometimes zygomorphic and heterostylic flowers, is characteristic of several groups of emergent, free-floating and floating-leaved hydrophytes. But numerous aquatic angiosperms appear to have discarded entomophily in favour of anemophily, with corresponding modifications of floral structure, whilst in a few genera self-pollination prevails.

The Nymphaeaceae. The eight genera of the Nymphaeaceae *sensu lato* are linked by certain vegetative characters and by their pendulous, anatropous, parietal ovules but in many features of floral structure they are quite distinct. In the nature of the corolla, androecium or gynoecium, the genera form a morphological series, advancing from numerous spiral parts to few cyclic parts. Differentiation of calyx and corolla is common to all genera but perhaps sharpest in *Cabomba*: in *Nuphar* the sepals are petaloid, and the petals reduced and bract-like.

The gradual structural transition between petals, staminodes and stamens in *Nymphaea* has been adduced as evidence that petals represent sterile stamens (Eames, 1961). Although Burtt (1961) voiced the necessity for caution in interpreting such homologies, it must be admitted that this concept of the origin of the corolla is stimulating, especially in the light of Moseley's (1958) exhaustive study of the androecium. Moseley concluded that the most primitive form of stamen in the family, represented by the central stamens of the polymerous *Victoria* and some species of *Nymphaea* (Fig. 9.6), is broad and dorsiventrally flattened, has a sterile distal appendage in which the median and two main lateral veins end, and has four, elongated, wall-less microsporangia embedded in sterile tissue and covered by a fibrous exothecium which extends also along the connective. The semi-laminar form, apical and marginal growth, and vascular supply suggest homology between the stamen and the sporophyll of lower vascular plants. Moseley argued that from this primitive stamen petals may have evolved by an expansion of the sterile parts and progressive loss of the fertile tissue. Constriction of the sterile proximal part into a narrow flat stalk and ultimately a terete filament, loss of the sterile distal appendage, retraction of the adjacent sterile tissue to form the walls of the microsporangia, migration of the microsporangia from an adaxial to a lateral and eventually an abaxial position, and loss of all but one vein would together yield the anther-plus-filament type of stamen in *Barclaya, Brasenia, Cabomba, Euryale* and *Nelumbo*. The typical stamens of *Nuphar, Nymphaea* and *Victoria* are variously intermediate between the primitive and derived forms (Fig. 9.6).

The morphology of the gynoecium (Fig. 9.7) is less clearly understood (Troll, 1934; Saunders, 1936). Some genera are apocarpous, with three carpels borne

10

on the receptacle (*Cabomba*) or many carpels uniquely sunk in the receptacle but still superior (*Nelumbo*): both these arrangements seem to be specialised modifications of a primitive gynoecial condition. In other genera the gynoecium is syncarpous and multilocular: it may be superior (*Nuphar*) or semi-inferior

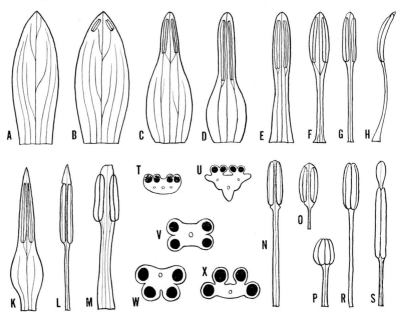

FIG. 9.6. Stamen form (A to S) and anatomy in transverse section (T to X) in the Nymphaeaceae. (Principal veins are shown in A to S and in transverse section in T to X: in the latter, sporangia are shown in black.) A to H and T, *Nymphaea odorata*: A, petal (× 0·8); B, C, outer stamens (× 1); D, E, central stamens (× 1·2); F, G, H, inner stamens (× 1·5); T, section of inner stamen: sporangia adaxial, dehiscence introrse (× 2). K to S, U to X, typical stamens of other taxa: K, *Nymphaea nouchali* (× 1); L, *N. caerulea* (× 1); M, U, *Nuphar lutea*: sporangia adaxial, dehiscence introrse (M, × 2·5; U, × 4); N, V, *Brasenia schreberi*: sporangia lateral, dehiscence latrorse (N, × 2·5; V, × 8); O, *Barclaya mottleyi* (× 6); P, *Euryale ferox* (× 6); R, W, *Cabomba aquatica*: sporangia abaxial, dehiscence extrorse (R, × 5; W, × 15); S, X, *Nelumbo nucifera*: sporangia obliquely lateral, dehiscence latro-introrse (S, × 1; X, × 5). (A to G, K to P, and S all show the adaxial face; H is a lateral view; R shows the abaxial face.) (Partly after Moseley, 1958.)

due to adnation of the stamens and petals (*Nymphaea*), or truly inferior, being sunk in the receptacle (*Euryale* and *Victoria*). Placentation is typically, and probably primitively, laminar: the many ovules are borne all over the adaxial surface of each carpel and receive their vascular supply from minor lateral veins. Reduction in ovule number is manifest in *Cabomba* (three or four per carpel), *Brasenia* (two per carpel) and *Nelumbo* (one per carpel). In these specialised types, placentation becomes submarginal and the vascular supply is derived from one or both of the major lateral veins. Throughout the family the ovules are notable for their massive nucellus, much of which persists after fertilisation to form the storage perisperm of the seeds (Khanna, 1964; Ramji and Padmanabhan, 1965). Moseley (1961, 1965) made a detailed study of floral development and gynoecial structure in numerous species of *Nymphaea* and *Nuphar*, and suggested how the gynoecium may have originated in these

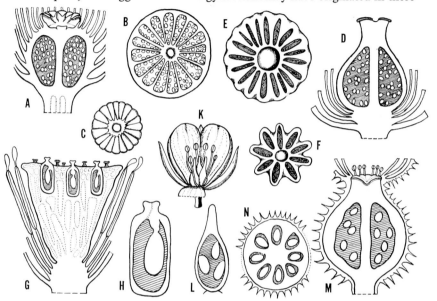

FIG. 9.7. The gynoecium of the Nymphaeaceae (all figures semi-diagrammatic). *Nymphaea odorata*: A, L.S. gynoecium, to show stigmatic lobes, loculi with many scattered ovules, lacunae of peduncle ending in receptacle (×1·5); B, T.S. gynoecium, to show berry-like structure and laminar placentation (×2); C, radiating stigmatic lobes, from above (×2). *Nuphar lutea*: D, L.S. gynoecium, to show flask shape and loculi with many scattered ovules (×0·6); E, stigmatic disc, from above (×2). *Nuphar pumila*: F, stigmatic disc, from above (×2). *Nelumbo nucifera*: G, L.S. gynoecium, to show carpels sunk in lacunate receptacle (×0·8); H, L.S. carpel, to show solitary pendulous ovule and button-shaped stigma (×2·5). *Cabomba caroliniana*: K, flower (with one petal deflected forwards), showing monocotyledon-like arrangement of free parts (×2); L, L.S. carpel, to show three scattered ovules (×6). *Euryale ferox*: M, L.S. gynoecium, to show stigmatic disc, loculi with few scattered ovules, and spiny armour (×1); N, T.S. fruit, to show eight loculi (×0·6).

genera. Van Leeuwen (1963) visualised the possible derivation of the carpel of *Nelumbo* by reduction from a gynoecium of the *Nymphaea* type. Both these authors commented on the strong morphological similarities between the gynoecia of the Nymphaeaceae and those of primitive woody Ranalians, such as the Degeneriaceae and Winteraceae.

In polymerous taxa the numbers of different floral parts are quantitatively varying characters. In *Nymphaea alba*, for example, the total ranges of variability and mean numbers of petals, stamens and carpels do not differ much between large areas of the species' natural range. Nor do they vary much in extensive lowland and lake districts where the habitats are often inter-connected and the breeding populations comprise several thousand individuals. But in isolated habitats the colonies often display great diversity in the numbers of floral organs and the size of leaves and flowers: in some isolated colonies the range of variability is conspicuously wider than in others. J. Heslop-Harrison (1953b) found singularly little variation in carpel number and similar characters in random samples of colonies of *N. alba* in Avinlochan (Inverness) but immense variation in colonies from South Uist (Outer Hebrides). The differences between colonies are generally greater than could be caused by chance variation and appear to be genetically rather than environmentally determined. Since the genetical variability of an isolated colony of a species will be a function of the heterozygosity of the pioneer colonists, until further colonists arrive or mutation occurs, the narrow range of variation in some isolated populations of *N. alba* is probably caused by the pioneer immigrants reproduc-ing mainly by vegetative methods, forming a closed community which inhibits further colonisation (Heslop-Harrison, J., 1953b; Heslop-Harrison, Y., 1955b, c).

The opening of the flower bud, anthesis, shows a more or less precise diurnal timing in several members of the Nymphaeaceae. Species of *Nuphar*, for example, and most species of *Nymphaea* in the northern hemisphere, such as *N. alba, N. mexicana, N. odorata* and *N. tetragona*, open their flowers during the day, either from 7 or 8 a.m. to about 1 p.m. or from about 10 a.m. to about 4 p.m. Of the tropical *Nymphaeas*, some are also day-flowering, e.g. *N. caerulea* (7 or 8 a.m. to as late as midnight), *N. ampla, N. elegans, N. micrantha* and *N. stellata*, whilst others, such as *N. amazonum, N. lotus* and *N. rubra*, are night-blooming. *Victoria amazonica* and the closely related (perhaps conspecific) *V. cruziana* and *V. trickeri* also bloom at night, anthesis in *V. amazonica* occurring soon after sunset (6 p.m.). Gessner (1960a) induced buds to open as early as 4 p.m. by darkening them with black paper for 30 min, but buds darkened any earlier than 4 p.m. maintained a natural rhythm and opened about 6 p.m. Exposure to light during the night delays anthesis during the succeeding few days, but eventually anthesis occurs even in continuous illumination. It seems likely that the natural periodicity of anthesis is controlled by an endogenous rhythm regulated by the preceding illumination timetable. Dianthesis has been described in *Brasenia schreberi*: the flowers appear above water, opening from about 6 a.m. to 9 a.m., and are then drawn back into the water, rising and opening again the following morning, when the anthers shed their pollen (Tokura, 1937). Cultivated specimens of *Victoria amazonica* behave in a similar way, the flower opening partly on the first evening, closing in the early morning, then re-opening fully on the second evening.

Almost all the Nymphaeaceae are protogynous and nectarless. They are pollinated by beetles, small flies and sweat-bees which crawl indiscriminately over the flowers, the beetles often biting and eating the organs. The principal attractions for these rather primitive pollinating agents are probably the smell and warmth of the opening flower and the food value of the stamens. (The conspicuousness of the corolla, often brilliant red, blue, yellow or white, is something of an enigma: it may become explicable when more is known of the vision of these particular insects.) *Victoria amazonica* evolves a strong scent, mainly from the carmine-red apical outgrowths of the carpels: heat is also generated, raising the temperature of the flower as much as 10°C above that of the atmosphere. The cockchafers and other night-flying insects attracted to the giant flower eat the stamens and often remain inside the flower when it closes, flying away when it reopens the next evening (Knoch, 1899; Knuth, 1906–9). Many of the tropical *Nymphaeas* are similarly fragrant, as is the North American *N. odorata*, and other taxa emit various odours, such as the strong alcoholic smell of the flowers of *Nuphar lutea*. Some north temperate members of the family, e.g. *Nymphaea alba* and *N. tetragona*, are not notably fragrant and may have abandoned cross-pollination: they are homogamous and self-fertile. The flowers of *Euryale* are usually cleistogamous (Khanna, 1964).

Nuphar, *Nymphaea* and *Nelumbo* are notable for their abundant natural and artificial hybrids (Fig. 9.8), most of which are sterile. Available chromosome counts suggest that the north temperate *Nuphar* is homoploid (2n = 34), and the existence of probable natural hybrids (e.g. *N. lutea* × *N. pumila*, *N. advena* × *N. sagittifolium*) led Beal (1956) to treat the 9 to 12 species as subspecific variants of the Eurasian *N. lutea*, a practice not followed by others in view of the reasonably discrete ecological and geographical differences between the taxa. Many species of *Nymphaea* differ in both the average size of the plant and flowers and in the chromosome number (which ranges from 2n = 28 to 2n = 224) but these characters may not be causally related since the pigmy of the genus (*N. tetragona*) and one of the largest-flowered (*N. gigantea*) both appear to be high polyploids. Different chromosome numbers have also been recorded within certain possibly aggregate taxa, e.g. the *N. odorata* complex (2n = 56 or 84) and the *N. alba* complex (2n = 84, 112 or 160) (Wood, 1959).

The Nymphaeaceae is certainly a very heterogeneous family. Some botanists, notably Li (1955), Hutchinson (1959), Takhtajan (1959b) and Tutin (1964), have chosen to rearrange the eight genera in from two to as many as five separate families, *Cabomba* and *Brasenia* usually being segregated as the Cabombaceae, *Nymphaea* and *Nuphar* as the Nymphaeaceae *sensu stricto*, *Euryale* and *Victoria* as the Euryalaceae, *Barclaya* as the Barclayaceae and *Nelumbo* as the Nelumbonaceae. Some of these families have been further elevated to the rank of orders. In view of the uncertainty which still surrounds numerous aspects of the comparative morphology of the group, this fine taxonomic breakdown seems somewhat premature. To avoid unnecessary confusion until such time as the relationships between the genera are understood more clearly, it appears preferable to retain the Nymphaeaceae *sensu lato* as a family within the Ranales, whilst acknowledging with Caspary (1856, 1888) and Wood (1959) that in several morphological characters *Cabomba* and *Brasenia* stand somewhat apart from the other genera, as also does *Nelumbo*, which is perhaps the most specialised of the whole family.

In some features, notably the scattered bundles of the stem and the laminar placentation of the ovules, the Nymphaeaceae appear transitional to the

FIG. 9.8. A, surface-floating flower of the hardy cultivated hybrid, *Nymphaea* 'Marliacea carnea', with large spreading petals, many stamens, and stigmatic lobes (×0·3); B, surface-floating, 'double' flower of another hardy hybrid, *Nymphaea* 'Mme. Wilfron Gonnère' showing globular form, large sepals and many petals (×0·3); C, well-elevated aerial flowers of the tropical hybrid, *Nymphaea* 'Mrs G. H. Pring', with the closed buds of the night-blooming species, *N. rubra*, beyond (×0·05); D, open aerial flower of *Nelumbo nucifera*, showing top of receptacle with protruding dark stigmas (×0·2).

Helobian monocotyledons: some earlier morphologists (e.g. Schaffner, 1904; Cook, 1906, 1909) did not perceive the connation of the cotyledons in certain species and so actually regarded the family as monocotyledonous (Conard, 1936). Comparative studies of the androecium and gynoecium strongly suggest that the Nymphaeaceae may have close affinities with the primitive woody Ranalians (Saunders, 1936; Moseley, 1958, 1961; Sastri, 1959; van Leeuwen, 1963). The heterogeneity of the group, the specialisation of all genera, and the evident restriction of some (e.g. *Euryale, Brasenia, Nelumbo* and *Victoria*) to floristically primitive tropical rain-forests and swamps (pp. 384, 403) support the idea of an ancient and primitive origin. The family may well comprise relict surviving descendants of early herbaceous dicotyledons which failed to compete with tropical forest vegetation and survived only in marginal subaquatic habitats (Corner, 1964). The Amazonian *Victoria*, with its massive spiny body constructed solely of primary tissues, has perhaps changed least from this primitive stock, whilst the slender dissected-leaved *Cabomba*, and *Nelumbo*, with its apocarpous gynoecium strangely sunk into the receptacle, show more derived vegetative and reproductive organisation.

The Alismaceae and Butomaceae. The floral morphology of both these families includes several features held by most authorities to be relatively unspecialised. These are hermaphrodite flowers (except in *Sagittaria*), apocarpous gynoecia (with slight basal connation of the carpels in some taxa, as *Butomus* and *Damasonium*), and the absence of fusion of the other floral parts. The Alismaceae displays a trend from crowded or spiral carpels, in *Luronium, Echinodorus* and *Sagittaria*, to a single whorl of carpels in *Alisma* and *Damasonium*. Generally having solitary basal ovules, the family appears more specialised than the Butomaceae, in which each carpel has several ovules scattered over its inner surface. Both families are relatively advanced in having a whorled perianth differentiated into an outer persistent calyx and an inner usually deciduous corolla (Salisbury, 1926; Lawrence, 1951; Eames, 1961).

The mainly temperate *Sagittaria* shows an interesting trend towards unisexual flowers, male in the upper and female in the lower whorls of the inflorescence (Bogin, 1955). Of the tropical and warm temperate species segregated in Bogin's subgenus *Lophotocarpus*, the pan-tropical *S. guayanensis* regularly produces female flowers with a whorl of functional stamens and male flowers with vestiges of abortive pistils. Of the American species, the tropical *S. rhombifolia* and *S. intermedia*, and the widespread *S. montevidensis* tend to have mostly hermaphrodite flowers in the lowest whorls but the warm temperate *S. sanfordii* and *S. subulata* have only occasional hermaphrodite flowers. In the mainly north temperate species, such as *S. cuneata, S. engelmanniana, S. graminea, S. latifolia* and the Old World *S. sagittifolia*, a still more discrete expression of unisexuality is apparent, and perfect flowers are rarely found.

Throughout both families the whorled aerial flowers are borne on erect or floating axes and are essentially terrestrial in structure: they display no features correlated with the aquatic habit of the plants. The corolla, though often small, is significant and attractive, and most genera are probably entomophilous, pollinated mainly by flies with perhaps beetles and snails playing some part, but direct evidence of the mode of pollination is sparse. *Alisma plantago-aquatica* secretes nectar, but each flower produces only about 0·06 mg of pollen: all the anthers on a plant dehisce more or less simultaneously, with the result that pollen is available for only a short period of from 30 min to 4 h, about 92 per cent of the pollen being released between 11 a.m. and 12 noon (Percival, 1965). Wind may also pollinate this species (Daumann, 1964, 1965).

Two tropical monotypes in the Butomaceae, *Tenagocharis latifolia* and *Limnocharis flava*, for which no pollinating agents have been recorded, are probably self-pollinated. After anthesis in *T. latifolia*, the wilting petals close in around the dehisced anthers, pressing them close against the stigmas, which consequently become coated in pollen. The flowers of *L. flava* close after opening for only a few hours, and the petals and stamens quickly become transformed into a mucilaginous mass (van Steenis, 1954).

The controversial opinions on possible natural affinities within and between the Alismaceae and Butomaceae urgently recall the crucial theoretical problem of what constitutes a significant phylogenetic criterion. Most genera appear primitive in some characters but advanced in others. The assessment of the relative evolutionary status of any one genus, and the precise taxonomic delimitation of the families, therefore depend largely on which structural and cytogenetic characters the phylogeneticist heeds and weighs and which he rejects. If as many characters as possible are taken into account, both these families appear heterogeneous and the evolutionary relationships between their genera are immensely difficult to discern.

Although *Alisma*, for example, seems relatively specialised in floral structure, with but a single whorl of carpels, it appears primitive on cytological grounds, having a basic complement of $n=7$ and mostly isobrachial chromosomes (Brown, 1946; Baldwin and Speese, 1955; Skalinska *et al.*, 1961; Pogan, 1961, 1963a, b). In contrast, *Echinodorus* and *Sagittaria* are unspecialised in basic floral organisation but appear cytogenetically more advanced. So far as is known, both these genera are homoploid, with $2n=22$. They are probably closely related, with *Sagittaria* the more specialised in its trend towards unisexuality and a temperate distribution (Wodehouse, 1935, 1936; Brown, 1946; Baldwin and Speese, 1955; Bogin, 1955). Anatomical studies suggest that *Wiesneria* is perhaps the least specialised genus and somewhat remote in affinity with other members of the Alismaceae (Stant, 1964).

Most members of the Butomaceae resemble the Alismaceae in gross floral structure, pollen morphology, embryo-sac development and general anatomical organisation. *Butomus* itself, however, stands aloof in certain cytological respects and by virtue of its sessile linear leaves (rather than petioled laminate ones), lack of laticiferous ducts, persistent rather than caducous petals, pollen grains with only one aperture (rather than many), anatropous rather than campylotropous ovules, monosporic *Polygonum*-type embryo sac (rather than the bisporic *Allium*-type), and straight rather than curved embryo (Holmgren, 1913; Narasimha Murthy, 1933; Wodehouse, 1936; Johri, 1935a, b, c, 1936a, b, 1938a, b; Maheshwari and Singh, 1943; Pichon, 1946; Roper, 1952; Rao,

1953). These differences have led some botanists to argue that the Butomaceae should comprise *Butomus* alone, the other four genera (*Limnocharis, Hydrocleys, Ostenia* and *Tenagocharis*) being assigned to the Alismaceae, as Pichon (1946) originally suggested, or segregated as a separate family—the Limnocharitaceae, as advocated by Takhtajan (1959b).

Although justified by the morphological distinctions cited, this taxonomic procedure ignores certain carpellary characters which are surely of evolutionary significance. All genera of the Butomaceae, including *Butomus,* differ from the Alismaceae in having many ovules scattered on the reticulate parietal placentas of each carpel. This type of placentation, which occurs elsewhere in the mono-cotyledons only in the Hydrocharitaceae, is probably primitive amongst living angiosperms and quite distinct from the basal or sub-basal placentation of the solitary ovule of the Alismaceae. The contrast may be seen again later in development, between the unspecialised, adaxially dehiscent follicle of the Butomaceae and the reduced indehiscent achene of the Alismaceae. On the basis of these carpellary features, Hutchinson (1959) retained the Butomaceae as a family of five genera and grouped it with the Hydrocharitaceae as the most primitive order (Butomales) of monocotyledons, preceding the Alis-maceae in his phylogenetic system. Stant (1964) considered this practice to be further justified by comparative anatomical evidence and regarded *Wiesneria* as the genus of the Alismaceae with the closest affinities to the Butomaceae.

During the past 70 years or so, numerous botanists have speculated upon the possible origin of the monocotyledons from primitive, herbaceous, Ranalian dicotyledons via the Alismaceae, Butomaceae and related families (Henslow, 1891, 1911; Arber and Parkin, 1907; Sargant, 1908; Bessey, 1915; Arber, 1920; Kuprianova, 1948; Hutchinson, 1959). In support of this phylogenetic notion, resemblances between the less specialised Helobian families and the Ranunculaceae and Nymphaeaceae have been seen in such morphological characters as perianth differentiation, polyandry, polycarpy, anatropous ovules and multiple archesporial cells, and in the trimery and scattered parietal placentation of the Butomaceae and *Cabomba,* the scattered vascular bundles and pseudo-solitary cotyledon of the Nymphaeaceae, and the *Ranunculus*-like appearance of the two species of *Ranalisma, R. rostratum* and *R. humile* (Alismaceae).

Despite these structural similarities there are numerous critical differences which negate the possibility that monocotyledons might have so originated. None of the Ranalians possesses the authentic helobial type of endosperm development manifest in many Helobian monocotyledons (p. 323). In the latter the endosperm is generally consumed during seed development whereas some of the tissue persists in the mature seeds of the Ranunculaceae and Nymphaea-ceae (except *Nelumbo*). Although the pollen of some of the woody Ranalians resembles that of the monocotyledons in being monocolpate (having a single germinal furrow), the pollen of the herbaceous Ranunculaceae is tricolpate (Eames, 1961). The Alismaceae further differ from the Ranunculaceae in features of tapetal development, microsporogenesis, nucellar structure, embryo-sac development and proembryo development (Maheshwari, 1964).

10*

Perhaps the most convincing evidence that the monocotyledons could not have evolved from herbaceous dicotyledons is provided by the clearly recent and independent origin and specialisation of vessels in monocotyledonous families (Cheadle, 1942, 1943a, b, 1944, 1953; Bailey, 1949, 1951). Whereas in the Ranunculaceae, vessels predominate in the xylem of all organs, in the Alismaceae vessels occur only in the roots. The xylem tracheary elements in the other organs comprise tracheids with spiral, annular or scalariform thickening and oblique end walls. The Alismaceae also differ anatomically from the Ranunculaceae in their stomatal structure, lacunar system, and in sometimes possessing latex, raphides and rod-shaped crystals. All these morphological distinctions militate against a close affinity between the two families. They do not completely exclude the possibility of descent from a common ancestral stock, but this seems highly unlikely and any such stock must have been extremely remote and ancient (Metcalfe, 1963; Stant, 1964). Finally, it should be noted that the presence of specialised simply-perforate vessels in the roots of the Alismaceae and Butomaceae renders highly improbable any suggestion that either of these families could have been ancestral to other Helobian monocotyledons.

The Mayacaceae and Pontederiaceae. Unspecialised aerial flowers and entomophily also characterise most members of these two monocotyledon families. The hermaphrodite and basically trimerous flowers are borne either solitarily, as in the Mayacaceae, or in a raceme or panicle subtended by a large sheath-like bract, as in most genera of the Pontederiaceae. The conspicuous corolla or petaloid perianth is commonly white, lilac or blue, or rarely yellow. The posterior perianth segment in blue- or lilac-flowered species, e.g. *Eichhornia crassipes* and *Pontederia cordata*, often bears a contrasting bright yellow mark, which may function as a 'honey guide' to visiting bees. In *Monochoria*, the perianth bears red spots and the anthers are differently coloured, five usually being yellow and the sixth larger one blue. Most taxa are actinomorphic but in the Pontederiaceae a trend towards zygomorphy may be described through *Monochoria* and *Heteranthera*, culminating in the heterostylic *Eichhornia*. Specialisation in the syncarpous gynoecium leads from a trilocular ovary, with many ovules in each loculus, as in *Monochoria* or *Eichhornia*, to a unilocular ovary, with a single ovule, the abortive carpels surviving as ridges on the ovary wall, as in *Pontederia* (Singh, 1962).

The floral biology of *Eichhornia crassipes* has been studied in some detail. Anthesis occurs soon after sunrise on bright days: on cloudy humid days it is often delayed (Agharkar and Banerji, 1930). Penfound and Earle (1948) found that the whole flowering cycle takes longer at lower temperatures and also noted that anthesis could be delayed by exposure to white light before midnight, or accelerated by similar exposure after midnight in the preceding dark period. These observations suggest that as in *Nymphaea* and *Victoria* anthesis may be controlled by a sensitive endogenous rhythm. The inflorescence spike comprises 2 to 35 or more, spirally-arranged, zygomorphic flowers. The androecium comprises three short and three long stamens. In India, Agharkar and Banerji (1930) described only mesostylic flowers, with the style inter-mediate in length between short and long stamens. Haigh (1936) found such flowers unusual in Ceylon: there, most flowers possess a style exceeding the long stamens. This latter type was encountered by Penfound and Earle (1948) in a small number of plants from Louisiana and Florida but over 99 per cent of plants in that area are mesostylic. Malaysian specimens appear to be exclusively mesostylic (Backer, 1951f). In none of these areas has the third type of flower, having a style shorter than the short stamens, been found.

The absence or extreme rarity of one type and the paucity of either of the remaining two types of flower in different areas suggest that cross-pollination must only rarely be achieved, and that the heterostylic condition must be disadvantageous to this species. In Indian habitats only about 35 per cent of flowers are successfully pollinated. In both India and the southern U.S.A. self-pollination frequently occurs, especially when the flowers wilt and the perianth segments become inflexed (Agharkar and Banerji, 1930; Penfound and Earle, 1948). In Malaysia, however, fruits are unknown (Backer, 1951f): this curious fact suggests that the mesostylic race here is perhaps self-incompatible.* It would be valuable to study the heterostyly of *E. crassipes* in other parts of its native and adventive range.

Amongst the insects recorded as pollinating agents for *Pontederia cordata* is one species of bee, *Dufourea novae-angliae*, which apparently visits no other plant, its annual emergence usually coinciding with the onset of flowering of *P. cordata* (Percival, 1965).

Entomophilous Dicotyledons. Numerous aquatic dicotyledons dispersed in the larger families show close affinities of floral morphology and pollination with related terrestrial genera. The principal entomophilous examples are the batrachian *Ranunculi* (resembling terrestrial relatives in the Ranunculaceae); *Neptunia* and some species of *Mimosa* (Mimosaceae-Leguminosae); the hetero-stylic *Hottonia* (Primulaceae); *Nymphoides* and the heterostylic *Menyanthes* (Menyanthaceae); *Bacopa*, *Dopatrium*, *Limnophila* and *Micranthemum* (Scrophulariaceae); aquatic species of *Utricularia* (Lentibulariaceae); species of *Asteracantha*, *Cardanthera*, *Hygrophila*, *Nomaphila* and *Synnema* (Acan-thaceae); *Lobelia dortmanna* (Lobeliaceae) and *Megalodonta beckii* (Com-positae). Certain aquatic dicotyledons, however, display slight floral reduction and appear to have discarded the entomophily or ornithophily of their close relatives. They retain the hermaphrodite state but their minute inconspicuous flowers lack petals, or very quickly shed them, and appear to be mainly self-pollinated. *Elatine* (Elatinaceae), *Peplis*, *Decodon* and some species of *Rotala* (Lythraceae), and *Ludwigia* (Onagraceae) are examples of such transitional taxa (Fassett, 1939a; Munz, 1944; Graham, 1964).

Floral Modification and Anemophily. The abandonment of entomophily in favour of anemophily, with concomitant reduction and specialisation of floral

---

*Adventive plants in central California also appear to be self-incompatible (Baker, 1965).

structure, probably occurred during the evolution of the monocotyledonous
Sparganiaceae and Typhaceae and dicotyledonous Hippuridaceae and Haloragaceae for these families now show only the result of the transition (Fig. 9.9).
In the unigeneric Sparganiaceae the unisexual flowers are borne in globose
heads on a simple or branched axis, male heads above and female below. The

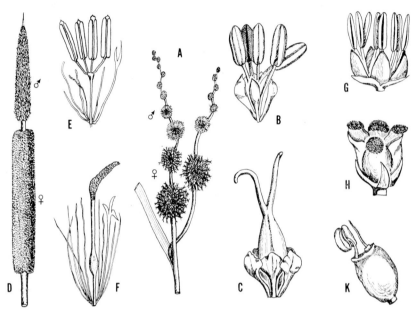

FIG. 9.9. Floral structure in certain anemophilous hydrophytes: *Sparganium eurycarpum*: A, inflorescence (×0·4); B, male flower (×6); C, female flower (×6). *Typha
angustifolia*: D, inflorescence (×0·3); E, male flower (×6); F, female flower (×4).
Myriophyllum spicatum: G, male flower (with petals separated) (×12); H, female
flower (×12). *Hippuris vulgaris*: K, flower (with style deflected away from anther
groove in which it normally lies) (×12).

perianth is reduced to three to six, linear or spatulate scales. Each male flower
has three to eight, mostly free stamens whilst each female flower possesses a
single sessile ovary with one or two loculi, each having but one ovule, and a
simple or forked style. There is fossil evidence of an irregular reduction in
number of loculi since Oligocene time (Cook, 1961a, b).

The Typhaceae show slight further reduction. The flowers are densely
crowded on a single cylindrical spadix. The perianth is represented by bristles
or hairs, which are long in the female flower and may aid the capture of the
wind-borne pollen. The stamens often have connate filaments. The ovary has
but one loculus with a single ovule: the style is filiform and bears a spatulate
stigma. Hybridisation occurs frequently between such widespread species as
Typha latifolia and *T. angustifolia* (Fassett and Calhoun, 1952; van Ooststroom
and Reichgelt, 1962c).

The flowers of the submerged or heterophyllous *Myriophyllum* are aerial and wind-pollinated like those of *Proserpinaca* and the subaquatic genera of the Haloragaceae. Sex distribution varies in different species. In some, e.g. *M. verrucosum*, all the flowers are hermaphrodite: in others, e.g. *M. heterophyllum*, they may be all hermaphrodite or all unisexual, the male arranged above the female. All three types are usually present in inflorescences of *M. spicatum* and *M. alterniflorum*, the hermaphrodite flowers borne between the male and female regions of the spike. In *M. verticillatum* all states may be found on different individuals, with sometimes a tendency towards dioecism, when one type of flower predominates (Pearsall, 1934; Brenan and Chapple, 1949; Clapham, 1962). Modification associated with anemophily is apparent in the inconspicuous lobed calyx which is small in male flowers and minute in female; the feebly coloured petals, which are often absent from female flowers; the relatively long well-exposed anthers, and the recurved or plumose stigmas (Fig. 9.9). Most species, especially those with hermaphrodite flowers, are protandrous.

The mostly hermaphrodite flowers of *Hippuris* are further simplified. The perianth is reduced to a vestigial rim round the apex of the ovary, the androecium to a single median stamen. The unilocular ovary has only one pendulous ovule. The style is filiform and bears receptive papillae along the whole of one side (Fig. 9.9).

Littorella has obvious affinities with the two terrestrial genera of the Plantaginaceae in such features as the tiny membranous corolla, exserted stamens, abundant powdery pollen, long hairy style, and anemophily. It is more specialised than *Plantago*, however, in having unisexual flowers, a unilocular ovary and a single ovule.

Amongst the advanced monocotyledons the isolated aquatic taxa, such as some species of *Carex, Cladium, Cyperus, Eleocharis, Scirpus, Schoenoplectus*, (Cyperaceae), and species of *Glyceria, Phalaris, Phragmites, Vossia, Zizania*, (Gramineae), closely resemble in floral morphology and anemophily the many terrestrial members of their families (Gilly, 1946; Lawrence, 1951; Bakker, 1954; Anderson, 1961; Hadac, 1961; Otzen, 1962; Koyama, 1962, 1963).

Floral Reduction Accompanying Vegetative Specialisation. In both the dicotyledonous Podostemaceae and the monocotyledonous Lemnaceae floral reduction accompanies vegetative specialisation.

The minute aerial flowers of the podostemads are hermaphrodite and basically trimerous. In the least specialised genera, e.g. *Indotristicha*, the regular flowers are usually fragrant and insect-pollinated. They possess a perianth of three, free or connate, bract-like segments with which the three free stamens alternate, and a trilocular ovary with three filiform styles (Fig. 9.10). In other genera the increasing dorsiventrality of the vegetative body also affects the bracts associated with the flowers and ultimately the stamens and gynoecium themselves. Fusion of the bracts at the base of each pedicel produces a cupule-like spathe enclosing the young flower-bud. One stamen is lost and the remaining two become situated ventral to the ovary, their filaments becoming fused and dorsiventrally flattened. In *Farmeria* and some species of *Dicraea* and *Podostemum* there is further reduction to a solitary stamen. The ovary tends to become flattened and bilocular, and the number of styles is concomitantly reduced to two. In *Farmeria* the ventral loculus usually aborts and instead of the many ovules characteristic of the family, the functional loculus has only two or four ovules. A few specialised genera, e.g. *Hydro-*

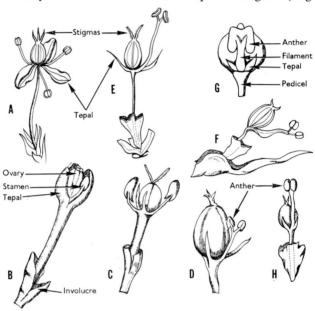

FIG. 9.10. Floral structure in the Podostemaceae: A, *Indotristicha ramosissima* (× 2·5); B, *Tristicha trifaria* (× 3·5); C, *Wettsteiniola accorsii* (× 2·5); D, *Mniopsis weddelliana* (× 10); E, *Dicraea stylosa* (× 2·5); F, *Podostemum subulatus* (× 2·5); G, *Torrenticola queenslandica* (× 7); H, *Cladopus nymani* (× 4). (A, E, F after Subramanyam, 1962; B, C, D after Accorsi, 1944, 1946, 1951; G, H after van Steenis, 1949d.)

bryopsis and *Zeylanidium*, retain two reduced perianth segments lateral to the stamens, but most, e.g. *Farmeria*, *Griffithella* and *Willisia*, have truly naked flowers (Fig. 9.10).

It is a remarkable feature of this strange family that the trend towards extreme zygomorphy (dorsiventrality), culminating in such genera as *Cladopus*, *Torrenticola* and *Farmeria*, is associated with the loss of entomophily and its replacement by anemophily. Yet the dorsiventrality of the flower, restricting the display of anthers and stigmas, must be a great handicap to a cross-pollinated plant (Willis, 1902, 1914, 1915). As if to compensate for this disadvantage, the flower of numerous specialised genera tends to grow erect, by curvature of the pedicel or even of the individual stamens and ovary. The marked tendency of some dorsiventral genera to discard anemophily in favour of autogamy is also probably correlated with the difficulty of achieving cross-pollination.

Willis (1914, 1915, 1926) was particularly impressed by the singular lack of adaptation throughout the Podostemaceae, despite the amazing spectrum of variation in their vegetative and floral morphology. Arber (1920) thought this absence of adaptive characters might be correlated, at least in part, with the uniformity and peculiar nature of the habitats of the family, and the consequent preclusion of competition and elimination of natural selection.

Most botanists now consider the Podostemaceae (and perhaps also the Hydrostachyaceae) to be very advanced and specialised derivatives of the terrestrial Saxifragaceae or Crassulaceae. The podostemads resemble the Saxifragaceae in numerous floral characters, such as the usually superior gynoecium, free styles, and numerous anatropous ovules (Warming, 1891; Engler, 1930). The Podostemaceae is most notable, however, for its complete lack of endosperm and vessels, and for its peculiar pseudo-embryo sac created by the breakdown of nucellar cells immediately beneath the female gametophyte (Magnus, 1913; Razi, 1949; Maheshwari, 1945, 1950, 1964). On the basis of these and other embryological features, the family seems to have closer affinities with the Crassulaceae, from which it may have been derived by further reduction along lines already manifest in the latter group. The submerged *Crassula aquatica* has the most reduced form of endosperm in its family and so appears to be a morphological link between the two groups.

The floral reduction of the Lemnaceae is most comprehensible when interpreted as the end-point of a morphological, and probably evolutionary, series extending through the free-floating *Pistia* from the emergent and terrestrial Araceae. In the evolution of the Araceae, a complete inflorescence appears to have become transformed into a compound insect-pollinated 'flower', the tiny individual flowers being densely crowded on a simple spadix enclosed in a large, herbaceous, and often brilliantly coloured spathe. Most emergent aroids closely resemble their terrestrial relatives: some, e.g. *Acorus*, *Calla* and *Orontium*, have hermaphrodite flowers with a perianth, numerous stamens, and a bi- or multilocular ovary, whilst others, e.g. *Anubias*, *Cryptocoryne* and *Lagenandra*, have naked unisexual flowers on the same spadix, the male above the female. In *Acorus* the spathe is absent whilst in *Orontium* it is reduced to a membranous scale at the base of the spadix.

Submerged species of *Cryptocoryne* are especially interesting for their obstinate retention of flowers adapted for aerial life and entomophily (Fig. 9.11). Most emergent species of the genus produce aerial inflorescences some 5 to 20 cm tall with brightly coloured spathes (de Wit, 1958a). The few habitually submerged species, e.g. *C. affinis*, *C. griffithii* and *C. longicauda* in fresh water and *C. ciliata* in tidal rivers, still produce the same type of inflorescence, but with the spathe growing up through the water, to 40 cm or more tall, and opening just above the surface. The failure of attempted self-pollination (Legro, 1955) and the tendency towards dioecism in such species as *C. lucens*, in which all examined inflorescences show reduction of either stamens or ovaries (de Wit, 1962), suggest that obligate cross-pollination prevails in *Cryptocoryne*.

Experiments have shown that generally the ovaries are ripe and the stigmas receptive for only the first day after the spathe opens whereas the anthers dehisce on the fourth and fifth days. In addition to successful intraspecific cross-pollination between inflorescences of suitable age, a surprising number of interspecific crosses have been achieved, between *C. beckettii* and *C. lutea*, *C. beckettii* and *C. nevillii*, and *C. lutea* and *C. wendtii*, all of which are emergents

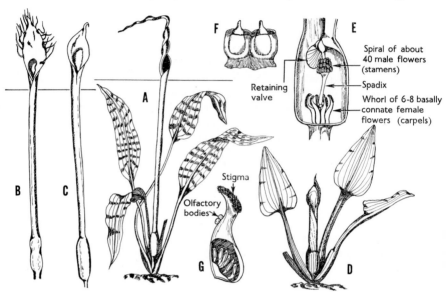

FIG. 9.11. Floral structure in the genus *Cryptocoryne*: A, habit drawing of the sub-merged *C. affinis*, in flower ($\times 0.25$); B, spathe of *C. ciliata* ($\times 0.25$); C, spathe of *C. griffithii* ($\times 0.4$); D, habit drawing of the emergent *C. versteegii*, in flower ($\times 0.4$); E, side view inside basal part of spathe of *C. scurrilis* ($\times 2.5$); F, Single stamen of *C. scurrilis* ($\times 20$); G, side view of single carpel of *C. scurrilis* showing brush-like stigma, olfactory bodies on style, and ovules (in part L.S.) ($\times 8$). (E, F, G, after de Wit, 1962.)

with mitotic chromosome counts of $2n = 28$. Of even greater interest are the successful crosses between *C. lutea* and an unidentified species (with $2n = 42$), and between *C. willisii* ($2n = 28$) and *C. petchii* ($2n = 42$), and also the fact that the submerged *C. affinis*, *C. griffithii* and *C. longicauda* (along with the emergent *C. versteegii*) all have $2n = 34$ (presumably derived from $2n = 35$). These have possibly originated by allopolyploidy from tetraploid ($2n = 28$) and hexaploid ($2n = 42$) emergent parents (Legro, 1960, 1963, *in litt.*).

These various data and the frequent presence of small flies in the inflo-rescences of species imported to Europe suggest that in natural habitats *Cryptocoryne* is cross-pollinated by flies, small moths and beetles in a manner similar to that of the temperate *Arum* and many tropical aroids. The insects probably slip down the spathe into the belly of the flower (i.e. under water in the submerged species) and remain there for a day or so, first shedding pollen on the stigmas, later collecting pollen as they brush past the dehiscing anthers on their way out of the spathe, when the retaining valve withers. According to McCann (1943), some species have translucent streaks on the shoulder of the spathe opposite the male flowers. Collection of pollen may be facilitated by the congregation of the flies in the upper part of the spathe in response to the light filtering through the translucent grille.

The inflorescence of the free-floating *Pistia* (Fig. 9.12) is typically aroid in form but is much reduced, with an unusually short spathe, only 1 to 2 cm long. There is just one whorl of three to eight male flowers, each comprising two connate stamens, and only a single female flower, comprising a unilocular ovary, obliquely adnate to the base of the spadix, with numerous anatropous ovules and a discoid stigma.

Many writers have commented on the apparent rarity of the flowers of most members of the Lemnaceae in natural habitats (Kurz, 1867a, b; Hegelmaier, 1868, 1896; Gillman, 1871; Guppy, 1894; Vuyck, 1895; Thompson, 1898; Saeger, 1929; Hicks, 1932a; Giardelli, 1935, 1939; Gilbert, 1937; Mason, 1938; Kurz and Crowson, 1948; Hillman, 1961c; Daubs, 1965). In only very few taxa, notably *Lemna perpusilla*, are the flowers and fruits relatively frequent. The flowers of several species are known from only one or two collections of herbarium material, whilst those of the warm temperate American *Wolffiella gladiata* have yet to be discovered. It is possible that in some regions the climate at the present time is less favourable for the flowering of certain species than it has been in the past. In the British Isles, for example, conspicuously high frequencies of pollen and seeds resembling those of *Lemna minor* have been observed in various deposits of the Boreal and Atlantic periods of post-glacial time, when the climate was warmer and milder than it is now (Beatson, 1955; Walker and Lambert, 1955).

Floral structure is highly reduced throughout the Lemnaceae (Fig. 9.12). The minute inflorescence of *Spirodela* and *Lemna* is borne in one of the two marginal pockets (often the left-hand one) near the base of the thallus. It comprises one female and two male flowers which protrude from the enclosing membranous spathe. In most species this spathe is open only at the apex, but in some (e.g. *S. oligorhiza* and *L. perpusilla*) it is open for the full depth of one side. Each male flower is a single stamen with a transversely dehiscent bilocular anther. The female consists of a single sessile carpel with a hollow cylindrical style and concave stigma. Species of either genus could be arranged in a series showing reduction in the number, and change in the orientation, of the ovules (Table 9.1).

The inflorescence of *Wolffiella* and *Wolffia* arises from a furrow on the upper exposed surface of the thallus (Fig. 9.12). The furrow is in the median plane in most species of *Wolffia* but lateral to it in *Wolffiella* and also *Wolffia hyalina* and *W. repanda*. *Wolffiella welwitschii* is exceptional in having two lateral furrows on each thallus. In both genera the inflorescence lacks a spathe and comprises merely one male flower and one female flower, the latter being nearer to the base of the thallus. The male is a single stamen with a bilocular or unilocular anther, which dehisces along a pigmented line across its top. In all species the solitary carpel representing the female flower contains just one orthotropous ovule.

The floral morphology of the four genera thus shows further reduction along lines already manifest in *Pistia*. However, it may briefly be noted, as Daubs (1965) remarked in his recent monograph, that had not the conviction of an affinity with the Araceae been so firmly held over the years and were it not now

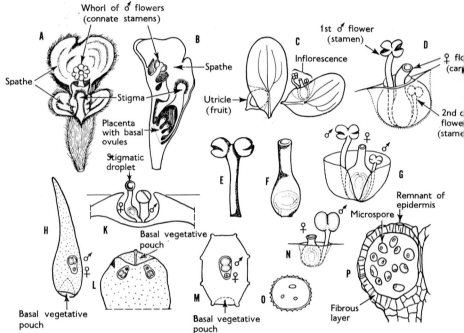

FIG. 9.12. Floral structure in *Pistia* and the Lemnaceae. *Pistia stratiotes*: A, anterior view of inflorescence (×3); B, diagrammatic median L.S. inflorescence (×3). *Lemna minor*: C, fertile thalli from above, with inflorescence and fruit protruding from marginal reproductive pouches (indicated by dotted lines) (×3·5); D, inflorescence surrounded by sac-like spathe (open only at apex) within reproductive pouch (×25); E, lateral view of male flower (stamen) (×30); F, lateral view of female flower (carpel) (×35). *Lemna valdiviana*: G, inflorescence surrounded by spathe (open fully on one side) (×20). *Wolffiella floridana*: H, punctate thallus from above, with inflorescence of one stamen (with bilocular anther) and one carpel in dorsal furrow to one side of median plane (×4·5); K, lateral view of inflorescence in dorsal furrow (note that this part of thallus emerges above water) (×15). *Wolffiella welwitschii*: L, basal half of punctate thallus from above, with inflorescences in furrows on both sides of median plane (×3·5). *Wolffia microscopica*: M, fertile thallus from above, with inflorescence in median dorsal furrow (×20); N, lateral view of inflorescence emerging from furrow (×30); O, echinate, three-nucleate microspore (×350); P, L.S. one loculus of anther, showing fibrous layer and ephemeral epidermis (×200). (Note: various degrees of transverse dehiscence of anthers in D, E and G; pigmented line of dehiscence across top of anther in K and N; female flower towards base of thallus in H, L and M; ovule orientation amphitropous in F, orthotropous in G, K and N); (G, H, K, L, after Daubs, 1965; M, N, O, P, after Maheshwari, 1954.)

supported by other evidence (see p. 290), the descriptive terms applied to the inflorescence of the Lemnaceae might well be different. No trace of an aroid spadix is visible in any species, and the spathe of *Spirodela* and *Lemna* could have been deemed a reduced perianth. Consistent with this notion, the inflorescence of all four genera could have been regarded as a reduced hermaphrodite flower, composed of one carpel and either one or two stamens.

Some earlier observers (see Arber, 1920) claimed that *Lemna minor* and other species are protandrous but certain recent authors (see Lawalrée, 1961) have alleged they are protogynous. In at least some species possessing three

TABLE 9.1   Number and orientation of ovules in *Spirodela* and *Lemna*

Species of Spirodela	Lemna	Number per carpel	Orientation
	L. gibba	2 to 6	anatropous
		1	amphitropous
S. intermedia		4	anatropous
S. polyrhiza		2	anatropous
		1	amphitropous
S. biperforata		2	anatropous
	L. disperma	2	amphitropous
S. oligorhiza	*L. minor*		
S. punctata	*L. obscura*	1	amphitropous
	L. trisulca		
	L. perpusilla	1	obliquely orthotropous
	L. trinervis		
	L. minima	1	orthotropous
	L. valdiviana		

(Table compiled from data in Daubs, 1965.)

flowers per inflorescence, floral development is actually phased. One stamen ripens first, then the carpel, and lastly the second stamen (Subramanyam, 1962). For such species neither protandrous nor protogynous is really an appropriate term. Species of *Wolffia*, in which the inflorescence is only two-flowered, do appear to be commonly protogynous (Maheshwari, 1954; Daubs, 1965).

Noting the short rigid nature of the stamens and carpels and the rather low output of microspores, which are echinate in all species, Arber (1920), McCann (1942) and others have concluded that the Lemnaceae are entomophilous. Rather than attach such significance to the products of drastic morphological reduction, it might be more realistic to regard the mode of pollination as quite unspecific. All species are highly gregarious plants, and wind or surface currents could easily bring the stiff curved stamens of any one thallus into direct contact with the stigma of another, as den Hartog (1964b) recently observed in colonies of *Lemna trisulca*. Pollen could equally be blown or splashed from plant to plant or carried by haphazardly scrambling weevils, flies and surface-dwelling aquatic insects.

It is now commonly believed, in agreement with Engler (1877), that the Lemnaceae have close natural affinities with the Araceae, from which they may have been derived by evolutionary reduction along a line represented amongst living plants by the series: Araceae→*Pistia*→*Spirodela*→*Lemna*→*Wolffiella*→ *Wolffia* (Arber, 1919c, 1920; Maheshwari, S. C., 1956b, 1958, 1959; Hutchinson, 1959; Corner, 1964; Maheshwari, P., 1964). A lone voice opposing this view has been that of Lawalrée (1943, 1945, 1952) who argued that *Lemna* evolved from *Wolffia* and that the family as a whole is derived from the Helobiales. Lawalrée failed to explain how the relatively complex vascular organisation of *Lemna* could have originated from *Wolffia* in which no such system is present. He homologised the flaps of the pockets of *Spirodela* with 'squamulae in:ravaginales' and alleged that the endosperm of *Lemna minor* is helobial. However, the investigations by Gupta (1935), Maheshwari (1954, 1956a, b, 1958), and Maheshwari and Kapil (1963a, b) have clearly shown that in both *Lemna* and *Wolffia* the endosperm is the cellular type, as in typical members of the Araceae, and not the helobial or nuclear types found in the Helobian monocotyledons. These studies also revealed similarities between the Lemnaceae and Araceae in microsporogenesis, pollen morphology, structure of the nucellus and integuments, and early embryogeny, and so strongly supported the idea that the Lemnaceae are much reduced and specialised descendants of an aroid stock. *Pistia stratiotes* is a reduced aroid, whilst *Spirodela polyrhiza* and *S. intermedia* are in certain features less specialised than the remaining Lemnaceae, and so these plants occupy a seemingly intermediate position in the hypothetical evolutionary series. Many botanists have commented on the similarity of adult *Spirodela* or *Lemna* to seedlings of *Pistia*; and Takhtajan (1959a, b) saw in this the interesting possibility that both have evolved from *Pistia* (or a *Pistia*-like stock) by neoteny. The morphological resemblance between adult *Wolffia* thalli and very young *Lemna* seedlings could be similarly interpreted.

CLEISTOGAMY AND SELF-FERTILISATION IN BUD

The cleistogamy of certain hydrophytes has been regarded as an evasion of the problems of elevating flowers above the water. The buds remain submerged and never open, so that self-pollination is enforced: pollen is presumed to be shed on the stigmas of the same flower through air retained within the clasped perianth. Cleistogamy has been recorded in numerous submerged and floating-leaved species, notably *Baldellia ranunculoides* (West, 1910), *Elatine triandra* (Backer, 1951a), *Euryale ferox* (Goebel, 1891–1893; Khanna, 1964), *Heteranthera graminea* (Wylie, 1917b), *Hydrothrix gardneri* (Goebel 1913), *Limosella aquatica* (Hooker, 1847), *Luronium natans* (Schenck, 1885), *Podostemum barberi* (Willis, 1902; Subramanyam, 1962), certain batrachian *Ranunculi* (Royer, 1881–1883), and *Trapella sinensis* (Oliver, 1888). It is also said to occur in *Hottonia palustris* (e.g. Tutin, 1962) although Prankerd (1911) found that supposedly cleistogamous flowers were merely abortive.

Cleistogamy has recently been studied in *Ottelia ovalifolia* (Ernst-Schwarzenbach, 1956). Specimens from New Caledonia cultivated for several years at

Zurich regularly produced normal aerial flowers in the summer, but in the spring or autumn, or in the summer if the plants were crowded, they bore only small submerged cleistogamous flowers in the axils of the leaf sheaths. Many of the cleistogamous specimens were dwarf juvenile plants with ribbon leaves. The cleistogamous flowers were found to have dwarfed but functional stamens and stigmas inside the reduced perianth. The anther walls did not dehisce in the normal way: they just degenerated wherever they were adjacent to the stigmas, so that microspores and stigmas came into direct contact. Fruits developing from cleistogamous flowers were smaller and had fewer seeds than those from normal flowers. It would be interesting to know whether the formation of cleisto- or chasmogamous flowers in *O. ovalifolia* and other hydrophytes is a response to photoperiod, as Borgström (1939) found in the terrestrial *Viola*.

A few hydrophytes exhibit a related phenomenon, slightly different from cleistogamy, which occurs also in certain terrestrial angiosperms, such as *Hordeum vulgare* (barley) and *Pisum sativum* (garden pea). Self-pollination occurs within the closed flower-buds, but these subsequently open. This happens quite frequently in *Subularia aquatica* (Hiltner, 1886), *Blyxa alternifolia* (den Hartog, 1957b) and *Ottelia alismoides* (Ernst-Schwarzenbach, 1956). The buds fail to emerge into the air, are self-pollinated, and then eventually open whilst still submerged (see also Fig. 9.13, D). Such flowers, unlike cleistogamous ones, are similar in size and structure to the normal aerial flowers of the species.

TRENDS CULMINATING IN HYDROPHILY

Trends of floral modification culminating in the development of submerged water-pollinated flowers are discernible amongst both monocotyledons and dicotyledons. The progressive floral reduction evident amongst the families in the Najadales is associated with both the transition from anemophily to hydrophily and the conquest of marine habitats. Numerous genera within the Hydrocharitaceae afford a similar morphological series. The Callitrichaceae displays reduction in flower structure in both wind- and water-pollinated species: structural reduction and hydrophily also occur in another isolated dicotyledonous family, the Ceratophyllaceae. These two families are restricted to fresh water, perhaps because they lack the extensive system of rhizomes and roots which seems essential for survival in the sea (Arber, 1919d, 1920).

Associated with the transition to hydrophily is an overall trend from actinomorphic hermaphrodite flowers (or reduced inflorescences) to zygomorphic dioecious flowers. The perianth becomes modified, greatly reduced, even lost. The number of stamens is reduced and the filament may disappear: the androecium of the most specialised taxa, e.g. *Najas* and *Zostera*, comprises only a solitary sessile anther. Carpel number and ovule number are also reduced: the solitary pendulous ovule of some highly modified taxa, e.g. the Zannichelliaceae and Zosteraceae (but not the Najadaceae), is orthotropous in contrast to the more common anatropous type.

The flowers of plants pollinated at the surface of the water are unusually mobile. When mature, male flowers may absciss from their pedicels and float freely, whilst the stigmas are brought to the surface by the elongation of the peduncle or the apex of the ovary. The waxy cuticle and air-trapping spines of their extine enable the microspores to float, although this is of adaptive value in a few taxa only, notably species of *Elodea*. In the wholly submerged flowers of truly hydrophilous plants the reduction of the anther wall and frequent absence of an endothecium are presumably associated with the fact that the normal mechanism of dehiscence, triggered by desiccation, cannot operate under water. The wall commonly comprises just an epidermis and hypodermis of thin-walled cells. Rarely, as in *Zostera*, a few feeble thickenings develop on the walls of the hypodermal cells but do not function in dehiscence. The microspores are liberated when the epidermis is ruptured by local swellings of the hypodermis. Submerged floating microspores generally lack an extine, are filiform in shape or united into long chains, and often show precocious germination (Wodehouse, 1935; van Campo, 1951). Many hydro-anemophilous and hydrophilous genera resemble anemophilous terrestrial angiosperms in their great pollen output compared with low ovule number (Jaeger, 1961).

Floral Modification and Pollination in the Najadales. Amongst the Najadales the least specialised flowers are probably those of the submerged and floating-leaved Aponogetonaceae (Figs. 9.13, 9.14). They are small, hermaphrodite, actinomorphic and borne on an aerial spike initially enveloped by a caducous basal hood. In most Asiatic and Australian species the spike is simple: in most African species it is forked once or more. Each flower has one to three persistent tepals, six to eighteen whorled stamens, and a gynoecium of three to six sessile carpels, each containing up to eight basal anatropous ovules. Some members of the family are probably ento- or anemophilous, others perhaps autogamous. Certain species tend towards unisexuality. In *Aponogeton loriae* the dense lower flowers are hermaphrodite but the remote upper ones are almost male, having reduced carpels and unusually long stamens (van Steenis, 1948). The *A. junceus* complex includes ssp. *natalensis*, with hermaphrodite flowers; ssp. *junceus*, with mostly hermaphrodite self-fertile flowers but also occasional female flowers having just six carpels and two tepals; and the permanently apomictic ssp. *rehmannii*, with flowers always female, their potential stamens being replaced by carpels (Obermeyer, 1966a, *in litt.*). Female flowers devoid of tepals occur in *A. nudiflorus* (Peter, 1938). The trend culminates in the dioecism of *A. troupini* and *A. dioecus*, whose male flowers have two tepals, six stamens and a pistillode of three abortive carpels, the naked female flowers comprising just three or four carpels (Bosser and Raynal, 1966).

Perhaps the most puzzling morphological feature of the flowers in the Aponogetonaceae is that whilst the androecium and gynoecium are regularly trimerous in basic arrangement, there is a frequent tendency for the perianth to consist of only two anteriolateral segments, as in *A. natans*, *A. crispus* and *A. stachyosporus*, or even just a single, enlarged, bract-like segment, as in *A.*

FIG. 9.13. The inflorescence of the Aponogetonaceae (*Aponogeton*). *A. distachyos*: A, flowering community, showing forked inflorescences with conspicuous tepals (smaller floating leaves belong to seedlings) ($\times 0.1$); B, opening inflorescence, showing hood ($\times 0.8$), (see also Fig. 9.14 F). *A. desertorum*: C, forked inflorescences ($\times 0.25$). *A. fenestralis*: D, submerged forked inflorescence with carpels ripening to follicles which ultimately liberated many seeds. (This inflorescence never emerged from the water: self-fertilisation presumably occurred in the bud; the carpels had already begun to swell by the time the hood was dropped ($\times 0.8$). *A. junceus* ssp. *rehmannii* (an apomict): E, aerial inflorescences with carpels beginning to swell ($\times 0.5$); F, submerged inflorescences: one young and still hooded (to right of leaves at centre bottom), one older but still possessing reduced tepals (at right) and one with elongated axes and carpels ripening to follicles (at left) ($\times 0.4$); G, older submerged inflorescence with clusters of 6 to 9 swelling carpels ($\times 0.5$).

distachyos. Such perianths are generally presumed to have originated by reduction from a basic trimerous type, yet Singh (1965c) was quite unable to find any evidence in the vascular anatomy of the flower to support this mode of derivation. Singh did find, however, another feature of anatomical interest; namely, the occasional presence of inversely orientated vascular bundles in the perianth segment of *A. distachyos*, suggesting that this organ, like the perianth segment of *Eichhornia crassipes* (see Singh, 1962) is phyllodial in nature.

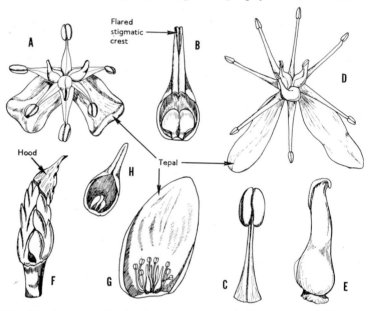

FIG. 9.14. Floral structure in the Aponogetonaceae (*Aponogeton*). *A. rigidifolius*: A, flower, anterior view (×8); B, carpel, adaxial surface and part L.S. to show ovules (×18); C, stamen, adaxial surface (×30). *A. stachyosporus*: D, flower, anterior view (×7); E, carpel, lateral view (×18). *A. distachyos*: F, opening inflorescence just before hood falls (×0·8); G, flower, anterior view (×3·5); H, carpel, adaxial surface and part L.S. to show ovules (×8).

The studies of von Eber (1934), Uhl (1947) and Singh (1965c) have revealed important morphological similarities between the Aponogetonaceae and the monotypic Scheuchzeriaceae (*Scheuchzeria palustris*) of the cool north temperate zone. In both families the gynoecium is basically trimerous; the follicular carpels are basally and adaxially connate and open whilst young; and each carpel is supplied by one dorsal and two ventral vascular bundles. These common (and relatively primitive) features suggest that the two families may have much closer affinities than Hutchinson (1959) recognised. He placed the Scheuchzeriaceae in his order Alismatales, regarding it as perhaps reduced from the Alismaceae, and put the Aponogetonaceae, as possible freshwater progenitors of the marine Zosteraceae, in another order, Aponogetonales. Singh (1965c) further pointed out that the vascularisation of the carpel lends no support to the notion of affinity between the Aponogetonaceae and Zostera-ceae, for it is quite different in the two groups.

Affinities may also exist between the Scheuchzeriaceae and the Juncagina-ceae (*Triglochin* and its relatives). Points of resemblance include the basically trimerous and hermaphrodite flowers, often basally connate carpels, basal anatropous ovules, racemose inflorescence, basally-sheathing linear leaves, emergent rhizomatous habit, protogyny and anemophily. The Juncaginaceae is perhaps more specialised in its tendency towards unisexuality in some species, occasional sterility of alternate carpels, reduction to a single ovule in each carpel, and predominantly halophytic habit.

The anemophilous emergent *Lilaea scilloides*, which occurs in alkali-rich lakes and temporary pools in Pacific North and South America, is somewhat anomalous in floral organisation. It bears two types of inflorescence: basal spikes enclosed in the sheathing leaf-bases and composed of hermaphrodite flowers except for a terminal male flower, and scapose spikes which comprise just female flowers. Each hermaphrodite flower has a bract-like perianth segment which is adnate to the base of the single stamen, and a single appressed carpel containing a solitary ovule. Singh (1965d) recently showed that the gynoecium is derived from an original trimerous type by suppression of two of the three carpels. His anatomical studies also led to the conclusion that each hermaphrodite flower is a true flower, and not a secondary inflorescence reduced to a combined male flower and female flower, as Uhl (1947) and Eames (1961) suggested. Furthermore, he demonstrated that the two long-styled female flowers which occur near the base of the peduncle receive, from the rhizome, vascular supplies quite separate from the supply to the inflore-scence, and are therefore morphologically equivalent to axillary shoots.

The taxonomic position of *Lilaea scilloides* has long been uncertain. Most botanists have tended to include it with the Juncaginaceae and/or Scheuch-zeriaceae. On the basis of embryological characters, Agarwal (1952) considered its affinities closer to *Triglochin* than to *Scheuchzeria*. The morphological and anatomical data presented by Uhl (1947) and Singh (1965d) support the notion that it is probably a descendant of a *Triglochin*-type of stock, but justify its segregation as a monotypic family, the Lilaeaceae, as in Hutchinson's classification.

In the Potamogetonaceae the flowers are borne on axillary or terminal spikes and appear to be hermaphrodite. The most puzzling feature of each flower is that each of the four so-called perianth segments is curiously adnate to a stamen (Fig. 9.15) and has been interpreted by some botanists to be an outgrowth of the staminal connective. However, developmental studies by Hegelmaier (1870), Uhl (1947) and Sattler (1965) have shown quite clearly that the stamen and corresponding perianth segment are initiated separately on the floral apex and later become basally united: each organ has a distinct vascular supply. Even so, there is still no general agreement about the morphological nature of the perianth. Uhl (1947) and later Eames (1961) chose to interpret each perianth segment as a sepaloid bract subtending and adnate to the correspond-ing stamen. On this hypothesis, they regarded the flower of the Potamogetonaceae as an inflorescence comprising four male flowers, each of a single stamen and its adnate bract, and four apetalous female flowers, each of a single carpel with one campylotropous ovule (Fig. 9.15). They therefore considered that the flower spike represents a reduced compound inflorescence. Singh (1965a), on the other hand, concluded from a comparative study of floral morphology and vascular anatomy in seven species of *Potamogeton* (together

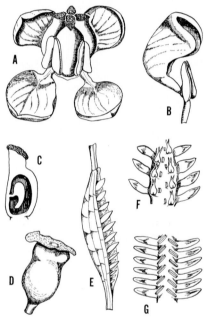

FIG. 9.15. Floral structure in *Potamogeton*, *Ruppia* and *Phyllospadix*. *Potamogeton natans*: A, flower, with two 'perianth segments' deflected forwards ($\times 8$); B, lateral view of 'perianth segment' and anther ($\times 12$); C, L.S. carpel to show ovule position ($\times 8$). *Ruppia maritima*: D, lateral view of carpel with peltate stigma ($\times 8$). *Phyllospadix scouleri*: E, Lateral view of leaf sheath with emerging inflorescence ($\times 0.6$); F, surface view of part of female inflorescence with bracts, sessile carpels, and rudimentary sessile anthers ($\times 1.2$); G, surface view of part of male inflorescence with bracts and sessile anthers ($\times 1.2$). (E, F, G, after Hutchinson, 1959.)

with one of *Ruppia* and one of *Zannichellia*) that the flower of *Potamogeton* is a normal flower with true perianth segments. Sattler (1965), however, frankly considered it impossible to categorise the flower as a true flower or as an inflorescence, since it displays characteristics of both. He very pertinently questioned the interpretive value of the orthodox morphological assumption that the flower and the inflorescence are mutually exclusive categories, and further emphasised the pressing need for critical studies of the floral morphology of many other Helobian genera.

Most members of the Potamogetonaceae produce erect spikes and are wind-pollinated. In some, as *Potamogeton natans* and *P. polygonifolius*, the spike is densely flowered; in others, as *P. pusillus* and *Groenlandia densa*, it bears only two to eight flowers: the carpels are reduced effectively to one in *P. trichoides*. The spike of a few species, e.g. *P. filiformis* and *P. pectinatus* (which often extend into brackish waters), floats on or near the water surface, each successive flower being lifted just above the surface. The pollen floats to the stigmas of the same or other inflorescences (Daumann, 1963). In these species, the stigmas bear larger receptive papillae than those of the anemophilous taxa. The Potamogetonaceae appear intermediate in the trend towards genuine hydrophily and the marine habit.

Further specialisation may be traced along several separate lines. The flowers of the unigeneric Ruppiaceae, a small family of brackish-water plants, are somewhat similar in structure to those of the Potamogetonaceae but are usually submerged and pollinated under water. Each spike bears two hermaphrodite flowers, each comprising two stamens between which lie six or more stipitate carpels, each with a campylotropous ovule. Singh (1965a) considered this to be a true flower rather than a reduced inflorescence, and regarded the triangular outgrowth from between the lobes of each stamen as homologous with the perianth segment of the *Potamogeton* flower. In *Ruppia maritima*, the stalks of the carpels elongate, so that the discoid peltate stigmas (Fig. 9.15) form a loose canopy some 2·5 to 3 cm above the anthers. The long reniform microspores, often adherent in strings, float upwards and are caught beneath the stigmatic canopy of the same or higher inflorescences. They tend to drift out from under the canopy, round its margins, to the receptive stigmatic surface, where some adhere and germinate (McCann, 1945).

True hydrophily is also attained in the marine Zosteraceae (*Zostera* and *Phyllospadix*). Each female flower of *Zostera* is reduced to a carpel with a single orthotropous ovule and two large stigmas whilst each male flower is represented by a single unilocular sessile anther. Male and female flowers alternate in two rows on a flattened axis enclosed by a leaf-sheath. All species seem to be protogynous, the carpels maturing between 1 and 3 days before the anthers (Clavaud, 1878; Tutin, 1936, 1962). The liberated microspores are filiform and of the same specific gravity as sea-water: they float in a cloudy mass at any depth and are caught by chance on the stigmas of other plants. In turbulent water much pollen must be wasted. *Phyllospadix* also has filamentous microspores, and carpels with two slender stigmas, but in contrast to *Zostera* it is usually dioecious (Fig. 9.15).

Specialisation is evident also in the marine Posidoniaceae (*Posidonia*) and in the fresh- or brackish-water and marine Zannichelliaceae (*Zannichellia*, *Althenia*, *Syringodium*, *Amphibolis*, *Cymodocea* and *Halodule*), the flowers of which are fully submerged and pollinated under water. *Posidonia* has branched spikes of hermaphrodite flowers, with or without a reduced perianth of three scales. The androecium of each flower comprises three or four sessile anthers and a unilocular ovary with a solitary parietal ovule and a feathery lacerate stigma (Fig. 9.16). In contrast, the floral organisation of the Zannichelliaceae appears more advanced, as a result of further reduction. The flowers are solitary or in cymose clusters and usually enclosed initially in membranous sheaths:

most genera seem to be monoecious, but *Althenia, Cymodocea* and *Halodule* are dioecious. A reduction series in androecial structure may be traced through the various genera from *Amphibolis* and *Cymodocea* which have two free anthers to *Halodule*, in which the two or three bilocular anthers are basally or wholly connate, and *Althenia*, in which there is but one unilocular anther. In the marine genera, pollination depends upon chance entanglement of the thread-like microspores amongst the simple or forked filamentous styles.

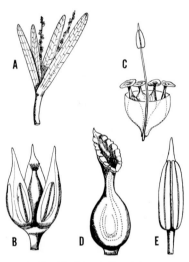

FIG. 9.16. Floral structure in *Posidonia* and *Zannichellia*. *Posidonia oceanica*: A, in-florescence subtended by reduced leaves (× 0·8); B, lateral view of flower, with anthers slightly deflected (× 15). *Zannichellia palustris*: C, four female flowers (carpels), each with peltate stigma, within spathe; and one male flower (stamen) (× 4); D, female flower (carpel) with lingulate stigma (stylar canal and ovule position shown by dotted lines) (× 10); E, anther (× 15). (A, B, after Hutchinson, 1959.)

In *Zannichellia* itself the flowers are unisexual and monoecious, one male and one or several females appearing to arise as a group in a leaf axil. The male flower is actually borne terminally on a short lateral stem in the axil of the lower of the two leaves at a node, whilst the female terminates the main axis, vegetative growth being maintained by an axillary shoot. The membranous cup-shaped spathe which usually surrounds the female flower(s) may be homologous with the tubular bract-like sheath around each node of the vegetative shoot. Each female flower comprises a single carpel with one orthotropous ovule. Each male flower usually comprises a single stamen, but stamens have been found which possess four lobes, eight microsporangia and a double vascular strand, suggesting that two original stamens have become fused into an apparently single organ (Singh, 1965a). The staminal filament elongates and raises the anther well above the carpels. The liberated microspores, as in the genus *Althenia*, are globose and of higher specific gravity than water. They sink on to the peltate or tongue-shaped stigmas and are said to slide down the stylar canal (Roze, 1887).

Singh's (1965a) study and interpretation of floral structure led him to visualise a morphological series from *Potamogeton* through *Ruppia* to *Zannichellia*, involving the change from hermaphroditism to unisexuality, the reduction and loss of the perianth, a decrease in the number of stamens, and the reduction of the carpellary vascular supply. In view of these apparent affinities, together with resemblances of vegetative structure (Singh, 1964), he argued that *Ruppia* and *Zannichellia* should be retained within the Potamogetonaceae, and not segregated in different families as Hutchinson (1959) maintained.

The hydrophilous Najadaceae, comprising one genus of fresh- and brackish-water plants, are probably the most reduced of all the Helobian monocotyledons. Most species are monoecious, with their minute flowers borne solitarily or in small groups. In typical species, e.g. *Najas graminea*, each flower appears axillary in position but the vascular anatomy of the nodal region shows that it is actually terminal on a much-reduced lateral branch (Singh, 1965b). Each male flower has but a single sessile anther which is borne aloft on a short stalk during anthesis. The anther is invested by a two-lipped envelope which is only two cells thick and is adnate basally, adherent above. This envelope is not present around the female flower, which comprises just a solitary sessile carpel containing a basal anatropous ovule. Although two stigmas are commonly present, there is no evidence in the vascular supply of the flower to suggest that the gynoecium originally comprised more than one carpel (Singh, 1965b).

According to the species, an outer, free, flask-shaped envelope may surround a solitary flower of either sex, or a cluster of flowers. This structure was used by Rendle (1899, 1900) to divide species into two subgenera: *Najas* (comprising only *N. marina*; Fig. 9.17), with the outer envelope present only in male flowers, and *Caulinia*, with the envelope present or absent in both types of flower.

The morphological nature of the floral envelopes has been obscure and controversial for many years. Both the inner and the outer have been variously designated as perianths, spathes or membranous sheathing bracts. From his anatomical investigations, Singh (1965b) concluded that the outer envelope, whether it surrounds a solitary flower or a cluster, is equivalent in origin, structure and vascularisation to the spathe of the Hydrocharitaceae, thus supporting Rendle's (1899) original contention. In a recent study of the Asiatic and Malaysian taxa of *Najas*, de Wilde (1961) encountered specimens of *N. graminea* (in which the flowers are usually naked) with some flowers possessing envelopes intermediate in structure between a typical spathe and a foliage leaf (Fig. 9.17). They resembled a spathe in the connation of their margins and lack of a midrib, but like a foliage leaf they were green, elongated, and possessed intravaginal scales. Amongst the female flowers of Indian specimens of *N. indica* de Wilde also found envelopes of intermediate structure (Fig. 9.17). The outer free envelope of the *Najas* flower is thus probably homologous with a normal foliage leaf. This interpretation is supported also by the fact that typical envelopes, intermediates and leaves all have a similar toothed apex. Since intermediates occur, the presence or absence of the outer envelope is not a reliable characteristic and is certainly inadequate for segregation at subgeneric level (de Wilde, 1962).

The inner envelope of the male flower and the curious absence of any corresponding structure from the female flower still present problems. Most authorities have followed Rendle (1899) in interpreting the envelope as the

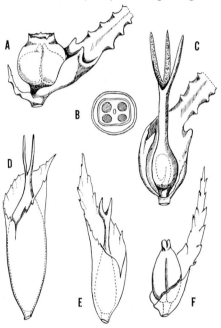

FIG. 9.17. Floral structure in the Najadaceae (*Najas*). *Najas marina*: A, male flower in leaf axil (form of anther shown by broken line; inner envelope not shown) (×18); B, diagrammatic T.S. male flower, showing two envelopes, four sporangia and vascular strand (×18); C, female flower in leaf axil (ovule position shown by broken line) (×18). *Najas indica*: D, Exceptional female flower (×14). *Najas graminea*: E, exceptional female flower (×18); F, exceptional male flower (×12); D, E, F, showing envelopes intermediate between typical spathe and typical foliage leaf. (D, E, F, after de Wilde, 1961.)

perianth (and in regarding the eventual stalk of the anther as a pedicel, not a filament) but there is little critical evidence in support of this view. Arber's (1920) argument that the envelope is not likely to be a morphologically normal perianth was based upon the speculative notion that the Najadaceae might have been derived from Potamogetonaceae stock. She presumed that the latter, together with the modern pondweeds, lacked a true perianth, but as noted earlier (p. 295) this is itself a very moot morphological point. Her other suggestion, that the envelope might be a cupule- or aril-like structure is not easily reconciled with its presence in the male rather than the female flower.

Although different organs rarely show parallel rates of evolutionary reduction it is surely strange that a complete investing perianth should have survived in one sex but not the other, and in a flower so profoundly reduced as that of *Najas*. Until the development and possible homologies of these structures are better understood, it might perhaps be politic to avoid morphological commitment, as Swamy and Lakshmanan (1962b) suggested, by referring to the inner envelope simply as the inner envelope, and the outer one as the sheath.

No detailed studies have been devoted to the pollination of *Najas*. The microspores are globular or ellipsoid, rich in starch and devoid of an extine: when liberated through the apex of the inner envelope they have often begun to germinate. Since the monoecious plants usually grow in dense masses male and female flowers are likely to be in close proximity. The floating microspores are probably caught haphazardly on the elongated stigmas (Roze, 1892). The partly-grown pollen tubes, increasing the effective surface of the microspores and thus substituting for the filamentous form of the pollen of other hydrophilous plants, may facilitate pollination.

The phylogenetic relationships between the various families of the Najadales are still profoundly obscure and are likely to remain so for some time. Taxonomic opinions on classification and evolutionary concepts of affinities within the order often differ in quite fundamental respects, largely because of different morphological interpretations of such structures as the flower of *Potamogeton* and the floral envelopes of *Najas*. At the present time, it seems preferable to keep all the families within one order and to refrain from phylogenetic speculation until the floral and vegetative morphology of all genera are much better understood. There is reasonable agreement, however, on certain general principles, such as the overall trends toward unisexuality, true hydrophily and marine habit, and the cardinal significance of evolutionary advance by morphological reduction. With these notions in mind, it seems valid to regard the Scheuchzeriaceae and Aponogetonaceae as the least specialised and perhaps genuinely primitive families, and the Zannichelliaceae and Najadaceae as the most highly advanced, the last having failed to colonise marine habitats probably only because of its lack of rhizomes and generally sparse roots. Beyond this, very little may be said, with any validity, on phylogenetic relationships. However, it is important to appreciate that there is no *a priori* reason to assume that all the families are closely allied and that the Najadales represents a homogeneous natural order. Indeed, present knowledge of the morphology of the group, inadequate though it may be, is sufficient to suggest that evolutionary specialisation has probably followed several quite distinct courses.

Floral Structure and Pollination in the Hydrocharitaceae. Great interest in the floral biology of the Hydrocharitaceae was evoked by early studies of the pollination mechanism of *Vallisneria*. Although nothing is known of the flowering behaviour of *Blyxa* and *Nechamandra*, or of numerous species in other genera, present knowledge reveals within the family a singularly fascinating transition series (Figs. 9.18, 9.19, 9.20).

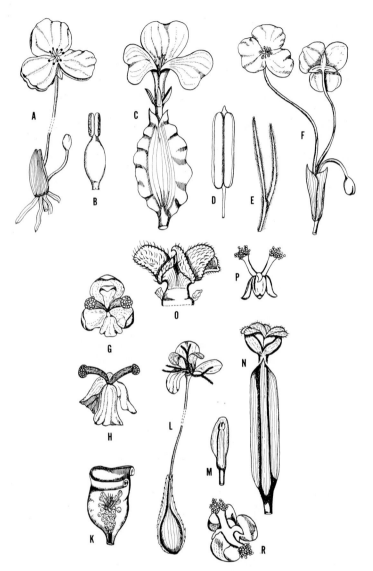

FIG. 9.18. Floral structure in the Hydrocharitaceae. *Egeria densa*: A, male spathe, bud
and open flower (×1); B, stamen (×7). *Ottelia alismoides*: C, flower and winged
spathe (×0·6); D, stamen (×6); E, style (×4). *Hydrocharis morsus-ranae*: F,
male spathe, bud, and two flowers, showing upper and lower surface (×0·75). *Nechamandra alternifolia*: G, young male flower, from above (×15); H, older male flower,
lateral view (×15); K, male spathe, with flower buds within (×5). *Lagarosiphon major*:
L, female flower and spathe (×10). *Vallisneria spiralis*: M, young female spathe
(×6); N, female flower at pollination time (lies horizontally) (×4); O, stigmatic
lobes of female flower (×10); P, male flower, lateral view (×12); R, male flower,
from above (×15). G, H, K, after Subramanyam, 1962; N, O, P, R, after Kausik,
1939.)

Certain free-floating and submerged taxa are entomophilous: *Hydrocharis*, *Limnobium* (except *L. stoloniferum*), *Ottelia*, *Stratiotes* and *Egeria*. Their aerial flowers are the least modified of the genus. They are quite large (1 to 4 cm in

FIG. 9.19. *Vallisneria spiralis*: A, two specimens with some outer leaves removed to show male spathes (arrowed): empty spathe on plant at left, intact spathe containing male flowers, with smaller developing spathe just beneath it, on plant at right ($\times 0.5$); B, base of female plant with leaves slightly displayed to show young female spathe (arrowed) on slender peduncle which is just starting to elongate ($\times 0.4$); C, view of female plant at later stage with spathe (arrowed) being borne up to the surface on filiform peduncle ($\times 0.3$).

diameter), actinomorphic, and trimerous, with a distinct calyx of herbaceous persistent sepals and a corolla of white, pink or yellow imbricate petals. The flowers are arranged in a spathe composed of a single entire bract, or two opposite bracts, which may be free or connate (Fig. 9.18).

Sex distribution varies. Some taxa have unisexual flowers: the male have three to twelve or more stamens (the outer sometimes sterile) and often one or more rudimentary ovaries, pistillodes; the female have an inferior unilocular

11

ovary, with parietal placentae and numerous scattered ovules, and staminodes are often present. *Hydrocharis* and *Limnobium* are probably monoecious, the two sexes occurring in different rosettes, i.e. at different nodes, joined by fragile stolons. The few records of dioecism are perhaps based on plants

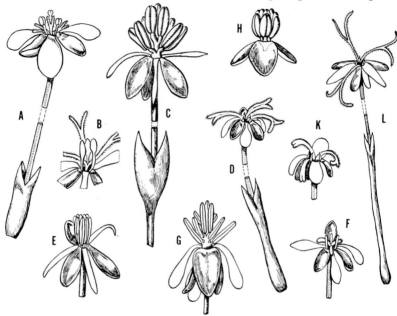

FIG. 9.20. Floral structure in the Hydrocharitaceae (continued): A to L: the genus *Elodea*. A, *E. granatensis*, hermaphrodite flower and spathe ($\times 5$); B, *E. nevadensis*, centre of female flower ($\times 4.5$); C, *E. canadensis*, male flower and spathe ($\times 2.5$); D *E. canadensis*, female flower and spathe ($\times 2.5$); E, *E. longivaginata*, male flower ($\times 2.5$); F, *E. longivaginata*, female flower ($\times 2.5$); G, *E. peruviensis*, male flower ($\times 2.5$); H, *E. nuttallii*, liberated male flower ($\times 5$); K, *E. nuttallii*, female flower ($\times 4$); L, *E. callitrichoides*, female flower and spathe ($\times 2.5$). (Note the range of spathe form in A, C, D and L; staminode and stigma form in B, D, F, K and L; stamen form and arrangement in A, C, E, G and H.) (A to L, redrawn from St. John, 1962b, 1963, 1964, 1965.) (M to S on p. 305.)

separated in handling (Lindberg, 1873). *Stratiotes* and *Egeria* are dioecious. According to Caspary (1875), only female specimens of *Stratiotes* occur throughout the northern part of its native range and mainly male specimens in the southern part, whilst both commonly occur in the intermediate area. This curious pattern of distribution is presumed still to exist. Certainly in Britain (in the north of its range) only female plants normally occur (Tutin, 1962): there are a few records of specimens with apparently hermaphrodite flowers (e.g. Geldart, 1906), although these may have been functionally female, with rudimentary stamens present. If the alleged sex distribution still prevails, reproduction of the species in the north and south of its range must be entirely or predominantly vegetative. It is also possible that vegetative reproduction may predominate in some parts of the range of *Egeria*. Female plants of one species, *E. densa*, seem to be extremely rare: cultivated specimens and most, if not all, herbarium specimens appear to be male. In the other species, *E. naias*, very few flowers of either sex have ever been seen (St. John, 1961).

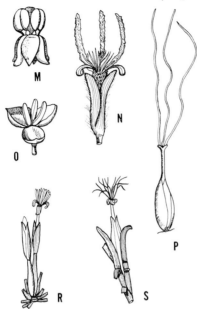

FIG. 9.20. Floral structure in the Hydrocharitaceae (continued): M to S: the marine genera. M, *Enhalus acoroides*, male flower ($\times 5$); N, *E. acoroides*, female flower protruding from spathe ($\times 1$); O, *Halophila ovalis*, male flower ($\times 4$); P, *H. ovalis*, female flower protruding from spathe ($\times 1.5$); R, *Thalassia hemprichii*, two male spathes—one with open flower ($\times 0.5$); S, *T. hemprichii*, female flower protruding from spathe amidst leaf bases ($\times 0.5$). (M to P, after Subramanyam, 1962; R and S, after Pascasio and Santos, 1930).

Both hermaphrodite and unisexual flowers occur in *Ottelia*. Certain taxa were formerly segregated as the genera *Bootia*, *Oligolobos* and *Xystrolobos* on the basis of hermaphrodite or unisexual flowers, monoecism or dioecism, and the number of flowers in a spathe, but Dandy (1934) pointed out that although these characters may be constant for species, they are artificial criteria for supra-specific classification. *O. alismoides*, the type species, and the Australian *O. ovalifolia* both have hermaphrodite flowers.

The female flowers of the five entomophilous genera, and the hermaphrodite flowers of some species of *Ottelia*, are usually borne solitarily in a spathe whereas the male ones are arranged in groups of two to many and are rarely solitary. Both types may be distinctly pedicelled as in *Hydrocharis*, but more commonly, as in *Ottelia* and *Stratiotes*, the males are pedicelled, the female sessile. The spathe is normally membranous and inconspicuous but in *Ottelia*, subgenus *Ottelia* it has five to ten prominent broad wings, in subg. *Dipteron*

it has two opposite wings, and in subg. *Bootia* no wings but usually six pro-
truberant ribs (Dandy, 1934).

Little is known of the specific pollinating agents. *Egeria densa* is apparently
pollinated by flies: these, together with small beetles and surface-dwelling
insects, are often seen scrambling about the flowers of other taxa. It would be
valuable to know whether wind may also effect pollination in any of these
plants. The occasional replacement of cross-pollination in *Ottelia* by cleistogamy or self-pollination in buds that subsequently open has been described
earlier (p. 290).

Anemophily occurs in the excepted species of *Limnobium*, i.e. *L. stoloniferum*
(*Hydromystria stolonifera*) which has long, hairy, branched styles protruding
above the floating rosette. According to Hauman-Merck (1915), transport of
pollen by water may also be effective when the styles wilt and touch the water.

A definite approach to hydrophily is shown by the submerged *Hydrilla*
verticillata, Vallisneria spiralis, Lagarosiphon muscoides and *Enhalus acoroides*
which produce floating female flowers pollinated at the surface (Figs. 9.18,
9.20). It is important to note, however, that the dry microspores are transferred to the stigmas, which also remain dry, through the air and not the water.
In the monotypic *Hydrilla verticillata* (Ernst-Schwarzenbach, 1945), the
unusually solitary male flower-bud abscisses from its short pedicel, deflects
the two apical lobes of the spathe and rises through the water to float on the
surface film for about an hour. The perianth parts then curve back and the three
anthers spring erect, explosively discharging the microspores around the
flower. The female flower is borne aloft on its elongating peduncle and only
when it reaches the surface do the perianth parts open, forming a funnel which
is quite dry inside, the three styles with their fringed stigmas being surrounded
by air, not water. Ernst-Schwarzenbach found that the turgidity of the
perianth is exceeded by forces of surface tension so that the flower is not inundated by a passing wave: it merely closes around the dry styles and reopens
when the surface again becomes stable. This behaviour obviously precludes the
possibility of pollen being carried by water into the female flower. Successful
pollination must therefore depend upon a male flower opening close by,
microspores being discharged into the female flower and landing upon the
stigmas. Pollen shed on the surface of the water is wasted.

In *Vallisneria spiralis* (Wylie, 1917a; Witmer, 1937) many minute flowers
are borne in umbellate fashion in a tubular, two-lipped spathe (Fig. 9.19):
each has a reduced perianth of three tepals, which remain sealed around the
two stamens until the flower, as in *Hydrilla*, has abscissed and risen to the
surface. There, the tepals become recurved and function as a sailing apparatus,
the two larger opposite ones entering the water as rudders, the third smaller
one remaining in the air as a tiny sail. As dehiscence of the anthers is not
explosive the microspores usually adhere to the tip of each stamen as a globular
mass. The perianth of the female flower is reduced to three, pinkish-white
sepals surrounding three, minute, rudimentary petals. At the megasporocyte
stage of ovule development, the flower, some 2 mm long, begins to rise on its

peduncle (Fig. 9.19), which grows slowly at first but later elongates at the rate of up to 2 cm per hour (Funke, 1938). This growth continues for 1 to 3 days and often seems curiously unrelated to the depth of water, so that ultimately the filiform peduncle is very much longer than is necessary to accommodate appreciable sudden rises in water level without immersion of the flower. Funke (1938) measured peduncles of 80 to 120 cm on European plants growing in water 27 and 45 cm deep. In Indian specimens, however, Kausik (1939) found a strict relation between the length of peduncle and depth of water. Whether excessive or not, the growth of the peduncle is achieved principally by cell elongation: most cells extend to 40 to 50 times their original length (Funke, 1938; Kausik, 1939).

Prior to pollination, the female flower, now 14 mm or more long, lies horizontally in a depression in the surface film created by its own weight. The sepals spread apart, exposing to the atmosphere the three, fleshy, bifid stigmas: these remain quite dry, even if submerged by waves, because air is trapped within the dense pile of hairs on their surfaces (Fig. 9.18). Pollination occurs when the surface is placid and is accomplished within 4 to 6 hours of anthesis. The male flowers are spread about on the surface by air and water currents. If they chance to encounter a female flower they inevitably slide down the sides of the depression, and the tips of the stamens, projecting beyond the recurved tepals, strike against the receptive inner surfaces of the stigmas, to which the sticky microspores adhere.

Vallisneria americana, V. asiatica and *V. aethiopica* are thought by some botanists to be just geographical races of *V. spiralis.* There is some evidence (Wylie, 1917a; Svedelius, 1932) that in *V. americana* the stamens are commonly erect and do not diverge beyond the recurved tepals, and so direct contact with the stigmas is probably precluded. It is suggested that the male flowers are captured inside the perianth of the female flower as it closes during temporary immersion by a wave. The pollen is probably rubbed off on the dry stigmas as the male flowers topple into the interior of the female. Pollen-tube growth and fertilisation show no significant differences from the majority of angiosperms (Wylie, 1941). Pollination behaviour has not been studied in *V. neotropicalis* or *V. gigantea.*

The behaviour of the sea-grass, *Enhalus acoroides,* is remarkably similar to that of *Vallisneria americana.* Kausik (1941) observed in the pedicels of mature male flowers a definite transverse abscission-zone in which the cells lacked the tannins characteristic of the rest of the pedicel and floral parts. The flowers absciss at low tide and are buoyed up to the surface, as in *Vallisneria* and *Hydrilla,* by the air they contain. At the surface the petals and sepals become sharply reflexed, exposing the three erect stamens, which may be derived by the splitting of an original one during development (Lakshmanan, 1963b). The female flower, borne up on its peduncle, rests horizontally on the surface and its long much-wrinkled petals extend beyond the spathe (Fig. 9.20). Troll (1931) attributed the opening of both male and female flowers to the marked rise in temperature in the shallow water at low tide.

Having a waxy cuticle the petals of both types of flower repel water: the free male flowers tend to drift in swarms and to cluster round any female flower they might encounter. Pollination cannot yet occur for the anthers are still erect, the stigmas still shrouded by the petals. As the tide rises, the female flowers are submerged and assume a roughly vertical position. Svedelius (1904) suggested that the anthers dehisce on the surface and that the microspores, heavily laden with starch, slowly fall through the water to the stigmas. But the stigmas are not in fact freely exposed under water. As each female flower is immersed, its hydrophobic petals close together pulling the male flowers inside them. Ernst-Schwarzenbach (1945) suggested that the anthers of the overturned captured males shed their pollen on the stigmas through the air imprisoned within the clasped female perianth.

Lagarosiphon muscoides and *Nechamandra alternifolia* both resemble *Vallisneria spiralis* in floral structure and mode of pollination (Ernst-Schwarzenbach, 1945; Lakshmanan, 1963b). Contact between the male flowers and the lobed stigmas occurs on the surface of the water and the act of pollination is essentially aerial. Each male flower of *Lagarosiphon* is supported on the surface film by its six reflexed perianth segments. The three long staminodes are joined at their tips and remain erect, functioning as a sail. Prior to pollination the filament of each of the three stamens becomes orientated parallel to the surface of the water and so holds out the anther, which hangs vertically, beyond the limits of the perianth (Wager, 1928; Obermeyer, 1964). In *Nechamandra* there are no staminodes but the perianth segments become reflexed as in *Lagarosiphon* and so raise the anthers into the air (Fig. 9.18). Although both *Nechamandra* and *Vallisneria* appear to have two stamens in each male flower, these in fact represent only one true stamen which splits into two halves during ontogeny (Lakshmanan, 1963b). In the female flowers of *Lagarosiphon* and *Nechamandra* the perianth tube becomes very elongated, to several centimetres, in raising the three bilobed stigmas to the surface (Fig. 9.18).

A further interesting advance towards hydrophily is shown by species of *Elodea*, in which the microspores float to the stigmas on the surface of the water. Throughout the genus the solitary flowers are borne in membranous, urn-shaped or globose, axillary spathes. Floral organisation is basically trimerous (Fig. 9.20). The biseriate perianth is well differentiated although reduced in size: there are three, greenish, concave sepals which are generally elliptic in shape and often striated with purple or black, and three, delicate, membranous, white or purplish petals which vary in shape from linear to elliptic or spatulate. The unilocular ovary is inferior, and, unlike that of *Vallisneria*, remains under water, surrounded by the spathe in the leaf axil. As each flower bud matures, the hypanthium enclosing the style above the ovary undergoes immense elongation, pushing the bud through the bifid apex of the spathe up to the surface of the water where anthesis occurs.

In three species—*E. granatensis*, *E. brandegeae* and *E. schweinitzii* (grouped together as the subgenus *Apalanthe* by St. John, 1962b, 1963, 1964, 1965)—the flowers are hermaphrodite, each having three stamens and three or four entire or bifid stigmas (Fig. 9.20). Their hypanthium usually elongates to a length of between 1·5 and 6 cm. The other fourteen species, constituting the subgenus *Elodea*, are functionally dioecious and so appear more specialised. Within the perianth of each male flower there are nine erect stamens on a common stalk, the six outer (lower) ones usually being whorled and the three inner (upper) ones elevated on a central compound filament. Rarely, the stamens may be attached in three sets of three each, as in *E. peruviensis*, or all nine may arise from one level at the top of the hypanthium, as in *E. longi-vaginata* (Fig. 9.20). Some indication of the ancestral hermaphrodite condition is still visible in the female flowers, which always possess three staminodes alternating with the petals. These staminodes are generally abortive and show progressive reduction in different species, from the apically expanded form in *E. columbiana* or *E. nevadensis* to the linear or acicular type in *E. bifoliata* or *E. canadensis* (Fig. 9.20). Each female flower has three spatulate or ligulate stigmas which have a papillose, receptive, upper surface and may be entire or deeply bifid. The hypanthium of both male and female flowers is filiform and perhaps generally rather longer than that of the hermaphrodite species. Typically, it elongates to between 5 and 15 cm: less commonly, it may reach about 23 cm, as in the female flower of *E. callitrichoides*, or 30 cm, as in the male *E. longivaginata*, or several decimetres in the exceptional instance of the female flower of *E. longivaginata*.

Although the male flowers are sometimes to be seen drifting freely on the surface of the water, as a result of accidental rupture of the hypanthium (Wylie, 1904, 1912), only in a single exceptional species are they actually liberated by the plant itself. In *E. nuttallii* each male flower-bud is sessile, and when mature it abscisses and rises out of the spathe to the surface. It further differs from that of the other dioecious species in having no petals. The female flowers of *E. nuttallii* are quite typical in both structure and behaviour (St. John, 1962b, 1965; see Fig. 9.20).

In all species of the genus anthesis occurs on the surface of the water, the unwettable sepals becoming reflexed and propping up the flower. Like that of *Vallisneria*, the female flower creates by its own weight a slight depression in the surface film and in this it lies obliquely, usually resting on two of the three water-repellent stigmas, all of which protrude beyond the perianth. The male flowers open suddenly and are buoyed up by the recurved perianth. The anthers remain more or less erect and dehisce explosively, spraying the microspores over the surrounding water. Isolated or still in tetrads, the microspores float due to the air trapped between the tiny spines of the extine, and are moved about on the water by both air currents and surface tension. Species of *Elodea* are highly gregarious and if both male and female flowers occur in the same vicinity there is probably a reasonable chance that some of the drifting microspores will contact receptive stigmas (Hauman-Merck, 1913; Ernst-Schwarzenbach, 1945). In *E. nuttallii* the chances of success-ful pollination may perhaps be increased by the greater mobility of the male flowers. Should pollination occur, the germinating pollen tubes must grow down the full length of the style, within the hypanthium, to reach the ovules.

The rarity of seeds in all species of the genus may not necessarily indicate that the mode of pollination is inefficient. It is more likely to be due to the great disparity in distribution of the two sexes. In some dioecious species only one type of flower is yet known: in *E. columbiana* and *E. nevadensis*, for example, the males have still to be discovered, and in *E. linearis* the females. Even amongst better-known species of wide geographical range, e.g. *E. canadensis*, the male plants are notoriously rare (St. John, 1965). Furthermore, fertility may be reduced. In *E. canadensis* and *E. nuttallii*, both of which are relatively specialised, only two to six ovules mature in each ovary and only one or two of each tetrad of microspores ever germinate (Ernst-Schwarzenbach, 1951). Finally, it may be noted that the geographical distribution of the genus is also somewhat curious. Eight of the seventeen species occur in warm temperate or tropical South America south of Panama, whilst the other nine are restricted to temperate North America north of Mexico. Not a single species has been found as an indigene anywhere in Central America. The only extensive North American species are the dioecious *E. canadensis* and *E. nuttallii*. The hermaphrodite *E. brandegeae* and *E. schweinitzii* are known only from single stations, in striking contrast to *E. granatensis* which is the only far-ranging species of South America, the seven dioecious species all being markedly restricted (St. John, 1962b, 1963, 1964, 1965).

The culmination of the trend is reached in the two marine genera *Halophila* and *Thalassia* (Fig. 9.20). Neither male nor female flowers ever ascend to the surface and pollination occurs under water. The filiform or feathery nature of the styles, and union of the globular or ellipsoid microspores into long chains, may be interpreted as adaptations to hydrophily (Pascasio and Santos, 1930; Kausik and Rao, 1942).

Of the two genera, *Halophila* has been more thoroughly studied. In *H. ovalis*, for example, the dioecious flowers are usually solitary, the male pedicelled and the female sessile on separate plants. The perianth is reduced in both sexes to three inconspicuous tepals. The ovary has usually three filiform styles, 25 mm or more long, which bear receptive papillae throughout their length. The male flower has three stamens with almost sessile, linear-oblong anthers (Fig. 9.20). The microsporocytes are long, narrow and regularly arranged in linear rows. They divide meiotically in transverse planes, forming linear tetrads of microspores. The tetrads do not separate. At maturity each sporangium therefore contains a bundle of parallel chains of microspores. Each bundle is released as a unit when the reduced anther wall ruptures. In the water the bundles tend to disintegrate into smaller clusters of microspore-chains which float freely at any depth. Chains drifting into the vicinity of a female plant become entangled amidst the exposed filiform styles (Kausik and Rao, 1942).

The Hydrocharitaceae is truly remarkable in providing, within the limits of a single closely-knit family, so nearly complete a morphological spectrum, from entomophily to hydrophily and from free-floating or often sparsely rooted freshwater species to wholly submerged rhizomatous marine plants. The family probably stands at a low phylogenetic level amongst the monocotyledons. This belief is engendered principally by the strange, and probably primitive, parietal placentation of the ovules and by other marked resemblances to the Butomaceae, from which the Hydrocharitaceae only really differs in having a more specialised and inferior ovary, a trend towards dioecism, and a reduction of the perianth associated with the trend towards hydrophily. The Hydrocharitaceae is one of the very few angiosperm families which has successfully invaded, and is now thoroughly committed to, both freshwater and marine habitats. The range of floral and vegetative habits, the prevalence of species in the tropics and subtropics, and the existence of several very small genera with disjunct distributions all suggest that the family is old. Fossil evidence of the evolutionary history of *Stratiotes* (Figs. 9.24, 9.25) and geographical evidence that the contemporary marine genera (which must be derived from freshwater ancestors) were already in existence at the beginning of the Tertiary Era (pp. 384–87) strengthen the concept of the family's ancient status.

Floral Structure and Pollination in the Callitrichaceae. Far-reaching floral reduction has evidently occurred in the evolution of the Callitrichaceae, a small isolated family of 25 or so species which display no obvious affinities with any other dicotyledons. The minute flowers are unisexual, actinomorphic and quite naked (Fig. 9.21). They are usually solitary: rarely, both a male and a female are produced in the same leaf axil. Each male flower is reduced to a reniform anther on a long slender filament. The female flower comprises a syncarpous, four-lobed ovary divided into four loculi by false septa, each loculus containing a solitary, pendulous, anatropous ovule. There are usually two free styles, filiform and papillose throughout their length.

With the exception of *Callitriche petriei*, a dioecious species described from New Zealand by Mason (1959), all taxa are monoecious. The female flowers often occur at lower nodes than the male. Numerous taxa are typically terrestrial or palustral. Fassett (1951) segregated eight such American species in a new section, *Microcallitriche*, but Mason (1959) noted that at least one criterion used by Fassett, the presence or absence of bracts, is not taxonomically reliable and therefore considered it better to keep these taxa with the amphibious ones in the section *Eucallitriche* of Hegelmaier (1864).

The various terrestrial species, e.g. *C. brachycarpa*, produce flowers at most nodes and appear to be anemophilous. When growing in water the amphibious species, e.g. *C. stagnalis* and *C. platycarpa*, bear flowers in the axils of only the uppermost leaves that form a floating rosette. Their stamens are generally longer than those of the terrestrial species, 2 to 5 mm or more compared with 0·2 to 1·2 mm, and typically mature before the ovaries. These species are probably anemophilous too, although they may also be pollinated by flies and other insects visiting or living on the surface. Their microspores, like those of the terrestrial taxa, have a cuticularised extine and will float (Moar, 1960). Although in most species the styles remain erect and so are unable to receive floating pollen, in a few (e.g. *C. stagnalis*) they soon become recurved and may be accessible to microspores drifting between the leaves of the floating rosette.

In the totally submerged species, e.g. *C. hermaphroditica* and *C. truncata*, which belong to Hegelmaier's section *Pseudocallitriche*, regions of male and

11*

female flowers sometimes alternate along the stems. The filaments of the stamens are short: the slender styles are spreading or reflexed. The microspores have an undifferentiated extine and commonly contain oil globules. Drifting at all depths, some may chance to strike against and adhere to the stigmatic papillae of female flowers. Submerged pollination is at best very haphazard, but particularly so in these species of *Callitriche* where the microspores are neither individually elongated nor united in strings, and the styles

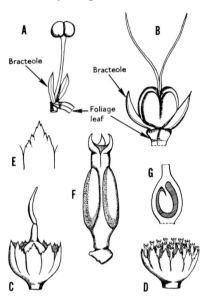

FIG. 9.21. Floral structure in the Callitrichaceae and Ceratophyllaceae. *Callitriche obtusangula*: A, male flower (stamen) in leaf axil (×3); B, female flower (ovary) in leaf axil (×5). *Ceratophyllum demersum*: C, female flower (×6); D, male flower (with some stamens removed) (×6); E, outline of free part of perianth segment (×12); F, stamen, showing laminar form and tricuspid extension of connective (×25); G, diagrammatic L.S. carpel showing ovule position (×6).

are not excessively long or branched. Yet pollination must often be successful: in Britain *C. hermaphroditica* is the most freely fruiting of all species (Clapham, 1962).

Cytological and geographical differentiation accompany morphological specialisation within the family. Members of the section *Eucallitriche* have a chromosome complement of n = 5, 10, or rarely 19 or 20, and are to be found on all continents. Species of *Pseudocallitriche*, however, have n = 3 and are restricted to cool temperate Europe and North America (Arber, 1920; Fassett, 1951). Some botanists, notably Hegelmaier (1864, 1867), Pax and Hoffman (1931) and Hutchinson (1959), have considered the Callitrichaceae to be allied to the Haloragaceae or to the terrestrial Euphorbiaceae or Caryophyllaceae. The studies of ovule-, endosperm- and embryo development by Jörgensen (1923,

1925) and Souèges (1952) evoke grave doubts of these affinities, and suggest rather that the Callitrichaceae is related to the dicotyledons of the Tubiflorae, especially the Verbenaceae.

Hydrophily in the Ceratophyllaceae. The few species of the single genus *Ceratophyllum*, e.g. *C. demersum*, are all submerged and monoecious, bearing the minute actinomorphic flowers solitarily in the axil of one leaf of a whorl, male and female usually at different nodes (Fig. 9.21). The unilocular sessile ovary of each female flower has just one, pendulous, anatropous ovule and a filiform oblique style. It is surrounded by ten to fifteen, bristle-pointed, basally connate, perianth segments. The male flower has a similar perianth and ten to twenty stamens, spirally arranged on a flat receptacle. Each stamen has a long subsessile anther, beyond which projects a tricuspid expansion of the connective. This acts as a float when the anther reaches maturity and the stamen abscisses: on reaching the surface the anther dehisces, and the microspores gradually sink downwards, some falling upon the stigmas of the female flowers in the leaf axils provided that the water is relatively static (Roze, 1892). The chances of pollination are probably enhanced by the highly gregarious habit of the species. In very deep, flowing or turbulent water, flowers are much less common.

The systematic position and natural affinities of the Ceratophyllaceae are utterly obscure. Extreme reduction, perhaps in association with the hydrophilous habit, is evident in the gynoecium, ovule and embryo (p. 322). The stamens, laminar in form and bearing abaxial microsporangia, appear remarkably similar to those of the primitive woody Ranales but whether or not this resemblance indicates genuine affinity is an open question. The family is usually thought to be more or less closely allied to the Nymphaeaceae, but its abaxial microsporangia and whorled leaves set it apart from all genera of the latter except *Cabomba*. Eames (1961) acknowledged the possibility that the Ceratophyllaceae may not even belong in the Ranales, despite the structure of its stamens. Arber (1920) regarded its submerged hydrophilous habit and apparently isolated position amongst the primitive Ranalian dicotyledons as evidence that its ancestors must have entered the water very early in the evolution of the angiosperms.

IV POST-FERTILISATION DEVELOPMENT IN AQUATIC ANGIOSPERMS

MOVEMENTS OF THE FLORAL ORGANS

Movements of the floral axis after fertilisation are common amongst hydrophytes but are in no way specifically associated with the aquatic habit. In many species the peduncle eventually curves downwards, bringing the developing fruits below water. In *Eichhornia crassipes*, for example, by the late afternoon of the third day after anthesis, the flowers have begun to wilt and the basal part of the peduncle bends outwards so that the inflorescence leans at an

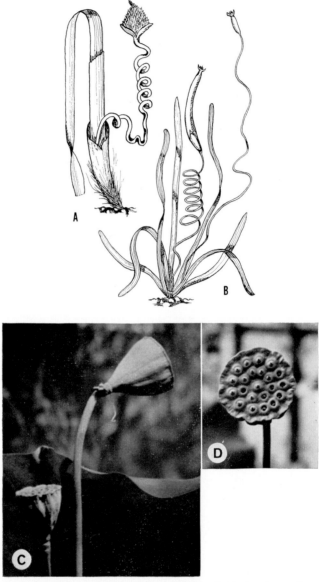

FIG. 9.22. Post-floral movements. A, *Enhalus acoroides*: habit drawing to show developing fruit pulled down by spiral coiling of peduncle (×0·3); B, *Vallisneria spiralis*: habit
drawing of plant bearing two ripening fruits of different ages being withdrawn from
surface by coiling peduncles (×0·3); C, *Nelumbo nucifera*: lateral view of two ripening
fruits; one at left has erect receptacle, one at right shows peduncle beginning to curve
and receptacle nearly horizontal (×0·15); D, *Nelumbo nucifera*: view of top of
receptacle showing protruding tips of ripening achenes (×0·2). (A, after Subramanyam, 1962.)

angle of about 45°. Later a sharp downward curvature occurs about 2 to 3 cm below the bracts of the inflorescence. Thus, the distal portion of the inflorescence makes an angle of about 90° with the basal portion, and provided that the surface is not densely crowded the developing fruits are immersed. By about 7 or 8 a.m. on the following morning the inflorescence becomes more or less horizontal beneath the surface of the water (Penfound and Earle, 1948).

Submerged fruit development as a result of curvature of the peduncle is also found in, amongst others, *Aldrovanda, Aponogeton, Brasenia, Cabomba, Hydrocharis, Limnobium, Nymphaea, Nymphoides, Ottelia*, most of the Pontederiaceae and Potamogetonaceae, the batrachian *Ranunculi, Trapa* and *Victoria*.

Vallisneria displays unusual post-floral behaviour. After fertilisation, its peduncle becomes spirally coiled (Fig. 9.22). This torsion is first manifest at the base of the elongated ovary. Later, numerous loose coils appear lower down the peduncle: these become progressively tighter and corkscrew-like. The developing fruit is thus pulled down into the water, slowly at first (less than 1 cm/h), more rapidly as the coils draw closer together (Kausik, 1939). The peduncle does not always form a perfect corkscrew: the coiling is frequently loose and irregular and sometimes scarcely manifest at all. Funke (1938, 1939) found that natural auxin, IAA, stimulates the coiling of the peduncle when applied in concentrations of 3 or 7·5 ppm to the water in which *V. spiralis* is growing. The most spectacular result he noted was the coiling of one peduncle, 85 cm long, into an almost perfect corkscrew less than 3 cm tall, in 3 days. Funke also found that NAA exerts a similar effect and that both IAA and NAA stimulate the development of parthenocarpic fruits, as has been noted in many terrestrial plants. These effects of externally applied auxin, together with the fact that torsion occurs first at the base of the ovary, suggest that the natural coiling of the peduncle may perhaps be regulated by auxin liberated from the germinating microspores or developing embryos. The peduncles of *Enhalus* (Fig. 9.22) and the stalks of the carpels of *Ruppia* may become similarly coiled after fertilisation.

Persistent retention of aerial fruit development is notably rare amongst submerged, floating-leaved and free-floating angiosperms. It is found, however, in *Hottonia, Lobelia dortmanna, Nuphar* and *Utricularia*, and inevitably in the Podostemaceae left stranded as the water recedes at the onset of the dry season.

Post-floral movements often occur in emergent hydrophytes but because of the height of the plant do not usually carry the fruits into the water or the soil. In *Nelumbo nucifera* (Fig. 9.22), for example, the erect receptacle containing the developing fruits is moved through an angle of 180° by curvature of the apical part of the peduncle and it points downwards before finally abscissing into the water.

TYPES OF FRUITS (Fig. 9.23)

As a result of the reduction of their gynoecium, many aquatics produce one-seeded indehiscent fruits: e.g. the nuts or drupes of *Littorella, Potamogeton*,

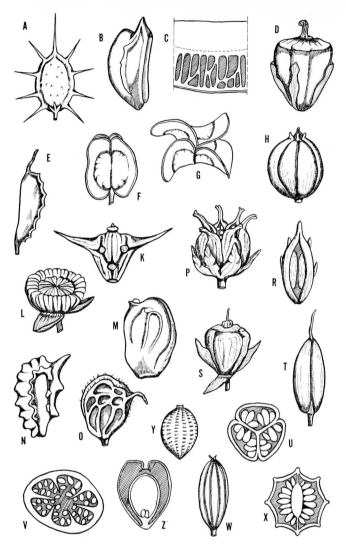

FIG. 9.23. Fruit structure in certain hydrophytes: A, *Ceratophyllum echinatum*, achene
(×2); B, *Potamogeton thunbergii*, achene (×14); C, *P. natans*, diagrammatic T.S. fruit
wall to show lacunae (shaded) in outer zone (×50); D, *Sparganium eurycarpum*, nut
with persistent perianth (×2·5); E, *Zannichellia palustris*, stipitate drupelet (×7);
F, *Callitriche hermaphroditica*, schizocarp (×7); G, *C. hermaphroditica*, schizocarp
from above (×9); H, *Myriophyllum verticillatum*, schizocarp (×8); K, *Trapa bicornis*,
nut (seed with spined endocarp) (×0·4); L, *Alisma plantago-aquatica*, head of
achenes (×4); M, *Echinodorus isthmicus*, achene (×7); N, *Sagittaria guayanensis*,
achene (×6); O, *Limnophyton obtusifolium*, achene (×3·5); P, *Butomus umbellatus*,
head of follicles (×2); R, *Aponogeton crispus*, beaked follicle (adaxial face) (×3);
S, *Mayaca fluviatilis*, capsule (×4·5); T, *Monochoria vaginalis*, capsule (×4); U, *M.
vaginalis*, diagrammatic T.S. capsule (×7); V, *Hydrocharis morsus-ranae*, diagrammatic T.S. berry (×5); W, *Zeylanidium olivaceum*, capsule (×10); X, *Z. olivaceum*,
diagrammatic T.S. capsule (×20); Y, *Nymphaea caerulea*, seed (×15); Z, *N. caerulea*,
diagrammatic L.S. seed to show thin aril and air space (shaded) (×20). (A, after
Muenscher, 1940; M, after Fassett, 1955; N, after Bogin, 1955; O, T, U, W, X,
after Subramanyam, 1962.)

the Ceratophyllaceae, Ruppiaceae, Zosteraceae, Sparganiaceae, Typhaceae; the achenes of *Groenlandia*, the Hippuridaceae, Najadaceae, Zannichelliaceae and the batrachian *Ranunculi*; and the utricles of *Pontederia* and the Lemnaceae. The schizocarps of the Callitrichaceae and *Myriophyllum* separate into single-seeded, indehiscent drupelets or nutlets. In the Alismaceae the apocarpous gynoecium typically develops into a head of achenes, whilst in *Nelumbo* the achenes are aggregated within the fleshy receptacle. In the Trapaceae the fruit is initially a one-seeded drupe, as in *Potamogeton*, but the fleshy exocarp is quickly lost, leaving a pyrene comprising the seed surrounded by the horned stony endocarp.

The adaxially dehiscent follicle, believed to be a primitive type of fruit, is found in the Aponogetonaceae, Butomaceae and Scheuchzeriaceae and also in *Cabomba*. Dehiscent capsules ripening above water are produced in certain groups: e.g. the three-valved capsules of the Eriocaulaceae, Mayacaceae, Xyridaceae and *Monochoria*; the septicidal capsules of the Elatinaceae, Podostemaceae and *Menyanthes*; and the variously dehiscent capsules of the aquatic Lythraceae, *Nuphar* and *Utricularia*.

Capsules developing under water are very uncommon. Structurally, they resemble the aerial capsules of related taxa but they become immersed early in development and ultimately dehisce in a different way. Obviously desiccation cannot cause the opening of the fruit: instead, dehiscence is usually wrought irregularly by pressure from within the fruit. The capsule of *Eichhornia*, for example, is structurally comparable with the explosively dehiscent fruit of *Monochoria*, its Old World emergent relative, but is split longitudinally, after floating for a day or so, by the pressure of swelling watery mucilage inside (Parija, 1934; Haigh, 1936). Internal swelling of mucilage, following absorption of water, also causes irregular splits in the pericarp of the berry-like capsules of *Nymphaea* and *Victoria*, and of *Nymphoides*, which are structurally comparable with the aerial capsules of, respectively, *Nuphar* and *Menyanthes* (Arber, 1920). The berry-like, many-seeded fruit of the Hydrocharitaceae is typically indehiscent, the seeds being liberated after the slow decay of the pericarp, but in *Hydrocharis* and *Stratiotes* the fruits are reported to burst due to the swelling of gelatinous pulp produced by the testas of the seeds (Goebel, 1891–1893). Fossil seeds of *Stratiotes* recovered from deposits dating back to the upper Eocene show gradual but remarkable changes of form during the evolution of the genus (Figs. 9.24, 9.25).

Fruit development is curiously retarded, even prevented, in a few species. *Alternanthera philoxeroides*, for example, rarely sets seed in Louisiana (Hitchcock *et al.*, 1950) and its fruits are unknown in Java, where it is an adventive (Backer, 1949). In Britain, Guppy (1894) observed during the hot summer of 1893 that fruits of *Ceratophyllum demersum* matured in a shallow pool in which the daily maximum temperature was 27 to 35°C but none developed in nearby waters that did not become as strongly heated. He later reported that even in Fiji, fruits ripened only in exposed and overheated shallow waters (Guppy, 1906). The rarity of fruiting has been remarked upon by many authors. However, whilst acknowledging that plants in deep or flowing water often fail to flower or set seed, Muenscher (1940) and van Steenis (1949a) considered that in the U.S.A. and Malaysia, successful reproduction is probably much more common in shallow exposed habitats than the rarity of flowers and fruits amongst herbarium specimens might suggest.

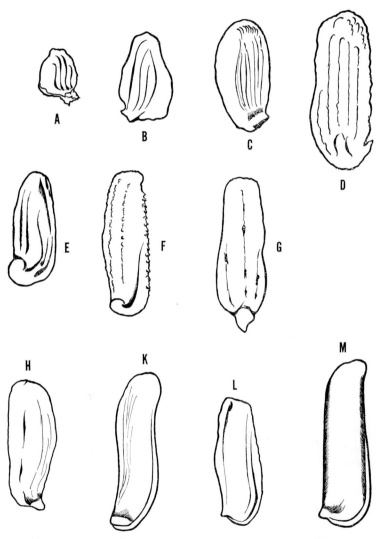

FIG. 9.24. Evolutionary series of fossil seeds of *Stratiotes*: A, B, *S. headonensis*; C, D, *S. acuticostatus*; E, *S. kaltennordheimensis*; F, G, *S. intermedius*; H, K, L, *S. aloides* (Pleistocene); M, *S. aloides* (recent). (all ×4·5). Note the transition from short and broad, rough-surfaced seeds A and B to long and narrow, smooth-surfaced seeds K and M. (See also Fig. 9.25.) (After Chandler, 1923.)

Hydrocharis morsus-ranae is also somewhat unpredictable in its behaviour. It often flowers, but in certain parts of its range it rarely fruits, although good fruiting has occasionally been recorded, as in Britain in 1947 (Gurney, 1949).

The fruits of *Acorus calamus* are quite unknown in many parts of its present range. Throughout northern, central and western Europe the species is represented by a sterile, triploid, adventive race which maintains itself by vegetative propagation (Wulff, 1954). Native specimens in eastern continental

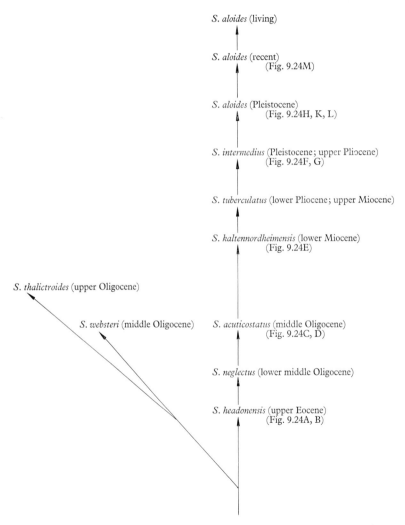

FIG. 9.25. Chandler's suggested phylogeny of the genus *Stratiotes*, based upon features of seed morphology and comprising eight extinct and one surviving species. (After Chandler, 1923.)

Asia and Japan appear to be tetraploid and fertile, yet in the north of this area seedlings had never been encountered until about 10 years ago. The apparent sterility here seems to be due to the failure of the seeds to ripen in the normally cold climate. Viable seedlings were found in 1954 near Harbin in northern Manchuria, and Baranov (1960) concluded that seeds are able to mature and germinate in years when the prevailing temperatures are sufficiently high. The North American race seems to comprise normally sexual diploid plants. Although seed is frequently set in the north-central United States, for many years there was great doubt of the ability of this race to reproduce successfully in the area east of the Appalachian Mountains (Buell, 1935). It has recently been noted that viable seeds are produced in warm and fairly moist summers, as in New Jersey in 1961 and 1962, but if there is a prolonged dry season fructification may be drastically reduced or completely suppressed. The extensive clones of the species known throughout the states of the Atlantic seaboard are presumably the products of sustained vegetative propagation in climatic conditions unfavourable for the development and germination of seeds (Jervis and Buell, 1964).

FEATURES OF EMBRYONIC STRUCTURE AND ENDOSPERM DEVELOPMENT

The development of the seed in aquatic angiosperms comprises the same structural and physiological events occurring in a wide variety of terrestrial angiosperms. In contrast to the juvenile or adult, the embryonic sporophyte seems to have undergone no major morphological modifications in reaction to the aquatic environment. With the exception of a few reduced or highly peculiar types, as in the Podostemaceae, the features of embryogeny and endosperm development are essentially comparable with those seen in terrestrial relatives, and so provide potentially reliable criteria of phylogenetic affinity. Although the gross characters of embryo and seed development are unremarkable in aquatic taxa, certain minor features are of special interest and merit brief description.

In many aquatic monocotyledons belonging to Helobian families, the early embryo is notable for its very prominent basal cell, the nucleus of which attains an exceptionally high ploidy, up to 128n having been reported in *Alisma lanceolatum* and *Groenlandia densa* (Baude, 1956; Hasitschka-Jenschke, 1959). The later embryo of, for example, *Alisma* and *Butomus* (Fig. 9.26) seems to be primitively simple rather than secondarily reduced (Eames, 1961). It has a poorly differentiated radicle and a cylindrical or ligulate cotyledon with no distinction into base and lamina. In these (and many other monocotyledonous) taxa, the cotyledon has often been regarded as terminal and the shoot axis as lateral to it. Critical study of the embryo of *Halophila, Ottelia, Najas, Potamogeton* and *Eichhornia* has shown that the topographical relationships between the cotyledon and epicotyl, and between the shoot apex and hypocotyl, are the same as in the embryo of a dicotyledon. The cotyledon and epicotyl arise side by side, the site of inception of each involving half of the active zone of the embryonic shoot apex (except in *Eichhornia* where the cotyledonary locus involves three-quarters and the epicotylary locus one-quarter of the active zone). The cotyledon, however, grows much more rapidly and forces the epicotyl and apex to one side. Hence in the later embryo the relatively massive cotyledon appears to be terminal, with its basal part sheathing the still feebly

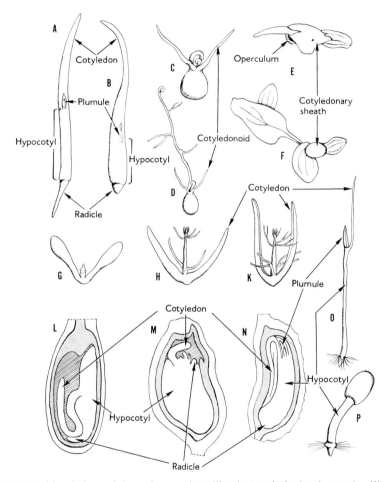

FIG. 9.26. Morphology of the embryo and seedling in certain hydrophytes: A, *Alisma plantago-aquatica*, embryo (× 12); B, *Butomus umbellatus*, embryo (× 12); C, *Utricularia gibba*, embryo (× 30); D, *U. gibba*, at later stage of germination (× 15); E, *Lemna trisulca*, lateral view of germinating seed (× 8); F, *L. trisulca*, seedling from above (× 6); G, *Ceratophyllum demersum*, embryo (× 4); H, *C. demersum*, seedling (× 1·2); K, *C. echinatum*, seedling (× 1·2); L, *Zostera marina*, L.S. fruit (testa shaded) (× 10); M, *Ruppia maritima*, L.S. fruit (testa shaded) (× 15); N, *Zannichellia palustris*, L.S. fruit (testa shaded) (× 12); O, *Z. palustris*, seedling (× 2·5); P, *Hippuris vulgaris*, germinating seed (× 5). (C, D, after Goebel, 1891–1893; E, F, after Hegelmaier, 1868; H, K, after Muenscher, 1940; L, M, N, O, after Raunkiaer, 1896; P, after Good, 1924.)

developed plumule (Haccius, 1952; Swamy and Lakshmanan, 1962a, b; Swamy and Parameswaran, 1962; Swamy, 1963, 1966). The embryo of *Sagittaria* is notable in having a curious vascularised outgrowth from the hypocotyl. This structure has sometimes been interpreted as the vestige of a second cotyledon by authors eager to establish the derivation of monocotyledons from dicotyledons.

Connation of the two cotyledons is an interesting feature of the embryo of several genera of the Nymphaeaceae and has misled some botanists (e.g. Schaffner, 1904) into treating the family as monocotyledonous. Species of *Nuphar*, in which one cotyledon is often smaller than the other, display stages in the process of connation. In *Nelumbo* the two cotyledons fuse to form a tubular organ enclosing the plumule.

The embryo of *Utricularia* is just a mass of scarcely differentiated cells containing starch and oil reserves. There is no vestige of radicle or plumule (Fig. 9.26). One or more main shoots develop laterally from a conical growth centre. In all except one aquatic species the first discrete structures to appear are tiny linear cotyledonoids, varying in number from two (e.g. *U. gibba*) to ten to twelve (e.g. *U. vulgaris*). *U. purpurea* has no cotyledonoids but produces three primary axes (Lloyd, 1942).

The embryo of the Lemnaceae is also remarkable for its lack of differentiation (Figs. 9.26, 9.27). Within the seed the only conspicuous structure is the chlorophyllous cotyledonary sheath. This emerges from the testa when the suspensor of the embryo dislodges the lignified operculum plugging the micropyle. The first true thallus appears from within the cotyledonary sheath. The embryo itself has no radicle: a single root subsequently develops from the node of the first thallus in *Spirodela* and *Lemna* but *Wolffiella* and *Wolffia* remain rootless (Hegelmaier, 1868; Rostowzew, 1905; Maheshwari, 1954, 1956; Narayanaswami, 1961; Maheshwari and Kapil, 1964).

The radicle is completely absent, or only very short-lived, in the embryo of numerous other hydrophytes, e.g. *Aldrovanda*, *Aponogeton*, *Ceratophyllum*—in which there is no hypocotyl either (Fig. 9.26), *Elatine*, *Hippuris*, the Hydrocharitaceae, Najadaceae, Podostemaceae (Fig. 9.29), Ruppiaceae, Trapaceae and Zannichelliaceae (Schleiden, 1838; Goebel, 1891–1893; von Wettstein, 1906; Arber, 1920). In some of these examples, that ultimately do lead a rooted existence, e.g. *Elatine*, *Hippuris* and *Zannichellia*, long root hairs develop from around the collet at the base of the hypocotyl (Fig. 9.26). This circlet of supporting hairs, seen also in certain radicle-less terrestrial seedlings, compensates for the absence of an anchoring root in keeping the seedling stable during the upward thrust of the plumule and expansion of the cotyledons (Good, 1924).

Numerous aquatic monocotyledons are notable in showing the so-called 'helobial' type of endosperm development. In contrast to the more common cellular and nuclear types, this involves the separation of the two nuclei formed by the first mitosis of the endosperm nucleus by a transverse wall, which thus divides the embryo sac into a chalazal cell and a (usually larger) micropylar cell. Free nuclear divisions then commonly occur in both cells, although much less frequently in the chalazal, which may even remain uninucleate in some plants.

After a coenocytic phase, the micropylar cell usually becomes transformed into a cellular tissue, although walls may not appear until very late in endosperm ontogeny in some plants.

Helobial endosperm was so named because of its frequency amongst genera belonging to Helobian families. It is known to be formed in the Aponogetonaceae (Afzelius, 1920; Stenar, 1935; Sâne, 1939), the Butomaceae (Johri,

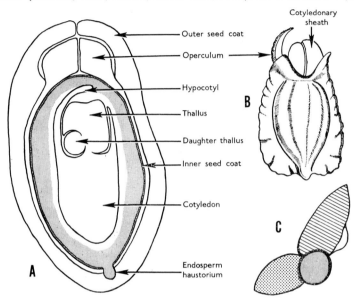

FIG. 9.27. *Lemna perpusilla*: A, diagrammatic L.S. seed containing mature embryo (cellular endosperm shaded) (× 50); B, lateral view of germinating seed, showing cotyledonary sheath emerging after dislodgement of operculum (× 25); C, diagram of young seedling, from above (cotyledonary sheath, shaded; first thallus, stippled; daughter thallus, lined; granddaughter thallus, clear) (× 15). (After Maheshwari and Kapil, 1964.)

1936b, 1938a, b; Maheshwari, 1943; Roper, 1952), the Scheuchzeriaceae and Potamogetonaceae (Stenar, 1935), in *Zannichellia* (Lakshmanan, 1965b), and in most, probably all, genera of the Hydrocharitaceae, notably *Blyxa* (Rangaswamy, 1941; Govindappa and Naidu, 1956; Lakshmanan, 1961), *Enhalus* (Kausik, 1940a), *Halophila* (Lakshmanan, 1963a), *Hydrilla* (Maheshwari, 1933; Lakshmanan, 1965a), *Ottelia* (Narasimha Murthy, 1935; Maheshwari, 1943; Islam, 1950), *Stratiotes* (Baude, 1956), *Vallisneria* (Witmer, 1937; Maheshwari, 1943) and *Nechamandra* (Lakshmanan, 1963b). In all these genera the chalazal endosperm cell remains uninucleate, and the micropylar chamber becomes cellular only very late in development. Some genera of the Alismaceae, namely *Echinodorus*, *Limnophyton* and *Sagittaria*, have helobial endosperm but *Alisma*, *Damasonium*, *Luronium* and *Machaerocarpus* apparently possess the nuclear type (Johri, 1935a, b, c, 1936a; Swamy and Parameswaran, 1963).

The Ruppiaceae may have helobial endosperm, although further study is needed for confirmation, but the Najadaceae seem to be of the free nuclear type, with cellular tissue sometimes formed at a very late stage (Swamy and Lakshmanan, 1962b). Of the aquatic monocotyledons outside the Helobiales, *Eichhornia, Heteranthera, Monochoria, Pontederia,* and probably the other genera of the Pontederiaceae have helobial endosperm (Banerji and Halder, 1942), whereas the Lemnaceae exhibit the cellular type (Maheshwari, 1954, 1956a, b, 1958; Maheshwari and Kapil, 1963b).

In their recent illuminating review, Swamy and Parameswaran (1963) pointed out that the helobial endosperm alleged to occur in certain dicotyledonous plants, including *Brasenia, Cabomba, Nuphar* and *Nymphaea* amongst the Nymphaeaceae (Cook, 1906, 1909), is a modified aberrant form of the normal cellular or nuclear types. They regarded the authentic helobial type as a distinctive monocotyledonous feature, perhaps even as useful a morphological criterion as the single cotyledon, typically trimerous flowers, monocolpate pollen, and generally scattered or multiseriate arrangement of the closed vascular bundles in the stem. They also emphasised that whilst helobial endosperm superficially appears to possess features of both the nuclear and cellular types, there is absolutely no reason to regard it as ontogenetically or phylogenetically intermediate.

DORMANCY AND GERMINATION

The seeds of an overwhelming majority of aquatic angiosperms exhibit prolonged dormancy. In most species this habit is due to the mechanical imprisonment of the embryo within the testa or pericarp. In the single-seeded, indehiscent achenes, nuts or drupes, the embryo is protected by the testa, which is usually hard, heavily cuticularised and tight-fitting, as in *Alisma, Halophila* and *Zostera,* and further by the pericarp, which is sometimes thin but tough, as in *Callitriche,* but more commonly has a hard, stony, scleridial endocarp as in *Hippuris, Littorella, Myriophyllum, Potamogeton* and *Sparganium.* The micropyle of the seed or the aperture in the protective endocarp is usually tightly sealed by a cuticularised or lignified plug formed from the integument or funicular tissue. Germination does not occur until this plug is dislodged or the endocarp is ruptured or has decayed. In natural habitats germination tends to be extremely erratic: some seeds germinate after their first winter or dry season, others remain dormant and viable for four or five years (Sauvageau, 1894; Fauth, 1903; Crocker, 1907; Crocker and Davis, 1914).

Drying of the seeds of some species seems to induce rupture of the testa or endocarp, so that absorption of water, prevented by the intact coat even when the seed is immersed, can take place and germination is promoted (Crocker, 1907). Ludwig (1886) found that seeds of *Mayaca fluviatilis,* for example, germinated promptly in water after 6 weeks' drying but seeds kept wholly immersed had not begun to germinate after even 12 weeks. In some species drying may reduce viability: the seeds of *Zizania aquatica* are killed by air-drying for 90 days (Simpson, 1966). Seeds of *Nymphoides peltata*, however, withstand drying for $2\frac{1}{2}$ years (Guppy, 1897), whilst those of *Sparganium erectum* remain viable for at least 4 years irrespective of whether they are kept wet or dry, at room temperature or in a refrigerator (Cook, 1962a). Guppy (1893, 1897) also found that fruits of *Alisma plantago-aquatica*, *Myriophyllum spicatum* and *Sagittaria sagittifolia*, and seeds of *Nuphar lutea* and *Nymphaea alba*, *inter alia*, retain their viability after being frozen in ice or mud for at least several weeks.

Extreme retention of viability is an oft-quoted attribute of the seeds of both lotuses, *Nelumbo lutea* and *N. nucifera*. During their maturation within the fleshy receptacle, the fruits individually shrink to as little as one-third of their former volume and the carpel wall and integuments form a very hard and impermeable coat around the seed. As in the seeds of the Leguminosae this coat resists bacterial and fungal attack and prevents imbibition for very long periods. Absorption of water, and subsequent germination, may be induced by treating the fruits or seeds with concentrated sulphuric acid, ammoniacal cupric sulphate, or fat solvents (Jones, 1928; Shaw, 1929; Meyer, 1930).

The seeds of the American *Nelumbo lutea* are reported to remain viable for at least 56 years (Mayer and Poljakoff-Mayber, 1963), but those of the Asiatic *N. nucifera* probably surpass even this achievement and are commonly regarded as the longest-lived of all angiosperm seeds.* One seed of this species, known to be at least 237 years old, germinated on a herbarium sheet accidentally flooded after the British Museum of Natural History was bombed in 1940 (Ramsbottom, 1942). Of perhaps even greater interest is the consistent germination of many allegedly ancient seeds of *N. nucifera* discovered in the moist peat of a drained lake-bed in the Pulantien basin of southern Manchuria (Ohga, 1926a). The age of these is not certainly known. Ohga (1926a) put forward estimates of at least 120 years (from observations of the trunks of willows now growing in the peat bed), 160 to 250 years (from the probable date of drainage of the lake), and more than 400 years (from observations of the extent to which a river had cut down through the exposed lake bottom). Libby (1951) obtained an estimate of about 1040 years by radioactive-carbon dating of a sample of Ohga's fruits, but Godwin and Willis (1964) were recently unable to confirm this. Their repeated determinations, using a different technique but with the same material, suggested an age of no more than about 100 years. These two workers thought the seeds could in fact be from quite modern plants and expressed the need for confirmatory estimations on further specimens collected from the same site.

Whatever their precise age, the Manchurian seeds showed nearly 100 per cent germination when their coats were made permeable by treatment with sulphuric acid (Ohga, 1926a, b). They developed equally well in either aerobic or anaerobic conditions, sufficient oxygen for germination still being present in the cavity and intercellular spaces within each fruit. Analysis of the 0·2 ml or so of gas in each fruit showed that on average the proportion of oxygen had

---

* However, Odum (1965) presented evidence that seeds of many terrestrial angiosperm weeds may remain viable for up to 600 years, or even longer.

decreased, and that of nitrogen had increased, by only about 0·6 per cent relative to the composition of the gas in fruits harvested from plants in 1924 (Ohga, 1926b). The catalase activity, respiration rate and growth rate of the ancient seeds during germination actually exceeded those of the modern seeds (Ohga, 1926c, d). The survival of these seeds for even 100 years is truly astonishing, for their respiration rate must have been incredibly low to have created so little change in their internal atmosphere and not to have depleted their food reserves. The irregular and delayed germination of the seeds of some species may be associated, as in such terrestrial plants as the tomato, with the persistence of a growth inhibitor in the embryo itself, the testa or the fruit tissue. Vose (1962) recently found that the sometimes prolonged dormancy of *Phalaris arundinacea* is caused by a water-soluble inhibitor present in either the caryopsis or the embryo. The inhibition is apparently quickly eliminated when the tissues of the fruit become well-aerated, as when the enclosing palea is punctured or removed.

Prolonged dormancy, even if not so phenomenal as in the lotuses, is presumably advantageous in permitting widespread dispersal away from parental competition, by either water-transport or carriage of the seeds through the air for a lengthy period, as on the plumage or feet of birds. It may also allow survival of the species through harsh winters or scorching dry seasons when streams and shallow pools may be frozen over or desiccated. Furthermore, it enables the seeds to germinate under more favourable conditions in the spring or the succeeding rainy seasons, when the chances of survival are rather better than if germination occurred immediately the seeds matured. In a few tropical genera which are sometimes described as viviparous, e.g. the marine *Enhalus* and *Thalassia*, the embryo has no dormant phase. Its development is continuous and the seeds may germinate before they are liberated by the disintegration of the pericarp, and even whilst still attached to the parent.

Most hydrophyte seeds will germinate in a suitable depth of water or on moist or flooded soil, provided that a suitable temperature and an oxygen supply are available (Muenscher, 1936). For the germination of brackish-water plants, e.g. *Triglochin maritima* and *T. palustris*, salinity may also be an important factor (Binet, 1961, 1962). A few freshwater species, e.g. *Rorippa nasturtium-aquaticum* and *Typha latifolia*, actually show better germination in low oxygen tensions (Morinaga, 1926a, b). Sifton (1959) showed that germination of *Typha latifolia* seeds is favoured, under normal experimental conditions on moist filter paper, by a reduced oxygen tension. Under water, where the oxygen concentration is naturally much lower than in air, the seeds require a light stimulus. It was observed microscopically that germination is initiated by the attraction of water to the colloidal proteins of the aleurone granules of the seed, the consequent swelling bursting the testa. Sifton explained the results of his experiments on the premise that certain wavelengths of light and the accumulated products of anaerobic respiration both increase the water-holding capacity of the aleurone colloids and thus promote germination. Vigorous aerobic respiration causes vacuolation in many cells of the seed and the increased turgor pressure compensates to a certain extent for the lack of aleurone swelling and causes some rupture of testas. Thus germination still occurs in aerobic conditions but not so favourably as in low oxygen concentrations.

Mayer and Poljakoff-Mayber (1963) interpreted the light requirement and the promotion of germination by anaerobic conditions to be of adaptational

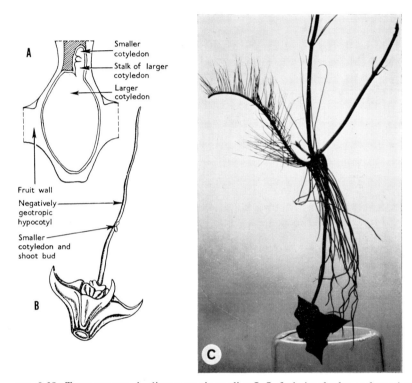

FIG. 9.28. *Trapa natans*: A, diagrammatic median L.S. fruit (seed plus endocarp) to show embryo ($\times$ 1·2); B, young seedling (larger cotyledon retained within seed) ($\times$ 0·6); C, older seedling, showing hypocotyl (growing up to left) with long, positively geotropic, early-formed roots and shorter, negatively geotropic, later-formed roots: to the right is an abortive shoot, in the centre is the vertical main shoot, and to its left a younger developing shoot ($\times$ 0·4).

significance in permitting germination to occur either in oxygen-deficient swamps and seasonally inundated marginal soils, or in relatively shallow water penetrated by light, whilst preventing it in deeper water beyond the photic zone where there would be little or no chance of survival. Promotion of germination by a daily regime of alternating low and high temperatures, as reported for the emergent *Zizania aquatica* by Simpson (1966), could also be advantageous to plants of shallow marginal waters, in which diurnal fluctuations of temperature may be quite wide during the spring and early summer.

Spence (1964) drew attention to the possibility that the range of suitable habitats available for successful germination of the seeds of many hydrophytes is significantly narrower than for the development of vegetative propagules and mature individuals. He found that seeds of the emergent *Phragmites communis* will not germinate when submerged (even at a depth of only 5 cm) although mature individuals will grow and spread by rhizomes in water as much as 1 m deep.

The seeds of some free-floating plants, e.g. *Eichhornia crassipes, Hydrocharis, Stratiotes* and *Trapa,* germinate on the substrate and become temporarily rooted. In *E. crassipes* the cotyledon and short hypocotyl appear first. Root hairs from the hypocotyl anchor the seed during the emergence and establishment of the radicle. A little later, when the first juvenile leaves have expanded, the seedling rises to the surface (Haigh, 1936; Hitchcock *et al.*, 1949; and Fig. 13.5). The seeds of *Trapa natans* (Fig. 9.28) and *T. bicornis* are usually fixed in the substrate by their own weight and by the spines of the fruit wall. The large functional cotyledon remains within the seed but the second abortive one is borne aloft on the negatively geotropic hypocotyl. Lateral roots grow down from the hypocotyl and firmly anchor the seedling in the soil. The plumule then begins to grow up to the surface, and a secondary shoot often arises in the axil of the abortive cotyledon. Soon after the apical rosette of foliage has developed, the lower part of each shoot decays and the plant becomes truly free-floating (Goebel, 1891–1893; Jankovič, 1955, 1956).

DISPERSAL OF FRUITS, SEEDS AND SEEDLINGS

Of the four principal agents of dispersal—water, wind, animals and man— water is of especial significance in the dissemination of many emergent hydrophytes which have buoyant fruits and seeds. The period of buoyancy, a few days to a month or more, is sufficient to allow the propagules to be carried well away from the competitive parental habitat. There is a good chance that many will have been stranded in favourable marginal sites by the time they become waterlogged. It is unlikely that the distances they are carried are great, but in short-range dispersal water-transport is probably a potent factor. Of course, the mobility endowed by power of flotation must be attended by a severe risk that floods will sweep the fruits and seeds on to adjacent terrestrial soils or into estuarine or coastal waters.

Ravn (1894), Guppy (1906) and Praeger (1913) collated voluminous data on the buoyancy of fruits, seeds and seedlings: their principal findings were later valuably summarised by Ridley (1930) in his classic book on plant dispersal. When liberated from the parent, the achenes (caryopses) of the aquatic grasses, such as *Glyceria, Phalaris* and *Zizania,* and the achenes or nutlets of the aquatic sedges, such as *Eleocharis* and species of *Cyperus* and *Scirpus,* usually remain enclosed by air within one or more associated bracts and therefore float freely until they become waterlogged. The most frequent anatomical modification endowing buoyancy is the development of subepidermal, air-filled, lacunate tissue, or just rather large intercellular spaces, either in the pericarp, as in the fruits of *Alisma, Cladium, Limnocharis, Mentha aquatica, Orontium, Pontederia, Potamogeton* (Fig. 9.23), *Sparganium*, and some species of *Scirpus* and *Scutellaria*, or in the testa, as in some species of *Aponogeton, Menyanthes, Calla, Scheuchzeria* and *Iris pseudacorus*, or in the dry receptacle of *Nelumbo*. The mericarps of species of *Oenanthe* and *Sium* owe their buoyancy to lateral masses of suberised corky tissue, whilst the achenes of *Sagittaria* and *Limnophyton* have comparable lateral wings (Fig. 9.23) containing lacunate parenchyma. The buoyancy of these fruits and seeds may be enhanced by oil in the cotyledons or pericarp, and by the waxy cuticularised epidermis of the testa or exocarp. The exact period of flotation varies considerably even within a species but is usually between 2 or 3 days, as in *Oenanthe* and *Orontium*, and 2 months or rarely longer, as in *Alisma* and *Menyanthes*.

The seeds and fruits of some emergents, e.g. *Baldellia ranunculoides, Lythrum salicaria, Scrophularia aquatica* and some species of *Juncus*, sink immediately they fall into the water. This disadvantage is compensated by the fact that the young seedlings rise to the surface and float for several weeks before becoming permanently rooted. Buoyant seedlings are also produced by a few submerged plants, e.g. *Hottonia palustris*. The seedling of the marine *Amphibolis antarctica* only breaks free of the parent when it is 7 to 10 cm long. It is enclosed by a basket-like structure bearing four spines. This 'grappling apparatus' keeps the seedling morphologically upright during its free-floating existence and easily becomes tangled in marine algae and shore debris, thereby aiding the establishment of the young plant in a suitable habitat (Osborn, 1914).

In contrast to those of emergents, the fruits and seeds of submerged and floating-leaved angiosperms generally have no great powers of flotation. They either sink at once, as in *Callitriche, Ceratophyllum, Groenlandia, Lobelia dortmanna* and most hydrophilous genera, or float for a few hours to a day, sufficient to facilitate dispersal from the environs of the parent, as in *Myriophyllum* and the batrachian *Ranunculi*. The loculi liberated when the aerial fruit of *Nuphar* splits irregularly, float for 2 to 3 days until their walls become waterlogged. The seeds of *Nymphaea* also float for a short period because of the air trapped within the aril (Fig. 9.23). The fruits or seeds of free-floating plants such as *Eichhornia, Lemna, Trapa* and *Wolffia* usually float for a day or so but the seeds of *Hydrocharis* and *Stratiotes* sink in a mass of gelatinous pulp when the fruit bursts.

The minute seeds of the Podostemaceae do not seem to be very widely dispersed. They are commonly found germinating on the vegetative residues of the parent, the pedicels of the fruits, the external and internal walls of the dehisced capsules (Fig. 9.29), and on bare rocks near the parent. Willis (1902, 1914, 1926) drew attention to the singular absence, from all members of this family, of any adequate mechanism for attachment of the seeds, which would be of tremendous adaptive value in their habitat. As it is, the generally torrential water must sweep away vast numbers of seeds and seedlings before they become established. The seeds do become loosely attached to a substrate by mucilage produced by their outer coats in contact with moisture. Adhesion becomes firmer if the seed dries out and the mucilage hardens. If remoistened, however, the mucilage liquefies again and so can be of no permanent value in attaching the seeds. Eventually, during germination, the hypocotyl and the thallus to which it gives rise by lateral expansion become anchored to the substrate by clinging hairs (Goebel, 1891–1893; Willis, 1902; Accorsi, 1944, 1946, 1951). The typically high output of seeds, 200 to 600 per capsule, may to some extent compensate for the great wastage. Only in one genus (*Farmeria*)

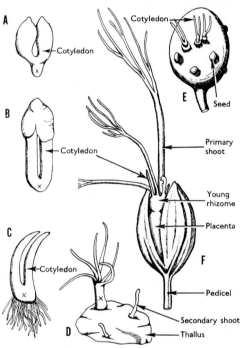

FIG. 9.29. Embryos and seedlings of the Podostemaceae: A, *Podostemum subulatus*, embryo (× 20); B, *Wettsteiniola accorsii*, germinating seed (× 25); C, *W. accorsii*, young seedling with absorptive hairs (× 20); D, *Dicraea stylosa*, seedling with first thallus formed from hypocotyl (× 10); E, *Mniopsis weddelliana*, seeds and seedlings emerging from fruit capsule (× 10); F, *Wettsteiniola accorsii*, seedling developing on placenta within fruit capsule (× 8). (In A to D the hypocotyl is marked X.) (A, D, after Willis, 1902; B, C, E, F, after Accorsi, 1944, 1946.)

is the number of seeds greatly reduced. The two seeds of *F. metzgerioides* are borne within an indehiscent fruit (not a capsule) and germinate *in situ* on the remains of the parent. Willis (1902, 1914) suggested that even this apparent adaptation may be no more than a fortuitous coincidence, for the indehiscent two-seeded fruit may be just another structural expression of the family's trend towards dorsiventrality, which is most extremely manifest in this species of *Farmeria*.

For estuarine plants the proximity to the sea and the fluctuating tidal currents must constitute sore hazards. The area within which successful dispersal of seeds may be achieved is very much smaller than for any other group of hydrophytes. The Indo-Malaysian aroid *Cryptocoryne ciliata* gives an interesting example of the behaviour of such tidal-mud plants (Ridley, 1930). Germination of its seeds usually starts before the surrounding capsule opens. By the time the seeds are liberated, the cotyledon has emerged as several linear filaments which act collectively as a floating organ. After only a few minutes, adequate to allow dispersal from the parent in the tidal current yet not long enough for the seedling to be swept right out to sea, the cotyledon abscisses and the developing embryo sinks to the mud.

In a recent review of the dispersal and survival of plants, Löve (1963) remarked that marine plants are naturally adapted to dispersal in sea-water. This is an unfortunate generalisation. One example she cited, *Zostera*, certainly possesses seeds with buoyant corky appendages but there is no critical evidence that the period of buoyancy is long enough to permit long-distance dispersal, as suggested. The seeds of *Halophila* (which are very similar in structure to those of *Zostera*) and of *Thalassia*, *Cymodocea* and other marine angiosperms sink immediately they are liberated, or float for only a few hours until the testa is cast off and the heavy embryo sinks, as in *Enhalus acoroides* (Kausik, 1940a, b), or remain *in situ* on the parent, partly buried in the substrate, as in *Cymodocea nodosa* (Bornet, 1864). Some species, it is true, have floating seedlings, but both these and the buoyant vegetative organs soon die if they fail to achieve a suitable anchorage. They are extremely vulnerable to destruction by the relentless wave-action and strong currents in many coastal habitats, as illustrated by the frequent stranding of their debris. Long-range dispersal of seeds, seedlings or vegetative fragments by sea-currents is not likely to be significant in the dispersal of marine angiosperms.

Some aerial-ripening fruits and seeds may be dispersed by wind, although the distance covered is unlikely to be more than a few metres or so in view of their mass and their general lack of structures aiding aerial transport. Wind dispersal cannot be of great advantage because of the likelihood that seeds will be blown to dry terrestrial soils as often as to aquatic sites. Wind presumably contributes to water-transport in blowing seeds and fruits some little way from the parent before they fall into the water.

Animals, and water-birds in particular, are unquestionably the prime agents in the short-range dispersal of hydrophytes of all life forms. Over a century ago, in *The Origin of Species*, Darwin surmised that the remarkably wide range of some freshwater plants had been achieved mainly by the carriage of seeds and vegetative fragments on the plumage and muddy feet of water-fowl. Direct observations of such dispersal are of course difficult to obtain, but many naturalists and ecologists, notably Reid (1892), Guppy (1893, 1897, 1906), Walker (1905), Godwin (1923), Gates (1927), Ridley (1930) and Samuelsson (1934), have amassed an enormous volume of circumstantial evidence for both exo- and endozoic transport of seeds and other propagules. There is no doubt that seeds and small fruits, adhering by mucilage or hairs to the feathers of water-fowl, or imprisoned in the mud upon their feet, are frequently carried from habitat to habitat in the course of the birds' ordinary flights. Similar accidental transport by amphibians, reptiles and small mammals frequenting aquatic sites may also contribute in some measure to their dissemination. Fruits and seeds of many freshwater plants are eaten in abundance, together with succulent vegetative organs, by a variety of water-fowl, marsh birds, shore birds, game birds, and by a few mammals and fishes. Although the effects of the animals' digestive enzymes have not been critically studied, analysis of the contents of crops, stomachs and intestines has revealed quantities of seeds— and also sporocarps of such plants as *Marsilea* (Malone and Proctor, 1965)— and it is likely that at least the more resistant types pass through the animal unharmed. Clearly the discharge of the faeces will often occur some distance from the site of ingestion. The seeds of *Enhalus*, *Thalassia* and other marine angiosperms may perhaps be conveyed in a similar way by certain sea-mammals (manatee and dugong), turtles and fishes (ballahoo) which often browse on these plants.

Although exo- and endozoic transport must be highly significant in the widespread dispersal and resulting ubiquity of many hydrophytes throughout discrete regions within a major land mass and throughout archipelagic areas, they are unlikely to be effective in long-range dispersal between continents. It has been suggested from time to time that seeds and fruits could be carried over the major oceans by migrating birds. As Löve (1963) explained, there are several critical reasons for doubting this possibility. Successful endozoic transport over such immense distances would entail retention of the propagules within the digestive tract for most, if not all, of the flight. Even in larger birds with a slower metabolic rate, such as ducks, geese and swans, the passage of food takes less than 7 h. Flight speeds over land are about 80 km/h but radar estimates for pintails and mallards suggest that over open sea the speeds are slower. It is also likely that metabolic rates increase during a strenuous migratory flight. In addition, it appears that many birds do not eat immediately before migrating and so it is improbable that seeds could be carried in this way for more than perhaps 100 to 300 km. Exozoic transport during migration is rendered less likely by the reported fastidious preening by the birds before taking off, although occasional seeds could conceivably still adhere to the feet. In the context of both exo- and endozoic carriage, it must also be remembered that most migratory flights occur in the spring, when propagules are less abundant, or in the late summer, often starting before temperate aquatic vegetation reaches its climax and before many fruits and seeds have ripened.

Finally it may be noted that man has certainly contributed to dispersal. Precise data are again sparse but it is likely that the seeds or fruits of various tropical species growing amongst irrigated crops such as rice and cotton are accidentally distributed with the seeds and other products of the harvested crop. Casual transport by boats and agricultural vehicles and the escape of seeds or vegetative parts from ornamental waters and botanic gardens have also assisted the adventive spread of several hydrophytes. The importance of vegetative propagules is discussed further in Chapters 10 and 13, and the relation of dispersal capacity to geographical range in Chapter 11.

Vegetative Reproduction
and Perennation

The relative uniformity of the aquatic environment encourages good vegetative growth. The abundance of water and carbon dioxide, and the insulation given by the water against intense illumination and violent fluctuations of temperature seem to be conducive to active photosynthesis and sustained development of foliage once the growing season has started. Many observers have endorsed Arber's (1920) opinion that 'the excessive vegetative activity of water plants acts, in all probability, as a deterrent to sexual reproduction.' Acknowledging that the growth of different organs is delicately correlated, this crude notion recognises an antithesis between vegetative and reproductive growth: an increasing number of vegetative meristems may be expected to exert a steadily greater demand on the plant's pool of nutrients, leaving less and less available for floral meristems. Common horticultural practice indicates that there is indeed some sort of inverse relationship between vegetative and reproductive growth, as between blooming and fruiting, but since growth processes may be initiated and influenced by photoperiod, temperature and perhaps other factors such a relationship cannot adequately be expressed in simple nutritional terms. Furthermore, it is important to appreciate that the vegetative growth of most aquatic vascular plants (except some perennial emergents), although often visually striking and exuberant, is not unusually luxuriant when measured by quantitative criteria.

Yet, despite these qualifications, it must be admitted that there is often a tendency amongst hydrophytes towards the replacement of sexual by vegetative reproduction. This phenomenon seems congruous with the fact that the floral reproductive organs of most species are singularly ill-adapted to aquatic life and have still to be raised into the air for pollination. A capacity for sustained vegetative propagation, thereby evading the hazards of elevating aerial flowers, might therefore be advantageous, especially to plants living in deeper water.

Although the frequency of vegetative reproduction may be higher in aquatic plants, the organs actually employed as propagules are essentially similar, in both morphological origin and mode of development, to those of herbaceous land plants. Fragmentation of the plant body, followed by regeneration from any small part bearing a bud, is a common phenomenon in the reduced free-floating plants and in those submerged hydrophytes whose stems are long and delicate. Regeneration from any fragment of the body containing meristematic tissue is also prevalent amongst members of the Podostemaceae. Gemmipary, the development of young plants from vegetative buds borne on the parent body, occurs in several wild and cultivated hydrophytes.

Colonisation by means of rhizomes, stolons and runners is widespread amongst all life forms and in numerous taxa these organs also store food reserves and function as hibernacula, enabling the plant to survive conditions unfavourable to vegetative growth. Although the higher temperatures and long frostless periods in subtropical climates permit sustained vegetative growth, organs of perennation are important in some habitats as a means of passing the dry season. In temperate hydrophytes the alliance between vegetative reproduction and perennation is especially close and the same organs regularly serve both functions.

Some temperate hydrophytes are exceptional in producing, in response to a depleted nutrient supply or abnormal conditions, organs which are not developed during normal vegetative growth, and which serve specifically for perennation. Towards the end of the growing season some species of *Sagittaria* and *Potamogeton*, for example, form small tubers on the ends of stolons or lateral branches, whilst some species of *Hydrocharis*, *Myriophyllum* and *Utricularia* develop specialised dwarf shoots, known as turions. Other plants bear rather less specialised structures: *Ceratophyllum*, for example, has dense shoot apices. Protected by mucilage or a thick cuticle, these various organs are loaded with food reserves and remain dormant throughout the winter.

Most types of vegetative propagule probably contribute significantly to the dissemination of species about the globe, as a result of the ease with which they are accidentally transported by floods, water-fowl, other animals and man. Vegetative reproduction is of paramount importance in the maintenance and spread of many hydrophytes, especially in conditions which prevent fructification or seedling development. For some species, *Elodea canadensis* and *Acorus calamus* being notable examples, it is the only method of reproduction throughout large sectors of their geographical range.

THE REPLACEMENT OF SEXUAL BY VEGETATIVE REPRODUCTION

Several instances of the trend towards suppression of normal sexual behaviour have already been described in an earlier chapter: notably, the formation of cleistogamous flowers, as in *Ottelia ovalifolia* (p. 290); self-fertilisation in bud, as in *Subularia aquatica* (p. 291); reduced fertility, as in *Elodea canadensis* and *E. nuttallii* (p. 310); and scarcity of viable seeds, as in *Stratiotes*, *Hydrocharis* and *Acorus calamus* (p. 319). There are many other examples of the tendency towards the substitution of sexual by vegetative reproduction. The following instances will illustrate this phenomenon.

Submerged specimens of amphibious plants are usually sterile. *Littorella uniflora*, for example, forms anemophilous flowers in abundance when it is emergent, but under water, especially when submerged at considerable depths, it spreads entirely by runners (West, 1905). Similarly, the pteridophytes *Marsilea* and *Pilularia* do not usually form reproductive organs in deep or flowing water, but spread by vigorous growth of their rhizomes (Schenck, 1885). Submerged plants may exhibit a similar trend: *Wettsteiniola accorsii* and other podostemads reproduce primarily by vegetative means in the Piraci-caba Fall in São Paulo, Brazil (Accorsi, 1944, 1946). Amongst the aquatic

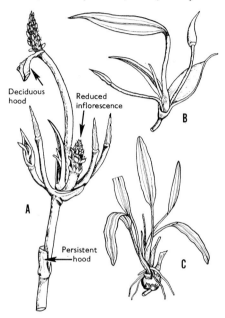

FIG. 10.1. *Aponogeton stachyosporus*: A, digitately branching, mixed inflorescence with a persistent basal hood and bearing much-reduced secondary inflorescences and young plants with deciduous hoods (×1); B, young plants developing from the inflorescence axis (×1·4); C, young plant at a later stage when a swollen tuberous stem has developed (×1). (After de Wit, 1958b.)

Utricularias the species with well-developed turions characteristically produce few or no flowers (Rossbach, 1939). In the emergent *Nelumbo nucifera*, this inverse relationship is evident in each individual, for only those last nodes of the horizontal shoot where flowers do not arise become thickened and modified as organs of vegetative propagation (Wang, 1956).

In addition to these various instances of extra-floral vegetative reproduction, there are numerous examples amongst hydrophytes of another apomictic phenomenon, pseudovivipary, in which vegetative propagules replace some or all of the normal sexual flowers in the inflorescence. Glück (1906) noticed that if an inflorescence of *Myriophyllum verticillatum* became submerged a turion was formed at the apex of the axis. Barber (1889) described the replacement of flowers by tubers in a cultivated variety of *Nymphaea lotus*: the tubers subse-

12

quently developed into independent plants. *Aponogeton stachyosporus* was described from Johore as forming a digitately branched axis which bears both reduced inflorescences and young plants (de Wit, 1958b; and see Fig. 10.1).

The family Alismaceae is rich in pseudoviviparous species. In the palaeo-tropical and warm temperate *Caldesia parnassifolia* and the Indian *C. grandis* the inflorescence axis bears whorls of turions instead of flowers, especially when the plants are growing in water of 50 cm or greater depth (Glück, 1905; den

FIG. 10.2. An aerial fruiting peduncle of *Echinodorus cordifolius* hanging vertically and bearing a sturdy young plant (arrowed) near its tip ($\times 0.4$).

Hartog, 1957a). The original herbarium specimen of the south-east Asiatic *Ranalisma rostratum* bears only one flower, the other potential flowers having been replaced by turions, each with one or a few leaves. The peduncle of the inflorescence appears to act as a stolon, bearing the turions away from the parent. The same phenomenon occurs in the tropical African *Ranalisma humile* and the European *Baldellia ranunculoides* and *Luronium natans* (den Hartog, 1957a). Several American species of *Echinodorus* likewise bear plantlets in place of flowers along the axis of their inflorescences: *E. brevipedicellatus*, *E. cordifolius* (Fig. 10.2) and *E. macrophyllus* produce both flowers and young plants quite freely, but the frequency of the latter is increased if the inflorescence is sub-merged. The inflorescence of *E. intermedius* and *E. tunicatus* sets seed above water but when submerged it tends to bear just plantlets. Plantlets appear in abundance on any inflorescence axis of *E. paniculatus*, in which species flowers rarely appear, even above water (de Wit, 1958a).

Pseudovivipary is by no means peculiar to aquatic angiosperms: it occurs in many terrestrial monocotyledons and dicotyledons, such as *Polygonum viviparum*, *Allium*, *Poa* and *Festuca* (Davis and Heywood, 1963). An analogous phenomenon is known in numerous terrestrial and aquatic pteridophytes. Here, the sporangia are partly or wholly replaced by young plantlets, as Goebel (1879) noticed in *Isoetes lacustris* and *I. setacea* growing in deep water in one of the Vosges lakes. Specimens of the amphibious fern, *Microsorium pteropus*, behave similarly when they are submerged (Fig. 10.3).

FIG. 10.3. Submerged leaves of *Microsorium pteropus*, one of which is bearing on its undersurface, in lieu of sporangia, a young plant (arrowed) with a developing rhizome and adventitious roots and two leaves, one as yet unexpanded (× 0·5).

REGENERATION AND GEMMIPARY

Consequent upon the reduction of their mechanical tissues and their dependence on turgor for internal support, the vegetative organs of almost all submerged hydrophytes are very brittle. The slender fragile stems of elongated flexuous species of *Ceratophyllum*, *Elodea*, *Myriophyllum* etc. are quickly broken and any violent disturbance of the water, by rapid currents, strong winds or foraging animals, shatters the plant body into a myriad fragments. Great masses of fragmentary material floating in the water or stranded upon the shores are left in the wake of floods and afford a common sight at the end of the growing season as communities decline and decay sets in. Reduced free-floating plants such as *Azolla*, *Lemna*, *Salvinia*, *Wolffia* and *Utricularia* are equally susceptible, the colonies breaking up at the slightest touch.

Almost any detached fragment, if it includes a bud or at least part of a node, can subsequently regenerate a new individual. In *Ceratophyllum*, *Egeria*, *Elodea*, *Hydrilla*, *Lagarosiphon*, *Myriophyllum* and other genera of similar habit, any part of the axis is viable and potentially capable of yielding a new plant if it bears a dormant lateral bud from which new growth can occur. In *Callitriche* any node together with a minute part of the adjacent internode is capable of growing into a new plant (Hegelmaier, 1864), whilst in the Lemnaceae any fragment which includes the vegetative bud pouch, and in *Salvinia* and *Azolla* the most minute part of the stem bearing an axillary bud, readily gives rise to new individuals. Fragmentation occurs especially during senescence, the rate of which may be regulated by an internal balance of growth substances. When added to the culture medium, 10 ppm or more of IAA increases the fragmentation of *Azolla mexicana*. Gibberellic acid, however, inhibits fragmentation in the same species by greatly depressing the rate of senescence. Moreover, 1 or 10 ppm gibberellic acid will suppress the promotion of fragmentation by 50 ppm IAA (Dusek and Bonde, 1965). The whorl of lateral shoots at the base of the inflorescence axis in *Hottonia* usually disintegrates after seed has been set and each shoot survives the winter and then forms an independent rooted or free-floating plant (Prankerd, 1911).

In some hydrophytes, as in numerous terrestrial plants, buds may be produced from foliar tissue (Goebel, 1908). This process of gemmipary is in some species natural and spontaneous but in certain others it may be induced by isolation of, or injury to, the leaf: in either case it is essentially a regeneration phenomenon. Since each leaf may bear several such buds, each capable of developing into a plantlet (or bulbil) which either drops off or becomes independent when the leaf decays, gemmipary is a prolific means of vegetative multiplication. In most gemmiparous species the plantlets arise at specific sites of cell-aggregates which naturally become meristematic, or may be induced to become so, with great facility. As Sinnott (1960) has remarked, it would be interesting to know how the cells at these sites differ physiologically from those throughout the remaining leaf tissue. In *Ceratopteris*, which produces plantlets in the vicinity of vein-endings at the base of marginal notches in the mature leaf (Fig. 10.4), the activity of the meristematic cell-aggregates seems to be influenced by diffusible growth substances. Excised meristems will produce healthy young plants if they are cultured on a nutrient medium to which adenine or IAA is added. Without either of these supplements, an excised meristem will yield a plantlet only if it is in contact with a vein of the leaf or if about a quarter or more of the leaf tissue is placed adjacent to it (Gottlieb, 1963).

The family Cruciferae is notably rich in examples of gemmipary, many of which, in such genera as *Cardamine*, *Dentaria* and *Rorippa*, have long been known to botanists (Goebel, 1908). Adventitious buds arise at the base of any detached simple leaf or of any isolated leaflet of a compound leaf: in some taxa even small fragments of a leaflet will eventually produce young plants. The axis of each bud elongates and from its lower nodes adventitious roots develop and soon anchor the new individual. Vast numbers of these gemmiparous plantlets may often be found amongst the disintegrating remains of the parents in the autumn. In the heterophyllous aquatic species, such as *Armoracia aquatica* (Foerste, 1889), gemmipary is especially common on the pinnately dissected submerged leaves.

Other examples of gemmipary are afforded by the tropical West African *Nymphaea micrantha* and by numerous tropical hybrid *Nymphaeas* of garden origin, such as *N.* × Daubeniana, *N.* × Talisman, *N.* × August Koch, *N.* × Peach Blow, *N.* × Mrs Woodrow Wilson and *N.* × Panama Pacific. In all these waterlilies, plantlets develop from buds at the junction of the petiole with the floating lamina and sometimes become sufficiently well-developed to flower whilst still attached to the parent leaf.

FIG. 10.4. Gemmipary in the free-floating *Ceratopteris cornuta*: A, rosette of leaves bearing numerous plantlets around the margins (× 0·4); B, plantlets liberated by decay of the parent leaf (× 0·5).

Conspicuous powers of regeneration are evident in such highly reduced submerged hydrophytes as species of *Utricularia* and the Podostemaceae. Most if not all cells in these species retain a meristematic capacity which becomes manifest in abnormal conditions or after injury. New shoots may develop from almost any part of the body of *Utricularia*, notably from the points of forking of old or detached leaves (Goebel, 1904; Glück, 1906) and from the axils of the scale leaves of excised inflorescences immersed in a culture medium (von Luetzelburg, 1910). So long as it is submerged, any portion of the thallus of podostemads such as *Mniopsis*, *Mourera*, *Terniola* and *Tristicha* will produce a new plant (Willis, 1902; Accorsi, 1944, 1946). In *Podostemum ceratophyllum* the decapitated part of a thallus is soon replaced by the derivatives of a group of dividing cells near the vascular tissue just behind the cut surface (Hammond, 1936, 1937).

THE GEOPHYTIC HABIT

Many rooted aquatic plants are geophytes, their resting vegetative organs and perennial stem apices being below the surface of the substrate. The great majority of emergent and floating-leaved species, together with a smaller proportion of submerged species, show this habit. The nature of the persistent organs surviving the unfavourable tropical dry season or temperate winter varies as widely as amongst terrestrial geophytes. *Nymphaea* and many emergent genera perennate by rhizomes, which may be tuberous, whilst in *Aponogeton* growth is renewed from a persistent corm-like rootstock. Stem tubers are produced by some species of *Cyperus*, *Potamogeton* and *Sagittaria*, and root tubers by some species of *Nymphaea* and *Nymphoides*. In most cases these organs serve also for vegetative reproduction since branching of rhizomes, division of rootstocks or production of several tubers by a single parent all yield an increase in numbers.

Rhizomes and Rootstocks. During the autumn in temperate waters, or when the water table falls at the onset of the dry season in the tropics, the foliage of many emergent hydrophytes dies back to the swollen, food-storing rhizome,

FIG. 10.5. Trailing epigeal rhizomes of the emergent *Calla palustris* exposed by death of the foliage in late autumn ($\times 0.2$).

the terminal and lateral buds of which remain dormant until conditions ameliorate. As was described more fully in Chapter 6, the structure of the rhizome varies considerably from genus to genus: it may be woody or herbaceous, spongy or firm, very swollen or quite slender, extensively creeping or somewhat abbreviated. *Acorus*, *Aglaonema*, *Anubias*, *Cryptocoryne*, *Eleocharis*, *Lagenandra*, *Marsilea*, *Peltandra*, *Pontederia*, *Phragmites*, *Scirpus* and *Typha* provide examples of the many forms (Fig. 10.5 and Fig. 6.1). The rhizomatous habit is also typical of most species of *Nuphar*, *Nymphaea* and *Victoria*, and several other floating-leaved plants such as *Potamogeton natans* and *Nymphoides aquatica*. Despite the variation in structure the principal function of perennation is evident in all types. Soluble carbohydrates translocated from the leaves are accumulated in insoluble reserve form in the parenchymatous ground tissue of the rhizome. The excessive swelling of some rhizomes is almost entirely due to hypertrophy of this storage tissue, the cells eventually becoming fully laden with starch grains. After dormancy, mobilisation of these reserves provides the simpler soluble molecules needed at the meristems of the buds for the synthesis of new cell constituents.

It will be recalled that the radical foliage of some rosette plants arises from an abbreviated axis situated in a more or less erect position at or just below soil level and known as a rootstock or crown. In most such plants the rootstock is herbaceous, compact and rather slender but in a few, such as *Aponogeton* and *Sagittaria*, it is swollen and either hard and corm-like or fleshy and bulb-like. In warmer waters the foliage is often retained throughout the year unless the habitat dries up, but in some genera inhabiting both tropical and temperate zones, such as *Aponogeton*, *Echinodorus*, *Limnophyton*, *Sagittaria* and *Tenagocharis*, there is usually a resting period, if only of short duration, and the foliage dies down, the rootstock serving for perennation. All types of rootstock, like horizontal rhizomes, store food reserves, especially starch, to a greater or lesser extent.

Formation of Stolons or Runners. Except for creeping rhizomatous genera, e.g. *Phragmites*, *Typha* and *Glyceria*, most plants with perennating underground stems remain in much the same position from year to year. They reproduce vegetatively and spread horizontally by means of runners, at or just above the soil surface, or stolons, growing underground. As in terrestrial plants each runner or stolon travels away from the parent for some distance, its growing apex eventually becoming erect and forming a new plant which is anchored by adventitious roots. A lateral bud on the abbreviated stem of the new plant may then develop into a secondary stolon which likewise produces at its tip a daughter rosette. Subsequently the connecting runners or stolons decay and the progeny become truly independent; sometimes the successive stems develop at such a rapid rate that whole chains of rosettes may be found still linked to the parent.

The formation of stems from a rhizome is exemplified by several species of *Cryptocorne*: more outstanding examples of the vigorous output of stolons or runners are *Hydrocleys nymphoides*, *Limosella aquatica*, *Littorella uniflora* (Fig. 10.6), *Lobelia dortmanna*, *Luronium natans*, *Nymphoides aquatica*, *Vallisneria spiralis* and such free-floating rosette plants as *Eichhornia crassipes* and *Pistia stratiotes*. The area colonised in this way is often considerable: by means of its slender runners with internodes often exceeding 1·5 m, *Nelumbo*, for example, can extend as much as 16 m radially in one growing season (Wood, 1959). It will be remembered that by virtue of their stoloniferous habit and ability to root in coarse substrates such plants as *Littorella* and *Lobelia* are ecologically important as pioneer colonists of eroded shores.

Both runners and stolons are generally short-lived and produced during optimal vegetative activity: their prime function is undoubtedly as organs of reproduction rather than perennation. There are, however, a few instances amongst hydrophytes of overwintering by either runners, e.g. *Limosella subulata* (Warburg, 1962) and *Sagittaria demersa* (Bogin, 1955), or stolons, e.g. *Justicia americana* (Penfound *et al.*, 1945).

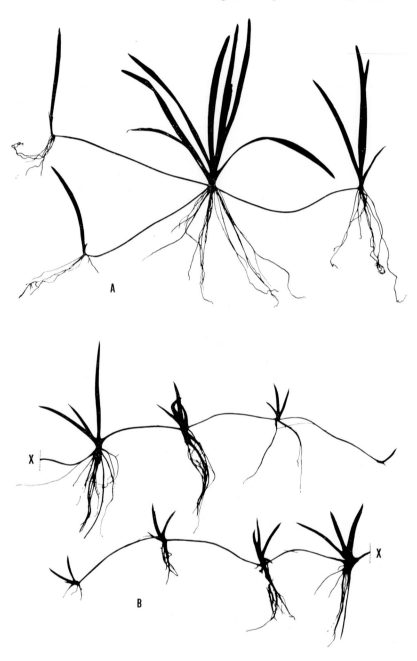

FIG. 10.6. Silhouettes of *Echinodorus tenellus* (A) and *Littorella uniflora* (B) showing formation of runners (runner in B broken at point X) (both ×0·5).

Stem Tubers. Although rarely functioning directly as perennating organs, stolons and runners may produce terminal swollen structures which remain dormant during adverse conditions and later grow into new plants. These structures vary in form, origin and development and do not fit into any of the accepted categories of storage organs. However, they are essentially swollen portions of stems, and those of successive years bear no constant relationship to their predecessors: they are therefore better regarded as stem tubers, rather than corms.

In *Nelumbo*, for example, towards the end of each growing season, the last one or two internodes at the tip of each runner become swollen with food reserves, forming a tuber some 8 to 28 cm long. This remains dormant, partly or completely buried in the substrate, and its terminal bud resumes growth the following spring (Wang, 1956; Wood, 1959).

The tropical *Scirpus grossus* exhibits a similar habit. In India, for example, creeping stolons which form new plants at their tips are produced throughout active vegetative growth. As the water recedes at the approach of the dry season and the foliage dies back, the tip of each stolon swells, due to hypertrophy of the parenchymatous ground tissue of the stele, and forms a hard, dark, globose tuber. Laden with starch, each tuber survives until the next monsoon when it sprouts forth, forming a new plant either directly at its apex or at the end of a short stolon (Mullan, 1945). Comparable rounded or ellipsoid tubers are formed by the swelling of several internodes of the slender creeping stolons in *Cyperus esculentus* and *C. rotundus* (Wild, 1961).

In some species of *Potamogeton*, e.g. *P. filiformis* and *P. pectinatus*, small tubers are formed from lateral buds of the rhizome which would normally develop into elongated leafy shoots. The two basal internodes of the bud become swollen by starch accumulation, the other internodes remaining condensed and undeveloped and functioning as a terminal bud. The whole tuber is sheathed in a scale leaf and is usually buried, at least partly, in the soil. After its period of dormancy the tuber forms a new rhizome from which erect shoots subsequently arise.

Several of the more widely distributed species of *Sagittaria*, such as *S. sagittifolia*, *S. subulata*, *S. graminea*, *S. cuneata* and *S. latifolia*, perennate by means of tubers in the cooler northerly parts of their range. *S. sanfordii*, endemic to the Great Valley of California, also perennates by tubers. During the normal growing season these species reproduce freely by means of long stolons which bear colourless scale leaves singly at their nodes and terminate in leafy buds which grow erect into new plants. In late summer and early autumn the stolons begin to show terminal tubers, each of which develops by an enlargement of the two short internodes posterior to the apical bud of the stolon (Arber, 1920). Each tuber, laden with starch and sheathed by enlarged scale leaves, is carried to some depth in the soil by the positive geotropic response of the stolon. When mature the tubers are from 3 to 5 cm long, ovoid or subcylindrical in shape, and often coloured in a specific way by epidermal anthocyanins: those of *S. sagittifolia*, for example, are usually bright blue spotted with yellow.

12*

During the winter the stolons decay and the tubers remain dormant. In the
spring, perhaps under the stimulus of a slight rise in temperature, the basal one
or two internodes of the apical bud elongate, carrying the rest of the bud up to

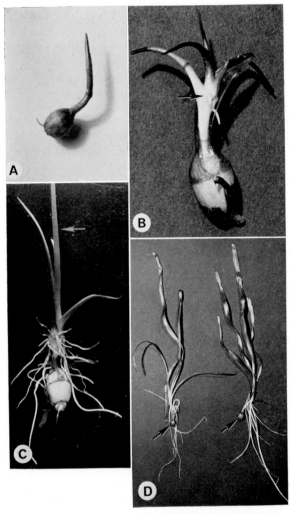

FIG. 10.7. Development of the stem tuber of *Sagittaria sagittifolia*: A, tuber just
breaking dormancy, with its apical bud beginning to elongate ($\times 0.3$); B, later stage,
when the sheathing leaves of the apical bud have expanded and the first adventitious
roots are emerging from the future rootstock or 'crown' (arrowed) ($\times 0.5$); C, still later
stage, with stronger root system. This tuber was grown in very shallow water and
quickly formed aerial leaves, the petiole of the first of these being arrowed ($\times 0.3$);
D, Two tubers (arrowed) of a similar age to that shown in C, but these were grown in
deep water and have produced the typical submerged ribbon leaves ($\times 0.2$).

the surface of the substrate (Fig. 10.7). Adventitious roots develop from the nodes and the first ribbon leaves of the new plant grow up into the water, the tuber gradually shrinking as its food reserves are mobilised and exhausted.

Root Tubers. Curious root tubers are produced by two closely related (perhaps conspecific) Atlantic North American species of *Nymphoides, N. aquatica* and *N. cordata*. Each of these floating-leaved plants has a permanent buried rootstock from which there arise long stems which trail through the water and gradually ascend to the surface. Short-petioled floating leaves develop from the terminal nodes of these stems, followed by clusters of aerial flowers borne on short curved stalks. Numerous adventitious roots also grow out from the node at the base of this floating rosette. Each root remains quite short but becomes swollen throughout most of its length due to the accumulation of food reserves in the cortical cells. In transverse section each mature root tuber shows an extremely wide zone of cortical storage parenchyma surrounding the tiny stele. Scattered sclereids probably give some support to the fleshy cortex, as in many succulent fruits. The epidermis and outermost part of the cortex usually contain chloroplasts. There is greater hypertrophy of the cortex on one side of the root than on the other so that each tuber is curved, and the consequent resemblance of the cluster of pendulous tubers to a hand of green bananas is reflected in the popular names of these species—'the underwater banana-plant' and 'the banana floating-heart' (Conard, 1937; Dress, 1954).

FIG. 10.8. Young specimen of *Nymphoides aquatica*, showing banana-like root tubers, juvenile submerged leaves and adventitious roots developing from the future rootstock (arrowed) (× 0·7).

The floating leaves and inflorescence eventually die back and the decay of the ascending stem liberates the cluster of tubers and its attached dormant apical bud. Their specific gravity usually being higher than that of water, the tubers normally sink to the substrate, but they occasionally remain floating. The tubers survive the winter unless they are frozen hard for any length of time and the following spring they provide the nutrients needed for the early development of the apical bud. Adventitious roots emerging from the basal nodes of the bud anchor the new young plant (Fig. 10.8), which first produces a few translucent submerged leaves, soon succeeded by floating foliage and flowering stems.

Nymphaea mexicana, which ranges from Florida through southern Louisiana and Texas to Mexico, perennates in some habitats by means of very similar banana-like tubers (Conard, 1905; Wood, 1959). During normal vegetative growth the species extends rapidly by long runners but towards the end of the season it forms clusters of fleshy, food-storing, adventitious roots at the terminal nodes of positively geotropic stems. These clusters of tubers survive the cold period partly or completely buried in the soil, their associated buds subsequently developing into new plants.

TURIONS, DORMANT APICES AND OTHER HIBERNACULA

In the cool temperate regions most submerged and floating plants which neither persist in a vegetative state throughout the year nor perennate by rhizomes, rootstocks or tubers, form hibernacula which are essentially modified buds, the leaves rather than the axis being the major components. Owing to the considerable spectrum of form shown by these organs no single term adequately covers all types. It seems preferable to describe the least specialised types, which are little more than dense clusters of apical leaves, as either dormant apices (e.g. in *Ceratophyllum* and *Elodea*) or offsets (e.g. in *Stratiotes*), and to employ the term turion for the more modified types, which have no exact terrestrial counterparts, and in which the leaves are specialised in form and quite unlike the normal foliage leaves (e.g. in *Hydrocharis*). (Some authors create unnecessary confusion by describing as a turion or winter-bud almost any perennating organ of any hydrophyte, including such essentially axial structures as the swollen tubers of *Sagittaria* and *Potamogeton pectinatus*.)

Dormant Apices and Offsets. Perennation by densely crowded apices is exemplified by *Ceratophyllum demersum* and *Elodea canadensis* (Fig. 10.9). During the autumn, the apices of lateral shoots in both species cease to elongate and come to bear tightly clustered dark green leaves, which contain much starch and are slightly more cuticularised than the normal foliage leaves. According to the rate at which the parent axis disintegrates, these apices may be liberated and sink to the substrate, or may remain attached throughout the winter. If the winter is exceptionally mild, the apices soon develop but otherwise they remain dormant until the spring, when the leaves expand, adventitious roots emerge from the lower nodes in *Elodea*, the axis elongates, and a new plant is formed.

The tips of shoots of the warm temperate and tropical *Hydrilla verticillata* are similarly densely clothed with acute, slightly fleshy, scale-like leaves. These apices are sometimes formed on subterranean branches of the main stems and then serve to carry the species through to the next rainy season should the habitat dry out.

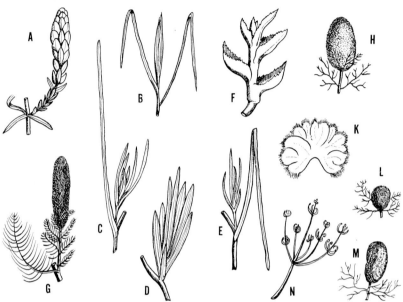

FIG. 10.9. Dormant apices (A to F) and turions (G to N) of various hydrophytes: A, *Elodea canadensis* (×0·6); B, *Potamogeton pusillus* (×1·5); C, *P. foliosus* (×1); D, *P. obtusifolius* (×1); E, *P. vaseyi* (×2); F, *P. crispus* (×1); G, *Myriophyllum verticillatum* (×0·5); H, *Utricularia intermedia* (×1·5); K, single leaf from turion of *U. intermedia* (×15); L, *U. geminiscapa* (×1); M, *U. vulgaris* (×0·8); N, *U. purpurea* (×2). In A, B, C, E, G, H, L and M a normal foliage leaf is also shown. (C, E, L and N after Fassett, 1957.)

Almost all the thirty-five or so species of *Najas* are annuals but *N. olivacea* is exceptional and in the U.S.A., where it occurs as a rare and local plant in Minnesota, New York and Wisconsin, it perennates by means of both the persistent lower nodes and the densely clustered apices of the main and lateral shoots (Rosendahl, 1939).

Throughout the summer *Stratiotes aloides* reproduces vegetatively by forming offsets (Fig. 10.10). These daughter rosettes first appear as small buds borne terminally on short stolons close to the parent rootstock. Each bud develops spinous foliage leaves and adventitious roots. When the stolon decays, the young plant is independent. Similar offsets formed late in the summer survive the winter without a prolonged dormant period, although of course development is slower than in the warmer months and the roots may take several weeks to emerge.

Numerous stages in the transition from dense shoot apices to quite specialised turions may be seen in the genus *Potamogeton* (Fig. 10.9), where the inter-specific differences in the structure of the perennating organs are sufficiently conspicuous to provide valuable taxonomic criteria (Hagström, 1916). In one group of species, e.g. *P. coloratus*, *P. foliosus*, *P. gemmiparus*, *P. polygonifolius* and *P. vaseyi*, the organs consist of fairly dense apices scarcely different from ordinary young leafy shoots, but in some linear-leaved submerged species the winter apices are more clearly differentiated. In *P. pusillus*, for example, they are mostly formed in the axils of both the lower and the upper leaves of the

FIG. 10.10. Side view of a rosette of *Stratiotes aloides*, with many of the older leaves removed, showing a terminal offset on a developing stolon (to the right) and a younger offset bud (arrowed) arising from the parent rootstock (× 0·5).

main shoots. Each apex is narrowly fusiform in shape, reaches 15 mm long by 0·5 mm wide, and consists of closely appressed young leaves enclosed by scales which represent stipules accompanied by rudimentary laminae (Arber, 1920). The winter apices of *P. berchtoldii* are relatively wider, those of *P. obtusifolius* fan-shaped and much longer, reaching 40 mm: in both species they are terminal in position, rather than axillary (Clapham, 1962). *P. acutifolius* and *P. com-pressus* provide similar examples but in the apices of the latter the inner leaves curiously protrude, by as much as 10 mm, beyond the outer ones. Associated with the general absence of perennating rhizomes from these linear-leaved species, the dormant apices are formed in vast numbers and, except in mild winters when some leafy shoots may persist, they are the only parts of the vegetative body to survive.

In yet another group of species, represented by *P. alpinus*, *P. lucens* and the hybrid *P. × fluitans*, dormant apices enclosed by scales, consisting solely of axillary stipules (the corresponding laminae being absent (Glück, 1906)), are formed mainly, sometimes exclusively, on the creeping rhizome system, which also serves for perennation. *Potamogeton crispus*, which is also rhizoma-tous, exhibits perhaps the most specialised perennating organs of the whole genus. They are up to 5 cm long and comprise three to seven small leaves, which are somewhat remote and stand out at an angle from the stem. Quite unlike the lanceolate, undulate, translucent foliage leaves, each leaf of the winter apex is roughly triangular in shape, thick and horny in texture and bears small firm spines along its margins (Clos, 1856). Although apparently resistant in structure these apices may be primarily organs of vegetative reproduction as they often develop as soon as they are formed. This possibility is accentuated by their peculiar mode of development, in which the main axis of the apex shows no elongation whatsoever: instead, lateral shoots grow out from the axils of the leaves and develop into either rhizomes or erect leafy stems. Thus each winter apex may yield as many as six or seven independent shoots.

Specialised Turions. *Myriophyllum verticillatum* and *M. exalbescens* are unusual amongst the temperate species of this genus in forming turions. Occurring on lateral branches, these are compact, club-shaped apices, 0·5 to 5 cm long, comprising dark green dwarfed leaves closely packed around the axis (Fig. 10.9). The leaf segments are fewer, shorter and thicker than in normal leaves and are very rich in starch. The turions become detached as the parent shoot system decays and either float or sink with waterlogged debris. They usually remain dormant throughout the winter until March or April when the dwarf leaves spread away from the axis and the apical bud begins to develop into an erect shoot with the typical finely dissected leaves: the new plant is anchored by spirally twisted adventitious roots from the basal nodes of the turion.

Morphologically similar turions are produced by *Aldrovanda vesiculosa* and some species of *Utricularia*. *Aldrovanda* perennates in this way only in the cooler parts of its range: in India and other parts of the tropics it grows vegetatively throughout the year. Amongst aquatic *Utricularia* spp. there is a similar pattern. Turions are not formed by tropical species or by such species as *U. biflora* and *U. fibrosa* which inhabit the warm Atlantic coastal plain of North America but they are produced by cool temperate species and in cold habitats at high altitudes in the tropics (Rossbach, 1939; Taylor, 1964).

The turions of *Aldrovanda* are about 6 to 8 mm in diameter and consist of up to thirty-two whorls of leaves tightly packed into a globular cluster on an abbreviated stem (Caspary, 1859, 1862). They contain much reserve starch and, because of this, usually sink when they break from the remains of the parent, rising to the surface again in spring when new young foliage is produced and the starch is converted to soluble sugars. However, Maisonneuve (1859) recorded that the developing plant may sometimes be weighted down on the substrate by the debris of the turion for several months, whilst Schoenefeld (1860) noted that in aquaria the turions may not sink at all but remain at the surface right until they germinate.

In *Utricularia vulgaris*, *U. intermedia*, *U. geminiscapa* and *U. minor*, spherical to ovoid turions, 3 to 20 mm long, are formed at the apices of the main and lateral axes. Each turion is enclosed in a layer of mucilage and comprises a highly condensed axis bearing many, reduced, concave, overlapping leaves, the outermost of which are scarcely divided, firm and leathery in texture, and in some species clothed with hairs (Fig. 10.9). Internal to these 'bud-scales' are several leaves which are normal foliage leaves in an early stage of development (Glück, 1906). The turions of *U. gibba* and *U. inflata* var. *minor* are similar but smaller, reaching a diameter of only 1 mm or even less (Rossbach, 1939).

The unique vegetative organisation of *Utricularia purpurea* has already been remarked: its turions are also quite distinct from those of other members of the genus. In this leafless species, there is no apical cluster: instead, the end of the axis becomes thickened and bears whorls of peculiarly remote, abbreviated and coiled branches (Fig. 10.9).

The turions of *Utricularia* may be dragged down to the substrate by the sinking waterlogged remains of the parent or they may break away and spend the winter floating at the surface. In the spring, the outer protective scale-like leaves bend away, the main axis shows great and rapid elongation, and apical growth produces the foliage of the new plant.

The predominantly tropical and warm temperate *Brasenia schreberi* resembles *Aldrovanda* in overwintering by means of turions in the cool northerly parts of its range, such as Maine in the U.S.A. In the autumn, the tip of each trailing stem becomes swollen with food reserves, the youngest leaves at the apex remain dwarf and their petioles also become thickened. These apical turions are reddish-brown, translucent, and, like the rest of the plant, sheathed in mucilage. They absciss and remain dormant on the substrate until the spring (Chrysler, 1938).

The turions of *Hydrocharis morsus-ranae* are really modifications of the buds which throughout the summer serve to propagate the plant. With the approach of autumn, buds produced terminally on slender stolons from the parent rosette do not unfold *in situ*: the two outer scale leaves of each remain tightly clasped around the rudimentary foliage leaves and their accompanying stipules. Growth of the adventitious roots is also apparently arrested for they do not emerge from the axis. The whole turion usually has a protective sheath of mucilage. Whereas the summer buds are usually upturned, both the turions and the stolons bearing them tend to droop in the water (Fig. 10.11), probably because of the greater weight of the turions, their abbreviated thick stem being laden with starch grains and their leaves largely devoid of air spaces. When the turion is ripe an abscission layer develops close to its base across the stolon. Only the least disturbance is required to detach the turions which then quickly sink to the bottom where they remain, like those of *Utricularia*, nicely upright, their centre of gravity being in the basal stalked region.

The turions remain dormant throughout the winter and indeed are still viable after as much as 2 years (Arber, 1920). In the spring, when conditions are suitable, the outer scale leaves unfold, the root rudiments develop and the apex of the turion becomes active. The first foliage leaves to appear are quite unlike those of the mature plant because their petioles are relatively long, their blades minute (Fig. 10.11). As the starch reserves are mobilised and air spaces begin to develop in the foliage, the specific gravity of the turion falls and the young plant rises to the surface. In the later leaves formed at the surface, the

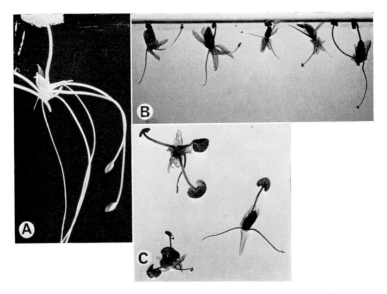

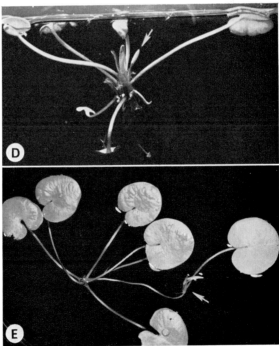

FIG. 10.11. Turion development in *Hydrocharis morsus-ranae*: A, side view of an almost decayed plant in autumn, showing two drooping stolons, each with a terminal turion. (×0·3); B, side view of young germinating turions after they have risen to the water surface in spring, showing the reflexed scale leaves and first rudimentary foliage leaves (×0·5); C, aerial view of three germinating turions at a similar stage to those in B (×0·8); D, side view of a young plant at a later stage showing the production of the first stolon (arrowed) (×0·7); E, later aerial view of the plant shown in D, showing a daughter rosette developing at the node of the stolon (arrowed) (×0·5).

length and width of the blade progressively increase and eventually the mature leaf form is attained (Fig. 10.12).

In concluding this survey of types of hibernacula, the perennating organs of some of the Lemnaceae may briefly be mentioned. These are really modified whole plants and so do not fit neatly into any of the previous categories. Those of *Spirodela polyrhiza* are brown reniform thalli, only about half the diameter of the normal plants, with very few air spaces but rich in starch. If detached from the parent thallus they sink to the substrate, rising to the surface again

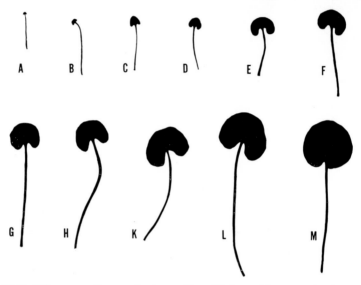

FIG. 10.12. Silhouettes of successive leaves (A to M) formed by a germinating turion of *Hydrocharis morsus-ranae*, showing the gradual attainment of the mature floating leaf form (all ×0·5).

in the spring when the first daughter thallus appears, absorbing the soluble products of starch hydrolysis and developing air spaces (Hegelmaier, 1868; Jacobs, 1947; Henssen, 1954). The winter thalli of *Lemna gibba* are dark green and lack the ventral mass of lacunate tissue. When they sink to the bottom mud they may become rooted. Several other species may form no modified organs, but their ordinary thalli accumulate reserves and sink to the substrate for the winter.

PHYSIOLOGICAL ASPECTS OF HIBERNACULA

Conditions Encouraging the Formation of Hibernacula. Prior to the experimental work of Goebel (1891–1893), Glück (1906) and others, turions, dormant apices, tubers and other hibernacula were treated as strictly adaptive structures with the specific functions of overwintering and propagation. It then became clear that they really represent the response of the plant to the presence of one or more unfavourable environmental factors, notably nutrient deficiency, water deficiency, low temperature and possibly low light intensity. It is possible that in natural temperate habitats hibernacula are initiated in response to diminishing photoperiods, as in numerous tuber- and bulb-forming terrestrial herbs (see Rees, 1966). It is important to note that although low nutrient supply, low temperature and low light intensity are characteristic of autumn they may prevail at other times of the year as a result of exceptional circumstances in the climatic rhythm, the structure of the plant community or the metabolism of the individual plant. Then the hibernacula are seen as structures associated not just with winter but with any conditions unfavourable to active vegetative growth.

Goebel (1891–1893) showed that when cultured in water alone, with no soil in which to root, turions of *Myriophyllum verticillatum* developed into erect, leafy stems, 30 cm and more long, which within a few weeks themselves formed turions. Similarly, whereas *M. verticillatum* can be grown satisfactorily in an aqueous nutrient medium, such as Sachs' or Knop's solution, specimens deprived of inorganic nutrients by culture in distilled or tap water soon react by developing turions. Turion formation at an exceptionally early date is also induced by severe competition in an overcrowded community (Glück, 1906).

Von Luetzelburg's (1910) experiments with *Utricularia minor* yielded comparable results. Turions germinated on sand developed into plants about 14 cm long in 17 days. After being transferred to a rich nutrient culture solution for 5 days, the now vigorously growing plants were starved by being returned to the sand, where, after 27 days, they had developed turions. These were harvested and the same experimental procedure repeated three times, further but smaller turions being induced each time by starvation. The four successive cycles of vegetative growth were accomplished in just over 7 months.

A poor nutrient supply similarly induces *Sagittaria sagittifolia* to form tubers. Debilitation of the plant by disease, the attacks of aphids, or being cultured in a pot-bound condition has the same consequences (Fig. 10.13).

Hibernacula are formed at an abnormally early stage in the land forms of *Hydrocharis morsus-ranae*, *Myriophyllum verticillatum* and *Sagittaria sagittifolia* (Glück, 1906), the turions in the first two species usually being formed underground. Glück found that in *M. verticillatum* each terrestrial specimen bore between four and ten turions by the beginning of August, whilst one specimen of *S. sagittifolia*, grown from the tuber stage in moist soil for about 8 months, produced only a few, poorly-developed, subterranean, ribbon leaves and four small tubers, each on a short stolon. The precocity of the hibernacula in these examples is attributable to the lack of water and generally unfavourable environment.

Arber (1920) noted that excessive water depth causes some species of *Potamogeton* to exhaust themselves in striving to reach the surface and likewise results in exceptionally early production of dormant apices.

It may be mentioned that *Spirodela polyrhiza* and *Lemna gibba* are somewhat exceptional in requiring for turion formation conditions favouring active growth, notably a high temperature and a good light intensity. Van Horen (1869) observed that turions are formed early by *S. polyrhiza* in brightly lit stagnant water, but much later in shady, presumably cooler habitats, whilst

FIG. 10.13. *Sagittaria sagittifolia*: A, side view of the base of a plant grown from the tuber shown in Fig. 10.7 C and allowed to become pot-bound. Only 7 weeks from germination of the tuber, this plant had itself started to form tubers; one in the centre, one at the right in the background, with a third developing stolon (arrowed) (×0·4); B, same plant as in A with the underground system unravelled, washed free of soil, and numerous roots removed, showing the three stolons (arrowed), all bearing scale leaves and two bearing fully formed tubers (×0·2); C, 6-week-old ribbon-leaved plant grown from a tuber rooted in sand in about 30 cm depth of distilled water, showing the formation of a single stolon with a terminal tuber (×0·2).

Guppy (1894) noted excessive turion production in water heated daily by the sun to about 27°C. Guppy also found that turions are produced by *L. gibba* after the flowering phase in hot summers, but not in cool summers when flowers rarely appear. These anomalies might perhaps be explained by the high volume of the turion relative to the parent thallus, necessitating active photosynthesis to accumulate the required mass of food reserves. In addition to light and temperature, factors which influence turion production in *S. polyrhiza* in culture include the total nutrient concentration and the concentrations of carbon dioxide, nitrate and sucrose. Under optimum conditions, the vegetative phase can be prolonged and turion formation delayed (Jacobs, 1947; Henssen, 1954; Czopek, 1964).

Dormancy and Germination of Hibernacula. Most types of turion, winter apex, tuber and rhizome exhibit a prolonged period of dormancy, the physiological control of which is as yet unexplained. It is not known whether external factors, such as low temperature, low light intensity and short photoperiod, are solely responsible or whether growth inhibitors are present in the hibernacula. This latter type of mechanism seems likely in view of the general similarity of the winter dormancy of vegetative buds to that of the embryonic sporophyte in seeds, and in view of the discovery of growth inhibitors in dormant buds of *Fraxinus, Prunus* and other woody plants (Heslop-Harrison, 1963; Eagles and Wareing, 1964). Should growth inhibitors be demonstrated in the hibernacula of hydrophytes, it would be interesting to investigate the factors influencing both their formation during the ripening of the organ, and their ultimate destruction during its germination. Those exceptional organs, such as the winter apices of *Potamogeton crispus*, which paradoxically often germinate without any dormant period, would also repay investigation.

Whilst they are dormant, the hibernacula show a certain resistance to adverse conditions which is endowed by their mucilaginous covering or protective scale-like outer leaves, but since they lack any hard, thick, impermeable coat this resistance is undoubtedly limited. Turions and winter apices which sink to the substrate thereby escape freezing in all but the shallowest waters and hardest winters, as do rhizomes, rootstocks and tubers buried at some considerable depth in the soil. Hibernacula which remain floating, even if not right at the surface, are more susceptible but little is definitely known of their capacity to tolerate freezing. Glück (1906) recorded that the turions of *Utricularia vulgaris* were still viable after being frozen for 12 days, but that those of *Hydrocharis morsus-ranae* and *Myriophyllum verticillatum* could only withstand such harsh conditions for less than 10 days, although Guppy (1893) had previously noted that the turions of *Hydrocharis* withstood freezing for several weeks.

The major physical factors influencing the germination of hibernacula are temperature and light intensity. The dormancy of the turions of *Spirodela polyrhiza, Myriophyllum verticillatum* and *Utricularia* spp., and of the winter apices of *Ceratophyllum, Elodea* and *Potamogeton* can be broken experimentally as early as November or December by keeping them indoors in the relatively warmer water of aquaria, and it is probable that in natural habitats germination is stimulated by the rising temperature (and perhaps also the increasing light intensity) in spring, but critical quantitative data on this point are lacking. In *Hydrocharis morsus-ranae*, light is perhaps the prime stimulus, for Terras (1900) found that a minimum intensity, especially of yellow and orange wavelengths, is required to induce germination and this influence overrides that of temperature. According to Kummerow (1958), a period at low temperature during the dormant phase is an essential prerequisite for activation of the turions of *Hydrocharis*, but this requirement is apparently overcome by treatment with the stimulant of cell division and bud formation, kinetin, whilst IAA counteracts this effect. Vegis (1965) emphasised the influence of temperature on the formation and dormancy of hibernacula, and noted that immersion in warm water promotes the growth of turions of *H. morsus-ranae* and offsets of *Stratiotes aloides*. Frank (1966) partially broke the strong dormancy of winter apices of *Potamogeton nodosus* by soaking them in solutions of fenac, NAA, sucrose or gibberellic acid. The complete breakage of dormancy achieved by immersion for 18 h in a solution of 1000 ppm IAA led Frank to wonder if low levels of this auxin in the apices might be the prime cause of the natural inhibition of their growth.

THE ROLE OF VEGETATIVE PROPAGULES IN THE DISPERSAL OF HYDROPHYTES

The remarkable rapidity of vegetative growth enables many hydrophytes to colonise enormous expanses of substrate. This vigour, together with the capacity to regenerate from small fragments, the abundant production of tubers, turions, dormant apices and offsets, and the ease with which all these propagules are dispersed accidentally by floods, water-fowl, man and other agents, are prime reasons for the successful penetration of many species into all available habitats in a given region (Darwin, 1859; Ridley, 1923, 1930; Salisbury, 1942). They are probably further responsible, with chance dispersal of seeds, for the curious appearance of some species in isolated habitats, such as small lakes at high altitudes, which have no surface connections with other bodies of water. In many such isolated habitats, the communities are often clones derived by vegetative reproduction from a few pioneer individuals.

Elongated, brittle, submerged hydrophytes and reduced free-floating plants may owe much of their widespread distribution to casual transport of vegetative fragments and perennating structures, as of fruits and seeds, by man, livestock, amphibians, and especially water-fowl. Emergent and floating-leaved hydrophytes are in general too large for viable portions of their body to be so carried over any appreciable distance. It is pertinent to remember that most submerged and free-floating plants are unable to survive out of water for more than a few hours, and so the distance over which viable organs may be dispersed by birds and other animals is not likely to be great, perhaps no more than 50 to 200 km. Turions and dormant apices are more resistant to desiccation than active fragments of the plant body: even so, they are not likely to be as significant in exozoic dispersal as the better-protected seeds and fruits. In archipelagic regions and extensive lake districts, the high frequency of suitable habitats may compensate to some extent for the loss and desiccation of vegetative propagules during transport.

Casual transport is probably highly significant in short-distance dispersal. Quantitative data on the subject are immensely difficult to obtain, but there is no shortage of qualitative evidence. In the literature there are innumerable scattered records of coots, moorhens, grebes, ducks, geese, ibis, flamingoes, herons and other birds that frequent aquatic habitats observed to be carrying lengths of *Ceratophyllum, Elodea, Lagarosiphon, Myriophyllum, Ranunculus* and similar flexuous submerged plants. Quantities of the scum-forming free-floating plants, such as *Azolla* and *Lemna*, adhere tenaciously to the plumage and feet of water-fowl and waders. More often than not, enough viable material will escape the bird's preening activities to ensure dispersal to some other habitat in the neighbourhood. Amphibians, small mammals and perhaps the larger, flying, aquatic insects, e.g. *Dytiscus* and *Notonecta*, may casually transport small fragments which cling to them as they emerge from the water. Both submerged and free-floating plants are also frequently dispersed by drinking cattle, agricultural equipment, boats and man himself. Saccardo (1892) commented on the spread of *Azolla* by humans and its frequent invasion of Italian ricefields fertilised with guano. Ridley (1930) also remarked on the common presence of *Azolla* and *Lemna* in ponds in Malaysia which are used for cultivating vegetable pig-food, whence they are accidentally transported into nearby ricefields.

Floods and normal river currents are perhaps the most potent agents in distributing vegetative propagules. Whole plants of all life forms, rooted rhizomes and tubers, vegetative fragments and turions are often torn away and carried for many miles, often to be stranded on adjacent land when the floods subside. Vast quantities of shattered colonies of emergent grasses, reeds and sedges, waterlilies and free-floating rosette plants are a common sight in the flood-waters of most tropical and temperate rivers. Ridley (1930) recalled an occasion in 1924 when a ditch densely populated with *Lemna minor*, situated alongside part of the Royal Botanic Gardens at Kew, was inundated by the rising River Thames: for more than a day the river was green with the millions of plants being swept away.

The rhizomes of waterlilies and emergents may be carried along river beds by normal undercurrents. Ridley (1930) drew attention to the possibility that rhizomatous and tuberous hydrophytes may be completely buried by alluvial deposits yet retain their viability and renew growth should they be re-exposed by the scouring of subsequent floods. He illustrated this by recounting that a pool which he excavated in the Singapore Botanic Gardens and planted with waterlilies eventually became so silted that it was almost dry land, the lilies becoming completely buried. He re-excavated it and allowed it to fill again with water. Soon after, the surface was again populated with the foliage and flowers of the lilies, whose rhizomes must have remained alive in the mud for several years. Millspough (in Perry, 1961), described a similar experience near Buffalo in the U.S.A. where the ploughing of an area of low-lying cultivated soil annually yielded large numbers of tuberous rhizomes. Grown in tubs of water these developed into deep pink waterlilies, identified as a variety of *Nymphaea odorata*. Just how long ago the area of land had been drained could not be precisely ascertained, but evidently a small lake had existed there, perhaps as much as a century before.

There is no doubt that vegetative reproduction is of the utmost importance in the maintenance and spread of many vascular hydrophytes, e.g. the various vegetative phases of *Sagittaria subulata* (Adams and Godfrey, 1961); the triploid clones of *Butomus umbellatus* (Löve, 1960); *Stratiotes aloides* (Samuelsson, 1934); most species of *Nuphar*, *Nymphoides* and *Nymphaea* (Heslop-Harrison, 1955a, b, c); *Enhalus, Halophila, Thalassia, Zostera* and other marine angiosperms (den Hartog, 1957b; Armiger, 1964; Conover, 1964); *Alternanthera philoxeroides, Glyceria maxima, Phragmites communis* and other common emergents (Lambert, 1947; Backer, 1949; Buttery and Lambert, 1965; Maheshwari, 1965). The rapid and insidious invasion of new territories by accidentally introduced hydrophytes provides further graphic examples of the reproductive capacity of the plant body. It is usually difficult to assess accurately the relative contributions of sexual and vegetative reproduction to such 'explosive' expansions of range. Both methods may be highly significant for certain adventives, e.g. *Eichhornia crassipes* (p. 460), whilst for others, e.g. *Azolla filiculoides* (see following section) and *Salvinia auriculata* (p. 473), fragmentation and regeneration may be more prevalent than development of sexual propagules. A few species are even vegetative apomicts throughout large sectors of their adventive range, e.g. the sterile triploid race of *Acorus calamus* in Europe: in some parts of North America, the diploid race of the same species often maintains itself vegetatively in conditions unsuitable for seed maturation. Perhaps the best-known example is *Elodea canadensis* which, though it undergoes normal sexual reproduction in its native American range, invaded many parts of Europe entirely by vegetative spread, the male plants being either absent or very rare (p. 360).

THE SPREAD OF *AZOLLA FILICULOIDES*

Formerly native to Europe, *Azolla filiculoides* became extinct in probably the last of the Ice Ages. It was reintroduced by a French botanist in 1880, but some 8 years before this the related species, *A. caroliniana*, had escaped from several continental botanic gardens and was already spreading in lakes, ponds and ditches. The history of the subsequent dispersal of the two species is in some places confused, because of the close morphological similarities and the absence, in many of the early records, of the fruiting material necessary for positive identification. As a result of this confusion, the evidence for the naturalisation of *A. caroliniana* in Britain and some localities of Europe is inadequate. The majority of the early records which were based upon examination of fruiting specimens proved to be *A. filiculoides*, and so the data for this species are more reliable.

For several years prior to 1879, the director of the botanic garden at Bordeaux had grown both species with eminent success and had observed the production of fertile material amongst the specimens of *A. caroliniana*. In Germany, this latter species had escaped from cultivation in the vicinity of Cassel in 1878 and had begun explosively rapid vegetative reproduction, quickly becoming a 'Wasserpest'. Similar vigorous growth ensued when, in 1879 and 1880, some of the specimens at Bordeaux were introduced into local waters. M. E. Roze

(1883), the botanist responsible, ingenuously reported that the climate of Bordeaux seemed fairly well suited to both species since portions of *A. caroliniana* (in 1879) and of *A. filiculoides* (in 1880) thrown here and there into ponds round the town had given birth to 'une légion innombrable' of plants, which had invaded almost all the ponds, lakes and ditches throughout the department of Gironde. He also remarked that in places the multiplication of *A. filiculoides* was so rapid that other floating plants, such as *Hydrocharis*, *Lemna* and *Salvinia natans*, were threatened with forcible extinction. *A. filiculoides* spread quickly over much of France, being common in western and northern districts by 1896; in 1900 it reached Italy (Marsh, 1914).

In England, Druce and Britton (1910) recorded *A. caroliniana* in a drain leading from a waterworks into the River Thames at Sunbury, near Hampton, but Marsh examined these specimens and identified them with *A. filiculoides*: this appears to be the earliest British record of the species. In 1911, Druce recorded *A. caroliniana* from a locality in Norfolk and from brackish water in a ditch adjoining a garden near Queenstown Junction, Cork, but Ostenfeld (1912) corrected one of these records : 'The *Azolla* growing in abundance and fruiting in a little pond near a garden at Woodbastwick, E. Norfolk is *A. filiculoides* Lam., not *A. caroliniana* Willd., as stated in Druce's notes.' He apparently did not collect specimens from the Cork station and so was unable to confirm or correct the identification there. Fruiting specimens of *A. filiculoides* were identified at Almondsbury, in west Gloucestershire, in 1912. These diffuse early records strongly suggest multiple introduction of the species.

Although the Sunbury station of 1910 provides the first unqualified British record, there is little doubt that *A. filiculoides* had become established on the Bure River before this time, possibly as early as 1898, since Palmer (1913) described its presence (he actually named it *A. caroliniana* and was corrected by Marsh, 1914) in a dyke near Horning Ferry, where it had apparently been known to local inhabitants for some fifteen years, although no evidence of its original introduction could be discovered. Severe floods in August 1912 carried vast quantities of the plant along the Bure, Ant, and Thurne Rivers, into several of the Norfolk Broads, where its increase during the ensuing 12 months was extraordinary.

In mid-October of 1913, *A. filiculoides* was discovered amongst duckweed in Jesus Ditch in Cambridge. Such was the increase of the colony that by the end of November it had become the dominant hydrophyte at one end of the ditch and was very abundant everywhere in the following February. The problem of its introduction remained unsolved: the nearest known site was the Norfolk Broads, and the Cambridge University botanic garden possessed specimens of *A. caroliniana* only (Marsh, 1914).

A. filiculoides is now widely naturalised in many midland and southern counties of England and in south Wales, where it was first recorded in 1922 at Goldcliff, near Newport in Monmouthshire (Hyde and Wade, 1954). Its extension northwards has been limited, probably by hard winter frosts. On the continental mainland it is naturalised in many places in Holland and Germany, in addition to France and Italy. In suitable habitats in a mild climate it spreads rapidly, often covering the entire surface of still water to the exclusion of other floating species. It is impossible to say how much of its spread over Europe has been wrought by fragmentation and how much by dispersal of the sporocarps, but its behaviour in culture and the likelihood of chance transport by birds suggest that the former has been more significant.

THE SPREAD OF *ELODEA CANADENSIS*

The spectacular manner in which the Canadian pondweed, indigenous to much of North America, spread throughout the waterways of Europe in the late nineteenth and early twentieth centuries is probably the most celebrated example of the consequences of introducing alien hydrophytes. The first appearance of *Elodea canadensis* in Europe was at Waringstown in County Down, Ireland, where one John Dew recorded it in 1836: there is also a less reliable report of its occurrence together with species of *Aponogeton* and other imported hydrophytes in a pond in Dublin in the same year. On the 3rd of August in 1842 Dr. G. Johnston, of Berwick-on-Tweed, found the species growing in the small loch in the grounds of Duns Castle in Berwickshire. The plant was subsequently found to be spreading in the River Whiteadder, about 1·6 km to the north-east, which it may have reached either by way of a small tributary from the Duns loch or by separate introduction. The station at Duns Castle is customarily regarded as the first in Great Britain, but there is a record, mentioned in Walker (1912), from Watford Locks on the Grand Union Canal in Northamptonshire and this is dated 1841, though doubts of its reliability have been expressed.

In 1847, 5 years after its appearance at Duns, *Elodea canadensis* was found in reservoirs adjacent to Foxton Locks on the canal near Market Harborough in Leicestershire, and also in a lake in Leigh Park in Hampshire. The exact manner of its introduction to these two places is unknown. It is said to have arrived at the Hampshire site in the company of ornamental aquatic plants from America. Marshall (1852) suggested that the Foxton specimens may have arrived, some time before their discovery, with American timber being used in the vicinity of Rugby for the construction and maintenance of the railways. It is fairly certain that they had not actually reached Foxton before 1845 because the reservoirs there, according to the Miss Kirby who discovered the plant at this site, had been cleaned out in that year. If the dubious 1841 record from Watford Locks near Welton railway station, about 11 km south-east of Rugby, was in fact genuine, then it is by no means impossible that specimens of the plant were accidentally transported from there along the Grand Union Canal north to Foxton.

As Marshall (1852) and more recently Salisbury (1961) have suggested, the geography and prosperity of the English canal system during the early decades of the nineteenth century confer great significance on the Foxton locality of the plant. After the canal boom reached its peak in 1793, there ensued a slump during which the only notable addition to the system of inland waterways was the extension of the Grand Union Company's main line from the Grand Junction Canal at Norton, linking with the Old Union Canal at Foxton, and so opening a direct water route between the R. Trent, Derby, Nottingham and London. This development involved a triumph of engineering at Foxton, where the Leicester section of the Grand Union Canal was made to descend from its 122 m summit level by means of a system of two staircases, each containing five locks. Shortly after the link was established in 1810, trade improved. By virtue of both its position on the main line to and from London and its general geographical situation, Foxton occupied a more or less central point in the system of waterways, and was very near to the line of the watershed dividing England into the four basins of the Rivers Trent, Ouse, Thames and Severn.

It is quite unwarranted to visualise all the subsequent spread of the species in the Midlands and southern England as resulting from the continuity of the inland waterways, but the possibility that most of the spread in the counties surrounding Leicestershire was so caused may not be disputed. Within 12 months of its discovery at Foxton, the species had become very abundant in parts of Northamptonshire and in the vicinity of Nottingham, and in the following year was noted to be spreading rapidly in Staffordshire, Warwickshire and Derbyshire. First recorded at Burton-on-Trent in 1849, it had almost blocked the river there only 2 years later. It is interesting to note in this context that the North American shrimp, *Crangonyx pseudogracilis*, which was introduced to Britain early in this century, has now become firmly established and is similarly extending its range via the inland waterways of the English Midlands. It has ventured into Wales along the Shropshire Union Canal and colonised a 30 to 35 km stretch of the River Dee downstream from its junction with the canal near Llangollen (Hynes, 1960).

One of the areas most severely affected by *Elodea canadensis* embraced the low-lying fens of Lincolnshire and Cambridgeshire, where the high frequency of slow-flowing rivers and ditches provided abundant habitats. The origin of the plant in this region is fairly well established. In 1847 specimens from Foxton were cultivated in a tub in the University botanic garden in Cambridge and in the following year the curator, a Mr. Murray, introduced a portion of living material into a stream flowing by the western boundary of the Garden (Marshall, 1852). This stream, known as Hobson's Conduit or the New River, was one of two ancient artificial schemes bringing water from the outskirts into the centre of the city. It was contrived in 1610 as a public utility providing water for drinking, scouring the drains and street cleansing, and although no longer in use it still provides a continuous flow from south of the city to the fountain in Market Hill and the ponds and swimming-pools in Emmanuel and Christ's Colleges (H.M.S.O., 1959). It is highly likely that fragments of the plant were carried from the Conduit along spillways draining surplus water across the Trumpington Road into Vicar's Brook, which flows north-west for about 700 m and then empties into the River Cam. Assuming this to have been its mode of introduction, the species must have spread rapidly downstream for in 1851 it was noticed by Marshall (1852) and others to be widespread and rampant in both the Cam and the Ouse, choking docks, sluices and sluggish reaches. The two rivers formed an important navigable waterway, from the port of King's Lynn to Cambridge, used for commercial traffic from as early as 1327, when white Yorkshire stone for King's College Chapel was thereby transported, until about the end of the nineteenth century. At the time of the *Elodea* invasion it still formed a route for barges carrying corn, coal and building materials, and Marshall (1852) was told that the river Cam along the Backs of the Colleges was so blocked that extra horses regularly had to be yoked to drag barges upstream to Foster's Mill (the King's Mill) which was just below the probable original entry of the weed. The average level of the river was said to have been raised some 10 cm and rowing and fishing were severely hampered. From 1850 to about 1857 the plant underwent explosively rapid vegetative reproduction, invading most fen districts and reaching a state of excessive abundance. Dykes were completely blocked and drainage hindered, and despite the Government's precipitous despatch of an adviser, a Mr. Rawlinson, to the Lincolnshire fens in 1852, no measures of prevention or eradication were found: dredging of the dykes quite failed to eliminate the weed.

Elsewhere in Britain, the species continued to spread and Marshall (1857) wrote that 10 years after its appearance at Foxton he found no symptoms of its invasion abating anywhere in the country. About 1855 it was first observed in Kent and Herefordshire, and had become abundant a few years later in Suffolk, the Isle of Wight, Gloucestershire, Cheshire, and southern Yorkshire. In the vicinity of Chester it attained maximum luxuriance during the 7 years from 1866 to 1873, and towards the end of this period was very troublesome in Dorset. Waterways in Lancashire, parts of the Lake District and the south-western counties were colonised during the 1870's and 1880's.

Ridley (1930) noted that the weed 'crossed' to France and Belgium by 1860. Of its introduction to France, little is known, but Devos (1870) recalled that in Belgium a certain Professor Scheidweiler had placed living specimens he received from England in a big lake at Ledeberg in 1858. In 1860 it was found near Gent and 2 years later was abundant in surrounding districts, at Dendermonde, and at Utrecht in Holland. It must have been introduced to Germany around this time because it was found spreading in many areas by 1865 (Bolle, 1867). By 1870 *Elodea canadensis* had spread throughout the Low Countries and in the remaining years of the nineteenth century it penetrated north through Denmark and Sweden to about 66°N, and east to Russia and Hungary. During this century it has become equally common in submerged floras throughout eastern and south-eastern Europe and western Siberia.

The species has also invaded rivers and standing waters in Victoria, Tasmania and much of lowland New Zealand (Thomson, 1922; Mason, 1960). Here again, the precise source, mode and time of introduction are not certainly known. The scanty records suggest that the plant arrived in these three regions of Australasia sometime during the 1860's, about the same time as it was making spectacular headway in Europe. According to Thomson (1922) it reached New Zealand from Tasmania several times in consignments of freshwater fish. There is also evidence that the species was first planted in 1868 in a fishpond at Christchurch, whence it probably escaped to the R. Avon, in which it was found to be spreading vigorously 4 years later. In South Island at the present time it is distributed throughout the plains and valleys of the eastern side, especially in Canterbury province where it is a frequent nuisance in drains, and it also occurs at Manapouri in the south and near Hokitika on the west coast. It has invaded suitable habitats throughout much of North Island from the lowlands south of Auckland to Cook Strait, except for Taranaki province and the western part of Wellington province north of the R. Rangitikei: it has also been found near Kaitaia in the far north of the North Auckland peninsula (Mason, 1960). Both Thomson (1922) and Mason (1960) commented on the fact that the invasion, although far-ranging, seemed to be less aggressive than in England and parts of Europe. They suggested that, at least in certain habitats such as shallow standing waters, *Elodea canadensis* probably met very strong competition from *Rorippa nasturtium-aquaticum*, which had been introduced earlier and was already spreading rapidly by the time *E. canadensis* began to establish itself.

It is remarkable that throughout the invasion of the British Isles, continental Europe, Tasmania and New Zealand the reproduction of *Elodea canadensis* has probably been exclusively vegetative. In 1879, Douglas (1880) discovered male flowers near Edinburgh and described and illustrated them. Apart from this solitary record, all flowering specimens collected from alien stations have proved to be female. It therefore seems reasonable to conclude that the production and dissemination of fruits and seeds have not contributed to the adventive spread of the species. It is interesting to note that two other submerged members of the Hydrocharitaceae, *Egeria densa* and *Lagarosiphon major*, similarly introduced to England, western Europe and New Zealand (p. 399), are also probably vegetative apomicts throughout their adventive range. All alien populations of *Egeria densa* appear to be male and, indeed, female plants are extremely rare even in the native range of this species. Flowers of either sex are very uncommon or as yet unknown in alien populations of *Lagarosiphon major*, as in areas of its native range. It is therefore clear that the adventive spread of all three of these submerged Hydrocharitaceae must have been accomplished through the dispersal of whole plants, viable fragments and dormant apices by water currents, seasonal floods, water-fowl and human agencies.

One interesting feature of the spread of *Elodea canadensis* in the British Isles and western Europe was first remarked upon by Siddall (1885), who had found in the Chester area that after a phase of active growth and colonisation, reaching its climax in 5 to 7 years, the vigour of the species appeared to wane. There was initiated in 1909 a survey of the contemporary status of the species in waterways throughout much of Great Britain and Ireland: information from representatives of corresponding Societies of Natural Science of the British Association was collated by Walker (1912) and presented by him to the Linnean Society of London. There was essential agreement between the reports from many counties: although still common in most waters, *Elodea canadensis* had decreased in frequency very markedly and had generally ceased to be troublesome. In Surrey, Kent, Devon, Worcestershire, Staffordshire, Shropshire, Herefordshire, Northamptonshire, and much of Ireland, the species was reported to be much less plentiful than previously. The frequency of the species had not diminished significantly in Middlesex, Yorkshire or Nottinghamshire and was apparently still increasing in Lancashire, Perthshire, Suffolk and parts of Lincolnshire. These latter reports are not surprising since they mainly represent the counties which had been colonised most recently. The abundance of the weed eventually decreased everywhere in the British Isles and similar behaviour has been observed in most countries of continental Europe.

It is apparent that in each locality it invaded, *Elodea canadensis* passed through a similar succession of growth phases. It would be erroneous to refer to this succession as a 'cycle' because the species subsequently became extinct in only very few places. After introduction the plant grew vigorously and reproduced vegetatively with remarkable rapidity, the population attaining maximum density in times varying from a few months to about 4 years. The phase of abundance often persisted for as many as 5 years, and then waned, sometimes gradually, sometimes very quickly. At the end of the phase of decline, the species ceased to be a troublesome weed. Throughout most of central and western Europe, including the British Isles, it remains as a frequent member of the hydrophyte flora of slow-flowing rivers and canals, ponds, and the shallower littoral regions of some lakes.

Many writers have argued that the natural decline of *Elodea canadensis* was due to the exclusively vegetative mode of reproduction and the consequent lack of genetic variability. This argument is effectively refuted by the repetition of the same rhythm of vigour, abundance and decline in each new habitat and by the sustained spread of the plant across Europe, largely or wholly in the absence of male specimens. The explanation advanced by Salisbury (1961), 'that some mineral nutrient or nutrients taken up by the plant became unduly depleted', is more plausible. It is pertinent to note that, firstly, during the phase of vigorous growth, no comparable increase was apparent in the rate of growth of other hydrophytes in the same habitat: secondly, when the alien declined, the other hydrophytes did not, but often increased slightly as competition for space became less severe. These facts suggest that a specific relationship between *Elodea canadensis* and the concentrations or relative proportions of certain nutrients might be involved. Perhaps in each habitat, as the supply of some limiting nutrient(s) was steadily depleted, the weed declined until an equilibrium was reached between the nutrient demand of a finite population frequency and the total amount or constituent proportions of the nutrient supply made continuously available by leaching or silt deposition. From laboratory and field experiments, Olsen (1954) concluded that the species grows vigorously, and increases its organic content significantly, only in those habitats where the substrate is anaerobic and its iron therefore in the ferrous state which can be absorbed, or where soluble and mobile iron-chelate complexes are available in the water. Although it is therefore conceivable that iron was, and is, the critical micronutrient for *Elodea canadensis* in many habitats, there does not seem to be any precise quantitative evidence for the type of dynamic equilibrium postulated above. Even so, the hypothesis remains interesting and could perhaps be tested with other aquatic weeds which are expanding their range at the present time.

Some Aspects of the Geography of Aquatic Vascular Plants

The geographical distributions of many vascular hydrophytes are intriguing and anomalous. It might be expected that because rivers, lakes and other waters are separated by tracts of land, aquatic plants would tend to be locally distributed in any one land mass, and that dispersal between continents would be prevented by the insurmountable barriers of the seas. Yet some hydrophytes extend so widely over several continents, reaching even remote oceanic islands, that they may justly be described as cosmopolitan. In *The Origin of Species* Charles Darwin was prompted to remark: 'Not only have many fresh-water species, belonging to quite different classes, an enormous range, but allied species prevail in a remarkable manner throughout the world.' Other than more or less ubiquitous species, not a few far-ranging hydrophytes are in fact north temperate taxa extending throughout most, if not all, of the circumpolar land surface, whilst certain others occur throughout the tropics of both Old and New Worlds.

About 40 per cent of hydrophytes display smaller ranges confined within the limits of a single continent or major land mass. In common with the more extensive types, many of these exhibit marked latitudinal penetration. Species confined longitudinally to some part of the tropics often extend into subtropical latitudes of one or both hemispheres, and some of them enter the cool temperate zone. Similarly, numerous species with the greatest intensity of their distribution in a temperate region penetrate the subtropics, and a few extend at moderate altitudes into the heart of the tropics. Such latitudinal extension, not so conspicuous amongst terrestrial herbs, is attributable primarily to the less violent variations of temperature and edaphic factors in the aquatic environment and perhaps also to the dissemination of seeds and vegetative propagules by migrant birds.

Although several authors, notably Ridley (1930), Good (1953, 1964) and Turrill (1958), have followed de Candolle (1855) and Darwin (1859) in commenting emphatically upon the great geographical ranges of many hydrophytes, they have not directed attention to the similarly high frequency of endemism. This is a surprising omission in view of their apt insistence upon the edaphic limitation of hydrophytes, for this is probably one of the main factors responsible for the high proportion of endemics (about 25 to 30 per cent of hydrophytes).

Most endemic hydrophytes are to be found in the tropics, numerous ecologically restricted members of the Podostemaceae being prominent amongst them. Some occur in the subtropics and the temperate zones. The minority of Eurasian and North American endemics corroborates the suggestion made by Good (1953) and others, on evidence from terrestrial plants, that the north temperate zone is remarkable for its floristic unity.

The ranges of a few temperate and tropical hydrophytes exhibit a curious discontinuity over and above that due to major land and sea configuration. These plants continue to attract speculation and discussion, much of which is fruitless since it is immensely difficult to confirm or negate any hypothesis of the origin of their peculiar distribution. Indeed, it is often difficult even to show that the discontinuity is genuine and that the plant has not in fact been introduced during historical times to certain parts of its present range.

Descriptions of the ranges occupied by particular species at a certain point in time inevitably leave only a static impression of plant geography. As a result of dispersal and colonisation, on the one hand, and the changing climatic, physical and edaphic factors of the environment, on the other, great migrations of species continue to occur as they have occurred during geological and historical time, and floras everywhere, aquatic no less than terrestrial, are always in a state of flux. The adventive spread and naturalisation of certain hydrophytes, and the extinction and post-glacial restriction of others, illustrate these dynamic aspects of plant geography.

EXTENSIVE HYDROPHYTES

The most widely distributed vascular hydrophytes are summarised in Table 11.1. It is conspicuous that the most widespread taxa (group A) are monocotyledons, with one exception, and include emergent, submerged and free-floating life forms. Some taxa have more extensive ranges than others. *Phragmites communis*, for example, has been called the most widely distributed angiosperm: extending north throughout Eurasia to 70°N it is a frequent member of reed-swamp communities; in a few tropical regions it is replaced by related species of more restricted latitudinal range, e.g. *P. mauritianus* in tropical Africa (Wild, 1961), and it is absent from the Amazon basin (Ridley, 1923). *Typha latifolia* and *T. angustifolia*, also common reed-swamp dominants, are almost as widespread, extending from the Arctic Circle to about 30°S, the former absent from Australia, Polynesia, central and southern Africa and southern Asia, the latter from Madagascar and South America (Tutin, 1962; Good, 1964).

Of the free-floating taxa *Lemna minor* is the most extensive, absent from only the polar regions and a few parts of the tropics: the ranges of the other species display notable gaps, *Spirodela polyrhiza* and *Lemna trisulca*, for example, being absent from South America and southern Africa. Despite the gaps, the ubiquity of these reduced hydrophytes is an astonishing testimony to their wide tolerance of temperature and the ease with which their thalli are accidentally dispersed. Of the submerged taxa, *Ceratophyllum demersum, Potamogeton*

(D indicates a dicotyledon; M – a monocotyledon; E – emergent; Fl – floating-leaved; Ff – free-floating; S – submerged)

A. Widespread Species

Species	
Ceratophyllum demersum	D S/Ff
Cladium mariscus	M E
Eleocharis acicularis	M E
E. palustris	M E
Lemna gibba	M Ff
L. minor	M Ff
L. perpusilla	M Ff
L. trisulca	M Ff
Najas marina	M S
Phragmites communis	M E
Potamogeton crispus	M S
P. pectinatus	M S
Ruppia spiralis	M S
Schoenoplectus lacustris	M E
Scirpus maritimus	M E
Spirodela polyrhiza	M Ff
Typha angustifolia	M E
T. latifolia	M E
Vallisneria spiralis	M S
Wolffia arrhiza	M Ff
Zannichellia palustris	M S

B. North Temperate Species

Species	
Calla palustris	M E
Carex lasiocarpa	M E
C. rostrata	M E
Elatine hydropiper	D S
Glyceria fluitans	M E
G. plicata	M E
Limosella aquatica	D E
Menyanthes trifoliata	D E
Myriophyllum verticillatum	D S
Naumbergia thyrsiflora	D E
Phalaris arundinacea	M E
Potamogeton alpinus	M S/Fl
P. berchtoldii	M S
P. filiformis	M S
P. friesii	M S
P. gramineus	M S/Fl
P. natans	M S/Fl
P. obtusifolius	M S
P. perfoliatus	M S
P. praelongus	M S
Ruppia maritima	M S
Scheuchzeria palustris	M E
Sparganium angustifolium	M Fl
S. emersum	M E/Fl
S. minimum	M Fl
Subularia aquatica	D S
Utricularia intermedia	D Ff
U. minor	D Ff

C. Pan-tropical Species

Species	
Ammannia auriculata	D E
Bacopa monnieri	D E
Cyperus difformis	M E
C. digitatus	M E
C. esculentus	M E
C. rotundus	M E
Echinochloa colona	M E
E. crus-galli	M E
Leersia hexandra	M E
Ludwigia adscendens	D E
Neptunia oleracea	D E
Pistia stratiotes	M Ff
Sagittaria guayanensis	M Fl
Sphenoclea zeylanica	D E
Utricularia gibba	D Ff

(Table compiled from data in many sources)

13

crispus and *P. pectinatus* are almost truly cosmopolitan. All three exhibit remarkable latitudinal penetration through the tropics (Dandy, 1937; Wild, 1961). *P. crispus*, like the floating *Wolffia arrhiza*, is absent from the New World. *Vallisneria spiralis* is primarily tropical and subtropical in distribution but is notable for its northward extension to parts of central France, whilst *Ruppia spiralis*, in contrast, is mainly temperate and subtropical, and occurs in the tropics only at high altitudes.

The continuity of vast areas of land surface in the north temperate zone, together with the similar succession of climatic changes in these areas during the Quaternary period, has endowed North America and Eurasia with outstanding floristic unity (Good, 1964). This is manifest in the high frequency of widely distributed species, aquatic as well as terrestrial. In this group of hydrophytes (Table 11.1, B) dicotyledons are better represented and the most extensive taxa, whose European range reaches North Africa, comprise in addition to the emergents *Glyceria fluitans* and *Menyanthes trifoliata*, several floating-leaved species, e.g. *Potamogeton alpinus* and *P. natans*. Of the remaining species, some, e.g. *Naumbergia thyrsiflora*, show a central and southern trend and are rare in the northern parts of their range, whilst others, e.g. *Scheuchzeria palustris*, *Sparganium angustifolium*, *Subularia aquatica* and *Utricularia intermedia* are distinctly northern plants. In North America, *Utricularia intermedia* is restricted to those northern, north-eastern and highland regions that were more or less glaciated at the time of the Wisconsin ice-cap (Rossbach, 1939). *Calla palustris* and *Elatine hydropiper* both display marked gaps, the former being absent from western and southern Europe, the latter from eastern Asia. *E. hydropiper* is also somewhat local: it is rare in Britain and does not seem to have substantially extended its Irish range in the 32 years since Praeger (1935) recorded its spread along canals and rivers eastward and southward from its apparent original stations in Loughs Neagh, Briclan and Shark.

Many authors have described *Myriophyllum spicatum* as a north temperate or circumpolar taxon, ignoring Fernald's (1919) differentiation of the North American plant as a separate species *M. exalbescens*. Löve (1961) has recently pointed out that although the European *M. spicatum* (*sensu stricto*) and *M. exalbescens* are both apparently hexaploid ($2n = 42$) they differ in the shape and length of the floral bracts, the shape and size of the bracteoles, the number of pairs of leaf-divisions and the fact that *M. exalbescens*, like *M. verticillatum*, forms turions whereas *M. spicatum* does not. These differences are greater than those delimiting many accepted species. Patten's (1954) claim, based on plants in New Jersey, that the two species intergrade and should therefore be recognised only as races of one species was challenged by Löve on the reasonable grounds that no cytological studies were made of the New Jersey material and the pollen and seed fertility were not observed. Löve concluded that *M. spicatum* (*sensu lato*) is only quasi-circumpolar since it is really an aggregate taxon comprising two valid species, morphologically and geographically distinct. It is probable that *Sagittaria sagittifolia* is also not truly circumpolar. Bogin (1955) treated *S. sagittifolia* as Eurasian and distinguished its North American equivalent as *S. cuneata* in view of the difference of bract structure and the absence of any intermediates between the two taxa. Den Hartog (1957a) recognised the *S. sagittifolia* of Malaysia and southern and eastern Asia as ssp. *leucopetala*, noting that it is quite distinct from the populations of Europe and northern Asia (ssp. *sagittifolia*) in geographical distribution and in having pure white petals with no purple basal spot, yellow rather than purple anthers,

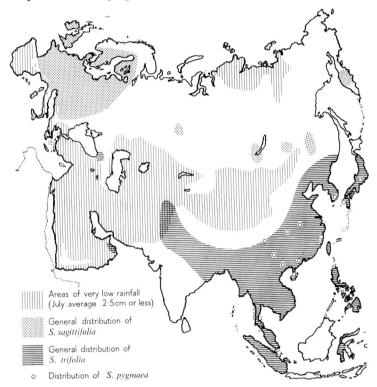

FIG. 11.1. The ranges of *Sagittaria sagittifolia* and *S. trifolia*, both occurring mainly in moist lowlands, and of *S. pygmaea*, a dwarfed annual species which may have evolved from *S. trifolia* (see p. 245). *S. sagittifolia* has been introduced to Scotland, and *S. trifolia* is similarly adventive in various parts of oceanic S.E. Asia, Australasia and the Pacific region (see Table 11.5). (Based on Lambert's Zenithal equal-area projection, and compiled from data in numerous sources.)

reflexed rather than appressed or spreading sepals, and very acute rather than blunt tips to the basal lobes of the leaf. More recent study (Dandy, *in litt.*) has shown that ssp. *leucopetala* ought to be placed in synonymy under *Sagittaria trifolia*, which is a good species. This treatment leaves *S. sagittifolia* as a species of Europe and northern Asia (Fig. 11.1).

Such pairs of allied but geographically discrete (i.e. allopatric) taxa have been loosely described by many authors as vicariads, but Löve (1954, 1955) proposed that this term should be used only for allopatric taxa that have probably become morphologically distinct after (and at least partly as a result of) geographical isolation. Such species are likely to have evolved gradually from a common ancestor and may not have become genetically distinct. *Myriophyllum exalbescens* and *M. spicatum* have the same chromosome number, as have *Sagittaria cuneata* and *S. sagittifolia*: these taxa may therefore constitute pairs of true vicariads. Löve further suggested that taxa which became differentiated before they penetrated separate regions should be deemed false vicariads: many of these are likely to have evolved abruptly, for example through polyploidy, and to be genetically distinct. The emergent *Triglochin maritima*, considered by many as a circumpolar taxon, comprises a series of polyploids (ranging from 2n = 12 to 2n = 144) and the north European, eastern Canadian, western American and Japanese plants are all cytologically, morphologically and ecologically distinct (Löve and Löve, 1958b; Löve and Leith, 1961; Hara, 1962; Packer, 1964). The two members of each of three other pairs of European and North American taxa, namely *Vallisneria spiralis* and *V. americana*, *Littorella uniflora* and *L. americana*, and *Nuphar lutea* and *N. advena*, have been described by some botanists as vicariads (in the loose sense) but have been regarded as conspecific by others (Heslop-Harrison, J., 1953b; Turrill, 1959; Good, 1964). Mulligan and Calder (1964) distinguished the Eurasian and North American *Subularia aquatica* as separate subspecies on morphological grounds.

Some of the pan-tropical hydrophytes (Table 11.1, C) exhibit notable extensions into subtropical and even warm temperate latitudes. *Pistia stratiotes*, which is continuously distributed except for tropical Australia, Micronesia and Polynesia, reaches south in Africa as far as southern Angola, Natal and Transvaal, whilst in the New World it extends both northward to south-western Arizona and the Gulf states and southward to Uruguay and Argentina. It is doubtful if the pan-tropical species listed, except the apparently primitive *Sagittaria guayanensis*, are truly indigenous in all parts of their range. Certain species, e.g. *Eichhornia crassipes*, have been excluded from the table because they are reliably known to have achieved their wide tropical range by adventive spread from a much smaller, initial, native area. The geography of most of the listed species, however, has yet to be thoroughly investigated. It is conspicuous that they are all important as weeds in some tropical countries (pp. 457–58). The possibility of their having been introduced to certain regions, perhaps in the company of subaquatic crops, cannot be ignored. No firm conclusions may be drawn from these somewhat uncertain data. It is worthy of note, however, that there do not appear to be any submerged hydrophytes of pan-tropical, rather than cosmopolitan, distribution.

HYDROPHYTES WITH CONTINENTAL RANGES

The proportion of aquatic vascular plants with distributions confined within one major land mass seems to be rather smaller than the proportion of similar terrestrial species: about 40 per cent compared with a significant majority. Within each continent innumerable variations in the pattern of distribution are discernible, but it must suffice here to notice just certain representative examples.

The most extensive type of Eurasian range is exemplified by *Sparganium erectum*, which penetrates north to the Arctic Circle, south to North Africa, and east to Siberia, but it should be noted that this is an aggregate species and although var. *microcarpum* displays the overall distribution, the other varieties are more restricted, both var. *erectum* and var. *neglectum*, for example, being distinctly southern and reaching no further north than southern Sweden (Cook, 1961a, 1962a; Tutin, 1962). *Hottonia palustris* is mainly central and northern in distribution, and is absent from the extreme north or south of Europe. In contrast, *Apium nodiflorum*, *Glyceria maxima* and *Nymphoides peltata* are central and southern lowland species with a very limited northward penetration, a trend visible in their British distribution (see Perring and Walters, 1962).

There are remarkably few hydrophytes widely distributed in Europe yet confined there and not extending appreciably into Asia. *Hydrocotyle vulgaris* is an example: it has a limited northern range, reaching just north of 60° in the coastal region of Norway (Godwin, 1956) but is extensive in the south, reaching Greece, Algeria, Morocco and Portugal (Tutin, 1962). *Isoetes lacustris* displays a northern European range centred on Scandinavia and northern Russia. Its extension south into warmer regions is restricted to stations at high altitudes, as in the eastern Pyrenees (Jermy, 1964). The emergent *Peplis portula*, which becomes more frequently submerged and fruitless towards the north of its range, comprises a spectrum of forms with unusual British distributions: var. *portula* is predominantly eastern and gives way westwards to intermediate forms and then finally to var. *longidentata*, which has a south-western 'Lusitanian' range, occurring elsewhere only in the Azores, Algeria and the Iberian Peninsula (Allen, 1954). Both *Oenanthe crocata* and *Ranunculus omiophyllus* show conspicuous oceanic western trends: their British distribution is more nearly continuous in the west than in the east and may be restricted to milder areas by intolerance of low winter temperatures (Perring and Walters, 1962).

The Asiatic hydrophyte flora includes many endemics and relatively few common widespread species. One of the most extensive is *Nelumbo nucifera*, which ranges from the Caspian Sea, Korea and Japan south through India and Malaysia to tropical northern Australia (Fig. 11.2). *Blyxa japonica*, *B. octandra*, *Hydrocharis dubia*, *Limnophila heterophylla*, *Monochoria vaginalis* and *Vallisneria gigantea* all have similar overall distributions (Backer, 1951f; den Hartog, 1957b). Certain other species may exhibit comparable latitudinal penetration but appear to be longitudinally restricted. *Philydrum lanuginosum*, for example, shows a north-south distribution extending from the Riu-Kiu islands and Formosa through Burma and Indo-China to north-east Australia (Skottsberg, 1948). *Saururus chinensis* has an essentially similar continental east Asiatic range: it penetrates further north, to Japan, but no further into the tropics than Luzon in Malaysia (van Steenis, 1949c). Numerous hydrophytes appear to be restricted to parts of the tropical rain-forest belt of India, Burma and Malaysia. *Barclaya longifolia*, a little known species of the Nymphaeaceae, for example, is an infrequent plant of the rain-forests of Burma, Cochinchina, Thailand and the Andaman Islands, whilst *Cryptocoryne ciliata*, an aroid of tidal rivers, together with *C. retrospiralis, C. wendtii* and *Synnema triflorum*, all extend from India through coastal Malaysia to Indonesia and possibly New Guinea (de Wit, 1958a, b). Although recorded from only one site in India, the submerged *Najas browniana* penetrates further east, through Java and southern New Guinea to the Northern Territory of Australia: *N. tenuifolia* has a comparable Malaysian-Australian range (de Wilde, 1962).

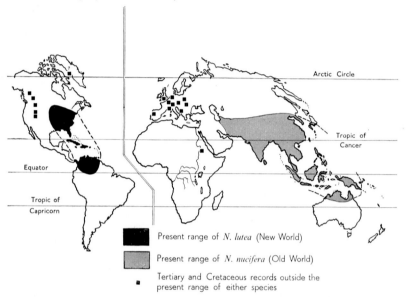

FIG. 11.2. The present distribution of the genus *Nelumbo* and the fossil records in regions where the plant is now extinct. Note that neither of the two existing species occurs in both Old and New Worlds, but both still extend significantly beyond the tropics into the north temperate zone. (Based on Bartholomew's Re-centred Sinusoidal equal-area projection, and compiled from data in many sources.)

Some of the indigenous hydrophytes of the New World are primarily tropical whilst others occur mainly in temperate latitudes, in either North or South America. As in other continents, innumerable different patterns of distribution are apparent as a result of various degrees of latitudinal or longitudinal restriction (Figs. 11.3, 11.4).

Alternanthera philoxeroides, Azolla mexicana, Mayaca fluviatilis and *Nelumbo lutea* (Fig. 11.2) are all centred on the tropical zone but extend into the subtropics and warm temperate regions of both North and South America: the northward penetration of *A. mexicana* is through the Pacific states to British Columbia whereas that of the other three species is over the Gulf and Atlantic coastal plains (Lawrence, 1951, Dittmer *et al.*, 1954, Wood, 1959). Other species extend northward or southward, but not both. *Echinodorus berteroi*, for example,

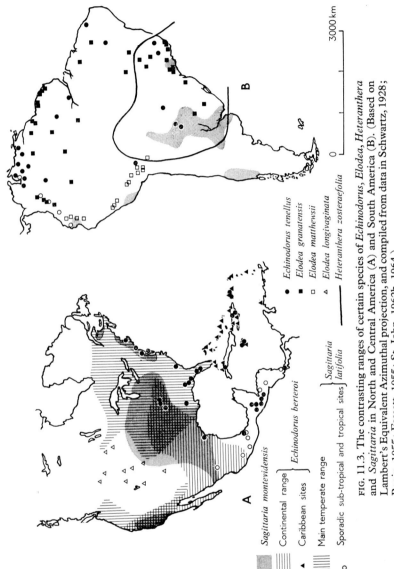

FIG. 11.3. The contrasting ranges of certain species of *Echinodorus, Elodea, Heteranthera* and *Sagittaria* in North and Central America (A) and South America (B). (Based on Lambert's Equivalent Azimuthal projection, and compiled from data in Schwartz, 1928; Bogin, 1955; Fassett, 1955; St. John, 1962b, 1964.)

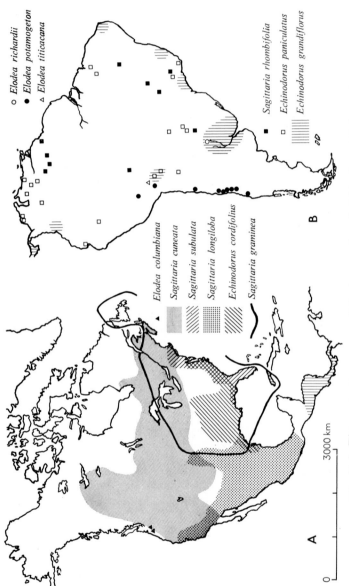

FIG. 11.4. The contrasting ranges of further species of *Echinodorus*, *Elodea* and *Sagittaria* in North and Central America (A) and South America (B). (Based on Lambert's Equivalent Azimuthal projection, and compiled from data in Bogin, 1955; Fassett, 1955; St. John, 1962b, 1963, 1964.)

extends from the Central American tropics only into North America, where it occurs in the central and southern United States. A contrasting southward extension through tropical and subtropical South America is shown by *Hydrocleys nymphoides, Eichhornia azurea* and *Echinodorus grandiflorus* (Schwartz, 1928; Fassett, 1955).

Azolla caroliniana and *Sagittaria montevidensis* are essentially warm temperate plants. Although rare or absent in many parts of the tropics, they both have immense latitudinal ranges, the former from Massachusetts to Brazil and the latter from Quebec to Chile (Svenson, 1944; Bogin, 1955; di Fulvio, 1961). *Lemna valdiviana* is equally far-ranging; it is frequent in tropical as well as temperate sites from about 43°N to 40°S (Daubs, 1965).

Of the many hydrophytes native in North America, *Sagittaria cuneata* and *Elodea canadensis* are two of the most extensive, ranging through 25 to 30° of latitude and covering the entire longitudinal span of the continent. Both *Sagittaria graminea* and *Elodea nuttallii* exhibit Atlantic North American ranges. The range of *S. graminea* shown in Fig. 11.4 is that of the aggregate species: within this are about six varieties, each having a small discrete range (Bogin, 1955). *E. nuttallii* is distributed from Quebec south to North Carolina and west to Minnesota, Nebraska and Kansas: isolated records to the south and west of this area, as in Alabama and northern Idaho, may represent specimens introduced or escaped from cultivation (St. John, 1965). *Wolffiella floridana, Echinodorus cordifolius* and *Sagittaria subulata* are also Atlantic but more restricted. The confinement of *S. subulata*, to fresh and tidal waters of the east coast of the U.S.A., is perhaps sufficiently marked for the species to be regarded as a local endemic. In contrast to these several Atlantic species, *Elodea longivaginata, Isoetes bolanderi* and *Marsilea vestita* have distributions centred on the Rocky Mountains or the Pacific coast, from British Columbia, Alberta and Saskatchewan south to California, Arizona and New Mexico (Stason, 1926; Dittmer *et al.*, 1954; St. John, 1962b).

South America seems to be relatively rich in endemics and poor in widespread hydrophytes (Figs. 11.3, 11.4; and see Table 11.4). Two fairly extensive, but essentially tropical species are *Echinodorus paniculatus* and *Sagittaria rhombifolia*. A third example, *Elodea granatensis*, is the only widely distributed member of its genus in South America: it ranges from the Andean valleys of Colombia eastward to French Guiana and southward to temperate southern Brazil and north-eastern Argentina (St. John, 1964).

Most of the far-ranging hydrophytes of Africa are tropical species, a fact which reflects the dearth of aquatic habitats in the northern- and southernmost regions of the continent where the land surface is arid desert except for certain valleys and the littoral plains. *Azolla africana, Ceratopteris cornuta* and *Najas pectinata* exemplify the most extensive type of range, from temperate South Africa north throughout the tropical zone of the continent, including Madagascar. *Azolla nilotica, Heteranthera callifolia, Nymphaea caerulea, Ottelia ulvifolia* and *Potamogeton thunbergii* show a rather less extensive latitudinal span, mainly between 10°N and 25°S, i.e. from Senegal and Ethiopia south to northern Transvaal (Schwartz, 1928; af Rantzien, 1951b; Wild, 1961). Some species

13*

are predominantly southern, e.g. *Lagarosiphon major* and *L. muscoides* in Rhodesia and South Africa, whilst others are western, e.g. *Anubias lanceolata*— occurring from Guinea to Cameroun and Gabon, or eastern, e.g. *Lagarosiphon crispus* and *Salvinia hastata*—found throughout much of tropical and sub-tropical East Africa (af Rantzien, 1951b; Obermeyer, 1964).

Vast tracts of the Australian continent, too, are devoid of aquatic habitats for much of the year. Many of the common indigenous hydrophytes are pan-tropical, Asiatic or Malaysian species which extend south-eastward into northern and eastern Australia. Amongst the few native hydrophytes which are peculiar to Australia are *Myriophyllum verrucosum*, and some species of *Cycnogeton, Haloragis* and *Maundia* (Schindler, 1905; Tuyama, 1940).

New Zealand is also relatively poor in hydrophytes that do not occur outside Australasia. There is a particular dearth of submerged freshwater species: only five hydrophilous indigenes are known, and four of these—*Lepilaena bilocularis**, *Potamogeton pectinatus, Ruppia spiralis* and *Zannichellia palustris*—occur mainly in brackish water. The last three, moreover, are cosmopolitan in range, not peculiar to Australasia. Since many freshwater habitats are not occupied by well adapted native species, it is perhaps not surprising that aliens, such as *Elodea canadensis, Egeria densa* and *Rorippa nasturtium-aquaticum*, have spread successfully throughout much of New Zealand (Table 11.5 and pp. 362, 369).

ENDEMISM AMONGST HYDROPHYTES

It is a working convention that by endemism is meant the possession of an abnormally confined geographical range that is clearly smaller than the average for the particular type of taxon. Families of plants occurring on just one con-tinent are frequently described as endemic because families generally occupy larger areas. To describe similarly distributed species as endemic, however, would be quite meaningless because the average range of such taxa is not so great. The term endemic is always applied in a comparative sense and there is an appreciable element of arbitrary choice in its use. Good (1953, 1964) considered as endemic those plants which are confined to one of his floristic regions. Since hydrophytes generally are more sporadic than terrestrial plants, the concept of an endemic applied here will be narrower, covering only those species which are very markedly restricted.

To establish the cause of endemism is important in studying the history and origins of the flora. Some light is shed on otherwise inexplicable local distribu-tions by the Theory of Generic Cycles, which is essentially a geographical life cycle of a taxon (Cain, 1944). It comprises four stages: (a) juvenility; (b) maturity; (c) decline; and (d) extinction. The theory is supported by cytological data and by palaeobotanical evidence of the origin of groups of plants, their dissemination and dominance, and their gradual eclipse and replacement by more highly organised types. During the phase of juvenility the range of a species or genus will expand, but at any given moment it will be more restricted in area than that of an established mature taxon. At the same time it will probably

---

* *L. bilocularis* belongs to the genus *Althenia* but its correct name has not yet been published.

be indistinguishable from the contracted range of a taxon which is declining and entering the phase of extinction. To decide whether an actual endemic species is a juvenile or relict taxon is immensely difficult and requires the fullest possible investigation of its morphological, cytological, reproductive and geographical affinities and, if possible, its fossil record.

Willis (1922) advanced the hypothesis that the area inhabited by a species is directly proportional to its age and that genera with many species are older than those containing few or a single species. In support of this, Willis assembled data from his unrivalled knowledge of such tropical families as the Podostemaceae. This large group of aquatic dicotyledons is especially rich in endemics (Weddell, 1872; Willis, 1902, 1914, 1917). The vast majority of species, belonging to such genera as *Apinagia, Castelnavia, Dicraea, Farmeria, Griffithella, Hydrobryopsis, Lophogyne, Mourera, Oenone, Oserya, Rhyncholacis* and *Weddellina*, are extremely local in distribution: in different parts of one Brazilian river, the Araguaya, were discovered no fewer than seven species of *Castelnavia*, a genus scarcely known elsewhere (Willis, 1914). This pattern of local ranges is typical of all parts of the tropics where the family occurs—Burma, India, Ceylon, Madagascar and Indonesia as well as tropical South America. Most podostemad genera are small; several are monotypic. Willis did not acknowledge the possibility that these small taxa could be ancient relics: he argued, on morphological grounds, that they are recently derived types and emphasised that whereas they are restricted in range, *Podostemum* and *Tristicha*, which he regarded as older and more primitive because of their simpler radially symmetrical organisation, are the only genera with extensive distributions. However, observations of north temperate floras suggest that the spread of a taxon depends more on suitable dispersal factors and on tolerance of edaphic and climatic variations than on age (Lawrence, 1951). Now the podostemads have no significant adaptations to dispersal and appear to be utterly committed to a very narrow ecological niche. It is more probable that they are all relatively old taxa.

The Podostemaceae is not the only aquatic family rich in endemics. Amongst the Alismaceae, *Sagittaria* and *Echinodorus* have numerous endemic species. The endemics in the genus *Echinodorus* are summarised in Table 11.2. Most species of *Sagittaria* are widespread, some exceptionally so, but there are a few strangely localised species. *S. sanfordii*, for example, occurs only in the Great Valley of California; *S. macrophylla* is apparently restricted to habitats around Mexico City, whilst *S. demersa* is known only from two districts some 800 km apart in the Mexican Highlands. Three other species have rather wider ranges but are still markedly local: *S. sprucei* in the Amazon Basin, *S. ambigua* in the southern Great Plains of the U.S.A., and *S. papillosa* along the Gulf Coast of Texas and further inland west of the Mississippi (Bogin, 1955). Both species of *Ranalisma* are also very local: *R. rostratum* in the Malay Peninsula (Selangor) and *R. humile* in parts of tropical Africa (den Hartog, 1957a). *Machaerocarpus californicus* is a Californian monotype, *Wiesneria triandra* is restricted to eastern India, and *W. filifolia*, *W. schweinfurthii*, and the monotypic *Burnatia enneandra* are sporadic tropical African plants (Carter 1960).

TABLE 11.2   Endemics in the genus *Echinodorus*

Of the twenty-four or so species of *Echinodorus* only five have extensive ranges: the tropical South American *E. grandiflorus* and *E. paniculatus*; *E. cordifolius* of the south-eastern United States; *E. berteroi* of the Caribbean islands, Yucatan, north-west Mexico and the south-eastern United States (except the Atlantic seaboard); and *E. tenellus*, which extends from the Atlantic United States and the Ozark Plateau through the Gulf States, Central America and the Greater Antilles into tropical South America.
All the remaining well-known species appear to be restricted to small areas in the American tropics:

E. andrieuxii	–	British Honduras, Guatemala, Pacific Mexico
E. bracteatus	–	Ecuador, Panama
⋆*E. brevipedicellatus*	–	Brazil
E. fluitans	–	Colombia
E. grisebachii	–	Cuba, Costa Rica
⋆*E. intermedius*	–	Brazil
E. isthmicus	–	Costa Rica, Panama
⋆*E. longipetalus*	–	Brazil
⋆*E. longistylis*	–	Brazil
E. macrophyllus	–	S.E. Brazil (Estados do Espirito Santo, Minas Gerais and São Paulo)
E. magdalenensis	–	Rio Magdalena basin and nearby Pacific Coast of Colombia
E. muricatus	–	N. Colombia, N. Venezuela and the Guianas
E. nymphaeifolius	–	Cuba, Yucatan
E. ovalis	–	W. Cuba
E. quadricostatus	–	N. Peru
E. sellowianus	–	Rio Paranaiba in the Estado de Minas Gerais in Brazil
E. trialatus	–	Colombia
E. tunicatus	–	Costa Rica, Panama
⋆*E. virgatus*	–	Pacific Coast of Central Mexico

NOTE: The distributions of species marked ⋆ need further study.
(Table compiled from data in Fassett, 1955; Duarte, *in litt.*)

Of the remaining groups of aquatic monocotyledons, the unigeneric families Najadaceae and Aponogetonaceae provide further examples of endemic plants. Taxonomic uncertainties preclude any comprehensive treatment of the Najadaceae, but it is nonetheless apparent, as Rendle (1899, 1900, 1901) noticed, that numerous probable species have extremely localised distributions. Guppy (1906, 1917) contrasted these with the more widely distributed species and postulated, in the terms of his Theory of Differentiation, that the local species had differentiated from a ubiquitous primitive stock, perhaps represented by the polymorphic *Najas marina*, which has more or less the full range of the genus. It is more probable, however, that at least some of the endemic plants are relatively primitive and perhaps relict members of the family, rather than advanced derived taxa. In Africa, for example, the only widely distributed species are *N. marina*, the palaeotropical *N. graminea*, the warm temperate and tropical *N. minor*, the central and southern African *N. interrupta*, and *N. pectinata*, which occurs throughout continental Africa and Madagascar. Almost all the remaining species appear to be strictly endemic: *N. australis*, *N. madagascariensis* and *N. setacea*, for example, occur only in the Madagascar–Mascarene region; *N. affinis* in Senegal; *N. baldwinii* in Liberia and Sierra Leone; *N. meiklei* in central Nigeria; *N. hagerupii* in Niger territory; *N. schweinfurthii* in southern Sudan; *N. testui* in northern Congo; *N. welwitschii* in Angola and Botswana; and *N. liberiensis*, which is disjunct between Liberia and Tchad. No fewer than six of these isolated species, namely *N. affinis*, *N. madagascariensis*, *N. meiklei*, *N. schweinfurthii*, *N. testui* and *N. welwitschii*, belong to Rendle's section *Spathaceae*, comprising those members of the family which seem most primitive in floral organisation (af Rantzien, 1952).

The geography of the Aponogetonaceae is most intriguing, for there is not a single species with a range anywhere approaching that of the whole family. The most extensive species are probably *Aponogeton natans*, ranging from Ceylon and India to subtropical China and perhaps eastern Australia; *A. desertorum*, which occurs in much of warmer Africa, from the eastern Cape, Natal and Transvaal north to Ethiopia and Somali in the east and Angola in the west; *A. junceus*, an aggregate species of southern, eastern, and perhaps parts of central Africa; and *A. subconjugatus* and *A. vallisnerioides*, which extend throughout tropical western Africa from Senegal eastwards to southern Sudan, the Congolese Republic and Uganda. The remaining species of the family appear to fall into several fairly discrete endemic groups, shown in Table 11.3, which display morphological affinities and differences between each other and together provide a remarkable palaeotropical series.

TABLE 11.3   Endemics in the genus *Aponogeton*

AUSTRALASIAN GROUP

A. elongatus	–	N. and E. Australia
A. loriae	–	Queensland, S.W. Celebes, New Guinea

SOUTH-EAST ASIATIC GROUP

A. stachyosporus	–	Malay Peninsula (Johore)
⋆A. luteus	–	Annam
⋆A. robinsonii	–	Annam
⋆A. eberhardtii	–	Annam
⋆A. lakhonensis	–	Laos

INDIAN GROUP

A. crispus	–	Ceylon
A. rigidifolius	–	S. Ceylon
A. undulatus	–	S.W. India (Malabar)
⋆A. echinatus	–	E. India (Bengal)
⋆A. microphyllus	–	E. India (Bhutan)

MADAGASCAN GROUP

A. bernieranus	–	Madagascar, Nossi-Bé
A. dioecus	–	Madagascar (Mt. Ankaratra)
A. fenestralis	–	Madagascar
⋆A. henckelianus	–	Madagascar
⋆A. quadrangularis	–	Madagascar
A. ulvaceus	–	Madagascar

TABLE 11.3—*continued*

CONTINENTAL AFRICAN GROUP

★*A. abyssinicus*	–	Tropical East Africa (Eritrea, Ethiopia, Somali)
A. angustifolius	–	S.W. Cape (winter rainfall region)
★*A. boehmii*	–	Equatorial Africa
A. distachyos	–	S.W. Cape (winter rainfall region)
A. nudiflorus	–	Tanzania
A. stuhlmannii	–	Tropical East Africa (Transvaal)
A. troupini	–	Tchad, N. Congo

NOTES: This table may at best be regarded as tentative. Although recent studies have clarified the understanding of several African species, the nomenclature and distributional data for most taxa in the genus are old, somewhat confused and greatly in need of revision. The taxa marked ★ are very poorly known. Detailed study might submerge them in synonymy, or reveal them to be valid species of wider distribution than is at present realised.

(Table compiled from data in Krause and Engler, 1906; Camus, 1923; Troupin, 1953; de Wit, 1958a, b; Wild, 1961; van Bruggen, 1962; Bosser and Raynal, 1966; Obermeyer, 1966a, *in litt.*; Podlech, 1966.)

In Table 11.4 are listed miscellaneous endemic hydrophytes belonging to other families.

TABLE 11.4   Miscellaneous endemic fresh water species

Family and species	**Distribution**
ISOETACEAE:	
Isoetes aequinoctialis	Angola
I. azorica	Azores
I. boryana	Coastal S.W. France
I. brochonii	E. Pyrenees
I. coromandelina	India
I. flaccida	Georgia, Florida
I. gardneriana	N. Brazil
I. habbemensis	W. New Guinea
I. heldreichii	C. Greece
I. hookeri	Tasmania
I. malinverniana	N.W. Italy
I. mexicana	W. Mexico
I. neoguineensis	E. New Guinea
I. philippinensis	Philippines
I. stuartii	Tasmania
I. triquetra	Peruvian Andes
CERATOPTERIDACEAE:	
Ceratopteris lockhartii	Trinidad, the Guianas
MARSILEACEAE:	
Marsilea deflexa	Brazil
M. macropoda	S. Texas
M. strigosa	S. Europe
Pilularia minuta	W. Mediterranean
Regnellidium diphyllum	Brazil

TABLE 11.4—*continued*

Family and species	Distribution
SALVINIACEAE:	
Salvinia herzogii	E. Argentina
S. martynii	Guyana, Mato Grosso
S. oblongifolia	N. Brazil
S. sprucei	N. Brazil, E. Venezuela, Trinidad
NYMPHAEACEAE:	
Cabomba aquatica	Amazon basin, the Guianas
C. australis	S. Brazil, N.W. Argentina
C. palaeformis	S. Mexico, Guatemala, British Honduras
C. pulcherrima	Coastal South Carolina, N. Florida
Nuphar fraternum	New Jersey
N. japonicum	Japan
N. ozarkanum	S. Missouri, N. Arkansas
N. sagittifolium	South Carolina
Nymphaea burtii	Tanzania
N. elegans	Texas, Mexico
N. liberiensis	Liberia, Cameroun
N. micrantha	Coastal W. Africa (Guinea)
CERATOPHYLLACEAE:	
Ceratophyllum floridanum	Florida Keys
C. muricatum	Egypt
C. tanaiticum	Ukraine, S. and E. Russia
RANUNCULACEAE:	
Ranunculus fluitans	W. and C. Europe
R. ololeucos	Portugal, W. France, Belgium, Netherlands
R. tripartitus	as above; also S. and W. British Isles
UMBELLIFERAE:	
Oenanthe fluviatilis	British Isles, Denmark, Germany
HALORAGACEAE:	
Myriophyllum ussuriense	Japan, Manchuria
CALLITRICHACEAE:	
Callitriche aucklandica	Auckland Islands
C. capricorni	Queensland
C. lusitanica	Iberian Peninsula
C. petriei	New Zealand
TRAPACEAE:	
Trapa acornis	E. China
HYDROCHARITACEAE:	
Blyxa novoguineensis	S. New Guinea
B. senegalensis	Senegal
Egeria densa	E. Argentina, S. Uruguay, S.E. Brazil

TABLE 11.4—*continued*

Family and species	Distribution
HYDROCHARITACEAE—*continued*	
E. naias	N.E. Argentina, Uruguay, S. Paraguay, E. Brazil
Elodea bifoliata	C. Arizona
E. brandegeae	E. California
E. callitrichoides	E. Argentina, S. Uruguay
E. columbiana	N.W. Oregon (see Fig. 11.4)
E. ernstiae	E. and N. Argentina
E. linearis	C. Tennessee
E. matthewsii	C. Ecuador, C. and S.E. Peru, W. Bolivia (see Fig. 11.3)
E. nevadensis	W. Nevada
E. peruviensis	S.E. Peru, W. Bolivia
E. potamogeton	S.E. Peru, W. Bolivia, coastal Chile (see Fig. 11.4)
E. richardii	N.E. Argentina (see Fig. 11.4)
E. schweinitzii	E. Pennsylvania
E. titicacana	W. Bolivia (see Fig. 11.4)
Hydrocharis chevalieri	C. Africa
Lagarosiphon ilicifolius	N. Botswana, W. Rhodesia, S. Zambia
L. madagascariensis	Madagascar
L. verticillifolius	S. Mozambique, Rhodesia, E. Transvaal, N. Natal
Ottelia mesenterium	S.E. Celebes
Vallisneria neotropicalis	W. Cuba, coastal Florida
MAYACACEAE:	
Mayaca vandellii	E. Brazil
PONTEDERIACEAE:	
Eichhornia paniculata	Cuba, Jamaica, N.E. Brazil
E. paradoxa	Coasts of N. Venezuela, N.E. and S.E. Brazil
Heteranthera potamogeton	Senegal
H. seubertiana	N.E. Brazil
H. sipcata	Cuba, Panama
H. zosteraefolia	Brazil, E. Bolivia (see Fig. 11.3)
Hydrothrix gardneri	N.E. Brazil
Pontederia heterantherimorpha	C. Brazil
ARACEAE:	
Anubias afzelii	Guinea, Sierra Leone
A. congensis	Guinea, Congo basin
A. nana	Cameroons
Cryptocoryne aponogetifolia	Philippines
C. balansae	Thailand
C. beckettii	Ceylon
C. blassii	Thailand
C. lutea	Ceylon
C. nevillii	Ceylon
C. pygmaea	Philippines

TABLE 11.4—*continued*

Family and species	Distribution
ARACEAE—*continued*	
C. siamensis	Thailand
C. thwaitesii	Ceylon
C. walkeri	Ceylon
Lagenandra insignis	S. India
L. koenigii	S. India
L. lancifolia	Ceylon
L. thwaitesii	Ceylon
LEMNACEAE:	
Spirodela punctata	Guyana (R. Essequibo)
Wolffia hyalina	Egypt (delta of R. Nile)
W. microscopica	India
W. repanda	Angola
Wolffiella denticulata	South Africa (Cape, Natal)

NOTES: This table has no pretensions to completeness: it comprises merely a selection of examples noticed in the literature. Numerous species listed are still known only from the type locality, i.e. whence they were originally described.

(Table compiled from data in many sources, principally Schwartz, 1928; Johnson and Chrysler, 1938; af Rantzien, 1951b; Fassett, 1953; den Hartog, 1957a, b; de Wit, 1958a; Alston, 1959b; Mason, 1959; Wood, 1959; Schotsman, 1961a; Wild, 1961; St. John, 1961, 1962b, 1963, 1964, 1965; de la Sota, 1962, 1963, 1964; Tutin, 1962, 1964; Cook, 1964b; Crabbe, 1964; Jermy, 1964; Nakano, 1964; Obermeyer, 1964, 1966b; Webb, 1964; Daubs, 1965.)

Although not exhaustive, the foregoing survey of species with conspicuously local ranges amply illustrates the rarely acknowledged fact that endemism is at least as common amongst hydrophytes as is the possession of an extensive distribution. The highest frequency of endemics seems to be in the tropics and subtropics of America, Africa and Asia: relatively fewer examples are known in temperate regions.

It is extremely difficult to discern the possible causes of endemism in the various groups of aquatic vascular plants. The local distribution of many of the Podostemaceae may be a consequence of their severe edaphic restriction and possible relict status. The Alismaceae and Butomaceae are likewise often regarded as old and primitive families (although both possess numerous characters acknowledged to be advanced) and the occurrence of endemics accords with this belief. The higher frequency of endemics in *Echinodorus*, as compared with the very closely related *Sagittaria*, is congruous with the probably more primitive status of the former genus. The Aponogetonaceae may also be an ancient family with primitive affinities. However, in view of the inevitable uncertainty which surrounds the origin and history of these and other families, any suggested association between the frequency of endemics and the age of the taxa is purely conjectural.

Whilst it is, of course, quite possible that more thorough botanical explorations and taxonomic revisions may reveal some endemics to be much more widespread and common than is now realised, the flora of certain areas of the tropics is sufficiently well understood for the ranges of many of the cited hydrophytes to be accepted as truly endemic. Den Hartog (1957a, b) further pointed out that numerous hydrophytes which are often considered to possess very extensive distributions are in fact extremely local in occurrence over quite large sectors of their range. He instanced *Aldrovanda vesiculosa, Blyxa japonica, Brasenia schreberi, Ceratophyllum submersum, Hydrocharis dubia, Najas marina, Nymphoides moonii, Tenagocharis latifolia*, and certain species of *Myriophyllum, Potamogeton, Sparganium, Trapa* and the Alismaceae, all of which are markedly rare in Malaysia. Jäger (1964), who noticed the similar rarity of some species of *Najas, Salvinia* and *Wolffia* in Europe, emphasised that areas of local and irregular distribution may not necessarily be relict sectors of the overall range: they may be created by one or more of a complex of climatic, edaphic and biotic factors.

The prevalence of endemic hydrophytes in Ceylon and parts of India may be partly due to the tropical rain-forests and coastal lowlands (in which most of the suitable aquatic habitats occur) being isolated from those of Africa and of continental and oceanic south-east Asia. However, it is doubtful if the high frequency of endemics and rarity of otherwise widespread hydrophytes within the East Indian Archipelago could similarly be attributed to physiographic circumstances, since the distances between islands are generally not great enough to constitute severe dispersal barriers. For the same reason, it is difficult to understand the conspicuous absence of many hydrophytes, e.g. the Alismaceae and some of the Nymphaeaceae, from the islands of Micro-, Macro- and Polynesia. Perhaps the endemic and very rare species of south-east Asia and other areas have only a narrow range of tolerance of edaphic factors. Den Hartog (1957a) noted that some of the species he cited seem to require waters with a particular mineral content whilst others appear to grow only in ancient swamps which have not suffered human interference. Although primarily controlled by the restricted existence of suitable potential habitats, the range of such plants is likely to be limited further by the strong competition from more adaptable species with a greater edaphic tolerance. It is also possible that some endemic and irregularly distributed hydrophytes, other than the Podostemaceae, lack efficient adaptations to dispersal.

In the context of endemism it is appropriate to mention also the marine angiosperms. Confined to relatively shallow coastal waters, these plants inevitably appear very local in distribution compared with many freshwater and terrestrial angiosperms. Yet the ranges of most marine species still seem remarkably limited even when due allowance is made for the narrow spectrum of potential habitats. The pronounced latitudinal restriction of most species, which probably reflects the prime influence borne by temperature in the otherwise relatively constant marine environment, was discussed in an earlier chapter (p. 35). It is pertinent to note here certain other interesting features of their geographical distribution which have been revealed by the studies of Ostenfeld (1915, 1927a, b), Miki (1932, 1933, 1934), Feldmann (1936), Bernatowicz (1952), Phillips (1960) and den Hartog (1957b, 1959, 1964a).

With very few exceptions, the marine angiosperms appear to be segregated between the tropical (and subtropical) and temperate zones and between the Old and the New Worlds. Of the temperate genera (*Althenia*, *Phyllospadix*, *Posidonia* and *Zostera*), only one species (*Zostera marina* in the northern hemisphere) has a really extensive range. Although taxonomic confusion prevents the construction of a clear geographical picture, all the remaining species of *Zostera* seem to have rather local ranges on the coasts of Atlantic Europe, eastern Asia, Australasia or South Africa. *Posidonia* has probably but two species: one is restricted to the Mediterranean coast of southern Europe and North Africa whilst the other frequents the Australian coasts. The species of *Phyllospadix* are segregated between the Pacific coasts of western North America and eastern Asia, and so afford an interesting marine example of the type of amphi-Pacific discontinuity found in the ranges of the emergent *Saururus* (van Steenis, 1949c) and numerous terrestrial genera (Hara, 1962; Good, 1964).

The various species of the tropical and subtropical genera (*Amphibolis*, *Cymodocea*, *Enhalus*, *Halodule*, *Halophila*, *Syringodium* and *Thalassia*) fall into two essentially distinct groups. One covers the Indo-Pacific coasts from eastern Africa, Madagascar and Mauritius to New Caledonia, Australia and the Pacific islands, with the greatest concentration of species in the Indo-Malaysian region. The other group is tropical American, being centred on the Caribbean with a limited northward extension along the subtropical coasts of the south-eastern U.S.A.

Even the few fairly extensive Indo-Pacific species, such as *Enhalus acoroides*, *Halodule pinifolia*, *Halodule tridentata* and *Thalassia hemprichii*, are not continuously distributed. The range of *Halodule pinifolia*, for example, extends from east Africa, Madagascar and the Red Sea eastwards to Australia and Tonga but is interrupted by conspicuous gaps: along the whole length of the coast of southern Asia the species occurs only in the Persian Gulf, Ceylon and the Gulf of Siam. Such curious disjunction is not easily explained: it may perhaps reflect the relatively ancient and primitive status of these species. Most other species of the Indo-Pacific group are markedly local. *Halophila beccarii*, for example, is a rare plant of Malaysian coasts extending east only as far as Borneo and the Philippines. A few species, however, may be slowly expanding their range. Since the Suez Canal was opened, *Halophila stipulacea*, a species of the Red Sea and western Indian Ocean, has spread into the Mediterranean and begun to colonise the coasts of Greece (den Hartog, 1957b, 1964a).

Almost all species of the tropical American group appear highly endemic. *Halodule bermudensis*, for example, is known only from the Bermudas, and *Halodule ciliata* only from the Caribbean coast of Panama, whilst *Halophila baillonis* and *Halophila engelmannii* are West Indian plants, the latter occurring also along the coast of Texas (den Hartog, 1959, 1964a).

Halodule, *Halophila*, *Syringodium* and *Thalassia* seem to be centred on, and may have originated in, the Indo-Malaysian region, for it is here that they have the highest species density, most apparently primitive species, or most nearly continuous distribution. The question of how and when the Caribbean representatives of these genera originated has therefore provoked much speculation. It is highly unlikely that ancestral or contemporary members of any of the four genera migrated from Indo-Malaysia to the Caribbean, either westward round South Africa and across the Atlantic Ocean or eastward across the Pacific Ocean and round South America. This would have involved dispersal over very long distances of open sea and none of the marine angiosperms seem to possess the requisite adaptations for such dispersal. Moreover, all four genera are conspicuously absent from the coasts of continental South America and (with the exception of one species of *Halodule*) from the coasts of South and West Africa too.

Ostenfeld (1915, 1927a, b) and den Hartog (1957b, 1964a) have argued that the genera may have migrated almost due east across the Pacific into what is now the Caribbean region prior to the formation of the isthmus of Panama. Certain geographical and morphological relationships between existing species may be cited in support of this interesting notion. The ranges of the two species of *Thalassia*, the Indo-Pacific *T. hemprichii* and the Caribbean *T. testudinum*, are discretely segregated by isthmian Central America. Although quite distinct, these two species have numerous morphological similarities and appear very closely related. They may therefore be vicariads which have evolved from a common parent whose range became split when the isthmus of Panama arose in Miocene time. As den Hartog (1964a) pertinently noted, the close resemblance of the twin species is not inconsistent with such an ancient origin: in view of the low frequency of sexual reproduction and relative uniformity of the marine environment, evolutionary changes are likely to be very conservative. The Indo-Pacific *Syringodium isoetifolium* and the Caribbean *S. filiforme* constitute a second pair of geographically isolated but morphologically similar species. The genus *Halodule* includes a third pair, the Indo-Pacific *H. uninervis* and the Caribbean *H. beaudettei*, but the latter occurs also on the Pacific side of the isthmus, and so, assuming this plant has not been carried across the isthmus by land or sea traffic, the evolution of these two discrete species must have occurred before Miocene time.

If the Caribbean species of *Halodule*, *Syringodium* and *Thalassia* did originate in this way, it is clear that these genera must already have been well established early in the Tertiary epoch. Since there is every reason to believe that these (and other) hydrophilous marine monocotyledons evolved from brackish- or freshwater ancestors and are amongst the most advanced aquatic angiosperms, the evolutionary lines which they terminate must reach back a very long way indeed, even perhaps to pre-Cretaceous time.

The major objection to the argument of Ostenfeld and den Hartog is that the migration to the Caribbean must have involved long-distance dispersal. To facilitate the immense journey across the Pacific it is of course tempting to imagine a land bridge or chain of islands stretching conveniently between Polynesia and the American continent. As den Hartog (1964a) pointed out, such connections have certainly not existed since the Tertiary and there is very little geological evidence that they could have existed in the Mesozoic era. The vast uninterrupted expanse of ocean must have been a severe barrier to migration. Dispersal of marine genera seems to be very slow, probably because of the low frequency of sexual reproduction, the lack of sustained buoyancy in fruits or seeds, and the poor survival of unattached seedlings or vegetative fragments (p. 331). Indeed, the lack of adaptations to long-distance dispersal, together with specific temperature relationships, is usually invoked as the prime reason for the geographical confinement of most marine angiosperms.

Finally, mention must be made of two marine plants which are quite exceptional in occurring in both the Old and the New Worlds. *Halophila decipiens* var. *pubescens* is widely distributed in the Caribbean as well as the Pacific islands and Indian Ocean. This immense disjunct range might perhaps have developed by trans-Pacific migration before the Panama isthmus was established (den Hartog, 1957b). The same interpretation could not be applied, however, to *Halodule wrightii*, whose range is most extraordinary for a species with (presumably) poor powers of dispersal. This plant occurs in the Caribbean and around the coasts of Florida and the Bermudas but has not been found anywhere on the coast of northern South America or on the Pacific side of the continent. In the Old World it is known only from tropical African waters, from Angola north to Senegal and from Madagascar and Mauritius north to Kenya and the Persian Gulf. Assuming that the populations are truly conspecific, the presence of this species on both the east and the west coasts of Africa is unique amongst marine angiosperms (den Hartog, 1964a).

DISCONTINUOUS DISTRIBUTION AMONGST HYDROPHYTES

The natural human inclination to concentrate attention on the strange and the anomalous is vividly reflected in the voluminous literature devoted to plants with discontinuous distributions. Good (1953, 1964), Heslop-Harrison (1953a) and others have rightly pleaded for caution in studying discontinuous taxa and stressed that they should preferably be investigated in association with the other less anomalous components of the flora. Good called for especial care in the discussion of taxa which appear to be discontinuous between the north and south temperate zones, because of the immense difficulty of establishing that in the southern hemisphere, notably Australasia, the plant is really native and has not been introduced during human settlement. Some indication of the pertinence of Good's warning is given by Allan's (1936) estimate of the number of species naturalised in New Zealand as 603, many of which are north temperate plants. It is clearly essential to prove conclusively that the plants occurring in several disjunct regions are truly indigenous and conspecific.

The use of the term 'discontinuous', like that of 'endemic', is always comparative. Any taxon is really discontinuous if the total range it occupies includes one or more regions from which it is absent. However, the range of a pan-tropical taxon, for example, is inevitably interrupted by oceans: for the same reason a south temperate taxon has an even more disjunct range. To describe such species as discontinuous would have little significance. It would also be meaningless to describe as discontinuous a hydrophyte whose range is interrupted by very small gaps, when aquatic habitats are obviously separated by greater or smaller tracts of land. By discontinuity, then, is meant the presence in a geographical range of gaps which are appreciable in area and contain apparently suitable habitats. Numerous phytogeographers cogently argue that discontinuity indicates the senescence of a taxon, a view derived from Cain's (1944) Theory of Generic Cycles. During the decline of a taxon, the gradual contraction of its range may occur earlier in some regions than in others, producing, sooner or later, a discontinuous distribution.

Myriophyllum elatinoides is an example of a discontinuous south temperate hydrophyte. It occurs in New Zealand, Tasmania, the Falkland Islands, Chile and Argentina, extending at fair altitudes into the New World tropics through northern Brazil as far north as Mexico and Oregon: it is curiously absent from the Australian continent and southern Africa (Fernald, 1919). Mason (1959) expressed doubt about certain records of *Callitriche antarctica* which has been alleged to range from Tasmania through the subantarctic islands to subantarctic South America: this species might also be discontinuous.

A good example of discontinuity amongst tropical hydrophytes, *Ceratopteris pteridoides*, only came to light several years ago. The genus *Ceratopteris* has long been taxonomically critical. Some authors have considered it monotypic, whilst Benedict (1909) distinguished four species but did not altogether exclude the possibility of others. DeVol (1957) noted confusion between *C. pteridoides* and *C. thalictroides* especially amongst Asiatic records, an observation of some interest because *C. pteridoides* had hitherto been regarded as a New World species. DeVol found that *C. pteridoides* differs in growth habit, leaf form and petiole structure. It has floating, not emergent, sterile leaves which are deltoid and simple rather than repeatedly pinnate, as in *C. thalictroides*. He also found that the petiole of *C. pteridoides* is short and fleshy, broader above and tapering below whereas that of *C. thalictroides* is long and slender and rarely tapers. He pointed out that the absence of a well-developed annulus, a taxonomic criterion used to describe *C. pteridoides* by Benedict and others, is not a reliable character because all the eastern Asiatic specimens he examined in fact had a marked annulus. From his investigations in herbaria and in the field, DeVol concluded that material previously collected from localities in central China and continental south-east Asia belonged to *C. pteridoides*.

In her studies of the genus in Malaya, Johnson (1961) realised that DeVol's criteria could only be used when sterile leaves were preserved: most Malayan herbarium specimens comprise only fertile material. Whilst confirming DeVol's criteria of petiole length and width for sterile and transitional leaves, she showed that they are not applicable to fertile leaves but she did find it possible to distinguish fertile leaves of the two species by the presence or absence of webbing at the base of the ultimate lobes and by the degree of revolution of the leaf margin. In Malaya *C. pteridoides* has only been recorded from Penang and Singapore though *C. thalictroides* is generally distributed and common in many parts of the Archipelago (Johnson, *in litt.*).

From the studies of DeVol, Johnson, and earlier authors, *C. pteridoides* emerged as discontinuous between America and Asia: its distribution extends south of the tropics in Paraguay and the Chaco area of northern Argentina, and north of the tropics to north-eastern Florida, and to Pukow in central China (Fig. 11.5).

Another diagnostic type of discontinuity within the tropics, between Africa and Asia, is exemplified by *Nymphaea lotus*. This white waterlily ranges over much of the African continent, from the delta of the Nile south to northern Angola, Malawi and Madagascar, and west to Senegal. It also occurs in tropical India, and extends through the Malay Peninsula to Java and perhaps further east to northern Australia. *Tenagocharis latifolia* and *Vossia cuspidata* are similarly

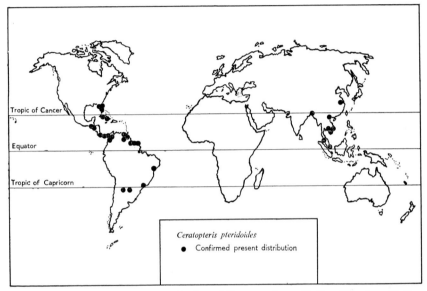

FIG. 11.5. The discontinuous distribution of *Ceratopteris pteridoides*. (Based on Mollweide's Interrupted Homolographic projection and compiled from data of DeVol, 1957, and Johnson, 1961.)

discontinuous between continental Africa and Asia, and absent from the New World tropics, but they differ from *Nymphaea lotus* in being absent also from Madagascar (af Rantzien, 1951b; van Steenis, 1954; Wild, 1961).

For 30 years or more, phytogeographers have intently focussed their gaze upon a group of amphi-Atlantic taxa which are apparently discontinuous between North America and Europe. These have been thoroughly discussed by, *inter alia*, Hultén (1958), Löve and Löve (1958a), Perring (1963) and by various contributors to a symposium in Reykjavik in 1962 (Löve and Löve, 1963). The attention of the earliest workers centred upon the so-called Hiberno–American hydrophytes which range widely in North America but are comparatively restricted, some extremely so, in western Europe: e.g. *Eriocaulon septangulare* which in Europe occurs only on the west coast of Ireland, and on Coll and Skye; *Potamogeton epihydrus*, confined to South Uist, off the west coast of Scotland (Heslop-Harrison, 1952); *Elodea nuttallii*, known from only two stations, in West Galway and the English Lake District (Bennett, 1914; Perring and Walters, 1962); and *Myriophyllum alterniflorum* var. *americanum*, recorded by Pugsley (1938) and Praeger (1938) in Loughs Neagh, Ree and Derg in Ireland but probably now present only in Lough Neagh and the adjacent Lough Beg (Clapham, 1962) (Fig. 11.6). With this group of taxa, some writers included three other western Irish species: the marsh plant *Sisyrinchium*

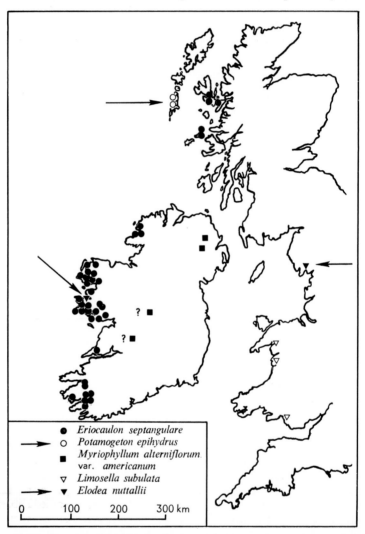

FIG. 11.6. The European (British) distribution of certain amphi-Atlantic hydrophytes. (Based on a Conical projection with two standard parallels, and compiled from data of Praeger, 1938; Heslop-Harrison, 1952; Hultén, 1958; Clapham, 1962; Perring and Walters, 1962.)

bermudiana (then known as *S. angustifolium*), which is naturalised elsewhere in Europe, the bog orchid *Spiranthes romanzoffiana*, native also in south Devon and a few sites in western Scotland, and the submerged *Najas flexilis*, which is also indigenous in the north-west of Britain and in north Germany, Sweden, Finland, Norway and central Russia (Fig. 11.11). Noting this fairly wide continental European range of *N. flexilis*, Heslop-Harrison (1953a) reasonably asked why *Lobelia dortmanna* should not be included in the group. This species has a northern and western distribution in the British Isles and ranges in continental Europe from about 68°N in Scandinavia south to western France (Tutin, 1962) (Fig. 11.7). *Limosella subulata* is another candidate for inclusion: in Europe it occurs only in a few stations in north and south Wales (Fig. 11.6) but in America extends from Labrador south to about 38°N, although it is absent from the Pacific States (Fassett, 1957; Warburg, 1962).

There are other amphi-Atlantic plants with the converse, 'mirror-image' type of asymmetrical distribution, i.e. extending throughout all or most of Europe but confined to the Atlantic coastal region of North America. Examples are *Potamogeton polygonifolius* which is widespread in Europe, including northwest Africa, but is confined to eastern North America, and the typical *Myriophyllum alterniflorum* which occurs throughout much of Europe east to central Russia, and in Iceland and Greenland, but in eastern North America is largely replaced by var. *americanum*. This group, like the Hiberno-American element, is not composed solely of hydrophytes: it also includes bog species such as *Drosera intermedia*. Moreover, its constituents vary in the extent of their American range, some being very narrowly confined, others more widely distributed. It is therefore apparent that the Hiberno–American plants form not an isolated anomalous group but part of a whole spectrum of distributional patterns, all discontinuous within the north temperate zone and showing various degrees of asymmetry across the Atlantic Ocean. It must also be realised that many more amphi-Atlantic taxa have attracted little curiosity since their distributions are more nearly symmetrical.

The possible origin of the unusual ranges of asymmetrical amphi-Atlantic plants has created tremendous argument. The fiercest controversy has raged around the question of whether the species have been present in the minor areas of their distribution since before or after the Ice Ages. So far as can be ascertained, all the taxa are truly native. *Eriocaulon septangulare* has been found in Quaternary fossil deposits of an age which eliminates the possibility of human introduction (Jessen, 1949). *Najas flexilis* and *Potamogeton polygonifolius* have been identified in deposits of inter-glacial as well as post-glacial age: *Myriophyllum alterniflorum* also may have survived the last glaciation (Backman, 1948; Godwin, 1956).

Most phytogeographers accept the idea of per-glacial survival and therefore regard the minor areas of these asymmetrical distributions as relics of more continuous ranges. Some writers have advocated that the plants may originally have migrated from the major area of their distribution across a hypothetical land bridge between Europe and America but Dahl (1963), Hultén (1958, 1963) and Einarsson (1964) have emphasised the paucity of geological and biological evidence that such a land connection could have existed in late Tertiary or Quaternary time. A second notion is that the European and North American ranges of amphi-Atlantic plants may have been linked through Siberia and Alaska during the great inter-glacial period. The adherents to both concepts

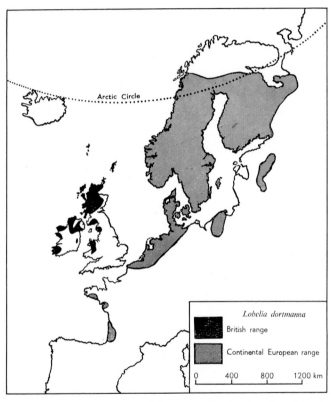

FIG. 11.7. The British and continental European distribution of *Lobelia dortmanna*. (Based on Bonne's projection, and compiled from data of Matthews, 1937, and Perring and Walters, 1962.)

ascribe the eventual disjunction of the range to the severe climate and ice sheets of the Pleistocene. Yet this hypothesis must apply to the symmetrical as well as the asymmetrical species. Now it may be argued that the symmetrical amphi-Atlantic plants existed through the Ice Ages in places south of the ice-sheets and then migrated northwards during the post-glacial period in both Europe and North America, attaining a similar range in each continent. However, the use of this reasonable argument for the asymmetrical species poses an awkward question: Why do these taxa not now occur outside the previously glaciated area in that continent where they have the minor part of their range ? (Heslop-Harrison, 1953a). *Najas flexilis*, for example, is distributed throughout both the Atlantic and Pacific regions of North America from about 50° to about 30°N, but in Europe its latitudinal range is from 62° to only about 51°N (Backman, 1948). If such species did survive the glacial period south of the ice-sheets it is indeed difficult to understand why they should persist at low latitudes in one continent but not in the other.

In the British sites, several of the asymmetrical species are abundant and vigorous, yet ecologically and geographically restricted. These paradoxical features suggest that in their minor areas these species could be races of low genetical variability. Heslop-Harrison (1953a) suggested that such races might be essentially local colonies derived from one or two pioneer individuals of recent (post-glacial) introduction, each colony thriving in habitats resembling those whence they originated but lacking the adaptability necessary for further adventive spread. He developed this thesis by reference to the migratory habits of the Greenland white-fronted goose, *Anser albifrons albifrons*, which breeds in summer in north-west Greenland and then migrates for the winter to Ireland or the basin of the St. Lawrence, occasionally to North Wales and north and west Scotland. Noting that these birds eat littoral aquatic plants, Heslop-Harrison considered it well within the bounds of possibility that seeds of various amphi-Atlantic species could be carried by the geese from North America via Greenland to western Europe and would there, in suitable habitats, give rise to local populations. In support of this he also drew attention to the fact that the most northerly station for *Sisyrinchium bermudiana* is within the Greenland breeding grounds of the geese.

From a very thorough appraisal of the evidence for the survival of plants and their dispersal by various agents, Löve (1963) recently concluded that very few species are likely to have been carried by birds across the Atlantic Ocean. Furthermore, she challenged the application of the long-distance dispersal hypothesis to *Eriocaulon* and *Sisyrinchium* on the interesting grounds that the Irish and American populations of each of these plants are distinct species. Some years ago, Godwin (1956) commented on the greater size of *Eriocaulon* pollen grains found in a western Irish fossil deposit by Jessen (1949) and produced by living Irish plants, compared with the grains of present American plants, and he suggested that the Irish and American plants might well belong to races of different chromosome number. The recent cytotaxonomical study by Löve and Löve (1958a) revealed that whereas the European *Eriocaulon septangulare* has a chromosome complement of 2n = 64, the North American plants have either 2n = 32, then distinguished as *E. pellucidum*, or 2n = 48, distinguished as *E. parkeri*. Similarly, Löve and Löve showed that whilst the North American specimens of *Sisyrinchium bermudiana* have 2n = 96, plants from Greenland have a complement of 2n = 32 and may belong to *S. albidum*, and those native in Ireland have 2n = 64 and might be segregated as *S. hibernicum*. It should be noted, however, that in a more recent study, Ingram (1964) found that Irish *S. bermudiana* is cytologically uniform with a complement of 2n = 88, which falls within the range 2n = 80 to 96 counted in American material of the species.

The conclusions reached by Godwin and the Löves are congruous with the notion of Praeger (1939) and Hultén (1958), that the western European populations probably survived the Ice Age in or near their present stations, not south of the glaciated area, and now represent relict endemic species, genetically impoverished by their per-glacial confinement and therefore ecologically restricted. On this hypothesis *Eriocaulon septangulare* and *Sisyrinchium bermudiana* would cease to be discontinuous taxa. Yet the evidence is not unequivocal. Some taxonomists do not accept *E. septangulare* (*sensu stricto*) and *S. hibernicum* as good species. Whether or not any of the other asymmetrical amphi-Atlantic taxa may comprise in its minor area a relict endemic species, truly distinct from its counterpart in the other continent, also remains to be established. The possibility seems very remote so far as *Limosella subulata* and *Najas flexilis* are concerned. Welsh and Canadian specimens of *L. subulata* are cytologically similar (with 2n = 20). British and European specimens of *N. flexilis* are apparently tetraploid (2n = 24), but tetraploids are also found, together with the less widespread diploids (2n = 12), amongst American populations of the species (Chase, 1947; Löve and Löve, 1958a).

Several hydrophytes exhibit discontinuous distributions which have no clearly defined pattern. *Aldrovanda vesiculosa* occurs in the warmer regions of Europe and north-east Asia, including Japan, and also in the Old World tropics, extending from central Africa through India and Timor to Australia. *Caldesia parnassifolia* has a somewhat similar range from warmer Europe and Egypt through India to the East Indies, China and northern Australia. The present anomalous distributions of *Brasenia schreberi*, *Salvinia natans* and *Trapa natans* are probably the result of extermination from certain areas during the glacial and post-glacial periods.

THE EXPANDING RANGES OF ADVENTIVE HYDROPHYTES

During historical time, especially the last hundred years or so, many aquatic vascular plants have been introduced to countries beyond their native range. The expansion of their adventive distribution, aided by various dispersal agents and sometimes accomplished by vegetative rather than sexual reproduction, has often had important biological and economic consequences. Some alien species have become naturalised throughout vast areas: their colonisation of new habitats, with which they are not in ecological equilibrium and in which indigenous competitors are sometimes deficient, has been insidious and often astoundingly rapid. Consequently these species have quickly become very serious weeds in many sites (see Chapter 13 for a further treatment of this topic). Numerous other aliens have not displayed so spectacular an expansion of range but their persistence, establishment and gradual spread are of no less phytogeographical and ecological interest.

A summary of the aquatic vascular plants recorded as aliens in various parts of the world is presented in Table 11.5.

TABLE 11.5   The adventive ranges of certain aquatic vascular plants[1]

Species	Adventive in:
A. Temperate Eurasian species introduced to North America and/or Australasia	
Apium nodiflorum	North America
Butomus umbellatus	E. Canada and N.E. United States
Callitriche intermedia	Australia and New Zealand
C. stagnalis	Australia and New Zealand
Glyceria maxima	Australia (Victoria) and New Zealand
Iris pseudacorus	Newfoundland, Canada, E. United States and New Zealand
Lythrum salicaria	E. Canada and N.E. United States
Najas minor	United States (Alabama, Tennessee, Illinois, West Virginia, New York)
Nymphoides peltata	E. United States (also Denmark and S. Sweden)
Potamogeton crispus	North America and New Zealand
†*Ranunculus aquatilis* (? *R. fluitans*)	New Zealand
Rorippa amphibia	North America
R. microphylla	Canada and N.E. United States
R. nasturtium-aquaticum	North America (also Central and South America), Australia (Victoria) and New Zealand
R. × sterilis	Canada and N.E. United States
Veronica anagallis-aquatica	E. United States
B. Temperate North American species introduced to Eurasia and/or Australasia	
Callitriche deflexa	Portugal
C. heterophylla	New Zealand
Eleocharis obtusa	N. Italy
E. olivacea	N. Italy
Elodea canadensis	British Isles, continental Europe, W. Siberia, Australia (Victoria, Tasmania) and New Zealand
Myriophyllum heterophyllum	England
Najas gracillima	N. Italy
Pontederia cordata	British Isles
‡*Potamogeton epihydrus*	England
Sagittaria rigida	England
Zizania aquatica	Japan, S.E. Asia and New Zealand
C. Neotropical or neotemperate species introduced to the Palaeotropics	
Alternanthera philoxeroides	W. Java, Burma and E. India
Bacopa erecta	Gambia, Guinea, Senegal and Sierra Leone
Eichhornia crassipes	Many parts of the palaeotropics (and California, S.E. United States, South Africa, Japan, E. Australia)

TABLE 11.5—*continued*

Species	Adventive in:
C. Neotropical or neotemperate species introduced to the Paleotropics—*continued*	
Hydrolea spinosa	W. Java
Limnobium stoloniferum	W. Java
Limnocharis flava	Ceylon, S. Burma, Thailand and W. Malaysia
Sagittaria lancifolia	W. Java
S. graminea var. *platyphylla*	Java
S. montevidensis	Tanzania and Java
S. subulata	Java
Salvinia auriculata	S. Asia and C. Africa (also S. Africa and warmer Europe)
D. Tropical and subtropical American species introduced to warm temperate America, Europe and/or Australasia	
Azolla caroliniana	W., C. and S. Europe
A. filiculoides	E. United States, S. England, Eire, W., C. and S. Europe
Egeria densa	Mexico, United States, England, France, Germany, Switzerland, Italy and New Zealand (also Kenya and Japan)
*Elodea ernstiae	England
Hydrocleys nymphoides	Warmer United States and New Zealand (also Japan)
Myriophyllum brasiliense	Warmer United States
Salvinia rotundifolia	Spain
E. Tropical and subtropical species of the Old World introduced to warm temperate America, Europe and/or Australasia	
Azolla pinnata	S. Europe
Blyxa japonica	N. Italy
Ceratophyllum muricatum	Bulgaria
Limnophila sessiliflora	Netherlands
Najas graminea	(England), N. Italy
Nelumbo nucifera	Mediterranean region and warmer United States
Ottelia alismoides	N. Italy
Salvinia natans	W. and S. Europe
Spirodela oligorhiza	United States (California, Florida, Louisiana, Illinois)
Trapa natans	N.E. United States and Australia
Vallisneria spiralis	England, Netherlands, Germany, France, Hungary, Australia and New Zealand

TABLE 11.5—*continued*

Species	Adventive in:
F. Southern African or Australasian species introduced to north and/or south temperate countries	
Aponogeton distachyos (S. African)	British Isles, W. Europe, Peru, Australia and New Zealand
Crassula helmsii (Australasian)	England
Lagarosiphon major (S. African)	England, Channel Islands, N.W. France, Switzerland, Italy and New Zealand
Myriophyllum verrucosum (Australian)	England
G. Miscellaneous other species	
Acorus calamus (native in S. and E. Asia and North America)	W., C. and N. Europe
Alisma plantago-aquatica (north temperate)	Australia, New Zealand, S. Africa, and Chile
Blysmus compressus (Eurasian)	Iraq
Calla palustris (north temperate except for W. Europe)	W. Europe
Carex acutiformis (north temperate)	Iraq
Lemna perpusilla (widespread)	Palestine and N. Italy
Mimosa pigra (tropical African and American)	Tropical Asia
Sagittaria trifolia (S. and E. Asiatic)	Australia, Hawaii, Fiji, Philippines, Borneo and Java
Stratiotes aloides (N.W. Asia and parts of Europe, including England and probably Wales)	Scotland, Ireland, France and Switzerland
Trapa bicornis (continental Asiatic)	W. Java
Wolffia arrhiza (Old World but very local)	Hungary

NOTES:

[1] Since no two species have exactly the same origin or adventive range, it is impossible to classify the species listed into really discrete groups. Thus, the arrangement in the above table is very arbitrary. Its only merit is that it perhaps reflects the climatic tolerance of many species and also the major migrations of human populations which may have aided the long-distance dispersal of some species.

† The identity of the *Ranunculus fluitans* mentioned by Allan (1936) and the *R. aquatilis* recorded by Cockayne (1921) as similarly alien in New Zealand in terms of the batrachian *Ranunculi* delimited by modern taxonomists is not clear.

‡ It remains to be demonstrated that the *Potamogeton epihydrus* introduced in northern England is truly conspecific with the native Hebridean populations of the species and with the *P. epihydrus* widely indigenous in North America. (See also pp. 389–94.)

* *Elodea callitrichoides* was recently recorded as naturalised in south-east England. Kent (1964) pointed out, however, that in the Longford River in Middlesex this plant is in fact the species distinguished by St. John (1963) as *E. ernstiae*, and suggested that other British populations are probably this species and not *E. callitrichoides*.

(Table compiled from data in Dunn, 1905; Cheeseman, 1906; Cockayne, 1921; Thomson, 1922; Allan, 1936, 1937; Backer, 1949, 1951b, f; Brenan and Chapple, 1949; van Steenis, 1949b, 1954; Koch, 1950, 1952; Howard and Lyon, 1951, 1952; Lawrence, 1951; af Rantzien, 1951b; Lohammar, 1955; Fassett, 1957; den Hartog, 1957a, b; Lousley, 1957b; Mason, 1959, 1960; Wood, 1959; Cody, 1961; Edwards, 1961; Hadac, 1961; Laundon, 1961; Schotsman, 1961a; St. John, 1961, 1963; Szaniszlo, 1961; Wild, 1961; Clapham, Tutin and Warburg, 1962; Daubs, 1962, 1965; Feuillade, 1962; Green, 1962; van Ooststroom and Reichgelt, 1962a, b, 1963; Wallace 1963, 1964; Corillion, 1964; Kent, 1964; Lawalrée, 1964; Tutin, 1964; Webb, 1964; Witmer, 1964; Maheshwari, 1965; Ant, 1966; Fore and Mohlenbrock, 1966; Winterringer, 1966).

Sufficient time has elapsed since certain species were first disseminated from their native range for them to have become firmly established in congenial habitats, often encroaching upon and even dominating the local aquatic indigenes. The extensive alien distribution which may be so attained is clearly exemplified by *Acorus calamus*, *Eichhornia crassipes*, *Elodea canadensis* and *Salvinia auriculata*, which are discussed fully elsewhere (pp. 360, 460, 473, 518). Certain other species of more recent introduction, such as *Alternanthera philoxeroides*, *Egeria densa*, *Lagarosiphon major* and *Limnocharis flava*, could become equally widely distributed in the near future if their present vigorous increase in several sites is any criterion.

In certain sites several aliens, such as *Egeria densa*, *Najas graminea* and *Vallisneria spiralis* in their British stations, have persisted for an appreciable time but have not spread further afield. *N. graminea*, for example, formed thriving colonies throughout a 0·4 km stretch of the Reddish Canal between Stockport and Manchester (Bailey, 1884) but did not spread from there and, indeed, subsequently became extinct (Weiss and Murray, 1909; Perring and Walters, 1962). It is pertinent to note that in the British sites colonised by these three aliens, the waters are, or were, artificially warmed by effluents discharged from nearby cotton-mills and factories. The confinement of the species to these unusual habitats is probably due to their inability to survive the low winter temperatures which generally prevail in natural waters elsewhere in the British Isles. Indeed, the average temperatures throughout the year in British waters are probably significantly lower than those experienced by these plants in their native tropical or warm temperate ranges.

The hypothesis that temperature is the prime factor controlling the distribution of these restricted aliens is supported by the observed behaviour of *Egeria densa* and *Myriophyllum verrucosum* in two British stations and by the successful spread of several species in European sites where the climate is notably milder. *E. densa* was first recorded as an alien in Britain in 1953, growing in a canal at Droylesden, near Manchester. Since then, one of the nearby cotton-mills has started to use electric power and in the absence of a warm-water effluent the temperature of the canal at this site has fallen and the colonies of *E. densa* no longer flower (Edwards, 1961). It will be interesting to see whether this species declines and disappears in the near future, as *Najas graminea* did just after the turn of the century. *Myriophyllum verrucosum*, an Australian species introduced to certain pools in a gravel-pit in southern England, also seems to be sensitive to low temperatures. Although it occurred in some quantity at this site in Bedfordshire during the years 1944 to 1946 it could not be found there again in 1947 or 1948, and Brenan and Chapple (1949) concluded it had probably suffered badly during the unusually severe frosts of the 1946–1947 winter.

In warmer localities in western Europe, however, *Egeria densa* and *Vallisneria spiralis*, and also the tropical and warm temperate *Limnophila sessiliflora* and *Lagarosiphon major* do thrive and spread in quite natural waters. *V. spiralis*, which extends as a native as far north as central France, has been known from 1955 in the R. Meuse near Liège. In 1960 it was found in the canal to Liège at Maastricht, and in 1962, to the north of this site, vast quantities of the plant were discovered in the overflow of the R. Meuse in the Bosscherveld (van Ooststroom and Reichgelt, 1962b, 1963). *Lagarosiphon major* is now known to occur in L. Maggiore, and in sites in the Channel Islands and north-western France. Since about 1944 it has also become established in the unheated water of gravel- and chalk-pits in warmer English counties, notably Middlesex, Bedfordshire, Surrey, Kent, Devon and Hampshire (Wallace, 1966; Dandy, *in litt.*; Westlake, *in litt.*). In the past 20 years, colonies of *Egeria densa* have become established in L. Maggiore, several German sites, and very recently in the R. Selune in Normandy and the valley of the Erdre (Loire) where they hinder navigation (Koch, 1950; Lousley, 1957b; Feuillade, 1962; Corillion, 1964).

Similar flourishing invasions by these last two adventives have been observed in the mild valleys and coastal plains of New Zealand (Mason, 1960). *Egeria densa* was first noticed in 1946 in the R. Waikato in North Island. By 1958 it had become the most common submerged plant in that river, forming extensive stands throughout a 56 km stretch downstream from Ngaruawahia, and also upstream in L. Whangape. In 1959 colonies were also seen scattered along part of the R. Thames near Hikutaia, to the north-east of Hamilton. *Lagarosiphon major* was first recorded as an alien in New Zealand in 1950, and during the subsequent 8 or 9 years seems to have spread rapidly from several probable sites of initial introduction. Mason (1960) found it to be especially common and sometimes very troublesome as a weed in the middle R. Waikato downstream of L. Hamilton, in the Rotorua district of South Auckland, in central Taranaki, in the Hutt valley near Wellington, and near Blenheim just across the Cook Strait in South Island. In commenting on the present aggression displayed by *E. densa* and *L. major* and their superior competitive powers against the older-established alien, *Elodea canadensis*, Mason suggested that the prevailing temperatures in New Zealand waters may be more nearly optimal for the former species than for the cool temperate *E. canadensis*. She partly attributed the adventive success of all three species, and of a fourth alien—*Potamogeton crispus*, to their ability to colonise deep, shaded or swift-flowing waters, to which habitats the sparse native flora of submerged angiosperms seems ill-adapted.

It is worthy of note that a few species have failed to expand their adventive range even in areas possessing suitable potential habitats and a prevailing climate closely resembling that of their indigenous range. *Potamogeton epihydrus*, discussed earlier as a possible amphi-Atlantic plant and native in the Outer Hebrides, has been established as an alien in the R. Calder and canals near Halifax in northern England for over 40 years but it has not spread significantly beyond these stations. Two similar examples are afforded by the temperate North American *Callitriche heterophylla* in New Zealand, and the warm temperate and tropical American *Sagittaria montevidensis* in Tanzania and Java. The concept of temperature sensitivity can scarcely be invoked to explain the confinement of these species. The alien populations may perhaps be clones or local biotypes of low genetical variability, lacking the dispersal adaptations, edaphic tolerance or competitive ability which might aid their invasion of habitats already occupied by indigenes. As an adventive in New Zealand,

14

Vallisneria spiralis was reported by Cockayne (1921) to occur only in L. Takapuna, near Auckland City, the abundant dense colonies being allegedly derived from a single plant introduced in 1885. It is conceivable that in its northern English alien stations, *Potamogeton epihydrus* may consist of genetically impoverished clones, as indeed it may in its possibly relict endemic range in the Hebrides. It is difficult, however, to believe that the same applies to *Callitriche heterophylla* or *Sagittaria montevidensis* for these are both notoriously plastic species of wide ecological amplitude in their native habitats. Furthermore, it must be acknowledged that enforced vegetative reproduction and clone formation has in no way curtailed the invasive powers of numerous other adventives, such as *Acorus calamus, Alternanthera philoxeroides, Egeria densa, Elodea canadensis* and *Lagarosiphon major*.

Little is known of the precise mode of introduction of most alien hydrophytes, or of the agents and environmental factors which facilitate their subsequent spread. Viable fruits or seeds of certain species may be accidentally transported with agricultural products. *Najas graminea*, for example, may have been introduced to northern Italy in the company of rice from Egypt: in both regions it is a ricefield weed (Ascherson, 1874). It is thought to have arrived at its British station, near Manchester, with Egyptian cotton, the fruits or seeds being separated from the raw cotton by the carding engines or in the blowing rooms and subsequently being swept, blown or drained into the adjacent canal. Bailey (1884) discovered that although Egyptian cotton was not commonly imported at that time to the Manchester and Stockport districts, one mill on the banks of the Reddish Canal did in fact use it. He also surmised that *N. graminea* and other alien species of the same genus might appear in mill-ponds and canals in the Bolton district, a few miles to the north, where Egyptian cotton was much more widely used, but there are no records of this having happened.

Propagules of numerous aliens may similarly have been dispersed to other continents with the irrigated crops amongst which they frequently grow. *Ceratophyllum muricatum, Alisma plantago-aquatica, Bacopa erecta, Blyxa japonica, Eleocharis obtusa, E. olivacea, Limnocharis flava, Mimosa pigra, Najas gracillima, Ottelia alismoides* and *Sagittaria graminea* var. *platyphylla* are all conspicuous weeds of rice-paddies and irrigation schemes in the warmer countries of the world (Koch, 1952; Wild, 1961). Fruits and seeds of aliens originating in America may have been introduced to the palaeotropics in packing materials during the Second World War, as Maheshwari (1965) suggested for the appearance of *Alternanthera philoxeroides* in India.

Myriophyllum verrucosum may have reached its British station as seeds imprisoned in the caked mud adhering to imported Australian wool. Waste shoddy from this source was apparently used by farmers and market gardeners in the vicinity of the Bedfordshire gravel-pits at the time the plant was introduced (Brenan and Chapple, 1949).

It is likely that many aquatic aliens have been introduced and further distributed as a result of accidental escape from cultivation or deliberate planting. *Acorus calamus*, for example, almost certainly reached many parts of western

Europe by virtue of its medicinal value and consequent propagation in physic gardens. In both temperate and tropical regions *Rorippa nasturtium-aquaticum, R. × sterilis, Sagittaria trifolia, Trapa* spp. and *Zizania aquatica* are grown locally as human food crops. Similarly, cultivation of *Limnocharis flava,* and species of *Sagittaria* and *Trapa,* along with *Azolla, Pistia* and *Eichhornia crassipes,* as fodder for pigs and other livestock has undoubtedly assisted the spread of these plants in lowland south-east Asia. Escape from botanic gardens is known or strongly suspected to have been the source of introduction of several species to particular regions, e.g. *Azolla caroliniana* and *A. filiculoides* to parts of France (p. 358); *Elodea canadensis* to certain English counties (p. 361); *Salvinia auriculata* to parts of Ceylon (p. 475); and *Eichhornia crassipes, Limnocharis flava, Sagittaria lancifolia* and *S. graminea* var. *platyphylla* which all spread through Java following their escape from the Buitenzorg (Bogor) Botanic Gardens (Backer, 1951f; van Steenis, 1954; den Hartog, 1957a).

The European *Iris pseudacorus* was originally introduced to Canada as a garden subject. From the establishment and propagation of rhizomes unearthed by floods or discarded in rubbish it has spread widely, aided by the production of abundant seeds, and now appears thoroughly naturalised in many freshwater and moist habitats. First recorded as an escaped adventive in 1911 in Newfoundland, it had appeared also in Nova Scotia by 1915 and during the next 25 years colonies were found established in British Columbia, Prince Edward Island, Quebec and Ontario. In 1953 it was discovered for the first time in Manitoba, at a site west of Winnipeg. In recent years it seems to have become particularly widespread in Ontario where it is now known to occur in eleven counties (Cody, 1961). It is also adventive in the eastern United States, from Massachusetts south to Virginia and west to Wisconsin (Fassett, 1957).

The introduction and dispersal of the Eurasian *Butomus umbellatus* in the St. Lawrence basin and around the Great Lakes may also have been aided by its cultivation as an ornamental plant. This species was first collected in 1905 from the St. Lawrence R. in Quebec, at which site it had probably occurred for at least 8 years. By 1930, colonies had become established around much of the southern end of L. Champlain east of the Adirondack Mountains, and at the western end of L. Erie. During the following two decades the plant appeared on the eastern shore of L. St. Clair and gradually spread along the southern shore of L. Erie, reaching the eastern (Ontario) end by 1948: it also extended further along the St. Lawrence to Montreal, along the Ottawa River and Rideau Canal in Ontario, around L. Champlain in Vermont, and in the area of Cayuga L. in New York State. Since 1950 it has become more firmly entrenched around Detroit, and has appeared and spread in various sites just south of the Strait of Mackinac in Michigan, further west in Wisconsin, and further south in Illinois and Indiana (Core, 1941; Gaiser, 1949; Witmer, 1964).

Aponogeton distachyos, Hydrocleys nymphoides, Lythrum salicaria, Nelumbo nucifera, Nymphoides peltata and *Pontederia cordata* are all frequently cultivated in ornamental lakes, pools and hothouses, whilst various species of *Azolla, Egeria, Elodea, Lagarosiphon, Lemna, Limnophila, Myriophyllum, Sagittaria, Salvinia, Spirodela* and *Vallisneria* are common aquarium subjects. Most of these plants have appeared as adventives in regions of the world where water gardening and the aquarium hobby are most popular. It seems very likely that the increasing traffic in such exotic plants will yield in the near future yet more additions to the already long list of aquatic aliens.

THE QUATERNARY HISTORY OF CERTAIN HYDROPHYTES IN
NORTH TEMPERATE COUNTRIES

(With Special Reference to Restriction of their British and European Ranges)

Most fossil plants, whether petrified or compressed, occur as intact or fragmentary leaves, stems, cones, seeds or spores which may have suffered considerable alteration of form during preservation. The identification of such fragmentary material is inevitably difficult and sometimes very much open to question, especially if based mainly or entirely on vegetative organs. The study and identification of fossil hydrophytes are further hindered by the deficiency of resistant woody parts. Soft vegetative organs and flowers rarely withstand preservation: three exceptional examples are the male flowers of *Myriophyllum alterniflorum* found in late-glacial deposits at Hawks Tor in Cornwall (Conolly *et al.*, 1950), the turions of *Potamogeton* sp. recovered at Kilteely in Co. Limerick (Jessen, 1949) and the fragmented shoots of *Myriophyllum* sp. found at Nazeing in Essex (Allison *et al.*, 1952). For the most part, however, hydrophytes occur in fossil deposits as the resistant and relatively hard fruits, seeds, pollen grains and spores. The mericarps of *Hippuris vulgaris*, the smooth seeds of *Menyanthes trifoliata* and the pyrenes of *Potamogeton* spp. are amongst the most abundant and characteristic of all Quaternary plant remains (Godwin, 1956). Owing to the possibility of dispersal of both wind- and water-borne propagules, the site of fossil material may not necessarily indicate that the species was a constituent of the contemporary flora of that precise locality. If the fossil remains are abundant in many widespread sites the range of the species in a particular geological period may be described with reasonable validity. Especial caution is required, however, when the remains are few and their sites isolated, and when the present distribution of the taxon is anomalous or markedly restricted: conclusions cannot be based solely on the absence of a plant from a particular region.

Cretaceous and early Tertiary records of hydrophytes are very scanty: one of the few reliable finds comprised reproductive organs of an extinct species of *Azolla* silicified in a block of chert from the Eocene Deccan beds of India (Sahni, 1941). In the north temperate zone little is known of aquatic angiosperms, or even aquatic pteridophytes, before the Eocene period. During this period and the subsequent Oligocene and Miocene, the climate of Europe and North America was tropical and warm temperate, and the overall floras consequently bore little resemblance to those of today. In the British Isles over 70 per cent of the Eocene genera were plants now typical of Malaysia, about 20 per cent are now West Indian and Central American and some 4 per cent now characterise southern Europe. However, the swamp communities of that time, revealed in the London clay deposits, did include four familiar aquatic genera: *Alisma*, *Phragmites*, *Potamogeton* and *Sparganium* (Matthews, 1955), and in the Headon beds, of late Eocene age, *Salvinia natans* and seeds of the now extinct *Stratiotes headonensis* were found (Chandler, 1923). In North America, *Equisetum*, *Lemna*, *Myriophyllum*, *Nymphaea*, *Pontederia*, *Potamogeton*, *Salvinia*, *Sparganium* and *Typha* have all been identified in the Eocene carbonaceous shales of Gosiute Lake in Wyoming (Bradley, 1963), and the horned fruits of *Trapa* have been recovered from the Eocene Wilcox beds in Alabama (Seward, 1933). During the Oligocene and Miocene, the flora changed but was still essentially exotic, some 71 per cent of the genera now occurring in China and Japan. However, the proportion of Mediterranean taxa increased and there appeared numerous genera now found in northern Europe. In the British Isles fossil deposits at Bembridge, Isle of Wight, have yielded several Oligocene hydrophytes, including *Aldrovanda*, *Azolla*, *Brasenia*, *Potamogeton*, *Sparganium* and *Stratiotes*. The Miocene flora is better known from central Europe than Britain: it apparently included the tropical genus *Nelumbo*, which also occurred in Hungary in Oligocene time and as far north as Canada in the Eocene period (Seward, 1933; and see Fig. 11.2).

During the Pliocene period in Europe and North America, the climate steadily deteriorated and the flora was profoundly redistributed. As conditions became colder the exotic species disappeared and species that are now still native increased, so that by the end of the Pliocene the flora of the British Isles and western Europe was markedly similar to that at the present time. Hydrophytes are well represented in Pliocene deposits: at Castle Eden and Pakefield in Suffolk, *Alisma plantago-aquatica*, *Ceratophyllum demersum*, *Hippuris vulgaris*, *Najas minor* and *N. marina*, *Nuphar lutea*, *Nymphaea alba*, several species of *Potamogeton* and batrachian *Ranunculus*, *Sparganium erectum*, *Trapa natans* and *Zannichellia palustris* have all been found, whilst *Brasenia schreberi*, *Najas flexilis*, *Sagittaria sagittifolia* and *Stratiotes aloides*, *inter alia*, are known from similar deposits near Frankfurt (Backman, 1951).

The Pliocene climatic changes culminated in the advance of the ice-sheets over north-west Europe and North America. Some hydrophytes probably became extinct on the first approach of glacial conditions: for example, the exotic *Nelumbo* disappeared from Europe and parts of North America, and both *Aldrovanda* and *Brasenia* vanished from Britain. Others persisted, perhaps surviving the vicissitudes of the Pleistocene Ice Ages in southern and western Europe, and migrating northwards again as the climate improved during each inter-glacial period. At some stage between successive glaciations the climate evidently became warmer than it is now, for inter-glacial deposits in both Britain and continental Europe have yielded the remains of several thermophilous hydrophytes. For instance, several extinct species of *Azolla* and *Euryale* have been found in the Tegelen clays in Holland, *Euryale ferox* at Lichvin in Russia, *Aldrovanda vesiculosa* and *Brasenia schreberi* in several continental deposits, and *Azolla filiculoides*, *Najas graminea*, *Najas minor*, *Salvinia natans* and *Trapa natans* at various British and continental sites (Backman, 1951; West, 1953; Godwin, 1956; and see Fig. 11.8). The more typical temperate hydrophytes such as *Ceratophyllum demersum, Myriophyllum spicatum, Nuphar, Nymphaea,* several species of *Potamogeton* and batrachian *Ranunculus* also occurred in inter-glacial floras.

During perhaps the most recent Ice Age, some of the thermophilous hydrophytes completely vanished from Europe whilst others were forced to retreat but managed to survive in the south and east. *Azolla, Brasenia, Euryale*

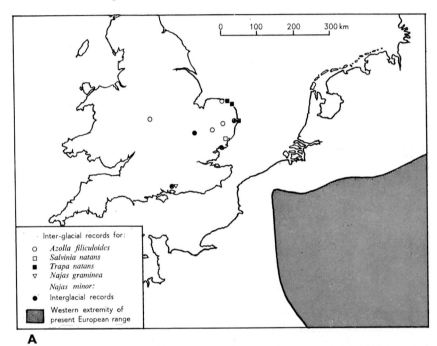

A

FIG. 11.8. A, The inter-glacial records of certain species now extinct in Britain, and the present western European distribution of one of these (*Najas minor*). (Based on a Conical projection with two standard parallels, and compiled from data of Reid, 1899; Backman, 1951; West, 1953; Godwin, 1956.) (B on facing page.)

and *Najas graminea,* for example, became extinct in Europe. Species of *Azolla* are now known only as aliens. *Najas graminea* has similarly been reintroduced to northern Italy and one temporary station in Britain, but as a native plant it is restricted to the tropics and subtropics of the Old World. Although eliminated from Europe, *Brasenia schreberi* survived in the New World, where it now extends north from central America and the West Indies through the southern United States to Alaska in the west and Prince Edward Island in the east—a remarkable latitudinal range, whilst in the Old World it is confined to the tropical and warm temperate regions of eastern Asia, Africa and Australia (Wood, 1959). *Euryale ferox* is today known only in India, southern and eastern Asia. *Aldrovanda vesiculosa* retreated but did not become extinct in Europe: it still extends eastward from southern France through Asia to Japan, but is now primarily tropical and subtropical. *Najas minor, Salvinia natans* and *Trapa natans* all disappeared from the British Isles but survived on the continental mainland. *Salvinia natans* is now indigenous in warmer regions of Europe,

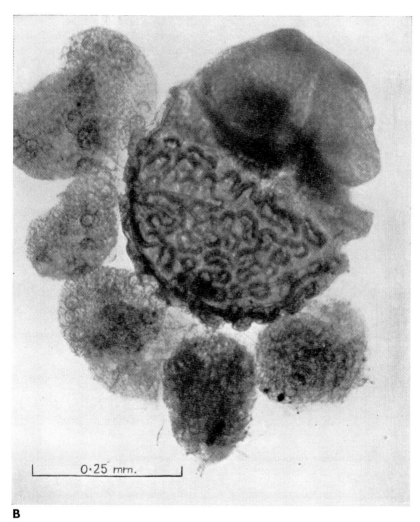

0·25 mm.

B

FIG. 11.8. B, Fossil megaspore of *Azolla filiculoides* from an inter-glacial deposit at Hoxne, Suffolk, England. The collapsed inner wall of the megaspore is visible beneath the sculptured perisporium. The lower half of the megaspore is surrounded by eight microsporic massulae with glochidia. Two of the three alveolar 'floats' of the megaspore are visible at the top of the photograph. (From West, 1953; by courtesy of the author, the editors of *New Phytologist*, and Blackwell Scientific Publications Ltd., Oxford.)

Algeria and Persia: some of its northerly stations, as in Holland, are due to reintroduction.

The history of the north temperate floras, especially those of the British Isles and western continental Europe, is incomparably better known for the recent period since the last glaciation than for all previous geological time. This is largely because of the very intensive studies of post-glacial fossil deposits by Godwin, Jessen, Erdtman, Iversen and Troels-Smith, *inter alia*, and the spectacular use these palaeobotanists have made of pollen analysis. With criteria of microspore morphology, it is now possible to make specific identification of many angiosperm remains from Quaternary deposits. These various researches have permitted the construction of a Quaternary time scale and revealed the principal floristic changes since the last Ice Age. The post-glacial period comprised three main phases: a phase of increasing warmth as the ice-sheets withdrew, a phase of maximum warmth (the post-glacial climatic optimum), and a phase of decreasing warmth culminating in the conditions of today; i.e. a climatic rhythm similar to that of each inter-glacial period. The nature of aquatic habitats and the conditions of preservation of fossil remains have so favoured hydrophytes that the post-glacial history of many species is now excellently documented. As the last ice-sheets disintegrated and retreated they left behind in the British Isles and on the continental mainland a multitude of lakes, ponds, bogs and fens in which there thrived a remarkably varied hydrophyte flora, some members of which had probably survived the last glaciation whilst a few may even have persisted from much older Tertiary floras (Table 11.6).

TABLE 11.6   Ancient indigenous hydrophytes of the British Isles

These species have been native in the British Isles since late-glacial time: some may have been per-glacial survivors.

Alisma plantago-aquatica	*Potamogeton obtusifolius*
Ceratophyllum demersum	*P. pectinatus*
Eleocharis palustris	*P. polygonifolius*
Hippuris vulgaris	*P. praelongus*
Isoetes lacustris	*P. pusillus*
Littorella uniflora	*Scheuchzeria palustris*
Menyanthes trifoliata	*Schoenoplectus lacustris*
Myriophyllum alterniflorum	*S. tabernaemontani*
M. spicatum	*Sparganium angustifolium*
M. verticillatum	*S. emersum*
Nuphar lutea	*S. erectum*
Nymphaea alba	*S. minimum*
Oenanthe aquatica	*Stratiotes aloides*
Phragmites communis	*Subularia aquatica*
Potamogeton alpinus	*Typha angustifolia*
P. gramineus	*T. latifolia*
P. natans	*Zannichellia palustris*

(Table compiled from data in Reid, 1899; Jessen & Farrington, 1938; Jessen, 1949; Conolly *et al.*, 1950; Mitchell, 1951, 1953; Godwin, 1956.)

The distribution of some indigenous species, which are apparently sensitive to increasing warmth or cold, has changed markedly during post-glacial time.

It is believed that *Potamogeton filiformis*, for example, prefers a cool temperate climate and that it retreated northwards as the British Isles became warmer early in the post-glacial period. At present *P. filiformis* does not occur in England: it is distributed in Scotland from Berwick and Ayr northwards and in Ireland north of about 53° 30′ N; it also occurs in Anglesey. Dandy and Taylor (1946) reported a new *Potamogeton*, named *P. × suecicus*, in the Rivers Ure, Wharf and Tweed, which appeared to be a hybrid of *P. pectinatus* and *P. filiformis*, although the latter is now absent from these rivers (Fig. 11.9). The apparent hybrid was also found in the Outer Hebrides and north-east Scotland, but these stations are all within the present range of *P. filiformis*. Using criteria such as the structure of the leaf apex, leaf sheath, endodermal cells and the number of vascular bundles in the stele, Bance (1946) compared the hybrid with its probable parents and her conclusions supported Dandy and Taylor's identification. The notion that *P. filiformis* suffered an early post-glacial northward restriction, suggested by its absence from the hybrid's stations in

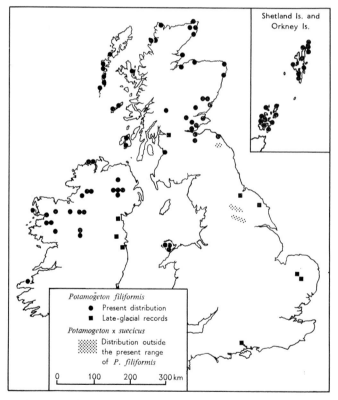

FIG. 11.9. The past and present British distribution of *Potamogeton filiformis*, and the occurrence of the hybrid *P. × suecicus* south of the present range of *P. filiformis*. (Based on a Conical projection with two standard parallels, and compiled from data of Dandy and Taylor, 1946; Godwin, 1956; Perring and Walters, 1962.)

14*

north-east England, is reinforced by the discovery of fossil material of *P. filiformis* in late-glacial deposits in Durham, Yorkshire, Norfolk, Hampshire and eastern Ireland, all south of its present range (Godwin, 1956; and see Fig. 11.9).

Nuphar pumila seems to have suffered similar northward restriction: it has become extinct in southern Europe except in montane or subalpine stations, as in the Vosges, where relict populations have survived in local cold microclimates. The same trend is apparent in the British Isles where the species is now largely confined to the Scottish Highlands, with two relict southern stations in Merioneth and Shropshire (Fig. 11.10). The hypothesis of post-glacial restriction is supported by the occurrence of presumed hybrids (*N.* × *spennerana*) between *N. pumila* and the more southern lowland *N. lutea*, in stations south of the present range of *N. pumila*. These hybrids could have originated from interbreeding as the range of *N. lutea*, immigrating from the south, temporarily overlapped that of *N. pumila*, retreating north as the climate ameliorated. In a few upland stations, such as Chartners Lough in Northumberland, where both parents are now absent, the conditions may subsequently have favoured neither parent and the intermediate nature of the hybrid may, together with vigorous vegetative reproduction, have been of adaptive value (Heslop-Harrison, Y., 1953, 1955b, c). Fossil evidence suggests that *Rumex*

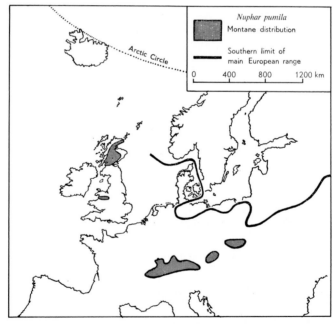

FIG. 11.10. The European distribution of *Nuphar pumila*. (Based on Bonne's projection, and compiled from data of Matthews, 1937; Heslop-Harrison, Y, 1953; Perring and Walters, 1962).

aquaticus may have retreated like *Nuphar pumila*. Its only native station in Britain appears to be the shores of Loch Lomond in Scotland, where it was discovered in 1935 (Lousley, 1939), but fossil remains have been unearthed south of this point (Godwin, 1956). *Sparganium angustifolium* and *Subularia aquatica* also withdrew northward in the British Isles during post-glacial time (Matthews, 1955; Godwin, 1956). It is interesting to note, in contrast, that another northern species, *Littorella uniflora*, was apparently unaffected by even

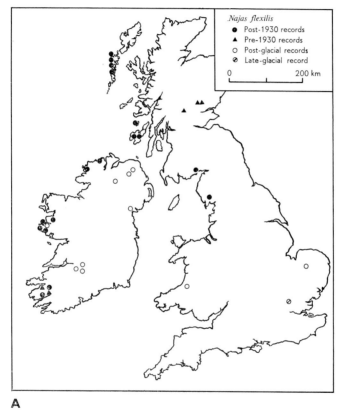

A

FIG. 11.11. A, The past and present distribution of *Najas flexilis* in the British Isles. (B on p. 410.)

the climatic optimum, as shown by Jessen's (1949) record of the species from a zone VI deposit in Londonderry and Blackburn's (1952) similar record from Neasham in Durham.

There is substantial evidence that the present narrow European range of *Najas flexilis*, noticed earlier in the context of amphi-Atlantic taxa, was created by post-glacial restriction. Scandinavian and British fossil records suggest that this species spread widely as the climate improved after the last glaciation, and reached its highest frequency and extent during the Boreal period. During subsequent time, as conditions became cooler, it retreated to areas where a more oceanic climate persists. Thus, whereas in the British Isles it withdrew northward and westward from Cardiganshire and east and central Ireland, its retreat in Scandinavia was southward and eastward towards the southern shores of the Baltic (Praeger, 1939; Backman, 1948; Deevey, 1949; and see Fig. 11.11).

Numerous species which are now rare in, or absent from, the north of the British Isles and continental Europe apparently migrated southwards during later post-glacial time, as the climatic optimum waned and conditions in the north became cooler. The fossil record of both *Ceratophyllum demersum* and *C. submersum* includes sites far to the north of their present northern limits (Backman, 1943). The distribution of *Nymphaea alba* seems to have contracted southwards in a similar way, since hybrids between it and the related *N. candida* have been found north of its present northern limit (Godwin, 1956).

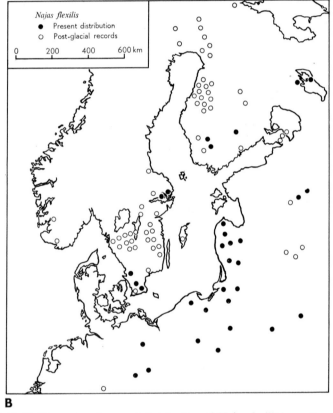

B

FIG. 11.11. B, The past and present distribution of *Najas flexilis* in north-west continental Europe. (Both A and B based on a Conical projection with two standard parallels, and compiled from data of Matthews, 1937; Backman, 1948; Godwin, 1956; Hultén, 1958; Perring and Walters, 1962.)

In continental Europe the thermophilous *Najas minor* and *Trapa natans*, eliminated from the British Isles by the glaciation, spread as conditions ameliorated, but as the climatic optimum waned they again suffered severe restriction. *Najas minor* retreated southwards from northern Russia and parts of Finland: it now extends from Russia through eastern and central Europe but reaches no further towards Britain than about 3°E in France (Backman, 1951; and see Fig. 11.8). *Trapa natans* also became restricted and now has a most anomalous distribution, occurring mainly in warmer stations in central and southern Europe, southern and eastern Asia, North Africa, and tropical Africa from Sudan and Portuguese Guinea south to Natal (Wild, 1961). Its extermination in parts of Europe was probably not solely due to climatic deterioration because although it disappeared from Belgium and Switzerland living plants still occurred in the nineteenth century in the north of Scania. These plants differed somewhat from the usual continental form and might have been relict local biotypes. The use of the fruits for food and the gradual drying-up of lakes and ponds may have contributed to the species' withdrawal in Europe (Areschoug, 1873). Heslop-Harrison and Blackburn (1946) found a single fruit of *T. natans* amidst debris of *Potamogeton pectinatus* on the shore of Loch Ceann a' Bhaigh on South Uist in the Outer Hebrides. They obtained from the peat adhering to the fruit a pollen count which agreed closely with that from zone VII in a peat profile sampled 3·2 km to the north-west. Heslop-Harrison and Blackburn therefore suggested that *Trapa natans* was in fact still living in the lowlands to the west during Atlantic time. Since at this time its range was contracting in Europe, and because the Hebridean specimen was enclosed in a *Sphagnum-Calluna* peat and not the calcareous mud that normally adheres to both fossil and living fruits, this Scottish record must be treated with great caution (Godwin, 1956).

Changes in the altitudinal distribution of plants have received far less study than changes in their areal distribution. It is likely that plants sensitive to cold achieved their greatest altitudinal range during the warmest phase of post-glacial time, and that subsequently they have retreated to lower stations whereas northern montane plants (e.g. *Nuphar pumila*) have ascended to greater heights. In Britain, for example, the vegetative organs of *Phragmites communis* have been found abundant in zone VI peat deposits at Malham in Yorkshire although this species does not now occur in the emergent flora of Malham Tarn. It now ascends no higher than about 420 m in the Pennines but fossil remains indicate that it reached at least 670 m during the post-glacial climatic optimum (Pigott and Pigott, 1963).

Three other hydrophytes which have apparently suffered post-glacial restriction merit brief consideration. The submerged *Najas marina*, almost cosmopolitan in overall distribution, now reaches no further north in continental Europe than the extreme south of Norway, southern Finland and southern Sweden. In both Scandinavia and the British Isles it achieved its most extensive northward and westward spread during the climatic optimum and since then has become severely restricted, surviving, like *Najas minor*, mainly in warmer southern and eastern stations (Backman, 1941). In the British Isles its eastward withdrawal resulted in its extinction in Ireland and survival only in the Norfolk Broads (Fig. 11.12). In contrast to similarly confined species, *Najas marina* was probably limited principally by its requirement of a high electrolyte concentration rather than by post-glacial climatic deterioration. From a comparison of one brackish-water and eight fresh water habitats in Sweden, Forsberg and Forsberg (1961) found the species cannot accumulate sufficient

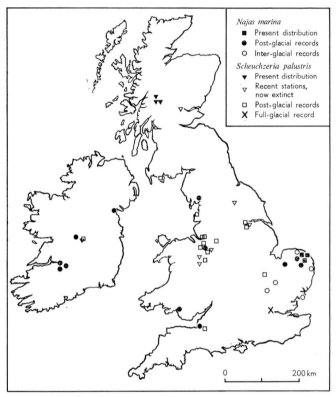

FIG. 11.12. The past and present British distributions of *Najas marina* and *Scheuchzeria palustris*. (Based on a Conical projection with two standard parallels, and compiled from data of Sledge, 1949; Barry & Jermy, 1952; Godwin, 1956; Perring and Walters, 1962; Tallis and Birks, 1965.)

electrolytes when the concentration falls below a certain minimum, approximately equivalent to an average conductivity of 300 μmho/cm^2. Barry and Jermy (1952) similarly observed that in Norfolk *Najas marina* occurs in water of mean pH about 8, with a salinity range 85 to 2800 ppm NaCl, and an alkalinity range 100 to 240 ppm CaCO$_3$—the minima of these ranges corresponding to a conductivity of about 300 μmho/cm^2.

Scheuchzeria palustris resembles *Potamogeton filiformis* and *Najas flexilis* in its recent northward retreat. It is a cold north temperate plant occurring sparsely north of the Arctic Circle in Finland and Scandinavia, but mainly distributed between 40° and 60°N. It reaches southward only at high altitudes as in the Pyrenees and the Alps. It is absent from western France, the Mediterranean region, most of the Iberian region, Iceland, Greenland, and areas of continental North America and eastern Asia, and is thus markedly discontinuous. Fossil evidence suggests that in Europe it spread during post-glacial time from an initial centre in the Netherlands (Jessen, 1935; Tallis and Birks, 1965). In the British Isles (Fig. 11.12) it now occurs only on Rannoch Moor in Scotland, having disappeared from Somerset and Huntingdonshire in southern England, from Shropshire, Cheshire, Derbyshire, Lancashire and Yorkshire in northern England, from Wigtown in Scotland and from Offaly in Ireland (Clapham and Godwin, 1948; Sledge, 1949; Tallis and Birks, 1965).

The autecology of *S. palustris* is not yet well understood. It is typically an emergent or semi-submerged plant of permanently wet peat bogs at low to moderate altitudes. Yet it often seems to succeed in only a few of the potentially suitable habitats in an area. Its water requirement seems to be so high that it cannot grow if the habitat dries out for even a very short period. The post-glacial and recent diminution of range have probably been caused by the increasing dryness of the habitats as a result of natural accumulation of organic matter and fall in the water table, and by the artificial drainage of many boggy areas (Sledge, 1949). The macroscopic remains of the cosmopolitan *Cladium mariscus*, like those of *S. palustris*, often form a diagnostic type of peat: they reached a high frequency in Atlantic time. In Scandinavia the species became restricted during Sub-boreal time with the onset of colder conditions, but it apparently persisted in the milder oceanic climate of the British Isles, although it has recently diminished, like *S. palustris*, as a result of reclamation of bogs and fens, and is now abundant only in Norfolk and parts of western and central Ireland (Conway, 1937, 1942; Godwin, 1956).

The ranges of several other vascular hydrophytes in the British Isles and continental Europe seem to be changing at the present time. *Baldellia ranunculoides, Damasonium alisma* and the calcicolous *Hydrocharis morsus-ranae* and *Stratiotes aloides* are all local and probably diminishing plants, whilst *Luronium natans* seems to be increasing, at least in Britain, where its original local range in Wales and north-west England has extended to Ayr and recently Argyll in Scotland (Wallace, 1964). These taxa clearly merit thorough autecological and geographical study.

12

The Growth of Hydrophyte Communities and their Interaction with the Aquatic Environment

There have been very few dynamic sociological studies of aquatic plant communities. Indeed, the preliminary vegetational surveys, on which any analysis of interaction between community and environment must be based, are still lacking for many types of aquatic habitat, especially in the tropics. Despite this inadequacy it must be admitted that ecological studies of the classical descriptive type, however detailed, create an unnaturally static and clear-cut impression of community structure, principally because of the inevitable imposition of some form of analytical classification upon a continuum of intergrading populations. This fault tends to be magnified by synoptic accounts, as in this book, where limitations of space allow only summaries of community types and preclude a comprehensive review of specific examples. Communities are rarely isolated discrete entities: they merge into an ecological spectrum of both species and life forms. The more gradual the transitions, the less conspicuous the gross zonation of vegetation in a habitat may appear. The natural flux in community composition from season to season, year to year and site to site becomes apparent only through extensive quantitative sampling of populations at regular intervals over a long period of time.

The probable influences of certain physical and chemical factors of the aquatic environment upon the life activities of vascular hydrophytes were examined in Chapter 2 and various examples of the resulting distribution and ecological zonation of aquatic vegetation were outlined. In subsequent chapters the biology of the different life forms has been discussed in some detail. It is now opportune to attempt, so far as available data permit, to assess the patterns of change in hydrophyte communities and the nature and extent of their influence upon the environment and the other organisms inhabiting it. In particular, it is of considerable interest to know whether the spatial sequence of vegetational zones typical of sheltered aquatic habitats truly represents a temporal succession of plant communities, as is often stated, and if so, to gain some idea of the speed of this succession and the nature of the associated edaphic changes. It is also pertinent to examine the seasonal floristic changes and rates of growth in particular communities and to estimate their annual productivity.

As a result of the relatively restricted volume of any inhabited body of water, aquatic vegetation exerts a much more profound influence upon its environment than does terrestrial vegetation. Through their photosynthesis and respiration, and their manner and rate of growth, vascular hydrophytes may have very significant effects upon such environmental factors as the concentrations of dissolved oxygen, carbon dioxide and ammonia, mineral nutrient supplies, pH value, light penetration, current velocity and rate of silting. These effects can wield a direct or indirect influence on the lives of other aquatic organisms, notably the microflora and fauna for which the hydrophytes may provide support, shelter or food. The impact of hydrophytes on the environment and on biotic relationships increases as the volume of the water-body diminishes: plants are most significant in ponds, canals and stagnant swamps, and in most rivers, which are usually shallow compared to lakes and so contain a relatively greater concentration of plants. Analysis of these ecological interactions presents a formidable problem: the tremendous variation in local edaphic and biotic conditions invalidates all but a very few generalisations.

THE NATURE AND SPEED OF CHANGES IN AQUATIC VEGETATION

It is often asserted that the zonation of hydrophyte communities parallel to the margins of standing waters and slow-flowing rivers represents a natural succession of vegetation, and hence that at any given time each life form, for example floating-leaved, exemplifies one stage in this hydrosere. In effect, it is assumed that a steady accumulation of inorganic sediment and organic debris gradually raises the substrate nearer and nearer to the level of the water table: submerged communities give way to floating-leaved; these are in turn replaced by reed-swamp emergents, which ultimately pass over into bog, fen, marsh and terrestrial formations when the substrate reaches the water table. The suggested correspondence between a spatial sequence of communities through decreasing depths of water and a temporal succession is probably in essence valid. But the application of this concept to all aquatic habitats, and the frequent assumption, or implication, that the successional changes are rapid, must both be questioned.

From his pioneer researches into the dynamic relationships between hydrophyte communities and their environment, Pearsall (1917, 1918a, 1920) concluded that in the English Lakes the succession of communities of different life forms is controlled primarily by an allogenic factor, the net accumulation of inorganic silt. He also presented evidence that the hydrosere may be arrested by wave action or modified by changes in the nature and rate of silting. Since plant debris remains largely undecomposed in the absence of bases, organic matter begins to accumulate if the influx of inorganic silt suddenly ceases, and communities thriving on silted soils are in time replaced by those typical of organic substrates. Renewed heavy deposition of inorganic silt causes the reverse change. However, it must be appreciated that such sudden modifica-

TABLE 12.1   Representative hydroseres

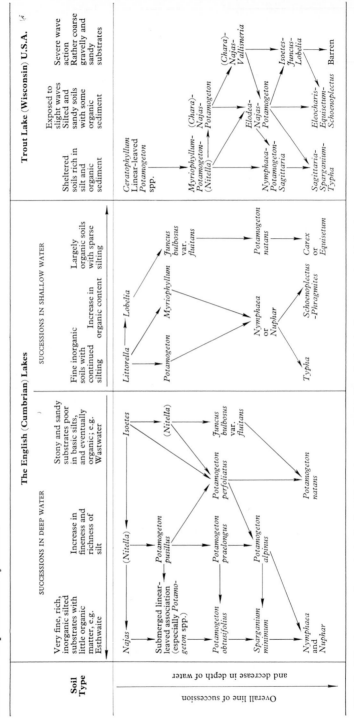

NOTE: In all the above successions, only the dominant(s) of each community is indicated. Algal dominants are enclosed in brackets. (Data for the English Lakes from Pearsall, 1920, and for Trout Lake, Wisconsin, from Wilson, 1941.)

tions, and the consequent rapid vegetational changes, are probably restricted to areas where tributaries enter or where there are very strong littoral currents. Pearsall and others have further suggested that in the ultimate stages of the hydroseres plant debris is less and less completely decomposed, eventually accumulating much more rapidly than silt. The substrate therefore becomes increasingly organic and acidic. In habitats where inorganic silt is relatively abundant the reed-swamp eventually gives way to marsh communities. Where the soil has a greater proportion of organic peaty remains but the reaction of the water is still neutral to alkaline, fen communities are the ultimate successors of the hydrophytes. In primitive lakes, often at moderate to high altitudes, with poor coarse substrates deficient in calcium and potash, the debris of plants undergoes scarcely any decay and builds up a highly organic peaty substrate: where this reaches the water table the emergent hydrophytes are gradually replaced by bog communities thriving on the acid peat.

Direct evidence for such postulated hydroseres is by no means as abundant as is often thought. Pearsall (1920) outlined three main types of succession amongst the deep-water communities of the English Lakes and two main types amongst the shallow-water communities. These are summarised in Table 12.1, together with three broadly comparable lines of succession recorded by Wilson (1941) from Trout Lake, Wisconsin. It should be noted that these are generalised trends constructed from locally variable successions, some of which were actually observed, others inferred on reasonable grounds.

It is becoming increasingly clear that in extensive lowland lakes, and lakes in hard rock regions, rapid successional changes are mainly restricted to delta sites where there is a relatively consistent influx of inorganic silt. An excellent example of this is to be found at the head of the eutrophic Esthwaite Water (in the English Lakes) where the vegetational succession, in the delta of the Black Beck, was extensively mapped by Pearsall in 1914–1915 and again in 1929 (see Tansley, 1949). In the course of a recent survey of the vegetation of Scottish lochs, Spence (1964) re-photographed numerous sites which had been photographed or described in detail over 50 years ago by West (1905, 1910). These preliminary comparisons also revealed evidence of moderately rapid succession in a few delta sites, notably at the western end of L. Meiklie and in Urquhart Bay, at the entry of the R. Urquhart into L. Ness (Fig. 12.1). Especially interesting, however, was the striking *absence* of succession in floating-leaved communities and marginal reed-swamp in most lochs of the palaeogenic Highlands, e.g. L. Kinord, L. a'Mheig, L. na Ba Ruaidhe and L. Tarff (Fig. 12.2). Spence attributed the absence or extreme slowness of vegetational change in these poor-water lakes to the lack of inwashed, inorganic silt and clay. A fine contrast, between the changes associated with silting at delta sites and the static vegetation of sites where there is no silting, emerged from the photographic comparisons of L. Uanagan (Figs. 12.3 and 12.4). A zone of *Schoenoplectus lacustris* on a broad fan of detritus dropped by an affluent stream in the south-west corner of the loch (Fig. 12.3) had obviously expanded in the 55 years since West's photographs, whereas no material change could be discerned in a marginal open stand of *Carex rostrata* situated some way from any inflow currents at the north-west corner (Fig. 12.4). Spence also presented evidence that even where the annual accumulation of the organic remains of a particular community provides debris favourable for autogenic succession, change is negligible in the absence of fine inorganic silts.

In poor- to moderately rich-water lakes of glacial origin in old hard rocks, colonisation is severely restricted or prevented in many sites by the steepness

A

FIG. 12.1. A, Urquhart Bay, looking south across part of the delta formed by the entry of the R. Urquhart into L. Ness, Scotland. *Menyanthes trifoliata* in foreground. *Phalaris arundinacea* on left and right. Groups of *Alisma plantago-aquatica* in centre; on the left of them *Carex rostrata*. *Alnus glutinosa* on both sides; same again in middle distance, with *Equisetum fluviatile*. Dead tree washed up on the shore. Cultivated land on opposite side of bay. (From West, 1905, by courtesy of the Council of the Royal Society of Edinburgh.) (B on facing page.)

and rockiness of the shore or the turbulence of the water. Yet even where colonisation is possible, on gradually sloping substrates in more sheltered sites, the rate of change in reed-swamp and floating-leaved communities, and probably submerged vegetation too, appears to be extremely slow. Rapid vegetational succession, as conventionally depicted in 'typical hydroseres', does not occur in the absence of inwashed inorganic sediments, even though the accumulation of plant debris may provide an organic substrate apparently favourable for succession. In lakes of this type the only sites likely to display substantial changes with passing time are the deltas of principal affluents where the substrate may receive a consistent supply of silt. Even in lakes of higher trophic status the importance of the silting factor is still evident in the discernibly greater rates of change in delta sites compared with marginal zones isolated from affluents.

The most rapid successions of aquatic vegetation are probably to be found in lowland ponds and lakes in kettle-holes in fluvio-glacial drift material of soft

FIG. 12.1. B, similar view to A, photographed by Spence in 1960. (Growth of shrubs to right of picture prevented photograph being taken at West's exact site.) The spit in the middle distance of West's photograph is now wooded while the pool in the foreground is now *Carex rostrata—Acrocladium* and *C. rostrata—Menyanthes trifoliata*. *Alisma plantago-aquatica* is much restricted. The pool is filled with sandy sediment, with only 6·1 per cent C, 0·1 per cent N. (From Spence, 1964, by courtesy of the author, the editor, and Oliver and Boyd, Edinburgh.)

sedimentary origin. In many of these habitats, the substrate possesses from its creation an abundance of fine inorganic material. Further inflow of silt and clay together with the accumulation of dead plant material permit rapid allogenic-autogenic succession. Similar rapid changes are characteristic also of ox-bow lakes and other standing waters associated with the lower reaches of rivers traversing flat plains, such as the broads of East Anglia which are inundated peat cuts adjacent to the main river channels. In ponds, ox-bows and smaller fertile lakes with few or no inlets and outlets, the succession of communities and transition to terrestrial vegetation may be very rapid, the raising of the substrate by the accumulation of silt and organic debris ultimately

A

B

FIG. 12.2. A, view of L. Tarff, Scotland, looking north-east, showing wooded islands and *Carex* associations in shallow places. (From West, 1905, by courtesy of the Council of the Royal Society of Edinburgh.) B, similar view photographed by Spence in 1960. The small effluent from this loch leaves in right foreground. The open *Carex rostrata* there and in the sheltered area behind the island has not developed at all since West's photograph. (From Spence, 1964, by courtesy of the author, the editor, and Oliver and Boyd, Edinburgh.)

A

FIG. 12.3. A, view from south-west to north-east over L. Uanagan, Scotland. (From West, 1905, by courtesy of the Council of the Royal Society of Edinburgh.) B, similar, but more restricted, view photographed by Spence in 1960. A stream enters the loch at left foreground and a detrital fan extends out to the *Schoenoplectus lacustris* stand. This has developed considerably since West's photograph, as has the open *Carex rostrata* sociation nearer the shore. The stream entry too has become silted up. (From Spence, 1964, by courtesy of the author, the editor and Oliver and Boyd, Edinburgh.)

A

B

FIG. 12.4. A, view over the west end of L. Uanagan, Scotland, with *Schoenoplectus lacustris* growing out in the water. *Eriophorum angustifolium, Carex* and other marsh plants in the foreground. (From West, 1905, by courtesy of the Council of the Royal Society of Edinburgh.) B, similar view photographed by Spence in 1960. The stream enters the loch beyond the right foreground. Further from this stream than the area shown in Fig. 12.3 B, there is little development of *Schoenoplectus lacustris*, while the marginal open *Carex rostrata* stand in the foreground has not developed at all since West's photograph. (From Spence, 1964, by courtesy of the author, the editor, and Oliver and Boyd, Edinburgh.)

obliterating the habitat. The greater the expanse of water and area of uncolonised substrate the longer the process of filling-up and obliteration may be expected to take. In the sluggish meandering reaches of rivers a spatial sequence of aquatic communities may develop as in a lake or pond, but the continuous current scours the bed and generally restricts the vegetation to marginal zones, precluding the raising of the substrate. Should the vegetation seriously obstruct the flow, the river may inundate the adjacent land, creating transient swamps and marshes, or cut a new course, thereby isolating ox-bow lakes.

In some tropical and subtropical rivers, lakes and swamps there may be found, in addition to communities of rooted life forms, dense aggregations of floating vegetation known collectively as sudd (sadd) or flotant. Sudd is especially common in wide slow-flowing rivers in predominantly flat open country, e.g. the White Nile, Niger, Brahmaputra, Ganges, Essequibo and Siak; in the extensive swampy deltas of such rivers; and in lakes and swamps often created by land subsidence or human activity, e.g. Bangweulu, Kariba and Lukanga in Africa, the Grand Lac system in Cambodia, and the Gran Chaco in South America. Sudd communities may arise in two essentially different ways. They may be pioneered by free-floating plants, such as *Eichhornia crassipes* and *Pistia stratiotes*, whose stoloniferous habit creates a compact floating mat spreading from sheltered marginal sites out over open water (Fig. 12.5). This mat of living plants and organic debris provides a favourable rooting medium for emergent hydrophytes, especially grasses and sedges, which invade from the shore and stabilise the mat of sudd still further with their intertwined rhizomes and roots. Ultimate invasion by marsh and terrestrial plants completes the succession. Sudd may also develop directly from thickets of emergent sedges which extend from the shore in calm shallows. The rhizomes and roots do not become anchored in the substrate: they form a stable raft floating at a depth of a few centimetres. Whichever the mode of origin, the resulting mass of sudd is virtually impenetrable and spreads with alarming rapidity. The fringes extending into open water are commonly torn away by fierce winds and strong currents, forming drifting islands which in suitable places may become re-established. As a result of their mode and speed of growth, sudd communities cause a critical weed problem on navigable waterways and on lakes used as fisheries, domestic reservoirs and sources of hydro-electric power (see Chapter 13).

· Typically, the flora of sudd communities varies in both life form and specific composition. In some localities the principal species are widespread, well-known and troublesome in many parts of the tropics, whilst in others they may be almost exclusively local in origin, the flora then reflecting, to a certain extent, the prevailing physiography and climate. In the Bengal swamps, for example, *Pistia stratiotes* is probably the main constituent of the platform of rotting vegetation, reported to attain a thickness of 15 to 60 cm. Other free-floating plants found in and above the mat include *Aldrovanda*, *Azolla*, *Ceratopteris*, *Salvinia* and *Trapa*. Species of *Nymphaea* may root in the mat whilst *Cyperus cephalotes*, *C. platystylis*, *Aeschynomene aspera* and *Hygroryza aristata* are the most common invading emergents (Ridley, 1930; Subramanyam, 1962). In many African habitats this flora is paralleled by local and adventive species of comparable growth habit. *Salvinia auriculata* provides the initial floating mats on L. Kariba: *Pistia stratiotes* is present but much less important than in Bengal. In the vanguard of the emergents come *Scirpus cubensis, Ludwigia adscendens*—which is not prevalent in sudd elsewhere in Africa—and *Vossia cuspidata* (Emmanuel, *in litt.*; Hattingh, unpubl.). In certain other African habitats, such as the White Nile in southern Sudan, the

FIG. 12.5. A, young colonies of *Eichhornia crassipes* (left foreground, right centre, and in distance) developing around submerged trees and spreading rapidly outwards: L. Apanás, Nicaragua, 1965; B, well-developed colonies of *Eichhornia crassipes* which are beginning to form floating sudd associations with invading emergent plants (example arrowed): L. Apanás, Nicaragua, 1965. (By courtesy of Dr. E. C. S. Little, A.R.C. Weed Research Organisation, Oxford, England.)

swamps fringing L. Victoria and occupying shallow valleys in Uganda, and the Niger delta, the pioneer sudd plant is the emergent *Cyperus papyrus*. *Aldrovanda, Azolla, Ottelia, Pistia, Trapa* and *Utricularia* are often dispersed in the water overlying the papyrus raft but are of only minor importance. The other common emergents are *Cyperus colymbetes, C. nudicaulis, Echinochloa pyramidalis, Herminiera elaphroxylon, Ipomoea aquatica, Phragmites communis, Typha australis* and *T. capensis*, and *Vossia cuspidata* (Hope, 1902; Ridley, 1930; Drar, 1951; Carter, 1955; Wild, 1961).

Sudd communities in the Essequibo, tributaries of the Amazon, and certain other South American rivers are rather different from those of the Old World. They are much less stable, principally because the dominant constituents are very buoyant aroids, e.g. *Montrichardia arborescens*, and grasses e.g. *Panicum elephantipes*, accompanied by light pithy leguminous shrubs. *Azolla, Pistia* and *Salvinia* also occur but are not usually significant in the establishment of the community (Rodway, 1895).

It has been stated by some writers that flotants build from the substrate upwards and that it is only when the saturated organic ooze, derived from waterlogged debris, accumulates to the bottom of the floating mat that the later invaders of the mat are able to take root and complete the succession. A different opinion was voiced by Penfound and Earle (1948) after studying floating vegetation in Louisiana. They found that peaty mats of *Eichhornia crassipes* or *Alternanthera philoxeroides* rarely exceeded 15 cm in depth: even well-developed flotants with a varied emergent flora were often separated from the substrate by as much as 2 m of water. They therefore surmised that sudd accumulates from the surface downwards. Over a 10-year period Penfound and Earle observed the development of *Eichhornia crassipes* mats and their invasion by, first, other floating and emergent hydrophytes (of which they recorded thirty-three different species), then marsh or bog plants (twenty-one spp.), followed by terrestrial types (nine spp.). In standing waters in the New Orleans area the sudd is ultimately succeeded by willow forest.

Although sudd is essentially a tropical phenomenon, communities comparable in structure though smaller in extent occur also in warm and cool temperate regions. The best-studied example is probably plav, the floating fen that often succeeds reed-swamp in the Danube delta of Rumania (Pallis, 1916). Unlike sudd, plav is usually a pure community. In the Danube the species involved is the common emergent, *Phragmites communis*. Plav differs from the normal reed-swamp of this species in being established from vertical, not horizontal, rhizomes. These and the matted roots retain great quantities of soil and silt. The community develops when the basal rhizomes of the plants die during the reed-swamp stage of growth and when the water is sufficiently deep for the living upper rhizomes and foliage not to reach the substrate. Pallis observed that the only serious competitor in the Danube delta is *Typha angustifolia* and that plav is succeeded by rooted sedges such as *Cladium mariscus* and *Carex* spp. The floating *Phragmites* fen described in parts of East Anglia is similar to plav in origin and structure but it exhibits much less variation in the size of the emergent shoots (Pallis, 1916).

In numerous north temperate waters, other normally rooted emergent hydrophytes may form sudd-like floating rafts, as Spence (1964) noted for *Carex lasiocarpa* and *C. rostrata* in certain lochans and the sheltered sites of larger lochs in Scotland.

COMPOSITIONAL CHANGES AND INTERSPECIFIC ANTAGONISM

Ecological surveys usually place considerable stress upon the status of a given species, as dominant, co-dominant, sub-dominant etc., within a community. Clearly, with growth forms as disparate as those of hydrophytes, the status of a species could differ according to the criteria employed to assess dominance. Assuming that a standard criterion (usually percentage areal cover) is applied, the specific composition of a community and the status of its various constituents are still likely to show seasonal variation: there is no reason to suppose that growth is finely synchronised throughout the population. Differential growth rates may change the status of one or more species during the growing season. Single visits to sites may provide descriptions of communities at a particular moment but are inadequate to reveal compositional flux.

In a quantitative study of the submerged vegetation of certain eutrophic Wisconsin lakes, Swindale and Curtis (1957) demonstrated a pattern of continual change in the composition of communities. Studying an English chalk stream, the R. Ivel, Edwards and Owens (1960) noted that throughout the summer of 1958 *Berula erecta* dominated the vegetation of the less heavily silted areas: *Hippuris vulgaris, Ranunculus pseudofluitans, Callitriche intermedia* and *C. obtusangula* were all initially sub-dominant. Between June and September, however, the *Ranunculus* and *Callitriche* spp. grew relatively more rapidly and their proportions of the total crop substantially increased. In 1959, in two other reaches of the same river, the proportion of *Ranunculus pseudofluitans* fell markedly between June and August, and in one reach the species lost its dominance to *Callitriche* spp. (Owens and Edwards, 1961).

Although such compositional changes may occur, it is apparent that numerous submerged, floating-leaved and reed-swamp plants tend to form extensive pure stands. These species assert their status early and attain a seasonal or permanent predominance. Of the numerous factors responsible, rates of vegetative reproduction and antagonism between species of similar or different life form are perhaps the most important. Vigorous vegetative spread, by means of rhizomes, stolons and tubers, is a typical attribute of several reed-swamp dominants, notably species of *Carex, Cyperus, Glyceria, Phalaris, Phragmites, Schoenoplectus, Typha* and *Vossia*. In a favourable site one species may gain an early initiative and increase much faster than any competitor. In mature reed-swamp communities, different species may ultimately show a significant negative association, i.e. may come to have mutually exclusive distributions, as Spence (1964) noted for *Carex rostrata* with *Glyceria maxima, Phragmites communis* or *Typha latifolia* in certain Scottish sites. The tendency to form pure closed communities inhibiting colonisation by potential competitors is also characteristic of numerous plants of other life forms. Notable examples are *Nelumbo, Nuphar* and *Nymphaea*, especially in isolated habitats (Heslop-Harrison, 1955c; and Fig. 12.8); *Potamogeton pectinatus* and *Zostera marina*, which typically form extensive meadows in brackish and saline waters (Turrill, 1963; Lewis, 1964); and species of *Ceratophyllum, Egeria, Elodea, Lagarosiphon, Myriophyllum, Najas* and *Stratiotes*, which often develop vigorous and highly homogeneous stands in suitable habitats (Forsberg, 1959, 1960; Mason, 1960; Stookey *et al.*, 1964).

Although the open fringes of reed-swamps are often penetrated by reduced floating and submerged plants (e.g. *Azolla, Lemna, Utricularia* and *Callitriche* spp.), most mature reed-swamps are so dense that they resist infiltration by larger free-floating rosettes and severely reduce the amount of light reaching the water, thus indirectly inhibiting the growth of invading submerged species. The vigorous *Eichhornia crassipes*, for example, is reported to be unable to penetrate very far into stands of *Echinochloa* spp. or *Vossia cuspidata* (C.C.T.A./ C.S.A., 1957). Conversely, some advancing emergents find it difficult to colonise floating mats of stoloniferous species: Hitchcock *et al.* (1949, 1950) commented upon the inability of *Alternanthera philoxeroides* to invade and compete effectively with *Eichhornia crassipes*. Antagonism may also be evident within communities of the same life form. Species competing for the same principal environmental factor are unable to persist together for an indefinite period. This is particularly manifest in communities of floating-leaved or free-floating species, for which optimal exposure to light, i.e. occupation of the maximum surface area, is the critical element of competition (Fig. 12.6). Clatworthy and Harper (1962) studied four reduced free-floating species in mixed cultures, each of two species: *Salvinia natans* and *Spirodela polyrhiza*; *Lemna gibba* and *S. polyrhiza*; *S. polyrhiza* and *L. minor*. Of the four, *S. natans* and *L. gibba* proved to be the most successful, perhaps partly because of the persistent elongating stem and protected lateral buds of the former and the buoyant lacunate parenchyma of the latter. The only two which seemed to reach an equilibrium when growing together were *L. minor* and *S. polyrhiza*. An example of interspecific antagonism under natural conditions is provided by the regression of colonies of *Pistia stratiotes* in the face of invading *Eichhornia crassipes*, observed on the R. Congo (C.C.T.A./C.S.A., 1957).

Buttery and Lambert (1965) have recently studied the antagonism between two emergent hydrophytes, *Glyceria maxima* and *Phragmites communis*, in the fens bordering Surlingham Broad in East Anglia. In this site, reproduction of both species is primarily vegetative, and each spring the *Glyceria maxima* grows rapidly, producing thick pure stands before the foliage of *Phragmites communis* has developed to any extent. The *Phragmites* is inhibited wherever the *Glyceria* remains vigorous and dense, but it manages to penetrate and compete in those areas where there is some reduction in the growth of *Glyceria*. Once established, the *Phragmites* competes more and more success-fully, mainly as a result of its taller and more erect foliage absorbing more and more of the incident light. Towards the back of the fen the growth of both species is conspicuously reduced (Table 12.3 and accompanying text), but

Phragmites appears to be much the more successful. Buttery *et al.* (1965) found no limitation of nutrient supply which might be invoked to explain the diminution in growth, but they did find that the substrate was substantially anaerobic. Noting that the roots of *Phragmites communis* contain an appreciably higher proportion of lacunate parenchyma than those of *Glyceria maxima*, they suggested that *Phragmites* might be more tolerant of low oxygen tensions in the

FIG. 12.6. Competition on the surface of the water: A, aerial view of part of L. Apanás in Nicaragua, 1965, showing *Eichhornia crassipes* (dark clumps) growing in a dense population of *Pistia stratiotes*. Dead trees (arrowed) indicate the shallow water. (By courtesy of Dr. E. C. S. Little, A.R.C. Weed Research Organisation, Oxford, England); B, a dense community of *Lemna gibba* competing very effectively with the floating foliage of *Nuphar lutea*. The latter has produced very few leaves (and even these are almost swamped by the *Lemna*) but has still managed to flower; canal in west Lancashire, England, 1964.

substrate and hence better fitted for the unfavourable conditions at the back of the fen.

In artificial reservoirs, dam basins, and natural sites with a fluctuating water level, changes in community composition and antagonism are probably faster and hence more conspicuous than in undisturbed waters. Minkina (1962) recently described the changes in submerged associations and the replacement of *Equisetum fluviatile* and *Phragmites communis* by *Potamogeton natans*, *Polygonum amphibium* and *Sparganium* spp. in a Karelian dam basin where water depth fluctuated.

THE PRODUCTIVITY OF HYDROPHYTE COMMUNITIES

Many writers have commented upon the rapid, often excessive, vegetative growth of numerous tropical and temperate hydrophytes. There are innumerable records of the vigour of specific organs, e.g. Caspary's (1856) measurement of an increase of 36·7 cm/day in the width of *Victoria amazonica* laminae, Schenck's (1885) observation of a batrachian *Ranunculus* with shoots 7 m long, Arber's (1920) records of a shoot system of *Polygonum amphibium* extending for about 13 m and of rates of elongation exceeding 5 cm/day attained by the roots of *Stratiotes aloides*, and Funke's (1938, 1939) notes on the rapid growth of *Vallisneria* peduncles. Whole populations provide arresting examples of such exuberant growth on a more conspicuous scale (Figs. 12.7 and 12.8). In 1868 Hegelmaier watched an expanse of water about 0·2 ha in area, initially fringed by a narrow border of *Lemna gibba*, become more or less completely covered by the plant in only 19 days. Comparable phenomena have been seen in the insidious spread of notorious weeds like *Eichhornia crassipes*, *Elodea canadensis*, *Pistia stratiotes* and *Salvinia auriculata*.

It should be realised that the notion thus evoked, that aquatic plants are unusually luxuriant and productive, is purely subjective and qualitative. Westlake (1963) recently emphasised that when judged by quantitative criteria most submerged and floating communities are in fact poorly productive. Visual impressions of luxuriance, as of the dominance of a certain species, are primarily determined by the apparent areal cover of the vegetation. So far as submerged plants are concerned such impressions are likely to be misleading because of the typically high volume/dry weight ratio of many species, the lack of substantial underground parts (compared with floating-leaved and especially emergent plants), the preference of certain plants (e.g. *Callitriche*, *Potamogeton* and *Ranunculus* spp.) for shallow waters, where the ratio of occupied volume of water to occupied surface area is small, and their habit of floating in masses with their long flexuous shoots trailing downstream in flowing water. So although the percentage areal cover of submerged communities may be high, their dry weight biomass per unit area is often small. An aerial photographic survey and crop sampling of a stretch of the shallow R. Ivel in England (Edwards and Brown, 1960; Edwards and Owens, 1960) showed that *Berula erecta* and *Hippuris vulgaris*, both of which tend to grow more or less erect, afforded 29·8 per cent and 12·1 per cent, respectively, of the total vegetation cover. Their contributions to the standing crop were, respectively, 37·6 and 15·7 per cent of the fresh weight and 28·6 and 21·7 per cent of the weight of organic carbon. *Callitriche intermedia, C. obtusangula* and *Ranunculus pseudofluitans*, in contrast, had large percentage covers in relation to their weights:

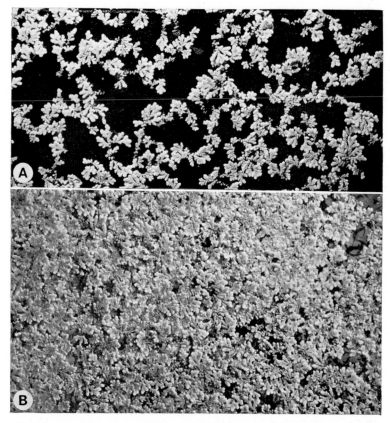

FIG. 12.7. A, part of a pure community of *Azolla filiculoides* on the water in a greenhouse tank; B, similar view, 10 days later, when the plant had formed an almost complete blanket on the surface (both × 0·2).

Callitriche spp. afforded 43·6 per cent of the total cover but only 35·7 per cent of the crop fresh weight and 35·8 per cent of the crop organic carbon, whilst *Ranunculus pseudofluitans*, with 14·5 per cent cover, contributed only 5·5 per cent of the fresh weight and 8·6 per cent of the organic carbon.

The extensive areal cover of a vigorous free-floating community may similarly engender an image of exceptional luxuriance whilst concealing the total absence of these plants below the surface. Since the population spreads only in the horizontal plane, the biomass per unit area will remain more or less constant once all available space is occupied, and it will tend to be lower for

FIG. 12.8. Colonisation by *Nelumbo lutea* of an extensive area of shallow water (to about 2·5 m deep) in north Alabama, U.S.A., during one growing season: A, *Saururus cernuus* in centre, *Nelumbo lutea* in deep water at back: 9 June, 1944; B, same site on 4 October, 1944. (From Penfound *et al.*, 1945, by courtesy of the authors and Duke University Press, Durham, North Carolina.)

15

species whose foliage rests mainly on the surface (e.g. *Hydrocharis morsus-ranae*) than for those with emergent leaves (e.g. *Eichhornia crassipes*). The same principles apply to floating-leaved rooted communities, although their biomass per unit area is likely to vary more because of interspecific differences in the volume and extent of their subterranean organs. Only in the case of reed-swamp emergents, which are often tall and bulky and have a relatively lower volume/dry weight ratio, are subjective visual pictures of luxuriance likely to tally with genuine productivity, which does indeed appear to be high.

Quantitative studies of the growth and productivity of aquatic (and terrestrial) vegetation have yielded data expressed in many different units and according to a variety of different concepts. Westlake (1963, 1965b) lucidly discussed the terminology of the subject and the problems of standardising published data in order to effect valid comparisons of the productivity of different plant communities. Most published data for aquatic communities refer to the standing crop, i.e. the mass of plant material harvested from a given area of a given habitat at a given time. Marginal emergents and the less accessible organs of sampled species, e.g. buried rhizomes and roots, may not be harvested. The disparity between estimates of standing crop and biomass (the total weight of plant material per unit area) may sometimes be great, for the underground organs may comprise from less than 10 per cent of the biomass (in brittle, sparsely rooted, submerged species) to as much as 80 to 90 per cent (in some geophytic emergents) (p. 152). For rootless submerged species and free-floating plants, standing crop estimates should be equivalent to the biomass.

Standing crops and biomass are most conveniently expressed as grams (or kilograms) dry weight per square metre of occupied area. The use of the dry weight criterion (as distinct from wet weight or fresh weight) eliminates interspecific variations attributable solely to differences in the amount of water adhering to freshly sampled material and in the water content of the material itself, differences which may be considerable amongst aquatic plants. The dry weight of many submerged plants and smaller emergents of soft texture usually represents about 10 to 15 per cent of the fresh weight. In the larger, more fibrous, emergent hydrophytes, however, dry matter accounts for about 25 per cent of the fresh weight, on average; perhaps up to even 40 per cent in some species (Westlake, 1965a). Estimates of dry weight still conceal disparities due to varying inorganic constituents. In many land plants the total inorganic (ash) weight may be as little as 5 per cent of the dry weight, and in some of the bulkier emergent hydrophytes it may be about 10 per cent. In other aquatic life forms (Table 12.2), inorganic constituents form a larger total proportion, varying more between species, sometimes exceeding 35 per cent of the dry weight in plants growing in calcareous waters where heavy encrustations of marl may be deposited on the foliage. In certain algae of such habitats, e.g. *Chara* and *Nitella*, the inorganic weight represents an even higher proportion, up to 40 to 60 per cent (Schuette and Alder, 1929b; Gortner, 1934; Forsberg, 1960).

TABLE 12.2   Proportion of inorganic matter in certain aquatic vascular plants

Species	Inorganic (ash) weight (as % of total dry weight)
EMERGENT:	
Arundo donax	2·5–7·4
Typha sp.	8·0–10·0
Mentha aquatica	16·0
Sparganium sp.	18·0
Myosotis scorpioides	20·0
FLOATING-LEAVED:	
Nuphar advena	8·0
Nymphaea odorata	11·2
FREE-FLOATING	
Salvinia auriculata	28·0
SUBMERGED (MAINLY OR EXCLUSIVELY):	
Groenlandia densa	12·0
Ranunculus pseudofluitans	12·0–21·9
Potamogeton pectinatus	13·0–19·0
Potamogeton praelongus	14·0
Hippuris vulgaris	15·0
Ceratophyllum demersum	15·7–23·7
Myriophyllum verticillatum	16·5–20·7
Rorippa nasturtium-aquaticum	17·0–23·0
Myriophyllum spicatum	17·1–20·3
Najas flexilis	17·3–23·9
Potamogeton amplifolius	18·3–38·8★
Potamogeton zosteriformis	18·4
Callitriche obtusangula	19·2
Elodea canadensis	22·0–30·7
Littorella uniflora	24·0
Berula erecta	24·0–27·0
Thalassia testudinum	24·8
Myriophyllum alterniflorum	25·0
Vallisneria spiralis	25·2–28·6
Heteranthera graminea	28·4
Potamogeton richardsonii	30·2
Potamogeton lucens	32·0

★ High value obtained from material encrusted with calcareous deposits.
Estimates obtained by different workers for the same species show reasonable agreement. There does not seem to be any great seasonal variation in either the inorganic (ash) content or the organic carbon content, which in all life forms represents 43 to 48 per cent of the *ash-free* dry weight. In hard waters, however, calcareous deposits may increase appreciably during active growth.
(Table compiled from data in Schuette and Hoffmann, 1921; Schuette and Alder, 1927, 1929a; Gortner, 1934; Juday, 1935; Nelson *et al.*, 1939; Williams, 1956; Perdue, 1958; Burkholder *et al.*, 1959; Edwards and Owens, 1960; Forsberg, 1960; D.S.I.R., 1962; Owens and Edwards, 1962; Westlake, 1965a. Most of these papers also give detailed analyses of the inorganic constituents. Virtually all the available data on the water content, ash content, and proximate composition of temperate species have recently been collated by Straškraba, 1966.)

Marl encrustations appear to be influenced by organic pollution. Owens and Edwards (1961) noticed in the R. Ivel, in which total hardness was equivalent to about 290 ppm calcium carbonate, that *Ranunculus pseudofluitans* was heavily encrusted with marl in unpolluted reaches but showed no such deposit below the entry of a sewage effluent. Above this effluent, dry matter comprised 16·4 per cent of the fresh weight of the *Ranunculus* crop, but downstream of the point of discharge only 10·7 per cent. The shells of the snail *Potamopyrgus jenkinsi*, abundant on hydrophytes in this river, were similarly seen to be encrusted above but not below the point of entry of the sewage. It is known that photosynthetic utilisation of carbon dioxide in water rich in bicarbonate ions tends to precipitate calcium carbonate when the pH rises above about 8·0, as it often may during bright summer days. In hard water at these fairly high pH values, certain organic substances in the sewage effluent (notably carboxy-methyl cellulose, a constituent of detergents) seem to prevent the precipitation of calcium carbonate on plants, mollusc shells, etc. (D.S.I.R., 1960; Edwards and Heywood, 1960, 1962).

Examples of standing crops of aquatic vegetation recorded in different habitats are shown in Table 12.3, with notes on the general environments and floras concerned. Perhaps the most outstanding disparity is between the lakes of south-east and those of north-east Wisconsin (entries 1 to 8). A further discrepancy becomes apparent when the depth distribution of the crop is examined. In five of the north-eastern lakes (entries 1 to 5) 60 to 70 per cent of the total crop was harvested from the shallowest zone (0 to 1 m depth): in Trout L., for example, 61 per cent of the crop came from this first zone, 23 per cent from 1 to 3 m depth, and 16 per cent from depths exceeding 3 m (Wilson, 1941). In contrast, the bulk of the crop in the two south-eastern lakes came from depths greater than 1 m: in L. Mendota, 30 per cent was harvested from 0 to 1 m, 45 per cent from 1 to 3 m, and 25 per cent from depths greater than 3 m, whilst in Green Lake these three depth zones yielded, respectively, 9, 40 and 50 per cent of the crop (Rickett, 1921, 1924). The exceptional north-eastern lake, Weber, more nearly resembled Mendota and Green in having only 29 per cent of the total crop in the uppermost zone (Potzger and van Engel, 1942).

Examination of the general features of the lakes and their flora permits some explanation of these disparities in standing crop and depth distribution. Wilson (1939) pointed out that the soft- to medium-hard water, north-eastern lakes lie in a sandy outwash plain and frequently have rather barren sandy soils colonised mainly by submerged rosette species (e.g. *Isoetes* spp.) which have comparatively little dry weight biomass and reach their highest population density in shallow water. The south-eastern lakes, in contrast, have more abundant silt and clay, and hard water. Although they do not have a significantly greater number of species or area of occupied bottom, the most frequent dominant plants (*Ceratophyllum, Myriophyllum, Potamogeton amplifolius, P. pectinatus, P. richardsonii, Vallisneria* and the alga *Chara*) are bulkier and have far greater dry weight biomass. The conspicuously greater proportion of the crop in depths greater than 3 m in Green L., compared with L. Mendota, is

TABLE 12.3   Standing crops of hydrophyte communities†

ENTRY	SITE	HABITAT TYPE	SEASON OR MONTH	*CROP DRY WT. g/m²	OCCUPIED DEPTH m	NO. OF SPP.	*NOTES ON FLORA, CROP, ETC.	SOURCE OF DATA
1	Trout L., NE Wisconsin	Soft- to medium-water lakes on sandy granite outwash	Summer	0·07	6·5	38	Crop data are summer averages, and include submerged angiosperms, *Chara*, and *Nitella*. *Chara* formed 50 per cent of the crop dry wt. in Green L.	Wilson, 1941
2	Silver L., NE Wisconsin			0·08	6·0	15		Wilson, 1935
3	Muskellunge L., NE Wis.			0·45	7·0	31		
4	Little John L., NE Wis.			0·52	3·0	13		Wilson, 1937
5	Sweeney L., NE Wis.	Hard-water lakes on calcareous drift		1·73	2·3	27		Potzger and van Engel, 1942
6	Weber L., NE Wisconsin			16·8	5·0	8		
7	Green L., SE Wisconsin			178	10·0	27		Rickett, 1924
8	L. Mendota, SE Wis.			202	6·5	20		Rickett, 1921
9	L. Gräsvarpet, Sweden	Shallow fertile lowland lakes: L. Gräsvarpet has periodic influx from Baltic Sea	July	280	2·0	1	*Ceratophyllum demersum*	Forsberg, 1959
10a	L. Ösby, Sweden		July	520				
10b	L. Ösby, Sweden		August	680			*Ceratophyllum demersum*	Forsberg, 1960
10c	L. Ösby, Sweden		October	590	3·5	1		
10d	L. Ösby, Sweden		July	200				
10e	L. Ösby, Sweden		August	240			*Myriophyllum verticillatum*	
10f	L. Ösby, Sweden		October	170	3·0	1		
11a	L. Rotorua, New Zealand	Shallow lakes in pasture land; Rotorua enriched by sewage	Summer	50‡	Deep	Few	Infestations of *Lagarosiphon major*: other species negligible. Crop in L. Rotoiti included many tough old stems—probably 2 or more years old	Fish, 1963
11b	L. Rotorua, New Zealand			550‡	Shallow			
11c	L. Rotoiti, New Zealand			1000‡	—			
12	Silver Springs, Florida	Fertile, subtropical spring-river		621		Few	Mainly *Sagittaria subulata*	Odum, 1957b

TABLE 12.3—continued

ENTRY	SITE	HABITAT TYPE	SEASON OR MONTH	*CROP DRY WT. g/m²	OCCUPIED DEPTH m	NO. OF SPP.	*NOTES ON FLORA, CROP, ETC.	SOURCE OF DATA
13a	R. Ivel, England	Fertile chalk stream, unpolluted reach	June	160	0·6 to 0·8	5	Berula erecta community with 6 per cent of September crop composed of marginal plants	Edwards and Owens, 1960
13b	R. Ivel, England		September	519		9		
14a	R. Ivel, England	Unpolluted reach shaded by trees	March	20	0·5 to 0·8	c.5	Mainly Berula erecta, Callitriche obtusangula, and C. intermedia	Owens and Edwards, 1961
14b	R. Ivel, England		June	107				
14c	R. Ivel, England		August	107				
15a	R. Ivel, England	Reach polluted by sewage and shaded by trees	March	19	0·5 to 0·8	c.5	As above, with Ranunculus pseudofluitans co-dominant	
15b	R. Ivel, England		June	138				
15c	R. Ivel, England		August	118				
16a	R. Ivel, England	Unshaded reach polluted by sewage	March	10	0·5 to 0·8	c.5	Ranunculus pseudo-fluitans community	
16b	R. Ivel, England		June	235				
16c	R. Ivel, England		August	70				
17a	R. Test, England	Clean fertile lowland river	April	119	0·3 to 0·6	c.6	Almost entirely Ranunculus pseudo-fluitans	
17b	R. Test, England		May	385				
17c	R. Test, England		August	195				
18	R. Chess, England	Disused watercress bed draining into chalk stream	July	322	0·3	3	Almost entirely Groenlandia densa	Owens and Edwards, 1962
19	R. Yare, England	Mildly polluted fen river	June	381	1·5	1	Potamogeton lucens	

	Location	Description	Month					Reference
20	R. Colne, England	Turbid sewage effluent channel draining into river	July	120	1·0	1	*Potamogeton pectinatus*	Westlake, 1961
21a	La Parguera, Puerto Rico	Shallow, well-illuminated saline channels, bays and inner margins of coral reefs	February	695	5·0	1	*Thalassia testudinum* community. Crop data are maximum values for each site: about 80 to 90 per cent of each crop comprised underground rhizomes and roots about 2 to 3 years old	Burkholder *et al*, 1959
21b	Las Palmas, Puerto Rico			4909				
21c	W La Cueva, Puerto Rico			5761				
21d	N La Cueva, Puerto Rico			7376				
22	New Orleans, Louisiana	Inland waterways and bayous	August to October	1472	—	1	*Eichhornia crassipes*: crop value is average biomass	Penfound and Earle, 1948
23	Cedar Creek, Minnesota		August	630	—	1	*Zizania aquatica*: about 8 to 9 per cent of crop comprised rhizomes and roots but these only that year's growth	
24a	Cedar Creek, Minnesota	Boggy area on sandy outwash plain	August	4090	—	Few	Almost entirely *Typha latifolia × angustifolia*: 60 to 65 per cent of crop comprised rhizomes and roots about 4 years old	Bray *et al*., 1959
24b	Cedar Creek, Minnesota		September	4640	—			

TABLE 12.3—*continued*

ENTRY	SITE	HABITAT TYPE	SEASON OR MONTH	*CROP DRY WT. g/m²	OCCU-PIED DEPTH m	NO. OF SPP.	*NOTES ON FLORA, CROP, ETC.	SOURCE OF DATA
25a	Surlingham Broad, England			800	—	Few	60 per cent of crop *Phalaris arundinacea*; rest almost entirely *Phragmites communis*	
25b	Surlingham Broad, England	Fen area bordering much-overgrown lake on peat and alluvium: lake has tidal ebb and flow of non-saline water		959	—	Few	*Glyceria maxima* and *Phragmites communis* co-dominant	Buttery and Lambert, 1965
25c	Surlingham Broad, England			1154	—	Few	About 85 per cent of crop *Glyceria maxima*: rest mainly *Typha latifolia* and *Solanum dulcamara* Crop values for all three communities include only aerial organs: rhizomes and roots were not harvested.	

NOTES: * All estimates of crop dry weight exclude underground organs, except where otherwise stated.
† This table is not exhaustive: further standing crop data for hydrophyte communities are given by, *inter alia*, Lindeman, 1941; Juday, 1942; Borutskiĭ, 1949, 1950; Shcherbakov, 1950; Hogetsu, 1953; Nygaard, 1955, 1958; Yamaguti, 1955; Seidel, 1955, 1956, 1959; Pearsall and Gorham, 1956a, b; Grøntved, 1958; Ekzertsev, 1958; Hejný, 1960; Zaki, 1960; Elster and Vollenweider, 1961; Straškraba, 1963; Westlake, 1966c.
‡ These values have been calculated, from Fish's published estimates of fresh weight, on the assumption that in this species the dry weight represents 10 per cent of the fresh weight.

probably related to the greater light penetration: 1 per cent of the average summer surface light intensity penetrates to only 4 m in Mendota but to 8 m in Green. *Ceratophyllum, Myriophyllum,* and also *Chara,* which provided 50 per cent of the total crop dry weight in Green, predominated in the deeper water (Rickett, 1924). In Juday's (1942) opinion, the size of crops in the north-eastern lakes may be limited more by the supply of carbon dioxide and perhaps dissolved organic factors than by deficiencies of mineral nitrogen and phosphorus. It is significant that amongst the north-eastern lakes the largest standing crops were recorded in Weber, where the water had been enriched with fertilisers. Mineral fertilisers added annually from 1932 to 1935 had no significant effects on the standing crop: the additions of soybean meal in 1936 and cottonseed meal in 1939, however, were both followed by marked increases in the crops of aquatic plants, and of plankton (Potzger and van Engel, 1942).

It will also be seen from Table 12.3 that the standing crops from fertile Swedish sites are of a similar order of magnitude to those of Lakes Mendota and Green and several English rivers. The maximum crop recorded by Forsberg (1960) in Lake Ösby (entry 10b) is the largest of all the freshwater submerged angiosperm communities, with the exception of the infestation of *Lagarosiphon major* sampled by Fish (1963) in one New Zealand lake (entry 11c). The greatest crop in temperate rivers is that sampled by Edwards and Owens (1960) at the time of the September maximum in the R. Ivel (entry 13b). The crops harvested from subtropical Floridan spring-river systems (entry 12; and see Natelson, in Penfound, 1956), where growth is continuous, are not significantly higher than those attained in fertile temperate rivers and lakes during the summer growing season, despite the generally greater annual solar radiation that the former habitats must receive. There is no evidence that crops are greater in flowing than standing waters. Nor is there any evidence that larger standing crops may be expected in polluted (entries 19, 20) than in unpolluted rivers (entries 12 to 14, 17, 18), as some authors have suggested. In a 12-month study of the R. Ivel from March 1959 to February 1960, Owens and Edwards (1961) found very similar maximum crops in two shaded reaches, one clean and the other polluted (entries 14, 15), despite the enrichment of the ammonia, nitrate and phosphate concentrations of the latter. In view of the much greater maximum crop recorded in a third unshaded reach (entry 16), they suggested that in this river the growth of aquatic vegetation is limited not by nutrient supplies but by the available solar radiation.

The tabulated data for the English rivers and Swedish lakes illustrate the seasonal variation in standing crops to be expected in cool temperate habitats where growth starts essentially in late spring and communities exhibit a marked decline in the autumn. They also illustrate the variation in the time of attainment of the maximum crop, which may be as early as May or June or as late as September. There is slight indication that maximum crops occur earlier in polluted than clean rivers. This might be due to premature loss of older foliage, which is more susceptible to pollutants, especially detergents, or to overall respiration exceeding photosynthesis by an earlier date, as a result of reduction of photosynthesis but not respiration in turbid water and when

15*

foliage is coated with silt-like solids (Westlake, 1960). However, these data are from comparatively few sites and the apparent differences may not be significant. In general, the dates of maximum crops might be expected to vary from place to place, according to local climatic and edaphic conditions, and from community to community, according to the particular growth cycles of the dominant species involved.

In Table 12.3 there are also estimates for a tropical marine submerged community (entry 21), a subtropical free-floating community (entry 22), and five temperate emergent communities (entries 23 to 25). The marine turtle-grass crops are notably large, and far in excess of most of the freshwater submerged communities, even if allowance is made for the fact that the under-ground parts of *Thalassia testudinum* form the bulk of the biomass and are probably about 2 years old whereas the freshwater crops are almost wholly 1 year's growth. The crop of free-floating *Eichhornia crassipes* is about two-to three-fold greater than the larger submerged crops in fresh waters or the crop of emergent *Zizania aquatica*, which is an annual. In contrast, the perennial emergents, with extensive rhizomes and roots, yield much larger crops. Had the underground organs been harvested, the crops at Surlingham Broad (entries 25a, b, c) would probably have been comparable with, perhaps rather smaller than, those at Cedar Creek (entries 24a, b). It is interesting to note that the largest standing crop at Surlingham Broad (entry 25c) was sampled only 7 m from open water, whereas the smallest (entry 25a) of the three crops was the furthest (actually 99 m) from open water (Buttery and Lambert, 1965). Buttery et al. (1965) suggested this decrease in crop size from the front to the back of the fen might be caused by the increasingly anaerobic nature of the substrate, progressively impairing absorption of nutrients and hence reducing growth.

As a result of seasonal and annual variations, standing crops provide only limited information on the growth of communities. More illuminating com-parisons may be drawn from estimates of productivity. The increase in biomass, corrected for losses due to death, disease and grazing, and expressed as dry organic (ash-free) weight per unit area per unit time, provides an estimate of the *net* primary productivity, or accumulation of organic substance in the plant body. (Additional correction for respiratory losses would give the *gross* primary productivity.)

Losses due to grazing vary according to the particular site and community. Many hydrophytes have been recorded as food plants for cattle, pigs, sheep and other mammals (p. 453): some types, especially certain emergent grasses such as *Echinochloa*, *Glyceria* and *Vossia*, are grazed more intensively than others. Consumption of vegetative and reproductive organs by birds, fishes, small aquatic mammals and invertebrates may also be significant in some shallow-water communities. Westlake (1963, 1965a) pointed out, however, that unless grazing losses are visually obvious it is probably not important to measure them accurately when estimating the productivity of the plant community.

Losses due to the natural death of plants also vary from site to site. In temperate waters such losses occur predominantly in the autumn and winter and are probably very small during the growing season, at least until the maximum biomass is attained (which is often at about the time of flowering). Generally, losses from the current year's crop probably do not amount to more than 2 to 10 per cent of the maximum biomass (Harper, 1918; Borutskiĭ, 1950; Westlake, 1965a). In subtropical and tropical habitats, however, deaths occur throughout the year, usually at much the same rate as new material is produced, so that the biomass remains more or less constant.

Losses due to disease are probably often small, although this aspect of the biology of hydrophytes has received remarkably little study. Various ascomycetes, basidiomycetes and other fungal parasites are known to infect the vegetative organs of emergents such as *Glyceria*, *Typha*, *Phragmites* and *Scirpus* (Lambert, 1947; Walker, 1966), but the only well-documented example is the curious wasting disease of the sea-grass, *Zostera marina*. Communities of this species in European and North American waters were severely ravaged during the period 1931–1934 and a spectacular decline in abundance was recorded from New Brunswick to North Carolina, along the coasts of France, Holland, Denmark and Sweden, and on the south coast of England (Cotton, 1933; Tutin, 1942). The two other species in these areas, *Z. angustifolia* and *Z. noltii*, were apparently unaffected and in some localities increased as competition diminished. The disease, recognised by the browning-off and subsequent death of large stands of plants, is almost certainly caused by a myxomycete, *Labyrinthula macrocystis* (Renn, 1936). Subsequent recolonisation in the north temperate waters has been slow and effected mainly by dissemination of seed (Tutin, 1938, 1942). Recently, the disease has begun to ravage New Zealand communities of *Zostera* species, which, although taxonomically confused, all belong to a different section (*Zosterella*) from *Z. marina* (sect. *Zostera*). Dying brown patches, again associated with infection of the plants by *Labyrinthula macrocystis*, were first noticed in communities in Okahu Bay, near Auckland, in 1961. The subsequent spread of the disease has been slightly retarded each winter but seems not to be abating: infected communities have been reported from Manukau Harbour and various bays near Auckland, from several sites on the east coast, and from Purau, near Christchurch (Armiger, 1964).

In estimating the annual productivity of communities of geophytes, corrections must be made for the persistence of underground organs for more than 1 year. Unfortunately, quantitative data on the life span and annual growth of rhizomes and root systems are very sparse. It has been estimated, or shown directly by marking experiments, that the rhizomes of *Glyceria maxima*, *Sparganium erectum* and *Typha latifolia* persist for less than 2 years, those of *Phragmites communis* for 2 to 3 or more years, and those of *Schoenoplectus lacustris* for at least 3 and perhaps as long as 7 years. Further detailed studies of this topic are needed (Westlake, 1965a).

In clearly healthy communities, where deaths and grazing losses are seen to be absent or negligible, the recorded increases in biomass up to the seasonal maximum generally provide a satisfactory basis for estimates of productivity. In certain communities, however, the use of this technique of estimation may be complicated by the unusual mode of growth of the plants. *Glyceria maxima* appears to be such an exception: between July and October old shoots die while newer shoots continue growth, with the result that the seasonal maximum of the community is obscured (Westlake, 1966c). If significant and variable losses do occur from the current year's growth, and if some organic material is translocated from dying foliage to underground organs, the estimation of productivity from biomass changes becomes very difficult (Westlake, 1965a).

Productivities may also be estimated from determinations of metabolic changes, e.g. photosynthetic oxygen production (and respiratory oxygen consumption) (Owens, 1965). Such techniques are useful for those marine and warm habitats where growth and decay are more or less continuous and the biomass of the community is relatively constant, as in the subtropical spring communities and marine vegetation studied by Odum (1957a, b; 1963), Odum and Wilson (1962) and Odum *et al.* (1959). Edwards and Owens (1962) applied this method to a shallow fertile stream in southern England. Wetzel (1964) estimated the productivity of a *Ruppia maritima* community in Borax Lake in the U.S.A. from measurements of the fixation of radioactive carbon.

From data in Rickett (1921), Yamaguti (1955) and Forsberg (1959, 1960), *inter alia*, Westlake (1963) estimated the annual net primary productivity of submerged macrophyte communities in fertile lakes to be 4 to 7 metric tons organic matter per hectare, but in poor-water lakes (from data of Potzger and van Engel, 1942; Nygaard, 1955, 1958; Westlake, 1960) only about 1 m.t./ha, occasionally up to 2·5 m.t./ha, and in temperate flowing waters about 1 to 6 m.t./ha (from data of Yamaguti, 1955; Westlake, 1961; Owens and Edwards, 1961, 1962; Edwards and Owens, 1962). Greater productivities were calculated for subtropical habitats, ranging from about 10 m.t. organic matter/ha year (from several sources, e.g. Penfound, 1956; Zaki, 1960; Elster and Vollenweider, 1961) to as much as 21 m.t./ha year, estimated from Odum's (1957a, b) data for a *Sagittaria subulata* community (with epiphytic algae constituting 30 per cent of the dry weight biomass) in a fertile Floridan spring. Tropical marine angiosperms may attain productivities of 30 m.t. organic matter/ha year, calculated from data of Burkholder *et al.* (1959) for a *Thalassia testudinum* community in Puerto Rican waters.

Numerous studies of fertile reed-swamps and marshes (Harper, 1918; Merinotti, 1941; Rasmussen *et al.*, 1948; Pearsall and Gorham, 1956a, b; Perdue, 1958; Bray *et al.*, 1959; Seidel, 1959; Hejný, 1960; Bray, 1962 and Straškraba, 1963) provided biomass and standing crop data from which Westlake (1963) estimated that temperate emergents, such as *Schoenoplectus* and *Typha*, may attain organic productivities of 20 to 46 m.t./ha year, whilst in tropical and warm temperate habitats even higher values, 40 to 75 m.t./ha year or more, may be reached by such species as *Arundo donax* and *Cyperus papyrus*.

There is an unfortunate deficiency of data relating specifically to floating-leaved and free-floating communities. Since these two life forms are in certain respects intermediate between the emergent, with essentially terrestrial foliage and extensive underground organs, and the submerged, with essentially aquatic foliage and sparse underground organs, comprehensive productivity studies might be of considerable interest. The tropical *Eichhornia crassipes* is often cited as an example of a notably luxuriant species in view of the serious weed problems it creates, yet the available data (e.g. from Penfound and Earle, 1948; Dymond, 1949) permit no more than a rough estimate of productivity of 11 to 33 m.t./ha year. However, there is some evidence from rates of increase observed in favourable infested habitats, as in Louisiana and on the Nile, that if grown in good conditions, with an optimal population density over the whole available area and a continual predominance of young plants, this species might produce as much as 110 to 150 m.t. organic matter/ha year (Westlake, 1963).

Lindeman (1942) suggested that the classical hydrosere, from truly submerged to truly terrestrial vegetation, is accompanied by an overall increase in productivity, but that productivity is minimal in the marginal amphibious zones. Yet Westlake's (1963) comparisons show quite clearly that reed-swamp vegetation is as productive as terrestrial vegetation, and in good conditions it may be more productive. In the temperate zones, the annual organic productivity of reed-swamp communities is comparable with that of perennial agricultural crops and coniferous forest, and significantly greater than that of deciduous forest or cultivated annuals. In the tropics, too, reed-swamps are probably amongst the most productive communities, equalled only by rain-forest and intensively cultivated perennials, such as *Saccharum officinarum* (sugar cane). The high productivity of reed-swamps is perhaps attributable to their having the best of both worlds, in the sense of more or less unrestricted supplies of gaseous carbon dioxide and light, and of water and dissolved nutrients. Yet shallow waters and waterlogged soil are far from ideal habitats: the underground organs may be embarrassed by oxygen deficiency and absorption may sometimes be hindered, even though nutrients may be more freely available in an anaerobic substrate.

Westlake's (1963) review also effectively disputes the notion advanced by many authors on inadequate data or inappropriate comparisons, that truly aquatic communities produce as much as or more than terrestrial communities. With the possible exception of tropical marine angiosperms, communities of submerged hydrophytes generally appear to be poorly productive, as Gessner (1959) suggested. Their average annual organic productivities in temperate regions lie within the same low range (1–7 m.t./ha year) as those of natural phytoplankton communities, and even if the somewhat higher values from subtropical sites are included, they are still very low compared to those of temperate and tropical reed-swamps, tropical crops and rain-forest. This poor productivity is perhaps associated with the lower intensities and differential penetration of light under water, and with the slower rates of diffusion in aqueous solution and hence less readily obtainable supplies of metabolites.

INTERACTIONS BETWEEN HYDROPHYTES, THEIR ENVIRONMENT AND OTHER AQUATIC ORGANISMS

Direct Effects of Plants on the Oxygen Balance: Photosynthesis and Respiration. The direct effects of submerged hydrophytes on the oxygen balance of the aquatic environment accrue from their photosynthetic and respiratory activities, productivity and decay. Photosynthetic fixation of an absorbed carbon source, be it gaseous or dissolved carbon dioxide or bicarbonate ions, is accompanied, in terms of the conventional photosynthetic equation yielding hexose, by evolution of an equivalent amount of oxygen. If the photosynthetic quotient $(\Delta O_2 / -\Delta CO_2)$ is unity, then for every 1 g carbon fixed, 2·67 g oxygen should be liberated. Under natural conditions, however, this relationship is unlikely to be valid for long periods. Assimilation normally involves the elaboration of fats, proteins and other substances from the initial photosynthetic product, hexose. Synthesis of fats and proteins creates higher photosynthetic quotients, up to about 1·6 when nitrate is the source of nitrogen and growth is rapid. Westlake (1963, *in litt.*) suggested that a more realistic average quotient would be 1·2 (1 g carbon $\equiv$ 3·2 g oxygen) for temperate communities with a seasonal growth periodicity, and 1·35 (1 g carbon $\equiv$ 3·6 g oxygen) for communities in tropical habitats where growth is more or less continuous. If the net organic carbon productivity of a particular community is known, these relationships may then be used to estimate the net oxygen output of the community over the same period of time.

Crop data from the Rivers Ivel, Test and Yare in England, for example, have provided estimates of average net productivities ranging from 0·04 to 2·30 g organic carbon/m² day, equivalent to 0·11 to 6·14 g oxygen/m² day (assuming a photosynthetic quotient of 1·0) or 0·13 to 7·36 g oxygen/m² day (assuming a quotient of 1·2) (Edwards and Owens, 1960; Owens and Edwards, 1961, 1962; Ministry of Technology, 1965). It should be noted that these are average daily values. Photosynthesis is of course restricted to daylight hours and its rate in the field is related more or less closely to the intensity of solar radiation (Edwards and Owens, 1962; Odum and Wilson, 1962). In good conditions in the middle of a warm bright summer's day the photosynthetic oxygen production rate may be as much as 1·5 to 2·0 g/m² h or even higher.

It must be remembered that estimations of net oxygen production derived from organic carbon productivities assume (a) a given average photosynthetic quotient, (b) that all the oxygen produced in photosynthesis is liberated from the plant body, and (c) that the oxygen is liberated into the water and not into the atmosphere. None of these assumptions is valid in all circumstances. Likely variations in the photosynthetic quotient have already been mentioned. It is not possible to estimate the proportion of photosynthetic oxygen that is retained within the intercellular spaces and cortical lacunae of the plant body, in order to make corrections for assumption (b). As described in Chapter 5 (p. 122), up to 7 per cent or more of the total daily oxygen production may be lost to the atmosphere in bubbles escaping from the plant surface. Some oxygen may also be lost directly to the atmosphere from partly emergent plants, such as *Berula erecta* and *Hippuris vulgaris*. Since rates of photosynthesis may well differ between aerial and submerged parts, as a result of different prevailing light intensities, and since some oxygen may diffuse from the aerial to the submerged parts, it is impossible to make corrections for assumption (c) based solely on the observed proportion of the crop which is above water. Values of photosynthetic oxygen production calculated from crop data are therefore only very approximate.

The physiological effects of plants on their environment may be assessed more accurately from *in situ* measurements of changes in the dissolved oxygen concentration, together with determinations of the rate of reaeration and of respiratory oxygen consumption. This technique was first used in attempts to determine productivity and energy budgets in lakes (Juday, 1940; Juday *et al.*, 1943), but has recently been modified and applied to rivers (Odum, 1956, 1957a, b). The principles of the technique were outlined in Chapter 2 and it must suffice here to reiterate that if in a reach which receives no tributaries or run-off water the flow, reaeration from the atmosphere, biochemical oxygen demand of the water and benthic oxygen demand are predictable, the photosynthetic oxygen production or respiratory oxygen consumption of the plants may be estimated from observed changes in dissolved oxygen concentration between an upstream and a downstream station. Respiration rates determined at night must be corrected for the temperature and oxygen changes occurring during the day.

This technique has been applied to two unpolluted reaches of the R. Ivel, measurements being made on several days in May, July and September of different years (Edwards and Owens, 1962; Ministry of Technology, 1965). On these summer days, gross photosynthetic oxygen production ranged from 10·1 to 17·6 g/m² day: community respiration varied from 7·7 to 15·4 g oxygen/m² day, of which about 30 per cent (3 to 4 g/m² day) was accounted for by mud respiration and about 70 per cent by plants. On all occasions gross photosynthesis exceeded respiration, the net photosynthetic oxygen production varying from 0·16 to 5·16 g/m² day. During the middle of the day the net oxygen production reached 0·7 g/m² h. On a sample day in October of one year, when solar radiation was much lower and plant communities were declining, community respiration exceeded gross photosynthesis by up to 3·5 g oxygen/m² day. Estimates of gross oxygen production in a polluted reach of the R. Lark in June and July (D.S.I.R., 1962; Owens and Edwards, 1963) were very similar to summer values in the Ivel, 13 to 14 g/m² day, but were well exceeded by community respiration, estimated at 19·6 to 24·4 g oxygen/m² day, of which only 6 to 9 g/m² day was accounted for by plants (including algae), illustrating that in a polluted habitat the major oxygen demand is exerted by the mud. In both the Ivel and the Lark the biochemical oxygen demand was an insignificant component of the total oxygen consumption. The data obtained from these two English rivers are similar to Hoskin's (1959) estimates of 9·8 and 21·5 g/m² day for the photosynthetic oxygen production and community respiration respectively, in streams in North Carolina, although in this study determinations of the oxygen concentrations were less frequent and no corrections were made for changing respiration rates during the day.

It has been suspected for some time that in flowing waters the photosynthesis of submerged hydrophyte communities might be directly responsible for diurnal amplitudes of as much as 230 per cent of the average dissolved oxygen concentration. Diurnal ranges of up to 18·5 ppm have been reported in rivers downstream of sources of organic pollution where the hydrophytes were displaying vigorous growth (Butcher *et al.*, 1930; Schroepfer, 1942). Laboratory studies of the optimal rates of photosynthesis achieved in flowing water (e.g. D.S.I.R., 1959) also suggest that hydrophytes might cause diurnal oxygen fluctuations of this magnitude, at least under ideal conditions. During the summer of 1963, surveys of dissolved oxygen concentration were made at 24 sites in certain clean and polluted English rivers with depths ranging from 0·46 to 4·0 m and velocities from about 6 to 72 cm/s (D.S.I.R., 1964; Owens and Edwards, 1964). At twelve of the sites there was a conspicuous diurnal oxygen rhythm of the classical type, concentrations being minimal just before dawn and maximal in the afternoon. A diurnal amplitude of more than 10 ppm was recorded in the R. Yare and R. Anker, both slow-flowing and densely populated with aquatic plants, the former being relatively clean at the sampling site, the latter polluted by industrial and sewage effluents. In seven other streams of various depths and flows the observed fluctuations of 3 to 5 ppm were similarly attributable to the photosynthesis of plant communities. The diurnal amplitude in three streams was only 2 ppm or less. No typical diurnal rhythm was found at the remaining 12 sites, which also varied in depth and flow, and the observed fluctuations in oxygen concentration could not be attributed to photosynthesis. Anomalous and not easily explained fluctuations were also observed in over 60 per cent of samples in a recent study by Gunnerson (1964). It must be appreciated that the impact of photosynthesis on the oxygen balance in rivers is by no means always great or clear-cut. It is also worthy of note that dense growths of benthic, epiphytic or planktonic algae, when present, may contribute relatively much more oxygen than the vascular hydrophytes (Fig. 12.9). In a subtropical community in Silver Springs, Florida, epiphytic algae comprised about 30 per cent of the total standing crop of plants but yielded about 70 per cent of the total daily photosynthetic oxygen production (Odum, 1957b).

Within the obvious limits of generalisation it may be concluded that during daylight hours at the height of the growing season the photosynthetic activities of vigorous plant communities may appreciably enrich the dissolved oxygen concentration of rivers and the shallow parts of sheltered lakes, provided that the benthic and biochemical oxygen demands are relatively insignificant and more or less constant. In polluted rivers, however, where these demands are generally greater and more variable, the effects of photosynthesis may be of little significance for the improvement of environmental conditions and the benefit of the aquatic fauna. The extent of oxygen enrichment at all sites will clearly vary from day to day with the changing light intensity and temperature and with the density and distribution of the plant populations. During the middle of a summer day photosynthetic oxygen production may be expected to be significantly greater under a bright warm sun than under a cloud cover: on a very dull cool day community respiration may exceed even the maximum photosynthetic rate. Rates of photosynthesis will also be higher in clear unpolluted rivers than in those turbid with suspended solids, either natural silt or particulate pollutants.

Much has yet to be learnt about the effects of self-shading within aquatic communities of different growth habits. Light penetration is markedly curtailed within stands of even such erect plants as *Hippuris vulgaris* and *Berula erecta* (Fig. 12.10). The floating apical rosettes of *Callitriche* spp. may provide so dense a cover that as little as 1 per cent of the surface light intensity reaches a depth of 5 cm, yet most of the biomass of the community will be below this

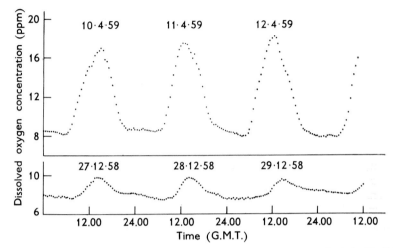

FIG. 12.9. Diurnal rhythms of dissolved oxygen concentration in a reach of the English R. Ivel on representative days in December 1958 and April 1959. The oxygen content was recorded at the downstream end of a slow-flowing reach containing communities of *Callitriche* spp. and *Hippuris vulgaris*. The conspicuous increase in the daily maximum dissolved oxygen concentrations in April 1959 reflects a heavy bloom of epiphytic diatoms (principally *Synedra, Fragilaria, Melosira, Navicula* and *Gomphonema*) which developed at this time. (From D.S.I.R., 1960, by courtesy of the Controller of Her Majesty's Stationery Office, London.)

level (Ministry of Technology, 1965). Westlake (1964, 1966b) pointed out that in communities of batrachian *Ranunculi* and some species of *Potamogeton*, whose elongated shoots also trail and form a similar canopy of floating foliage, maximal rates of photosynthesis are attained near the water surface. Such communities may produce, on a net daily basis per unit area, significantly more oxygen than do more uniformly distributed communities, in which respiration probably exceeds photosynthesis at the lower depths during most of the day. In dense stands of plants in stagnant waters, where mixing is absent or minimal, the dissolved oxygen concentration may fall sharply with depth and become markedly stratified (Buscemi, 1958). In the littoral zone of a backwater of the R. Elbe, where the foliage of dense populations of *Hydrocharis, Nuphar, Ceratophyllum* and *Myriophyllum* was aggregated near or on the water surface, Straškraba (1965) found a pronounced stratification of temperature and of chemical factors, the variations of oxygen concentration, pH and alkalinity being clearly dependent on the photosynthesis and respiration of the plants.

If during warm bright days the water becomes supersaturated, photosynthetic oxygen may be lost, especially where the flow is disturbed at weirs and rapids. During the later hours of daylight, photosynthesis wanes and is eventually exceeded by respiration which reaches a maximum during darkness. In polluted or very densely populated reaches, therefore, day-time photosynthesis may temporarily improve conditions but night-time respiration, added to the respiratory demand of the mud and the biochemical oxygen demand, may

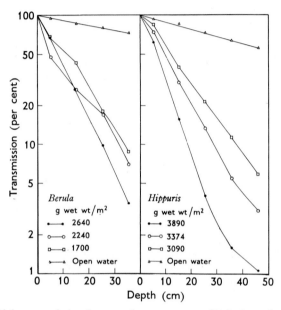

FIG. 12.10. Light transmission (expressed as percentage of light intensity immediately below water surface) through open water and through beds of *Berula erecta* and *Hippuris vulgaris*, of varying standing crop. (From Ministry of Technology, 1965, by courtesy of the Controller of Her Majesty's Stationery Office, London.)

seriously deplete the oxygen supply, even reducing it to levels critical for the aquatic fauna (Westlake, 1960).

In temperate waters the production of photosynthetic oxygen probably increases gradually from the onset of the growing season until the optimum population density is attained. Further increase in the standing crop may accrue but because of shading effects may not be accompanied by an increase in oxygen production per unit area. After the maximum crop is reached, the gradual decrease in solar radiation and increase in old dying plants will be accompanied by a fall in the daily oxygen output of the community. Oxygen will ultimately be consumed in the decay of the dead plants. If decay is complete and aerobic throughout, as much oxygen should be consumed in the decomposition of this organic matter as was earlier liberated in its production. However, this theoretically valid relationship will rarely hold in natural temperate habitats. In all but truly annual species some organic matter synthesised in each growing season may persist for several years in underground organs. Floods in late summer and autumn may carry old and decaying plants to deeper water in lakes or well downstream in rivers, towards estuaries and the sea or over adjacent land. In certain conditions plant debris may accumulate in sediments, especially in lakes, and undergo little or no decay. Accumulated debris may be partly or wholly decomposed within mud deposits by anaerobic processes, yielding methane and hydrogen sulphide. Even if the bulk of the annual crop is retained within the same water-system and decay is principally aerobic, the rate of decomposition will be retarded as the water cools and the oxygen demand will be extended throughout the winter. So far as submerged communities are concerned, therefore, vigorous oxygen production may benefit the aquatic fauna during the summer when temperatures are high and oxygen relatively scarce, whilst consumption of oxygen in decay will be spread over a period of 6 months or more when the fauna is less active and oxygen more plentiful due to lower temperatures and higher rates of reaeration and flow. This favourable balance may be disturbed, however, in habitats possessing marginal communities. The vast bulk of the photosynthetic oxygen of emergent hydrophytes is either lost directly to the atmosphere or retained within their tissues and so in no way benefits the aquatic fauna. Yet most of their foliage decays within the water at the expense of dissolved oxygen. The accumulated debris of emergents may therefore exert a significant net oxygen demand at certain seasons and the aquatic fauna may then suffer from oxygen scarcity. Other animals may also be indirectly affected. According to Hawker *et al.* (1960), the decomposing vegetation in shallow stagnant ponds in the vicinity of the salt lakes of Utah forms during the hot summer months a metabolic substrate for the anaerobic *Clostridium botulinum*. The potent exotoxin produced by this bacterium poisons thousands of ducks feeding at the ponds.

Indirect Effects on the Oxygen Balance: Effects on Flow, Silting and Light Penetration. Through their growth habit, stands of hydrophytes tend to modify the physical nature of their environment. Vigorous plant populations may occupy 1 to 4 per cent, or rarely up to 10 per cent, of the total volume of a river, and are known to reduce the maximum velocity of the current to less than 75 per cent of that in uncolonised reaches, causing the water to rise more than 1 cm/day to as much as 70 to 80 cm above the normal level (Hillebrand, 1950).

The resistance to the flow may also increase the rate of deposition of silt, although the magnitude of this effect varies according to local conditions (Butcher, 1933; Schulz, 1961; Kopecký, 1965). In swift and deep rivers carrying little suspended matter, plant populations will have little impact on the rate of silting. In shallower rivers, however, especially those with abnormally wide courses, the average velocity will be much lower and silt may be abundant. Then, stands of plants may locally reduce the flow and accelerate the building of densely colonised beds of silt, between which will be fast-flowing silt-free channels, with sandy or gravelly substrates.

It is probable that the entry of oxygen from the atmosphere is increased by the aerial foliage of marginal plants and inflorescences of submerged and floating-leaved species which increase turbulence at the surface of the water. This advantage is likely to be lost, however, in densely populated reaches because of the decrease in reaeration caused by the increase in water depth and the decrease in current velocities. Furthermore, the resistance offered by plant communities will increase the average retention time for a particular reach: dissolved and suspended matter will be confined there for longer, and a greater proportion of sediment will settle over a given area of river bed, than if the current were unimpeded. Through their effects upon flow and silting, therefore, extensive plant populations may significantly reduce the oxygen supply and in polluted rivers could cause great local increase in the biochemical oxygen demand and mud respiration.

It was noted earlier that hydrophyte communities may reduce their photosynthetic efficiency by self-shading when the optimal population density is exceeded. Oxygen enrichment by algal photosynthesis may likewise be reduced or inhibited because of shading and nutrient depletion by submerged vascular plants. Hasler and Jones (1949) studied the population changes amongst the phyto- and rotifer plankton in four silo-ponds, all of which had the same water and had received the same inoculum of plankton. Two ponds were otherwise bare but the remaining two were densely planted with *Elodea canadensis* and *Potamogeton foliosus*. There was unequivocal evidence in both years of the experiment that the growth of both planktonic algae and rotifers was markedly suppressed in the ponds containing vascular hydrophytes, due probably to the restricted penetration of light and depletion of nutrients. However, it is worth noting that this antagonism may also operate in the reverse direction. The complete elimination of submerged hydrophytes from Lake Lingby Sø has been attributed to the great increase in phytoplankton density brought about by increasing enrichment of the waters with sewage from the heavily populated catchment area (Olsen, 1964)*.

Through its shading, surface cover and hindrance to currents, floating vegetation is generally antagonistic to all other aquatic plant life, and, through its creation of oxygen deficiency, to aquatic animals too. In the waterlily zone fringing L. Victoria, Carter (1955) found that the clusters of petioles and shoots within the water hindered mixing and created a marked stratification of oxygen concentration: at less than 2 m depth there was only 32 per cent saturation. Severe oxygen depletion, associated with rapid decay of abundant vegetation, has also been found in the warm waters of the Gran Chaco swamps of South America (Carter and Beadle, 1931) and the tropical rain-forests of Guyana (Carter, 1934). Conditions are often worse under floating mats. In L. Victoria, Carter (1955) found that oxygen was absent or in very low supply in the water beneath floating rafts of *Cyperus papyrus*. There is often a similar dearth or complete absence of oxygen beneath floating mats of *Eichhornia*

---

* The recent disappearance of most submerged hydrophytes from L. Leven in Scotland is also probably due to extinction of light by persistant blue-green algal blooms (Morgan, 1966).

crassipes, as noted by Lynch *et al.* (1957) in the southern United States, and Hickling (1961) in Java. Similarly, Yount (1963) reported the absence of oxygen at only a few centimetres' depth in the isolated pools on surface limestone in Florida which are thickly covered with *Lemna, Pistia, Salvinia* and sometimes *Eichhornia*. Floating mats drastically curtail the penetration of light and so inhibit the growth and photosynthesis of phytoplankton and submerged vascular plants. They also shelter the surface from the wind, minimising turbulence and retarding reaeration, and hinder thermal water currents, preventing mixing and accelerating stratification. Most or all of the little available oxygen is consumed by mud deposits and rotting organic debris.

Effects of Photosynthetic Activities upon pH value, and Dissolved Carbon Dioxide, Ammonia, etc. There is evidence that for many aquatic animals, especially fishes, pH, carbon dioxide concentration and ammonia concentration are more critical factors than the oxygen supply, at least until this is reduced to low limiting levels. Fishes, for example, may tolerate a substantial fall in the oxygen concentration provided that the concentration of free carbon dioxide is also reduced. It is important, therefore, that the chemical effects of plant populations on their environment should not be envisaged solely in terms of the oxygen balance. Unfortunately there have so far been very few quantitative studies of the influence of aquatic plant communities upon the daily fluctuations in pH value and ammonia and carbon dioxide concentrations in natural habitats. The possible nature of the influence may be surmised, but the magnitude of it in particular circumstances cannot yet be accurately assessed.

In addition to increasing the dissolved oxygen supply, photosynthesising communities will also deplete the carbon dioxide concentration: for every rise of 2 ppm in the oxygen concentration the total carbon dioxide concentration should drop by 2·75 ppm; the pH will rise and the toxic free form of carbon dioxide will be correspondingly reduced. Although it is likely that during periods of photosynthesis the carbon dioxide concentration will be maintained well below levels critical for the fauna, the simultaneous rise in pH and concentration of toxic un-ionised ammonia may have serious consequences, especially in waters that are heavily polluted with sewage, liquors from gas- and coke-works, and other effluents rich in ammonia. It has recently been shown that the toxicity of un-ionised ammonia to fish is influenced not only by pH, temperature and oxygen but also by the chemical composition of the water (D.S.I.R., 1959, 1960). The toxicity is significantly greater in a well-buffered water because excretion of respiratory carbon dioxide by the fish alters very little the pH value of the water at the gill surface and the concentration of un-ionised ammonia there is much the same as in the bulk of the water; whereas in an unbuffered water of similar alkalinity, excretion of carbon dioxide considerably reduces the pH, and hence the concentration of un-ionised ammonia, at the gill surface. Over a fairly wide pH range, reduction in the concentration of un-ionised ammonia at the gills relative to that in the bulk of the water accompanies reduction in the concentration of free carbon dioxide in the water.

High pH values may themselves be lethal. Sensitivity to pH probably varies considerably between different species of fishes: roach, for example, appear to be more resistant than rainbow trout to alkaline pH values (D.S.I.R., 1963). Most adult fishes probably tolerate pH values of 9·0 to 9·5 for short periods of a few hours: spawning fishes and fry may well be much more susceptible. It is unlikely that even adult specimens can survive for long at a pH of 10·0 to 10·5: an exposure of 1 h at pH 11·0 can be lethal to trout. High values above pH 9·0 are by no means uncommon during the day in waters densely populated with hydrophytes, especially when large algal populations are also present (Zakharenkov, 1962; D.S.I.R., 1962, 1963, 1964).

The Place of Hydrophytes in Biotic Relationships. Many vascular hydrophytes occupy key positions in biotic relationships (U.S.D.A., 1937; Frohne, 1938; Hotchkiss, 1941; Penfound, 1956). Their soil-binding roots, rhizomes and stolons help to reduce erosion and facilitate colonisation by benthic algae and invertebrates. Their foliage offers shelter, support and, at least during daylight, a locally enriched oxygen supply, and consequently often bears a rich and varied epiphytic microflora and fauna. Hydrophytes of all life forms provide a direct or indirect source of food for an immense variety of aquatic invertebrates and fishes, and for those birds and mammals that frequent aquatic habitats. A summary of the more common hydrophyte genera important to fishes, birds and mammals is presented in Table 12.4.

All submerged organs, especially the dissected leaves of such plants as *Cabomba, Ceratophyllum* and *Myriophyllum,* may carry dense communities of epiphytic desmids, diatoms and filamentous algae and of zooplankton (Straškraba, 1965). Using photographic methods, Edwards and Owens (1965) showed that for entire shoots of species of *Berula, Callitriche, Hippuris* and *Sparganium* 1 mg dry weight is approximately equivalent to 1 cm² of plant surface. Assuming this relationship to hold for all rooted aquatic plants, Edwards and Owens calculated that the ratio of plant surface area to substrate surface area in four shallow fertile streams was about 30:1 between April and September, and they suggested that it may exceed 50:1 in some flowing waters during the summer growing season. Hydrophytes thus present a vast potential area for colonisation by micro-organisms. The standing crop of algal epiphytes on shoots of *Hippuris vulgaris* in an English river one spring was estimated as $3·8 \times 10^{10}$ cells/m² of river bed (D.S.I.R., 1962). Westlake (1965a) suggested that the biomass of luxuriant growths of epiphytes may reach between 100 and 500 g dry weight/m² of substrate, but pointed out that such dense populations do not normally persist for long periods.

Epiphytic algae, and the bacteria, protozoans and rotifers which they support, provide abundant food for the aquatic crustaceans, molluscs, annelids and insect larvae on which carnivorous fishes, in turn, depend. On submerged plants the average biomass of animals, per unit area of substrate, may be at least three- or four-fold greater than that on silt and fifteen-fold greater than that on rock or gravel (Needham, 1938). Molluscs and insects of various types may eat the tissues of submerged and emergent plants, together with the epiphytes

Genera	Organs	Sea-mammals	Hippopotamus	Muskrat	Beaver, Deer, Moose, Porcupine etc.	Goats & Sheep	Pigs	Cattle	Game birds	Shore birds	Marsh birds (waders)	Grebes & Swans etc.	Coots & Geese etc.	Ducks	Spawning medium	Shade & shelter	Food producer	Direct food
Acorus, Calla	Rhizomes																	
Alisma, Bacopa, Brasenia, Carex, Echinodorus, Eleocharis, Glyceria, Hippuris, Leersia, Nelumbo, Nuphar, Nymphaea, Nymphoides, Sparganium	Fruits & seeds / Foliage / Rhizomes & tubers			*	*		*	+	*	*	*	*	*	+		*	*	*
Coix, Cyperus, Echinochloa, Hygroryza, Paspalidium, Sagittaria, Scirpus, Schoenoplectus, Zizania	Fruits & seeds / Foliage / Rhizomes & tubers			*	*	*	+	+				+*	+*	+	+	*	*	*
Ischaemum, Oryza, Vossia	Foliage		+	+	+		+	+						*	*			
Limnocharis, Ludwigia, Menyanthes, Monochoria, Pontederia, Phragmites, Typha	Fruits & seeds / Vegetative parts		+	+		*	+	+	*		*	+	+	+		*	*	
Azolla, Lemna, Spirodela, Salvinia, Wolffia	Whole plants			+			+	*				+		+		+	+	+
Ceratopteris, Eichhornia, Pistia	Foliage & roots						+	*								+	+	
Aldrovanda, Utricularia	Whole plants							*								*	*	
Cabomba, Ceratophyllum, Myriophyllum, Najas, Proserpinaca, linear-leaved *Potamogeton*	Foliage / Fruits & seeds								+	+	+	+	+	*	+	+	+	*
Callitriche, Elatine, Podostemaceae	Foliage								+	+	*	+	+	+	*	*	*	*
Elodea, Ruppia, Vallisneria, Zannichellia	All parts			+								+	+	+		+	+	+
Isoetes, Marsilea, Pilularia	All parts			+		+	+	+	+	+		*	*	+		*	+	
Amphibolis, Cymodocea, Enhalus, Halodule, Halophila, Syringodium, Thalassia, Zostera	Foliage, fruits & seeds	+					+	+										+

NOTE: *denotes moderate importance; †denotes great importance

(Table compiled from data in Titcomb, 1909; Moore, 1913; McAtee, 1915, 1939; Mabott, 1920; Oberholtzer and McAtee, 1920; Pfeiffer, 1922; Seton, 1929; Terrell, 1930; Gortner, 1934; Aitken, 1936; U.S.D.A., 1937; Frohne, 1938; de Gruchy, 1938; Penfound & Hathaway, 1938; Hamerstrom & Blake, 1939; Martin & Uhler, 1939; Nelson *et al.*, 1939; Moyle & Hotchkiss, 1945; Penfound & Schneidau, 1945; Penfound, 1957; Yocom, 1951; van Steenis, 1954; Fassett, 1957; den Hartog, 1957a, b; Burkholder *et al.*, 1959; Allsopp, 1960; Perry, 1961; Wild, 1961; Hickling, 1961, 1962; Lewis, 1964; Malone and Proctor, 1965.

and detritus on their surface (McGaha, 1952; Smirnov, 1958; Macan, 1965): up to 7·5 per cent of the biomass of the community may be so consumed per day (Smirnov, 1961). Smaller fragile and succulent hydrophytes, notably the reduced *Lemna*, *Utricularia* and *Wolffia* and some of the linear-leaved submerged species, are eaten directly by such vegetarian fishes as *Ctenopharyngodon idella* and *Tilapia* species. There is some indication that hydrophytes may have specific odours distinguishable by certain fishes. One minnow (*Pimephales notatus*) is apparently capable of detecting, and differentiating between, over a dozen submerged hydrophytes, even when their odours are diluted or masked by aqueous extracts of different species (Walker and Hasler, 1949). Dense stands of dissected- and linear-leaved submerged species also provide natural spawning media for gastropod and nudibranch molluscs, and for egg-scattering and nesting fishes, and subsequently afford the protection, shade and microparticulate food needed by the fry (de Gruchy, 1938; Hickling, 1961, 1962).

The fruits and seeds of widespread emergent and submerged plants— *Ceratophyllum*, *Echinochloa*, *Najas*, *Peltandra*, *Potamogeton*, *Sagittaria*, *Scirpus* and *Zizania* foremost among them—provide the most important food of many types of water-fowl (e.g. coots, ducks, geese, grebes and swans) and are also commonly eaten by marsh birds (e.g. bittern, gallinule and heron), shore birds (e.g. plover, sandpiper and snipe) and game birds (e.g. grouse, partridge and pheasant). Many birds take also the succulent young shoots and turions, and the reduced free-floating plants (McAtee, 1939; Moyle and Hotchkiss, 1945; Penfound, 1949; Fassett, 1957). Fine testimony to the importance of hydrophytes is given by Forsberg's (1964) study of L. Tåkern. The water-fowl populations of this shallow Swedish water, once famous for its birds, are now rapidly diminishing, following the recent decline of the submerged angiosperm vegetation. The starch-, inulin- or oil-containing tubers and rhizomes, and the green foliage, often rich in sugar, of such emergents as *Acorus*, *Carex*, *Cyperus*, *Echinochloa*, *Glyceria*, *Isoetes*, *Nelumbo*, *Oryza*, *Phragmites* and *Typha*, and of the floating-leaved Nymphaeaceae, figure prominently in the diet of those mammals most associated with aquatic habitats, e.g. beaver, cows, deer, hippopotamus, moose, muskrat and pigs (Gortner, 1934; Frohne, 1938; Hamerstrom and Blake, 1939; Nelson *et al.*, 1939; Fassett, 1957; Wild, 1961). Submerged marine angiosperms, such as *Thalassia* and *Zostera*, provide important food for numerous animals, notably turtles, dugong and manatee (den Hartog, 1957b; Burkholder *et al.*, 1959; Allsopp, 1960).

Some hydrophytes, rich in metabolic by-products, may have deleterious effects if they are frequently eaten. Noting that *Menyanthes trifoliata* is grazed by sheep and cattle only in late summer when other fodder is scarce, Hewett (1964) suggested that the species is not normally relished because of the glucoside, menyanthin, which it contains. The intensely acrid latex juices of species of *Alisma* are reported to be harmful to cattle (Perry, 1961). Several methylated tryptamine alkaloids present in *Phalaris arundinacea* and *P. tuberosa* are probably responsible for the sudden collapse and death, or chronic neurological degeneration (the 'phalaris staggers' syndrome), sometimes exhibited by sheep that have grazed these emergent grasses (Gallagher *et al.*, 1964).

It is of considerable medical and economic importance that the conditions created in warm standing or flowing waters by dense plant populations and accumulated debris are unfortunately favoured as breeding habitats by the vectors of certain critical diseases. Certain freshwater molluscs, such as *Bulinus, Biomphalaria* and *Oncomelania,* are the intermediate hosts of two species of *Schistosoma* which cause bilharziasis, one of the most critical insidious diseases of the tropics and subtropics. In the submerged and marginal plant communities of irrigation canals and other waterways, these snails find admirable sheltered microhabitats with rich supplies of their microbial foods and suitable surfaces for oviposition (W.H.O., 1965). Two other prominent examples are *Anopheles* and *Mansonia* mosquitoes, carrying the parasites responsible for malaria and rural filariasis, respectively (Hinman, 1938; Williams, 1956). The hydrophytes most frequently implicated in the creation of favourable breeding habitats include *Alternanthera philoxeroides, Eichhornia crassipes, Justicia americana, Nelumbo lutea, Pistia stratiotes, Saururus cernuus* and *Typha* spp., e.g. *T. australis* and *T. capensis* (Hall, 1940; Penfound, 1940a, b; Hall and Penfound, 1944; Hess and Hall, 1945; Penfound, 1953a; Williams, 1956; Wild, 1961). The seasonal development of the hydrophyte community sometimes appears temporally related to the habits of the disease vector. Penfound *et al.* (1945) found in Alabama, for example, that each year *Nelumbo lutea* produced its first leaves and *Nuphar advena* and *Salix nigricans* both flowered about 2 weeks before *Anopheles quadrimaculatus* started to breed in the habitats. Closer investigation of such relationships could clearly aid the timely execution of control programmes.

13

The Problem of Aquatic Weeds

One of the major consequences of the luxuriant vegetative growth and vigorous adventive spread of hydrophytes is that numerous species attain prime importance as insidious weeds. Indeed, since about 1850 almost the only interest in these hydrophytes has been the desire to extirpate them. The list of species recognised as weeds in some part of their native or adventive range is very long and includes all life forms. Submerged plants are generally least troublesome, choking small lakes, dams and irrigation channels but rarely creating any gross permanent obstruction. The most severe problems are caused by stoloniferous free-floating species, occurring either as extensive pure colonies or as constituents of sudd communities. They form vast impenetrable floating mats which quickly block drainage channels, sluices and hydro-electric installations and render navigation and fishing impossible on both lakes and rivers. The concomitant financial losses incurred by farmers, traders, fisheries and public utilities are often considerable.

EMERGENT WEEDS

Many emergent hydrophytes create local problems by forming dense pure stands in slow-flowing rivers, at the margins of lakes and reservoirs, in the shallow waters of irrigation channels and drainage furrows, and amongst tropical subaquatic crops. Such extensive colonies impede the current, accelerate the deposition of silt, and, by so raising the substrate, eventually cause flooding. On fertile irrigated soils their more rapid growth chokes the less vigorous crops. The total number of troublesome species is very large; almost every emergent hydrophyte has been reported at some time or another as a local nuisance, most frequently in tropical countries.

In North Carolina and the Gulf Coastal states of North America, for example, alligator weed (*Alternanthera philoxeroides*) infests small rivers, pools and irrigation channels and often encroaches on navigable waters, sometimes even replacing the free-floating water hyacinth, *Eichhornia crassipes*, as the dominant weed. In many respects *Alternanthera philoxeroides* typifies emergent weeds. It cannot survive unless its roots are firmly anchored in the substrate or some other submerged medium suitable for root growth, such as a mat of rotting vegetable debris. Its growth is therefore limited to water sufficiently shallow to allow anchorage of the roots and it is rarely found in water deeper than 1·5 to 2·5 m. It spreads by prostrate growth of the stems, which root at the nodes and eventually become erect and aerial. When a pure colony encroaches outwards from the margin of the water, the advancing plants cease growth and become chlorotic when they encounter a depth of over about 2·5 m. The outermost fringe of plants is then broken by wind or waves, swift currents or passing boats, and the dispersed clumps regenerate elsewhere, provided they reach shallow water and remain there long enough for the roots to become anchored.

As a result of its different habit of growth, alligator weed does not compete with *Eichhornia crassipes* or other floating weeds unless it is firmly anchored in a suitable substrate, although it will rapidly colonise sufficiently shallow water which has just been cleared of *Eichhornia*. Although *A. philoxeroides* flowers in profusion in natural habitats, seeds are very rarely set, and the spread of the weed is almost entirely due to vigorous vegetative reproduction.

Alligator weed was first found in the Old World in 1875, when it was seen growing near Djakarta, and has since become naturalised in standing and slow-flowing waters throughout much of western Java (Backer, 1949). It may have been introduced to the mainland of south-east Asia early in this century: the first certain record is from the man-made Victoria (Inya) Lake in the Rangoon district of Burma in 1932 (Maheshwari, 1965). In recent years the weed has been seen in an increasing number of pools and lakes in Bihar and West Bengal. Noting the fact that its first appearance in eastern India was near an aerodrome at Calcutta, Maheshwari (1965) suggested that viable seeds may have been introduced accidentally with packing material from America sometime during the Second World War. In view of its rapid multiplication elsewhere, the weed could undoubtedly present a severe threat to shallow waterways and irrigation channels in other parts of India, and also in warmer Africa, should it ever become naturalised there.

Species of *Alisma*, *Glyceria*, *Schoenoplectus* and *Sparganium*, common dominants in reed-swamp communities, occasionally cause local problems in slow-flowing rivers and drainage ditches throughout North America and Eurasia. Species of *Phragmites*, *Sagittaria* and *Scirpus* occur as weeds through-out the world: for example, *Phragmites mauritianus* in various parts of Africa, *Sagittaria guayanensis* in Malaysian ricefields, and *Scirpus juncoides* in rice paddies in Madagascar, Malaysia and the Philippines. Similarly some species of *Typha* occur as ricefield weeds in the southern U.S.A. and Portugal, whilst others form immense colonies in wide lowland rivers, such as the Senegal, and are becoming increasingly troublesome in sudd communities in the tropics (Wild, 1961). So extensive is the range of *Phragmites* and *Typha*, and so vigorous is their rhizomatous habit, that their menace as weeds is ubiquitous.

Several species of *Cyperus* are harmful throughout the world in natural waters, irrigation systems and subaquatic crops. Foremost among them is *C. papyrus*, widely distributed in Africa and adventive elsewhere. It closes navigable channels, hinders hydro-electric projects, and obstructs fishing by encroaching on open water from the shallow margins, the colonies extending largely by rhizomes. Wild (1961) noted that in Africa it is troublesome in this way in the

Okovango river system of Botswana, Lake Bangweulu in Zambia, and in Uganda. *C. esculentus* and *C. rotundus*, probably indigenous to most of the warmer regions of the world, are very troublesome in African and Indian ricefields. According to Wild (1961), one or other species, sometimes both, is of major importance in Angola, Central Africa, the Congo, Egypt, Madagascar, Mozambique, South Africa and the Sudan. *C. difformis* is a nuisance in rice paddies in Madagascar, the Philippines and Portugal, and *C. digitatus* in irrigated crops in Gambia.

Miscellaneous tropical emergents, such as *Echinochloa colona*, *E. stagnina*, *Ischaemum rugosum*, *Mimosa pigra*, *Neptunia oleracea*, *Oryza perennis*, *Pycreus mundtii* and *Vossia cuspidata*, are likewise important as weeds of subaquatic crops and irrigation schemes in west tropical Africa, Madagascar, the Sudan, Ceylon and India, Malaysia and the Philippines, and some Pacific Islands. They are also potentially dangerous as constituents of sudd.

SUBMERGED AND FLOATING-LEAVED WEEDS

Submerged and floating-leaved weeds are often of only local importance. Even so, their effects are frequently drastic if their vigorous growth is unchecked. They block small rivers and irrigation channels, reducing the flow of water and eventually causing wastage by flooding. They also infest ponds and lakes, hindering the culture of fish and reducing the recreational amenities of the water. Examples of such submerged weeds are provided by *Aponogeton ulvaceus* in Madagascan ricefields, *Myriophyllum spicatum* in Portugal, southern Africa and the R. Kafue in Zambia, many species of *Najas* in irrigation schemes in subtropical America, Portugal, tropical Africa and Asia (Wild, 1961). Extensive colonies of *Ceratophyllum demersum*, floating off-shore beneath the surface of the water, have gradually developed in L. Volta since the formation of the lake began in May 1964, but they have not yet presented any serious problem (Ewer, 1966). Species of *Callitriche*, *Ceratophyllum*, *Hippuris*, *Myriophyllum*, *Potamogeton*, *Ranunculus* and *Zannichellia* are similarly occasional nuisances in many north and south temperate countries. *Ranunculus pseudofluitans* and other submerged plants have to be cut annually (or even more frequently) in many English chalk streams, at appreciable expense to the river authorities and fishery owners (Westlake, *in litt.*).

Sometimes the weeds are aliens which seem to reproduce and spread more vigorously than in their native range. The classic example is the North American *Elodea canadensis* which attained the status of a critical weed throughout much of the British Isles, continental Europe and New Zealand (p. 360). Other submerged members of the same family, the Hydrocharitaceae, also appear potentially dangerous. Vigorous adventive populations of the South American *Egeria densa*, for example, are now known in numerous sites in the United States, Europe and New Zealand (Koch, 1950; Mason, 1960; Feuillade, 1962; Corillion, 1964). Species of *Lagarosiphon* are locally troublesome as indigenes in southern Africa (Wild, 1961), and one of these—*L. major*, which is a common aquarium plant—has been recorded as a thriving alien in several European and New Zealand stations (Koch, 1950; Lousley, 1957b; Mason, 1960; Corillion,

1964). In New Zealand, where it was first observed in 1950, particularly heavy infestations have developed in L. Rotorua and L. Rotoiti in South Auckland, threatening angling and other sporting activities and evoking innumerable public complaints, which culminated in a law suit against the local authority in 1952. The excessive growth of the weed has been attributed to the favourable local climate and the enrichment of the water by sewage as the drainage area became increasingly developed. The infestations show no sign of waning and unfortunately appear to be resistant to herbicidal treatment with sodium arsenite (Mason, 1960; Fish, 1963; and see p. 500).

Amongst floating-leaved hydrophytes, several species of *Nuphar, Nymphaea* and *Potamogeton* are regarded as weeds in north temperate countries and parts of tropical Africa and Asia, although they rarely threaten navigable rivers, lakes or large reservoirs because of their edaphic restriction to fairly shallow waters up to 3 m deep. Even so, the leaves of *Nymphaea caerulea* and *Potamogeton thunbergii* may completely blanket small dams or farm ponds in two seasons, hindering the culture of fish and the use of water for irrigation or domestic purposes (Wild, 1961). *Aponogeton desertorum* similarly infests small dams throughout much of southern Africa. Three other floating-leaved plants present a potential menace in view of their frequent cultivation as ornamental subjects and their vigorous spread whenever they escape to suitable natural habitats. These are *Hydrocleys nymphoides* in warm temperate and tropical regions of the Old World, *Nymphoides peltata* in temperate Europe and America, and *Nymphoides indica* in warmer Africa, Asia and Australia.

FREE-FLOATING WEEDS

The magnitude of the problem set by free-floating weeds varies to some extent with their size and habits of growth. The fragile reduced species of *Lemna* and *Wolffia* may create a trivial nuisance as scums on ponds, slow-flowing canals and ditches; they may block the grids of small domestic dams. They are almost ubiquitous but are especially troublesome amongst irrigated crops in Ceylon, India, Malaysia, Portugal and the southern U.S.A. where the higher temperatures encourage superabundant growth. They are occasionally aggressive in temperate sites too. An 'explosive' increase of *Lemna minor* during the late summer has choked several kilometres of the sluggish Sudbury River in eastern Massachusetts annually since 1936. An infestation of the same species also appeared suddenly in 1936 and 1937 in the Charles R., which is in the same area but has no surface connection with the Sudbury. It is possible that the continued abnormal abundance of the species each year in the Sudbury is related to some environmental change which occurred in the mid-1930's, perhaps an increase in soluble nitrogen and a shift towards slight alkalinity resulting from pollution by sewage (Eaton, 1947). Species of *Azolla* and *Utricularia* are also an occasional nuisance in pools, small lakes, drainage ditches and rice-paddies, although *Utricularia* spp. are not of widespread importance, probably because of their edaphic preference for waters of low pH value. Generally these various reduced genera are too small and brittle to create any major permanent obstacle.

It is the larger, vigorous, stoloniferous species that cause the greatest damage. In conditions favouring vegetative growth, *Trapa natans*, for example, reproduces rapidly by stolons. The colonies of connected rosettes quickly form quite a stable surface-floating mat which hinders navigation in the littoral regions of lakes and on slow-moving rivers. The species is troublesome in this way on the River Danube in Rumania and is potentially dangerous in many parts of Africa and in the north-eastern United States, to which it has been extensively introduced. In the Sudbury R. in Massachusetts, for example, it suddenly increased and seriously choked long stretches in the summer of 1945, although for many years before this it had grown there and given no trouble (Eaton, 1947).

Pistia stratiotes is more widespread in tropical waters. Its native range, like that of many apparently pan-tropical hydrophytes, is not accurately known: Ridley (1930) doubted that the plant is indigenous to Malaysia. The possibility that it is adventive in numerous areas is enhanced by its ancient medicinal use in the treatment of erysipelas and the healing of abrasions. Although abundant stolons are produced by this weed, it seems likely that dissemination of the seeds, which are minute and liberated in great numbers, contributes significantly to its spread over large areas. Little is known of the ecology of *P. stratiotes*. Its tolerance of salinity seems to be low: Ridley (1930) observed that rosettes floating down the river at Batu Pahat, in Johore, began to die on reaching brackish water and disappeared in sea water. *Pistia stratiotes* resembles *Trapa natans* and *Eichhornia crassipes* in forming floating obstacles. It is very troublesome on the Upper White Nile which from the foot of the Murchison Falls, some 80 km from the Karuma Falls, becomes a broad, quiet, slow-moving stream covered with millions of the floating rosettes (Moorehead, 1960). It also causes problems in Dahomey, Guinea, the Ivory Coast, Mali, Mauretania, Gambia, Senegal, Nigeria, Cameroun, the Congolese Republic and coastal Angola (Wild, 1961). Soon after L. Volta began to fill, scattered colonies of *P. stratiotes* appeared, especially along the eastern shore. These increased markedly during 1965 and in the westward Afram arm of the lake formed dense mats invaded by other plants (Ewer, 1966). The species is also a weed in the Grand Lac region of Cambodia and in Ceylon (Williams, 1956; Hickling, 1961). From time to time, it is troublesome in parts of India, Malaya and subtropical America.

Neither *Pistia stratiotes* nor *Trapa natans* is as critically dangerous a weed as *Eichhornia crassipes* or *Salvinia auriculata*, both of which have caused immense problems in various warmer parts of the world. The spread and effects of each of these two species merit detailed consideration.

THE ADVENTIVE SPREAD OF THE WATER HYACINTH, *EICHHORNIA CRASSIPES*

Although Hildebrand (1946) considered *Eichhornia crassipes* to have been introduced from Japan about 1876, it is actually a true indigene of tropical South America and does not occur as a native anywhere in Asia. Originally described (as *Pontederia crassipes*) from Brazil by von Martius in 1823, it has an extensive range centred on northern Brazil and Venezuela and is particularly abundant in the Pernambuco region, the Amazon basin and the lower Orinoco. It may also extend as a native into parts of Central America and the larger Caribbean islands, although some of its stations in this area might be due to early introduction. In South America, *E. crassipes* is accompanied by *E. azurea*, a species of very similar overall range, by the more restricted *E. paniculata* and *E. paradoxa*, and by *E. natans* in most tropical parts of the continent. It is very remarkable that whilst these other neotropical members of the genus, and also the exclusively African *E. diversifolia*, have all apparently remained more or less within the limits of their native range, *E. crassipes* has spread far and wide during the past 80 years (Fig. 13.1), becoming perhaps the most renowned of all aquatic weeds.

Just when the dissemination of *E. crassipes* about the globe actually began is not clear. Some authors, notably Ridley (1930), have suggested that the plant was introduced to the palaeotropics about 1829 but the most reliable evidence points to a later date, during the last decade of the nineteenth century. According to Backer (1951f), the plant was introduced in 1894 to the Buitenzorg (Bogor) Botanic Gardens in Java. Not long after, as a result of the nuisance it rapidly caused, immense amounts of living specimens were summarily dumped into the Tji Liwung flowing through the Gardens. This river doubtless conveyed the plant down to the coastal plains, throughout which innumerable local infestations were soon evident. By 1902 water hyacinths had been found in several sites in continental South-East Asia, and about 1905 they first appeared in Ceylon. In Africa, the species seems to have been introduced to Egypt sometime between 1879 and 1892 (Tackhölm and Drar, 1950) and to Natal in the early years of this century (Wild, 1961). It is interesting to note that the original manner of introduction in Java parallels the escape of several other aliens, notably *Limnocharis flava* and species of *Sagittaria*, from the very same Botanic Gardens (see p. 401) and the liberation of *Elodea canadensis* from the Cambridge Botanic Garden in England (p. 361). Very little is known of the precise mode of introduction of *Eichhornia crassipes* to the other sites in the Asian and African tropics.

Opinions differ as to how *E. crassipes* was introduced to the U.S.A. but the most reliable accounts suggest that, at an international Cotton Exposition held at New Orleans in 1884, members of the delegation from the Japanese Government distributed as souvenirs water hyacinths which had been imported from the lower Orinoco in Venezuela (Hildebrand, 1946). The plants were aesthetically prized for their beautiful exotic blooms and from New Orleans were taken to surrounding districts and cultivated in garden pools and farm ponds. It is likely that when their prodigious rate of increase was eventually discovered, vast numbers of excess plants were merely dumped in nearby streams and drains (Klorer, 1909). Shortly afterwards, in 1890, the species appeared in Florida and soon after the turn of the century it was becoming naturalised in all the south-eastern coastal states as far north as Virginia, and also in California (Penfound and Earle, 1948).

The subsequent spread of *Eichhornia crassipes* has been spectacular and disastrous everywhere. In Florida, for example (Fig. 13.2, A), it became particularly troublesome in the St. Johns River which provided magnificently suitable habitats. As a result of the very slight gradient of its course, a tidal effect being apparent even 220 km inland, the current throughout is sluggish and thus enabled the hyacinths to colonise the shallow margins without being swept

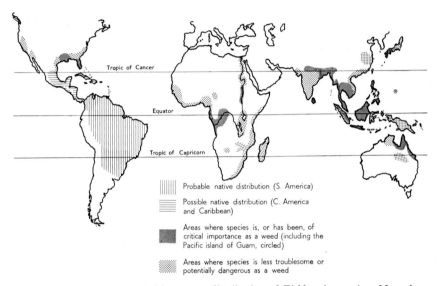

Tropic of Cancer

Equator

Tropic of Capricorn

|||||| Probable native distribution (S. America)

Possible native distribution (C. America and Caribbean)

Areas where species is, or has been, of critical importance as a weed (including the Pacific island of Guam, circled)

Areas where species is less troublesome or potentially dangerous as a weed

FIG. 13.1. Map of the probable present distribution of *Eichhornia crassipes*. Note the thorough invasion of most of the regions of the Old World tropics which possess a high frequency of aquatic habitats, and also the extension into subtropical latitudes on all continents. (Based on Mollweide's Interrupted Homolographic projection, and compiled from data in many sources: since precise distributional data are lacking in several parts of both the native and adventive ranges, this map ought to be regarded as tentative.)

away. Dense colonies in creeks and backwaters acted as foci in the insidious invasion. By 1895, colonies varying in width from 8 to 70 m extended along each bank of the main river for over 160 km. The weather during the summer of 1896 was stormy, and gale-force winds drove the mats of hyacinth upstream from Lake George, creating a blockage some 40 km long. The mass of vegetation could not be penetrated by boats, and it became impossible to float logs down the river; the annual loss to the lumber trade was estimated at 55 000 dollars (Arber, 1920).

Throughout the twentieth century the species has increased as a pest in the slow-flowing rivers and irrigation ditches of the Gulf coastal states and also in parts of California (Fig. 13.1). In Louisiana, several infested areas developed to the north, near Shreveport and Monroe, but the species achieved its highest intensity in the complicated system of tributaries of the Mississippi in the south-central part of the state (Fig. 13.2, B). In 1948 this area of critical infestation extended from Franklin eastward to Point à la Hache and southward from Alexandria to Houma. It included several large bayous, the Atchafalaya River, the lower reaches of the Red River, and all the freshwater lakes and current Mississippi deltas. Transport by water is still a vital f:ctor in the economy of this area of the state, since corn, rice, cane and cotton, together with fish, citrus fruits, salt, oil, lumber and other products, are all thereby carried. The *Eichhornia* invasion thus had disastrous consequences, and it has been estimated that the annual loss incurred in Louisiana through the effects of the weed amounted to an average of 5 million dollars; in some years it was as much as 15 million (Penfound and Earle, 1948).

In Ceylon in 1909, 4 years after the species had been initially introduced, an Ordinance was enacted which made it a punishable offence to cultivate the plant, import it or fail to destroy it. Despite this measure the plant spread relentlessly through the slow-flowing parts of rivers, irrigation channels, drains, lagoons, tanks and swamps, and had become by 1925 a serious menacing weed in Southern Province where infestations were common, especially at sea-level (C.D.A., 1926; Haigh, 1936). By October 1936 the only areas which remained

FIG. 13.2. A, Map of peninsular Florida showing lakes, waterways and principal sites referred to in the text. (B on p. 464.)

16

uninfested were in the Northern, North-Central and Eastern Provinces (C.D.A., 1938).

From its initial stations in south-east Asia, it spread (Fig. 13.1), aided by further introductions and cultivation as an ornamental. It is now a frequent weed in Victoria, New South Wales, Queensland, Borneo, the Philippines, Guam

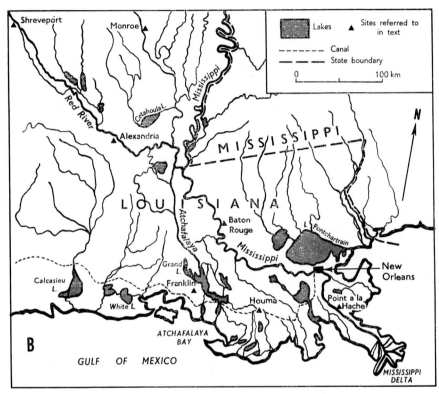

FIG. 13.2. B, Map of central and south-eastern Louisiana showing lakes, waterways and principal sites referred to in the text.

(the Micronesian island east of the Philippines), Sumatra, and Java, where it ascends from the coastal plains to an altitude of about 1600 m (Backer, 1951f). On the mainland it has spread through the Malay Peninsula and extended its range north to parts of Thailand, China and Japan. In these areas it was, and still is, cultivated in ponds, along with *Pistia* and other floating plants, as fodder for pigs. Carried about in pails of this pig-food, it must frequently have escaped into the irrigated ricefields, though Ridley (1930) noted that it did not thrive in the rivers around Singapore, probably because of their brackish water. It is extremely abundant in the Grand Lac region of Cambodia and in some Malayan rivers where its packed colonies choke reed- and chicken-wire fences and often cause flooding (Hickling, 1961). It has invaded much of lowland Burma and India, becoming a notorious pest in the valleys and deltas of the Brahmaputra, Ganges and Mahanadi in the provinces of Assam, West Bengal, Bihar, Uttar Pradesh and Orissa.

In Africa (Fig. 13.1) the water hyacinth is at present notably troublesome in the lowland areas of Angola, equatorial Africa and the Congolese Republic, the principal rivers involved being the Congo and its tributaries—the Kasai, the Ubangui, the Sanga, the Itimbiri, and the Mongala. The immense scale of the infestation is shown vividly by the fact, quoted by Lebrun (1959), that in 1956–1957, 152 400 kg (150 tons) of *Eichhornia* per hour were being swept through Leopoldville by the Congo river, even with attempted control measures costing 50 million Belgian francs. The species also constitutes local hindrances in the eastern Cape, Madagascar, Mozambique, Natal, Rhodesia, and Tanganyika (C.C.T.A./C.S.A., 1957; Wild, 1961). Wild considered it to be potentially dangerous in the upper basin of the Nile, the basins of the Kagera, Logone, Niger, Senegal and Zambezi, the Okovango system in Botswana, the Sabi system in Rhodesia, Lakes Victoria and Albert and their tributaries. Parts of several rivers in the Guinean region are in fact slightly contaminated, and the menace to the Nile has been realised, for in the last few years the plant has taken hold on the Upper White Nile, in the Sudd region, insidiously colonising the sluggish streams from the banks and steadily spreading, despite the ravaging effect of passing steamers (Moorehead, 1960).

Water hyacinths were first seen on the White Nile in March 1958, at a point near Aba Island some 300 km south of Khartoum, but were probably present further south between Adok and Bor, in the Sudd region (Fig. 13.3), in 1956 or early 1957. It seems likely that colonies were swept downstream on the White Nile flood of 1957, their northward advance being halted when the prevailing winds became northerly in September of that year, and maintained at about Kosti, just downstream of Aba Island, until the southerly winds returned in March 1958 (Gay, 1958). At this time there were two principal infested areas: from Kosti upstream to El Jebelein, and further south, from Malakal upstream to the confluence of the Bahr el Zeraf and Bahr el Jebel. Throughout the summer these reaches remained the foci but the weed spread downstream, as expected, under the influence of the southerly winds, and by October 1958 the infested length of river had increased by nearly 50 per cent. Quite unexpectedly, however, the weed spread upstream too, in the Bahr el Jebel and Bahr el Ghazal. Clearly, this feature of the weed's expansion of range could not have been caused by the prevailing wind, still less by the river current. Gay (1960) held the Nile steamers responsible, as specimens of *Eichhornia* were frequently seen to be entangled amidst the numerous barges lashed each side and forward of the driving unit of the steamers. Indeed, the weed creates an appreciable problem by obstructing entry to the steamers' cooling systems. In support of his conclusion, Gay cited the fact that whereas the weed is common in the main navigational channel of the Bahr el Ghazal, it is absent from adjacent lagoons and tributaries through which the steamers do not pass.

By July 1959 a dense infestation had developed at the Jebel Aulia Dam, south of Khartoum (Figs. 13.4, 14.1). In the Jebel Aulia basin, conditions in the river are magnificently suited to the accumulation of weed. The velocity of the current is minimal, having progressively decreased from the point where

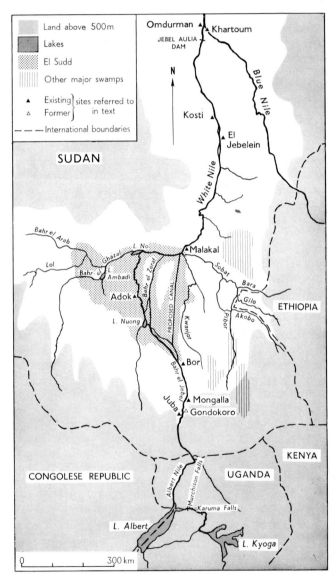

FIG. 13.3. Map of the basin of the White Nile, showing El Sudd and the various lakes rivers and principal sites referred to in the text.

the Bahr el Jebel enters the Sudd just north of Bor, over 1500 km upstream: the river is also wide (up to 7 km across) and fully exposed to the wind, which raises waves up to 2 m high and tends to bank up the floating weed into serious obstacles. From the Jebel Aulia Dam infestations now occur as far south as Juba on the Bahr el Jebel (Fig. 13.3), on the weak-flowing Bahr el Ghazal and

FIG. 13.4. A, Mr. Salah el Din Hassan Ahmed (left), the Senior Inspector of Water Hyacinths of the Ministry of Agriculture in the Sudan, standing on the Jebel Aulia Dam and inspecting a typical specimen of *Eichhornia crassipes* which has been stopped by the dam from floating into the lower Nile, September 1964. (B and C on p. 468.)

Bahr el Zeraf, and also to an incompletely known extent on the Sobat and Pibor rivers (Pettet, 1964). Being relatively slow-flowing, shallow, and fertile, and having only a narrow diurnal amplitude of temperature, the waters of the Nile in the affected areas would seem to afford an excellent habitat for the weed. There is little doubt that if unchecked, the infestations could easily block the navigational channels of the White Nile as disastrously as they were blocked by sudd communities on innumerable occasions up to the end of the nineteenth century. Floods may easily carry the weed into secondary channels and into irrigation systems. Gay (1960) considered that future spread upstream into Uganda is likely to be prevented by the several cataracts south of Juba.

Eichhornia crassipes has not yet appeared on L. Kariba or L. Volta, but the possibility that it may invade these lakes, and similar future projects such as

FIG. 13.4. B, Long islands (one arrowed) of *Eichhornia crassipes* mixed with *Cyperus papyrus* drifting down the White Nile in the Sudan, September 1964. Such islands have seriously interfered with navigation. C, large floating mats of *Eichhornia crassipes* spreading across L. Apanás in Nicaragua, with smaller colonies around partly submerged trees in the right foreground, May 1965. Extensive mats elsewhere have blocked the lake from bank to bank. All the growth has occurred within about two years. (By courtesy of Dr. E. C. S. Little, A.R.C. Weed Research Organisation, Oxford, England.)

the Nigerian L. Kainji, cannot be ignored. The weed has actually infested three new man-made lakes in the neotropics. By the middle of 1965, expanses of the weed had developed along about 70 km of the shoreline of Brokopondo L. in Surinam, which only began to fill in February 1964 (Leentvaar, 1966). L. Rio Lempa in El Salvador has existed since 1957 and now possesses a dense marginal infestation of water hyacinths which is apparently tolerated by the project's engineers, despite the significant wastage of water which it probably causes by displacement and transpiration (Little, 1966). The small and winding L. Apanás in Nicaragua reached its maximum level in 1964. By June 1965, extensive mats of *E. crassipes* had developed at one end of the lake and were spreading rapidly; invasion by sudd-forming emergents had begun in some sites (Figs. 12.5, 13.4). At the other end of the lake dense populations of *Pistia stratiotes* had become established, whilst in the middle region the two weeds were competing for space (Fig. 12.6).

The relative importance of vegetative and sexual reproduction in the spread of *Eichhornia crassipes* in different areas is very difficult to assess. Some eight years ago, a symposium on the problems of the weed in Africa deplored the shortage of information on the processes of fruiting, germination, and dissemination of seeds and vegetative fragments (C.C.T.A./C.S.A., 1957). Past reports, from south-east Asia, Ceylon and other places, that seed is never set or that cross-pollination is rarely successful (p. 281) seem to have inculcated the widespread belief that reproduction by seed is not an important factor. Certainly, it is true that the weed spreads very quickly by means of stolons and regeneration from viable fragments: floating mats, solitary drifting plants and accumulated fragments are all too readily distributed by water currents, strong winds and passing boats. But certain experimental studies of the life cycle of the plant, together with recent observations in infested reaches of the Nile, strongly suggest that the dissemination and development of seeds may be far more significant than has hitherto been acknowledged.

Haigh (1936) found that neither drying of the seeds nor a prolonged dormant period is necessary for subsequent germination, but concluded that a high temperature and/or intense light are necessary, this being consistent with the observation that in nature seedlings are often absent from shaded habitats and more abundant in bright than cloudy weather. Haigh found it hard to culture seedlings beyond the two-leaf stage and only succeeded by placing the seedlings on mud kept wet but not deeply flooded: even then, however, growth was only very slow. He concluded that germination is most likely to occur in shallow water warmed by intense sunlight and that the possibility of spread by seeds is real and permanent.

It has been observed in many infested rivers, ditches and tanks that after being exposed and hardened during prolonged dry weather the banks have become covered with *Eichhornia* seedlings when the waters have again risen. This suggests that although desiccation may not be necessary for germination the seeds are able to tolerate a long dry period and yet remain viable. Hitchcock *et al.* (1949) showed that dried seeds take approximately twice as long (4 months) to germinate as seeds kept wet from the time of collection. The percentage germination after air-dry storage in the laboratory for 69 days at 22°C was only 84 to 96 whereas after storage for an identical period in water at the same temperature it was 100. Seeds were found to withstand storage at a temperature as low as $-5°C$ for one week and still show 50 per cent germination, a result of no little significance in assessing the possible survival of the species under extreme conditions in natural habitats. The same workers obtained 100 per cent germination of seeds when the water temperature was 28 to 36°C in the middle of the day, the air temperature varying from 21 to 27°C in the course of each day. It is worthy of note that these experiments, which confirmed in all major respects those of Haigh (1936), were performed in Petri dishes or wide-mouthed bottles, containing tap water to a depth of up to 5 cm: several earlier workers had been unable to germinate seeds under water but Hitchcock *et al.* pointed out that their failure was probably due to too low a temperature and insufficient light. Prompted by the fact that hyacinth seeds sink to the substrate when liberated from the fruit, Hitchcock *et al.* (1950) investigated germination under water of 2·5, 10, 20, 30 and 40 cm depth and found that the rate of germination increases consistently with increasing volume and depth of water. They suggested that this is due to a less marked temperature decrease in the larger volumes of water during the night. Parija's (1934) observation that a greater number of seedlings appears in water tanks with steep sides than in those with sloping sides could be similarly interpreted.

Although these various experiments amply demonstrated the potential of the water hyacinth for spreading by seed, Hitchcock and his colleagues observed during 1948 and 1949 that despite the production of huge numbers of seeds by plants in the waterways of Louisiana, remarkably few seedlings could be found. In 1948 no seedlings whatsoever could be seen either in open water or on the fringes of mature colonies: seedlings were found only on one exposed part of a floating mat. During April 1949 the normal frequent rains fell, the water table was high, and seedlings were found on the wet banks of the experimental pits and canals, which were exposed to direct sunlight and must have been at a sufficiently high temperature for germination. Widespread mortality ensued in May, when dry weather stranded most of the seedlings in hard soil. During the same two months, the temperature of the water at or near the surface of a mat of hyacinths was found to vary between 17 and 21°C, well below that required for germination, and it is significant that when much of the aerial foliage was removed, seeds on the section of the floating mat thereby exposed to direct sunlight germinated within 7 days. These survived provided that the mat did not sink but remained exposed for 3 to 4 weeks. Clearly, in natural habitats, the only factor likely to reduce the rate of germination is shading by aerial foliage, with its consequent depression of the temperature of the water at or near the surface of the floating mat. Having reached the seedling stage, the young plants require anchorage in a wet, yet relatively solid medium for about 4 weeks, until they can grow as floating plants (Fig. 13.5). It has also been suggested that ligulate-leaved juvenile plants have different nutritional requirements from mature floating rosettes. Hitchcock *et al.* (1950) concluded that the development of mature individuals from seed is likely to be limited by unfavourable growing conditions rather than conditions unsuitable for germination, and they surmised that the development of seedlings was of negligible significance in the rapid spread of the weed in Louisiana.

More recent observations suggest that far from being just a potential menace, germinating seeds are a real and dangerous source of infestation in certain areas of the tropics. Immense numbers of seedlings were discovered in November 1963 along the banks of the White Nile between Jebel Aulia and Kosti. Ironically, it is probable that the control measures at present in operation are creating conditions encouraging rapid growth of the seedlings. Many hyacinth plants, dying after being sprayed with 2,4-D, are swept on to the banks by the wind and the current and there they decay into a layer of peat-like remains, often mixed with *Cyperus papyrus* and species of *Typha* and forming a conspicuous 'strand-line' at the water's edge. Both ligulate- and floating-leaved seedlings are found most abundantly on the richest, most decomposed debris: they do not occur where the banks are just ordinary sandy soil. These facts suggest, firstly, that seeds may be concentrated along the water line by the accumulation of decaying plants, and, secondly, that the debris is especially suitable for subsequent growth of the seedlings (Pettet, 1964).

The severity of the threat presented by such seedlings will be influenced by the state of the river, for if the waters should subside fairly rapidly, most if not all the seedlings will be completely stranded and desiccated. Rising waters will liberate the seedlings and those which have reached the independent floating-leaved stage will not only survive but be dispersed, perhaps over a considerable distance. Wherever the fluctuation of water level is small, as it is upstream of Kosti (Pettet, 1964), the seedlings' chances of survival are greater still.

The strand-line of dying *Eichhornia* could well accelerate infestation of irrigation systems as well as the river itself. Accumulated seeds could easily be dispersed in the water withdrawn at the banks and pumped into the irrigation channels. Pettet (1964) surmised that small colonies of hyacinths he observed in numerous channels on both sides of the White Nile had originated in this way. He also commented upon the discovery, several times since April 1962, of seedlings rooted in the substrate in fairly shallow water in the main river *below* the Jebel Aulia dam. These must have developed from seeds carried down through the sluices of the dam. This conclusion raises the alarming possibility of eventual infestation of the main Nile down past Khartoum into the future L. Nasser and of the Gezira cotton scheme via the Blue Nile, threats thought to have been alleviated by the herbicidal control of plants on the upper river.

In habitats where the water is shallow, exposed and at a high enough temperature for germination, and where the rooting medium is suitable for the initial development of the seedlings, propagation by seeds may contribute significantly to the spread of *Eichhornia crassipes* and could be a potent source of reinfestation of cleared areas. The development and maintenance of the colonies, and perhaps the gross adventive spread in some areas, are undoubtedly achieved by vegetative reproduction and dispersal of the mature plants by strong currents and high winds. By virtue of the spongy lacunate tissue in all the

16*

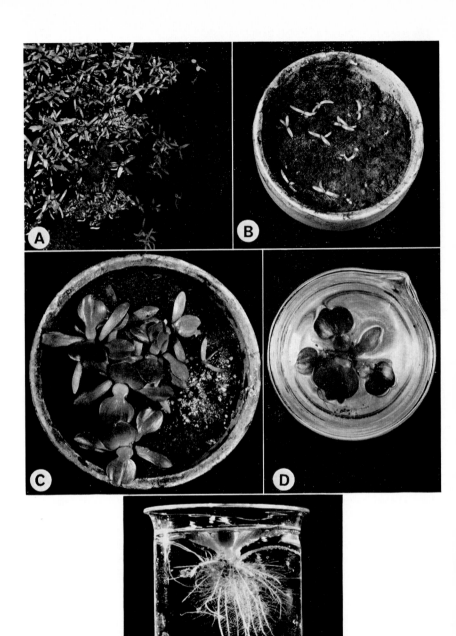

organs, and the sail-like attitude of the leaf blades, the rosettes are very buoyant and easily swept along by wind, even against an appreciable surface current. The vigorous stoloniferous habit and the presence of thick pendulous clusters of profusely branched roots are mainly responsible for the creation of densely interwoven, mat-like colonies. In a suitable habitat during active growth the plants can double their numbers every 2 weeks, the floating mat extending by as much as 0·5 to 0·75 m/month. Penfound and Earle (1948) calculated that at this rate of multiplication ten individuals would have produced 655 360 plants, equivalent to a solid acre, during one growing season, which in Louisiana extends from at least March 15 to about November 15. They also found that the total wet weight of an 8-year-old hyacinth mat varied from 50 600 kg/ha (123 tons/acre) in winter to 75 700 kg/ha (184 tons/acre) in summer.

THE ADVENTIVE SPREAD OF *SALVINIA AURICULATA*

With the exception of its invasions of Ceylon and part of central Africa this free-floating fern has caused much less damage as an alien than *Eichhornia crassipes*. This innocuousness may be illusory for it must be remembered that *Salvinia* is of more recent introduction than *Eichhornia* and may yet make its presence felt in an equally disastrous way. Like other alien weeds, it is not in equilibrium with its new environments and if climatic and edaphic factors are favourable, natural competitors are absent and no preventive measures are taken, it may still spread and invade new areas.

Originally described from Guiana by Aublet, *Salvinia auriculata* has a wide native range in the neotropics extending from Mexico and the Galapagos Islands through Central America and the Antilles and most of tropical South America as far as southern Brazil (Herzog, 1935, 1938). Populations identified as *S. auriculata* from warm temperate Argentina south to the Rio de la Plata are probably *S. herzogii* (de la Sota, 1962). *S. auriculata* is accompanied throughout much of its range by another extensive native species, *S. rotundifolia*, and in small areas of South America by various endemic species, *S. oblongifolia*, *S. martynii* and *S. sprucei* (de la Sota, 1962, 1963, 1964; and see Table 11.4). Similarly, in various parts of its adventive range, *S. auriculata* is accompanied by one or more native palaeotropical species which are sometimes important as weeds. In Africa there are two indigenous species: *S. hastata* occurs widely in tropical east Africa and Madagascar (Wild, 1961), and *S. nymphellula* is

FIG. 13.5. Development of seedlings of *Eichhornia crassipes*: A, about 700 seedlings growing in saturated soil which slopes into shallow water at right, those partly or wholly immersed being somewhat retarded in growth compared with those wholly exposed (at left); B, young seedlings germinated in water and photographed 10 days after planting in wet soil; C, same seedlings as in B one month later, showing transition to leaves with floats, at which stage they grow better in water; D, seedling removed from pot in C, seen from above after a further 16 days, i.e. 56 days after germination, showing transition from spatulate leaves to ones with inflated petioles; E, Same seedling as in D seen from side, showing inflated petioles and a root system which developed in water during the 16-day period. (From Hitchcock *et al.*, 1949, by courtesy of the Boyce Thompson Institute for Plant Research, Yonkers, New York.)

common in tropical west Africa (Alston, 1959a). Frequent in areas of southern
Asia are *S. cucullata*, which is also indigenous in Australia, and *S. natans*, a
subtropical and warm temperate species which extends from Bengal to north
China and also occurs in southern Europe (Herzog, 1935, 1938).

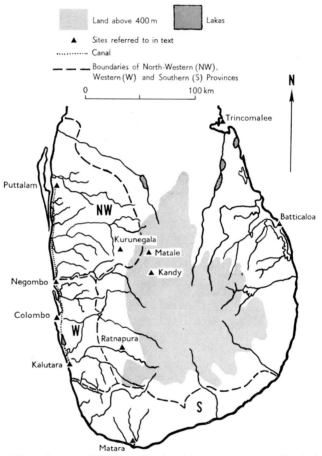

FIG. 13.6. Map of most of Ceylon, showing lakes, waterways and principal sites
referred to in the text.

S. auriculata is considered to have been introduced to the Old World from
tropical America but of the manner, time or precise source of the introductions
almost nothing is known. It is often cultivated, like several other alien hydrophytes, in botanic gardens, aquaria and ornamental lakes, and may have escaped
or been deliberately introduced from one or more of these sources.

In Ceylon (Fig. 13.6) during the last 20 years *Salvinia auriculata* has infested
thousands of acres of the richest paddy lands, throughout the length of the
western seaboard. The weed was first recorded in 1942 when the Divisional

Agricultural Officer of Western Province, a Dr. Paul, observed quantities of it near Kolonnawa, a suburb of Colombo. It seems that specimens of *S. auriculata* were sent in 1933 from Germany to the Royal Botanical Gardens in Calcutta and from here in 1939 living material was despatched together with specimens of *S. cucullata* and *S. natans* to Colombo University for use in botanical studies. Subsequently, unwanted specimens somehow got into nearby waters where they survived and multiplied beyond all expectation (Senaratna, 1952a; Williams, 1956).

In August 1943 a few juvenile plants were found scattered in a water channel adjacent to the experimental ricefields at Usvetakeyyava, and a few hundred metres away sparse colonies were seen in the slow-flowing water of the Negombo Canal. According to labourers and local inhabitants these plants had been swept along the canal during the previous month: upstream towards Colombo the infestations were heavier. In the same month a dense infestation of much-branched adult plants was discovered at the Stanley Power Station at Kolonnawa. In 4 months this mass had covered about 95 m^2 of water surface, blocking the inlet through which water was withdrawn to cool the machinery. A thorough survey revealed that the weed was fortunately restricted to Western Province, but that the infestations were scattered from Werahera north to Negombo Lagoon, an area permeated by a system of waterways connecting Negombo to Bolgoda Lake (Senaratna, 1943). It was all too clear that the current in the canals and drainage channels distributed plants and built up blockages wherever there was a barrier to the flow, the colonies multiplying in quiet backwaters and stagnant pools.

One waterway in particular probably facilitated the spread of the plant. Running near the coast, from Puttalam, some 130 km north of Colombo, to Kalutara, 40 km south of the capital, the San Sebastian Canal built during the Dutch occupation serves for both transport and irrigation. In the abnormally heavy rains of 1947 the canal reached its highest level ever and overflowed for several kilometres, carrying the infestations of *S. auriculata* over the adjacent land. Several years later, colonies of weed extended almost the whole length of the canal (Williams, 1956). By 1952 waterways had become infested throughout the Western, North-Western and Southern Provinces from Puttalam as far south as Matara and east to Kurunegala. The linkage of all the principal zones of infestation in this area by the canal and river systems suggests that passive dispersal by flowing water was the prime agent of the weed's invasion. In each local area buffaloes and other mammals, water-fowl and man probably helped spread the weed through the irrigation channels and adjacent paddy fields. Water-fowl may well have carried fragments and juvenile plants some distance inland for soon after 1950 infestations appeared in the districts of Ratnapura and Matale, and even on the eastern coast in the vicinity of Batticaloa (Senaratna, 1952a). A survey of the whole of Ceylon in 1954 revealed the immense extent of the invasion: since its appearance twelve years before, *Salvinia auriculata* had infested at least 810 ha (2000 acres) of waterways and approximately 8910 ha (22000 acres) of cultivable ricefields (Williams, 1956).

A similar problem has recently arisen in Africa (Hattingh, 1961; Schelpe, 1961; Boughey, 1963). In 1959 fragments of *Salvinia auriculata* were observed on the rising waters of Lake Kariba in the Zambezi valley (Fig. 13.7). The species was known to occur on the Zambezi as early as 1949 when it was found

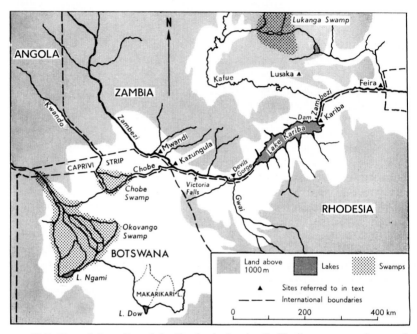

FIG. 13.7. Map of the valley of the Zambezi, showing L. Kariba, swamps, rivers and principal sites referred to in the text.

at Katombora, about 55 km upstream from the Victoria Falls: colonies were subsequently observed along 100 km of the river from the Falls to Kazungula. The swift current prevented these colonies creating any permanent obstacle and much of the weed perished in its tumble over the Falls. If any fragments survived and established colonies lower down the river, the regular floodwaters probably washed them away.

The present problem owes its origin to the building of the Kariba Dam and the impounding of the river, which began in December 1958. When the maximum reservoir level was reached in 1963 the lake was 190 km long by 10 to 32 km wide, with a surface area of about 4500 km², and it therefore formed a magnificent sink of still water on which the *Salvinia* could establish itself. The weed underwent explosive vegetative reproduction and only 13 months after its appearance it had formed extensive littoral colonies covering a total area of 195 to 390 km². During 1962 the colonies extended along almost the entire shoreline of 3200 km, and achieved a peak coverage of 900 to 1000 km² (Emmanuel, *in litt.*). Infestations were especially heavy in the upper (western) reaches of the lake, notably the Milibizi area, but later the species became more established at the lower end. Since the prevailing wind is from the east, these colonies near Kariba itself could easily reinfest cleared areas in the upper reaches (Hattingh, unpubl.).

It was originally hoped that the *Salvinia* invasion might be just a transient phenomenon induced by a temporarily high nutrient concentration in the young lake. It is certainly true that the flooding of land in the Zambezi valley as the lake rose created a particularly fertile water (Jackson, 1960; Harding, 1961); but the consequent high productivity is likely to persist, because about one-third of the total volume of the lake is replaced annually by inflowing rivers which drain a catchment area extending into not only Zambia and Rhodesia but also Angola, Botswana and South-West Africa. Furthermore, thorough analyses made before impounding of the Zambezi began, and over the subsequent 3½ years, revealed no fundamental change in the composition of the water (Hattingh, unpubl.). Hattingh concluded that the damming of the river and the creation of sheltered habitats with more or less static water were the principal factors encouraging the sudden rapid spread of the weed.

The origin of the infestations on Lake Kariba provides a remarkable testimony to the astonishing power of regeneration and vegetative reproduction possessed by this free-floating species. Although known to be upstream of the Victoria Falls, the prime source of the weed has not yet been traced but is quite probably the Chobe Swamps in Botswana, since the Chobe River is known to be infested where it separates Botswana from the Caprivi Strip (Wild, 1961). These infestations block parts of the main Chobe channels and extend some 55 km to near Nogoma, which is about 190 km from the Victoria Falls. The Zambezi itself is infested from at least Mwandi, perhaps even upstream of here, right down to the Falls, some 130 km away (Hattingh, unpubl.). It might be thought that *Salvinia* swept along in the swift-flowing Zambezi would be totally destroyed by the natural hazard of the Victoria Falls, but despite the prodigious drop, from a height of some 112 m, with a colossal mass of water, fragments of weed must survive and regenerate. For some 110 km downstream from the Falls only apparently dead *Salvinia* is visible, but in the stretch from the point where the Gwai joins the Zambezi in Devil's Gorge to the western extremity of Lake Kariba, live regenerating colonies appear amongst the floating marginal masses of debris. It is from this critical reach of the river that the lake is directly infested (Hattingh, unpubl.).

The nature of the infestation varies with the habitat. On open water the floating masses of plants remain relatively diffuse. Although buoyant, highly mobile, and therefore easily drifted along by wind to infest new areas, these unstabilised mats present no serious hindrance to navigation. In the littoral zones of the lake, however, winds and wave action are tempered by both the dissected nature of the shoreline and the remains of partly submerged trees. Around these latter the mats become stabilised: in the sheltered conditions, growth of the weed is excessive and the dense compact mats of foliage and debris may exceed 15 cm in depth.

As originally feared, the situation on Lake Kariba became more critical in certain protected areas along the shoreline, through the invasion of stabilised mats by the sedge *Scirpus cubensis*, two species of *Ludwigia*—*L. adscendens* and *L. leptocarpa*, and many other emergent species, forming dense thick masses of sudd (Boughey, 1963). The long stolons of the *Ludwigia* and *Scirpus* bind the *Salvinia* colonies into a compact thick platform which gives the emergents support, their roots extending into the water beneath. So vigorously does *Scirpus* grow that a single pioneer plant may eventually produce an infestation 12 m in diameter and up to 1·25 m in height, which may be sufficiently firm and stable to support the weight of a man (Hattingh, unpubl.). *Cyperus papyrus*, prevalent in sudd communities elsewhere, is fortunately less important on Kariba (Emmanuel, *in litt.*). Additional problems are, however, created by *Pistia stratiotes* which occurs as pure floating mats or in association with *Salvinia auriculata*. Since 1962 the total area of the infestations seems to have decreased to about 500 km², approximately 10 per cent of the lake's surface (Mitchell, in Little, 1966).

Attempts to resist the increasing invasion in both Ceylon and Lake Kariba have been sadly handicapped by the lack of knowledge of the autecology of this fern. One of the most crucial questions, as yet not fully resolved, is the possible significance of sporocarps in the spread of the weed. Sporocarps are formed abundantly on the submerged dissected leaves in crowded mats which have been stationary for several weeks. In Ceylon sporocarps are most evident from August to November, when vegetative growth is least, and Senaratna (1943) remarked that reproduction by spores is probably a prolific means of multiplication. However, the development of spores and the subsequent sexual phase of reproduction have not been observed, either in Ceylon or Africa, and research workers have been totally unable to germinate the spores *in vitro* (Williams, 1956; Hattingh, unpubl.). So it is assumed that spore formation and sexual reproduction are of negligible importance in the natural dissemination of the weed. It seems probable that in a favourable environment vigorous apical growth, fragmentation and regeneration are wholly responsible for the maintenance and spread of infestations.

Outside Ceylon and Lake Kariba, *Salvinia auriculata* is not yet of critical economic importance, but it must obviously be regarded throughout most of the warmer regions of the Old World as a plant of immense potential danger. Its recent ominous appearance on the R. Congo has increased the likelihood of future invasions of central and western equatorial Africa (Little, 1965). It has also been reported from the Umtali-Inyazura area of Rhodesia, from the Jonkershoek and Knysna regions in Cape Province, from Natal and Kenya, but in these districts it is mainly restricted to small waterways, irrigation ditches and farm dams (Wild, 1961). Williams (1956) recorded that in the Calcutta Botanical Gardens the weed has invaded the various lakes, eliminating most of the other hydrophytes, but it has not been allowed to escape and spread. Though rarely troublesome, the species is also common in some Malayan waters, where it is probably spread by heavy rains and floods. It is grown in the lake of the University of Singapore for use in botanical classes, and during flood periods colonies have been washed away and found floating on the nearby Bukit Timah Road (Johnson, *in litt.*). Even so, *S. auriculata* has not become established in the waterways of Singapore Island and Johnson pointed out that whereas in Africa, especially Lake Kariba, heavy infestations occur in water with a pH range of 6·8 to 9·5 (7·4 in Kariba) and a high calcium concentration, the Malayan waters where the weed occurs, in Singapore and South Johore, have an average pH of about 5·2. The weed has not so far spread to limestone areas of northern Malaya where the pH is higher. Johnson also observed that propagation in Singapore is entirely vegetative for although abundant sporocarps are produced, they all mature into microsporocarps. The absence of megasporocarps thus raises an interesting parallel between the spread of *S. auriculata* here and the spread of *Elodea canadensis* in western Europe, where, due to the extreme rarity or absence of the microsporangiate organs (i.e. the male flowers), reproduction is also necessarily vegetative. It would be valuable to know whether in any other areas of the Old World tropics the fruiting bodies of the *Salvinia* communities are exclusively micro- or megasporocarps.

THE PROBLEM OF SUDD OBSTACLES

In many tropical countries sudd infestations are a frequent nuisance in shallow, stagnant or slow-flowing water. The most critically affected areas in central and southern Africa are the Niger delta, parts of the Congo, L. Bangweulu and the Lukanga swamp in Zambia, the fringes of Lakes Tanganyika and Victoria, and the Okovango river system in Botswana. The main locality of sudd in India is the vast swamp which covers the deltas of the Brahmaputra, Ganges and Surma. Hope (1902) and Ridley (1930) noted that this Bengal sudd differs from that of the major African river systems in growing in almost stationary water. So vast is the expanse of the main river channels that when swept into them during the annual floods the sudd rarely constitutes any great obstacle. Ridley (1930) further observed that comparatively few Malaysian rivers become blocked by sudd, though large quantities of vegetation are swept down through the sandy littoral regions of the eastern Malay Peninsula. Surviving plants aggregate into temporary islands but are later washed out to sea in the rainy season. Most of the rivers of tropical South America are too wide and deep and have too swift a current for sudd to become permanently established. Temporary obstructions occur, however, on smaller rivers, such as the Essequibo in Guyana, and some tributaries of the Amazon, such as the Solimões. According to Rodway (1895), in the dry season when the river is low and the current weak, the sudd extends from the margins and may block the channel for a short while, but the eventual floods rip the mats to pieces, sweeping great islands, 15 m or more in diameter, away downstream.

Until about 1900, formidable obstructions were often created by sudd communities in that part of southern Sudan where the upper reaches of the White Nile percolate northwards through an immense blanket of swamps, known collectively as El Sudd (Fig. 13.3). In the rainy season El Sudd spreads over an area as large as England, a desolate and sinister maze inhabited only by hippopotamuses, crocodiles, strange water-birds and lower forms of life, the air plagued with mosquitoes and other disease-carrying insects. El Sudd is neither land nor water—just an endless expanse of transient pools and ephemeral streams amidst the stagnant ooze and drifting forest of floating vegetation. Moorehead (1960), who recently journeyed the length of the Nile, remarked: 'The Sudd can still be a slight ordeal for a traveller even though he now passes through it on the deck of a paddle steamer with wire netting around him to keep the mosquitoes at bay. By the end of the first day . . . he will understand very well how Baker came to write "during the dead calms in these vast marshes the feeling of melancholy produced is beyond description. The White Nile is a veritable Styx".'

The great river of Africa was known to the Ancient Egyptians as far south as the site of what is now Khartoum: they may also have known something of the lowest reaches of the Blue Nile but were wholly ignorant of the course of the White Nile. About 460 B.C. Herodutus penetrated up the Nile to the first cataract at Aswan, and confessed: '. . . of the sources of the Nile no one can give any account—it enters Egypt from parts beyond'. In the middle of the 1st century A.D., about the year 57, the Emperor Nero despatched two centurions and a body of praetorian troops to explore the Nile and find its source. This Roman expeditionary force somehow scaled all the cataracts, and, quite remarkably, forged on past Napata, Meroe and the site of the present Khartoum far into the Nubian interior, but was eventually halted by El Sudd. On returning to Rome the two centurions related their experience to Seneca (*Quaestiones Naturales*, Book VI, 8): 'We came indeed to huge marshes, the limit of which even the natives did not know, and no one else could hope to know; so completely was the river entangled with vegetable growth, so impassable the waters by foot, or even by boat . . .'

Explorations in the nineteenth century revealed the vastness of the Sudd region. Lying in a great land depression, with a latitudinal span of nearly $5°$, it extends from the vicinity of Juba and Mongalla northward to just beyond L. No and eastward almost to Malakal. The expanse of swamp covers not only a meandering 800 km stretch of the main White Nile (Bahr el Jebel or Mountain Nile) but also two principal tributaries, the Bahr el Zeraf and the Bahr el Ghazal. Upstream of Malakal the Sobat flows in from the Ethiopian highlands and the White Nile at last emerges from the Sudd and follows a more regular course for some 720 to 800 km north through the desert to Khartoum.

For some time prior to 1863 both the Bahr el Jebel and the Bahr el Zeraf were navigable. In December 1862, whilst searching for the explorers Speke and Grant, Baker accomplished the 1600 km voyage from Khartoum to Gondokoro in 40 days, having had a fairly easy passage through the Sudd. In March 1863, however, the river downstream of the entry of the western tributary, the Bahr el Ghazal, was found to be blocked by sudd, and 2 years later Baker's party, returning triumphant from the discovery of Lake Albert, was tragically trapped for weeks, many deaths ensuing from the plague which broke out (Hope, 1902; Moorehead, 1960).

The situation deteriorated and when Baker ventured up the Nile again in 1870, he found that the Bahr el Jebel had almost disappeared under the spongy drifting mass of sudd. As he and his party hacked their way through the tangled vegetation the current brought down more and more floating debris, packing it solidly ahead of them and closing the channel again behind them. In 2 months they pressed forward only a few kilometres and at the beginning of April withdrew to firm ground for 8 months until the annual flood. Conditions were still appalling as they vainly toiled once more and by February 1871 they had advanced only a pitiful distance along the Bahr el Jebel. One by one, their boats either sank or became stranded in the cloying mud. In the humid atmosphere and tremendous heat many men fell down with sunstroke and fever: none could avoid the pernicious attacks of mosquitoes. In the middle of March, more than a year after they had first been imprisoned, they eventually escaped by constructing a dam behind the remaining boats (Moorehead, 1960).

In 1874 the main route along the Bahr el Jebel was cleared, and it took General C. G. Gordon only 25 days to journey by steamer from Khartoum south to Gondokoro to take up his new appointment as Governor of the province of Equatoria. However, an unusually high flood in 1878 swept away most of the debris from the banks and obstacles were again established. Yet another vivid glimpse of the magnitude of the blockage is afforded by the much-quoted fact that in 1881 Romolo Gessi Pasha, Gordon's right-hand man and the Governor of Bahr el Ghazal province, journeying downstream on his way to Khartoum, was obstructed by the sudd for $3\frac{1}{2}$ months. In that time he travelled a distance normally covered in 5 hours: there were reported to be twenty separate obstacles on the Bahr el Ghazal between the point where the Bahr el Arab enters and the confluence with the Bahr el Jebel. By the time rescue came, the majority of the Governor's escort of 400 men had perished from starvation and some survivors had turned cannibal (Hope, 1902; Moorehead, 1960).

Permanent channels were at last opened up in 1899 and the years immediately after. The Herculean task of clearance was accomplished under the guidance of Sir William Garstin, deputed by the Egyptian Government to consider possible irrigation projects in the basin of the Upper Nile (MacMichael, 1934). Although the Bahr el Jebel, which is the main route for regular navigation, is now generally clear, obstacles still develop at times in the Zeraf Cuts, and on the upper reaches of the Bahr el Ghazal and Pibor (Gay, 1960).

The Nile infestations spread in the way typical of sudd communities. Dense floating thickets of *Cyperus papyrus* extend from the shallow muddy margins, the compact mat of roots and rotting foliage allowing anchorage of other emergent species, notably the um-soof reed—*Vossia cuspidata*, *Phragmites communis*, *Typha australis*, *Echinochloa stagnina*, and the ambatch—*Herminiera elaphroxylon*, and also plants such as *Ottelia alismoides* which normally root in the substrate but appear to float amidst the sudd community. *Pistia stratiotes*, *Aldrovanda vesiculosa*, and species of *Azolla*, *Ceratopteris*, *Trapa* and *Utricularia*, brought down from the lakes of central Africa, Lake Nuong and Lake Ambadi, also occur in variable quantities amongst the emergents. The explorer Georg Schweinfurth (1873) maintained that the ambatch was the major constituent of the floating obstacles but Garstin, in his first report sent to London by Lord Cromer, the Consul-General in Cairo, and officially published in 1901, took a different view. He considered the papyrus, and to a lesser extent the um-soof reed, to be the most important weeds and emphasised that the ambatch was not prevalent in the vicinity of the Bahr el Jebel (Hope, 1902). The dominant role of papyrus has been confirmed by many observers (Drar, 1951). Describing his impressions of the Sudd, Moorehead (1960) remarked: 'The papyrus reed when seen for the first time, or carved in stone upon some Egyptian monument, is a beautiful plant with delicate arching fronds making an hieratic pattern against the sky. But when it is multiplied to madness, hundreds of square miles of it spreading away like a green sea on every side, the effect is claustrophobic and sinister . . .'.

THE BIOLOGICAL AND ECONOMIC EFFECTS OF FLOATING WEED
INFESTATIONS

Extensive floating mats of vegetation, composed of either pure colonies of a single free-floating species or mixed sudd communities of free-floating and emergent plants, have far-reaching biological and economic consequences. The severity of the problems created and the magnitude of the economic losses incurred are difficult to appreciate in the cool temperate countries where inland waterways are often of declining importance in trade and communication and where comparable weeds are almost unknown. On all affected tropical waters floating weed infestations threaten a multitude of local and even national interests.

First and foremost of the manifold effects is the direct mechanical hindrance to navigation. Even if the floating mats are not completely impenetrable, the networks of stolons and rhizomes and clustered masses of roots quickly become entangled around boat propellers so that sooner or later craft are marooned in the midst of the weed. Wind and water currents bank up free-floating islands of vegetation into thick stabilised mats which accumulate in upstream reservoirs, behind dams and in hydro-electric installations, clogging the grids and sluices.

Infestation of irrigated paddy fields by *Salvinia auriculata* or *Eichhornia crassipes* sorely hinders both sowing and reaping, and may quite prevent the rice emerging into the air. If the fields are left fallow for some months the unchecked spread of the weed may necessitate complete abandonment of the land.

When masses of sudd or pure colonies occlude rivers and irrigation channels the velocity of the current is drastically reduced and the rate of deposition of silt correspondingly increased, necessitating expenditure on dredging, disrupting cultivation programmes and increasing the likelihood of flooding. Although the White Nile rises in the tropical forests, lakes and swamps of central Africa and Ethiopia and is fed by heavy rains, it eventually contributes only about 29 per cent of the total Nile discharge. The Atbara and Blue Nile, draining the Ethiopian highlands, have a short but very intense flood, little infesting vegetation and swamp-free courses, and they contribute, respectively, 14 per cent and about 57 per cent. As much as half the water of the Upper White Nile is utterly wasted. It was estimated in 1933 that approximately $27 \cdot 5 \times 10^9$ m³ of water pass Mongalla each year: as much as 14×10^9 m³ of this is lost through overflow, transpiration and evaporation in the sudd of the Bahr el Jebel and Bahr el Zeraf. Further gross wastage of the water so vital to Lower Egypt is caused by the sudd through which the Bahr el Ghazal flows (MacMichael, 1934). It is small wonder that in his efforts to improve the regulation, conservation and distribution of the water of the Nile, Sir William Garstin strongly recommended the canalisation of El Sudd.

In addition to causing loss of crops, cattle, and water for domestic and power supplies, flooding is itself a potent force in breaking up mats of vegetation, dispersing the floating fragments far downstream to form new foci from which infestations again develop.

Apart from these several mechanical effects, floating mats reduce gaseous exchange between the water and the atmosphere and curtail the penetration of light so that submerged hydrophytes and phytoplankton, and the organisms which they support, are unable to develop. The oxygen concentration beneath the mats usually falls to levels inadequate for fishes and most invertebrates, and the soluble nutrients in the water are severely depleted. The blankets of weed thus offer a dire threat to the establishment of commercial inland fisheries, as on Lake Kariba, because of both the creation of a shallow-water environment totally unsuitable for fish to breed in and the immense physical obstruction to boats and nets in water where some fish might be able to survive (C.D.A., 1926; Lynch *et al.*, 1947; Penfound and Earle, 1948; C.C.T.A./C.S.A., 1957; Hattingh, unpubl.).

The stagnant conditions, shallow water and foliage canopy of the mats together provide a magnificent breeding habitat for mosquitoes (and see p. 455). *Mansonia* mosquitoes, the vectors of rural filariasis, lay their eggs in abundant large masses on the underside of the leaves of *Pistia stratiotes* and the larvae subsequently attach themselves to the roots. Egg masses have also been found on *Salvinia auriculata* but they are generally small and sparse. Williams (1956) suggested that the much denser canopy of foliage, as compared with *Pistia* colonies, probably denied the mosquitoes access to the underside of the leaves for oviposition, and that, in consequence, *Salvinia* infestations would not maintain the rich mosquito population needed to spread the disease. In the southern U.S.A. and certain other subtropical and tropical areas persistent infestations of *Eichhornia crassipes* and of sudd communities have impeded control programmes against anopheline mosquitoes. This hazard to health is especially acute in heavily populated districts where the weeds also interfere with sewage disposal and drainage.

14

The Control of Aquatic Weeds

Although the desire to control nature may be censured by the purist as an attitude of mind conceived in arrogance, it unquestionably reflects a contemporary economic and agricultural necessity. If resources of land and water are to be efficiently exploited in the provision of food, other natural products, power and communications, an effort must clearly be made to resist and, if possible, eliminate biological factors which would otherwise quickly thwart this aim. To acknowledge this need is not to condone such clumsy and short-sighted attempts to control weeds and pests as have in recent years evoked proper public outrage at the use of certain herbicides and insecticides.

The purpose of the following brief discussion is to emphasise the relationships between the biology of aquatic weeds, the nature of aquatic habitats, and the choice of appropriate control methods, and to draw attention to the precautions, disadvantages and virtues of certain techniques. Readers desiring further information and practical data should consult the textbook by Robbins *et al.* (1954) and the relevant journals, such as *Weed Research, Hyacinth Control Journal* and *Pesticides Abstracts and News Summary, Sections B and C.* Important contributions to the study of herbicidal and other control techniques for ponds, lakes, rivers and irrigation schemes in temperate and tropical regions have been made by Smith and Swingle (1941a, b); Speirs 1948; Surber (1949); Hitchcock *et al.* (1949, 1950); MacKenthun (1950, 1955, 1960); Clark (1954); Dunk and Tisdall (1954); Huckins (1955); Timmermans (1955); Greenwald (1956, 1957); Hooper and Cook (1957); Chancellor (1958); Lawrence (1958); Seaman (1958); Snow (1958); Walker (1959, 1964); Allsopp (1960); Westlake (1960); Burdick (1961); Wild (1961); Frank *et al.* (1963); Seaman and Porterfield (1964); Wilkinson (1964); and Hattingh (unpubl.). The examples cited in this chapter have been drawn largely from these original sources.

SOME GUIDING PRINCIPLES

The control of aquatic weeds presents many specialised problems. So immense is the range of growth habits that a method of control appropriate to one species is often completely unsuitable for another species growing in the same place. Moreover, techniques are most frequently required to control not pure colonies but mixed communities comprising several weeds of different life form. Greater difficulties than are met in the control of terrestrial weeds arise from the simple fact that troublesome hydrophytes grow in various depths of water and may also have extensive rhizomes and root systems buried in the substrate. If all the growing regions, submerged and rooted as well as aerial, are not destroyed, new foliage is soon produced and the weed problem eventually recreated. In flowing waters control is further hindered by the current which rapidly dilutes any herbicide, carries it beyond the weed-infested zone, and may distribute it over adjacent agricultural land during flood periods. The control of agricultural weeds, terrestrial or aquatic, demands a selective agent, in order that the crop is not itself destroyed. This problem is especially acute in tropical and warm temperate countries where irrigated crops are infested with aquatic weeds which closely resemble the cultivated species in morphological structure, ecological behaviour and natural affinity. An even greater complication presents itself in some tropical waterways and irrigation schemes, where it may be essential to control not only the aquatic weeds themselves but also disease-transmitting animals which occupy microhabitats within the plant community, such as the bulinid and planorbid snails which transmit the species of *Schistosoma* that cause bilharziasis. Mechanical weed control runs the risk of distributing the animals rather than eradicating them, and unfortunately very few chemical compounds are yet known to be lethal to both the animals and the plants.

Most streams, rivers, canals, and natural and man-made lakes differ fundamentally from drainage channels, irrigation systems and inundated ricefields in serving more than one vital purpose. A weed infestation may affect these several purposes in quite different ways. Consequently the problem is not simply one of destroying all weeds: it is usually far more complex. In this context it is perhaps pertinent to note that the frequent colloquial description of aquatic plants in general as 'water-weeds' encourages much too easily the belief that in a body of water any plants at all are undesirable. This is not so. In tackling weed problems in multi-purpose waters it is important, firstly, to consider how much weed is necessary to maintain edaphic stability and to support breeding populations of fish or water-fowl; secondly, to consider how little weed is necessary for efficient drainage and fishing and to avoid depletion of dissolved oxygen and nutrients; thirdly, to decide the amount of weed that will achieve a practical balance between these opposing requirements; and fourthly, to decide how the weed may be efficiently maintained at the selected level at an economic cost. The aim is thus control rather than eradication.

Many living weeds drastically reduce the oxygen concentration and increase the carbon dioxide content of the water, creating an environment unsuitable for plankton, other invertebrates and fishes. Inefficient disposal of killed weed aggravates this problem, because of the great absorption of oxygen and evolution of carbon dioxide and hydrogen sulphide during the processes of decay. It also increases the risk of reinfestation from viable fragments of weed. Speedy removal of chopped or dead vegetation is clearly vital to successful control.

It is rarely possible to tackle particular aquatic weed problems in a routine manner. Each problem ought to be treated as unique, and all the local factors thoroughly investigated before a control technique is chosen. Since the treatment of aquatic habitats, especially flowing waters, is often likely to affect many surrounding agricultural, commercial or domestic interests, it is clearly advantageous to attempt control as early as possible, before the weed problem becomes critical, to avoid the use of drastic techniques. Efforts to control the most serious aquatic weeds have been intensive but often unsuccessful. The search for methods of control and prevention is frequently retarded by the inadequate knowledge of the autecology of many species.

There are four potential ways of dealing with aquatic weeds: (a) mechanical control; (b) chemical control; (c) biological control; (d) actual use of the weed for some economic purpose. For many years, infestations were removed exclusively by manual or mechanical techniques, low in efficiency and high in labour and equipment costs. Although still widely practised in numerous places, these methods have been gradually supplanted in many temperate countries by the use of various inorganic and organic herbicides. With these chemical controls, moderate success has been achieved, mainly in shocking ignorance of the possible long-term side effects on other members of the aquatic communities. The field of selective biological control unfortunately remains largely unexplored.

CONTROL BY MECHANICAL (INCLUDING MANUAL) METHODS

Effective removal by mechanical means is possible if the growth of weed is in a reasonably early stage of development. The co-ordinated use of a mechanical method, such as the burning of emergent foliage, and the application of a suitable herbicide is sometimes more effective than either method practised alone. *Phragmites communis*, for example, has been successfully controlled by burning off the aerial foliage and then applying dalapon after an interval of up to 20 weeks.

Persistent weeding and cutting by hand is perhaps still the most economical method of removing isolated groups of plants and the small marginal populations of ditches, canals and ponds. These methods are apparently still practised in attempts to eradicate *Pistia stratiotes* in the Nile Delta and Nigeria, *Cyperus papyrus* and other weeds on small farms. In the ricefields of Portugal, India, Malaysia, and parts of Africa, species of *Azolla, Lemna, Salvinia* and *Wolffia* are removed by raking.

The drying out of lakes, ditches, ponds, and irrigated fields is widely used, but is satisfactory only in countries with a prolonged dry season or elsewhere in habitats which are easily drained (Surber, 1949; Clark, 1954; Walker, 1959). The technique has been moderately successful in the ricefields of tropical countries as a means of eradicating *Cyperus esculentus, Cyperus rotundus, Elodea canadensis, Marsilea* spp., *Najas* spp., *Myriophyllum* spp., *Potamogeton* spp., and other submerged hydrophytes: it is often supplemented by ploughing the dry soil with disks reaching to a depth of about 25 cm. It may be noted that the converse technique, flooding the ricefields before cultivation, together with dense sowing of the crop, has been used in Portugal and the Philippines to reduce infestations of *Alisma plantago-aquatica* and *Cyperus difformis* (Wild, 1961).

In parts of North America special barges are used which cut the weeds and also remove them from the water. The weeds of chalk streams in southern England are cut regularly, sometimes by means of a cutting machine mounted on a boat. The cut weed floats downstream to booms where it accumulates and is removed by a grab (Westlake, *in litt.*).

Dragging is often recommended for use in small lakes, canals, narrow rivers, and small dams, and has been reasonably successful in Africa for eradicating species of *Aponogeton, Nymphaea, Nymphoides*, and *Potamogeton* (Wild, 1961). A heavy chain or rake bearing downward-projecting teeth is dragged along the substrate by means of a power winch or two tractors, one on each bank. If a large area is to be dragged, the accumulated weeds may be removed periodically and raked up the banks. An elaboration of this method, dredging, may be used for larger lakes and rivers, and it incidentally removes some of the mud and silt which encourages the profuse growth of many weeds.

Mechanical mowing and rolling are widely practised in the control of weeds of irrigation ditches (Dunk and Tisdall, 1954; Seaman, 1958). The blades of the mower chop the plants away from the banks and the substrate, and the heavy roller presses much of the debris and the weeds on the substrate into the mud. With the concomitant risk of new growth from some of the rolled vegetation, the efficiency of this method is low.

Numerous important disadvantages are inherent, to a greater or lesser degree, in all mechanical methods of control. First, there is the risk of incomplete coverage of the infested area, either as a result of missing parts of the substrate, or through cutting or dragging off just the foliage, leaving rhizomes, stolons, runners and root systems intact. Efficient eradication depends upon extracting complete plants from their anchorage, a task which in deep water or with stubbornly rooted hydrophytes needs expensive equipment and labour. Second, there is the risk of reinfestation by seeds or vegetative fragments which escape collection or are deliberately left in piles of debris too close to the water: this risk is especially critical in areas liable to be flooded, and when the weed has great powers of regeneration. Until about the end of 1954 *Salvinia auriculata*, for example, was removed manually from affected waters in Ceylon: no great problems were encountered in harvesting the weed and dumping it on the land to decompose (Senaratna, 1943). In 1952 a 'Salvinia Week' was inaugurated by the Government in an effort to clear several thousand acres of infestations. The floating mats were swept along by nets and booms to suitable spots and then removed by hand and heaped in great piles on the nearby land. Due to fragmentation of the plants as they were removed, complete reinfestation had occurred a few months later and certain areas just had to be abandoned (Williams, 1956). Hitchcock *et al.* (1950) reported abundant regeneration within a month from chopped material of *Alternanthera philoxeroides* and *Eichhornia crassipes* floating in experimental pits. The third disadvantage of mechanical methods is the need for frequent repetition of the treatment. Fourth, there is the risk of greatly disturbing the aquatic environment: during hot weather when the oxygen concentration is low there is the danger of suffocating fish populations through stirring up vast quantities of mud and silt. Fifth, there is the high cost of labour and equipment. Annual expenditure on mechanical weed control in the Gezira irrigation scheme in the Sudan, for example, amounts to more than 143 500 dollars (W.H.O., 1965). However, it must be admitted that mechanical methods have to be used to curb certain weeds which are resistant to herbicides, e.g. numerous species of floating-leaved *Potamogeton*, *Nuphar* and *Nymphaea*. Moreover, although expensive, mechanical methods are usually the most convenient to control weed populations at a selected level in multi-purpose waters.

CONTROL BY HERBICIDES

The recent qualified progress in controlling aquatic weeds with various organic and inorganic herbicides has been made primarily in the United States, western Europe, Australia and New Zealand: in tropical countries, mainly because of lack of opportunity and facilities, exploration of the field of chemical control has been very slow and there are many serious weeds for which no fully satisfactory herbicides are known. Herbicides which have shown notable promise include 2,4-D, monuron, dalapon, MCPA and TCA (for emergents); simazine, diquat, paraquat and PCP (for surface-floating plants); sodium arsenite and aromatic solvents (for submerged weeds) (Timmermans, 1955; Chancellor, 1958; Snow, 1958; Wild, 1961). The recently developed compound, Aqualin, which is based on acrolein as the active ingredient, is also notable since in field trials it has effectively controlled not only submerged aquatic vegetation but also the herbivorous freshwater molluscs which act as secondary hosts for schistosome parasites. It could therefore be of great value in bilharziasis areas where both problems are often combined (W.H.O., 1965).

The Choice of Herbicide. The selection of an appropriate herbicide is influenced by many factors, notably the morphology and physiology of the weed and the location, nature and uses of the habitat. The greatest problem presented by the habits of aquatic weeds is the inaccessibility of some or all the vegetative organs: the lower foliage of emergents is often submerged, if only in shallow water, and their underground organs are often stout and resistant, extensively creeping, or buried at considerable depth. Most of the foliage of floating-leaved weeds and, except during flowering, all the foliage of submerged weeds is shielded by the water. Hitchcock *et al.* (1950) noted that *Alternanthera philoxeroides*, for example, growing in the Mississippi delta, could not be controlled by spraying with 2,4-D because of regeneration from the rootstocks which were periodically buried under 30 cm or more of silt. The best herbicides for emergent and floating-leaved species are those administered to the soil near the underground organs, by 'injection' in tablet form, or those which, when sprayed on the foliage, are absorbed and rapidly translocated to the subterranean growing points. Of the latter type, dalapon shows probably the greatest potential value: applied at rates of 11·2 to 44·8 kg/ha (10–40 lb/acre) it has given good, often complete, eradication of species of *Carex*, *Glyceria*, *Phragmites*, *Sparganium* and *Typha*, and it may well soon replace TCA and similar compounds hitherto used less successfully to eradicate these deep- and strongly-rooted hydrophytes.

In the tropics and subtropics, the weeds of irrigation schemes are usually of very similar structure and close natural affinity to the crops. Unfortunately all the common selective herbicides destroy broad-leaved weeds, which are rarely important in subaquatic cultivation, except in ill-drained areas, such as south of Kelani Ganga in Ceylon. The dominant weeds of paddy lands are grasses and sedges and it has recently been admitted (*Trop. Agric.*, 1959) as unlikely that selective herbicides will be useful in tackling the weeds in areas of swamp rice culture in Ceylon for several years. Meanwhile, weeding must inevitably remain largely mechanical.

Submerged weeds can be controlled only from within the water. Sodium arsenite, used at rates of 2 to 5 ppm (calculated as As_2O_3), is the only chemical of widespread application to submerged species in static water (MacKenthun, 1950, 1955, 1960; Hooper and Cook, 1957). It is cheap, simple to apply, and successful against species of *Callitriche, Ceratophyllum, Elodea, Myriophyllum, Najas, Potamogeton, Ranunculus* and *Vallisneria. Myriophyllum spicatum* and a few other submerged plants have also been eradicated by phygon-XL, applied at a rate of 16·82 kg/ha (15 lb/acre). There are no wholly satisfactory herbicides for eradicating submerged weeds in flowing water. Petroleum, coal-tar naphthas, and aromatic solvents, such as the chlorinated benzenes and TCBA, are commonly used to clear irrigation ditches and similar running waters in America, but all are extremely expensive and highly toxic, which prohibits their use in habitats where the fish population and other fauna are to be conserved (Burdick, 1961).

Free-floating weeds form an especially troublesome group: the immense variation of habit necessitates the selection of separate techniques for individual types. Submerged free-floating hydrophytes, e.g. some species of the Lemnaceae and *Utricularia*, absorb nutrients over their whole surface and are most susceptible to herbicides applied to the water as soluble salts, e.g. sodium arsenite at 5 ppm. Surface-floaters are similarly susceptible, since they absorb substances through either their roots or the lower surface of their leaves, but they may also be treated by sprays since much of their foliage is exposed to aerial attack. Diuron (at a rate of 5 to 10 ppm) and simazine (at 0·6 g/m²) have successfully controlled some of these types, e.g. species of *Lemna* and *Wolffia*, and *Pistia stratiotes*.

It is regrettably true that *Eichhornia crassipes* and *Salvinia auriculata* are the only major weeds that have been really thoroughly studied from the point of view of control measures. It is deplorable that many weed problems do not receive the official recognition, financial resources and intensive study necessary for their solution until they reach critical proportions. Concentrated attention was directed to the water hyacinth problem only after the Second World War. Hildebrand (1946) chose 2,4-D for her experiments since it had already been used successfully on broad-leaved terrestrial weeds. Various tests performed on infestations in a stream with an appreciable current and in a pond with relatively quiet water showed that 2,4-D could completely kill water hyacinths. In experiments performed in artificial pits, canals, bayous and other waterways in Louisiana during 1948–1949, Hitchcock *et al.* (1949, 1950) showed that at any time throughout the year mats of hyacinths could be killed and sunk within 2 to 3 months by a dosage of 9 kg 2,4-D/ha (8 lb/acre). The related compound 2,4,5-T was found to be less effective, as were all the non-hormone herbicides, none of which significantly improved the control when added to 2,4-D. Although expensive, 2,4-D has become generally accepted as the best herbicide for *Eichhornia crassipes* and is used in control programmes throughout infested areas in Africa, notably the Congo and the Upper Nile, and in the southern U.S.A. Unfortunately, as noted in Chapter 13 (p. 471), the control technique may sometimes encourage development of the seeds liberated from decaying plants stranded at the water line or heaped on the banks. As a further complication to control measures, 2,4-D and related compounds do not appear to be lethal to certain sudd-forming emergents often associated with *Eichhornia crassipes*, notably *Cyperus papyrus* (Fig. 14.1).

In recent years, extensive infestations of *Eichhornia crassipes* in Louisiana have been cleared by concerted programmes of herbicidal and mechanical treatment (Wunderlich, 1964). In Africa, limited success has been achieved in destroying the weed on parts of the Nile, Congo, Itimbiri, Kasai, Sanga and Ubangui, and conditions of navigation on these rivers have improved. Yet it is unlikely that this notorious pest will be satisfactorily controlled for some time. The use of 2,4-D is expensive and may not be wholly effective because of the dispersal and dormancy of seeds. Unfortunately, the nutrient regime and temperature appear to be optimal for this weed in many palaeotropical rivers, lakes and swamps. Furthermore, the sheer magnitude of the areas contaminated or vulnerable to invasion demands a vast and highly co-ordinated

FIG. 14.1. A mass of *Eichhornia crassipes* held back by the Jebel Aulia Dam on the White Nile in the Sudan, September 1964. Spraying with 2,4-D amine has killed all these plants, but amongst them there remain clumps of living *Cyperus papyrus* (one arrowed) unaffected by the herbicide. (By courtesy of Dr. E. C. S. Little, A.R.C. Weed Research Organisation, Oxford, England.)

system of control, and the physical nature of many equatorial regions greatly hinders the detection of sources of infestation and the penetration of control units. These difficulties emphasise the supreme importance of resisting such weeds as soon as they appear and thereby eliminating the danger of large-scale invasions.

In Ceylon, trials of possible herbicides for *Salvinia auriculata* were initiated in the early 1950's, when the inadequacy of manual and mechanical controls had been fully appreciated (Senaratna, 1952a). Both 2,4-D and 2,4,5-T were reported as promising but four sprays at intervals of several days were necessary for effective kill (Senaratna, 1952b). Eventually, all the tested herbicides based on 2,4-D and the related MCPA were rejected because of their low efficiency, as were several mineral oils which not only had to be applied several times but also caused gross pollution. Finally, PCP was found to be effective, first against young plants and subsequently, at higher concentrations, against mature colonies (Chow *et al.*, 1955). Within 3 weeks of the second of two sprays, each at a dose of 28 kg PCP/ha (25 lb/acre), floating mats had been killed and sunk. It was found that paddy seed could be sown within 3 days of the second spraying, so the treatment caused no major setback to programmes of cultivation. Accordingly, in January 1955 the Government inaugurated a Salvinia Eradication Campaign, operating continuously except during the monsoon (Williams, 1956).

A second, independent search for a control for *Salvinia auriculata* began in October 1960 at Lake Kariba. Over sixty possible herbicides were screened for effectiveness in long, narrow, artificial pools near the lake. Of the substituted phenols, PCP was found to be less effective than DNBP, but both were rejected because of their high cost and toxicity to fish. Amongst the majority of compounds which failed to give acceptable and economical control were the acetamides, such as Dicryl, Karsil and Solan; *s*-triazines, such as simazine, atrazine, propazine, and their methoxy- and methyl-mercapto-substituted analogues; phenoxy compounds, such as 2,4-D, 2,4-DB, 2,4-DP, 2,4,5-T, kuron, MCPA and MCPP; and miscellaneous others, such as amitrole, dalapon, 2,6-DBN, endothal and TCBA. Four herbicides showed especial promise, warranting field trials. These were sodium arsenite—hitherto not used for floating weeds; dodecyl hexamethyleneimine—a rather new herbicide whose side effects are not yet well known; and the dipyridyl compounds, diquat and paraquat—both rapidly absorbed and translocated, producing an early response, and detoxified when they enter soil; paraquat being about eight times more active than diquat. *Salvinia auriculata* proved to be much more sensitive to sodium arsenite than are submerged weeds, a dose of 3·4 to 6·7 kg/ha (3 to 6 lb/acre; approx. 0·5 to 1·0 ppm in water 0·6 m deep) giving 90 per cent control over a test period of 6 weeks. The unusual sensitivity of the plant was thought to be due to dual uptake of the herbicide, the spray being absorbed by first the aerial and then the submerged leaves as it fell on the surface and diffused down through the water. Field trials showed that either paraquat (applied at 0·56 kg active cation/ha; 0·5 lb/acre) or sodium arsenite (at 11·2 kg/ha; 10 lb/acre) would completely control both the mats of *Salvinia* and also the sudd-forming emergents which invade them (Hattingh, unpubl.; and see Figs. 14.2 and 14.3). Despite Hattingh's detailed recommendations, no organised programme of control has yet been started on L. Kariba, principally because of the awkward political situation in this part of Africa.

Finally, it may be noted that there are numerous troublesome aquatic weeds, e.g. *Alternanthera philoxeroides*, *Cyperus papyrus*, *Hydrocleys nymphoides*, *Vossia cuspidata*, and several species of *Nymphaea*, for which no fully satisfactory herbicidal controls have yet been discovered.

FIG. 14.2. A, View of an extensive mature mat of *Salvinia auriculata* at Siavonga West on Lake Kariba, October 1962. The photograph shows the boundary (arrowed) between an untreated area of the mat (lighter, to right) and an area sprayed with 0·56 to 1·12 kg paraquat/ha (0·5 to 1·0 lb/acre) from a helicopter; B, view of the same site as in A showing the mat breaking up 6 weeks after the application of the herbicide. (From colour prints in Hattingh, unpubl.; by courtesy of the Lake Kariba Co-ordinating Committee.)

Application of the herbicide. The manner, time and number of applications of the appropriate herbicide depend upon several factors, all of which ought to be considered when deciding how to tackle a particular problem. These factors include the nature of the compound, the type of weed, the nature of the habitat and the physiography of the surroundings.

Some herbicides, such as monuron, which is used to control emergents such as *Echinochloa*, *Phragmites* and *Sagittaria*, and submerged species of *Ceratophyllum*, *Elodea*, *Najas* and *Potamogeton*, are made in the form of tablets or large granules. These may be dropped into the water to form a concentrated solution in the vicinity of the roots and to reduce the likelihood of damaging shore vegetation which might be sensitive to windswept sprays. A less efficient variation of the tablet technique is often used in applying cupric sulphate by towing a sack containing the crystals through the water. Most herbicides are applied as solutions or emulsions sprayed over emergent foliage (e.g. 2,4-D) or over the water surface (e.g. sodium arsenite), the aim in the latter instance being to produce a uniform concentration of the active component throughout the entire depth of water. The various aromatic acids, e.g. 2,4-D, 2,4-DB,

2,4,5-T, dalapon, kuron and MCPA, are normally applied as solutions of their sodium or amine salts, or as emulsions of their ethyl, isopropyl, butyl, isoctyl or propylene-glycol-butyl-ether esters. These forms often differ slightly in effectiveness. Different dosages of most herbicides have vastly different effects, and so accuracy in the preparation of the solution is essential, especially when the chemical is toxic.

FIG. 14.3. View of a mat of *Salvinia auriculata* and various sudd-forming emergent species in Loteri Bay on Lake Kariba, April 1963. Photograph taken 6 weeks after spraying with 11·2 kg sodium arsenite (as As_2O_3)/ha (10 lb/acre) from a helicopter, and showing the killing of the sudd species (lighter patches) as well as the *Salvinia*. (From colour print in Hattingh, unpubl.; by courtesy of the Lake Kariba Co-ordinating Committee.)

The effectiveness of a particular treatment may be influenced by the structure of the weed. Three features of *Salvinia auriculata*, for example, hinder the penetration of a spray: the more or less vertical attitude of the leaves during the mature phase of growth, the dense felt of liquid-repellent hairs on the upper surface of each leaf, and the shelter given to the shoot buds by the apical clusters of young growing leaves (Williams, 1956). In the trials on Lake Kariba, wetting agents failed to enhance the activity of either paraquat or sodium arsenite, perhaps because they increase, rather than reduce, the rate of run-off from the repellent hairs, or perhaps because the prime route of absorption is the lower, rather than the upper, surface of the aerial leaves (Hattingh, unpubl.). Hitchcock *et al.* (1950) found the rate of sinking of killed hyacinths (*Eichhornia crassipes*) varied with the age and structure of the floating mats. Tightly packed flotants, 6 months or more old, with a mat of debris and roots up to about 12 cm thick around the rootstocks of the living plants, took between 30 and 40 days more to sink than floating mats less than 3 months old.

It is impossible to generalise the influence borne by the habitat and the physiography of the region upon the method of control. Weeds in rivers, irrigation ditches and other flowing waters, where the current can carry the herbicide miles downstream, require different techniques of application from weeds in ponds, lakes and static waters. Local small infestations may often be sprayed from the bank or from a small boat by means of a knapsack sprayer or stirrup pump, the efficiency of these methods being largely determined by the operator's dexterity. Spraying machines fitted to extensible booms mounted on tractors or on boats may be used for larger infestations on canals, small lakes and similar habitats (Figs. 14.4 and 14.5). For the most severe weed problems, notably in the tropics and warmer regions, these techniques are usually wholly inadequate, for several reasons. The infestation is frequently too vast to be reached by sprays from the shore and may be impenetrable by even high-powered boats. The shoreline may be extremely dissected, with hidden bays and overhanging trees harbouring infestations, and it may be sheltered by dense vegetation, such as rain-forest or thick scrub, reaching right to the water's edge. Access to marginal areas of weed from either the land or the water may be denied.

Aerial application therefore becomes essential in many habitats. Fixed-wing aircraft are rarely practicable, because of high operating costs, lack of landing strips, and the immense variation in the area and shape of the infested areas. Although by no means always ideal, helicopters are more suitable and have been adopted in numerous regions, such as Louisiana, the Congo, and Lake Kariba (Figs. 14.2 to 14.6). Low or high pressure spraying equipment is fitted to the helicopter and the most efficient flying height and air speed then ascertained by extensive trials: in Louisiana, for example, spraying with low pressure equipment exerting less than $10·55$ kg/cm^2 (150 lb/in^2) at a height of about 13 m and an air speed of 48 km/h, was found most suitable for covering *Eichhornia crassipes* infestations (Zimmerman *et al.*, 1950). Despite its obvious value in otherwise inaccessible regions, aerial spraying has several dis-advantages. Complete coverage of infestations is rarely possible because of the hindrance of marginal trees and brush, and the irregularities of the shoreline. A high degree of coverage is only obtained with an experienced pilot, provided with guiding markers to avoid both the wastage caused by overlapping areas already sprayed and the reinfestation which will surely occur from areas missed.

The most suitable time for the herbicide to be applied must be considered in relation to the growth and life cycle of the weed and the local weather conditions. To minimise the danger of dispersing seeds, the herbicide should be applied before the production of flowers. The longer the treatment is delayed after flowering, the greater is the risk of some seeds ripening before all the plants are completely killed, especially in the case of weeds such as *Eichhornia crassipes* which are left in the water to sink. To those species which rarely flower, the chemicals are best applied before the period of most vigorous growth, e.g. late spring in temperate countries. The vulnerability of many weeds seems to vary with the state of growth of their vegetative organs. *Salvinia auriculata*, for example, which grows best in diffuse light and high relative humidity at temperatures of 18 to 25°C, quickly becomes scorched under light of high intensity at higher temperatures. Patches of brownish depauperate plants have been noticed frequently in cultivation and amidst mats of young green colonies in natural habitats. On Lake Kariba the weed grows best in the cooler autumn and winter: from August to November it is badly scorched and shows a different response to herbicides (Hattingh, unpubl.). Amongst healthy colonies the primary juvenile plants are generally easier to control than the tertiary mature ones.

FIG. 14.4. Killing and sinking of tightly packed *Eichhornia crassipes* (30 to 60 cm tall) in a pit in Louisiana, resulting from treatment in January 1949 with 1 per cent 2,4-D alkanolamine salt delivered at the rate of 11·2 kg/ha (10 lb/acre) by means of a pressure spray gun operated from both banks: A, appearance of dead hyacinths when sinking started, 7 weeks after application of the herbicide; B, appearance 4 weeks later, at the end of March, when about 50 per cent of the treated plants had sunk. (From Hitchcock *et al.*, 1949, by courtesy of the Boyce Thompson Institute for Plant Research, Yonkers, New York.)

17

FIG. 14.5. A, view of a canal about 15·25 m wide in Louisiana, solid with dead *Eichhornia crassipes* and lined on each bank with tall overhanging trees. Photograph taken 50 days after spraying with a 40 per cent concentrate of 2,4-D from a helicopter. Note the complete killing of hyacinths from bank to bank, including plants under the trees. B, a large borrow pit in Louisiana, about 91·5 to 122 m wide and 6·5 km long, completely cleared of *Eichhornia crassipes* by an amine salt of 2,4-D applied by boat-mounted spray equipment in April 1949, followed by one patrol maintenance spray 2 months later. Photograph taken at the end of July 1949. (From Zimmerman *et al.*, 1950, by courtesy of the Boyce Thompson Institute for Plant Research, Yonkers, New York.)

Almost all herbicidal sprays are rendered ineffective if rain falls soon after application, before sufficient time has elapsed for the spray to dry or to be absorbed. Hildebrand (1946) and subsequently Hitchcock *et al.* (1949) found that the degree of control of *Eichhornia crassipes* by 2,4-D is greatly reduced

FIG. 14.6. A, dense floating mat of *Eichhornia crassipes* in a borrow pit located on the Bonnet Carré Spillway Reservation in Louisiana being sprayed with a 40 per cent concentrate of 2,4-D from a Bell 47-D type helicopter in July 1949; B, aerial view of the same part of the borrow pit as in A photographed 7 weeks later, showing 90 per cent of the area cleared and only a narrow remaining fringe composed of hyacinths not contacted by a lethal dose of the spray and dead plants which had not yet sunk. (From Hitchcock *et al.*, 1950, by courtesy of the Boyce Thompson Institute for Plant Research, Yonkers, New York.)

by rainfall or wave action during the first 3 hours after spraying. Eradication programmes in the tropics must be curtailed during heavy rain, especially in monsoon countries.

A single application of a herbicide is rarely sufficient to eradicate a serious weed. In dense emergent stands or floating mats, young plants and sheltered apical buds and rhizomes may escape the first treatment, especially if the herbicide is not thoroughly translocated. 2,4-D, for example, is efficiently translocated from the leaves to other organs within a single individual plant of *Eichhornia crassipes*, but very little is transported through the connecting stolons to daughter rosettes with fairly well-developed roots (Penfound and Minyard, 1947; Hitchcock *et al.*, 1949). If reinfestation from fringe plants protected by littoral vegetation, from viable rhizomes and submerged parts, and from incompletely disintegrated floating mats is to be prevented, a second, and sometimes a third, application after a short interval is absolutely essential. Further annual treatment for two to four years is advisable because although the initial sprays may eradicate the weed from a given habitat they do not prevent invasion from adjacent areas or the dispersal and subsequent development of seeds.

The programme of application must be organised, not haphazard. Hattingh (unpubl.) recommended that on L. Kariba, for example, priority should be given to clearing fish-breeding grounds, harbours and the regions of domestic outflow: subsequently, the sheltered littoral regions could be tackled. Of course, control on the lake itself would be of little value without simultaneous control of the influx of *Salvinia* from above the Victoria Falls, and Hattingh therefore advised the erection of a boom in the Sebungwe Narrows, to halt the invasion, and the destruction of as much weed as possible from this point upstream in Devil's Gorge. Ill-organised application of a herbicide to any habitat inevitably results in inadequate control and heavy financial loss.

Toxicity of herbicides. The toxity of numerous herbicides necessitates stringent precautions for their use in aquatic habitats. It is an appalling and terrifying truth that all too many aquatic herbicides have come into general use despite colossal ignorance of their toxicology and biological side-effects. Although the situation is not perhaps quite as devastating as that created by the indiscriminate use of certain insecticides in the U.S.A. and Europe, it is nevertheless deplorable. The principal dangers inherent in the use of toxic herbicides for eradicating aquatic weeds are: (a) the hazard, to the persons applying the chemical or to others in the vicinity, of oral intake or cutaneous absorption; (b) the contamination of domestic water supplies; (c) the poisoning of plankton, invertebrates, fish and animals living in or around the water; and (d) the contamination of surrounding land bearing sensitive food crops or grazing livestock. Ingram and Tarzwell (1954) compiled a useful bibliography of work on the harmful effects of herbicides and insecticides on aquatic life.

Some crops are very susceptible to herbicidal sprays: cotton, banana and possibly cassava trees, for example, are highly sensitive to 2,4-D (C.C.T.A./ C.S.A., 1957). Several triazine compounds, such as atrazine, simazine and propazine, are toxic to pine and other gymnosperm seedlings, especially when they become incorporated in the soil layers penetrated by roots (Kozlowski, 1965). The possibility that mortality may be delayed enhances the need to study the toxicity of herbicides over long as well as short periods. This is of paramount importance with compounds such as monuron and the triazines, which persist in soil and mud and are not readily leached, inactivated or decomposed. At the normal dosages used to control aquatic weeds, certain herbicides, such as dalapon, monuron, TCA and 2,4-D, are not poisonous to man or to farm livestock, and probably have no harmful effects on most common fishes, although there may be unpleasant side-effects, such as the phenolic flavour of fish flesh and water after spraying with 2,4-D (Chancellor, 1958). Some compounds, however, are notably hazardous because of their powerful oxidising capacity and the consequent danger of fire (e.g. sodium chlorate) or their extreme toxicity to fish and/or other organisms (e.g. sodium arsenite, DNBP, coal-tar naphthas and chlorinated benzenes). As little as 0·1 to 0·325 g sodium arsenite is lethal to man, 0·38 to 0·64 g to sheep, and 1·92 to 3·84 g to cattle and horses (Timmermans, 1955). Many fish species are said to tolerate up to 18 ppm arsenic: at Kariba, 10 ppm As_2O_3 was found to be safe for *Tilapia melanopleura*, but in the presence of 15 ppm an average mortality of 20 per cent was observed amongst young fingerlings of this species (Hattingh, unpubl.).

The threat of universal contamination of ground-water is unlikely to be alleviated unless all aquatic herbicides are more thoroughly investigated and their application is performed only by qualified experts. The use of sodium arsenite and other herbicides is governed by State legislation and executed only by licenced personnel in certain of the United States, notably Arkansas, Massachusetts, Michigan, New York and Wisconsin. In all too many places, however, it is regrettably still possible for unqualified persons to attempt herbicidal control without any documentation or supervision of the project. In one of the few far-sighted studies of an aquatic weed problem, Hattingh (unpubl.) recommended that sodium arsenite, though effective and highly economical, should not be used to control *Salvinia auriculata* on Lake Kariba until the hazard to health could be eliminated, and that even then it should not be sprayed inshore, to avoid contaminating littoral vegetation. He further recommended that where herbicides are sprayed near outflows of domestic water, medical authorities should stipulate the safety precautions.

The ignorance of the biological side-effects of herbicides is more alarming than the knowledge that many are toxic. The determination of dosages toxic to man and other animals obviously provides invaluable data but is not an end in itself: to leave the matter there is merely to evade the real problem. As Carson (1963) recently emphasised, chemical controls may often have been tested against certain individual species, but their possible effects on complex ecosystems are rarely, if ever, investigated. Deplorably little is known of the effects aquatic herbicides have upon the composition, interrelationships and productivity of different types of community. Which members of the fauna and remaining flora are also affected? What happens to those organisms for which the weed normally provides food or shelter? Does the destruction of one weed allow another species to become dominant? Similarly, the effects of the herbicide upon the physical nature of the environment are glibly ignored. Even if a particular herbicide causes no apparent harm in a clean habitat it may have deleterious effects when added to water which already contains other chemical, domestic or radioactive wastes. Each individual herbicide and pollutant may well be innocuous but few are chemically inert: the interactions between them when they are indiscriminately mixed in the aquatic environment are completely unpredictable. There is always the possibility that carcinogenic or other toxic compounds could then be generated.

Although elaborate regulations may attend the application of a herbicide and great care may be taken to ensure that dosages are within a prescribed safe range, there remains the quite separate danger of compounds eventually being accumulated to toxic levels. Accumulation may occur in mud deposits, decaying organic matter, or living tissues. For instance, Hattingh (unpubl.) found that *Salvinia* accumulates arsenic: plants sampled one month after being sprayed with sodium arsenite contained 102 ppm As_2O_3 as compared with 0·1 ppm in control plants. It is interesting to note in this context that sodium arsenite has failed to control infestations of *Lagarosiphon major* in Lakes Rotorua and Rotoiti in New Zealand. Analysis of the bottom muds has revealed the presence of 6·5 to 57·0 ppm arsenic; this high level is probably a consequence of geothermal activity on the lake shores. The weed itself has been found to contain 22 to 111 ppm arsenic and so may well have acquired resistance to arsenical herbicides (Fish, 1963).

Aquatic herbicides and insecticides may be absorbed by plankton and accumulated to a high level through the successive organisms of food chains. To illustrate the possible extent of this accumulation, the use of the insecticide TDE in Clear Lake, California, may be mentioned. This insecticide, recently shown to destroy the adrenal cortex of man and several experimental mammals (Zimmermann *et al.*, 1956), was used to control a species of *Chaoborus* which bred in the lake. This small gnat caused no serious problem, spread no disease, but it did irritate those who used the lake for angling and recreation. In 1949 TDE was applied at the rate of 1 part per 70 million parts of water: further treatments in 1954 and 1957 were at the rate of 1 part TDE per 50 million parts of water. Shortly after each of these two applications large numbers of western grebes, which bred on the lake, died. Their adipose tissues were found to have a TDE content of 1600 ppm. The level of TDE in the tissues of herbivorous fish was between 40 and 300 ppm, higher still in carnivorous species— one bullhead analysed having 2500 ppm, and even in 1959, by which time all trace of the insecticide had long disappeared from the water itself, the plankton still retained up to 5·3 ppm (Hunt and Bischoff, 1960). Recent experiments in England, too, demonstrated the efficiency of TDE in controlling midges with mud-dwelling larvae and also showed that lethal concentrations of the substance may be accumulated in adipose and other tissues in fish, even when the initial rate of application is only 1·121 kg/ha (1 lb/acre) (D.S.I.R., 1962, 1963, 1964). The phenomenon of accumulation renders any concept of a safe dosage utterly meaningless.

BIOLOGICAL CONTROL

Many recent conferences on the control of aquatic weeds (e.g. C.C.T.A./ C.S.A., 1957) and numerous individual authors (e.g. Chancellor, 1958; Wild, 1961) have directed attention to the paucity of successful methods of biological control and urged that intensive research be initiated. It is a conspicuous fact that several major adventive weeds, such as *Eichhornia crassipes* and *Salvinia auriculata*, create problems in areas where closely related native species, such as *E. diversifolia* and *S. cucullata*, behave as normal harmless members of aquatic communities. Studies should be made of the biotic relationships of these native species as well as the weeds.

Several promising examples of biological control merit brief description. It may become practicable to control some emergent weeds by the introduction of terrestrial competitors or by direct infection with parasites. Wild (1961) noted that troublesome growths of *Cyperus rotundus* may be reduced by the planting of eucalyptus, and also mentioned Italian experiments on the control of *Echinochloa crus-galli* by the smut fungus, *Sorosporium bullatum*.

Floating-leaved and submerged weeds present a greater problem, as a result of their immersion in the water, but some measure of control might be achieved in certain habitats through the antagonistic effects of phytoplankton blooms. Periodic applications of fertiliser to the water from early in the season promote dense blooms of planktonic algae which may reduce the penetration of light so drastically as to inhibit the growth of submerged weeds and of seedlings of other life forms. The rooted plants may also be smothered by benthic algae. This technique will successfully control such submerged weeds as *Najas guadalupensis* and prevent colonisation by floating-leaved species of *Nuphar* and *Nymphaea*, but it is practicable only in fish ponds and small lakes (Smith and Swingle, 1941a, b; Wild, 1961).

The practicability of control by aquatic herbivores is currently being investigated in numerous countries. Amongst the animals being tested are such fishes as the African cichlids, *Tilapia melanopleura* and *T. mossambica*, and the Chinese grass carp, *Ctenopharyngodon idella*, and such molluscs as *Marisa cornuarietis** (Seaman and Porterfield, 1964). The value of these animals will depend on the biomass and rate of growth of the weed infestation, the frequency of animals introduced, their rate of weed consumption and of breeding, and their vulnerability to predators. These considerations apply also to large tropical aquatic mammals of herbivorous habit, such as the manatee, *Trichechus manatus*. The manatee occurs naturally in coastal rivers as well as the sea, and eats great amounts of floating and rooted vegetation. Unfortunately, it is rare and difficult to catch and transport. Moreover, it does not breed when introduced to fresh waters, although it lives quite well. Consequently its probable potentiality as a clearer of weed cannot yet be economically exploited. Its use in experiments is very expensive, and the numbers of animals which would be necessary to control extensive infestations simply are not available. This is a great pity in view of the efficient weed control brought about by manatees in small-scale experiments conducted in irrigation and drainage schemes (Allsopp, 1960; Bertram and Bertram, 1962).

*In addition to successful experimental control of several submerged weeds, for which it has a voracious appetite, *M. cornuarietis* has also shown an ability to compete with, and reduce populations of, another herbivorous aquatic snail, *Australorbis glabratus*, which is medically important in the neotropics as a host of *Schistosoma mansoni*.

The control of aquatic weeds

ECONOMIC USE OF WEEDS

It has often been argued that it would be better to find a use for weeds than to lavish expenditure on their destruction. *Salvinia auriculata* has been used as a mulch in cocoa, rubber and coconut plantations but there is a considerable risk of its being spread by heavy rains into irrigation schemes and local water-ways (Hickling, 1961). It has also been investigated as a source of protein and of medicinal principles, and as an organic manure, a cattle food, a constituent of compressed fibre hardboard and a stabiliser for road-surfacing materials (Senaratna, 1952a; Emmanuel, *in litt.*). *Eichhornia crassipes* and *Pistia stratiotes* are used locally throughout eastern and southern Asia as fodder for ducks and pigs, and *E. crassipes* has also been examined as a potential cattle food, vegetable manure and source of protein (Pirie, 1960). However, the exploitation of weeds in these various ways is not yet commercially profitable: nor is it advisable because of the risk of disseminating seeds or spores during the processing, distribution and use of the products.

15

The Aesthetic and Economic Value of Aquatic Vascular Plants

Aquatic vascular plants are of limited economic value in the modern world. Generally herbaceous and fragile in structure, most species yield no commercially useful fibrous elements. As sources of food they have now been largely discarded, except in parts of the tropics or in times of famine, in favour of more productive and nutritious terrestrial crops. Their benefit to man now resides mainly in wild-life conservation practices, where they provide food for water fowl and other animals and protection for spawning fish, and in horticulture, as purely ornamental plants. Yet it is apparent from a multitude of sources that in the past aquatic plants have been cultivated for an astonishing diversity of medicinal, nutritional and decorative purposes. Their aesthetic and material significance to the peoples of the Orient, the Near East and the early European civilisations is vividly revealed in Sanskrit, Chinese, Greek and Roman literature and in the appearance of numerous species as motifs in ancient architecture, painting, pottery and metalwork. From the first century A.D. little is known of the use of hydrophytes in Europe until the revival of learning in the Renaissance when the herbalists documented the medicinal value of several native and imported plants. Although the nutritional and medicinal importance of most hydrophytes has subsequently declined, their aesthetic value has achieved renewed recognition in the last hundred years.

AQUATIC VASCULAR PLANTS IN RELIGION, ART AND ARCHITECTURE

In India, China and Japan several decorative water plants have been held in the highest esteem since the earliest times. The immense admiration of the beautiful flowers of lotuses and waterlilies, above all others, is reflected in their frequent portrayal on fabrics and tapestries, pottery and metalwork, monuments and tombs, temples and public buildings, and in their adoration in prose and verse. In India the native lotus, *Nelumbo nucifera*, has always had especial significance for the Hindu and Buddhist. 'In Indian mythology, the lotus occupies a position that cannot possibly be surpassed by any other flower. It is a symbol of cosmic creativeness' (Bhadri and Desai, 1962). There are abundant references to it in the Sanskrit literature of the Brahmins: it is known as *padma*

17*

in Hindu prayer. Brahma, the Creator, is visualised as reigning from the lotus flower, whilst the flower stalk is interpreted as the navel cord of Vishnu, the Preserver, a male deity who became, with the decline in the worship of Brahma, the object of more popular devotion. For centuries the lotus has figured in religious symbols and statues. One of the earliest surviving representations of Brahma, in the rock-hewn temple-caves of Elephanta Island in the harbour of Bombay, is a splendid sculptured figure of the four-faced god upon a lotus.

Ever since the doctrine of the heavenly Buddha Amitābha, the transcendental equivalent of the historical Buddha, was introduced in India in the middle of the sixth century B.C., the lotus has been revered as the emblem of purity, arising unsoiled from murky stagnant waters, and its flower is identified as the sacred throne of the Buddha, attended by the Bodhisattvas and the souls of the redeemed. The native blue waterlily, *Nymphaea stellata* (described as *utpala* and *kamala* in Sanskrit), and white waterlily, *Nymphaea lotus* (*kumuda* and *pundarîka*), were also much admired by both Brahmins and Buddhists but probably had no religious associations (Conard, 1905). Together with the sacred lotus they appear in paintings decorating the walls of excavated early Buddhist temples and monasteries, notably the chaitya halls of Ajanta, Karli and Nasik. Most of these paintings date from the Gupta period (A.D. 320– c. 600), a few from the beginning of the Christian era or even earlier. All three species have been illustrated consistently throughout subsequent periods of Indian art, as in the brilliant tempera paintings of the Rajput school in the late sixteenth and early seventeenth centuries.

So primal is its status in the scale of creation, the lotus has come to be regarded as symbolic of India itself. Lotus flowers appeared in the collar of the insignia of two Victorian orders of knighthood: the Order of the Star of India and the Order of the Indian Empire.

In China and Japan the lotus is also symbolic of summer and of the month of July. One of the Eight Immortals of Taoism, Ho Hsien-ku (or Kasenko)—who is reputed to have lived in the seventh century A.D. and is the patroness of housewives, is depicted as a girl with a lotus stalk in her hand.

As Buddhism spread through eastern Asia the lotus was increasingly portrayed in the art and architecture of Tibet, China and Japan. Lotus motifs and naturalistic representations of lotus pools appear on roof tiles and other remains from Japanese temples and palaces of the Nara period (eighth century), on the beautifully lacquered boxes of the Fujiwara period (ninth to eleventh centuries) and on religious Japanese metalwork, such as reliquaries, silver aureoles, long-handled censers and standing incense-burners (Feddersen, 1962) (Fig. 15.1). In addition to the lotus, the arrowhead—*Sagittaria trifolia*, the water chestnut—*Trapa* spp., the cultivated varieties of pond-iris, and the Asiatic equivalent of the water hyacinths—*Monochoria* spp., also appear in Japanese lacquer and metalwork designs (Fig. 15.2). Chinese silks woven during the Yuan and early Ming dynasties (1279–c. 1400) often bore lotus designs. Some of these fabrics were brought to Europe and used in ecclesiastical robes: one of the oldest examples, the gold vestment in which Pope Benedict XI was buried in 1304, bears a pattern of lotus-wreaths. Similar designs appear on Chinese porcelain, fourteenth-century silk damasks, and on the highly ornate silk and metal-thread K'o-ssŭ tapestries (Fig. 15.3) of the late Ming (c. 1400-1644) and early Ch'ing (1644 to nineteenth century) dynasties. Some of the Chinese designs are so stylised that the lotus resembles more closely the Japanese chrysanthemum. One of the principal fourteenth-century Chinese designs, in

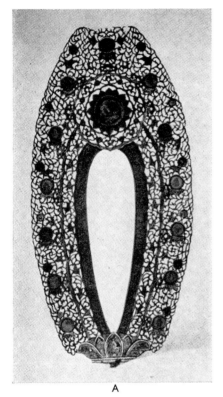

A

B

FIG. 15.1. A, silver aureole from the late Fujiwara period, bearing thirteen Bodhisattvas (in circles) surrounding a lotus flower; B, Buddhist standing incense-holder from the Tokugawa period, decorated with lotus motifs (Museum für Kunst und Gewerbe, Hamburg). (From Feddersen, 1962, by courtesy of the author and Messrs. Klinkhardt and Biermann, Brunswick.)

which lotus flowers occupy pointed oval panels formed by their stems, is the probable origin of several later designs on European textiles, such as the pomegranate patterns of the Gothic designers (Feddersen, 1961).

Most archaeologists and botanists agree that the lotus represented on the monuments and tombs of Ancient Egypt is not *Nelumbo nucifera* but probably either *Nymphaea caerulea* or *N. lotus*. The true sacred lotus is not indigenous in Africa. It may have been introduced from Persia, where it is native, when King Cambyses and the Persians conquered Egypt in 525 B.C. It does not figure in Egyptian art until the Roman period (Conard, 1905). Although neither the blue *N. caerulea* nor the white *N. lotus* was sacred, the beauty of both plants and the value of their rhizomes and seeds as food were widely appreciated.

The blue lily was the emblem of upper Egypt. It was commonly offered to the gods and was depicted in front of Osiris at the judgment of the dead (Conard, 1905). According to Wilkinson (1883), the custom at a nobleman's banquet was for each guest to be garlanded with the flowers and to pass into the

FIG. 15.2. Sixteenth-century Japanese sword guard of pierced iron, showing an arrow-head-leaf motif (Museum für Kunst und Gewerbe, Hamburg). (From Feddersen, 1962, by courtesy of the author and Messrs. Klinkhardt and Biermann, Brunswick.)

reception room holding a flower and with a single bloom draped over his fore-head. Both lilies were used in extravagant floral decorations inside houses and temples, and, especially during the XIX–XXI dynasties, in wreaths and bouquets filling the sarcophagi of notable figures. Flowers of both species were found by the explorer Georg Schweinfurth (1883, 1884) in the wreaths buried with the mummies of Amen Hotep I, Rameses II and Ahmes I. The wreaths of Amen Hotep probably date from nearly 2000 B.C.: those of Rameses were renewed about 1100 B.C. when the sarcophagus was broken during its removal to the Valley of the Kings in Western Thebes for protection from marauding desert hordes. Schweinfurth was unable to detect any significant differences between these magnificently preserved flowers and the flowers of living African plants of the two species. This remarkable morphological similarity has been adduced as evidence that Egypt has not experienced any profound climatic changes in the last 4000 years (Conard, 1905).

WATER GARDENING AND AQUARIUM PLANTS

The cultivation of ornamental aquatic plants had an obscure, undatable and probably hybrid origin. It may have arisen as an incidental feature of the very ancient arts of pisciculture and landscape horticulture which can be traced back to at least 2500 B.C. in Egypt, Assyria and Persia. It is probable that just as the fish bred in the ponds of temples and palaces were valued as cheap, plentiful and nourishing food, so the waterlilies, reeds and other hydrophytes were cultivated in ancient times primarily as economic plants rather than as pure

FIG. 15.3. Ornate K'o-ssŭ tapestry from the Ch'ing dynasty, with a design incorporating a lotus motif (Schleswig-Holsteinisches Landesmuseum, Schleswig). (From Feddersen, 1961, by courtesy of the author and Messrs. Klinkhardt and Biermann, Brunswick.)

ornaments. The Chinese have also grown *Euryale ferox* and other species for their nutritious seeds and rhizomes for probably 3000 years or more.

Clearer emphasis was placed on the aesthetic, as opposed to the utilitarian, value of water plants with the rise of Buddhism, when formal lotus pools became an integral feature of the gardens of all Buddhist temples. Throughout the Orient water has always been the principal motif of garden design, because of both the practical necessity of irrigation and the civilised appreciation of the tranquil beauty of lakes and pools, skilfully sited to enhance the visual impact of buildings and trees and to create a peaceful atmosphere conducive to meditation. In eastern Asia water gardening reached a peak of excellence through the supreme artistry and symbolic intricacy of the designs of Chinese and especially Japanese landscape gardeners. Their renowned achievements established criteria by which all other water garden designs are judged. In India, as a result of the indifference of both Muslims and British, water gardens eventually lost much of their significance and attraction and are now largely neglected, although isolated examples of the former art survive in the precincts of a few temples in the south (Bhadri and Desai, 1962).

The ancient Greeks do not seem to have practised either pisciculture or the cultivation of ornamental plants: perhaps, as a sea-faring people, they set greater store by accessible and abundant sea-foods. The Romans did breed fish for both consumption and ornament, having possibly learnt the techniques from Chinese traders by way of Parthia, but there is no evidence that they devoted great attention to aquatic plants in either the lakes and canals of public parks or the pools of patrician villas.

It was much later that the art of water gardening spread through the western world (Hervey and Hems, 1958). Moorish influences carried the decorative use of water in garden design to Spain and there mingled with the legacies of Roman architectural styles to create garden-palaces famed for their fountains, cascades and pools. The formal gardens of the Alhambra and Generalife at Granada, built in the thirteenth and fourteenth centuries, are probably the most notable examples. In Italy ponds and fountains featured prominently in Renaissance gardens, as at the Villa d'Este at Tivoli, the Villa Alodebrandini at Frascati and the Villa Pratolino at Florence. Italian taste also strongly influenced the French sixteenth-century gardens, as seen at the Palace of Fontainebleau. During Louis XIV's extravagant reign ornamental water gardens landscaped by the master hand of André Le Nôtre reached new standards of perfection. Le Nôtre and his disciples eliminated the immense avenues and vistas of Renaissance gardens and designed vast geometrical patterns of woods, pools, lawns and paths. The classic example is undoubtedly the garden of the Palace of Versailles, on which the parks of San Souci at Potsdam were later modelled. Aquatic plants were not, however, a dominant feature of these grandiose designs: they would undoubtedly have distracted attention from the mathematical precision and formal contrasts.

In England in the middle of the eighteenth century, when the creations of the rising naturalistic gardeners were beginning to oust the derived versions of Italian and French designs (Hadfield, 1960), people began to grow aquatic plants in water-filled wooden troughs lined with lead. After the fragrant *Nymphaea odorata* was introduced as an ornamental from North America in 1786 the cultivation of waterlilies became very fashionable.

Of the large eighteenth- and nineteenth-century English estates, Woburn and Chatsworth were justly famous for their water gardens. Chatsworth is of particular horticultural note as the place where the gigantic *Victoria amazonica* flowered for the first time in cultivation (Fitch and Hooker, 1851; and see Stearn, 1965). This remarkable plant was first discovered in 1801, by the botanist Haenke and a Spanish missionary, Fr. La Cueva, in marshes adjacent to the Rio Mamoré, a small Bolivian tributary of the upper Amazon. Numerous other travellers later reported seeing the plant elsewhere in tropical South America but no efforts to cultivate it were made for some 45 years. Eventually, two plants were raised at the Kew Botanic Garden in 1846, from seeds collected in Bolivia by Thomas Bridges, but both had died by the end of the year. Further material was collected in 1848, from the R. Essequibo in Guyana but this proved to be dead on arrival at Kew. In February of the following year viable seeds were received from Georgetown, and by the end of March these had germinated.

Early in August 1849, Joseph Paxton, then in the service of the Duke of Devonshire, obtained one of the seedlings from Kew, and only three months later he had the plant in full bloom at Chatsworth. In the twelve months following this sensational event the plant produced no fewer than 150 leaves and 126 flowers. Flowering specimens were also cultivated successfully in 1850 at Kew and at the Duke of Northumberland's seat at Syon, and it was from these that Fitch prepared his magnificent folio illustrations of the species (in Fitch and Hooker, 1851). Raised annually from seed, the specimen of *V. amazonica* has since been one of the major tropical specialities to be seen at the Kew Botanic Garden.

Popular enthusiasm for water gardening in Britain has grown apace since 1900 (Figs. 15.4, 15.5, 15.6). It has been fostered partly by the splendid examples set in the stylish pools and lakes of such estates as Bodnant, in the Conway valley, and Sheffield Park, in Sussex, and partly by the personal achievements of William Robinson, Gertrude Jekyll, Edward Bowles and other great gardeners who devoted considerable labour to the cultivation of water-lilies and other aquatic plants. Due tribute must also be paid to Amos Perry whose manual, *Water, Bog and Moisture Loving Plants*, became a compact classic and whose nurseries have pioneered the commercial propagation of both hardy and tropical hydrophytes. His daughter-in-law, Frances Perry, has made further notable and energetic contributions, her *Water Gardening* (1938) also becoming a standard work, whilst in the U.S.A. the cultivation of orna-mental species has been actively promoted by Albert Greenberg and the Everglades Aquatic Nurseries of Tampa, Florida.

Amongst the plants most commonly grown in water gardens (Perry, 1938, 1961, 1962) are natural species of all life forms, but emphasis is understand-ably laid on the more decorative and imposing types, notably emergents such as *Butomus, Cyperus, Menyanthes, Nelumbo, Pontederia, Sagittaria, Typha* and numerous aroids; floating-leaved species of *Aponogeton, Hydrocleys, Nuphar, Nymphaea* and *Nymphoides*; and free-floating plants like *Azolla, Ceratopteris, Eichhornia, Pistia, Salvinia, Stratiotes* and *Trapa*. Pride of place is naturally awarded to the waterlilies. Since the 1860's, the remarkable achievements of Latour Marliac, of Temple-sur-Lot in the south of France, George Pring (1934) and the staff of the Missouri Botanic Gardens, and several other breeders have created an immense variety of beautiful *Nymphaea* hybrids. These showy forms, comprising single- and double-flowered, hardy and tropical, and day- and night-flowering plants, offer a wide spectrum of colours, from white and yellow through pink and copper to red, blue and purple, and are naturally preferred to some of the less startling wild species.

Since the First World War there has also been a marked burst of enthusiasm in the U.S.A., south-east Asia, the European countries and Russia for th

FIG. 15.4. A, Blenheim Palace, Oxfordshire, England: the magnificent terrace of formal pools, laid out in 1925, which links the house with the great lake and park, landscaped by 'Capability' Brown in the late eighteenth century. B, Westbury Court, Gloucestershire, England: the head of the T-shaped canal (with a statue of Neptune), a very fine example of a formal water garden in the early eighteenth-century style. (By courtesy of *Country Life*, London.)

FIG. 15.5. A, Leonardslee, Sussex, England: a 'hammer' pond, with marginal aquatic plants, in the valley of this beautiful woodland garden. B, Julians, Hertfordshire, England: the circular waterlily pool with its bronze statue of a seal, on which is centred the walk through the old walled garden beyond. (By courtesy of *Amateur Gardening*, London.)

FIG. 15.6. Bodnant, Denbighshire, Wales: the major feature of this garden is the series of five great terraces overlooking the R. Conway, which were constructed out of a sloping lawn between 1905 and 1914. A, B, the large pool on the third terrace, its formal design broken by the luxuriant waterlilies and marginal plants. C, the severely formal, rectangular pool, with waterlilies at each end, on the fifth terrace—looking towards the open-air stage with its wings and background of clipped yew flanked by cypresses in the classical Italian style of the eighteenth century.

cultivation of plants in cold-water and tropical aquaria (François, 1951; Wendt, 1952–1955; de Wit, 1958a; Makhlin, 1961; Sculthorpe, 1962, 1965, 1966; Roe, 1966). Plants are grown in cold or electrically heated tanks, with a rooting medium of gravel, sand, or a loam or clay compost. Given adequate space and rooting depth, many species thrive for long periods under fluorescent, tungsten or natural illumination and some flower quite freely even in such artificial habitats. Propagation is accomplished through seed in certain genera

FIG. 15.7. Some representative bog plants which tolerate immersion as aquarium subjects: A, *Acorus gramineus* var. *pusillus* (×0·6); B, *Aglaonema simplex* (×0·3); C, *Bacopa monnieri* (×0·5); D, *Cryptocoryne beckettii* (×0·25). (E to H on p. 514.)

but more frequently by natural and artificial vegetative methods. In addition to the genuine submerged hydrophytes, such as the linear-leaved *Sagittaria, Vallisneria, Elodea, Lagarosiphon,* and the dissected-leaved *Cabomba, Ceratophyllum, Myriophyllum* and *Limnophila,* many small emergent and amphibious plants that will tolerate immersion are also grown in aquaria. Notable examples

FIG. 15.7. Some representative bog plants which tolerate immersion as aquarium subjects: E, *Echinodorus longistylis* (×0·2); F, *E. muricatus* (×0·2); G, *Ludwigia repens* (×0·25); H, *Samolus floribundus* (×0·5).

are species of *Acorus, Bacopa, Cardamine, Cryptocoryne, Echinodorus, Heteranthera, Hygrophila, Lagenandra, Micranthemum, Nomaphila, Rorippa, Samolus* and *Synnema* (Fig. 15.7). The increasing importation of hydrophytes collected in the tropics, to satisfy the appetite of aquarists for new and exotic subjects, has incidentally helped to redirect the attention of temperate botanists to such poorly understood genera as *Aponogeton, Anubias, Cryptocoryne, Echinodorus* and *Lagenandra,* and has revealed several hitherto undescribed species (de Wit, 1958b, 1962; van Bruggen, 1962).

HYDROPHYTES AS SOURCES OF FOOD

There occur in hydrophytes two principal types of organ which by virtue of their accumulated food reserves are of potential nutritional value to man: seeds (or fruits) and swollen vegetative perennating organs. Various fruits and seeds rich in oil, starch or protein may be eaten raw, or dried and ground to flour which can be baked with water or milk to give quite palatable bread. Many rhizomes and tubers are similarly rich in carbohydrate, especially starch, sugar and mucilage, and are perfectly edible when raw or cooked. The foliage of a few hydrophytes provides acceptable salad ingredients or cooked vegetable dishes.

In ancient times the mighty River Nile was worshipped as a god, Hâpi, by the Egyptians. Then, as now, the nature of the landscape, the productivity of lower Egypt and the lives of its people were moulded by this vital stream of fertile water stretching north through half Africa. For most of the year lower Egypt lay arid and barren; the hand-built irrigation canals did little to regulate the distribution of water and alleviate the drought. The expectation of any year's growth and harvest depended solely on the height of the annual flood in late summer, when, below Memphis, the force of the Nile was dissipated and the water roamed unchecked over the desolate thirsty soil, eventually flooding most of lower Egypt and enriching the land with its fertile alluvium. 'The people are overjoyed the more', wrote Seneca (A.D. 63–4), 'the less they can see of their country . . . The river possesses this wonderful characteristic: while all other rivers wash away and exhaust land, the Nile, though so much larger than the rest, far from eating away or rubbing off soil, actually adds to its vigour; it contains very little that injuriously affects the soil, for by the mud it brings down, it soaks and binds the sands. Egypt, in fact, owes to the river not merely the fertility of the soil, but also the soil itself.'

It is evident from many sources that the banks of the Nile were shrouded by dense growths of reeds and grasses, and the marginal waters covered with the foliage and flowers of waterlilies and other aquatic plants. It is also certain that in the precarious economy of lower Egypt these aquatic plants were so valuable that they were intensively cultivated and regularly reaped. Herodotus (c. 484–425 B.C.) described from first-hand experience the annual harvest of waterlilies (probably *N. caerulea* and *N. lotus*) when the Nile was in spate and the plains were flooded, and he related that after the plants were dried in the sun the seeds were ground and bread was made from the flour. Some seeds were kept and sown by rolling them individually in tiny balls of clay which were then thrown into the water, a practice which together with the making of bread has been put forward as the origin of the biblical text (*Ecclesiastes xi*. 1): 'Cast thy bread upon the waters: for thou shalt find it after many days.' A further passage of Herodotus, describing lily-like plants with edible fruits, about the size of an olive stone, contained within a structure resembling a wasp's nest, almost certainly refers to *Nelumbo nucifera* which had probably been introduced by the time Herodotus travelled up the Nile (c. 460 B.C.). The ripe carpels of the lotus were apparently eaten both raw and dried. The baking of bread from the ground millet-like seeds of a *Nymphaea*, probably *N. lotus*, mixed with milk or water, was also described by Dioscorides (who flourished about A.D. 50) in his *De Materia Medica* and by Pliny (A.D. 77) who remarked that the bread was especially light and wholesome whilst it was hot but regrettably stodgy and indigestible when cold. Both Herodotus and Dioscorides revealed that the Egyptians also ate the sweet, quince-like rhizomes of *N. lotus* which when cooked resembled egg-yolks, and Theophrastus (370–c. 285 B.C.) recorded that *Cyperus papyrus* also 'is of very great use in the way of food. For all the natives chew the papyrus [culms] both raw boiled and roasted; they swallow the juice and spit out the quid.'

Elsewhere the lotus and waterlilies have been used in similar ways (Irvine and Trickett, 1953). In the Orient *Nelumbo nucifera* has been widely cultivated and its fruits and rhizomes used in a variety of cooked and fresh dishes for many centuries, as also have the rhizomes of *Sagittaria trifolia*, the farinaceous seeds of *Euryale ferox*, and the starch- and fat-laden horned fruits of *Trapa* spp. The Chinese probably introduced *S. trifolia* to Hawaii, Indonesia and the Philippines on account of its food value (Porterfield, 1940; den Hartog, 1957a). The fruits of *Trapa bicornis*, *T. natans* and *T. incisa* form a staple food in continental Asia, Malaysia and India. In addition to cultivating their own crop several countries in this area, such as Indonesia, also import the fruits directly from China (van Steenis, 1949b). *T. natans* is also cultivated on a smaller local scale in parts of the Mediterranean region and fruits are shipped from here and from the Orient to Chinese communities in Europe and the U.S.A.

The cultivated rice, *Oryza sativa*, provides the paramount example of a subaquatic food crop throughout tropical and warm temperate regions of the world. Its wild relative, *O. perennis*, is also occasionally used as a grain food in parts of Africa (Wild, 1961). The Canadian wild rice, *Zizania aquatica*, has been eaten by the North American Indians for over 300 years, and is being grown on a commercial scale at the present time in parts of the U.S.A., notably Minnesota (Simpson, 1966). It is also cultivated in China, Japan and Tonkin (Lohammar, 1955).

The starch-rich seeds and vegetative organs of many other species have formed vital constituents of the diet in historical time and are still eaten where food is scarce or native peoples remain isolated. The principal examples in the tropics of America, Africa, India and Malaysia are the seeds and rhizomes, and sometimes the petioles and peduncles, of *Nymphaea caerulea*, *N. capensis*, *N. lotus* and other lilies, the seeds of *Enhalus acoroides*, *Victoria amazonica* and *V. cruziana*, the swollen tubers of *Aponogeton* species and *Cyperus esculentus*, and the rhizomes of *Typha latifolia* and *T. angustifolia*. The rhizomes of several species of *Sagittaria* and the rhizomes and seeds of *Nelumbo lutea* and *Orontium aquaticum* have been an important carbohydrate source for the North American Indians. The dried and powdered rhizomes of *Butomus umbellatus*, *Calla palustris* and *Menyanthes trifoliata* have been extensively used to make bread by the Eskimoes and other people of northern Eurasia.

Comparatively few hydrophytes are grown for their green herbaceous foliage. In India, young leaves, stems and roots of *Ipomoea aquatica* are eaten, and both there and throughout Malaysia the foliage of *Ottelia alismoides* and all the organs of *Monochoria hastata* and *M. vaginalis*, except the roots, furnish a relished dish (Backer, 1951f; den Hartog, 1957b; Subramanyam, 1962). In

Java juvenile plants of *Limnocharis flava* form a common and much-esteemed vegetable which van Steenis (1954) regretted is not adequately appreciated elsewhere. Several species of *Ceratopteris* are cultivated as a green salad crop in parts of Africa and tropical Asia (Copeland, 1942). The only prominent temperate example is the watercress, of which two types are cultivated, *Rorippa nasturtium-aquaticum* (which is always green) and *R. nasturtium-aquaticum* × *R. microphylla* (in which hybrid the leaves become brown in the autumn). Brown cress is often attacked by black ring spot virus, and is more vulnerable than green cress to infection by crook root disease: green cress is thus economically the more profitable (Bleasdale, 1964). Ingestion of fresh, inadequately washed vegetation from stagnant or slow-flowing waters, especially in the tropics, may contribute significantly to the spread of typhoid and other epidemic diseases. The metacercarial stage of the sheep liver fluke can be acquired by man, in areas where this parasite is prevalent, through consumption of watercress and other aquatic plants (Penfound, 1953a).

THE MEDICINAL USE OF HYDROPHYTES

To judge from Greek and Roman literature and the writings of European herbalists, there are remarkably few external or internal disorders of the human body that have not responded to treatment by some distillation, powder, liniment or poultice compounded of hydrophytes. Just how far the success of the treatment was achieved through genuine curative properties rather than superstition and psychological reassurance is an open question. In very few instances has the therapeutic use of hydrophyte organs been acknowledged over a period of centuries. In yet fewer cases has any medicinal principle been isolated and identified from the organs used. The medicinal application of aquatic plants has gradually waned but in places where native customs survive it apparently persists, as in India (Chopra *et al.*, 1956).

One of the best-known species, accorded a therapeutic value by numerous races, is *Acorus calamus*, the sweet flag, of which the rhizome has been used medicinally since at least the time of Hippocrates (c. 460–377 B.C.). References to fragrant reed-like plants from which sacred perfumes and ointments were compounded are frequent in ancient literature. Sweet calamus (translated from the Hebrew *kaneh bosem*) is mentioned in *Exodus xxx*. 23, and sweet cane (from *kaneh hattobh*) in *Jeremiah vi*. 20. The traffic in calamus in the market of Tyre is described by *Ezekiel* (*xxvii*. 19): 'Dan also and Javan going to and fro, occupied in thy fairs; bright iron, cassia, and calamus were in thy market.' The *kaneh*, and the aromatic *calamos* described by Hippocrates and Dioscorides, have been identified by some authorities with a fragrant oil-containing grass (a species of *Andropogon*) of central India. Celsus referred in *De Medicina* (c. A.D. 14–37) to another plant, *Calamus alexandrinus*, introduced from India to the Red Sea. But it is apparent from the works of Theophrastus and Pliny, and from Columella's *De Re Rustica* (c. A.D. 60) that there grew on the margins of lakes in the vicinity of Antioch and the upper valley of the Orontes (Asi) River another fragrant plant which may be identified more confidently as *Acorus calamus*. The greater accessibility of this region and the reported abundance of the plant strongly favour the belief that *Acorus calamus* was the fragrant species brought to the markets of Tyre and Damascus.

Since these ancient times *Acorus calamus* has been employed throughout much of Eurasia for a variety of medicinal and related purposes. An infusion of the rhizome has been used to treat eye diseases, dyspeptic flatulence, indigestion, toothache, coughs and colds. The reputation it earned as a general stimulant and tonic cure for ague persisted into modern times in certain places, such as East Anglia (Perry, 1961). In Tudor England the leaves (together with various reeds and rushes) were commonly strewn on the floor: when trampled underfoot, they gave off a fragrance which freshened the atmosphere of domestic rooms and combatted the malodours of church congregations. This practice was described by Erasmus of Rotterdam whose passionate desire for purity and cleanliness has been remarked by many historians. In view of the extreme physical discomfiture he experienced during his sojourn in damp and stagnant mediaeval Cambridge (Porter, 1958), it is understandable that he should have protested with vigour and disgust, in a letter to Cardinal Wolsey's physician (Allen, 1918): 'Then the floors are generally covered with clay, and then with marsh rushes, which are later renewed in such a way that the bottom sometimes remains for twenty years, fomenting under it spittle, spilt beer, the remains of fish, and other unmentionable filth. When the weather changes this gives forth a kind of vapour which in my opinion is scarsely healthy for the human body.' He was probably guilty of exaggeration in this unflattering account for there is evidence from the records of wealthier Elizabethan households that the floors were re-strewn as regularly as once a month (Byrne, 1961). The pleasant fragrance of the organs of *A. calamus* is due to a volatile oil, savouring strongly of tangerines, which is emitted more powerfully when the plant is crushed, warmed or dried. By virtue of their fragrance the dried and ground rhizomes and leaves were also used at times to flavour beer, gin and other drinks and to scent hair pomades and cosmetics.

There is little doubt that the medicinal and other uses of the plant have assisted its impressive adventive spread. It is a native of southern and eastern Asia (and probably also North America) but has become so thoroughly naturalised throughout Europe that it has often been thought indigenous there as well. Linnaeus described it as the only native aromatic plant of northern climates and many other European botanists of the eighteenth and nineteenth centuries, such as Babington, Hooker and Watson, agreed with him. Bromfield (1850), however, confessed to '. . . a lurking suspicion that the Sweet Flag may not be aboriginal to Britain', and Devos (1870) viewed its continental European status with similar doubt. Trimen (1871) reviewed the contemporary British distribution of the species and drew attention to the relevent remarks of the herbalists: Turner had been quite sure in 1548 that the plant did not grow in England; in his herbal of 1551 and 1568 he merely described the rhizome, which was regularly imported from the Levant. There was likewise no mention of the species occurring wild in England in the later herbals of Gerarde (1597, 1633) or Parkinson (1640). Trimen argued, as Bromfield had suggested, that the herbalists and simplers could hardly have overlooked a plant of such medical esteem had it in fact been native.

The appearance of living specimens in different parts of Europe has been traced by Mücke (1908), Wein (1939, 1942) and others. A Flemish diplomat called Augier Busbecque, in the service of the Emperors Karl V and Ferdinand I, visited Asia Minor in 1557 on a mission to Sultan Soliman I, the Magnificent, and his physician, one Wilhelm Quackelbeen, despatched specimens of *Acorus calamus* he collected from a lake near Nicomedia to the botanist Matthioli at Prague. Seventeen years later Charles de l'Écluse (Clusius) received living specimens from Istanbul which he cultivated in the botanic garden at Vienna. He published an illustration of the living inflorescence in his *History of Pannonic Plants* (1583) and sent specimens from his rapidly increasing stock to other European gardens. Bauhin grew it in 1590 in the Elector's gardens at Montbéliard, as did Sebitz in his garden at Strasbourg and Robin in the Jardin du Roi at Paris in 1591. Sebitz apparently introduced the plant to habitats near Strasbourg, where it had become very abundant by 1710, and Bauhin naturalised it around Montbéliard and Belfort.

Amongst the other gardens to which de l'Écluse sent material was one at Liège, from where in 1575 de l'Obel described the living rhizome and leaves. De l'Obel certainly visited England about this time for he recorded in his *Kruydtboeck* (1581) having seen '*Plantago aquatica minor*' (*Baldellia ranunculoides*) and other plants in aquatic habitats in England (Raven, 1947). Whether he actually brought from Liège living specimens of *Acorus calamus* as a gift for his friend Gerarde is not clear but in 1597 the sweet flag was included in the catalogue of Gerarde's garden in Holborn, London. How it was distributed in England is obscure: the first record of its growing wild appeared in John Ray's *Catalogus Plantae Angliae* (1670) which described the plant as occurring at Norwich in 1660. There, and around other large English towns it was reported as common by Bromfield (1850). It has subsequently become abundant in many parts of southern and central England and has also appeared in Ireland and Scotland (Perring and Walters, 1962; Kenneth and Wallace, 1964).

So remarkably complete is the naturalisation of the species in many regions of Europe that several writers have been reluctant to accept escape and introduction from botanic and physic gardens as solely responsible for its westward spread. Devos (1870) suggested that the Romans may have introduced it to Belgium, recognising its stimulant properties in a cool climate, and cited in support of his argument the abundance of the plant at the ancient Roman city of Trèves and along the banks of the Moselle. Another suggestion, offered by several authors, is that the plant was introduced to Poland by the Tartars about the middle of the thirteenth century.

Pistia stratiotes has been used medicinally for many centuries. Pliny (A.D. 77) described its use in Egypt for the treatment of diffusive inflammations of the skin in erysipelas and for the healing of abrasions. An external preparation, obtained by boiling the leaf-juice in coconut oil, is similarly used in India to treat chronic skin diseases, whilst a medicine compounded from the leaves, together with sugar and rosewater, is taken for coughs and asthma, and a poultice of leaves is recommended for haemorrhoids. The roots are said to provide a laxative and diuretic: ringworm may be treated by rubbing the ashes of the plant into the scalp (Chopra *et al.*, 1956).

Innumerable other species have been stated, at one time or another, to possess curative properties. The precise methods of application are often shrouded in decent but intriguing obscurity, as in Theophrastus' observation that a floating plant (probably *Ottelia alismoides*) was used by physicians 'for the complaints of women and for fractures'. Infusions of the seeds of *Euryale ferox*, *Nelumbo nucifera* and *Nymphaea stellata*, of the leaves of *Limnophila rugosa*, *Rorippa nasturtium-aquaticum* and *Vallisneria spiralis*, and of the rhizomes of *Menyanthes trifoliata* and *Cyperus articulatus* have acquired reputations as invigorating tonics. Preparations of various species are said to be useful in treating gastric and intestinal disorders: e.g. the powdered rhizomes or tubers of *Nelumbo nucifera*, *Nymphaea nouchali* and *Scirpus grossus* for piles, dyspepsia and dysentery; the leaves of *Ipomoea aquatica*, *Limnophila rugosa*, *L. indica*, *Asteracantha longifolia* and *Ceratophyllum demersum* as purgatives, diuretics and remedies for biliousness and jaundice. Other extracts are mixed with oily or mucilaginous bases and applied externally to treat elephantiasis, pestilent fevers, rheumatism, sores, sunburn and skin complaints: such liniments are prepared from, *inter alia*, the seeds of *Nelumbo nucifera*, the fruits of *Trapa* spp., and the foliage of *Asteracantha longifolia*, *Bacopa monnieri*, *Ceratophyllum demersum*, *Limnophila aromatica* and *L. indica*, *Hydrolea zeylanica*, and *Ludwigia adscendens*. Remarkable virtues have been claimed by herbalists for even the commonest of plants, as witness Culpeper's (1661) remarks on the white waterlily, *Nymphaea alba*: '. . . the leaves both inwards and outwards are good for agues, the syrup of the flowers produces rest and settles the brain of frantic persons.'

Some of the hydrophytes employed medicinally may contain active principles: about fifteen different alkaloids have been isolated from members of the Nymphaeaceae (Hegnauer, 1966). The long-established use of the leaves of *Nuphar* as styptics and of infusions of the rooted parts as a lotion for eruptive skin ailments probably owes its success to the high concentration of tannic acid in these organs. The presence of toxic or anaesthetic substances may perhaps explain the unfortunate effects of some species used in the past. The treatment of hydrophobia, tetanus and rattlesnake poisoning by the administration of the acrid extracts of *Alisma plantago-aquatica* was often followed by the complete paralysis of the patient, whilst narcotic poisoning usually attended the use of *Oenanthe aquatica* for fevers, ulcers and asthma (Perry, 1961). Describing the occurrence of *Oe. crocata* in the R. Thames in his revision of Gerarde's herbal (1633), Johnson exclaimed: 'Pernitious and not excusable is the ignorance of some of our time that have bought and (as one may probably conjecture) used the roots of this plant instead of those of Peionie; and I know they are dayly by the ignorant women in Cheape-side sold to people more ignorant than themselves by the name of Water Lovage; *Caveat Emptor!*'

MISCELLANEOUS COMMERCIAL USES

From time to time various hydrophytes have supplied useful products worthy of mention. The rhizomes of *Nymphaea alba* and *Nuphar* species, by virtue of their gallic acid or tannic acid, both of which have mordanting properties, have been employed in several European countries in dyeing and tanning, and also in brewing. The leaves of *Menyanthes trifoliata* have similarly been used as a substitute for hops in brewing beer (Hewett, 1964). The Indian emergent *Aeschynomene aspera* provides abundant supplies of a soft pith-like material (secondary xylem), light in texture and somewhat similar to balsa, which is employed in the making of such varied items as artificial flowers, toys, sunhats, life-belts and swimming jackets: it also provides a tropical counterpart of the temperate botanist's elder-pith for embedding plant organs for section-cutting (Subramanyam, 1962). The strong fibrous culms or leaves of species of *Cyperus*, *Schoenoplectus* and *Typha* are used still in many parts of the world in the weaving of mats, screens and chair-bottoms, in thatching and coarse basket-work, and in the construction of barrels and casks, whilst the fine plush afforded by the hairs of female *Typha* flowers was formerly used in stuffing pillows (Backer, 1951d; Seidel, 1955, 1959; Zhadin and Gerd, 1963). In India, New Guinea and the Moluccas the fairly strong fibres of the leaves and rhizomes of the marine *Enhalus acoroides* are woven into fishing nets (den Hartog, 1957b; Subramanyam, 1962). Species of *Azolla*, *Lemna*, *Salvinia* and *Utricularia*, together with *Eichhornia crassipes*, *Pistia stratiotes*, *Hydrilla verticillata*, *Limnocharis flava* and *Sagittaria trifolia* are commonly collected in vast quantities and used as manure or fodder for cattle and pigs in tropical Africa, India and south-east Asia. The culms of *Arundo donax*, a frequent plant along the margins of canals, ditches and lakes in the subtropical and warm temperate regions, have provided reeds for woodwind instruments for probably 5000 years. This plant has also yielded cellulose for the manufacture of rayon, and has been considered at several times, notably during the war periods, as a possible source of paper pulp. Its culms and fibrous leaves, like those of *Typha* spp., have also been widely employed in weaving and thatching, and in the making of walking sticks and fishing rods (Perdue, 1958). In various coastal areas of the northern hemisphere, the foliage of the indigenous sea-grasses, *Zostera* spp., provides an insulating, upholstering and packing medium. Since it is rich in the micro-organisms on which larval oysters feed, stranded debris of *Zostera* is greatly valued in oyster culture in Japan (Armiger, 1964).

The most productive and historically significant species in the marginal flora of the Nile was undoubtedly the papyrus, *Cyperus papyrus*, which was the emblem of lower Egypt. This plant is probably indigenous only in tropical Africa and may have been introduced to lower Egypt in ancient times from the Nubian region (now southern Sudan). Its present occurrence in southern Italy and Sicily has developed almost certainly by adventive spread, possibly from specimens originally sent by Ptolemy Philadelphus in 250 B.C. as a gift to Hieronymus II, King of Syracuse. The Ancient Egyptians constructed boats or skiffs of papyrus, believing the plant to be abhorred by the crocodiles with which the Nile seethed. The papyrus is thought by some commentators to be the biblical bulrush (*Exodus ii*, 3) but this may perhaps have been a species of *Scirpus* or *Vossia cuspidata*. From the outer fibrous parts of the culms of papyrus the Egyptians also made ropes and baskets, and wove mats and canvas for floor- and furniture-coverings and for boat-sails. The manufacture of paper from the pith of the culms dates from at least 2400 B.C. After the superficial fibrous material had been peeled off, the pith was sliced longitudinally into wafer-like strips. These were arranged side by side on a flat surface, moistened with water and stuck together under heavy pressure. When dry the broad papyrus sheets were cut and rolled as required.

As a final contrast to the almost universal decline in the economic value of papyrus and other historically important species, it is interesting to note the recent spectacular expansion of a Rumanian industry based on the reeds of the Danube delta. The delta, a vast complex of rivers, lakes, swamps and dry land, covers about 434 000 ha (1675 square miles). More than 60 per cent of this area bears dense populations of emergent reeds, predominantly *Phragmites communis* with some *Typha angustifolia* (see p. 425). For many centuries this great wealth of plants was tapped on only a very local scale, for peasant crafts, thatching, fences and wind-breaks. It was only in 1956 that the government initiated organised farming and industrial use of the reeds. As a result of botanical, hydrobiological and engineering studies at an experimental station at Maliuc, the growth of the reed-beds is now being carefully controlled and their productivity increased (Rudescu, 1965). Harvesting, storage and transportation are gradually being mechanised, with equipment specially developed for operation in the difficult deltaic terrain. Harvested reeds are converted to pulp in the mills of Brăila, a short distance inland. From this pulp are derived printing paper, cellophane, cardboard, and various synthetic fibres. The raw reeds and pulp-mill wastes yield a variety of other products, notably cemented reed-blocks and compressed fibre boards; furfural, alcohol and fuel; insulation material and fertiliser. With an annual harvest amounting to hundreds of thousands of tons, the farming of the Danube reeds has become a vital component of the modern Rumanian economy.

Nature does not reveal all her secrets at once. We imagine we are initiated in her mysteries: we are, as yet, but hanging around her outer courts. Those secrets of hers are not opened to all indiscriminately . . . Of one of them this age will catch a glimpse, of another, the age that will come after.
                                                                    LUCIUS ANNAEUS SENECA
                                          Book VII of Quaestiones Naturales (A.D. 63–64)

BIBLIOGRAPHY AND INDEX OF AUTHORS

Bibliography and Index of Authors

This bibliography provides an index of authors: in square brackets at the end of each reference are the numbers of the pages on which that work is cited in the text of this book (including tables and legends to illustrations). The titles of periodicals are abbreviated as in the *World List of Scientific Periodicals* (edn 4; Butterworth, London; 1964, 1965). Volume numbers are set in bold type; series numbers (or letters) and part numbers are given only if required to locate the reference. The following abbreviations and contractions are used: Appx—appendix; ed.—edited by; edn—edition; imprn—impression; p.—pages; repr.—reprinted (by); rev.—revised (by); ser.—series; Suppl.—supplement, Anhang or Beiblatt; transln—translation (by).

An extensive annotated list of references to the older literature will be found in Arber (1920). In addition to the treatments of groups of hydrophytes in standard floras, valuable descriptive manuals and check-lists, some with identification keys for use in the field, have been compiled for certain temperate and tropical regions by Hotchkiss (1936), Eyle and Robertson (1944), Muenscher (1944, 1959), Moyle and Hotchiss (1945), Rytschin (1948), Funke (1951), Brünner (1953), Voronichin (1953), Biswas and Calder (1955), Matsumura and Harrington (1955), Mason (1957), Fassett (1957), Wild (1961), Chancellor (1962), Subramanyam (1962), Zhadin and Gerd (1963), Bursche (1963) and Steward *et al.* (1963). The only major work to discuss aquatic plants from a physiological (and ecological) standpoint is the treatise by Gessner (1955, 1959). Books describing the cultivation and propagation of aquatic plants in botanic gardens, pools and aquaria have been written by Perry (1938, 1961, 1962), François (1951), Wendt (1952–1958), Hoehne (1955), de Wit (1958a, 1964), Bhadri and Desai (1962), Sculthorpe (1962, 1965, 1966), Brünner (1964) and Roe (1966).

AARIO, L. (1933) Vegetation und postglaziale Geschichte des Nurmijarvi-Sees. *Suomal. eläin-ja kasvit. Seur. van. kasvit. Julk.*, **3** (2), 132 p. [152, 155]

ABEL, P. & DENFFER, D. VON (1962) Über den Zusammenhang zwischen Zell- und Organpolarität bei der Ausbildung des Zellteilungsmusters auf der Blaseninnenwand von *Utricularia vulgaris. Beitr. Biol. Pfl.*, **37**, 77–84. [215]

ACCORSI, W. R. (1944, 1946, 1951) Contribuição para o estudo biológico e ecológico das Podostemonaceae do Salto de Piracicaba, I, II and III. *Anais Esc. sup. Agric. 'Luiz Queiroz'*, **1**, 59–106; **3**, 400–24; **8**, 748–68. [110–11, 284, 330, 335, 339]

ADAMS, P. & GODFREY, R. K. (1961) Observations on the *Sagittaria subulata* complex. *Rhodora*, **63**, 247–66. [100, 358]

ADANSON, M. (1763) *Familles des plantes.* Paris. [192]

AFZELIUS, K. (1920) Einige Beobachtungen über die Samenentwicklung der Aponogetonaceae. *Svensk bot. Tidskr.*, **14**, 168–75. [323]

AGARWAL, J. S. (1952) The embryology of *Lilaea subulata* H.B.K. with a discussion on its systematic position. *Phytomorphology*, **2**, 15–29. [19, 295]

AGHARKAR, S. P. & BANERJI, I. (1930) Studies in the pollination and seed formation of water hyacinth (*Eichhornia speciosa* Kunth). *Agric. J. India*, **35**, 286–96. [280–81]

AITKEN, W. W. (1936) Introduction of aquatic plants into artificial lakes of Iowa. *Proc. Iowa Acad. Sci.*, **43**, 133–37. [453]

ALEXANDER, E. J. (1937) Pontederiaceae. *N. Am. Flora*, **19**, 51–60. [20]

ALEXANDER, W. B., SOUTHGATE, B. A. & BASSINDALE, R. (1935) Survey of the River Tees. II. The estuary—chemical and biological. *Tech. Pap. Wat. Pollut. Res. D.S.I.R.*, **5**, 171 p. [33]

ALLAN, H. H. (1936) Indigene versus alien in the New Zealand plant world. *Ecology*, **17**, 187–93.   [387, 397]
— (1937) The origin and distribution of the naturalised plants of New Zealand. *Proc. Linn. Soc. Lond.*, **150**, 25–46.   [397]
ALLEN, D. E. (1954) Variation in *Peplis portula* L. *Watsonia*, **3**, 85–91.   [371]
— (1963) Report of the Midland regional meeting of the B.S.B.I. for 1961. *Proc. bot. Soc. Br. Isl.*, **5**, 66–67.   [221]
ALLEN, P. S. (1918) *Selections from Erasmus*. London.   [518]
ALLENBY, K. G. (1966) The manganese and calcium content of some aquatic plants and the water in which they grow. *Hydrobiologia*, **27**, 498–500.   [—]
ALLISON, J., GODWIN, H. & WARREN, S. H. (1952) Late-glacial deposits at Nazeing in the Lea Valley, North London. *Phil. Trans. R. Soc.*, ser. B, **236**, 169–240.   [402]
ALLSOPP, A. (1951) *Marsilea* spp.: materials for experimental study of morphogenesis. *Nature, Lond.*, **168**, 301.   [233, 249]
— (1952) The effect of various physiologically active substances on the development of *Marsilea* in sterile culture. *Ann. Bot.*, **16**, 165–83.   [157, 233]
— (1953a) Investigations on *Marsilea*. 2. Induced reversion to juvenile stages. *Ann. Bot.*, **17**, 37–55.   [233]
— (1953b) Investigations on *Marsilea*. 3. The effect of various sugars on development and morphology. *Ann. Bot.*, **17**, 447–63.   [233]
— (1954a) Juvenile stages of plants and the nutritional status of the shoot apex. *Nature, Lond.*, **173**, 1032–33.   [233, 235]
— (1954b) Investigations on *Marsilea*. 4. Anatomical effects of changes in sugar concentration. *Ann. Bot.*, **18**, 449–61.   [233]
— (1955) Investigations on *Marsilea*. 5. Culture conditions and morphogenesis, with special reference to the origin of land and water forms. *Ann. Bot.*, **19**, 247–64.
                                                                                                     [218, 233, 243]
— (1956a) Morphogenetic effects of 3-indolylacetonitrile on sporelings of *Marsilea* in aseptic culture. *J. exp. Bot.*, **7**, 1–13.   [236]
— (1956b) Apical dominance in *Marsilea*, with particular reference to the effects of 3-indolylacetic acid, 3-indolylacetonitrile, and coumarin on lateral bud development. *J. exp. Bot.*, **7**, 14–24.   [95]
— (1959) Effects of gibberellic acid on juvenility in *Marsilea* and certain other plants. *Nature, Lond.*, **184**, 1575–76.   [236]
— (1962) The effects of gibberellic acid on morphogenesis in *Marsilea drummondii* A. Br. *Phytomorphology*, **12**, 1–10.   [236]
— (1963) Morphogenesis in *Marsilea*. *J. Linn. Soc. (Bot.)*, **58**, 417–27.   [235]
— (1964) Shoot morphogenesis. *A. Rev. Pl. Physiol.*, **15**, 223–54.   [142, 235]
— (1965a) Heteroblastic development in cormophytes. *Handb. PflPhysiol.*, **15** (1), 1172–221.   [218, 235]
— (1965b) Land and water forms: physiological aspects. *Handb. PflPhysiol.*, **15** (1), 1236–55.   [218]
ALLSOPP, W. H. L. (1960) The manatee: ecology and use for weed control. *Nature, Lond.*, **188**, 762.   [453–54, 484, 501]
ALSTON, A. H. G. (1959a) *Ferns and fern allies of west tropical Africa*. Suppl. to edn 2 of *Flora of west tropical Africa*. Crown Agents for Oversea Governments and Administrations, London.   [16, 474]
— (1959b) Isoetaceae. *Flora Malesiana*, ser. 2, **1**, 63–64.   [16, 257]
ALSTON, R. E. (1966) Chemotaxonomy or biochemical systematics? In: *Comparative phytochemistry*, ed. Swain, T., 33–56. Academic Press, London and New York.
                                                                                                             [20, 202]
ALSTON, R. E. & TURNER, B. L. (1963) *Biochemical systematics*. Prentice-Hall, New York.
                                                                                                                  [202]
AMSTUTZ, E. (1957) *Stylites*, a new genus of Isoetaceae. *Ann. Mo. bot. Gdn*, **44**, 121–23.
                                                                                                             [16, 256]
ANDERSON, D. E. (1961) Taxonomy and distribution of the genus *Phalaris*. *Iowa St. Coll. J. Sci.*, **36**, 1–96.   [283]
ANDREWS, H. N. (1961) *Studies in paleobotany*. Wiley, New York and London.
                                                                                                            [167, 257–58]
ANGELSTEIN, U. (1911) Über die Kohlensäureassimilation submerser Wasserpflanzen in Bikarbonat- und Karbonatlösungen. *Beitr. Biol. Pfl.*, **10**, 87–117.   [115, 120]
ANT, H. (1966) *Vallisneria spiralis* (Hydrocharitaceae) in der Lippe. *Arch. Hydrobiol.*, **61**, 537–39.   [397]

ARBER, A. (1914) On root development in *Stratiotes aloides* L. *Proc. Camb. phil. Soc. biol. Sci.*, **17**, 369–79.   [160, 190, 192]
— (1918) The phyllode theory of the monocotyledonous leaf, with special reference to anatomical evidence. *Ann. Bot.*, **32**, 465–501.   [61–63, 187]
— (1919a) On heterophylly in water plants. *Am. Nat.*, **53**, 272–78.   [218]
— (1919b) Aquatic angiosperms and their systematic distribution. *J. Bot., Lond.*, **57**, 83–86.   [24]
— (1919c) On the vegetative morphology of *Pistia* and the Lemnaceae. *Proc. R. Soc.*, ser. B, **91**, 96–103.   [201, 290]
— (1919d) The 'Law of Loss' in evolution. *Proc. Linn. Soc. Lond.*, **131**, 70–78.   [291]
— (1920) *Water plants: a study of aquatic angiosperms.* University Press, Cambridge. Repr. (1963) with an introduction by Stearn, W.T., as *Historiae Naturalis Classica*, **23**. Cramer, Weinheim.   [7, 24, 66–67, 71, 82, 100, 127–28, 137, 141, 145, 149–50, 156, 167, 175, 180, 182, 187, 212–13, 215, 218, 223–24, 228–29, 245–46, 253, 279, 285, 289–91, 300, 312–13, 317, 322, 333, 343, 348, 350, 353, 429, 462]
— (1921) Leaves of the Helobieae. *Bot. Gaz.*, **72**, 31–38.   [97]
— (1922a) Leaves of the Farinosae. *Bot. Gaz.*, **74**, 80–94.   [63, 187]
— (1922b) Studies on intrafascicular cambium in monocotyledons. *Ann. Bot.*, **36**, 251–56.   [137]
— (1923) On the 'squamulae intravaginales' of the Helobieae. *Ann. Bot.*, **37**, 31–41. [149]
— (1924) Leaves of *Triglochin. Bot. Gaz.*, **77**, 50–62.   [97]
— (1925a) On the 'squamulae intravaginales' of the Alismataceae and Butomaceae. *Ann. Bot.*, **39**, 169–73.   [149]
— (1925b) *Monocotyledons: a morphological study.* University Press, Cambridge. Repr. (1961) as *Historiae Naturalis Classica*, **21**. Cramer, Weinheim.   [97]
ARBER, E. A. N. & PARKIN, J. (1907) On the origin of angiosperms. *J. Linn. Soc. (Bot.)*, **38**, 29–80.   [279]
ARENS, K. (1930) Zur Kenntnis der Karbonatassimilation der Wasserpflanzen. *Planta*, **10**, 814–16.   [132]
— (1933) Physiologisch polarisierter Massenaustausch und Photosynthese bei submersen Wasserpflanzen. I. *Planta*, **20**, 621–58.   [132]
— (1936a) Physiologisch polarisierter Massenaustausch und Photosynthese bei submersen Wasserpflanzen. II. Die Ca(HCO$_3$)$_2$ Assimilation. *Jb. wiss. Bot.*, **83**, 513–60.   [115, 132]
— (1936b) Photosynthese von Wasserpflanzen in Kalziumbikarbonatlösungen. *Jb. wiss. Bot.*, **83**, 561–66.   [132]
— (1938a) Manganablagerungen bei Wasserpflanzen als Folge des physiologisch polarisierten Massenaustausches. *Protoplasma*, **30**, 104–29.   [132]
— (1938b) Lokaler Nachweis von Kalzium in den Membranen des *Elodea*-Blattes mittels Natriumoleat. *Protoplasma*, **31**, 508–17.   [132]
ARESCHOUG, F. W. C. (1873) On *Trapa natans* L., especially the form now living in the southernmost part of Sweden. *J. Bot., Lond.*, **2**, 239–46.   [411]
ARISZ, W. H. (1953) Active uptake, vacuole secretion, and plasmatic transport of chloride ions in leaves of *Vallisneria spiralis. Acta bot. neerl.*, **1**, 506–15.   [135]
— (1954) Transport of chloride in the 'symplasm' of *Vallisneria* leaves. *Nature, Lond.*, **174**, 223.   [135]
— (1958) Influence of inhibitors on the uptake and the transport of chloride ions in leaves of *Vallisneria spiralis. Acta bot. neerl.*, **7**, 1–32.   [136, 149]
— (1963) Influx and efflux of electrolytes by leaves of *Vallisneria spiralis*. I. Active uptake and permeability. *Protoplasma*, **57**, 5–26.   [135]
— (1964) Influx and efflux of electrolytes. II. Leakage out of cells and tissues. *Acta bot. neerl.*, **13**, 1–58.   [135, 136]
ARISZ, W. H. & SCHREUDER, M. J. (1956) The path of salt transport in *Vallisneria* leaves. *Proc. K. ned. Akad. Wet.*, **59**, 454–60.   [137]
ARISZ, W. H. & SOL. H. H. (1956) Influence of light and sucrose on the uptake and transport of chloride in *Vallisneria* leaves. *Acta bot. neerl.*, **5**, 218–46.   [135]
ARMAND, L. (1912) Recherches morphologiques sur le *Lobelia dortmanna* L. *Revue gén. Bot.*, **24**, 465–78.   [114]
ARMIGER, L. C. (1964) An occurrence of *Labyrinthula* in New Zealand *Zostera. N.Z. Jl Bot.*, **2**, 3–9.   [358, 441, 521]
ARMSTRONG, W. (1964) Oxygen diffusion from the roots of some British bog plants. *Nature, Lond.*, **204**, 801–02.   [161]

18

ARNOLD, A. (1931) Der Verlauf der Assimilation von *Helodea canadensis* unter konstanten Aussenbedingungen. *Planta*, **13**, 529–74.   [117]
ARNOLD, C. A. (1947) *An introduction to palaeobotany*. McGraw-Hill, New York and Maidenhead.   [193]
ARNOLDI, W. (1910) Beiträge zur Morphologie der Keimung von *Salvinia natans*. *Flora*, *Jena*, **100**, 121–39.   [263, 265]
ASCHERSON, P. (1874) Vorläufiger Bericht über die botanischen Ergebnisse der Rohlfs' schen Expedition zur Erforschung der libyschen Wüste. (Schluss.). *Bot. Ztg*, **32**, 641–47.   [400]
ASCHERSON, P. & GRAEBNER, P. (1907) Potamogetonaceae. *Pflanzenreich*, **31** (IV.11), 184 p.   [19]
ASHBY, E. (1929a) The interaction of factors in the growth of *Lemna*. III. The inter-relationship of intensity and duration of light. *Ann. Bot.*, **43**, 333–54.   [204]
— (1929b) The interaction of factors in the growth of *Lemna*. IV. The influence of minute quantities of organic matter upon growth and reproduction. *Ann. Bot.*, **43**, 805–16.   [204]
— (1948a) Studies in the morphogenesis of leaves. I. An essay on leaf shape. *New Phytol.*, **47**, 153–76.   [236]
— (1948b) Studies in the morphogenesis of leaves. II. The area, cell size and cell number of leaves of *Ipomoea* in relation to their position on the shoot. *New Phytol.*, **47**, 177–95.   [236]
— (1950) Some effects of length of day upon leaf shape in *Ipomoea caerulea*. *New Phytol.*, **49**, 375–87.   [242]
ASHBY, E., BOLAS, B. D. & HENDERSON, F. Y. (1928) The interaction of factors in the growth of *Lemna*. I. Method and technique. *Ann. Bot.*, **42**, 771–82.   [204]
ASHBY, E. & OXLEY, T. A. (1935) The interaction of factors in the growth of *Lemna*. VI. An analysis of the influence of light intensity and temperature on the assimilation rate and the rate of frond multiplication. *Ann. Bot.*, **49**, 309–36.   [204]
ASHBY, E. & WANGERMANN, E. (1949) Senescence and rejuvenation in *Lemna minor*. *Nature, Lond.*, **164**, 187.   [204]
ASHBY, E., WANGERMANN, E. & WINTER, E. J. (1949) Studies in the morphogenesis of leaves. III. Preliminary observations on vegetative growth in *Lemna minor*. *New Phytol.*, **48**, 374–81.   [207]
ASHIDA, J. (1934) Studies on the leaf movement of *Aldrovanda vesiculosa* L. I. Process and mechanism of the movement. *Mem. Coll. Sci. Kyoto Univ.*, ser. B, **9**, 141–244.
                                                                                   [209, 211]
— (1935) Studies on the leaf movement of *Aldrovanda vesiculosa* L. II. Effects of mechanical, electrical, thermal, osmotic and chemical influences. *Mem. Coll. Sci. Kyoto Univ.*, ser. B, **11**, 55–113.   [211]
— (1937) Studies on the leaf movement of *Aldrovanda vesiculosa* L. III. Reaction time in relation to temperature. *Bot. Mag.*, *Tokyo*, **51**, 505–13.   [211]
ASKENASY, E. (1870) Ueber den Einfluss des Wachsthumsmediums auf die Gestalt der Pflanzen. *Bot. Ztg*, **28**, 193–201, 209–19, 225–31.   [150, 239]
ATKINSON, L. R. (1943) A preliminary report of fertilisation in *Marsilea vestita*. *Am.J. Bot.*, **30**, 401–04.   [261]

BACHMANN, H. (1896) Submerse Blätter von *Nymphaea alba*. Landformen von *Nymphaea alba*. *Ber. schweiz. bot. Ges.*, **6**, 11–12.   [90]
BACHMANN, R. W. (1961) *Uptake of radioactive heavy metals by aquatic plants*. Thesis, University of Michigan.   [41]
BACKER, C. A. (1949) Amaranthaceae. *Flora Malesiana*, ser. 1, **4**, 69–98.
                                                                              [317, 358, 397, 457]
— (1951a) Elatinaceae. *Flora Malesiana*, ser. 1, **4**, 203–06.   [17, 290]
— (1951b) Hydrophyllaceae. *Flora Malesiana*, ser. 1, **4**, 207–09.   [397]
— (1951c) Sparganiaceae. *Flora Malesiana*, ser. 1, **4**, 233–34.   [20, 34]
— (1951d) Typhaceae. *Flora Malesiana*, ser. 1, **4**, 242–44.   [20, 33, 521]
— (1951e) Callitrichaceae. *Flora Malesiana*, ser. 1, **4**, 251–52.   [34]
— (1951f) Pontederiaceae. *Flora Malesiana*, ser. 1, **4**, 255–61.   [5, 20, 33,
                                                              254, 281, 371, 397, 401, 461, 464, 516]
BACKMAN, A. L. (1941) *Najas marina* in Finnland während der Postglazialzeit. *Acta bot. fenn.*, **30**, 1–38.   [411]
— (1943) *Ceratophyllum submersum* in Nordeuropa während der Postglazialzeit. *Acta bot. fenn.*, **31**, 1–38.   [410]

BACKMAN, A. L. (1948) *Najas flexilis* in Europa während der Quartärzeit. *Acta bot. fenn.*, **43**, 1–44.   [391, 393, 410]
— (1951) *Najas minor* All. in Europa einst und jetzt. *Acta bot. fenn.*, **48**, 1–32.
[403–04, 411]
BAILEY, C. (1884) Notes on the structure, the occurrence in Lancashire, and the source of origin, of *Naias graminea* Delile var. *Delilei* Magnus. *J. Bot.*, *Lond.*, **22**, 305–33.
[113, 398, 400]
BAILEY, I. W. (1949) Origin of the angiosperms: need for a broadened outlook. *J. Arnold Arbor.*, **30**, 64–70.   [14, 280]
— (1951) The use and abuse of anatomical data in the study of phylogeny and classification. *Phytomorphology*, **1**, 67–70.   [14, 280]
— (1953) Evolution of the tracheary tissue of land plants. *Am. J. Bot.*, **40**, 4–8.   [14]
BAITY, H. G. (1938) Some factors affecting the aerobic decomposition of sewage sludge deposits. *Sewage Wks J.*, **10**, 539–68.   [49]
BAKER, H. G. (1965) Characteristics and modes of origin of weeds. In: *The genetics of colonizing species*, ed. Baker, H. G. and Stebbins, G. L., 147–68. Academic Press, London and New York.   [281]
BAKKER, D. (1954) Miscellaneous notes on *Scirpus lacustris* L. *sensu lat.* in the Netherlands. *Acta bot. neerl.*, **3**, 425–45.   [283]
BALDWIN, J. T. & SPEESE, B. M. (1955) Chromosomes of taxa of the Alismataceae in the range of Gray's Manual. *Am. J. Bot.*, **42**, 406–11.   [18, 278]
BANCE, H. M. (1946) A comparative account of the structure of *Potamogeton filiformis* Pers. and *P. pectinatus* L. in relation to the identity of a supposed hybrid of these species. *Trans. Proc. bot. Soc. Edinb.*, **34**, 361–67.   [407]
BANERJI, I. & HALDER, S. (1942) A contribution to the morphology and cytology of *Monochoria hastaefolia* Presl. *Proc. Indian Acad. Sci.*, ser. B, **16**, 91–106.   [324]
BARANOV, A. (1960) On the case of sprouting of the seeds of *Acorus calamus* in North Manchuria. *Phyton, Horn*, **9**, 21–23.   [320]
BARBER, C. A. (1889) On a change of flowers to tubers in *Nymphaea lotus* var. *monstrosa*. *Ann. Bot.*, **4**, 105–16.   [335]
BARBER, D. A. (1961) Gas exchange between *Equisetum limosum* and its environment. *J. exp. Bot.*, **12**, 243–51.   [64, 159, 162]
BARNHART, J. H. (1916) Segregation of genera in the Lentibulariaceae. *Mem. N.Y. bot. Gdn*, **6**, 39–64.   [208, 214]
BARRATT, K. (1916) The origin of the endodermis in the stem of *Hippuris*. *Ann. Bot.*, **30**, 91–99.   [120, 147]
BARRETT, M. J., GAMESON, A. L. H. & OGDEN, C. G. (1960) Aeration studies at four weir systems. *Wat. & Wat. Engng*, **64**, 407–13.   [46]
BARRY, D. H. & JERMY, A. C. (1952) Observations on *Najas marina* L. *Trans. Norfolk Norwich Nat. Soc.*, **17**, 294–97.   [412]
BAUDE, E. (1956) Die Embryoentwicklung von *Stratiotes aloides* L. *Planta*, **46**, 649–71.
[320, 323]
BAUER, L. (1952) Studien zum Heterophyllieproblem. I. Mitteilung. *Planta*, **40**, 515–28.
[218]
BEADLE, L. C. (1963) Anaerobic life in a tropical crater lake. *Nature, Lond.*, **200**, 1223–24.
[32, 52]
BEAL, E. O. (1956) Taxonomic revision of the genus *Nuphar* Sm. of North America and Europe. *J. Elisha Mitchell scient. Soc.*, **72**, 317–46.   [17, 275]
BEATSON, M. E. (1955) Sub-fossil pollen of *Lemna* in Quaternary deposits. *New Phytol.*, **54**, 208.   [287]
BEEFTINK, W. G. (1962) Conspectus of the phanerogamic salt-plant communities in the Netherlands. *Biol. Jaarb.*, **30**, 325–62.   [13]
BEER, SIR G. DE (1958) *Embryos and ancestors.* edn 3. Clarendon Press, Oxford.   [245]
BELAJEFF, W. (1898) Über die männlichen Prothallien der Wasserfarne (Hydropterides). *Bot. Ztg*, **56**, 141–94.   [266]
BENEDICT, R. C. (1909) The genus *Ceratopteris*: a preliminary revision. *Bull. Torrey bot. Club*, **36**, 463–76.   [16, 388]
BENNETT, A. (1914) *Hydrilla verticillata* Casp. in England. *J. Bot., Lond.*, **52**, 257–58.
[390]
BERG, K. (1948) Biological studies on the river Susaa. *Folia limnol. scand.*, **4**, 1–318. [28]
BERNATOWICZ, A. J. (1952) Marine monocotyledonous plants of Bermuda. *Bull. mar. Sci. Gulf Caribb.*, **2**, 338–45.   [14, 384]

BERTRAM, G. C. L. & BERTRAM, C. K. R. (1962) Manatees of Guiana. *Nature, Lond.*, **196**, 1329. [501]

BESSEY, C. E. (1915) The phylogenetic taxonomy of flowering plants. *Ann. Mo. bot. Gdn*, **2**, 109–64. [279]

BHADRI, B. B. SINGH, & DESAI, B. L. (1962) *Water plants.* Indian Council of Agricultural Research, New Delhi. [503, 508, 523]

BHAMBIE, S. (1962) Studies in pteridophytes. II. A contribution to the anatomy of the axis of *Isoetes coromandelina* L. and some other species. *Proc. Indian Acad. Sci.*, ser. B, **56**, 56–76. [167]

BINET, P. (1961) Rapports entre l'eau de mer et la germination des semences de *Triglochin maritimum* L. *Bull. Soc. linn. Normandie*, sér. 10, **1**, 117–32. [326]

— (1962) Les semences de *Triglochin palustre* L. et de *Triglochin maritimum* L.: étude comparée de leur germination. *Bull. Soc. linn. Normandie*, sér. 10, **2**, 148–60. [326]

BIRGE, E. A. & JUDAY, C. (1927) Organic content of lake water. *Bull. Bur. Fish., Wash.*, **42**, 185–205. [38]

— & — (1934) Particulate and dissolved organic matter in inland lakes. *Ecol. Monogr.*, **4**, 440–74. [38]

BISWAS, K. & CALDER, C. C. (1955) *Handbook of common water and marsh plants of India and Burma.* edn 2. *Hlth Bull., Simla*, **24**. [523]

BLACKBURN, K. B. (1952) The dating of a deposit containing an elk skeleton found at Neasham, near Darlington, County Durham. *New Phytol.*, **51**, 364–77. [409]

BLACKMAN, F. F. & SMITH, A. M. (1911) Experimental researches on vegetable assimilation and respiration. IX. On assimilation in submerged water plants and its relation to the concentration of carbon dioxide and other factors. *Proc. R. Soc.*, ser. B, **83**, 389–412. [117]

BLACKMAN, G. E. (1956) Influence of light and temperature on leaf growth. In: *The growth of leaves*, ed. Milthorpe, F. L., 151–69. Butterworth, London. [197, 204]

BLACKMAN, G. E. & BLACK, J. N. (1959) Physiological and ecological studies in the analysis of plant environment. XII. The role of the light factor in limiting growth. *Ann. Bot.*, **23**, 51–63. [152]

BLACKMAN, G. E. & SARGENT, J. A. (1959) The uptake of growth substances. II. The absorption and accumulation of 2,3,5-triiodobenzoic acid by the root and frond of *Lemna minor*. *J. exp. Bot.*, **10**, 480–503. [206]

BLACKMAN, G. E., SEN, G., BIRCH, W. R. & POWELL, R. G. (1959) The uptake of growth substances. I. Factors controlling the uptake of phenoxyacetic acids by *Lemna minor*. *J. exp. Bot.*, **10**, 33–54. [206]

BLANC, M. LE (1912) Sur les diaphragmes des canaux aérifères des plantes. *Revue gén. Bot.*, **24**, 233–43. [125]

BLEASDALE, J. K. A. (1964) The flowering and growth of watercress (*Nasturtium officinale* R.Br.). *J. hort. Sci.*, **39**, 227–33. [250, 517]

BLOCH, R. (1943) Differentiation in red root tips of *Phalaris arundinacea*. *Bull. Torrey bot. Club*, **70**, 182–83. [152]

BODMER, H. (1928) Beiträge zur Anatomie und Physiologie von *Lythrum salicaria* L. *Beih. bot. Zbl.*, **45**, 1–58. [70–71]

BOGIN, C. (1955) Revision of the genus *Sagittaria* (Alismataceae). *Mem. N.Y. bot. Gdn*, **9**, 179–233. [18, 33, 100, 222, 224–25, 277–78, 316, 341, 368, 373–75, 377]

BOKORNY, T. (1890) Weitere Mittheilung über die wasserleitenden Gewebe. *Jb. wiss. Bot.*, **21**, 505–19. [64]

BOLLE, C. (1865) Eine Wasserpflanze mehr in der Mark. *Verh. bot. Ver. Prov. Brandenb.*, **7**, 1–15. [362]

— (1867) Weiteres über die fortschreitende Verbreitung der *Elodea canadensis*. *Verh. bot. Ver. Prov. Brandenb.*, **9**, 137–47. [362]

BONNET, A. L. M. (1955) Contribution à l'étude des Hydroptéridées: recherches sur *Salvinia auriculata* Aublet. *Annls Sci. nat. (bot.)*, sér. 11, **16**, 529–600. [16, 196]

— (1958) Contributions à l'étude des Hydroptéridées. IV. Commentaires et conclusions générales. *Naturalia monspel. (Bot.)*, **8**, 37–104. [16, 266]

BONOMI, G. (1964) Un nuovo aspetto dell'evoluzione del Lago di Varese: La comparsa di situazioni meromittiche. *Memorie Ist. ital. Idrobiol.*, **17**, 231–46. [47]

BORGSTRÖM, G. (1939) Formation of cleistogamic and chasmogamic flowers in wild violets as a photoperiodic response. *Nature, Lond.*, **144**, 514–15. [291]

BORNET, E. (1864) Recherches sur le *Phucagrostis major* Cavol. *Annls Sci. nat. (bot.)*, sér. 5, **1**, 5–51. [331]

BORNKAMM, R. (1965a) Die Rolle des Oxalats im Stoffwechsel höherer grüner Pflanzen. Untersuchungen an *Lemna minor* L. *Flora, Jena*, ser. A, **156**, 139–71. [204]
— (1965b) Zur Oxalatsynthese von *Lemna minor* L. unter verschiedenen Anzuchtbedingungen. *Ber. dt. bot. Ges.*, **77**, 177–93. [204]
— (1966) Ein Jahresrhythmus des Wachstums bei *Lemna minor* L. *Planta*, **69**, 178–86. [207]
BORODIN, J. (1870) Ueber den Bau der Blattspitze einiger Wasserpflanzen. *Bot. Ztg*, **28**, 841–51. [148]
BORUTSKIĬ, E. V. (1949) Changes in the growth of the macrophytes in Lake Beloic at Kossino from 1888 to 1938. (In Russian) *Trudȳ vses. gidrobiol. Obshch.*, **1**, 44–56. [438]
— (1950) Data on the dynamics of the biomass of macrophytes of lakes. (In Russian) *Trudȳ vses. gidrobiol. Obshch.*, **2**, 43–68. [155, 438, 441]
BOSSER J. & RAYNAL, J. (1966) Sur deux *Aponogeton* dioiques d'Afrique et Madagascar. *Adansonia*, **6**, 153–59. [19, 292, 380]
BOSTRACK, J. M. & MILLINGTON, W. F. (1962) On the determination of leaf form in an aquatic heterophyllous species of *Ranunculus*. *Bull. Torrey bot. Club*, **89**, 1–20. [241–43]
BOTTOMLEY, W. B. (1917) Some effects of organic growth-promoting substances (auximones) on the growth of *Lemna minor* in mineral culture solutions. *Proc. R. Soc.*, ser. B, **89**, 481–507. [204]
— (1920) The growth of *Lemna* plants in mineral solutions and in their natural media. *Ann. Bot.*, **34**, 345–52. [204]
BOUBY, H. (1961) Observations sur les 'Utricularia' de la Forêt de Fontainebleau. *Bull. Ass. Nat. Vall. Loing*, **37**, 72–74. [212]
BOUGHEY, A. S. (1963) The explosive development of a floating weed vegetation on Lake Kariba. *Adansonia*, **3**, 49–61. [476, 478]
BOULTER, D., COULT, D. A. & HENSHAW, G. G. (1963) Some effects of gas concentrations on the metabolism of the rhizome of *Iris pseudacorus* L. *Physiologia Pl.*, **16**, 541–48. [162]
BOURNAUD, M. (1963) Le courant, facteur écologique et éthologique de la vie aquatique. *Hydrobiologia*, **21**, 125–65. [58]
BOWER, F. O. (1923, 1926, 1928) *The ferns*, **1**, **2**, and **3**. University Press, Cambridge. [16, 259, 266–67]
— (1930) *Size and form in plants*. MacMillan, London. [95]
— (1947) *Botany of the living plant*. edn 4. MacMillan, London. [95]
BRADLEY, W. H. (1963) Paleolimnology. In: *Limnology in North America*, ed. Frey, D. G., 621–52. University of Wisconsin Press, Madison, Wisconsin. [403]
BRADSHAW, A. D. (1965) Evolutionary significance of phenotypic plasticity in plants. *Adv. Genet.*, **13**, 115–55. [218, 246]
BRAUN-BLANQUET, J. & TÜXEN, R. (1943) Übersicht der höheren Vegetationseinheiten Mitteleuropas. *Communs Stn int. Géobot. médit. alp.*, **84**. [13]
BRAVO, H. (1930) Los Lemnaceas del Valle de Mexico. *An. Inst. Biol. Univ. Méx.*, **1**, 7–32. [20]
BRAY, J. R. (1962) Estimates of energy budgets for a *Typha* (cattail) marsh. *Science, N.Y.*, **136**, 1119–20. [442]
BRAY, J. R., LAWRENCE, D. B. & PEARSON, L. C. (1959) Primary production in some Minnesota terrestrial communities for 1957. *Oikos*, **10**, 38–49. [437, 442]
BRENAN, J. P. M. & CHAPPLE, J. F. G. (1949) The Australian *Myriophyllum verrucosum* Lindley in Britain. *Watsonia*, **1**, 63–70. [150, 283, 397–98, 400]
BRIGGS, G. E. (1959) Bicarbonate ions as a source of carbon dioxide for photosynthesis. *J. exp. Bot.*, **10**, 90–92. [116]
BRIGGS, G. E., HOPE, A. B. & ROBERTSON, R. N. (1961) *Electrolytes and plant cells*. Blackwell, Oxford. [136]
BRITTON, N. L. (1909) Scheuchzeriaceae. *N. Am. Flora*, **17**, 41–42. [19]
BROCHER, F. (1911) La problème de l'*Utriculaire*. *Annls Biol. lacustre*, **5**, 33–46. [210]
BROMFIELD, W. A. (1850) A catalogue of the plants growing wild in Hampshire, with occasional notes and observations on some of the more remarkable species. *Phytologist* **3**, 1002–20. [518–19]
BROOKS, J. S. (1940) *The cytology and morphology of the Lemnaceae*. Thesis, Cornell University. [20, 199]
BROWN, R. (1956) Contribution to the discussion in Jones (1956). [241]

BROWN, W. H. (1911) The plant life of Ellis, Great, Little, and Long Lakes in North Carolina. *Contr. U.S. natn. Herb.*, **13**, 323–41. [13]
— (1913) The relation of the substratum to the growth of *Elodea. Philipp. J. Sci.*, ser. C, **8**, 1–20. [174]
BROWN, W. V. (1946) Cytological studies in the Alismaceae. *Bot. Gaz.*, **108**, 262–67. [278]
BRUGGEN, H. W. E. VAN (1958) *Mayaca* spp. *Aquarium, Den Haag*, **28**, 151–54. [20]
— (1962) *Aponogeton rigidifolius* sp. nov. *Meded. bot. Tuinen Belmonte Arbor. Landb-Hoogesch., Wageningen*, **6**, 88–91. [15, 19, 102, 380, 514]
BRÜNNER, G. (1953) *Wasserpflanzen.* Wenzel, Brunswick. [523]
— (1964) *Aquarienpflanzen.* Kosmos-Verlag; Keller, Stuttgart. [523]
BRUYNE, C. DE (1922) Idioplastes et diaphragmes des Nymphéacées. *C. r. hebd. Séanc. Acad. Sci., Paris*, **175**, 452–55. [125]
BUCHENAU, F. (1865) Morphologische Studien an deutschen Lentibularieen. *Bot. Ztg*, **23**, 61–66, 69–71, 77–80, 85–91, 93–99. [213]
— (1903) Scheuchzeriaceae; Alismataceae; Butomaceae. *Pflanzenreich*, **16** (IV. 14, IV. 15, IV. 16), 20 p., 66 p. and 12 p. [18, 19]
BUELL, M. F. (1935) *Acorus calamus* in America. *Rhodora*, **37**, 367–69. [320]
BUGNON, F. (1963) La notion de concrescence congénitale et le cas des bourgeons 'extra-axillaires' du *Zostera marina* L. *Mém. Soc. bot. Fr.*, 1963, 92–101. [—]
BUGNON, F. & JOFFRIN, G. (1962) Recherches sur la ramification de la pousse chez le *Vallisneria spiralis* L. *Mém. Soc. bot. Fr.*, 1962, 61–72. [95]
— (1963) Ramification de la pousse chez l'*Hydrocharis morsus-ranae* L.; comparison avec le cas du *Vallisneria spiralis* L. *Bull. Soc. bot. Fr.*, **110**, 34–42. [188]
BURDICK, G. E. (1961) Chemical control of aquatic vegetation in relation to the conservation of fish and wildlife. *Proc. NEast Weed Control Conf.*, **15**, 485–91. [484, 489]
BURGERSTEIN, A. (1904) *Die Transpiration der Pflanzen.* Jena. [145]
BURKE, K. (1963) Dissolved gases in East African lakes. *Nature, Lond.*, **200**, 1308. [52]
BURKHOLDER, P. R., BURKHOLDER, L. M. & RIVERO, J. A. (1959) Some chemical constituents of turtle-grass, *Thalassia testudinum. Bull. Torrey bot. Club*, **86**, 88–93. [14, 154, 433, 437, 442, 453–54]
BURNS, G. P. (1904) Heterophylly in *Proserpinaca palustris. Ann. Bot.*, **18**, 579–87. [239, 243–44]
BURR, G. O. (1941) Photosynthesis of algae and other aquatic plants. In: *A symposium on hydrobiology*, by Needham, J. G., *et al.*, 163–81. University of Wisconsin Press, Madison, Wisconsin. [116]
BURSCHE, E.-M. (1963) *Wasserpflanzen: Kleine Botanik der Wassergewächse.* edn 3. Neumann Verlag, Radebeul, Germany. [523]
BURTT, B. L. (1961) Interpretive morphology (a review of Eames, 1961). *Notes R. bot. Gdn Edinb.*, **23**, 569–72. [271]
BUSCEMI, P. A. (1958) Littoral oxygen depletion produced by a cover of *Elodea canadensis. Oikos*, **9**, 239–45. [447]
BÜSGEN, M. (1890) Untersuchungen über normale und abnorme Marsilienfrüchte. *Flora, Jena*, **73**, 169–82. [259]
BUTCHER, R. W. (1927) A preliminary account of the vegetation of the River Itchen. *J. Ecol.*, **15**, 55–65. [12]
— (1933) Studies on the ecology of rivers. I. On the distribution of macrophytic vegetation in the rivers of Britain. *J. Ecol.*, **21**, 58–91. [12, 27, 59, 449]
BUTCHER, R. W., LONGWELL, J. & PENTELOW, F. T. K. (1937) Survey of the River Tees. III. The non-tidal reaches—chemical and biological. *Tech. Pap. Wat. Pollut. Res. D.S.I.R.*, **6**, 189p. [12]
BUTCHER, R. W., PENTELOW, F. T. K. & WOODLEY, J. W. A. (1930) Variations in composition of river waters. *Int. Revue ges. Hydrobiol. Hydrogr.*, **24**, 47–80. [12, 446]
—, — & — (1931) A biological investigation of the River Lark and the effect of beet sugar pollution. *Fishery Invest., Lond.*, **3** (3), 112p. [12]
BUTLER, J. L. (1963) Temperature relations in shallow turbid ponds. *Proc. Okla. Acad. Sci.*, **43**, 90–95. [33]
BUTTERY, B. R. & LAMBERT, J. M. (1965) Competition between *Glyceria maxima* and *Phragmites communis* in the region of Surlingham Broad. I. The competition mechanism. *J. Ecol.*, **53**, 163–81. [358, 427, 438, 440]
BUTTERY, B. R., WILLIAMS, W. T. & LAMBERT, J. M. (1965) Competition between *Glyceria maxima* and *Phragmites communis* in the region of Surlingham Broad. II. The fen gradient. *J. Ecol.*, **53**, 183–95. [161, 428, 440]

BUVAT, R. (1955) Le méristème apical de la tige. *Année biol.*, **31**, 595–656. [94]
BYRNE, M. ST. CLARE (1961) *Elizabethan life in town and country.* edn 8. Methuen, London. [518]

CAIN, S. A. (1944) *Foundations of plant geography.* Harper & Brothers, New York. [376, 388]
CAMPBELL, D. H. (1892) On the prothallium and embryo of *Marsilia vestita. Proc. Calif. Acad. Sci.*, ser. 2, **3**, 183–205. [262, 265]
— (1893) On the development of *Azolla filiculoides* Lam. *Ann. Bot.*, **7**, 155–87. [266]
— (1897) A morphological study of *Najas* and *Zannichellia. Proc. Calif. Acad. Sci.*, ser. 3, **1**, 1–61. [22]
— (1904) Affinities of the Marsiliaceae and Ophioglossaceae. *Am. Nat.*, **38**, 761–75. [16]
— (1905) *The structure and development of mosses and ferns.* edn 2. New York. [259]
CAMPO, M. VAN (1951) Remarques sur les grains de pollen de quelques plantes aquatiques *Bull. Soc. Bot. N. Fr.*, **4** (2), 36–39. [292]
CAMUS, A. (1923) Le genre *Aponogeton* L.f. *Bull. Soc. bot. Fr.*, **70**, 670–76. [19, 380]
CANDOLLE, ALPHONSE P. DE (1855) *Géographie botanique.* Paris. [365]
CANDOLLE, AUGUSTE P. DE (1827) *Organographie végétale.* Paris. [61]
CARL, G. C. (1937) Flora and fauna of brackish water. *Ecology*, **18**, 446–53. [41]
CARPENTER, K. E. (1926) The lead mine as an active agent in river pollution. *Ann. appl. Biol.*, **13**, 395–401. [39]
— (1928) *Life in inland waters.* Sidgwick & Jackson, London. [26–27]
CARSON, R. (1963) *Silent spring.* Hamish Hamilton, London. [499]
CARTER, G. S. (1934) Results of the Cambridge Expedition to British Guiana, 1933. The freshwaters of the rain-forest areas of British Guiana. *J. Linn. Soc. (Zool.)*, **39**, 147–93. [450]
— (1955) *The papyrus swamps of Uganda.* Heffer, Cambridge. [425, 450]
CARTER, G. S. & BEADLE, L. C. (1931) Reports of an expedition to Brazil and Paraguay. The fauna of the swamps of the Paraguayan Chaco. I. Physico-chemical nature of the environment. *J. Linn. Soc. (Zool.)*, **37**, 205–58. [450]
CARTER, S. (1960) Alismataceae. In: *Flora of tropical East Africa*, ed. Turrill, W., Milne-Redhead, E. and Hubbard, C. E. 16p. Crown Agents for Oversea Governments and Administrations, London. [18, 377]
CASPARY, R. (1856) Les Nymphéacées fossiles. *Annls Sci. nat. (bot.)*, sér. 4, **6**, 199–222. [275, 429]
— (1859, 1862) *Aldrovanda vesiculosa* Monti. *Bot. Ztg*, **17**, 117–50; **20**, 185–206. [209, 349]
— (1875) Die geographische Verbreitung der Geschlechter von *Stratiotes aloides* L. *Sber. Ges. naturf. Freunde Berl.*, 1875, 101–06. [304]
— (1888) Nymphaeaceae. *Natürl. PflFam.*, edn 1, **3** (2), 1–10. [17, 275]
CASTELLANOS, A. (1958) Las Pontederiaceae de Brasil. *Archos Jard. bot., Rio de J.*, **16**, 149–216. [20]
C.C.T.A./C.S.A. (1957) (COMMISSION FOR TECHNICAL CO-OPERATION IN AFRICA SOUTH OF THE SAHARA/SCIENTIFIC COUNCIL FOR AFRICA SOUTH OF THE SAHARA) Report of the symposium on *Eichhornia crassipes*, Leopoldville, 1957. *C.C.T.A./C.S.A. Publs*, **27**, 1–31. [42, 427, 465, 469, 483, 498, 500]
CEDERKREUTZ, C. (1947) Die Gefässpflanzenvegetation der Seen auf Aland. *Acta bot. fenn.*, **38**, 1–77. [13]
C.D.A. (1926) (CEYLON DEPARTMENT OF AGRICULTURE) The water hyacinth pest. *Leafl. Dep. Agric. Ceylon*, **40**. [463, 483]
— (1938) The water hyacinth weed. *Leafl. Dep. Agric. Ceylon*, **132**. [464]
CHANCELLOR, A. P. (1958) *The control of aquatic weeds and algae.* H.M.S.O., London. [484, 488, 499–500]
CHANCELLOR, R. J. (1962) The identification of common water weeds. *Bull. Minist. Agric. Fish. Fd., Lond.*, **183**, 48p. [523]
CHANDLER, M. E. J. (1923) The geological history of the genus *Stratiotes*: an account of the evolutionary changes which have occurred within the genus during Tertiary and Quaternary times. *Q. Jl geol. Soc. Lond.*, **79**, 117–38. [318–19, 403]
CHAPMAN, V. J. (1964) *Coastal vegetation.* Pergamon Press, Oxford. [43]
CHASE, S. S. (1947) Polyploidy in an immersed aquatic angiosperm. *Am. J. Bot.*, **34**, 581–92. [19, 394]
CHASSAT, J. F. (1962) Recherches sur la ramification chez les Nymphaeacées. *Mém. Soc. bot. Fr.*, 1962, 72–95. [254]

CHEADLE, V. I. (1942) The occurrence and types of vessels in the various organs of the plant in the Monocotyledoneae. *Am. J. Bot.*, **29**, 441–50.
[86, 141, 144–45, 168–69, 203, 280]
— (1943a) The origin and certain trends of specialisation of the vessel in the Mono-cotyledoneae. *Am. J. Bot.*, **30**, 11–17. [280]
— (1943b) Vessel specialisation in the late metaxylem of the various organs in the Monocotyledoneae. *Am. J. Bot.*, **30**, 484–90. [280]
— (1944) Specialisation of vessels within the xylem of each organ in the Monocotyle-doneae. *Am. J. Bot.*, **31**, 81–92. [280]
— (1953) Independent origin of vessels in the monocotyledons and dicotyledons. *Phytomorphology*, **3**, 23–44. [280]
CHEADLE, V. I. & WHITFORD, N. B. (1941) Observations on the phloem in the Mono-cotyledoneae. I. The occurrence and phylogenetic specialisation in structure of the sieve tubes in the metaphloem. *Am. J. Bot.*, **28**, 623–27. [148]
CHEESEMAN, T. F. (1906) *Manual of the New Zealand flora*. Wellington. [397]
CHODAT, R. & VISCHER, W. (1917) La végétation du Paraguay. VI. Podostemonacées. *Bull. Soc. bot. Genève*, sér. 2, **9**, 165–96. [18, 114]
CHOPRA, R. N., NAYAR, S. L. & CHOPRA, I. C. (1956) *Glossary of Indian medicinal plants*. Council of Scientific and Industrial Research, New Delhi. [517, 520]
CHOW, C. Y., THEVASAGAYAM, E. S. & WAMBEEK, E. G. (1955) Control of *Salvinia*. *Bull. Wld Hlth Org.*, **12**, 365–69. [491]
CHRISTENSEN, C. (1938) Filicinae. In: *Manual of pteridology*, ed. Verdoorn, F. Nijhoff, The Hague. [16, 259, 266]
CHRISTIANSEN, W. (1934) Das pflanzengeographische und soziologische Verhalten der Salzpflanzen mit besonderer Berücksichtigung von Schleswig-Holstein. *Beitr. Biol. Pfl.*, **22**, 139–54. [13]
CHRYSLER, M. A. (1907) The structure and relationships in Potamogetonaceae and allied families. *Bot. Gaz.*, **44**, 161–88. [19, 139, 144, 268]
— (1938) The winter buds of *Brasenia*. *Bull. Torrey bot. Club*, **65**, 277–83. [350]
CHRYSLER, M. A. & JOHNSON, D. S. (1939) Spore production in *Regnellidium*. *Bull. Torrey bot. Club*, **66**, 263–79. [16, 262]
CHUA, S. E. & DICKSON, M. H. (1964) The effect of flashing light, supplemented by con-tinuous red and far-red light, on the growth of *Lemna minor* L. in the presence of growth regulators. *Can. J. Bot.*, **42**, 57–64. [207]
CHURCHILL, M. A., ELMORE, H. L. & BUCKINGHAM, R. A. (1962) The prediction of stream reaeration rates. *Int. J. Air Wat. Pollut.*, **6**, 467–504. [45]
CLAPHAM, A. R. (1962) In: *Flora of the British Isles*, by Clapham, A. R., Tutin, T. G. & Warburg, E. F. edn 2. University Press, Cambridge.
[109, 222, 283, 312, 348, 390]
CLAPHAM, A. R. & GODWIN, H. (1948) Studies of the post-glacial history of British vege-tation. VIII. Swamping surfaces in peats of the Somerset Levels. *Phil. Trans. R. Soc.*, ser. B, **232**, 233–49. [413]
CLAPHAM, A. R., TUTIN, T. G. & WARBURG, E. F. (1962) *Flora of the British Isles*, edn 2. University Press, Cambridge. [397]
CLARK, W. F. (1954) Controlling weeds and algae in farm ponds. *Ext. Bull. Cornell agric. Exp. Stn*, **910**. [484, 486]
CLARK, N. A. & ROLLER, E. M. (1931) The stimulation of *Lemna major* by organic matter under sterile and non-sterile conditions. *Soil Sci.*, **31**, 299–308. [204]
CLASON, E. W. (1964) Potamogetonaceae. *Flora Neerlandica*, **1** (6), 37–79. [19]
CLATWORTHY, J. N. & HARPER, J. L. (1962) The comparative biology of closely related species living in the same area. V. Inter- and intraspecific interference within cultures of *Lemna* spp. and *Salvinia natans*. *J. exp. Bot.*, **13**, 307–24. [427]
CLAUSEN, R. T. (1936) Studies in the genus *Najas* in the northern United States. *Rhodora*, **38**, 333–45. [19]
CLAVAUD, A. (1878) Sur le véritable mode de fécondation du *Zostera marina*. *Act. Soc. linn. Bordeaux*, **32**, 109–15. [297]
CLEMENS, H. P. & FINNELL, J. C. (1957) Biological conditions in a brine-polluted stream in Oklahoma. *Trans. Am. Fish. Soc.*, **85**, 18–27. [42]
CLOËZ, S. (1863) Observations sur la nature des gaz produits par les plantes submergées sous l'influence de la lumière. *C. r. hebd. Séanc. Acad. Sci.*, *Paris*, **57**, 354–57. [120]
CLOS, D. (1856) Mode de propagation particulier au *Potamogeton crispus* L. *Bull. Soc. bot. Fr.*, **3**, 350–52. [349]

CLOWES, F. A. L. (1959) Adenine incorporation and cell division in shoot apices. *New Phytol.*, **58**, 16–19. [94]
— (1961) *Apical meristems.* Blackwell, Oxford. [94, 192, 196]
COCKAYNE, L. (1921) The vegetation of New Zealand. In: *Die Vegetation der Erde*, ed. Engler, A. and Drude, O. Engelmann, Leipzig; Stechert, New York. [397, 400]
CODY, W. J. (1961) *Iris pseudacorus* L.—escaped from cultivation in Canada. *Can. Fld Nat.*, **75**, 139–42. [397, 401]
COHN, F. (1875) Ueber die Function der Blasen von *Aldrovanda* und *Utricularia*. *Beitr. Biol. Pfl.*, **1** (3), 71–92. [209–10]
COKER, R. E. (1954) *Streams, lakes, ponds.* University of North Carolina Press, Chapel Hill, N. Carolina. [26]
COLE, G. A. (1963) The American southwest and middle America. In: *Limnology in North America*, ed. Frey, D. G., 393–434. University of Wisconsin Press, Madison, Wisconsin. [34, 43]
COMBES, R. (1947) Le mécanisme de l'action du milieu aquatique sur les végétaux. Rôle du facteur température. *Revue gén. Bot.*, **54**, 249–70. [242]
COMPTON, R. H. (1909) The morphology and anatomy of *Utricularia brachiata* Oliver. *New Phytol.*, **8**, 117–30. [215]
— (1916) The botanical results of a fenland flood. *J. Ecol.*, **4**, 15–17. [67]
CONARD, H. S. (1905) The waterlilies: a monograph of the genus *Nymphaea*. *Publs Carnegie Instn*, **5**, 279 p.
[17, 85, 123–24, 137, 149, 160, 170, 269–70, 346, 504, 506]
— (1936) Water-lilies; monocots or dicots? *Am. Bot.*, **42**, 104–07. [277]
— (1937) The banana floatingheart (*Nymphoides aquaticum*). *Proc. Iowa Acad. Sci.*, **44**, 61–64. [345]
CONOLLY, A. P., GODWIN, H. & MEGAW, E. M. (1950) Studies in the post-glacial history of British vegetation. XI. Late-glacial deposits in Cornwall. *Phil. Trans. R. Soc.*, ser. B, **234**, 397–469. [402, 406]
CONOVER, J. T. (1964) The ecology, seasonal periodicity, and distribution of benthic plants in some Texas lagoons. *Botanica mar.*, **7**, 4–41. [14, 41–42, 358]
CONWAY, V. M. (1937) Studies in the autecology of *Cladium mariscus* R. Br. III. The aeration of subterranean parts of the plant. *New Phytol.*, **36**, 64–96.
[64, 157, 159, 413]
— (1942) Biological flora of the British Isles: *Cladium mariscus* (L.) R. Br. *J. Ecol.*, **30**, 211–16. [157, 413]
COOK, C. D. K. (1961a) *Sparganium* in Britain. *Watsonia*, **5**, 1–10. [20, 282, 371]
— (1961b) Die bayerischen *Sparganium*-Arten. *Ber. bayer. bot. Ges.*, **34**, 7–10.
[20, 282]
— (1962a) Biological flora of the British Isles: *Sparganium erectum* L. *J. Ecol.*, **50**, 247–55. [64, 69, 155, 157, 325, 371]
— (1962b) Studies in *Ranunculus* subgenus *Batrachium* (DC.) A. Gray. I. Chromosome numbers. *Watsonia*, **5**, 123–26. [222]
— (1963) Studies in *Ranunculus* subgenus *Batrachium* (DC.) A. Gray. II. General morphological considerations in the taxonomy of the subgenus. *Watsonia*, **5**, 294–303.
[5, 109, 149, 222, 242]
— (1964a) Hybrid water crowfeet. *Proc. bot. Soc. Br. Isl.*, **5**, 374. [246]
— (1964b) *Ranunculus* subg. *Batrachium* (DC.) A. Gray. *Flora Europaea*, **1**, 237–38.
[383]
— (1966) Studies in *Ranunculus* subgenus *Batrachium* (DC.) A. Gray. III. *Ranunculus hederaceus* L. and *R. omiophyllus* Ten. *Watsonia*, **6**, 246–59. [—]
COOK, M. T. (1906) The embryology of some Cuban Nymphaeaceae. *Bot. Gaz.*, **42**, 376–92. [277, 324]
— (1909) Notes on the embryology of Nymphaeaceae. *Bot. Gaz.*, **48**, 56–60.
[277, 324]
COPE, B. T., BOSE, S., CRESPI, H. L. & KATZ, J. J. (1965) Growth of *Lemna* in H_2O–D_2O mixtures: enhancement by kinetin. *Bot. Gaz.*, **126**, 214–21. [204]
COPELAND, E. B. (1942) Edible ferns. *Am. Fern J.*, **32**, 121–26. [517]
CORE, E. L. (1941) *Butomus umbellatus* in America. *Ohio J. Sci.*, **41**, 79–85. [18, 401]
CORILLION, R. (1964) *Elodea densa* (Planch.) Casp. ((Hydrocharitacée)=*Egeria densa* Planch.) en Bretagne. *Bull. Soc. scient. Bretagne*, **37**, 81–84. [397, 399, 458]
CORMACK, R. G. H. (1937) The development of root hairs by *Elodea canadensis*. *New Phytol.*, **36**, 19–25. [156–57]

18*

CORMACK, R. G. H. (1949) The development of root hairs in angiosperms. *Bot. Rev.*, **15**, 583–612.																																																	[157]
— (1962) Development of root hairs in angiosperms, II. *Bot. Rev.*, **28**, 446–64.			[157]
CORNER, E. J. H. (1964) *The life of plants.* Weidenfeld & Nicolson, London.
[260, 277, 290]
COSTANTIN, J. (1884) Recherches sur la structure de la tige des plantes aquatiques. *Annls Sci. nat. (bot.)*, sér. 6, **19**, 287–331.																										[71, 123, 185]
— (1885a) Observations critiques sur l'epiderme des feuilles des végétaux aquatiques. *Bull. Soc. bot. Fr.*, **32**, 83–88.																																[114]
— (1885b) Influence du milieu aquatique sur les stomates. *Bull. Soc. bot. Fr.*, **32**, 259–64.																																											[114]
— (1886) Études sur les feuilles des plantes aquatiques. *Annls Sci. nat. (bot.)*, sér. 7, **3**, 94–162.																									[88, 223, 229, 232, 244]
COTTON, A. D. (1933) *Zostera marina* in Britain. *Rep. botl Soc. Exch. Club Br. Isl.*, **10**, 623–24.																																							[441]
COULT, D. A. (1964) Observations on gas movement in the rhizome of *Menyanthes trifoliata* L., with comments on the role of the endodermis. *J. exp. Bot.*, **15**, 205–18.
[128, 157, 159, 161–62]
COULT, D. A. & VALLANCE, K. B. (1951, 1958) Observations on the gaseous exchanges which take place between *Menyanthes trifoliata* L. and its environment, I and II. *J. exp. Bot.*, **2**, 212–22; **9**, 384–402.																						[64, 159]
CRABBE, J. A. (1964) *Marsilea* L.; *Pilularia* L. Flora Europaea, **1**, 23–24.							[16, 383]
CRISP, D. J., WESTLAKE, D. F. & LE CREN, E. D. (*in litt.*) Personal correspondence, 1966.
[33]
CROCKER, W. (1907) Germination of seeds of water plants. *Bot. Gaz.*, **44**, 375–80.		[324]
CROCKER, W. & DAVIS, W. E. (1914) Delayed germination in seed of *Alisma plantago*. *Bot. Gaz.*, **58**, 285–321.																																[324]
CULPEPER, N. (1661) *The Herbal.* London.																																	[520]
CURTIS, J. T. (1959) *The vegetation of Wisconsin: an ordination of plant communities.* University of Wisconsin Press, Madison, Wisconsin.																	[12, 13, 35]
CUTTER, E. G. (1957a) Studies of morphogenesis in the Nymphaeaceae. I. Introduction: some aspects of the morphology of *Nuphar lutea* (L.) Sm. and *Nymphaea alba* L. *Phytomorphology*, **7**, 45–56.																						[83–84, 253–55]
— (1957b) Studies of morphogenesis in the Nymphaeaceae. II. Floral development in *Nuphar* and *Nymphaea*: bracts and calyx. *Phytomorphology*, **7**, 57–73.				[254]
— (1958) Studies of morphogenesis in the Nymphaeaceae. III. Surgical experiments on leaf and bud formation. *Phytomorphology*, **8**, 74–95.												[84]
— (1959) Studies of morphogenesis in the Nymphaeaceae. IV. Early floral development in species of *Nuphar*. *Phytomorphology*, **9**, 263–75.										[254]
— (1961) The inception and distribution of flowers in the Nymphaeaceae. *Proc. Linn. Soc. Lond.*, **172**, 93–100.																												[254–55]
— (1963) Experimental modification of the pattern of organogenesis in *Hydrocharis*. *Nature, Lond.*, **198**, 504.																												[188]
— (1964) Observations on leaf and bud formation in *Hydrocharis morsus-ranae*. *Am. J. Bot.*, **51**, 318–24.																											[95, 188]
— (1965) Recent experimental studies of the shoot apex and shoot morphogenesis. *Bot. Rev.*, **31**, 7–113.																												[255]
CZOPEK, M. (1964) Przeglad wyników badań nad powstawaniem turionów *Spirodela polyrrhiza*. *Wiad. bot.*, **8**, 59–78.																						[355]

DAHL, E. (1963) Plant migrations across the North Atlantic Ocean and their importance for the palaeogeography of the region. In: *North Atlantic biota and their history*, ed. Löve, A and D., 173–88. Pergamon Press, Oxford.																	[391]
DALE, H. M. (1951) Carbon dioxide and root hair development in *Anacharis (Elodea)*. *Science, N.Y.*, **114**, 438–39.																											[157]
— (1957a) Developmental studies of *Elodea canadensis* Michx. I. Morphological development at the shoot apex. *Can. J. Bot.*, **35**, 13–24.										[94, 120, 144]
— (1957b) Developmental studies of *Elodea canadensis* Michx. II. Experimental studies on morphological effects of darkness. *Can. J. Bot.*, **35**, 51–64.					[94, 120]
D'ALMEIDA, J. F. R. (1942) A contribution to the study of the biology and physiological anatomy of Indian marsh and aquatic plants. *J. Bombay nat. Hist. Soc.*, **43**, 92–96.
[155, 157–58]

DANDY, J. E. (1934, 1935) Notes on Hydrocharitaceae, I and II. *J. Bot., Lond.*, **72**, 132–39;
73, 209–17. [18, 305–06]
— (1937) The genus *Potamogeton* L. in tropical Africa. *J. Linn. Soc. (Bot.)*, **50**, 507–40.
[19, 222, 368]
— (*in litt.*) Personal correspondence, 1966. [369, 399]
DANDY, J. E. & TAYLOR, G. (1938–1942) Studies of British *Potamogetons*, I–XVIII.
J. Bot., Lond., **76**, 89–92, 166–71, 239–41; **77**, 56–62, 97–101, 161–64, 253–59,
277–82, 304–11, 342–43; **78**, 1–11, 49–66, 139–47; **79**, 97–101; **80**, 21–24, 117–20,
121–24. [19, 222]
— & — (1946) An account of *Potamogeton × suecicus* Richt. in Yorkshire and the Tweed.
Trans. Proc. bot. Soc. Edinb., **34**, 348–60. [407]
DARWIN, C. (1859, 1894) *The origin of species, by means of natural selection*. edns 1 and 6.
London. [356, 365]
— (1875) *Insectivorous plants*. London. [211]
DAUBS, E. H. (1962) The occurrence of *Spirodela oligorhiza* (Kurz) Hegelm. in the
United States. *Rhodora*, **64**, 83–85. [397]
— (1965) A monograph of Lemnaceae. *Illinois biol. Monogr.*, **34**, 118p. University of
Illinois Press, Urbana, Illinois. [20, 199–202, 287–89, 375, 383, 397]
DAUMANN, E. (1963) Zur Frage nach dem Ursprung der Hydrogamie zugleich ein
Beitrag zur Blütenökologie von *Potamogeton*. *Preslia*, **35**, 23–30. [297]
— (1964) Zur Morphologie der Blüte von *Alisma plantago-aquatica* L. *Preslia*, **36**,
226–39. [278]
— (1965) Insekten- und Windbestäubung bei *Alisma plantago-aquatica* L. *Öst. bot. Z.*,
112, 295–310. [278]
DAVID, R. W. (1958) An introduction to the British species of *Callitriche*. *Proc. bot. Soc.
Br. Isl.*, **3**, 28–32. [17, 221]
DAVIE, R. C. (1913) *Stratiotes aloides* Linn., near Crieff. *Trans. Proc. bot. Soc. Edinb.*,
26, 180–83. [182]
DAVIS, G. J. (1956) *The effects of certain environmental and chemical factors on hetero-
phylly in aquatic angiosperms*. Thesis, University of North Carolina. [242]
DAVIS, J. H. (1937) Aquatic plant communities of Reelfoot Lake. *J. Tenn. Acad. Sci.*,
12, 96–103. [14]
DAVIS, P. H. & HEYWOOD, V. H. (1963) *Principles of angiosperm taxonomy*. Oliver and Boyd,
Edinburgh and London. [14, 218, 222, 242, 246, 337]
DEAN, E. B. (1933) Effect of soil type and aeration upon root systems of certain aquatic
plants. *Pl. Physiol., Lancaster, Pa*, **8**, 203–22. [161]
DEEVEY, E. S. (1949) Biogeography of the Pleistocene. I. Europe and North America.
Bull. geol. Soc. Am., **60**, 1315–416. [410]
DEMALSY, P. (1953) Le sporophyte d'*Azolla nilotica*. *Cellule*, **56**, 7–60. [16, 194, 263]
DENNISTON, R. H. (1922) A survey of the larger aquatic plants of Lake Mendota. *Trans.
Wis. Acad. Sci. Arts Lett.*, **20**, 495–500. [13, 30]
DEVA, R. C. (1953) The anatomy of the floats of *Utricularia flexuosa* Vahl. *J. Indian bot.
Soc.*, **32**, 142–44. [270]
DEVAUX, H. (1889) Du mécanisme des échanges gazeux chez les plantes aquatiques
submergées. *Annls Sci. nat. (bot.)*, sér. 7, **9**, 35–179. [120]
DEVOL, C. E. (1957) The geographic distribution of *Ceratopteris pteridoides*. *Am. Fern J.*,
47, 67–72. [16, 388–89]
DEVOS, A. (1870) Les plantes naturalisées ou introduites en Belgique. *Bull. Soc. r. Bot.
Belg.*, **9**, 5–122. [362, 518–19]
DICKSON, H. (1938a) The occurrence of long and short cycles in growth measurements of
Lemna minor. *Ann. Bot.*, **2**, 97–106. [207]
— (1938b) Sampling as the cause of the apparent growth cycles of *Lemna minor*. *Ann.
Bot.*, **2**, 793–806. [207]
DICKSON, M. H. & CHUA, S. E. (1963) The effect of flashing light on plant growth. *Nature,
Lond.*, **198**, 305. [207]
DIOSCORIDES, P. (fl. c.50 A.D.) *De materia medica*, ed. Sprengel, C., Leipzig, 1829;
ed. Gunther, R. W. T., Oxford, 1934. [515]
DITTMER, H. J., CASTETTER, E. F. & CLARK, O. M. (1954) The ferns and fern allies of New
Mexico. *Univ. New Mex. Publs Biol.*, **6**, 139 p. [16, 372, 375]
DOIGNON, P. (1963) Cinquante ans de phytosociologie dynamique à la Mare aux Fées
(Forêt de Fontainebleau). *Bull. Ass. Nat. Vall. Loing*, **39**, 6–10. [13]

DONSELAAR, J. VAN (1961) On the vegetation of former river beds in the Netherlands. *Wentia*, **5**, 1–85. [13]

DORMER, K. J. & CUTTER, E. G. (1959) On the arrangement of flowers on the rhizomes of some Nymphaeaceae. *New Phytol.*, **58**, 176–81. [255]

DOUDOROFF, P. & KATZ, M. (1950) Critical review of literature on the toxicity of industrial wastes and their components to fish. I. Alkalis, acids and inorganic gases. *Sewage ind. Wastes*, **22**, 1432–58. [52]

DOUGLAS, D. (1880) Notes on the water thyme (*Anacharis alsinastrum* Bab.). *Sci. Gossip*, **16**, 227–29. [363]

DOWNING, A. L., MELBOURNE, K. V. & BRUCE, A. M. (1957) The effect of contaminants on the rate of aeration of water. *J. appl. Chem., Lond.*, **7**, 590–96. [46]

DRAR, M. (1951) The problem of the sudd in relation to stabilising and smothering plants. *Bot. Notiser*, 1951, 32–46. [425, 482]

DRESS, W. J. (1954) The identity of the aquatic 'banana plant'. *Baileya*, **2**, 19–21. [345]

DRUCE, G. C. (1911) The international phytogeographical excursion in the British Isles. III. The floristic results. *New Phytol.*, **10**, 306–28. [359]

DRUCE, G. C. & BRITTON, C. E. (1910) Notes on *Azolla caroliniana* Willd. *Rep. botl Soc. Exch. Club Br. Isl.*, **2**, 609. [359]

D.S.I.R. (1955) (DEPARTMENT OF SCIENTIFIC AND INDUSTRIAL RESEARCH) *Water pollution research, 1954*. H.M.S.O., London. [46]

— (1958) *Water pollution research, 1957*. H.M.S.O., London. [39, 46]

— (1959) *Water pollution research, 1958*. H.M.S.O., London. [28–29, 33, 39–41, 44, 46–47, 446, 451]

— (1960) *Water pollution research, 1959*. H.M.S.O., London. [39, 41, 434, 447, 451]

— (1962) *Water pollution research, 1961*. H.M.S.O., London. [39, 130, 433, 445, 452, 500]

— (1963) *Water pollution research, 1962*. H.M.S.O., London. [36, 39, 44–45, 48–49, 116, 119, 122, 452, 500]

— (1964) *Water pollution research, 1963*. H.M.S.O., London. [36, 39, 49–50, 446, 452, 500]

DUARTE, P. (*in litt.*) Personal correspondence, 1964. [378]

DUCHARTRE, P. (1872) Quelques observations sur les caractères anatomiques des *Zostera* et *Cymodocea*, à propos d'une plante trouvée près de Montpellier. *Bull. Soc. bot. Fr.*, **19**, 289–302. [92, 102]

DUNK, W. P. & TISDALL, A. L. (1954) Weed control in irrigation channels and drains. *Tech. Bull. St. Rivers Wat. Supply Commn Vict.*, **8**. [484, 487]

DUNN, S. T. (1905) *Alien flora of Britain*. London. [397]

DUSEK, W. A. & BONDE, E. K. (1965) Effects of gibberellic acid, indoleacetic acid, and maleic hydrazide on *Azolla mexicana*. *Phyton, B. Aires*, **22**, 51–54. [338]

DUTROCHET, M. (1837) *Mémoires pour servire à l'histoire anatomique et physiologique des végétaux et des animaux*. Brussels. [120]

DUVAL-JOUVE, J. (1872) Diaphragmes vasculifères des monocotylédones aquatiques. *Mém. Acad. Sci. Lett. Montpellier*, **8**, 157–76. [125]

DYMOND, G. C. (1949) The water hyacinth: a Cinderella of the plant world. In: *Soil fertility and sewage*, by van Vuren, 221–27. London. [443]

EAGLES, C. F. & WAREING, P. F. (1964) The role of growth substances in the regulation of bud dormancy. *Physiologia Pl.*, **17**, 697–709. [355]

EAMES, A. J. (1936) *Morphology of vascular plants (lower groups)*. McGraw-Hill, New York and Maidenhead. [194, 255–57, 260, 262–63, 266]

— (1953) Floral anatomy as an aid in generic limitation. *Chronica bot.*, **14**, 126–32. [14, 21]

— (1961) *Morphology of the angiosperms*. McGraw-Hill, New York and Maidenhead. [14, 271, 277, 279, 295, 313, 320]

EATON, R. J. (1947) *Lemna minor* as an aggressive weed in the Sudbury River. *Rhodora*, **49**, 165–71. [459–60]

EBER, E. VON (1934) Karpellbau und Plazentationsverhältnisse in der Reihe der Helobiae. *Flora, Jena*, **127**, 273–330. [294]

EDWARDS, P. ST. J. & ALLSOPP, A. (1956) The effects of changes in the inorganic nitrogen supply on the growth and development of *Marsilea* in aseptic culture. *J. exp. Bot.*, **7**, 194–202. [233]

EDWARDS, R. W. (1957) Vernal sloughing of sludge deposits in a sewage effluent channel. *Nature, Lond.*, **180**, 100. [51]
— (1958) The effect of larvae of *Chironomus riparius* Meigen on the redox potentials of settled activated sludge. *Ann. appl. Biol.*, **46**, 457–64. [50]
— (1962) Some effects of plants and animals on the conditions in fresh-water streams with particular reference to their oxygen balance. *Int. J. Air Wat. Pollut.*, **6**, 505–20. [45, 49–50]
EDWARDS, R. W. & BROWN, M. W. (1960) An aerial photographic method for studying the distribution of aquatic macrophytes in shallow waters. *J. Ecol.*, **48**, 161–63. [28, 30]
EDWARDS, R. W. & HEYWOOD, J. (1960) The effect of a sewage effluent discharge on the deposition of calcium carbonate on shells of the snail *Potamopyrgus jenkinsi* (Smith). *Nature, Lond.*, **186**, 492–93. [434]
— & — (1962) Some aspects of the ecology of *Potamopyrgus jenkinsi* Smith. *J. Anim. Ecol.*, **31**, 239–50. [434]
EDWARDS, R. W. & OWENS, M. (1960) The effects of plants on river conditions. I. Summer crops and estimates of net productivity of macrophytes in a chalk stream. *J. Ecol.*, **48**, 151–60. [426, 429, 433, 436, 439, 444]
— & — (1962) The effects of plants on river conditions. IV. The oxygen balance of a chalk stream. *J. Ecol.*, **50**, 207–20. [47–48, 117, 442, 444–45]
— & — (1965) The oxygen balance of streams. In: *Ecology and the industrial society*, ed. Goodman, G. T., Edwards, R. W. and Lambert, J. M., *Symp. Br. ecol. Soc.*, **5**, 149–72. Blackwell, Oxford. [122, 452]
EDWARDS, R. W., OWENS, M. & GIBBS, J. W. (1961) Estimates of surface aeration in two streams. *J. Instn Wat. Engrs*, **15**, 395–405. [45]
EDWARDS, R. W. & ROLLEY, H. L. J. (1965) Oxygen consumption of river muds. *J. Ecol.*, **53**, 1–19. [47, 49–50]
EDWARDS, W. F. (1961) More interesting plants of our local canals. *Athene*, **1**, 44–46. [397–98]
EINARSSON, T. (1964) On the question of Late Tertiary or Quaternary land connections across the North Atlantic, and the dispersal of biota in that area. *J. Ecol.*, **52**, 617–25. [392]
EKAMBARAM, T. (1916) Irritability of the bladders in *Utricularia*. *Agric. J. India*, **11**, 72–79. [210]
EKZERTSEV, V. A. (1958) The production of littoral vegetation of the Ivan'kovskoyo Reservoir. (In Russian) *Byull. Inst. Biol. Vodokhran.*, **1**, 19–21. [13, 438]
— (1963) The plant formation in the intermittently flooded zone of the Kuibyshev Reservoir. (In Russian) *Mat. nauchno-technich. soveshch. Kuibyshevskogo Vodokhran.*, **3**, 133–35. [13]
EKZERTSEV, V. A. & EKZERTSEVA, V. V. (1963) A study of the flora of the Ivan'kovskoyo Reservoir. (In Russian) *Mat. biol. gidrol. Volzhskikh Vodokhran. Akad. Nauk. SSSR*, 1963, 6–10. [13]
ELSTER, H. J. & VOLLENWEIDER, R. (1961) Beiträge zur Limnologie Ägyptens. *Arch. Hydrobiol.*, **57**, 241–343. [13, 438, 442]
EMMANUEL, A. J. (*in litt.*) Personal correspondence, 1962. [424, 477–78, 502]
EMOULD, M. (1921) Recherches anatomiques et physiologiques sur les racines respiratoires. *Mém. Acad. r. Belg. Cl. Sci.*, ser. 2, **6**, 52 p. [163]
ENGLAND, W. H. & TOLBERT, R. J. (1964) A seasonal study of the vegetative shoot apex of *Myriophyllum heterophyllum*. *Am. J. Bot.*, **51**, 349–53. [94, 142, 241]
ENGLER, A. (1877) Vergleichende Untersuchungen über die morphologischen Verhältnisse der Araceae. II. Ueber Blattstellung und Sprossverhältnisse der Araceae. *Nova Acta Acad. Caesar. Leop. Carol.*, **39**, 159–232. [199, 201, 290]
— (1879) Notiz über die Befruchtung von *Zostera marina* und das Wachsthum derselben. *Bot. Ztg*, **37**, 654–55. [21]
— (1888) Ceratophyllaceae. *Natürl. PflFam.*, edn 1, **3** (2), 10–12. [17]
— (1889) Lemnaceae. *Natürl. PflFam.*, edn 1, **2** (3), 154–64. [20]
— (1930) Podostemonaceae. *Natürl. PflFam.*, edn 2, **18a**, 3–68. [18, 111, 144, 285]
EPSTEIN, E. & LEGGETT, J. E. (1954) The absorption of alkaline earth cations by barley roots: kinetics and mechanism. *Am. J. Bot.*, **41**, 785–91. [133]
ERDTMAN, G. (1952) *Pollen morphology and plant taxonomy. I. Angiosperms.* Almqvist and Wiksell, Stockholm; Chronica Botanica, Waltham, Massachusetts. [23]
ERIKSEN, C. H. (1963) The relation of oxygen consumption to substrate particle size in two burrowing mayflies. *J. exp. Biol.*, **40**, 447–54. [49]

ERNST, A. (1872) Ueber die Anschwellung des unter Wasser befindlichen Stammtheiles von *Aeschynomene hispidula* H.B.K. *Bot. Ztg*, **30**, 586–87. [66]

ERNST-SCHWARZENBACH, M. (1945) Zur Blütenbiologie einiger Hydrocharitaceen. *Ber. schweiz. bot. Ges.*, **55**, 33–69. [18, 306, 308–09]

— (1951) Die Ursachen der verminderten Fertilität von *Elodea*-Arten. *Planta*, **39**, 542–69. [18, 310]

— (1953) Zur Kompatibilität von Art- und Gattungs-Bastardierungen bei Hydrocharitaceen.*Öst. bot. Z.*, **100**, 403–23. [18]

— (1956) Kleistogamie und Antherenbau in der Hydrocharitaceen—Gattung *Ottelia*. *Phytomorphology*, **6**, 296–311. [18, 254, 290–91]

ESAHI, Y. & ODA, Y. (1964) Effects of light intensity and sucrose on the flowering of *Lemna perpusilla*. *Plant Cell Physiol.*, *Tokyo*, **5**, 513–16. [252]

ESAU, K. (1953, 1965) *Plant anatomy*. edns 1 and 2. Wiley, New York and London. [94]

ESAU, K., CHEADLE, V. I. & GIFFORD, E. M. (1953) Comparative structure and possible trends of specialisation of the phloem. *Am. J. Bot.*, **40**, 9–19. [148]

ESENBECK, E. (1914) Beiträge zur Biologie der Gattungen *Potamogeton* und *Scirpus*. *Flora, Jena*, **7**, 151–212. [232]

EVANS, G. C. & HUGHES, A. P. (1961) Plant growth and the aerial environment. I. Effect of artificial shading on *Impatiens parviflora*. *New Phytol.*, **60**, 150–80. [149]

EWER, D. W. (1966) Biological investigations on the Volta Lake, May 1964 to May 1965. In: *Man-made lakes*, ed. Lowe-McConnell, R. H. *Symp. Inst. Biol.*, **15**, 21–31. Institute of Biology and Academic Press, London. [458, 460]

EYLES, D. E. & ROBERTSON, J. L. (1944) *A guide and key to the aquatic plants of the south-east United States*. U.S. Government Printing Service, Washington, D.C. [523]

FAIR, G. M., MOORE, E. W. & THOMAS, H. A. (1941) The natural purification of river muds and pollutional sediments. *Sewage Wks J.*, **13**, 270–307, 756–99, 1209–28. [49]

FAROOQ, M. & SIDDIQUI, S. A. (1966) Anatomy of the floats of *Utricularia inflexa* Forsk. var. *inflexa* Taylor. *Bull. Torrey bot. Club*, **93**, 301–05. [—]

FASSETT, N. C. (1930) The plants of some northeastern Wisconsin lakes. *Trans. Wis. Acad. Sci. Arts Lett.*, **25**, 155–68. [13, 30]

— (1939a) Notes from the Herbarium of the University of Wisconsin. XVII. *Elatine* and other aquatics. *Rhodora*, **41**, 367–77. [6, 17, 221, 222, 281]

— (1939b) Notes from the Herbarium of the University of Wisconsin. XVIII. *Podostemum* in North America. *Rhodora*, **41**, 524–29. [18, 111]

— (1951) *Callitriche* in the New World. *Rhodora*, **53**, 137–55, 161–82, 185–94, 209–22. [6, 17, 221, 311–12]

— (1953) A monograph of *Cabomba*. *Castanea*, **18**, 116–28. [15, 17, 107, 228, 268, 383]

— (1955) *Echinodorus* in the American tropics. *Rhodora*, **57**, 133–56, 174–88, 202–12. [15, 18, 222, 226, 316, 373–75, 378]

— (1957) *A manual of aquatic plants*. edn 2 (with a revision appendix by Ogden, E.C.) University of Wisconsin Press, Madison, Wisconsin. [6, 68, 70, 110, 199, 221, 228, 347, 391, 397, 401, 453–54, 523]

FASSETT, N. C. & ARMITAGE, K. B. (1961) Aquatic plants of El Salvador. Unpublished manuscript cited in Cole (1963). [2, 34, 43]

FASSETT, N. C. & CALHOUN, B. (1952) Introgression between *Typha latifolia* and *Typha angustifolia*. *Evolution, Lancaster, Pa*, **6**, 367–79. [282]

FAUTH, A. (1903) Beiträge zur Anatomie und Biologie der Früchte und Samen einiger einheimischer Wasser- und Sumpfpflanzen. *Beih. bot. Zbl.*, **14**, 327–73. [324]

FEDDERSEN, M. (1961) *Chinese decorative art*. Faber and Faber, London. [505, 507]

— (1962) *Japanese decorative art*. Faber and Faber, London. [504–06]

FELDMANN, J. (1936) Les monocotylédones marines de la Guadeloupe. *Bull. Soc. bot. Fr.*, **83**, 604–13. [384]

FELFÖLDY, L. J. M. (1960) Apparent photosynthesis of *Potamogeton perfoliatus* L. in different depths of Lake Balaton. *Annls Inst. biol. Tihany*, **27**, 201–08. [117]

FENNER, C. A. (1904) Beitrag zur Kenntnis der Anatomie, Entwicklungsgeschichte und Biologie der Laubblätter und Drüsen einiger Insectivoren. *Flora, Jena*, **93**, 335–434. [216]

FERNALD, M. L. (1917) The genus *Elatine* in eastern North America. *Rhodora*, **19**, 10–15. [17]

FE℈NALD, M. L. (1919) Two new *Myriophyllums* and a species new to the United States. *Rhodora*, **21**, 120–24. [17, 368, 388]
— (1922) Notes on *Sparganium*. *Rhodora*, **24**, 26–34. [20]
— (1924) *Myriophyllum magdalenense*, a correction. *Rhodora*, **26**, 198. [17]
— (1932) The linear-leaved North American species of *Potamogeton*, section *Axillares*. *Mem. Am. Acad. Arts Sci.*, **17**, 1–183. Repr. as *Mem. Gray Herb.*, **3**. [19]
— (1941) *Elatine americana* and *E. triandra*. *Rhodora*, **43**, 208–11. [17]
— (1946) The North American representatives of *Alisma plantago-aquatica*. *Rhodora*, **48**, 86–96. [18]
FERNALD, M. L. & GRISCOM, L. (1935) *Proserpinaca palustris* and its varieties. *Rhodora*, **37**, 177–78. [17]
FEUILLADE, J. (1962) Une plante aquatique nouvelle pour la France, *Elodea densa* (Planch.) Casp. *Bull. Soc. linn. Normandie*, sér. 10, **2**, 47–51, 185–88. [397, 399, 458]
FISH, G. R. (1963) Observations on excessive weed growth in two lakes in New Zealand. *N.Z. Jl Bot.*, **1**, 410–18. [435, 439, 459, 500]
FITCH, W. H. & HOOKER, W. J. (1851) *Victoria regia, or Illustrations of the Royal Water-lily, in a series of figures chiefly made from specimens flowering at Syon and at Kew*. London. [77–78, 508–09]
FLEURY, E. (1966) Contribution à l'étude de la dominance apicale chez le sporophyte du *Marsilea drummondii* A. Br. (Filicinées, Marsileacées). *Revue gén. Bot.*, **73**, 360–95. [95]
FLORIN, R. (1940) Zur Kenntnis einiger fossiler *Salvinia*-Arten und der früheren geographischen Verbreitung der Gattung. *Svensk bot. Tidskr.*, **34**, 265–92. [193]
FOERSTE, A. F. (1889) Botanical notes. *Bull. Torrey bot. Club*, **16**, 266–68. [338]
FOGG, G. E. (1959) Dissolved organic matter in oceans and lakes. *New Biol.*, **29**, 31–48. [37]
FOGG, G. E. & WESTLAKE, D. F. (1955) The importance of extracellular products of algae in freshwater. *Verh. int. Verein. theor. angew. Limnol.*, **12**, 219–32. [38]
FORD, S. O. (1902) The anatomy of *Ceratopteris thalictroides* L. *Ann. Bot.*, **16**, 95–121. [167, 192]
FORE, P. L. & MOHLENBROCK, R. H. (1966) Two new naiads from Illinois and distributional records of the Naiadaceae. *Rhodora*, **68**, 216–20. [19, 397]
FORSBERG, B. & FORSBERG, C. (1961) The freshwater environment for *Najas marina* L. in Scandinavia. *Svensk bot. Tidskr.*, **55**, 604–12. [37, 412]
FORSBERG, C. (1959) Quantitative sampling of subaquatic vegetation. *Oikos*, **10**, 233–40. [13, 427, 435, 442]
— (1960) Subaquatic macrovegetation in Ösbysjön, Djursholm. *Oikos*, **11**, 183–99. [13, 427, 432–33, 435, 439, 442]
— (1964) The vegetation changes in Lake Tåkern. *Svensk bot. Tidskr.*, **58**, 44–54. [13, 56, 454]
FOSTER, A. S. (1936) Leaf differentiation in angiosperms. *Bot. Rev.*, **2**, 349–72. [94]
— (1956) Plant idioblasts: remarkable examples of cell specialisation. *Protoplasma*, **46**, 184–93. [85]
FOSTER, A. S. & GIFFORD, E. M. (1959) *Comparative morphology of vascular plants*. Freeman, San Francisco. [114, 255]
FRANÇOIS, M. (1951) *Décors exotiques et plantes d'aquariums*. François, Argenteuil, France. [513, 523]
FRANK, A. B. (1872) Ueber die Lage und die Richtung schwimmender und submerser Pflanzentheile. *Beitr. Biol. Pfl.*, **1** (2), 31–86. [180]
FRANK, P. A. (1966) Dormancy in winter buds of American pondweed, *Potamogeton nodosus* Poir. *J. exp. Bot.*, **17**, 546–55. [356]
FRANK, P. A. & HODGSON, R. H. (1964) A technique for studying absorption and translocation in submersed plants. *Weeds*, **12**, 80–82. [174–75]
FRANK, P. A., HODGSON, R. H. & COMES, R. D. (1963) Evaluation of herbicides applied to soil for control of aquatic weeds in irrigation canals. *Weeds*, **11**, 124–28. [484]
FREY, D. G. (ed.) (1963) *Limnology in North America*. University of Wisconsin Press, Madison, Wisconsin. [26]
FROHNE, W. C. (1938) Limnological role of higher aquatic plants. *Trans. Am. microsc. Soc.*, **57**, 256–68. [452–54]
FRYER, A. (1887) Notes on pondweeds. VI. On land forms of *Potamogeton*. *J. Bot., Lond.*, **25**, 306–10. [90]
FRYER, A., BENNETT, A. & EVANS, A. H. (1898–1915) *The Potamogetons (pond weeds) of the British Isles*. London. [19]

FULVIO, T. E. DI (1961) Sobre el episporio de las especies Americanas de *Azolla* con especial referencia a *A. mexicana* Presl. *Kurtziana*, **1**, 299–302.   [16, 375]
FUNKE, G. L. (1931) On the influence of light of different wavelengths on the growth of plants. *Recl Trav. bot. néerl.*, **28**, 431–85.   [232]
— (1937, 1938, 1939) Observations on the growth of water plants, I, II and III. *Biol. Jaarb.*, **4**, 316–44; **5**, 382–403; **6**, 334–50.   [81–82, 307, 315, 429]
— (1951) *Waterplanten*. Noorduijn, Gorinchem, Netherlands.   [523]

GAISER, L. O. (1949) Further distribution of *Butomus umbellatus* in the Great Lakes region. *Rhodora*, **51**, 385–90.   [401]
GALLAGHER, C. H., KOCH, J. H., MOORE, R. M. & STEEL, J. D. (1964) Toxicity of *Phalaris tuberosa* for sheep. *Nature, Lond.*, **204**, 542–45.   [455]
GAMESON, A. L. H. (1957) Weirs and the aeration of rivers. *J. Instn Wat. Engrs*, **11**, 477–90.
                                                                                                        [46]
GAMESON, A. L. H. & TRUESDALE, G. A. (1959) Some oxygen studies in streams. *J. Instn Wat. Engrs*, **13**, 175–87.   [45]
GAMESON, A. L. H., TRUESDALE, G. A. & DOWNING, A. L. (1955) Re-aeration studies in a lakeland beck. *J. Instn Wat. Engrs*, **9**, 571–94.   [45–46]
GAMS, H. (1927) Die Gattung *Trapa* L. *Pflanzenareale*, **1** (3), 39–41 (map nos. 25–27).
                                                                                                        [17]
GARDNER, G. (1846) *Travels in the interior of Brazil*. London.   [214]
GATES, F. C. (1927) Establishment of plant associations. *Ecology*, **8**, 339–40.   [331]
GAUDET, J. J. (1960) Ontogeny of the foliar sclereids in *Nymphaea odorata*. *Am. J. Bot.*, **47**, 525–32.   [86, 123]
— (1964a) Morphology of *Marsilea vestita*. I. Ontogeny and morphology of the submerged and land forms of the juvenile leaves. *Am. J. Bot.*, **51**, 495–502.   [237]
— (1964b) Morphology of *Marsilea vestita*. II. Morphology of the adult land and submerged leaves. *Am. J. Bot.*, **51**, 591–97.   [237]
— (1965a) Morphology of *Marsilea vestita*. III. Morphogenesis of the leaves of etiolated plants. *Am. J. Bot.*, **52**, 716–19.   [238]
— (1965b) The effect of various environmental factors on leaf form of the aquatic fern *Marsilea vestita*. *Physiologia Pl.*, **18**, 674–86.   [237]
GAUTHIER, R. & RAYMOND, M. (1949) Le genre *Elatine* dans le Québec. *Contr. Inst. bot. Univ. Montréal*, **64**, 29–35.   [17]
GAY, P. A. (1958) *Eichhornia crassipes* in the Nile of the Sudan. *Nature, Lond.*, **182**, 538.
                                                                                                        [465]
— (1960) Ecological studies of *Eichhornia crassipes* Solms. in the Sudan. I. Analysis of spread in the Nile. *J. Ecol.*, **48**, 183–91.   [465, 467, 481]
GEHU, J.-M. (1960) Quelques observations sur la végétation et l'écologie d'une station réputée de l'Archipel de Chausey: Isle aux Oiseaux. *Bull. Lab. marit. Dinard*, **46**, 78–93.   [13]
GELDART, A. M. (1906) *Stratiotes aloides* L. *Trans. Norfolk Norwich Nat. Soc.*, **8**, 181–200.
                                                                                                        [304]
GERARDE, J. (1597) *The Herball*. (Rev. and ed. Johnson, T., 1633) London.   [518, 520]
GERM, H. (1951) Scheinbare Traumabewegungen von *Nymphaea*-Blattstielen. *Verh. zool.-bot. Ges. Wien*, **92**, 245–59.   [82]
GESSNER, F. (1937) Untersuchungen über Assimilation und Atmung submerser Wasserpflanzen. *Jb. wiss. Bot.*, **85**, 267–328.   [132]
— (1938) Die Beziehung zwischen Lichtintensität und Assimilation bei submersen Wasserpflanzen. *Jb. wiss. Bot.*, **86**, 491–526.   [116–17]
— (1940) Beiträge zur Biologie amphibischer Pflanzen. *Ber. dt. bot. Ges.*, **58**, 2–22.
                                                                                                        [243]
— (1945) Über die Wasseraufnahme emerser Wasserpflanzen. *Ber. dt. bot. Ges.*, **67**, 340–43.   [64–65, 89]
— (1950) The ecological importance of current speed in flowing waters and its measurement in a very small space. *Arch. Hydrobiol.*, **43**, 159–65.   [58]
— (1955) *Hydrobotanik: die physiologischen Grundlagen der Pflanzenverbreitung im Wasser. I. Energiehaushalt*. VEB Deutscher Verlag der Wissenschaften, Berlin.
                                                                                      [26, 28, 116, 523]
— (1956) Der Wasserhaushalt der Hydrophyten und Helophyten. *Handb. PflPhysiol.*, **3**, 854–901.   [93, 145]

GESSNER, F. (1959) *Hydrobotanik: die physiologischen Grundlagen der Pflanzenverbreitung im Wasser. II. Stoffhaushalt.* VEB Deutscher Verlag der Wissenschaften, Berlin.
[26, 82, 116, 129, 443, 523]
— (1960a) Die Blütenöffnung der *Victoria regia* in ihrer Beziehung zum Licht. *Planta,* **54**, 453–65. [274]
— (1960b) Höhere Wasserpflanzen. *Handb. PflPhysiol.,* **5**, 506–20. [—]
GESSNER, F. & PANNIER, F. (1958) Der Sauerstoffverbrauch der Wasserpflanzen bei verschiedenen Sauerstoffspannungen. *Hydrobiologia,* **10**, 323–51. [129]
GESSNER, F. & WEINFURTER, F. (1952) Die geotrope Krümmung der *Nymphaea*-Blattstiele. *Ber. dt. bot. Ges.,* **65**, 46–50. [82]
GIARDELLI, M. L. (1935) Las flores de *Wolfiella oblonga. Revta argent. Agron.,* **2**, 17–20. [287]
— (1939) El florecimiento de *Spirodela intermedia* W. Koch. *Notas Mus. La Plata (Bot.),* **4**, 317–22. [287]
GILBERT, H. C. (1937) Lemnaceae in flower. *Science, N.Y.,* **86**, 308. [287]
GILLMAN, H. (1871) *Lemna trisulca* in flower; *Lemna polyrrhiza* in flower. *Am. Nat.,* **5**, 651–53. [287]
GILLNER, V. (1960) Vegetations- und Standortsuntersuchungen in den Strandwiesen der schwedischen Westküste. *Acta phytogeogr. suec.,* **43**, 1–198. [13]
GILLY, C. L. (1946) The Cyperaceae of Iowa. *Iowa St. Coll. J. Sci.,* **21**, 55–151. [283]
GIN, A. (1909) Recherches sur les Lythracées. *Trav. Lab. Matière méd.,* Paris, **6**, 166p. [123, 141]
GLÜCK, H. (1905) *Biologische und morphologische Untersuchungen über Wasser- und Sumpfgewächse. I. Die Lebensgeschichte der europäischen Alismaceen.* Fischer, Jena.
[70, 123, 232, 336]
— (1906) *Biologische und morphologische Untersuchungen über Wasser- und Sumpfgewächse. II. Untersuchungen über die mitteleuropäischen Utricularia-Arten, über die Turionenbildung bei Wasserpflanzen, sowie über Ceratophyllum.* Fischer, Jena.
[108, 213, 216–17, 335, 339, 348, 350, 352–53, 355]
— (1911) *Biologische und morphologische Untersuchungen über Wasser- und Sumpfgewächse. III. Die Uferflora.* Fischer, Jena. [67, 70, 123, 229]
— (1913) Contributions to our knowledge of the species of *Utricularia* of Great Britain, with special regard to the morphology and geographical distribution of *Utricularia ochroleuca. Ann. Bot.,* **27**, 607–20. [213]
— (1924) *Biologische und morphologische Untersuchungen über Wasser- und Sumpfgewächse. IV. Submerse und Schwimmblattflora.* Fischer, Jena. [123, 232]
— (1940) Die Gattung *Trapella. Bot. Jb.,* **71**, 267–336. [184]
GODWIN, H. (1923) Dispersal of pond floras. *J. Ecol.,* **11**, 160–64. [12, 331]
— (1956) *The history of the British flora.* University Press, Cambridge.
[371, 391, 393–94, 402–04, 406–13]
GODWIN, H. & WILLIS, E. H. (1964) The viability of lotus seeds (*Nelumbium nucifera,* Gaertn.). *New Phytol.,* **63**, 410–12. [325]
GOEBEL, K. (1879) Ueber Sprossbildung auf *Isoëtes*blättern. *Bot. Ztg,* **37**, 1–6. [337]
— (1880) Beiträge zur Morphologie und Physiologie des Blattes. *Bot. Ztg,* **38**, 833–45]
[232.
— (1882) Ueber die 'Frucht' von *Pilularia globulifera. Bot. Ztg,* **40**, 771–78. [262]
— (1891–1893) *Pflanzenbiologische Schilderungen.* Marburg.
[66, 84, 105, 114, 120, 123, 145, 150, 184, 199, 209, 212–15, 232, 267, 290, 317, 321–22, 328, 330, 352–53]
— (1895) Ueber die Einwirkung des Lichtes auf die Gestaltung der Kakteen und anderer Pflanzen. *Flora, Jena,* **80**, 96–116. [232]
— (1896) Über Jugendformen von Pflanzen und deren künstliche Wiederhervorrufen. *Sber. bayer. Akad. Wiss.,* **26**, 447–97. [232]
— (1898–1901) *Organographie der Pflanzen.* Jena. [215, 219, 232]
— (1904) Morphologische und biologische Bemerkungen. 15. Regeneration bei *Utricularia. Flora, Jena,* **93**, 98–126. [339]
— (1908) *Einleitung in die experimentelle Morphologie der Pflanzen.* Leipzig.
[232, 243, 338]
— (1913) Morphologische und biologische Bemerkungen. 22. *Hydrothrix gardneri. Flora, Jena,* **105**, 88–100. [290]
— (1921) Zur Organographie der Lemnaceen. *Flora, Jena,* **114**, 278–305. [199]

GOOD, R. (1924) The germination of *Hippuris vulgaris* L. *J. Linn. Soc. (Bot.)*, **46**, 443–48. [321–22]

— (1953, 1964) *The geography of the flowering plants.* edns 2 and 3. Longmans Green, London. [365–66, 368, 370, 376, 385, 387]

GOOR, A. C. J. VAN (1921) Die *Zostera*-Assoziation des holländischen Wattenmeeres. *Recl Trav. bot. néerl.*, **18**, 103–23. [13]

GORHAM, E. (1958) The influence and importance of daily weather conditions in the supply of chloride, sulphate and other ions to fresh waters from atmospheric precipitation. *Phil. Trans. R. Soc.*, ser. B, **241**, 147–78. [36]

— (1961) Factors influencing the supply of major ions to inland waters, with special reference to the atmosphere. *Bull. geol. Soc. Am.*, **72**, 795–840. [36]

GORHAM, P. R. (1941) Measurement of the response of *Lemna* to growth promoting substances. *Am. J. Bot.*, **28**, 98–101. [204, 206–07]

— (1950) Heterotrophic nutrition of seed plants with particular reference to *Lemna minor* L. *Can. J. Res.*, ser. C, **28**, 356–81. [204]

GORTNER, R. A. (1934) Lake vegetation as a possible source of forage. *Science, N.Y.*, **80**, 531–33. [432–33, 453–54]

GOTTLIEB, J. E. (1963) Control of marginal leaf meristem growth in *Ceratopteris*. *Am. J. Bot.*, **50**, 614. [338]

GOVINDAPPA, D. A. & NAIDU, T. R. B. (1956) The embryo sac and endosperm of *Blyxa oryzetorum* Hook. f. *J. Indian bot. Soc.*, **35**, 417–22. [323]

GRAEBNER, P. (1900) Typhaceae, Sparganiaceae. *Pflanzenreich*, **2** (IV. 8, IV. 10), 18 p. and 26 p. [20]

GRAHAM, S. A. (1964) The genera of Lythraceae in the southeastern United States. *J. Arnold Arbor.*, **45**, 235–50. [66, 281]

GRAINGER, J. (1947) Nutrition and flowering of water plants. *J. Ecol.*, **35**, 49–64. [249, 255, 267]

GREEN, P. S. (1962) Watercress in the New World. *Rhodora*, **64**, 32–43. [397]

GREENWALD, M. (1956, 1957) *List of references on control of aquatic plants including algae.* Chipman Chemical Co., Bound Brook, New Jersey. [484]

GREENWOOD, D. J. & NELDER, J. A. (1964) The effect of drugs on the growth of *Lemna minor*. *Ann. Bot.*, **28**, 711–15. [207]

GRENDA, A. (1926) Über die systematische Stellung der Isoetaceen. *Bot. Arch.*, **16**, 268–96. [16]

GRIFFITHS, B. M. (1932) The ecology of Butterby Marsh, Durham. *J. Ecol.*, **20**, 105–27. [12]

— (1936) The limnology of the Long Pool, Butterby Marsh, Durham: an account of the temperature, oxygen-content and composition of the water. *J. Linn. Soc. (Bot.)*, **50**, 393–416. [12]

GRØNTVED, J. (1954) Typhaceernes og Sparganiaceernes Udbredelse i Danmark. *Bot. Tidsskr.*, **50**, 209–38. [20]

— (1958) Underwater macrovegetation in shallow coastal waters. *J. Cons. perm. int. Explor. Mer*, **24**, 32–42. [438]

GRUCHY, J. H. B. DE (1938) A preliminary study of the larger aquatic plants of Oklahoma with special reference to their value in fish culture. *Tech. Bull. Okla. agric. Exp. Stn*, **4**, 31 p. [13, 453–54]

GRÜSS, J. (1927) Die Luftblätter der Nymphaeaceen. *Ber. dt. bot. Ges.*, **45**, 454–58. [90]

GUERN, J. (1963a) Caractéristiques de la croissance des frondes de *Lemna trisulca*. L. *C. r. hebd. Séanc. Acad. Sci.*, Paris, **256**, 2220–22. [207]

— (1963b) Modifications expérimentales de l'intensité de la dominance entre frondes de *Lemna trisulca* L. *C. r. hebd. Séanc. Acad. Sci.*, Paris, **256**, 2686–88. [207]

— (1965) Corrélations de croissance entre frondes chez Lemnacées. *Annls Sci. nat. (bot.)*, sér. 12, **6**, 1–156. [207]

GUNNERSON, C. G. (1964) Diurnal and random variations of dissolved oxygen in surface waters. *Verh. int. Verein. theor. angew. Limnol.*, **15**, 307–21. [446]

GUPPY, H. B. (1893) The River Thames as an agent in plant dispersal. *J. Linn. Soc. (Bot.)*, **29**, 333–46. [325, 331, 355]

— (1894) On the habits of *Lemna minor*, *L. gibba*, and *L. polyrhiza*. *J. Linn. Soc. (Bot.)*, **30**, 323–30. [201, 217, 287, 317, 354]

— (1897) On the postponement of the germination of the seeds of aquatic plants. *Proc. R. phys. Soc. Edinb.*, **13**, 344–59. [325, 331]

GUPPY, H. B. (1906) *Observations of a naturalist in the Pacific between 1826 and 1899. II. Plant dispersal.* London. [71, 317, 328, 331]
— (1917) *Plants, seeds and currents in the West Indies and Azores.* London. [378]
GUPTA, B. L. (1935) Studies in the development of the pollen grains and embryo sac of *Wolffia arrhiza. Curr. Sci.*, **4**, 104–05. [290]
GURNEY, R. (1949) Notes on frogbit (*Hydrocharis*) and hair-weed (*Potamogeton pectinatus*). *Trans. Norfolk Norwich Nat. Soc.*, **15**, 381–85. [319]
GWYNNE-VAUGHAN, D. T. (1897) On some points in the morphology and anatomy of the Nymphaeaceae. *Trans. Linn. Soc. Lond.*, ser. 2, **5**, 287–99. [167, 224]

HABERLANDT, G. (1914) *Physiological plant anatomy.* Transln by Drummond, J. M. F. London. [88, 184]
HACCIUS, B. (1952) Die Embryoentwicklung bei *Ottelia alismoides* und das Problem des terminalen Monokotylen-Keimblattes. *Planta*, **40**, 433–60. [322]
HADAC, E. (1961) The family Cyperaceae in Iraq. *Bull. Coll. Sci. Iraq*, **6**, 1–28. [283, 397]
HADFIELD, M. (1960) *Gardening in Britain.* Hutchinson, London. [508]
HAGSTRÖM, J. O. (1916) Critical researches on the *Potamogetons. K. svenska VetenskAkad. Handl.*, **55**, 1–281. [19, 348]
HAIGH, J. C. (1936) Notes on the water hyacinth (*Eichhornia crassipes* Solms) in Ceylon. *Ceylon J. Sci.*, ser. A, **12**, 97–107. [191, 281, 317, 328, 463, 469–70]
HALL, T. F. (1940) The biology of *Saururus cernuus* L. *Am. Midl. Nat.*, **24**, 253–60. [455]
HALL, T. F. & PENFOUND, W. T. (1944) The biology of the American lotus, *Nelumbo lutea* (Willd.) Pers. *Am. Midl. Nat.*, **31**, 744–58. [455]
HAMERSTROM, F. N. & BLAKE, J. (1939) Central Wisconsin muskrat study. *Am. Midl. Nat.*, **21**, 514–20. [453–54]
HAMMANN, A. (1957) Assimilationszahlen submerser Phanerogamen und ihre Beziehung zur Köhlensäureversorgung. *Schweiz. Z. Hydrol.*, **19**, 579–612. [116]
HAMMOND, B. L. (1936) Regeneration of *Podostemon ceratophyllum. Bot. Gaz.*, **97**, 834–45. [339]
— (1937) Development of *Podostemum ceratophyllum. Bull. Torrey bot. Club*, **64**, 17–36. [339]
HANNIG, E. (1911) Über die Bedeutung der Periplasmodien. II. Die Bildung der Massulae von *Azolla. Flora, Jena*, **102**, 243–78. [266]
— (1912) Untersuchungen über die Verteilung des osmotischen Drucks in der Pflanze in Hinsicht auf die Wasserleitung. *Ber. dt. bot. Ges.*, **30**, 194–204. [147]
HARA, H. (1962) Racial differences in widespread species with special reference to those common to Japan and North America. *Am. J. Bot.*, **49**, 647–52. [19, 370, 385]
HARADA, I. (1952) Chromosome studies of some dicotyledonous water plants. *Jap. J. Genet.*, **27**, 117–20. [—]
HARDER, R. (1963) Blütenbildung durch tierische Zusatznahrung und andere Faktoren bei *Utricularia exoleta* R. Braun. *Planta*, **59**, 459–71. [249–50]
HARDING, D. (1961) Limnological trends in Lake Kariba. *Nature, Lond.*, **191**, 119–21. [477]
HARPER, R. M. (1918) Some dynamic studies of Long Island vegetation. *Pl. Wld*, **21**, 38–46. [441–42]
HARRIS, B. B. & SILVEY, J. K. G. (1940) Limnological investigation on Texas reservoir lakes. *Ecol. Monogr.*, **10**, 111–43. [14]
HARTOG, C. DEN (1957a) Alismataceae. *Flora Malesiana*, ser. 1, **5**, 317–34. [18, 254, 336, 369, 377, 383–84, 397, 401, 453, 516]
— (1957b) Hydrocharitaceae. *Flora Malesiana*, ser. 1, **5**, 381–413. [18, 22, 42, 291, 358, 371, 383–87, 397, 453–54, 516, 521]
— (1959) A key to the species of *Halophila* (Hydrocharitaceae) with descriptions of the American species. *Acta bot. neerl.*, **8**, 484–89. [18, 384–85]
— (1963) Einige waterplantengemeenschappen in Zeeland. *Gorteria*, **1**, 155–64. [13]
— (1964a) An approach to the taxonomy of the sea-grass genus *Halodule* Endl. (Potamogetonaceae). *Blumea*, **12**, 289–312. [19, 384–87]
— (1964b) Over de oecologie van bloeiende *Lemna trisulca. Gorteria*, **2**, 68–72. [289]
HARTOG, C. DEN & SEGAL, S. (1964) A new classification of the water-plant communities. *Acta bot. neerl.*, **13**, 367–93. [5, 7, 13, 172–73]
HARVEY, H. W. (1957) *The chemistry and fertility of sea waters.* edn 2. University Press, Cambridge. [26]

HASITSCHKA-JENSCHKE, G. (1959) Bemerkenswerte Kernstrukturen im Endosperm und im Suspensor zweier Helobiae. *Öst. bot. Z.*, **106**, 301–14. [320]
HASLER, A. D. & JONES, E. (1949) Demonstration of the antagonistic action of large aquatic plants on algae and rotifers. *Ecology*, **30**, 359–64. [450]
HASMAN, M. & INANÇ, N. (1957) Investigations on the anatomical structure of certain submerged, floating and amphibious hydrophytes. *İstanb. Üniv. Fen Fak. Mecm.*, ser. B, **22**, 137–53. [61, 113, 123, 145, 168, 171, 183, 187, 192]
HATTINGH, E. R. (1961) The problem of *Salvinia auriculata* Aubl. and associated aquatic weeds on Kariba Lake. *Weed Res.*, **1**, 303–06. [476]
— (unpubl.) *Unpublished reports on investigations into the control of Salvinia auriculata on Lake Kariba.* I (89 p. with 28 appendices), 1962; II (18 p. with 3 appendices), 1963.
[196–97, 424, 477–78, 483–84, 492–95, 498–500]
HAUMAN-MERCK, L. (1913) Observations éthologiques et systématiques sur deux espèces argentines du genre *Elodea*. *Recl Inst. bot. 'Léo Errera'*, **9**, 33–39. [309]
— (1915) Note sur *Hydromystria stolonifera* Mey. *An. Mus. nac. Hist. nat. B. Aires*, **27**, 325–31. [306]
HAWKER, L. E., LINTON, A. H., FOLKES, B. F. & CARLILE, M. J. (1960) *An introduction to the biology of micro-organisms.* Edward Arnold, London. [449]
HAWKES, H. A. (1957) Biological aspects of pollution. In: *Aspects of river pollution*, ed. Klein, L., 191–251. Butterworth, London. [59]
HAYES, F. R. & MACAULAY, M. A. (1959) Lake water and sediment. V. Oxygen consumed in water over sediment cores. *Limnol. Oceanogr.*, **4**, 291–98. [49]
HAYES, F. R. & PHILLIPS, J. E. (1958) Lake water and sediment. IV. Radiophosphorus equilibrium with mud, plants and bacteria under oxidised and reduced conditions. *Limnol. Oceanogr.*, **3**, 459–75. [52]
HAYES, F. R., REID, B. L. & CAMERON, M. L. (1958) Lake water and sediment. II. Oxidation-reduction relations at the mud-water interface. *Limnol. Oceanogr.*, **3**, 308–17. [52]
HEGELMAIER, F. (1864) *Monographie der Gattung Callitriche.* Stuttgart.
[17, 150, 311–12, 338]
— (1867) Zur Systematik von *Callitriche*. *Verh. bot. Ver. Prov. Brandenb.*, **9**, 1–40.
[17, 312]
— (1868) *Die Lemnaceen: eine monographische Untersuchung.* Leipzig.
[20, 199, 203, 287, 321–22, 352, 429]
— (1870) Ueber die Entwicklung der Blütentheile von *Potamogeton*. *Bot. Ztg*, **28**, 281–89, 297–305, 313–19. [295]
— (1896) Systematische Übersicht der Lemnaceen. *Bot. Jb.*, **21**, 268–305.
[20, 199, 287]
HEGNAUER, R. (1966) Comparative phytochemistry of alkaloids. In: *Comparative phytochemistry*, ed. Swain, T., 211–30. Academic Press, London and New York. [520]
HEJNÝ, S. (1957) Ein Beitrag zur ökologischen Gliederung der Makrophyten der tschechoslowakischen Niederungsgewässer. *Preslia*, **29**, 349–68. [7, 13]
— (1960) *Ökologische Characteristik der Wasser- und Sumpfpflanzen in den slowakischen Tiefebenen (Donau- und Theissgebiet).* Vdyavatel'stvo Slovenskej Akádemie Vied., Bratislava. [7, 13, 152, 155, 438, 442]
HENSHAW, G. G., COULT, D. A. & BOULTER, D. (1961) Cytochrome-c oxidase, the terminal oxidase of *Iris pseudacorus* L. *Nature, Lond.*, **192**, 579. [162]
—, — & — (1962) Organic acids of the rhizome of *Iris pseudacorus* L. *Nature, Lond.*, **194**, 579–80. [162]
HENSLOW, G. (1891) A theoretical origin of endogens from exogens through self-adaptation to an aquatic habit. *J. Linn. Soc. (Bot.)*, **29**, 485–528. [279]
— (1911) The origin of monocotyledons from dicotyledons through self-adaptation to a moist or aquatic habitat. *Ann. Bot.*, **25**, 717–44. [279]
HENSSEN, A. (1954) Die Dauerorgane von *Spirodela polyrhiza* (L.) Schleid. *Flora, Jena*, **141**, 523–66. [352, 355]
HERODOTUS (c. 484–425 B.C.) *Works.* Transln by Cary, H. from text of Baehr. London, 1891. [515]
HERRIG, F. (1915) Beiträge zur Kenntnis der Blattentwicklung einiger phanerogamer Pflanzen. *Flora, Jena*, **107**, 327–50. [94]
HERVEY, G. F. & HEMS, J. (1958) *The book of the garden pond.* Stanley Paul, London. [508]
HERZOG, R. (1935) Ein Beitrag zur Systematik der Gattung *Salvinia*. *Hedwigia*, **74**, 267–84. [16, 196, 473–74]
— (1938) Geographische Verbreitung der Gattungen *Salvinia* und *Azolla*. *Bot. Arch.*, **39**, 219–25. [16, 473–74]

HESLOP-HARRISON, J. W. (1952) Occurrence of the American pondweed *Potamogeton epihydrus* Raf. in the Hebrides. *Nature, Lond.*, **169**, 548. [389–90]
— (1953a) The North American and Lusitanian elements in the flora of the British Isles. In: *The changing flora of Britain*, ed. Lousley, J. E. Botanical Society of the British Isles, London; Buncle, Arbroath, Scotland. [387, 391, 393]
HESLOP-HARRISON, J. (1953b) *New concepts in flowering-plant taxonomy*. Heinemann, London. [245, 274, 370]
— (1963) Plant growth substances. In: *Vistas in botany*, **3**, ed. Turrill, W. B., 104–94. Pergamon Press, Oxford. [355]
HESLOP-HARRISON, J. W. & BLACKBURN, K. B. (1946) The occurrence of a nut of *Trapa natans* L. in the Outer Hebrides. *New Phytol.*, **45**, 124–31. [411]
HESLOP-HARRISON, Y. (1953) *Nuphar intermedia* Ledeb., a presumed relict hybrid, in Britain. *Watsonia*, **3**, 7–25. [408]
— (1955a) Biological flora of the British Isles: *Nuphar* Sm. *J. Ecol.*, **43**, 342–64. [253, 358]
— (1955b) Biological flora of the British Isles: *Nymphaea* L. em. Sm. (*nom. conserv.*). *J. Ecol.*, **43**, 719–34. [253, 274, 358, 408]
— (1955c) British water-lilies. *New Biol.*, **18**, 111–20. [91, 274, 358, 408, 427]
HESS, A. D. & HALL, T. F. (1945) The relation of plants to malaria control on impounded waters with a suggested classification. *J. natn. Malar. Soc.*, **4**, 20–46. [7, 455]
HEVLY, R. H. (1961) Notes on aquatic flowering plants with four additions to the Arizona flora. *Plateau*, **33**, 115–19. [14]
HEWETT, D. G. (1964) Biological flora of the British Isles: *Menyanthes trifoliata* L. *J. Ecol.*, **52**, 723–35. [454, 521]
HICKLING, C. F. (1961) *Tropical inland fisheries*. Longmans Green, London. [451, 453–54, 460, 465, 502]
— (1962) *Fish culture*. Faber and Faber, London. [453–54]
HICKS, L. E. (1930) Physiological experiments with the Lemnaceae. *Proc. Ohio Acad. Sci.*, **8**, 393–94. [204]
— (1932a) Flower production in the Lemnaceae. *Ohio J. Sci.*, **32**, 115–31. [287]
— (1932b) Ranges of pH-tolerance of the Lemnaceae. *Ohio J. Sci.*, **32**, 237–44. [204]
— (1937) The Lemnaceae of Indiana. *Am. Midl. Nat.*, **18**, 774–89. [20]
HIERN, W. P. (1872) A theory of the floating leaves in certain plants. *Proc. Camb. phil. Soc. biol. Sci.*, **2**, 227–36. [73]
HILDEBRAND, E. M. (1946) Herbicidal action of 2,4-dichlorophenoxyacetic acid on the water hyacinth, *Eichhornia crassipes*. *Science, N.Y.*, **103**, 477–79. [460–61, 489, 497]
HILDEBRAND, F. (1885) Über *Heteranthera zosteraefolia*. *Bot. Jb.*, **6**, 137–45. [155]
HILLEBRAND, D. (1950) Verkrautung und Abfluss. *Besond. Mitt. dt. gewässerk. Jb.*, **2**, 1–30. [449]
HILLMAN, W. S. (1958) Photoperiodic control of flowering in *Lemna perpusilla*. *Nature, Lond.*, **181**, 1275. [251]
— (1959a) Experimental control of flowering in *Lemna*. I. General methods. Photoperiodism in *L. perpusilla* 6746. *Am. J. Bot.*, **46**, 466–73. [251]
— (1959b) Experimental control of flowering in *Lemna*. II. Some effects of medium composition, chelating agents and high temperatures on flowering in *L. perpusilla* 6746. *Am. J. Bot.*, **46**, 489–95. [251]
— (1960a) Effects of gibberellic acid on flowering, frond size, and multiplication rate of *Lemna perpusilla*. *Phyton, B. Aires*, **14**, 49–54. [253]
— (1960b) Growth promotion by kinetin of *Wolffia columbiana* grown in excessively concentrated medium. *Phyton, B. Aires*, **14**: 43–46. [206]
— (1961a) Experimental control of flowering in *Lemna*. III. A relationship between medium composition and the opposite photoperiodic responses of *L. perpusilla* 6746 and *L. gibba* G3. *Am. J. Bot.*, **48**, 413–19. [251]
— (1961b) Test-tube studies on flowering: experiments with the Lemnaceae, or duckweeds. *Bull. Torrey bot. Club*, **88**: 327–36. [251]
— (1961c) The Lemnaceae, or duckweeds. A review of the descriptive and experimental literature. *Bot. Rev.*, **27**, 221–87. [20, 204, 251, 287]
— (1961d) Photoperiodism, chelating agents, and flowering of *Lemna perpusilla* and *L. gibba* in aseptic culture. In: *Light and life*, ed. McElroy, W. D. and Glass, B., 673–86. John Hopkins Press, Baltimore. [251]
— (1962a) Experimental control of flowering in *Lemna*. IV. Inhibition of photoperiodic sensitivity by copper. *Am. J. Bot.*, **49**, 892–97. [251]

HILLMAN, W. S. (1962b) *The physiology of flowering*. Holt, Rinehart and Winston, New York. [251]
HILTNER, L. (1886) Untersuchungen über die Gattung *Subularia*. *Bot. Jb.*, **7**, 264–72. [291]
HINMAN, E. H. (1938) Biological effects of fluctuation of water level on anopheline breeding. *Am. J. trop. Med.*, **18**, 483–95. [455]
HITCHCOCK, A. E., ZIMMERMAN, P. W., KIRKPATRICK, H. & EARLE, T. T. (1949) Water hyacinth: its growth, reproduction, and practical control by 2,4-D. *Contr. Boyce Thomson Inst. Pl. Res.*, **15**, 363–401.
                        [191, 250, 328, 427, 469–70, 473, 484, 490, 495, 497–98]
—, —, — & — (1950) Growth and reproduction of water hyacinth and alligator weed and their control by means of 2,4-D. *Contr. Boyce Thompson Inst. Pl. Res.*, **16**, 91–130.
                        [317, 427, 470, 484, 487–88, 490, 493, 497]
H.M.S.O. (1959) *Royal Commission on Historical Monuments. Inventory of the City of Cambridge*. H.M.S.O., London. [361]
HOCHREUTINER, G. (1896) Études sur les phanérogames aquatiques du Rhône et du Port de Genève. *Revue gén. Bot.*, **8**, 158–67, 188–200, 249–65. [146]
HOEHNE, F. C. (1955) *Plantas aquáticas*. Instituto de botânica, São Paulo. [523]
HOGETSU, K. (1939) Untersuchungen über die Lage des Kompensationspunktes der Wasserpflanzen im Kizakisee. *Bot. Mag., Tokyo*, **53**, 432–42. [116]
— (1941) Pflanzenökologische Untersuchungen über die höheren Wasserpflanzen des Suwasees, besonders im Herbst. *Bot. Mag., Tokyo*, **55**, 66–78. [13]
— (1953) Studies on the biological production of Lake Suwa. V. The standing crop of rooted aquatic plants. *Misc. Rep. Res. Inst. nat. Resour., Tokyo*, **30**, 4–9. [13, 438]
HÖHN, K. & AX, W. (1961) Untersuchungen über Wasserbewegung und Wachstum submerser Pflanzen. *Beitr. Biol. Pfl.*, **36**, 273–98. [146–47, 174]
HOLDEN, A. V. (1961) Concentration of chloride in freshwaters and rain water. *Nature, Lond.*, **192**, 961. [36]
HOLMGREN, I. (1913) Zur Entwicklungsgeschichte von *Butomus umbellatus* L. *Svensk bot. Tidskr.*, **7**, 58–77. [278]
HOLTTUM, R. E. (1949) The classification of ferns. *Biol. Rev.*, **24**, 267–96. [16, 259]
HOMÈS, M. & SCHOOR, G. VAN (1937) La présence de substances de croissance chez *Elodea canadensis*. *Bull. Acad. r. Belg. Cl. Sci.*, **23**, 183–93. [95]
HOOKER, J. D. (1847) *The botany of the Antarctic voyage of H.M. Discovery ships Erebus and Terror. I. Flora Antarctica*. London. [290]
HOOPER, F. F. & COOK, A. B. (1957) Chemical control of submerged water weeds with sodium arsenite. *Pamph. Fish Div. Mich. Dep. Conserv.*, **16**. [484, 489]
HOPE, C. W. (1902) The sudd of the upper Nile. *Ann. Bot.*, **16**, 495–516. [425, 479–82]
HOREN, F. VAN (1869) Observations sur la physiologie des Lemnacées. *Bull. Soc. r. Bot. Belg.*, **8**, 15–88. [199, 201, 354]
HOSKIN, C. M. (1959) Studies of oxygen metabolism in streams of North Carolina. *Publs Inst. mar. Sci. Univ. Tex.*, **6**, 186–92. [445]
HOTCHKISS, N. (1936) Check-list of marsh and aquatic plants of the United States. *Wildl. Res. Mgmt Leafl.*, B 5, **72**, 27p. [523]
— (1941) The limnological role of the higher plants. In: *A symposium on hydrobiology*, by Needham, J. G., *et al.*, 152–62. University of Wisconsin Press, Madison, Wisconsin. [452]
HOTCHKISS, N. & DOZIER, H. L. (1949) Taxonomy and distribution of North American cattails. *Am. Midl. Nat.*, **41**, 237–54. [20]
HOUGHTON, G. U. (1963) Contribution to the discussion in Owens & Edwards (1963). [36]
HOWARD, H. W. & LYON, A. G. (1951) Distribution of the British watercress species. *Watsonia*, **2**, 91–92. [397]
— & — (1952) Biological flora of the British Isles: *Nasturtium officinale* R. Br. *J. Ecol.*, **40**, 228–45. [397]
HUCKINS, R. K. (1955) Aquatic weed control studies in New Jersey: a progress report. *Proc. NEast Weed Control Conf.*, **9**, 519–34. [484]
HUET, M. (1954) Biologie, profils en long et en travers des eaux courantes. *Bull. fr. Piscic.*, **175**, 41–53. [27]
HULBARY, R. I. (1944) The influence of air spaces on the three-dimensional shapes in cells in *Elodea* stems and a comparison with pith cells in *Ailanthus*. *Am. J. Bot.*, **31**, 561–80. [120]

HULTÉN, E. (1958) The amphi-Atlantic plants and their phytogeographical connections. *K. svenska VetenskAkad. Handl.*, ser. 4, **7**, 1–340. [389–91, 394, 410]
— (1963) Phytogeographical connections of the North Atlantic. In: *North Atlantic biota and their history*, ed. Löve, A. and D., 45–72. Pergamon Press, Oxford. [391]
HUNT, E. G. & BISCHOFF, A. I. (1960) Inimical effects on wildlife of periodic DDD applications to Clear Lake. *Calif. Fish Game*, **46**, 91–106. [500]
HURLIMANN, H. (1951) Zur Lebensgeschichte des Schilfs am den Ufern der Schweizer Seen. *Beitr. geobot. Landes-aufn. Schweiz.*, **30**, 1–232. [154]
HUTCHINSON, G. E. (1957) *A treatise on limnology. I. Geography, physics and chemistry.* Wiley, New York and London. [26]
HUTCHINSON, J. (1959) *The families of flowering plants. I. Dicotyledons, II. Monocotyledons.* edn 2. Clarendon Press, Oxford. [20, 23, 275, 279, 290, 294–96, 298–99, 312]
HYDE, H. A. & WADE, A. E. (1954) *Welsh ferns: a descriptive handbook.* edn 3. National Museum of Wales, Cardiff. [16, 359]
HYNES, H. B. N. (1959) The biological effects of pollution. In: *The effects of pollution on living material*, ed. Yapp, W. B., *Symp. Inst. Biol.*, **8**, 11–24. Institute of Biology, London. [39, 46, 59]
— (1960) *The biology of polluted waters.* University Press, Liverpool.
[26, 39, 43, 46, 59, 361]

IKEDA, T. & UEDA, R. (1964) Light and electron-microscope studies on the senescence of chloroplasts in *Elodea* leaf cells. *Bot. Mag., Tokyo*, **77**, 336–41. [113]
ILLIES, J. (1955) Der biologische Aspekt der limnologischen Fliesswassertypisierung. *Arch. Hydrobiol. (Suppl.)*, **22**, 337–46. [27]
IMAMURA, S. J. (1929) Über *Hydrobrium japonicum* Imamura, eine neue Podostemonacee in Japan. *Bot. Mag., Tokyo*, **43**, 332–39. [18, 144]
IM THURN, E. F. & OLIVER, D. (1887) The botany of the Roraima Expedition of 1884. *Trans. Linn. Soc. Lond.*, ser. 2, **2**, 249–300. [214]
INANÇ, N. (1960) Investigations upon the physiological and the histological changes occurring in the structures of certain well adapted and least adapted submerged aquatic plants under the action of growth regulating compounds. *Istanb. Univ. Fen Fak. Mecm.*, ser. B, **25**, 93–144. [95–96, 156]
INGRAM, R. (1964) *Sisyrinchium* in Ireland. *Tenth Int. bot. Congr., Abstr. Pap.*, 390. [393]
INGRAM, W. M. & TARZWELL, C. M. (1954) Selected bibliography of publications relating to undesirable effects upon aquatic life by algicides, insecticides, weedicides. *Publ. Hlth Biblphy Ser.*, **13**, 1–28. [498]
IRVINE, F. R. & TRICKETT, R. S. (1953) Water lilies as food. *Kew Bull.*, **3**, 363–70. [516]
ISLAM, A. S. (1950) A contribution to the life history of *Ottelia alismoides* Pers. *J. Indian bot. Soc.*, **29**, 79–91. [323]
ITO, T. (1899a) Some remarkable marine monocotyledons in Japan. *Ann. Bot.*, **13**, 464–65. [100]
— (1899b) Floating-apparatus of the leaves of *Pistia stratiotes* L. *Ann. Bot.*, **13**, 466. [185, 187]
IVERSEN, J. (1936) *Biologische Pflanzentypen als Hilfsmittel in der Vegetationsforschung.* Thesis, University of Copenhagen. [5]
IVLEV, V. S. (1945) The biological productivity of waters. (In Russian) *Usp. sovrem. Biol.*, **19**, 98–120. [152]

JACKSON, R. N. B. (1960) Hydrobiological research at Kariba. *New Scient.*, (April 1960), 877–80. [477]
JACOBS, D. L. (1947) An ecological life-history of *Spirodela polyrhiza* (greater duckweed) with emphasis on the turion phase. *Ecol. Monogr.*, **17**, 437–69. [199, 201, 352, 355]
JAEGER, P. (1961) *The wonderful life of flowers.* Harrap, London. [292]
JÄGER, E. (1964) Zur Deutung des Arealbildes von *Wolffia arrhiza* (L.) Wimm. und einiger anderer ornithochorer Wasserpflanzen. *Ber. dt. bot. Ges.*, **77**, 101–11. [384]
JAGER, G. (1958) The influence of salts on protoplasmic streaming generated by light in sub-epidermal cells of *Vallisneria* leaves. *Acta bot. neerl.*, **7**, 635–53. [137]
JAMES, W. O. (1928) Experimental researches on vegetable assimilation and respiration. XIX. The effect of variations of carbon dioxide supply upon the rate of assimilation of submerged water plants. *Proc. R. Soc.*, ser. B, **103**, 1–42. [117]

548   *Bibliography and index of authors*

JANKOVIČ, M. (1955, 1956) Beitrag zur Kenntnis der individuellen Entwicklung der Wassernuss (*Trapa* L.), I, II & III. *Arh. biol. Nauka*, **7**, 17–23; **8**, 9–19, 81–86.
[17, 180, 184, 328]
JAVALGEKAR, S. R. (1960) Sporogenesis and prothallial development in *Ceratopteris thalictroides*. *Bot. Gaz.*, **122**, 45–50. [16, 259]
JENNINGS, D. H. (1963) *The absorption of solutes by plant cells*. Oliver and Boyd, Edinburgh and London. [136]
JENTSCH, R. (1960) Zur Kenntnis des Sprossvegetationspunktes von *Hippuris* and *Myriophyllum*. *Flora, Jena*, **149**, 308–19. [94, 241]
JERMY, A. C. (1964) *Isoetes* L. *Flora Europaea*, **1**, 5–6. [16, 371, 383]
JERVIS, R. A. & BUELL, M. F. (1964) *Acorus calamus* in New Jersey. *Bull. Torrey bot. Club*, **91**, 335–36. [320]
JESCHKE, W. D. & SIMONIS, W. (1965) Über die Aufnahme von Phosphat- und Sulfationen durch Blätter von *Elodea densa* und ihre Beeinflussung durch Licht, Temperatur und Aussenkonzentration. *Planta*, **67**, 6–32. [134]
JESSEN, K. (1935) Archaeological dating in the history of north Jutland's vegetation. *Acta archaeol.*, **5**, 185–214. [413]
— (1949) Studies in late Quaternary deposits and flora-history of Ireland. *Proc. R. Ir. Acad.*, ser. B, **52**, 85–290. [391, 393, 402, 406, 409]
JESSEN, K. & FARRINGTON, A. (1938) The bogs at Ballybetagh, near Dublin, with remarks on late-glacial conditions in Ireland. *Proc. R. Ir. Acad.*, ser. B, **44**, 205–60. [406]
JIMBÔ, T., TAKAMATSU, M. & KURAISHI, H. (1955) Notes on the aquatic vegetation of Lake Towada. *Ecol. Rev., Sendai*, **14**, 1–9. [13, 30]
JOHNSON, A. (1961) The genus *Ceratopteris* in Malaya. *Gdns' Bull., Singapore*, **18**, 76–81. [16, 388–89]
— (*in litt.*) Personal correspondence, 1962 and 1963. [388, 479]
JOHNSON, D. S. (1933) The curvature, symmetry, and homologies of the sporocarps of *Marsilea* and *Pilularia*. *Bull. Torrey bot. Club*, **60**, 555–63. [259, 262]
JOHNSON, D. S. & CHRYSLER, M. A. (1938) Structure and development of *Regnellidium diphyllum*. *Am. J. Bot.*, **25**, 141–56. [16, 167, 259, 383]
JOHNSON, G. V., MAYEUX, P. A. & EVANS, H. J. (1966) A cobalt requirement for symbiotic growth of *Azolla filiculoides* in the absence of combined nitrogen. *Pl. Physiol., Lancaster, Pa*, **41**, 852–55. [194]
JOHNSON, K. R. (1941) Vegetation of some mountain lakes and shores in northwestern Colorado. *Ecology*, **22**, 306–16. [13–14]
JOHRI, B. M. (1935a) Studies in the family Alismaceae. I. *Limnophyton obtusifolium* Miq. *J. Indian bot. Soc.*, **14**, 49–66. [18, 278, 323]
— (1935b) Studies in the family Alismaceae. II. *Sagittaria sagittifolia* L. *Proc. Indian Acad. Sci.*, ser. B, **1**, 340–48. [18, 278, 323]
— (1935c) Studies in the family Alismaceae. III. *Sagittaria guayanensis* HBK. and *Sagittaria latifolia* Willd. *Proc. Indian Acad. Sci.*, ser. B, **2**, 33–48. [18, 278, 323]
— (1936a) Studies in the family Alismaceae. IV. *Alisma plantago* L., *A. plantago-aquatica* L. and *Sagittaria graminea* Mich. *Proc. Indian Acad. Sci.*, ser. B, **4**, 128–38. [18, 278, 323]
— (1936b) The life history of *Butomopsis lanceolata* Kunth. *Proc. Indian Acad. Sci.*, ser. B, **4**, 139–62. [18, 278, 323]
— (1938a) The embryo sac of *Limnocharis emarginata* L. *New Phytol.*, **37**, 279–85. [18, 278, 323]
— (1938b) The embryo sac of *Hydrocleis nymphoides* Buch. *Beih. bot. Zbl.*, **48**, 165–72. [18, 278, 323]
JONES, E. N. (1925) *Ceratophyllum demersum* in West Okoboji Lake. *Proc. Iowa Acad. Sci.*, **32**, 181–88. [13]
— (1931) The morphology and biology of *Ceratophyllum demersum*. *Stud. nat. Hist. Iowa Univ.*, **13**, 11–55. [17, 94, 149]
JONES, H. (1955a) Heterophylly in some species of *Callitriche*, with especial reference to *Callitriche intermedia*. *Ann. Bot.*, **19**, 225–45. [218, 224, 239]
— (1955b) Further studies on heterophylly in *Callitriche intermedia*: leaf development and experimental induction of ovate leaves. *Ann. Bot.*, **19**, 369–88. [239, 243]
— (1955c) Notes on the identification of some British species of *Callitriche*. *Watsonia*, **3**, 186–92. [17, 219–21, 224, 239]
— (1956) Morphological aspects of leaf expansion, especially in relation to changes in leaf form. In: *The growth of leaves*, ed. Milthorpe, F. L., 93–106. Butterworth, London. [224, 239–40]

JONES, J. A. (1928) Overcoming delayed germinations of *Nelumbo lutea*. *Bot. Gaz.*, **85**, 341–43. [325]

JONES, J. R. E. (1949) An ecological study of the river Rheidol: north Cardiganshire, Wales. *J. Anim. Ecol.*, **18**, 67–88. [59]

JONGH, S. E. DE & HEGNAUER, R. (1963) *Montia fontana* L. in een stadstuintje. *Gorteria*, **1**, 131–32. [5, 223]

JÖRGENSEN, C. A. (1923) Studies on Callitrichaceae. *Bot. Tidsskr.*, **38**, 81–126. [17, 312]

— (1925) Zur Frage der systematischen Stellung der Callitrichaceen. *Jb. wiss. Bot.*, **64**, 404–42. [17, 312]

JUDAY, C. (1934) The depth distribution of some aquatic plants. *Ecology*, **15**, 325. [30]

— (1935) Chemical composition of large aquatic plants. *Science, N.Y.*, **81**, 273. [433]

— (1940) The annual energy budget of an inland lake. *Ecology*, **21**, 438–50. [445]

— (1942) The summer standing crop of plants and animals in four Wisconsin lakes. *Trans. Wis. Acad. Sci. Arts Lett.*, **34**, 103–35. [13, 438–39]

JUDAY, C. & BIRGE, E. A. (1932) Dissolved oxygen and oxygen consumed in the lake waters of northeastern Wisconsin. *Trans. Wis. Acad. Sci. Arts Lett.*, **27**, 415–86. [45]

JUDAY, C., BIRGE, E. A. & MELOCHE, V. W. (1935) The carbon dioxide and hydrogen ion content of the lake waters of northeastern Wisconsin. *Trans. Wis. Acad. Sci. Arts Lett.*, **29**, 1–82. [52]

JUDAY, C., BLAIR, J. M. & WILDA, E. F. (1943) The photosynthetic activities of the aquatic plants of Little John Lake, Vilas County, Wisconsin. *Am. Midl. Nat.*, **30**, 426–46. [13, 445]

JUMELLE, H. (1936) Aponogétonacées (23e famille) In: *Flore de Madagascar (Plantes vascullaires)*, ed. Humbert, H. 15p. L'Imprimerie Officielle, Tananarive. [19]

JUST, T. (1946) The use of embryological formulas in plant taxonomy. *Bull. Torrey bot. Club*, **73**, 351–55. [17, 21]

KAÁRET, P. (1953) Wasservegetation der Seen Orlången und Trehörningen. *Acta phytogeogr. suec.*, **32**, 1–50. [13]

KADEJ, A. R. (1966) Organisation and development of apical root meristem in *Elodea canadensis* (Rich.) Casp. and *Elodea densa* (Planch.) Casp. *Acta Soc. Bot. Pol.*, **35**, 143–58. [155]

KAMURO, S. (1957) The plant ecological studies of lakes and marshes having a period of drainage. III. On the amphiphyte-zone in artificial reservoirs. *Bot. Mag., Tokyo*, **70**, 305–12. [13]

KANDELER, R. (1955) Über die Blütenbildung bei *Lemna gibba* L. I. Kulturbedingungen und Tageslängenabhängigkeit. *Z.Bot.*, **43**, 61–71. [251]

— (1956) Über die Blütenbildung bei *Lemna gibba* L. II. Das Wirkungsspektrum von blühförderndem Schwachlicht. *Z.Bot.*, **44**, 153–74. [252]

— (1962) Die Aufhebung der photoperiodischen Steuerung bei *Lemna gibba*. *Ber. dt. bot. Ges.*, **75**, 431–42. [252]

— (1964) Zweifache Wirkung von Bikarbonat auf die Lichtsteuerung der Blütenbildung von *Lemna gibba*. *Ber. dt. bot. Ges.*, **77**, 140–42. [252]

KÁRPÁTI, V. (1963) Die zönologischen und ökologischen Verhältnisse der Wasservegetation des Donau-Überschwemmungsraumes in Ungarn. *Acta bot. hung.*, **9**, 323–85. [13]

KARSTEN, G. (1888) Ueber die Entwicklung der Schwimmblätter bei einigen Wasserpflanzen. *Bot. Ztg*, **46**, 565–78, 581–89. [82]

KAUSIK, S. B. (1938) Pollen development and seed formation in *Utricularia coerulea* L. *Beih. bot. Zbl.*, **58**, 365–78. [216]

— (1939) Pollination and its influences on the behaviour of the pistillate flower in *Vallisneria spiralis*. *Am. J. Bot.*, **26**, 207–11. [302, 307, 315]

— (1940a) A contribution to the embryology of *Enhalus acoroides* (L. fil.) Steud. *Proc. Indian Acad. Sci.*, ser. B, **11**, 83–99. [323, 331]

— (1940b) Vascular anatomy of the pistillate flower of *Enhalus acoroides* (L. fil.) Steud. *Curr. Sci.*, **9**, 182–84. [331]

— (1941) Structure and development of the staminate flower and the male gametophyte of *Enhalus acoroides* (L. fil.) Steud. *Proc. Indian Acad. Sci.*, ser. B, **14**, 1–16. [307]

KAUSIK, S. B. & RAO, P. K. V. (1942) The male gametophyte of *Halophila ovata* Gaudich. *Half-yrly J. Mysore Univ.*, ser. B, **3**, 41–49. [310]

KAWAMATU, S. (1962) Electronmicroscopy of the root-cap of *Azolla imbricata* Nakai. *Bot. Mag., Tokyo*, **75**, 114. [196]

KAWAMATU, S. (1963) Electron microscope observations on the root hair cell of *Azolla imbricata* Nakai. *Cytologia*, **28**, 12–20.   [196]
— (1965a) Electron microscope observations on blue-green algae in the leaf of *Azolla imbricata* Nakai. *Cytologia*, **30**, 75–79.   [194]
— (1965b) Electron microscope observations on the leaf of *Azolla imbricata* Nakai. *Cytologia*, **30**, 80–87.   [194]
KEMP, P. H. (1963) Geological effects on surface waters in Natal. *Nature, Lond.*, **200**, 1085.   [36]
KENNETH, A. G. & WALLACE, E. C. (1964) Plant records. *Proc. bot. Soc. Br. Isl.*, **5**, 239.   [519]
KENT, D. H. (1964) Plant notes: *Elodea*. *Proc. bot. Soc. Br. Isl.*, **5**, 232.   [397]
KHAN, R. (1954) A contribution to the embryology of *Utricularia flexuosa* Vahl. *Phytomorphology*, **4**, 80–117.   [216]
KHANNA, P. (1964) Morphological and embryological studies in Nymphaeaceae. I. *Euryale ferox* Salisb. *Proc. Indian Acad. Sci.*, ser. B, **59**, 237–43.   [17, 273, 275, 290]
KING, L. J. (1943) Response of *Elodea densa* to growth-regulating substances. *Bot. Gaz.*, **105**, 127–51.   [95, 155–56]
KLORER, J. (1909) The water hyacinth problem. *J. Ass. Engng Socs*, **42**, 33.   [461]
KNIEP, H. (1915) Über den Gasaustausch der Wasserpflanzen: ein Beitrag zur Kritik der Blasenzählmethode. *Jb. wiss. Bot.*, **56**, 460–510.   [120]
KNOCH, E. (1899) Untersuchungen über die Morphologie, Biologie und Physiologie der Blüte von *Victoria regia*. *Biblthca bot.*, **47**, 1–60.   [275]
KNÖPP, H. (1960) Untersuchungen über das Sauerstoff-Produktions Potential von Flussplankton. *Schweiz. Z. Hydrol.*, **22**, 152–66.   [47]
KNOWLES, G., EDWARDS, R. W. & BRIGGS, R. (1962) Polarographic measurement of the rate of respiration of natural sediments. *Limnol. Oceanogr.*, **7**, 481–84.   [48]
KNUTH, P. (1906–1909) *Handbook of flower pollination*. (Transln by Davis, R. A.) Oxford.   [275]
KOCH, W. (1950) Floristiche Mitteilungen. II. *Lagarosiphon major* (Ridley) Moss und *Elodea densa* (Planch.) Caspary, zwei im Lago Maggiore eingebürgerte Hydrocharitaceen. *Ber. schweiz. bot. Ges.*, **60**, 320–23.   [397, 399, 458]
— (1952) Zur Flora der ober italienischen Reisfelder. *Ber. schweiz. bot. Ges.*, **60**, 628–63.   [397, 400]
KOPECKÝ, K. (1961) Fytoekologický a fytocenologický rozbor porostů *Phalaris arundinacea* L. na náplavech Berounky. *Rozpr. čsl. Akad. Věd.* (*mat. přírod. Věd.*), **71** (6), 1–105.   [13]
— (1965) Einfluss der Ufer- und Wassermakrophyten-Vegetation auf die Morphologie des Flussbettes einiger tschechoslowakischer Flüsse. *Arch. Hydrobiol.*, **61**, 137–60.   [13, 449]
KOPECKÝ, K. & HEJNÝ, S. (1965) Allgemeine Charakteristik der Pflanzengesellschaften des *Phalaridion-arundinaceae*-Verbandes. *Preslia*, **37**, 53–78.   [13]
KORNAŚ, J. (1959) Sea bottom vegetation of the Bay of Gdańsk off Rewa. *Bull. Acad. pol. Sci. Cl. II Sér. Sci. biol.*, **7**, 5–10.   [13]
KORNAŚ, J., PANCER, E. & BRZYSKI, B. (1960) Studies on sea bottom vegetation in the Bay of Gdańsk off Rewa. *Fragm. flor. geobot.*, **6**, 3–92.   [13]
KOSTYCHEV, S. & SOLDATENKOW, S. (1926) Der tägliche Verlauf und die specifische Intensität der Photosynthese bei Wasserpflanzen. *Planta*, **2**, 1–9.   [116]
KOTSCHY, T. (1858) Eine neue Leguminose vom weissen Nil. *Öst. bot. Z.*, **8**, 113–16.   [66]
KOYAMA, T. (1962) The genus *Scirpus* Linn.; some North American aphylloid species. *Can. J. Bot.*, **40**, 913–37.   [283]
— (1963) The genus *Scirpus* Linn.; critical species of the section *Pterolepis*. *Can. J. Bot.*, **41**, 1107–31.   [283]
KOZHOV, M. (1963) Lake Baikal and its life. *Monographiae biol.*, **11**. W. Junk, The Hague.   [13]
KOZLOWSKI, T. T. (1965) Variable toxicity of triazine herbicides. *Nature, Lond.*, **205**, 104–05.   [498]
KRAMER, P. J. (1951) Causes of injury to plants resulting from flooding of soil. *Pl. Physiol.*, Lancaster, Pa, **26**, 722–35.   [71]
KRAUSE, K. & ENGLER, A. (1906) Aponogetonaceae. *Pflanzenreich*, **24** (IV. 13), 24p.   [19, 103, 380]
KUBITZKI, K. & BORCHERT, R. (1964) Morphologische Studien an *Isoëtes triquetra* A. Braun und Bemerkungen über das Verhältnis der Gattung *Stylites* E. Amstutz zur Gattung *Isoëtes* L. *Ber. dt. bot. Ges.*, **77**, 227–33.   [16, 256]

KUMMEROW, A. (1958) Beiträge zur Kenntnis der Ruheperiode von Winterknospen und Samen. *Beitr. Biol. Pfl.*, **34**, 293–314. [356]

KUNDT, A. (1910) Die Entwicklung der Micro- und Macrosporangien von *Salvinia natans*. *Beih. bot. Zbl.*, **27**, 26–51. [263]

KUPRIANOVA, L. A. (1948) Morphology of the pollen of the monocotyledons. (In Russian) *Trudȳ bot. Inst.*, *Baku*, ser. 1, **7**, 163–262. [279]

KURZ, H. & CROWSON, D. (1948) The flower of *Wolffiella floridana*. *Q. Jl Fla Acad. Sci.*, **11**, 87–98. [287]

KURZ, L. (1960) Anatomische und entwicklungsphysiologische Untersuchungen an *Utricularia*. *Beitr. Biol. Pfl.*, **35**, 111–35. [215]

KURZ, S. (1867a) Enumeration of Indian Lemnaceae. *J. Linn. Soc. (Bot.)*, **9**, 264–68. [20, 287]

— (1867b) Enumeration of Australian Lemnaceae. *J. Bot., Lond.*, **5**, 115. |20, 287|

KUTYURIN, V. M., ULUBEKOVA, M. V. & NAZAROV, N. M. (1964) Influence of the oxygen concentration on the rate of photosynthesis and respiration of aquatic plants. (In Russian) *Dokl. Akad. Nauk. SSSR*, **157**, 223–26. [129]

LAETSCH, W. M. (1962) Photomorphogenetic responses of sporelings of *Marsilea vestita*. *Pl. Physiol.*, *Lancaster, Pa*, **37**, 142–48. [—]

— (1963) Correlative inhibition and the primary organs of *Marsilea vestita*. *Bot. Gaz.*, **124**, 317–24. [—]

LAETSCH, W. M. & BRIGGS, W. R. (1961) Kinetin modification of sporeling ontogeny in *Marsilea vestita*. *Am. J. Bot.*, **48**, 369–77. [—]

LAING, H. E. (1940a) Respiration of the rhizomes of *Nuphar advenum* and other water plants. *Am. J. Bot.*, **27**, 574–81. [162]

— (1940b) Respiration of the leaves of *Nuphar advenum* and *Typha latifolia*. *Am. J. Bot.*, **27**, 583–85. [64, 84]

— (1940c) The composition of the internal atmosphere of *Nuphar advenum* and other water plants. *Am. J. Bot.*, **27**, 861–67. [64, 159]

— (1941) Effect of concentration of oxygen and pressure of water upon growth of rhizomes of semi-submerged water plants. *Bot. Gaz.*, **102**, 712–24. [84, 161, 162]

LAKSHMANAN, K. K. (1961) Embryological studies in the Hydrocharitaceae. I. *Blyxa octandra* Planch. *J. Madras Univ.*, ser. B, **31**, 133–42. [18, 323]

— (1963a) Embryological studies in the Hydrocharitaceae. II. *Halophila ovata* Gaudich. *J. Indian bot. Soc.*, **42**, 15–18. [18, 323]

— (1963b) Embryological studies in the Hydrocharitaceae. III. *Nechamandra alternifolia* (Roxb.) Thw. *Phyton, B. Aires*, **20**, 49–58. [18, 307–08, 323]

— (1965a) Embryological studies in the Hydrocharitaceae. IV. Post-fertilisation development in *Hydrilla verticillata* Royle. *Phyton, B. Aires*, **22**, 45–50. [18, 323]

— (1965b) Note on the endosperm formation in *Zannichellia palustris* L. *Phyton, B. Aires*, **22**, 13–14. [323]

LAMARCK, J. B. P. A. (1809) *Philosophie zoologique*, **1**. Paris. [244]

LAMARLIÈRE, L. G. DE (1906) Sur les membranes cutinisées des plantes aquatiques. *Revue gén. Bot.*, **18**, 289–95. [113]

LAMBERT, J. M. (1947) Biological flora of the British Isles: *Glyceria maxima* (Hartm.) Holmb. *J. Ecol.*, **34**, 310–44. [358, 441]

LAMOTTE, C. (1933) Morphology of the megagametophyte and the embryo sporophyte of *Isoetes lithophila*. *Am. J. Bot.*, **20**, 217–33. [256]

LANDOLT, E. (1957) Physiologische und ökologische Untersuchungen an Lemnaceen. *Ber. schweiz. bot. Ges.*, **67**, 271–410. [204]

LANG, W. H. (1915) Studies in the morphology of *Isoetes*. *Mem. Proc. Manchr lit. phil. Soc.*, **59**, 1–57. [166]

LANGENDONCK, H. J. VAN (1935) Étude sur la flore et la végétation des environs de Gand. *Bull. Soc. r. Bot. Belg.*, **68**, 117–80. [13]

LASSER, H. (1924) Zur Entwicklungsgeschichte des Prothalliums und des Embryos bei *Salvinia natans*. *Flora, Jena*, **117**, 173–220. [265]

LASSUS, A. DE (1861) Analyse du mémoire de Gaëtan Monti sur l'*Aldrovandia* suivie de quelques observations sur l'irritabilité des follicules de cette plante. *Bull. Soc. bot. Fr.*, **8**, 519–23. [209]

LAUNDON, J. R. (1961) An Australasian species of *Crassula* introduced into Britain. *Watsonia*, **5**, 59–63. [397]

LAWALRÉE, A. (1943) La multiplication végétative des Lemnacées, en particulier chez *Wolffia arrhiza. Cellule*, **49**, 335–82. [199, 290]
— (1945) La position systématique des Lemnacées et leur classification. *Bull. Soc. r. Bot. Belg.*, **77**, 27–38. [20, 290]
— (1952) L'embryologie des Lemnacées. Observations sur *Lemna minor* L. *Cellule*, **54**, 303–26. [20, 290]
— (1961) La pollinisation de *Lemna minor. Naturalistes belg.*, **42**, 164–65. [289]
— (1964) *Salvinia* Adanson; *Azolla* Lam. *Flora Europaea*, **1**, 24–25. [16, 397]
LAWRENCE, G. H. M. (1951) *Taxonomy of vascular plants.* MacMillan, New York.
[277, 283, 372, 377, 397]
LAWRENCE, J. M. (1958) Methods for controlling aquatic weeds in fish ponds with emphasis on the use of chemicals. *Rep. Ala. agric. Exp. Stn*, **69**, 8p. [484]
LEAVITT, R. G. (1902) The root-hairs, cap, and sheath of *Azolla. Bot. Gaz.*, **34**, 414–19.
[196]
LEBRUN, J. (1959) La lutte contre le developpement de l'*Eichhornia crassipes. Bull. agric. Congo Belge*, **50**, 251–52. [465]
LEENTVAAR, P. (1966) The Brokopondo research project, Surinam. In: *Man-made lakes,* ed. Lowe-McConnell, R. H., *Symp. Inst. Biol.*, **15**, 33–42. Institute of Biology and Academic Press, London. [469]
LEEUWEN, W. A. M. VAN (1963) A study of the structure of the gynoecium of *Nelumbo lutea* (Willd.) Pers. *Acta bot. neerl.*, **12**, 84–97. [17, 273, 277]
LEGRO, R. A. H. (1955) Bloei experiment met *Cryptocoryne nevillii* Trimen. *Aquarium, Den Haag*, **26**, 40–42. [250, 285]
— (1960) De generatieve vermenigvuldiging van *Cryptocorynen. Aquarium, Den Haag*, **30**, 219–20. [286]
— (1963) Kunstmatige vrucht- en zaadvorming bij *Cryptocorynen. Aquarium, Den Haag*, **33**, 180–83. [286]
— (*in litt.*) Personal correspondence, 1963. [286]
LEGRO, R. A. H. & WIT, H. C. D. DE (1956) Enkele aantekeningen over *Cryptocorynen. Aquarium, Den Haag*, **27**, 148–53. [250]
LEWIS, J. R. (1964) *The ecology of rocky shores.* English Universities Press, London.
[26, 427, 453]
LI, H. L. (1955) Classification and phylogeny of the Nymphaeaceae and allied families. *Am. Midl. Nat.*, **54**, 33–41. [17, 275]
LIBBY, W. F. (1951) Radiocarbon dates, II. *Science, N.Y.*, **114**, 291–96. [325]
LIEBIG, J. (1931) Ergänzungen zur Entwicklungsgeschichte von *Isoëtes lacustris* L. *Flora, Jena*, **125**, 321–58. [256]
LINDBERG, S. O. (1873) Is *Hydrocharis* really dioecious? *Trans. Proc. bot. Soc. Edinb.*, **11**, 389. [304]
LINDEMAN, R. L. (1941) Seasonal food-cycle dynamics in a senescent lake. *Am. Midl. Nat.*, **26**, 636–73. [438]
— (1942) The trophic-dynamic aspect of ecology. *Ecology*, **23**, 399–418. [443]
LINDSEY, A. A. (1938) Anatomical evidence for the Menyanthaceae. *Am. J. Bot.*, **25**, 480–85. [17, 21]
LIPIN, A. N. & LIPINA, N. N. (1950) Macroflora of standing waters in relation to their macrofauna. (In Russian) *Trudy vseross. nauchno-issled. Inst. prudov. choziasist.*, **5**, 1–270. [13]
LISTER, G. (1903) On the occurrence of *Tristicha alternifolia*, Tul., in Egypt. *New Phytol.*, **2**, 15–18. [149]
LITTLE, E. C. S. (1965) The discovery of *Salvinia auriculata* on the Congo. *Nature, Lond.*, **208**, 1111–12. [478]
— (1966) The invasion of man-made lakes by plants. In: *Man-made lakes*, ed. Lowe-McConnell, R. H., *Symp. Inst. Biol.*, **15**, 75–86. Institute of Biology and Academic Press, London. [469, 478]
LLOYD, F. E. (1942) *The carnivorous plants.* Chronica Botanica, Waltham, Massachusetts.
[2, 208–209, 211, 213–15, 322]
LOHAMMAR, G. (1938) Wasserchemie und höhere Vegetation schwedischer Seen. *Symb. bot. upsal.*, **3** (1). [13]
— (1955) The introduction of foreign water plants, with special reference to conditions in northern Europe. *Verh. int. Verein. theor. angew. Limnol.*, **12**, 562–68. [397, 516]
LÖHMEYER, W. (1962) Contribution à l'unification du système phytosociologique pour l'Europe moyenne et nord-occidentale. *Melhoramento*, **15**, 137–51. [13]

LOISEAU, J. E. & GRANGEON, D. (1963) Variations phyllotaxiques chez *Ceratophyllum demersum* L. et *Hippuris vulgaris* L. *Mém. Soc. bot. Fr.*, 1963, 76–91.   [94]
LOISEAU, J. E. & NOUGARÈDE, A. (1963) Comportement de l'apex des rosettes flottantes et processus de ramification chez *Hydrocharis morsus-ranae* L. (Hydrocharidacées). *C. r. hebd. Séanc. Acad. Sci.*, *Paris*, **256**, 3340–43.   [188]
LONDO, G. (1964) *Limosella aquatica* L. in de duinen bij Zandvoort. *Gorteria*, **2**, 1–4.   [—]
LOOS, W. (1962) Einfluss der Gibberellinsäure auf die vegetative Vermehrung und das Wurzelwachstum von *Lemna minor* L. *Phyton*, *B. Aires*, **18**, 133–36.   [206]
LOUIS-MARIE, PERE (1931) Flore-manuel de la province de Québec. *Contr. Inst. agric. Oka*, **23**, 320p.   [14]
LOUSLEY, J. E. (1939) *Rumex aquaticus* L. as a British plant. *J. Bot.*, *Lond.*, **77**, 149–52.   [409]
— (1957a) *Alisma gramineum* in Britain. *Proc. bot. Soc. Br. Isl.*, **2**, 346–53.   [18, 70]
— (1957b) The British flora during 1956. *Nature*, *Lond.*, **179**, 351–53.   [397, 399, 458]
LÖVE, A. (1954) Cytotaxonomical evaluation of corresponding taxa. *Vegetatio*, **8**, 212–20.   [369–70]
— (1955) Biosystematic remarks on vicariism. *Acta Soc. Fauna Flora fenn.*, **72**, 1–14.   [369–70]
— (1960) Biosystematics and classification of apomicts. *Reprium nov. Spec. Regni veg.*, **62**, 136–48.   [358]
— (1961) Some notes on *Myriophyllum spicatum*. *Rhodora*, **63**, 139–45.   [17, 368]
— (1962) Cytotaxonomy of the *Isoetes echinospora* complex. *Am. Fern J.*, **52**, 113–23.   [16]
LÖVE, A. & LÖVE, D. (1958a) The American element in the flora of the British Isles. *Bot. Notiser*, **111**, 376–88.   [389, 393–94]
— & — (1958b) Biosystematics of *Triglochin maritimum* agg. *Naturaliste can.*, **85**, 156–65.   [19, 370]
— & — (ed.) (1963) *North Atlantic biota and their history*. Pergamon Press, Oxford.   [389]
LÖVE, D. (1963) Dispersal and survival of plants. In: *North Atlantic biota and their history*, ed. Löve, A and D., 189–205. Pergamon Press, Oxford.   [331–32]
LÖVE, D. & LEITH, H. (1961) *Triglochin gaspense*, a new species of arrow grass. *Can. J. Bot.*, **39**, 1261–72.   [19, 370]
LOWENHAUPT, B. (1956) The transport of calcium and other cations in submerged aquatic plants. *Biol. Rev.*, **31**, 371–95.   [133–35]
LUDWIG, F. (1886) Ueber durch Austrocknen bedingte Keimfähigkeit der Samen einiger Wasserpflanzen. *Biol. Zbl.*, **6**, 299–300.   [324]
LUETZELBURG, P. VON (1910) Beiträge zur Kenntnis der Utricularien. *Flora*, *Jena*, **100**, 145–212.   [208, 210, 217, 339, 353]
LUND, J. W. G. (1950) Studies on *Asterionella formosa* Hass. II. Nutrient depletion and the spring maximum. *J. Ecol.*, **38**, 1–14.   [36]
LUNDH, A. (1951) Some aspects of the higher aquatic vegetation in the lake Ringsjön in Scania. *Bot. Notiser*, 1951, 21–31.   [13]
LUTHER, H. (1949) Vorschlag zu einer ökologischen Grundeinteilung der Hydrophyten. *Acta bot. fenn.*, **44**, 1–15.   [7, 13]
— (1951) Verbreitung und Ökologie der höheren Wasserpflanzen im Brackwasser der Ekenäs-Gegend in Südfinnland. *Acta bot. fenn.*, **49**, 1–231; **50**, 1–370.   [13, 42]
LÜTTGE, U. (1964) Mikroautoradiographische Untersuchungen über die Funktion der Hydropoten von *Nymphaea*. *Protoplasma*, **59**, 157–63.   [89]
LYNCH, J. J., KING, J. E., CHAMBERLAIN, T. K. & SMITH, H. L. (1947) Effects of aquatic weed infestations on the fish and wildlife of the Gulf States. *Spec. scient. Rep. U.S. Fish Wildl. Serv.*, **39**, 1–71.   [450, 483]
LYR, H. & STREITBERG, H. (1955) Die Verbreitung der Hydropoten in verschiedenen Verwandtschaftskreisen der Wasserpflanzen. *Wiss. Z. Martin-Luther-Univ. Halle-Wittenb.*, **4**, 471–83.   [132]

MABBOTT, D. C. (1920) Food habits of seven species of American shoal water ducks. *Bull. U.S. Dep. Agric.*, **862**.   [453]
MACAN, T. T. (1958) The temperature of a small stony stream. *Hydrobiologia*, **12**, 89–106.   [33]
— (1963) *Freshwater ecology*. Longmans Green, London.   [26]

MACAN, T. T. (1965) The fauna in the vegetation of a moorland fishpond. *Arch. Hydrobiol.*, **61**, 273–310.   [454]
MACAN, T. T. & MAUDSLEY, R. (1966) The temperature of a moorland fishpond. *Hydrobiologia*, **27**, 1–22.   [33]
MACAN, T. T. & WORTHINGTON, E. B. (1951) *Life in lakes and rivers*. Collins, London.   [26]
MACDOUGAL, D. T. (1914) The determinative action of environic factors upon *Neobeckia acquatica* Greene. *Flora, Jena*, **106**, 264–80.   [227]
MACKENTHUN, K. (1950) Aquatic weed control with sodium arsenite. *Sewage ind. Wastes*, **22**, 1062–67.   [484, 489]
— (1955) The control of submergent aquatic vegetation through the use of sodium arsenite. *Proc. NEast Weed Control Conf.*, **9**, 545–55.   [484, 489]
— (1960) Some limnological investigations on the long term use of sodium arsenite as an aquatic herbicide. *Proc. A. NCentr. Weed Control Conf.*, **17**, 30–31.   [484, 489]
MACMICHAEL, SIR H. (1934) *The Anglo-Egyptian Sudan*. Faber and Faber, London.   [481, 483]
MÄGDEFRAU, K. (1931) Zur Morphologie und phylogenetischen Bedeutung der fossilen Pflanzengattung *Pleuromeia*. *Beih. bot. Zbl.*, **48**, 119–40.   [257]
MAGNIN, A. (1893) Recherches sur la végétation des lacs du Jura. *Revue gén. Bot.*, **5**, 241–57, 303–16.   [13, 33]
MAGNUS, W. (1913) Die atypische Embryosackentwicklung der Podostemaceen. *Flora, Jena*, **105**, 275–336.   [285]
MAHABALÉ, T. S. (1954) The genus *Salvinia* and evolutionary problems related to it. *Eighth Int. bot. Congr.*, **7/8**, 304–06.   [16, 197, 265]
MAHESHWARI, J. K. (1965) Alligator weed in Indian lakes. *Nature, Lond.*, **206**, 1270.   [358, 397, 400, 457]
MAHESHWARI, P. (1933) A note on the life history of *Hydrilla verticillata* Presl. *Curr. Sci.*, **2**, 13.   [323]
— (1943) The mode of endosperm formation in *Vallisneria*, *Ottelia* and *Limnocharis*. *Proc. natn. Acad. Sci. India*, ser. B, **13**, 260–63.   [323]
— (1945) The place of angiosperm embryology in research and teaching. *J. Indian bot. Soc.*, **24**, 25–41.   [285]
— (1950) *An introduction to the embryology of angiosperms*. McGraw-Hill, New York & Maidenhead.   [285]
— (1964) Embryology in relation to taxonomy. In: *Vistas in botany*, **4**, ed. Turrill, W. B., 55–97. Pergamon Press, Oxford.   [21, 279, 285, 290]
MAHESHWARI, P. & SINGH, B. (1943) Studies in the family Alismaceae, V. *Proc. natn. Inst. Sci. India*, **9**, 311–22.   [18, 278]
MAHESHWARI, S. C. (1954) The embryology of *Wolffia*. *Phytomorphology*, **4**, 355–65.   [20, 200, 288–90, 322, 324]
— (1956a) Endosperm and seed of *Wolffia*. *Nature, Lond.*, **178**, 925–26.[20, 290, 324]
— (1956b) The endosperm and embryo of *Lemna* and systematic position of the Lemnaceae. *Phytomorphology*, **6**, 51–55.   [20, 290, 324]
— (1958) *Spirodela polyrhiza*: the link between the aroids and the duckweeds. *Nature, Lond.*, **181**, 1745–46.   [20, 290, 324]
— (1959) Systematic position of the family Lemnaceae. *Ninth Int. bot. Congr.*, **2**, 246–47.   [20, 290]
MAHESHWARI, S. C. & CHAUHAN, O. S. (1963) In vitro control of flowering in *Wolffia microscopica*. *Nature, Lond.*, **198**, 99.   [251–52]
MAHESHWARI, S. C. & KAPIL, R. N. (1963a) Morphological and embryological studies on the Lemnaceae. I. The floral structure and gametophytes of *Lemna paucicostata*. *Am. J. Bot.*, **50**, 677–86.   [20, 199, 290]
— & — (1963b) Morphological and embryological studies on the Lemnaceae. II. The endosperm and embryo of *Lemna paucicostata*. *Am. J. Bot.*, **50**, 907–14.   [20, 290, 324]
— & — (1964) Morphological and embryological studies on the Lemnaceae. III. The seed and seedling of *Lemna paucicostata*. *J. Indian bot. Soc.*, **43**, 270–77.   [20, 322–23]
MAHESHWARI, S. C. & VENKATARAMAN, R. (1966) Induction of flowering in a duckweed—*Wolffia microscopica*—by a new kinin, zeatin. *Planta*, **70**, 304–06.   [252]
MAISONNEUVE, D. DE (1859) *Aldrovandia*. *Bull. Soc. bot. Fr.*, **6**, 399–401.   [349]
MAJUMDAR, G. P. (1938) A preliminary note on polystely in *Limnanthemum cristatum* and *Ottelia alismoides*. *Curr. Sci.*, **6**, 383–85.   [268]

MAKHLIN, M. D. (1961) On some important aquarium plants. (In Russian) *Bot. Zh. SSSR*, **46**, 898–908. [513]

MALAVIYA, M. (1962) A study of sclereids in three species of *Nymphaea. Proc. Indian Acad. Sci.*, ser. B, **56**, 232–36. [86, 123]

— (1963) Study of sclereids in *Nymphoides cristatum* (Roxb.) O. Kuntze. *Proc. Indian Acad. Sci.*, ser. B, **57**, 223–29. [86, 123]

MALONE, C. R. & PROCTOR, V. W. (1965) Dispersal of *Marsilea mucronata* by water birds. *Am. Fern J.*, **55**, 167–70. [332, 453]

MANNING, W. M., JUDAY, C. & WOLF, M. (1938) Photosynthesis of aquatic plants at different depths in Trout Lake, Wisconsin. *Trans. Wis. Acad. Sci. Arts Lett.*, **31**, 377–410. [117]

MANTON, I. (1950) *Problems of cytology and evolution in the Pteridophyta.* University Press, Cambridge. [16, 100, 256]

MARIE-VICTORIN, FRÈRE (1931) L'*Anacharis canadensis.* Histoire et solution d'un imbroglio taxonomique. *Contr. Lab. Bot. Univ. Montréal*, **18**, 1–43. [18]

— (1943) Les *Vallisnéries* américaines. *Contr. Inst. bot. Univ. Montréal*, **46**, 1–38. [18]

MARSH, A. S. (1914) *Azolla* in Britain and in Europe. *J. Bot., Lond.*, **52**, 209–13. [12, 359]

MARSHALL, E. S. (1911) Note on *Isoetes lacustris* L., forma *longifolia strictior* Caspary. *Rep. botl Soc. Exch. Club Br. Isl.*, **3**, 145. [100]

MARSHALL, W. (1852) Excessive and noxious increase of *Udora canadensis. Phytologist*, **4**, 705–15. [360–62]

— (1857) The American water-weed, *Anacharis alsinastrum. Phytologist*, ser. 2, **2**, 194–97. [362]

MARTIN, A. C. & UHLER, F. M. (1939) Food of game ducks in the United States and Canada. *Tech. Bull. U.S. Dep. Agric.*, **634**, 156p. [453]

MASON, H. L. (1938) The flowering of *Wolffiella lingulata* (Hegelm.) Hegelm. *Madroño*, **4**, 241–51. [287]

— (1957) *A flora of the marshes of California.* University of California Press, Berkeley, California. [14, 523]

MASON, R. (1959) *Callitriche* in New Zealand and Australia. *Aust. J. Bot.*, **7**, 295–327. [15, 17, 311, 383, 388, 397]

— (1960) Three waterweeds of the family Hydrocharitaceae in New Zealand. *N.Z. Jl Sci.*, **3**, 382–95. [362–63, 397, 399, 427, 458–59]

MASSART, J. (1902) L'accomodation individuelle chez le *Polygonum amphibium. Bull. Jard. bot. État Brux.*, **1**, 73-95. [6, 70, 221]

MATREYEV, V. I. (1963) On the flowering of *Lemna gibba.* (In Russian) *Bot. Zh. SSSR*, **48**, 272. [251]

MATSUMURA, Y. & HARRINGTON, H. D. (1955) The true aquatic vascular plants of Colorado. *Tech. Bull. Colo. agric. Exp. Stn*, 1955. [523]

MATTHEWS, J. R. (1914) The White Moss Loch: a study in biotic succession. *New Phytol.*, **13**, 134–48. [12, 175]

— (1937) Geographical relationships of the British flora. *J. Ecol.*, **25**, 1–90. [392, 408, 410]

— (1955) *Origin and distribution of the British flora.* Hutchinson, London. [403, 409]

MATTHIESEN, FR. J. (1908) Beiträge zur Kenntnis der Podostemonaceen. *Biblthca bot.*, **68**, 1–55. [110, 131, 145]

MATZKE, E. B. & DUFFY, R. M. (1955) The three-dimensional shape of interphase cells within the apical meristem of *Anacharis densa. Am. J. Bot.*, **42**, 937–45. [144]

— & — (1956) Progressive three-dimensional shape changes in dividing cells within the apical meristem of *Anacharis densa. Am. J. Bot.*, **43**, 205–25. [144]

MAYER, A. M. & POLJAKOFF-MAYBER, A. (1963) *The germination of seeds.* Pergamon Press, Oxford. [325, 327]

MAYR, F. (1915) Hydropoten an Wasser- und Sumpfpflanzen. *Beih. bot. Zbl.*, **32**, 278–371. [89, 131]

MAZIA, D. (1938) The binding of Ca, Sr, and Ba by *Elodea* protoplasm. *J. cell. comp. Physiol.*, **11**, 193–203. [132–33]

MCATEE, W. L. (1915) Eleven important wild-duck foods. *Bull. U.S. Dep. Agric.*, **205**. [453]

— (1939) *Wildfowl food plants.* Collegiate Press, Ames, Iowa. [453–54]

MCCALLUM, W. B. (1902) On the nature of the stimulus causing the change of form and structure in *Proserpinaca palustris. Bot. Gaz.*, **34**, 93–108. [239, 243]

MCCANN, C. (1942) Observations on Indian duckweeds, Lemnaceae. *J. Bombay nat. Hist. Soc.*, **43**, 148–62.   [289]
— (1943) Light-windows in certain flowers (Asclepiadaceae and Araceae). *J. Bombay nat. Hist. Soc.*, **44**, 182–84.   [287]
— (1945) Notes on the genus *Ruppia* (Ruppiaceae). *J. Bombay nat. Hist. Soc.*, **45**, 396–402.   [19, 297]
MCCLURE, J. W. & ALSTON, R. E. (1964) Patterns of selected chemical components of *Spirodela oligorhiza* formed under various conditions of axenic culture. *Nature, Lond.*, **201**, 311–13.   [202]
MCCOMB, A. J. (1965) The control of elongation in *Callitriche* shoots by environment and gibberellic acid. *Ann. Bot.*, **29**, 445–58.   [244]
MCCULLY, M. E. & DALE, H. M. (1961a) Variations in leaf number in *Hippuris*: a study of whorled phyllotaxis. *Can. J. Bot.*, **39**, 611–25.   [94, 154, 222, 229, 241]
— & — (1961b) Heterophylly in *Hippuris*: a problem in identification. *Can. J. Bot.*, **39**, 1099–116.   [17, 222, 241, 243]
MCGAHA, Y. J. (1952) The limnological relations of insects to certain aquatic flowering plants. *Trans. Am. microsc. Soc.*, **71**, 355–81.   [454]
MEEUSE, A. D. J. (1961) Marsileales and Salviniales—'living fossils'? *Acta bot. neerl.*, **10**, 257–60.   [16, 266–67]
MEHTA, A. S. (1964) A study of the primary phloem of the petiole of *Nymphoides peltatum* (Gmel.) O. Kuntze. *J. Indian bot. Soc.*, **43**, 257–61.   [148]
— (1965) Electron microscopic demonstration of plasmodesmata in phloem parenchyma cells of the petiole of *Nymphoides peltatum* (Gmel.) O. Kuntze. *J. Indian bot. Soc.*, **44**, 271–75.   [—]
MEHTA, A. S. & SPANNER, D. C. (1962) The fine structure of the sieve tubes of the petiole of *Nymphoides peltatum* (Gmel.) O. Kuntze. *Ann. Bot.*, **26**, 291–99.   [148]
— & — (1963) Electron microscopic study of the sieve plate of *Nymphoides peltatum* (Gmel.) O. Kuntze. *J. Indian bot. Soc.*, **42**, 233–37.   [148]
MENDIOLA, N. B. (1919) Variation and selection within clonal lines of *Lemna minor*. *Genetics*, **4**, 151–82.   [204]
MER, É. (1882) De la végétation à l'air des plantes aquatiques. *C. r. hebd. Séanc. Acad. Sci., Paris*, **94**, 175–78.   [90]
MERINOTTI, F. (1941) L'utillazione della canna gentile *Arundo donax* per la produzione autarchica di cellulosa nobile per raion. *Chimica Ind., Milano*, **8**, 349–55.   [442]
MESCHKAT, A. (1937) Abwasserbiologische Untersuchungen in einen Buhnenfeld unterhalb Hamburgs. *Arch. Hydrobiol.*, **31**, 399–432.   [47]
METCALFE, C. R. (1963) Comparative anatomy as a modern botanical discipline. *Adv. bot. Res.*, **1**, 101–47.   [23, 280]
METCALFE, C. R. & CHALK, L. (1950) *Anatomy of the dicotyledons, I & II.* Clarendon Press, Oxford.   [63, 66, 90, 113–14, 123, 128, 137, 142, 149–50, 152, 171, 184, 192]
MEUNIER, A. (1888) La *Pilularia*. Étude anatomico-génétique du sporocarpe chez la *Pilularia globulifera*. *Cellule*, **4**, 319–400.   [262]
MEYER, B. S. (1939) The daily cycle of apparent photosynthesis in a submerged aquatic. *Am. J. Bot.*, **26**, 755–60.   [116–17]
MEYER, B. S. & HERMITAGE, A. C. (1941) Effect of turbidity and depth of immersion on apparent photosynthesis in *Ceratophyllum demersum*. *Ecology*, **22**, 17–22.   [117]
MEYER, B. S., BELL, F. H., THOMPSON, L. C. & CLAY, E. I. (1943) Effect of depth of immersion on apparent photosynthesis in submerged vascular aquatics. *Ecology*, **24**, 393–99.   [117]
MEYER, N. R. (1964) Palynological studies in Nymphaeaceae. (In Russian) *Bot. Zh. SSSR*, **49**, 1421–29.   [17]
MEYER, W. C. (1930) Dormancy and growth studies of the American lotus, *Nelumbo lutea*. *Pl. Physiol., Lancaster, Pa*, **5**, 225–34.   [325]
MIETTINEN, J. K. & WARIS, H. (1958) A chemical study of the neomorphosis induced by glycine in *Oenanthe aquatica*. *Physiologia Pl.*, **11**, 193–99.   [247]
MIKI, S. (1932) On the sea grasses new to Japan. *Bot. Mag., Tokyo*, **46**, 774–88.   [384]
— (1933) On the sea grasses in Japan. I. *Zostera* and *Phyllospadix*. *Bot. Mag., Tokyo*, **47**, 842–62.   [19, 384]
— (1934) On the sea grasses in Japan. II. Cymodoceaceae and marine Hydrocharitaceae. *Bot. Mag., Tokyo*, **48**, 131–42.   [18–19, 35, 384]
— (1937) The origin of *Najas* and *Potamogeton*. *Bot. Mag., Tokyo*, **51**, 290–480.   [19]
— (1952) *Trapa* of Japan with special reference to its remains. *J. Inst. Polytech. Osaka Cy Univ.*, ser. D, **3**, 1–29.   [17, 21]

MILLER, G. S. & STANDLEY, P. C. (1912) The North American species of *Nymphaea. Contr. U.S. natn. Herb.,* **16**, 109p. [17]
MINDEN, M. VON (1899) Beiträge zur anatomischen und physiologischen Kenntnis wasser-seciernierender Organe. *Biblthca bot.,* **46**, 1–76. [148, 185]
MINISTRY OF HOUSING (AND LOCAL GOVERNMENT). (1956) *Report of the committee on synthetic detergents.* H.M.S.O., London. [39]
MINISTRY OF TECHNOLOGY. (1965) *Water pollution research, 1964 (with index for 1952–1964).* H.M.S.O., London. [46, 121–22, 444–45, 447–48]
MINKINA, E. A. (1962) Some observations on the dynamics of higher aquatic vegetation of the Konchezersk group of islands in Karelia. (In Russian) *Gidrobiol. Issled., Tallinn,* **3**, 68–70. [13, 429]
MISRA, R. D. (1938) Edaphic factors in the distribution of aquatic plants in the English Lakes. *J. Ecol.,* **26**, 41–51. [13, 52, 175]
MITCHELL, G. F. (1951, 1953) Studies in Irish Quaternary deposits, VII and VIII. *Proc. R. Ir. Acad.,* ser. B, **53**, 111–206; **55**, 225–82. [406]
MOAR, N. T. (1960) Studies in pollen morphology. II. The pollen of the New Zealand and of two Australian species of *Callitriche* L. *N.Z. Jl Sci.,* **3**, 415–21. [17, 311]
MOELLER, J. (1879) *Aeschynomene aspera* Willd. (Papilionaceen). *Bot. Ztg,* **37**, 720–24. [66]
MOHANTY, P. K. & MISHRA, D. (1963) Stomatal distribution in relation to xeromorphy in aquatic plants. *Nature, Lond.,* **200**, 909–10. [6, 70]
MONOYER, A. (1926) Sur les stipules des *Potamogeton. C. r. Ass. Fr. Avanc. Sci.,* 1926, 1–3. [98]
MONTESANTOS, N. (1913) Morphologische und biologische Untersuchungen über einige Hydrocharideen. *Flora, Jena,* **105**, 1–32. [182, 185]
MOORE, D. M. (1963) The subspecies of *Montia fontana* L. *Bot. Notiser,* **116**, 16–30. [223]
MOORE, E. (1913) The *Potamogetons* in relation to pond culture. *Bull. Bur. Fish., Wash.,* **33**, 255–91. [453]
MOOREHEAD, A. (1960) *The White Nile.* Hamish Hamilton, London. [460, 465, 480–82]
MORGAN, A. H. (1930) *Field book of ponds and streams: an introduction to the life of fresh water.* Putnam, New York. [26]
MORGAN, N. C. (1966) Contribution to a discussion in: *Man-made lakes,* ed. Lowe-McConnell, R. H., *Symp. Inst. Biol.,* **15**, 155. Institute of Biology and Academic Press, London. [450]
MORINAGA, T. (1926a) Germination of seeds under water. *Am. J. Bot.,* **13**, 126–40. [326]
— (1926b) The favourable effect of reduced oxygen supply upon the germination of certain seeds. *Am. J. Bot.,* **13**, 159–65. [326]
MORTIMER, C. H. (1941, 1942) The exchange of dissolved substances between mud and water in lakes, I and II, III and IV. *J. Ecol.,* **29**, 280–329; **30**, 147–201. [52–53]
MOSELEY, M. F. (1958) Morphological studies in the Nymphaeaceae. I. The nature of the stamens. *Phytomorphology,* **8**, 1–29. [17, 271–72, 277]
— (1961) Morphological studies of the Nymphaeaceae. II. The flower of *Nymphaea. Bot. Gaz.,* **122**, 233–59. [17, 273, 277]
— (1965) Morphological studies on the Nymphaeaceae. III. The floral anatomy of *Nuphar. Phytomorphology,* **15**, 54–84. [17, 273]
MOYLE, J. B. (1945) Some chemical factors influencing the distribution of aquatic plants in Minnesota. *Am. Midl. Nat.,* **34**, 402–20. [13, 43]
MOYLE, J. B. & HOTCHKISS, N. (1945) The aquatic and marsh vegetation of Minnesota and its value to waterfowl. *Tech. Bull. Minn. Dep. Conserv. Div. Fish Game,* **3**, 1–122. [13, 453–54, 523]
MÜCKE, M. (1908) Über den Bau und die Entwicklung der Früchte und über die Herkunft von *Acorus calamus* L. *Bot. Ztg,* **61**, 1–23. [519]
MUENSCHER, W. C. (1936) Storage and germination of seeds of aquatic plants. *Bull. Cornell Univ. agric. Exp. Stn,* **652**, 1–17. [326]
— (1940) Fruits and seedlings of *Ceratophyllum. Am. J. Bot.,* **27**, 231–33. [17, 224, 316, 318, 321]
— (1944) *Aquatic plants of the United States.* Comstock Publ. Co., Ithaca, New York. [6, 523]
— (1959) Vascular plants. In: *Freshwater biology,* by Ward, H. B. and Whipple, G. C., edn 2, rev. Edmondson, W. T., 1170–93. Wiley, New York and London. [523]

19

MULLAN, D. P. (1932, 1933) Observations on the biology and physiological anatomy of some Indian halophytes. *J. Indian bot. Soc.*, **11**, 103–18, 285–302; **12**, 165–82, 235–53. [163]
— (1945) The biology and anatomy of *Scirpus grossus* L.f. *J. Bombay nat. Hist. Soc.*, **45**, 402–07. [343]
MÜLLER, TH. & GÖRS, S. (1960) Pflanzengesellschaften stehender Gewässer in Baden-Württemberg. *Beitr. naturk. Forsch. SüdwDtl.*, **19**, 60–100. [13]
MULLIGAN, G. A. & CALDER, J. A. (1964) The genus *Subularia* (Cruciferae). *Rhodora*, **66**, 127–35. [370]
MUNZ, P. A. (1944) Studies in Onagraceae. XIII. The American species of *Ludwigia*. *Bull. Torrey bot. Club*, **71**, 152–65. [281]

NAKANO, H. (1911) The vegetation of lakes and swamps in Japan. I. Teganuma (Tega-Swamp). *Bot. Mag., Tokyo*, **25**, 35–51. [13]
— (1964) Further studies on *Trapa* from Japan and its adjacent countries. *Bot. Mag., Tokyo*, **77**, 159–67. [17, 383]
NAKAYAMA, S. (1952) Experimental researches on photoperiodism. I. Photoperiodic responses of *Salvinia*. *Bot. Mag., Tokyo*, **65**, 274–79. [253]
— (1958) Studies on the dark process in the photoperiodic response of *Pharbitis* seedlings. *Sci. Rep. Tohuku Univ.*, ser. 4, **24**, 137–83. [252]
NARASIMHA MURTHY, S. K. (1933) Cytological and morphological studies in *Limnophyton obtusifolium* Miq. *Half-yrly J. Mysore Univ.*, **7**, 1–32. [278]
— (1935) The life history of *Ottelia alismoides*. *Proc. Indian Acad. Sci.*, ser. B, **2**, 59–66. [323]
NARAYANASWAMI, S. (1961) Morphology of the embryo in the monocotyledons. *Mem. Indian bot. Soc.*, **3**, 179–87. [322]
NEEDHAM, J. G. & NEEDHAM, P. R. (1962) *A guide to the study of freshwater biology.* edn 5. Holden-Day, San Francisco. [26]
NEEDHAM, P. R. (1938) *Trout streams.* Comstock Publ. Co., Ithaca, New York. [452]
NELSON, I. W., LINDSTROM, H. V., PALMER, L. S., SANDSTROM, W. M. & WICK, A. N. (1939) Nutritive value and chemical composition of certain freshwater plants of Minnesota. *Tech. Bull. Univ. Minn. agric. Exp. Stn*, **136**, 1–47. [433, 453–54]
NEUHÄUSL, R. (1959) Die Pflanzengesellschaften des südöstlichen Teiles des Witting-auer Beckens. *Preslia*, **31**, 115–47. [13]
NICKELL, L. G. (1958) Physiological studies with *Azolla* under aseptic conditions. I. Isolation and preliminary growth studies. *Am. Fern J.*, **48**, 103–08. [194]
NIEMI, A. (1962) En förekomst av växande *Zostera marina* L. öster om Helsingfors. *Memo. Soc. Fauna Flora fenn.*, **37**, 8–11. [13]
NINAN, C. A. (1956) Studies on the cytology and phylogeny of the pteridophytes. IV. Systematic position of *Ceratopteris thalictroides* (L.) Brongn. *J. Indian bot. Soc.*, **35**, 252–56. [16, 259]
— (1958) Studies on the cytology and phylogeny of the pteridophytes. V. Observations on the Isoetaceae. *J. Indian bot. Soc.*, **37**, 93–102. [16]
NOIRFALISE, A. & SOUGNEZ, N. (1961) Les forêts riveraines de Belgique. *Bull. Jard. bot. État Brux.*, **31**, 199–287. [3, 13]
NOLTÉ, E. F. (1825) *Botanische Bemerkungen über Stratiotes und Sagittaria.* Copenhagen. [181]
NYGAARD, G. (1955) On the productivity of five Danish waters. *Verh. int. Verein. theor. angew. Limnol.*, **12**, 123–33. [438, 442]
— (1958) On the productivity of the bottom vegetation in Lake Grane Langsø. *Verh. int. Verein. theor. angew. Limnol.*, **13**, 144–55. [438, 442]

OBERHOLZER, H. C. & MCATEE, W. L. (1920) Waterfowl and their food plants in the Sandhill region of Nebraska. *Bull. U.S. Dep. Agric.*, **794**. [453]
OBERMEYER, A. A. (1964) The South African species of *Lagarosiphon*. *Bothalia*, **8**, 139–46. [15, 18, 308, 376, 383]
— (1966a) Aponogetonaceae. In: *Flora of southern Africa*, **1**. Department of Agricultural Technical Services, Pretoria. [19, 292, 380]
— (1966b) A note on two rarely seen minute flowering plants, *Wolffiella denticulata* and *W. welwitschii*. *S. Afr. J. Sci.*, **62**, 277–78. [383]
— (*in litt.*) Personal correspondence, 1964 and 1965. [292]
ODA, Y. (1962) Effect of light quality on flowering of *Lemna perpusilla* 6746. *Pl. Cell Physiol., Tokyo*, **3**, 415–17. [252]

ODUM, H. T. (1956) Primary production in flowing waters. *Limnol. Oceanogr.*, **1**, 102–17. [445]

— (1957a) Primary production measurements in eleven Florida springs and a marine turtle-grass community. *Limnol. Oceanogr.*, **2**, 85–97. [442, 445]

— (1957b) Trophic structure and productivity of Silver Springs, Florida. *Ecol. Monogr.*, **27**, 55–112. [117, 122, 435, 442, 445–46]

— (1963) Productivity measurements in Texas turtle grass and the effects of dredging an intracoastal channel. *Publs Inst. mar. Sci. Univ. Tex.*, **9**, 48–58. [14, 442]

ODUM, H. T., BURKHOLDER, P. R. & RIVERO, J. (1959) Measurements of productivity of turtle-grass flats, reefs and the Bahia Fosforescente of southern Puerto Rico. *Publs Inst. mar. Sci. Univ. Tex.*, **6**, 159–70. [14, 442]

ODUM, H. T. & WILSON, R. F. (1962) Further studies on reaeration and metabolism of Texas bays, 1958–1960. *Publs Inst. mar. Sci. Univ. Tex.*, **8**, 23–55. [117, 442, 444]

ODUM, S. (1965) Germination of ancient seeds. Floristical observations and experiments with archaeologically dated soil samples. *Dansk bot. Ark.*, **24** (2), 70p. [325]

OES, A. (1913) Über die Assimilation des freien Stickstoffs durch *Azolla*. *Z. Bot.*, **5**, 145–63. [194]

OGDEN, E. C. (1943) The broad-leaved species of *Potamogeton* of North America and Mexico. *Rhodora*, **45**, 57–105, 119–216. [19]

— (1953) Key to the North American species of *Potamogeton*. *Circ. N.Y. St. Mus.*, **31**, 11p. [19]

OHGA, I. (1926a) On the structure of some ancient, but still viable fruits of Indian lotus, with special reference to their prolonged dormancy. *J. Jap. Bot.*, **3**, 1–20. [325]

— (1926b) The germination of century-old and recently harvested Indian lotus fruits, with special reference to the effect of oxygen supply. *Am. J. Bot.*, **13**, 754–59. [325–26]

— (1926c) A comparison of the life activity of century-old and recently harvested Indian lotus fruits. *Am. J. Bot.*, **13**, 760–65. [326]

— (1926d) A double maximum in the rate of absorption of water by Indian lotus seeds. *Am. J. Bot.*, **13**, 766–72. [326]

OLIVER, F. W. (1888) On the structure, development and affinities of *Trapella* Oliv., a new genus of Pedalineae. *Ann. Bot.*, **2**, 75–115. [184–85, 290]

— (1889) On a new form of *Trapella sinensis*. *Ann. Bot.*, **3**, 134. [216]

OLSEN, C. (1953) The significance of concentration for the rate of ion absorption by higher plants in water culture. IV. The influence of hydrogen ion concentration. *Physiologia Pl.*, **6**, 848–58. [134]

— (1954) Hvilke betingelser må vaere opfyldte for at *Helodea canadensis* kan opnå den optimale udvickling, der er årsag til dens massevise optraeden i naturen? *Bot. Tidsskr.*, **51**, 263–73. [364]

OLSEN, S. (1950) Aquatic plants and hydrospheric factors, I and II. *Svensk bot. Tidskr.*, **44**, 1–34, 332–73. [13]

— (1964) Vegetationsaendringer i Lingby Sø. Bidrag til analyse af kulturpavirkninger pa vand- og sumpplantevegetationen. *Bot. Tidsskr.*, **59**, 273–300. [450]

OOSTEN, J. VAN (1957) Great Lakes fauna, flora and their environment. *Publs Gt Lakes Res. Inst.*, 1957, 86p. [14]

OOSTSTROOM, S. J. VAN & REICHGELT, T. J. (1962a) Aanwinsten voor de Nederlandse adventief-flora, III. *Gorteria*, **1**, 49–53. [397]

— & — (1962b) Een Nederlandse vondst van *Vallisneria spiralis* L. *Gorteria*, **1**, 61–62. [397, 399]

— & — (1962c) *Typha angustifolia* L. × *T. latifolia* L.(*T.* × *glauca* Godr.) in Nederland. *Gorteria*, **1**, 90–92. [282]

— & — (1963) Nogmaals *Vallisneria spiralis* L. *Gorteria*, **1**, 95–96. [397, 399]

— & — (1964a) Alismataceae; Butomaceae; Hydrocharitaceae; Scheuchzeriaceae; Juncaginaceae. *Flora Neerlandica*, **1** (6), 1–36. [18, 19]

— & — (1964b) Ruppiaceae; Zannichelliaceae; Zosteraceae. *Flora Neerlandica*, **1** (6), 80–92. [19]

— & — (1964c) Lemnaceae; Sparganiaceae; Typhaceae. *Flora Neerlandica*, **1** (6), 221–42. [20]

OSBORN, T. G. B. (1914) Botany and plant pathology. 27p. repr. from *Handbook of South Australia*. Adelaide. [329]

— (1922) Some observations on *Isoetes Drummondii*, A. Br. *Ann. Bot.*, **36**, 41–54. [166–67, 256]

OSTENFELD, C. H. (1912) The international phytogeographical excursion in the British Isles. VI. Some remarks on the floristic results of the excursion. *New Phytol.*, **11**, 114–27. [359]
— (1915) On the geographical distribution of the seagrasses. *Proc. R. Soc. Vict.*, **27**, 179–91. [384, 386]
— (1927a) Meeresgräser. I. Marine Hydrocharitaceae. *Pflanzenareale*, **1** (3), 35–38 (map nos. 21–24). [18, 384, 386]
— (1927b) Meeresgräser. II. Marine Potamogetonaceae. *Pflanzenareale*, **1** (4), 46–50 (map nos. 34–39). [2, 19, 384, 386]
OTIS, C. H. (1914) The transpiration of emersed water plants: its measurements and its relationships. *Bot. Gaz.*, **58**, 457–94. [64, 89]
OTZEN, D. (1962) Chromosome studies in the genus *Scirpus* L., section *Schoenoplectus* Benth. et Hook., in the Netherlands. *Acta bot. neerl.*, **11**, 37–46. [283]
OWENS, M. (1965) Some factors involved in the use of dissolved-oxygen distributions in streams to determine productivity. *Memorie Ist. ital. Idrobiol.*, **18** (Suppl.), 209–24. [442]
OWENS, M. & EDWARDS, R. W. (1961) The effects of plants on river conditions. II. Further crop studies and estimates of net productivity of macrophytes in a chalk stream. *J. Ecol.*, **49**, 119–26. [426, 434, 436, 439, 442, 444]
— & — (1962) The effects of plants on river conditions. III. Crop studies and estimates of net productivity of macrophytes in four streams in southern England. *J. Ecol.*, **50**, 157–62. [36, 433, 436, 442, 444]
— & — (1963) Some oxygen studies in the River Lark. *Proc. Soc. Wat. Treat. Exam.*, **12**, 126–45. [36, 46–49, 445]
— & — (1964) A chemical survey of some English rivers. *Proc. Soc. Wat. Treat. Exam.*, **13**, 134–44. [32, 47, 446]
OWENS, M., EDWARDS, R. W. & GIBBS, J. W. (1964) Some reaeration studies in streams. *Int. J. Air. Wat. Pollut.*, **8**, 469–86. [46]
OWENS, M. & MARIS, P. J. (1964) Some factors affecting the respiration of some aquatic plants. *Hydrobiologia*, **23**, 533–43. [129–30]

PACKER, J. G. (1964) Chromosome numbers and taxonomic notes on western Canadian and arctic plants. *Can. J. Bot.*, **42**, 473–94. [370]
PAGEAU, G. (1959) *Étude descriptive structurale et fonctionelle de la végétation aquatique supérieure du lac Saint-Louis dans la Grande Anse de l'île Perrot, province de Québec.* Thesis, University of Montréal. [14]
PAL, N. & PAL, S. (1962) Studies on morphology and affinity of the Parkeriaceae. I. Morphological observations of *Ceratopteris thalictroides*. *Bot. Gaz.*, **124**, 132–43. [16, 109, 167, 183–84, 192, 258]
— & — (1963) Studies on morphology and affinity of the Parkeriaceae. II. Sporogenesis, development of the gametophyte, and cytology of *Ceratopteris thalictroides*. *Bot. Gaz.*, **124**, 405–12. [16, 258–59]
PAL, S. (1959) Chromosome number in *Ceratopteris siliquosa* (L.) Copel. *Curr. Sci.*, **28**, 455–56. [16, 258]
PALLIS, M. (1916) The structure and history of plav: the floating fen of the delta of the Danube. *J. Linn. Soc. (Bot.)*, **43**, 233–90. [152, 425]
PALMER, W. E. (1913) *Azolla* in Norfolk. *Nature, Lond.*, **92**, 233. [359]
PALMKRANTZ, P. J. (1952) Über Züchtung von *Elodea densa*. *Beitr. Biol. Pfl.*, **29**, 220–31. [—]
PANNIER, F. (1957, 1958) El consumo de oxigeno de plantas acuaticas en relacion a distintas concentraciones de oxigeno. *Acta cient. venez.*, **8**, 148–61; **9**, 2–13. [129]
— (1960) Physiological responses of Podostemaceae in their natural habitat. *Int. Revue ges. Hydrobiol. Hydrogr.*, **45**, 347–54. [131]
PANT, D. D. & SRIVASTAVA, G. K. (1962) Genus *Isoetes* in India. *Proc. natn. Inst. Sci. India*, ser. B, **28**, 242–80. [16]
— & — (1965) Cytology and reproduction of some Indian species of *Isoetes*. *Cytologia*, **30**, 239–51. [16, 256]
PARIJA, P. (1934) Physiological investigations on water-hyacinth (*Eichhornia crassipes*) in Orissa with notes on some other aquatic weeds. *Indian J. agric. Sci.*, **4**, 399–429. [317, 470]
PARKINSON, J. (1640) *Theatrum Botanicum.* London. [519]

PASCASIO, J. F. & SANTOS, J. K. (1930) A critical morphological study of *Thalassia hemprichii* Aschers. from the Philippines. *Nat. appl. Sci. Bull. Univ. Philipp.*, **1**, 1–19.
[305, 310]
PATTEN, B. C. (1954) The status of some American species of *Myriophyllum* as revealed by the discovery of intergrade material between *M. exalbescens* Fern. and *M. spicatum* L. in New Jersey. *Rhodora*, **56**, 213–25. [17, 368]
PAX, F. & HOFFMANN, K. (1931) Callitrichaceae. *Natürl. PflFam.*, edn 2, **19c**, 236–40.
[17, 114, 142, 312]
PEARL, R. (1907) Variation and differentiation in *Ceratophyllum*. *Publs Carnegie Instn*, **58**, 136p. [94–95]
PEARSALL, W. H. (1917, 1918a) The aquatic and marsh vegetation of Esthwaite Water. *J. Ecol.*, **5**, 180–202; **6**, 53–74. [13, 30, 54, 56, 156, 175, 415]
— (1918b) On the classification of aquatic plant communities. *J. Ecol.*, **6**, 75–84. [13]
— (1920) The aquatic vegetation of the English Lakes. *J. Ecol.*, **8**, 163–201.
[13, 30, 34, 37, 56, 91, 175, 415–17]
— (1921a) A suggestion as to factors influencing the distribution of free-floating vegetation. *J. Ecol.*, **9**, 241–53. [35, 177]
— (1921b) The development of vegetation in the English Lakes, considered in relation to the general evolution of glacial lakes and rock-basins. *Proc. R. Soc.*, ser. B, **92**, 259–84. [13]
— (1930) Phytoplankton in the English Lakes. I. The proportions in the waters of some dissolved substances of biological importance. *J. Ecol.*, **18**, 306–20. [36]
— (1933) The British species of *Myriophyllum*. *Rep. botl Soc. Exch. Club Br. Isl.*, **10**, 619–21. [17]
— (1934) The British species of *Callitriche*. *Rep. botl Soc. Exch. Club Br. Isl.*, **10**, 861–71. [17, 221, 283]
PEARSALL, W. H. & GORHAM, E. (1956a) Production ecology. I. Standing crops of natural vegetation. *Oikos*, **7**, 193–201. [438, 442]
— & — (1956b) Production ecology. III. Shoot production in *Phragmites* in relation to habitat. *Oikos*, **7**, 206–14. [438, 442]
PEARSALL, W. H. & HANBY, A. M. (1925) The variation of leaf form in *Potamogeton perfoliatus*. *New Phytol.*, **24**, 112–20. [242]
— & — (1926) Factors affecting the development and form of leaves. *Ann. Bot.*, **40**, 85–103. [239]
PEARSALL, W. H. & HEWITT, T. (1933) Light penetration into fresh water. II. Light penetration and changes in vegetation limits in Windermere. *J. exp. Biol.*, **10**, 306–12.
[30]
PEARSALL, W. H. & ULLYOTT, P. (1933) Light penetration into fresh water. I. A thermionic potentiometer for measuring light intensity with photo-electric cells. *J. exp. Biol.*, **10**, 293–305. [28]
— & — (1934) Light penetration into fresh water. III. Seasonal variations in the light conditions in Windermere in relation to vegetation. *J. exp. Biol.*, **11**, 89–93. [30–31]
PENFOUND, W. T. (1940a) The biology of *Dianthera americana* L. *Am. Midl. Nat.*, **24**, 242–47. [455]
— (1940b) The biology of *Achyranthes philoxeroides* (Mart.) Standley. *Am. Midl. Nat.*, **24**, 248–52. [455]
— (1949) Vegetation of Lake Chicot, Louisiana, in relation to wildlife resources. *Proc. La Acad. Sci.*, **12**, 47–56. [14, 453–54]
— (1952a) An outline for ecological life histories of herbaceous vascular hydrophytes. *Ecology*, **33**, 123–28. [7]
— (1952b) Southern swamps and marshes. *Bot. Rev.*, **18**, 413–46. [14]
— (1953a) The relation of plants to public health. *Econ. Bot.*, **7**, 182–90. [455, 517]
— (1953b) Plant communities of Oklahoma lakes. *Ecology*, **34**, 561–83. [13]
— (1956) Primary production of vascular aquatic plants. *Limnol. Oceanogr.*, **1**, 92–101.
[439, 442, 452]
PENFOUND, W. T. & EARLE, T. T. (1948) The biology of the water hyacinth. *Ecol. Monogr.* **18**, 447–72. [41, 177, 184–85, 188, 280–81, 315, 425, 437, 443, 461, 463, 473, 483]
PENFOUND, W. T., HALL, T. F. & HESS, A. D. (1945) The spring phenology of plants in and around the reservoirs in North Alabama with particular reference to malaria control. *Ecology*, **26**, 332–52. [13, 341, 431, 455]
PENFOUND, W. T. & HATHAWAY, E. S. (1938) Plant communities in the marshlands of southeastern Louisiana. *Ecol. Monogr.*, **8**, 1–56. [14, 453]

PENFOUND, W. T. & MINYARD, V. (1947) Relation of light intensity to effect of 2,4-dichloro-phenoxyacetic acid on water hyacinth and kidney bean plants. *Bot. Gaz.*, **109**, 231–34.   [498]
PENFOUND, W. T. & SCHNEIDAU, J. D. (1945) The relation of land reclamation to aquatic wildlife resources in southeastern Louisiana. *Trans. N. Am. Wildl. Conf.*, **10**, 308–18.
                                                                                      [14, 453]
PENTELOW, F. T. K. & BUTCHER, R. W. (1938) Observations on the condition of the Rivers Churnet and Dove in 1938. *Rep. Trent Fish. Distr.*, **1** (Appx).   [39]
PENTELOW, F. T. K., BUTCHER, R. W. & GRINDLEY, J. (1938) An investigation of the effects of milk wastes on the Bristol Avon. *Fishery Invest.*, *Lond.*, **4**, 80p.   [48]
PERCIVAL, E. & WHITEHEAD, H. (1929) A quantitative study of the fauna of some types of stream bed. *J. Ecol.*, **17**, 282–314.   [28]
PERCIVAL, M. S. (1965) *Floral biology*. Pergamon Press, Oxford.   [278, 281]
PERDUE, R. E. (1958) *Arundo donax*—source of musical reeds and industrial cellulose. *Econ. Bot.*, **12**, 368–404.   [433, 442, 521]
PERRING, F. H. (1963) The Irish problem. *Proc. Bournemouth nat. Sci. Soc.*, **52**, 36–48.
                                                                                      [389]
PERRING, F. H. & WALTERS, S. M. (ed.) (1962) *Atlas of the British flora*. Botanical Society of the British Isles; Nelson, London.
                            [371, 390, 392, 398, 407–08, 410, 412, 519]
PERRY, F. (1938, 1961) *Water gardening*. edns 1 and 3. Country Life, London.
                            [357, 453–54, 509, 518, 520, 523]
— (1962) *Water gardens*. Penguin Books, Harmondsworth, England.   [509, 523]
PETCH, T. (1928) Notes on *Cryptocoryne*. *Ann. R. bot. Gdns Peradeniya*, **11**, 11–26.
                                                                                      [68, 70]
PETER, A. (1938) Flora von Deutsch-ÖstAfrika: Aponogetonaceae. *Reprium nov. Spec. Regni veg.*, **40** (1), 116–17; Suppl., 9–10.   [292]
PETERSON, W. H., FRED, E. B. & DOMOGALLA, B. P. (1925) The occurrence of amino acids and other organic nitrogen compounds in lake waters. *J. biol. Chem.*, **63**, 287–95.
                                                                                      [38]
PETTET, A. (1964) Seedlings of *Eichhornia crassipes*: a possible complication to control measures in the Sudan. *Nature, Lond.*, **201**, 516–17.   [467, 471]
PFEIFFER, N. E. (1922) Monograph of the Isoetaceae. *Ann. Mo. bot. Gdn*, **9**, 79–232.
                                                                                      [16, 453]
PFEIFFER, W. M. (1907) Differentiation of sporocarps in *Azolla*. *Bot. Gaz.*, **44**, 445–54.
                                                                                      [263]
PHELPS, E. B. (1944) *Stream sanitation*. Wiley, New York.   [46]
PHILLIPS, R. C. (1960) Observations on the ecology and distribution of the Florida sea-grasses. *Prof. Pap. Ser. mar. Lab. Fla*, **2**, 1–72.   [14, 384]
PICHI-SERMOLLI, R. E. G. (1959) Pteridophyta. In: *Vistas in botany*, **1**, ed. Turrill, W. B., 421–93. Pergamon Press, Oxford.   [16, 256, 263, 266]
PICHON, M. (1946) Sur les Alismatacées et les Butomacées. *Phanérogamie*, **12**, 170–83.
                                                                                      [18, 278–79]
PIETERS, A. J. (1894) The plants of Lake St. Clair. *Bull. Mich. Fish Commn*, **2**, 10 p.
                                                                                      [14]
— (1902) Contributions to the biology of the Great Lakes. The plants of western Lake Erie, with observations on their distribution. *Bull. U.S. Fish Commn*, **21**, 57–79.
                                                                                      [14]
PIGOTT, C. D. & PIGOTT, M. E. (1963) Late-glacial and post-glacial deposits at Malham, Yorkshire. *New Phytol.*, **62**, 317–24.   [411]
PILGER, R. (1930) Mayacaceae. *Natürl. PflFam.*, edn 2, **15a**, 33–35.   [20]
PIRIE, N. W. (1960) Water hyacinth: a curse or a crop? *Nature, Lond.*, **185**, 116.   [502]
PIRSON, A. & GÖLLNER, E. (1953) Beobachtungen zur Entwicklungsphysiologie der *Lemna minor* L. *Flora, Jena*, **140**, 485–98.   [207]
PIRSON, A. & SEIDEL, F. (1950) Zell- und stoffwechselphysiologische Untersuchungen an der Wurzel von *Lemna minor* L. unter besonderer Berücksichtigung von Kalium- und Kalziummangel. *Planta*, **38**, 431–73.   [204]
PLINY, C. S. (A.D. 77) *Naturalis Historiae*. Transln by Holland, P. London, 1634.
                                                                                      [515, 519]
PLUMSTEAD, E. P. (1956) Bisexual fructifications on *Glossopteris* leaves from South Africa. *Palaeontographica*, ser. B, **100**, 1–25.   [267]
PODLECH, D. (1966) Aponogetonaceae. In: *Prodromus einer Flora von SüdWestAfrika*, ed. Merxmüller, H., no. 8, family 143. Cramer, Weinheim.   [19, 380]

POGAN, E. (1961) Oddrebnóśc gatunkowa i próba wyjaśnienia genezy *Alisma lanceolatum* With. *Acta Soc. Bot. Pol.*, **30**, 667–718. [18, 278]

POGAN, E. (1963a) Rangu systematyczna *Alisma subcordatum* Raf. i *Alisma triviale* Pursh. *Acta biol. cracov.*, **6**, 185–202. [18, 278]

— (1963b) Taxonomic value of *Alisma triviale* Pursh and *Alisma subcordatum* Rafin. *Can. J. Bot.*, **41**, 1011–13. [18, 278]

POLUNIN, N. (1959) *Circumpolar arctic flora.* University Press, Oxford. [17, 222]

POND, R. H. (1905) Contributions to the biology of the Great Lakes. The biological relation of aquatic plants to the substratum. 43 p. University of Michigan, Ann Arbor. [156, 174]

POPLAWSKAJA, G. I. (1948) Plant ecology. (In Russian) *Sov. Nauka*, 1948, 295 p. [5, 7]

PORSCH, O. (1905) *Der Spaltöffnungsapparat im Lichte der Phylogenie.* Jena. [115]

PORTER, H. C. (1958) *Reformation and reaction in Tudor Cambridge.* University Press, Cambridge. [518]

PORTERFIELD, W. M. (1940) Sagittaria as a food-plant among the Chinese. *Jl N.Y. bot. Gdn*, **41**, 45–47. [516]

POTZGER, J. E. & ENGEL, W. A. VAN (1942) Study of the rooted aquatic vegetation of Weber Lake, Vilas County, Wisconsin. *Trans. Wis. Acad. Sci. Arts Lett.*, **34**, 149–66. [13, 30, 434–35, 439, 442]

PRAEGER, R. L. (1913) On the buoyancy of the seeds of some Britannic plants. *Scient. Proc. R. Dubl. Soc.*, **14**, 13–62. [328]

— (1935) Recent advances in Irish field botany. *J. Bot., Lond.*, **73**, 42–46. [368]

— (1938) A note on Mr. Pugsley's *Myriophyllum alterniflorum* var. *americanum*. *J. Bot., Lond.*, **76**, 53–54. [390]

— (1939) The relations of the flora and fauna of Ireland to those of other countries. *Proc. Linn. Soc. Lond.*, **151**, 192–213. [394, 410]

PRANKERD, T. L. (1911) On the structure and biology of the genus *Hottonia*. *Ann. Bot.*, **25**, 253–67. [268, 290, 338]

PRASAD, R. & BLACKMAN, G. E. (1964) Studies in the physiological action of 2,2-dichloropropionic acid. I. Mechanisms controlling the inhibition of root elongation. *J. exp. Bot.*, **15**, 48–66. [206]

— & — (1965a) Studies in the physiological action of 2,2-dichloropropionic acid. II. The effect of light and temperature on the factors responsible for the inhibition of growth. *J. exp. Bot.*, **16**, 86–106. [206]

— & — (1965b) Studies in the physiological action of 2,2-dichloropropionic acid. III. Factors affecting the level of accumulation and mode of action. *J. exp. Bot.*, **16**, 545–68. [206]

PRIESTLEY, J. H. & NORTH, E. E. (1922) Physiological studies in plant anatomy. III. The structure of the endodermis in relation to its function. *New Phytol.*, **21**, 113–39. [147]

PRILLIEUX, E. (1864) Recherches sur la végétation et la structure de l'*Althenia filiformis* Petit. *Annls Sci. nat. (bot.)*, sér. 5, **2**, 169–90. [144]

PRIME, C. T. (1952) The 'Elodea' Experiment'. *Science Masters' Book*, ser. 3, part III, 214–23. [120]

PRING, G. H. (1934) Hybrid *Nymphaeas. Bull. Mo. bot. Gdn*, **22**, 47–90, 93–108. [17, 509]

— (1966) Tropical water-lilies. (with a note by Forsyth, J. and Brooks, A. V.) *Jl R. hort. Soc.*, **91**, 165–76. [—]

PRINGSHEIM, E. G. & PRINGSHEIM, O. (1962) Axenic culture of *Utricularia. Am. J. Bot.*, **49**, 898–901. [211, 249–50]

PRINGSHEIM, N. (1869) Über die Bildungsvorgänge am Vegetationskegel von *Utricularia vulgaris. Mber. K. Akad. Wiss.*, 1869, 92–116. [213]

— (1888) Ueber die Entstehung der Kalkincrustationen an Süsswasserpflanzen. *Jb. wiss. Bot.*, **19**, 138–54. [182]

PUGSLEY, H. W. (1938) A new variety of *Myriophyllum alterniflorum* DC. *J. Bot., Lond.* **76**, 51-53. [390]

PURI, V. (1962) Classification and phylogeny. *Bull. bot. Surv. India*, **4**, 167–72. [14]

— (1965) Disappointments of a morphologist. *J. Indian bot. Soc.*, **44**, 7–14. [14]

PURI, V. & GARG, M. L. (1953) A contribution to the anatomy of the sporocarp of *Marsilea minuta* L., with a discussion of the nature of the sporocarp in the Marsileaceae. *Phytomorphology*, **3**, 190–209. [259]

PURVES, W. K. (1961) Dark reactions in the flowering of *Lemna perpusilla* 6746. *Planta*, **56**, 684–90. [252]

RAALTE, M. H. VAN (1943) On the oxidation of the environment by the roots of rice (*Oryza sativa* L.). *Syokubutu-Iho, Buitenz.*, **1**, 2603. [161]

RABINOWITCH, E. I. (1945, 1951) *Photosynthesis and related processes*, **1** and **2**. Interscience Publishers, New York. [116]

RACIBORSKI, M. (1894) Die Morphologie der Cabombeen und Nymphaeaceen. *Flora, Jena*, **78**, 244–79; **79**, 92–108. [224]

RAM, M. (1956) Floral morphology and embryology of *Trapa bispinosa* Roxb. with a discussion on the systematic position of the genus. *Phytomorphology*, **6**, 312–23. [17, 21]

RAMJI, M. V. & PADMANABHAN, D. (1965) Developmental studies on *Cabomba caroliniana* Gray. I. Ovule and carpel. *Proc. Indian Acad. Sci.*, ser. B, **62**, 215–23. [17, 273]

RAMSBOTTOM, J. (1942) Recent work on germination. *Nature, Lond.*, **149**, 658. [325]

RAMSHORST, J. D. VAN. (1957a) Bermerkungen über die 'Hydropoten' einiger Wasserpflanzen. *Bull. aquat. Biol.*, **1**, 5–8. [132]

— (1957b) De bloeiwijze van *Cryptocoryne versteegii*. *Aquarium, Den Haag*, **28**, 33–34. [250]

RAMSHORST, J. D. VAN & FLORSCHÜTZ, P. A. (1956) A new variety of *Cabomba caroliniana* Gray. *Acta bot. neerl.*, **5**, 342–43. [109]

RANGASWAMY, K. (1941) A morphological study of the flower of *Blyxa echinosperma* Hook. *J. Indian bot. Soc.*, **20**, 123–33. [323]

RANTZIEN, H. HORN AF (1951a) Macrophyte vegetation in lakes and temporary pools of the alvar of Öland, South Sweden, I and II. *Svensk bot. Tidskr.*, **45**, 72–120, 484–97. [13]

— (1951b) Certain aquatic plants collected by Dr. J. T. Baldwin Jr. in Liberia and the Gold Coast. *Bot. Notiser*, 1951, 368–98. [375–76, 383, 389, 397]

— (1952) Notes on some tropical African species of *Najas* in the Kew Herbarium. *Kew Bull.*, 1952, 29–40. [19, 379]

RAO, Y. S. (1953) Karyo-systematic studies in Helobiales. I. Butomaceae. *Proc. natn. Inst. Sci. India*, **19**, 563–81. [18, 278]

RASMUSSEN, H. B., BJERROSØ, G., BÖCHER, T. W. & ILVER, K. (1948) Rørsumpvegetationen i Danmark. *Ingvidensk. Skr.*, **1**, 104 p. [442]

RASTETTER, V. (1963) Contribution à l'étude de la végétation du Haut-Rhin. Les étangs du Sandgau. *Bull. Soc. bot. Fr.*, **110**, 142–46. [13]

RAUH, W. & FALK, H. (1959) *Stylites* E. Amstutz, eine neue Isoëtacee aus den Hochanden Perus. *Sber. heidelb. Akad. Wiss.*, 1959, 1–160. [16, 256–57]

RAUNKIAER, C. (1896) *De Danske Blomsterplanters Naturhistorie. I. Helobieae*. Copenhagen. [321]

— (1903) Anatomical *Potamogeton*-studies and *Potamogeton fluitans*. *Bot. Tidsskr.*, **25**, 253–80. [139]

— (1934) *The life forms of plants and statistical plant geography*. Clarendon Press, Oxford. [3]

RAVEN, C. E. (1947) *English naturalists from Neckam to Ray*. University Press, Cambridge. [519]

RAVN, F. K. (1894) Om Flydeevnen hos Frøene af vore Vandog Sumpplanter. *Bot. Tidsskr.*, **19**, 143–88. [328]

RAZI, B. A. (1949) Embryological studies of two members of the Podostemaceae. *Bot. Gaz.*, **111**, 211–18. [285]

REAMS, W. M. (1953) The occurrence and ontogeny of hydathodes in *Hygrophila polysperma* T. Anders. *New Phytol.*, **52**, 8–13. [63, 66]

REED, C. F. (1954) Index Marsileata et Salviniata. *Bolm Soc. broteriana*, ser. 2, **28**, 5–61. [16, 266]

— (1962) Marsileaceae, Azollaceae e Isoetaceae de Portugal. *Bolm Soc. broteriana*, ser. 2, **36**, 73–94. [16]

REED, E. L. (1930) Vegetation of the playa lakes in the Staked Plains of western Texas. *Ecology*, **11**, 597–600. [14]

REES, A. R. (1966) The physiology of ornamental bulbous plants. *Bot. Rev.*, **32**, 1–23. [353]

REESE, G. (1962) Systematik und Cytologie der *Ruppia maritima*. *Ber. dt. bot. Ges.*, **75**, 365. [19]

REID, C. (1892) On the natural history of isolated ponds. *Trans. Norfolk Norwich Nat. Soc.*, **5**, 272–86. [12, 331]

— (1899) *The origin of the British flora*. London. [404, 406]

REID, G. K. (1961) *Ecology of inland waters and estuaries.* Reinhold, New York. [6, 26]
RENDLE, A. B. (1899, 1900) A systematic revision of the genus *Najas*; supplementary notes on the genus *Najas*. *Trans. Linn. Soc. Lond.*, ser. 2, **5**, 379–444.
[19, 299–300, 378]
— (1901) Naiadaceae. *Pflanzenreich*, **7** (IV. 12), 21 p. [19, 22, 378]
— (1930, 1953) *The classification of flowering plants. I. Gymnosperms and monocotyledons.* edn 2 and repr. University Press, Cambridge. [22]
RENN, C. E. (1936) The wasting disease of *Zostera marina*. I. A phytological investigation of the diseased plant. *Biol. Bull. mar. biol. Lab.*, *Woods Hole*, **70**, 148–58. [441]
RENNER, O. (1910) Beiträge zur Physik der Transpiration. *Flora, Jena*, **100**, 451–547. [89]
RICHARDSON, R. E. (1929) The bottom fauna of the middle Illinois River, 1913–25; its distribution, abundance, valuation and index value in the study of stream pollution. *Bull. Ill. St. nat. Hist. Surv.*, **17**, 387–475. [48]
RICKER, W. E. (1937) An ecological classification of certain Ontario streams. *Univ. Toronto Stud. biol. Ser.*, **37**, 114 p. [28]
RICKETT, H. W. (1921) A quantitative study of the larger aquatic plants of Lake Mendota, Wisconsin. *Trans. Wis. Acad. Sci. Arts Lett.*, **20**, 501–27.
[13, 30, 149, 175, 216, 434–35, 442]
— (1924) A quantitative study of the larger aquatic plants of Green Lake, Wisconsin. *Trans. Wis. Acad. Sci. Arts Lett.*, **21**, 384–414. [13, 30, 175, 434–35, 439]
RIDLEY, H. N. (1923) The distribution of plants. *Ann. Bot.*, **37**, 1–29. [356, 366]
— (1930) *The dispersal of plants throughout the world.* Reeve, Ashford, England.
[328, 331, 356–57, 362, 365, 424–25, 460–61, 464, 479]
RIEDE, W. (1921) Untersuchungen über Wasserpflanzen. *Flora, Jena*, **114**, 1–118. [103]
RIETZ, E. G. DU (1939) Zur Kenntnis der Vegetation des Sees Tåkern. *Acta phytogeogr. suec.*, **12**, 1–65. [13]
ROBBINS, W. W., CRAFTS, A. S. & RAYNOR, R. N. (1954) *Weed control.* edn 2. McGraw-Hill, London and New York. [484]
ROBERTS, F. W. (1959) Contribution to the discussion in Hynes (1959). [39]
RODHE, W. (1949) The ionic composition of lake waters. *Proc. int. Ass. theor. appl. Limnol.*, **10**, 377–86. [35]
RODWAY, J. (1895) *In the Guiana forest.* London. [425, 479]
ROE, C. D. (1966) *A manual of aquarium plants.* edn 3. Shirley Aquatics Ltd., Solihull, England. [513, 523]
ROPER, R. B. (1952) The embryo sac of *Butomus umbellatus* L. *Phytomorphology*, **2**, 61–74. [18, 278, 323]
ROSCOE, M. V. (1927) Cytological studies in the genus *Typha*. *Bot. Gaz.*, **84**, 392–406. [20]
ROSENDAHL, C. O. (1939) Additional notes on *Najas* in Minnesota. *Rhodora*, **41**, 187–89. [347]
ROSHARDT, P. A. (1915) Schwimm- und Wasserblätter von *Nymphaea alba* L. *Ber. dt. bot. Ges.*, **33**, 499–507. [88]
— (1922) Zahl und Verteilung der Spaltöffnungen in ihrer Abhängigkeit vom Licht beobachtet am Blatt von *Nymphaea alba* L. *Ber. schweiz. bot. Ges.*, **30/31**, 22–25. [88]
ROSSBACH, G. B. (1939) Aquatic *Utricularias*. *Rhodora*, **41**, 113–28.
[213, 335, 349–50, 368]
ROSTOWZEW, S. (1905) Zur Biologie und Morphologie der Wasserlinsen. (In Russian) *Izv. mosk. sel'.-khoz. Inst.*, **11**, 1–222. [20, 322]
ROYEN, P. VAN (1951, 1953) The Podostemaceae of the New World, I and II. *Meded. bot. Lab. Rijks-Univ. Utrecht*, **107** and **115**. [18]
— (1959a) Nomenclatural notes on the genera *Dalzellia*, *Lawia*, *Mnianthus*, and *Terniola* (Podostemaceae). *Acta bot. neerl.*, **8**, 473–76. [18]
— (1959b) A new species of *Rhyncholacis* (Podostemaceae). *Acta bot. neerl.*, **8**, 477–78. [18, 112]
ROYER, C. (1881–1883) *Flore de la Côte d'Or avec déterminations par les parties souterraines*, **1** and **2**. Paris. [4, 290]
ROZE, M. E. (1883) Contribution à l'étude de la fécondation chez les *Azolla*. *Bull. Soc. bot. Fr.*, **30**, 198–206. [358]
— (1887) Le mode de fécondation du *Zannichellia palustris* L. *J. Bot.*, *Paris*, **1**, 296–99. [299]
— (1892) Sur le mode de fécondation du *Najas major* Roth et du *Ceratophyllum demersum* L. *Bull. Soc. bot. Fr.*, **39**, 361–64. [301]

RUDESCU, L. (1965) Neue biologische Probleme bei den *Phragmites*kulturarbeiten im Donaudelta. *Arch. Hydrobiol.* (*Suppl.*), **30** (2), 80–111. [522]
RUTTNER, F. (1926) Ueber die Kohlensäureassimilation einiger Wasserpflanzen in verschiedenen Tiefen des Lunzer Untersees. *Int. Revue ges. Hydrobiol. Hydrogr.*, **15**, 1–30. [117]
— (1947, 1948) Zur Frage der Karbonatassimilation der Wasserpflanzen, I & II. *Öst. bot. Z.*, **94**, 265–94; **95**, 208–38. [115]
— (1953) Die Kohlenstoffquellen für die Kohlensäureassimilation submerser Wasserpflanzen. *Scientia, Bologna*, **88**, 20–27. [115]
— (1962, 1963) *Grundriss der Limnologie.* edn 3. W. de Gruyter, Berlin. Transln as *Fundamentals of limnology* by Frey, D. G. and Fry, F. E. J. University Press, Oxford; University Press, Toronto. [26, 32, 52–53]
RYDBERG, P. A. (1903) Sparganiaceae. *N. Am. Flora*, **17**, 5–10. [20]
RYTSCHIN, J. V. (1948) *Flora of hydrophytes.* (In Russian) Izdatelstvo 'Sovietskaya Nauka', Moscow. [523]

SACCARDO, P. A. (1892) De diffusione *Azollae carolinianae* per Europam. *Hedwigia*, **31**, 217–18. [357]
SAEGER, A. (1925) The growth of duckweeds in mineral nutrient solutions with and without organic extracts. *J. gen. Physiol.*, **7**, 517–26. [204]
— (1929) The flowering of Lemnaceae. *Bull. Torrey bot. Club*, **56**, 351–58. [20, 287]
— (1930) A method of obtaining pure cultures of *Spirodela polyrrhiza. Bull. Torrey bot. Club*, **57**, 117–22. [204]
— (1933) Manganese and the growth of Lemnaceae. *Am. J. Bot.*, **20**, 234–45. [204]
SAHNI, B. (1941) Indian silicified plants. I. *Azolla intertrappea* Sah. and H. S. Rao. *Proc. Indian Acad. Sci.*, ser. B, **14**, 489–501. [402]
SALISBURY, D. S. C. (1926) Floral constitution in the Helobiales. *Ann. Bot.*, **40**, 419–45. [277]
SALISBURY, E. J. (1942) *The reproductive capacity of plants.* Bell, London. [356]
— (1961) *Weeds and aliens.* Collins, London. [360, 364]
SALISBURY, F. B. (1963) *The flowering process.* Pergamon Press, Oxford. [252]
SAMANTARAI, B. (1938) Respiration of amphibious plants. I. *Scirpus articulatus* Linn. *J. Indian bot. Soc.*, **17**, 195–204. [64, 159]
SAMUELSSON, G. (1932) Die Arten der Gattung *Alisma* L. *Ark. Bot.*, **24**, 1–46. [18]
— (1934) Die Verbreitung der höheren Wasserpflanzen in Nord-Europa. *Acta phytogeogr. suec.*, **6**, 1–211. [331, 358]
SÂNE, Y. K. (1939) A contribution to the embryology of the Aponogetonaceae. *J. Indian bot. Soc.*, **18**, 79–92. [323]
SANIO, C. (1865) Einige Bemerkungen in Betreff meiner über Gefässbündelbildung geäusserten Ansichten. *Bot. Ztg*, **23**, 184–87, 191–93, 197–200. [139, 141, 144]
SANTOS, J. K. (1923) Differentiation among chromosomes in *Elodea. Bot. Gaz.*, **75**, 42–59. [—]
— (1924) Determination of sex in *Elodea. Bot. Gaz.*, **77**, 353–76. [—]
SARGANT, E. (1908) The reconstruction of a race of primitive angiosperms. *Ann. Bot.*, **22**, 121–86. [279]
SARGENT, J. A. (1956) Factors controlling differentiation of the vascular system of *Lemna minor* L. In: *The growth of leaves*, ed. Milthorpe, F. L., 205–06. Butterworth, London. [203]
SARGENT, J. A. & WANGERMANN, E. (1959) The effect of some growth regulators on the vascular system of *Lemna minor. New Phytol.*, **58**, 345–63. [203]
SASTRI, R. L. N. (1959) The vascularisation of the carpel in some Ranales. *New Phytol.*, **58**, 306–09. [277]
SATTLER, R. (1965) Perianth development of *Potamogeton richardsonii. Am. J. Bot.*, **52**, 35–41. [19, 295–96]
SAUER, F. (1937) Die Makrophytenvegetation ostholsteinischer Seen und Teiche. *Arch. Hydrobiol.* (*Suppl.*), **6**, 431–592. [13]
SAUNDERS, E. R. (1936) Some morphological problems presented by the flower of the Nymphaeaceae. *J. Bot., Lond.*, **74**, 217–21. [271, 277]
SAUVAGEAU, C. (1889a) Sur la racine du *Najas. J. Bot., Paris*, **3**, 3–11. [169, 172]
— (1889b) Contribution à l'étude du système mécanique dans la racine des plantes aquatiques: les *Potamogetons*; les *Zostera, Cymodocea*, et *Posidonia. J. Bot., Paris*, **3**, 61–72, 169–81. [154, 169, 172]
— (1890) Sur la feuille des Hydrocharidées marines. *J. Bot., Paris*, **4**, 269–75, 289–95. [92, 102, 113–14]

SAUVAGEAU, C. (1891) Sur les feuilles de quelques monocotylédones aquatiques. *Annls Sci. nat.* (*bot.*), sér. 7, **13**, 103–296. [92, 102, 113–14, 124, 146, 148]
— (1893) Sur la feuille des Butomacées. *Annls Sci. nat.* (*bot.*), sér. 7, **17**, 295–326. [90]
— (1894) Notes biologiques sur les *Potamogetons. J. Bot., Paris*, **8**, 1–9, 21–43, 45–58, 98–106, 112–23, 140–48, 165–72. [139, 324]
SAVIDGE, J. P. (1960) The experimental taxonomy of European *Callitriche. Proc. Linn. Soc. Lond.*, **171**, 128–30. [17, 221]
SCHADE, C. & GUTTENBERG, H. VON (1951) Über die Entwicklung des Wurzelvegetationspunktes der Monocotyledonen. *Planta*, **40**, 170–98. [192]
SCHAEPPI, H. (1935) Untersuchungen über die Blattentwicklung bei *Ceratophyllum, Cabomba* und *Limnophila. Planta*, **24**, 755–69. [227]
SCHAFFNER, J. H. (1904) Some morphological peculiarities of the Nymphaeaceae and Helobiae. *Ohio Nat.*, **4**, 83–92. [277, 322]
SCHELPE, E. A. C. (1961) The ecology of *Salvinia auriculata* and associated vegetation on Kariba Lake. *Jl S. Afr. Bot.*, **27**, 181–87. [476]
SCHENCK, H. (1884) Ueber Structuränderung submers vegetierender Landpflanzen. *Ber. dt. bot. Ges.*, **2**, 481–86. [71]
— (1885) Die Biologie der Wassergewächse. *Verh. naturh. Ver. preuss. Rheinl.*, **42**, 217–380. [4, 7, 90, 109, 150, 199, 290, 335, 429]
— (1886) Vergleichende Anatomie der submersen Gewächse. *Biblthca bot.*, **1**, 1–67. [113, 139, 142, 150, 157, 172, 203, 216]
— (1889) Ueber das Aërenchym, ein dem Kork homologes Gewebe bei Sumpfpflanzen. *Jb. wiss. Bot.*, **20**, 526–74. [65–66, 162–63]
SCHILLING, A. J. (1894) Anatomisch-biologische Untersuchungen über die Schleimbildung der Wasserpflanzen. *Flora, Jena*, **78**, 280–360. [84]
SCHINDLER, A. K. (1904) Die Abtrennung der Hippuridaceen von den Halorrhagaceen. *Bot. Jb.*, **34**, Suppl. 77, 1–77. [17]
— (1905) Halorrhagaceae. *Pflanzenreich*, **23** (IV. 225), 133 p. [17, 376]
SCHLEIDEN, M. J. (1838) Berichtungen und Nachträge zur Kenntnis der Ceratophylleen. *Linnaea*, **12**, 344–46. [224, 322]
SCHLOSS, H. (1913) Zur Morphologie und Anatomie von *Hydrostachys natalensis* Wedd. *Sber. Akad. Wiss. Wien*, **122**, 339–59. [18, 268]
SCHOENEFELD, W. DE (1860) Sur le mode de végétation de l'*Aldrovandia vesiculosa* en hiver et au printemps. *Bull. Soc. bot. Fr.*, **7**, 389–92. [349]
SCHOMER, H. A. (1934) Photosynthesis of water plants at various depths in the lakes of northeastern Wisconsin. *Ecology*, **15**, 217–18. [117]
SCHOTSMAN, H. D. (1954) A taxonomic spectrum of the section *Eu-Callitriche* in the Netherlands. *Acta bot. neerl.*, **3**, 313–84. [17, 221–22]
— (1958) Beitrag zur Kenntnis der *Callitriche*-Arten in Bayern. *Ber. bayer. bot. Ges.*, **32**, 128–40. [17]
— (1961a) Notes on some Portuguese species of *Callitriche. Bolm Soc. broteriana*, ser. 2, **35**, 95–128. [17, 383, 397]
— (1961b) Races chromosomiques chez *Callitriche stagnalis* Scop. et *Callitriche obtusangula* Le Gall. *Ber. schweiz. bot. Ges.*, **71**, 5–16. [17, 221]
— (1961c) Contribution à l'étude des *Callitriche* du Canton de Neuchâtel. *Bull. Soc. neuchâtel. Sci. nat.*, **84**, 89–101. [17]
— (1962) Note préliminaire sur les *Callitriches* du Sud-Ouest. *Bull. Cent. Étud. Rech. scient., Biarritz*, **4**, 205–09. [17]
SCHRENK, J. (1888) On the histology of the vegetative organs of *Brasenia peltata* Pursh. *Bull. Torrey bot. Club*, **15**, 29–47. [84, 90, 123, 149]
— (1889) On the floating tissue of *Nesaea verticillata* (L.) HBK. *Bull. Torrey bot. Club*, **16**, 315–23. [66–67]
SCHROEPFER, G. J. (1942) An analysis of stream pollution and stream standards. *Sewage Wks J.*, **14**, 1030–63. [446]
SCHUETTE, H. A. & ALDER, H. (1927) Notes on the chemical composition of some of the larger aquatic plants of Lake Mendota. II. *Vallisneria* and *Potamogeton. Trans. Wis. Acad. Sci. Arts Lett.*, **23**, 249–54. [433]
— & — (1929a) Notes on the chemical composition of some of the larger aquatic plants of Lake Mendota. III. *Castalia odorata* and *Najas flexilis. Trans. Wis. Acad. Sci. Arts Lett.*, **24**, 135–39. [433]
— & — (1929b) A note on the chemical composition of *Chara* from Green Lake, Wisconsin. *Trans. Wis. Acad. Sci. Arts Lett.*, **24**, 141–45. [432]

SCHUETTE, H. A. & HOFFMANN, A. E. (1921) Notes on the chemical composition of some of the larger aquatic plants of Lake Mendota. I. *Cladophora* and *Myriophyllum*. *Trans. Wis. Acad. Sci. Arts Lett.*, **20**, 529–31.   [433]
SCHULZ, A. G. (1961) Nota sobre la vegetatión acuática chaqueña. *Boln Soc. argent. Bot.*, **9**, 141–50.   [449]
SCHUMACHER, A. (1963) Quantitative aspekte der Beziehung zwischen Stärke der Tubificiden besiedlung und Schichtdicke der Oxydationszone in den Süsswasserwatten der Unterelbe. *Arch. FischWiss.*, **14**, 48–50.   [50]
SCHUSTER, J. (1907) Zur Systematik von *Castalia* und *Nymphaea*. *Bull. Herb. Boissier*, **7**, 853–68, 901–16, 981–96; **8**, 65–74.   [17]
SCHWARTZ, O. (1927) Zur Systematik und Geographie der Pontederiaceen. *Bot. Jb.*, **61**, Suppl. 139, 28–50.   [20]
— (1928) Die Pontederiaceen. *Pflanzenareale*, **2** (2), 13–14 (maps nos. 11–17).
                                                                                   [20, 373, 375, 383]
— (1930) Pontederiaceae. *Natürl. PflFam.*, edn 2, **15a**, 181–88.   [20]
SCHWEINFURTH, G. (1873) *The heart of Africa*. London.   [481]
— (1883) The flora of ancient Egypt. *Nature, Lond.*, **28**, 109–14.   [506]
— (1884) Ueber Pflanzenreste aus altaegyptischen Gräbern. *Ber. dt. bot. Ges.*, **2**, 351–71.
                                                                                   [506]
SCHWOERBEL, J. & TILLMANNS, G. C. (1964a) Untersuchungen über die Stoffwechseldynamik in Fliessgewässern. I. Die Rolle höherer Wasserpflanzen: *Callitriche hamulata* Kütz. *Arch. Hydrobiol.* (*Suppl.*), **28**, 245–58.   [134]
— & — (1964b) Untersuchungen über die Stoffwechseldynamik in Fliessgewässern. II. Experimentelle Untersuchungen über die Ammoniumaufnahme und pH-Änderung im Wasser durch *Callitriche hamulata* Kütz. und *Fontinalis antipyretica* L. *Arch. Hydrobiol.* (*Suppl.*), **28**, 259–67.   [134]
SCOTT, D. H. & HILL, T. G. (1900) The structure of *Isoetes Hystrix*. *Ann. Bot.*, **14**, 413–54.
                                                                                   [166]
SCOTT, L. I. & PRIESTLEY, J. H. (1928) The root as an absorbing organ. I. A reconsideration of the entry of water and salts in the absorbing region. *New Phytol.*, **27**, 125–40.
                                                                                   [147]
SCULTHORPE, C. D. (1962, 1965, 1966) A guide to aquarium plants and their cultivation. 93 p. In: *Exotic tropical fishes*, ed. Axelrod, H. R. and Vorderwinkler, W. T. F. H. Publications Inc., Jersey City, New Jersey. Monthly supplements in *Trop. Fish Hobby.*, **13**, **14** and **15**.   [513, 523]
SEAMAN, D. E. (1958) Aquatic weed control. *Proc. Soil Crop Soc. Fla*, **18**, 210–15.
                                                                                   [484, 487]
SEAMAN, D. E. & PORTERFIELD, W. A. (1964) Control of aquatic weeds by the snail *Marisa cornuarietis*. *Weeds*, **12**, 87–92.   [484, 501]
SEDDON, B. (1963) A lake flora survey of Wales. *Proc. bot. Soc. Br. Isl.*, **5**, 173. [13]
— (1964) Aquatic plants of Welsh lakes. *Nature Wales*, **9**, 3–8.   [13]
— (1965) Occurrence of *Isoetes echinospora* in eutrophic lakes in Wales. *Ecology*, **46**, 747–48.   [37]
SEIDEL, K. (1955) Die Flechtbinse (*Scirpus lacustris*). *Binnengewässer*, **21**, 216 p.
                                                                                   [13, 438, 521]
— (1956) *Scirpus lacustris* im eutrophen See. *Z. Fisch.*, **7/8**, 553–67.   [13, 438]
— (1959) *Scirpus*-Kulturen. *Arch. Hydrobiol.*, **56**, 58–92.   [13, 438, 442, 521]
SENARATNA, J. E. (1943) *Salvinia auriculata* Aublet—a recently introduced, free-floating water-weed. *Trop. Agric. Mag. Ceylon agric. Soc.*, **99**, 146–49.   [475, 478, 487]
— (1952a) Preliminary trials for the control of the water fern (*Salvinia*). *Trop. Agric. Mag. Ceylon agric. Soc.*, **108**, 49–50.   [475, 491, 502]
— (1952b) *Salvinia* in Ceylon. *Trop. Agric. Mag. Ceylon agric. Soc.*, **108**, 194–95. [491]
SENECA, L. A. (A.D. 63-64) *Quaestiones Naturales*. Transln as *Physical Science in the time of Nero*, by Clarke J. (with notes by Geikie, Sir A.) London, 1910. [480, 515, 522]
SERGUÉEFF, M. (1907) Contribution à la morphologie et la biologie des Aponogétonacées. *Thès. Inst. Bot. Univ. Genève*, sér. 7, **8**, 132 p.   [103–05]
SETCHELL, W. A. (1920) Geographical distribution of the marine spermatophytes. *Bull. Torrey bot. Club*, **47**, 563–79.   [35]
SETON, E. T. (1929) *Lives of game animals*. Doubleday, Garden City, New York.   [453]
SEVERIN, C. F. (1932) Origin and structure of secondary roots of *Sagittaria*. *Bot. Gaz.*, **93**, 93–99.   [157, 160]
SEWARD, A. C. (1910) *Fossil plants*. University Press, Cambridge.   [193]
— (1933) *Plant life through the ages*. edn 2. University Press, Cambridge.   [403]

SHAPIRO, J. (1957) Chemical and biological studies on the yellow organic acids of lake water. *Limnol. Oceanogr.*, **2**, 161–79. [38]
— (1958) Yellow acid-cation complexes in lake waters. *Science, N.Y.*, **127**, 702–04. [38]
— (1960) The cause of a metalimnetic minimum of dissolved oxygen. *Limnol. Oceanogr.*, **5**, 216–27. [51]
SHARP, L. W. (1914) Spermatogenesis in *Marsilia*. *Bot. Gaz.*, **58**, 419–31. [262]
SHAW, M. T. (1929) A microchemical study of the fruit coat of *Nelumbo lutea*. *Am. J. Bot.*, **16**, 259–76. [325]
SHCHERBAKOV, A. P. (1950) Productivity of the littoral macrovegetation of Lake Glubokoie. (In Russian) *Trudȳ vses. gidrobiol. Obshch.*, **2**, 69–78. [13, 438]
SHIBATA, O. (1958) Studies on photoperiodic responses of *Salvinia natans*. I. Role of carbon dioxide in photoperiodic responses. *J. Fac. lib. Arts Sci. Shinshu Univ.*, **8**, 7–12. [253]
— (1959) Studies on photoperiodic responses of *Salvinia natans*. II. The influences of organic acids of the citric acid cycle on photoperiodic responses. *Bot. Mag.*, *Tokyo*, **72**, 462–65. [253]
— (1961) Studies on photoperiodic responses of *Salvinia natans*. V. Effects of some inhibitory treatments under the influence of certain organic acids. *J. Fac. lib. Arts Sci. Shinshu Univ.*, **11**, 43–48. [253]
SHINOBU, R. (1952) Studies on the stomata of *Potamogeton*. *Bot. Mag.*, *Tokyo*, **65**, 56–60. [88–89, 114]
SHIRLEY, H. L. (1935, 1945) Light as an ecological factor and its measurement, I and II. *Bot. Rev.*, **1**, 355–81; **11**, 497–532. [28]
SHULL, G. H. (1905) Stages in the development of *Sium cicutaefolium*. *Publs Carnegie Instn*, **30**, 28 p. [227–28]
SIDDALL, J. D. (1885) The American water weed, *Anacharis alsinastrum* Bab.: its structure and habit; with some notes on its introduction into Great Britain. *Proc. Chester Soc. nat. Sci.*, **3**, 125–34. [363]
SIEGEL, S. M. (1962) *The plant cell wall*. Pergamon Press, Oxford. [144, 186, 197]
SIFTON, H. B. (1945, 1957) Air-space tissue in plants, I and II. *Bot. Rev.*, **11**, 108–43; **23**, 303–12. [125, 157]
— (1959) The germination of light-sensitive seeds of *Typha latifolia*. *Can. J. Bot.*, **37**, 719–39. [326]
SIGLER, W. F. (1948) Aquatic and shore vegetation of Spirit Lake, Dickinson County, Iowa. *Iowa St. Coll. J. Sci.*, **23**, 103–24. [13]
SIMON, T. (1960) Contribution à la connaissance de la végétation du delta Danube. *Annls Univ. Scient. bpest. Rolando Eötvös, ser. biol.*, **3**, 307–33. [13]
SIMPSON, G. M. (1966) A study of germination in the seed of wild rice (*Zizania aquatica*). *Can. J. Bot.*, **44**, 1–9. [325, 327, 516]
SINGH, V. (1962) Vascular anatomy of the flower of some species of the Pontederiaceae. *Proc. Indian Acad. Sci.*, ser. B, **56**, 339–53. [20, 280, 294]
— (1964) Morphological and anatomical studies in Helobiae. I. Vegetative anatomy of some members of Potamogetonaceae. *Proc. Indian Acad. Sci.*, ser. B, **60**, 214–31. [19, 299]
— (1965a) Morphological and anatomical studies in Helobiae. II. Vascular anatomy of the flower of Potamogetonaceae. *Bot. Gaz.*, **126**, 137–44. [19, 268, 296–99]
— (1965b) Morphological and anatomical studies in Helobiae. III. Vascular anatomy of the node and flower of Najadaceae. *Proc. Indian Acad. Sci.*, ser. B, **61**, 98–108. [19, 299]
— (1965c) Morphological and anatomical studies in Helobiae. IV. Vegetative and floral anatomy of Aponogetonaceae. *Proc. Indian Acad. Sci.*, ser. B, **61**, 147–59. [19, 294]
— (1965d) Morphological and anatomical studies in Helobiae. V. Vascular anatomy of the flower of *Lilaea scilloides* (Poir.) Hamm. *Proc. Indian Acad. Sci.*, ser. B, **61**, 316–25. [19, 295]
SINNOTT, E. W. (1960) *Plant morphogenesis*. McGraw-Hill, New York and Maidenhead. [218, 236, 242, 338]
SKALIŃSKA, M., BANACH-POGAN, E., PIOTROWICZ, M., SOKOŁOWSKA-KULCZYCKA, A. & WCISŁO, H. (1957, 1959, 1961) Further studies in chromosome numbers of Polish angiosperms. *Acta Soc. Bot. Pol.*, **26**, 215–46; **28**, 487–529; **30**, 463–89. [278]
SKENE, M. (1947) *The biology of flowering plants*. rev. imprn 4. Sidgwick and Jackson, London. [175, 215]
SKOTTSBERG, C. (1948) Philydraceae. *Flora Malesiana*, ser. 1, **4**, 5–6. [371]

SKUTCH, A. F. (1928) The capture of prey by the bladderwort: a review of the physiology of the bladders. *New Phytol.*, **27**, 261–97.   [210]
SLEDGE, W. A. (1949) The distribution and ecology of *Scheuchzeria palustris* L. *Watsonia*, **1**, 24–35.   [19, 412–13]
SMALL, J. K. (1909) Alismaceae. *N. Am. Flora*, **17**, 43–62.   [18]
— (1931) The water-lilies of the United States. *Jl N.Y. bot. Gdn*, **32**, 117–21.
                                                                                   [17, 269]
SMIRNOV, N. N. (1958) Some data about food consumption of plant production of bogs and fens by animals. *Verh. int. Verein. theor. angew. Limnol.*, **13**, 363–68.   [454]
— (1961) Consumption of emergent plants by insects. *Verh. int. Verein. theor. angew. Limnol.*, **14**, 232–36.   [454]
SMITH, A. C. (1937) Mayacaceae. *N. Am. Flora*, **19**, 1–2.   [20]
SMITH, E. V. & SWINGLE, H. S. (1941a) The use of fertiliser for controlling the pond-weed *Najas guadalupensis*. *Trans. N. Am. Wildl. Conf.*, **6**, 245–51.   [484, 501]
— & — (1941b) Control of spatterdock (*Nuphar advena* Ait.) in ponds. *Trans. Am. Fish. Soc.*, **70**, 363–68.   [484, 501]
SMITH, G. M. (1938) *Cryptogamic botany. II. Bryophytes and pteridophytes*. McGraw-Hill, New York and Maidenhead.   [167, 193, 196, 255, 257, 260–61, 265–67]
SMITH, R. W. (1900) Structure and development of the sporophylls and sporangia of *Isoetes*. *Bot. Gaz.*, **29**, 225–58, 323–46.   [255–56]
SNELL, K. (1908) Untersuchungen über die Nahrungsaufnahme der Wasserpflanzen. *Flora, Jena*, **98**, 213–49.   [146, 174]
— (1912) Der Transpirationsstrom der Wasserpflanzen. *Ber. dt. bot. Ges.*, **30**, 361–62.
                                                                                       [147]
SNOW, J. R. (1958) A preliminary report on the comparative testing of some of the newer herbicides. *Proc. A. Conf. SEast. Ass. Game Fish Commn*, **11**, 125–32.   [484, 488]
SNOW, L. M. (1914) Contribution to the knowledge of the diaphragms of water plants. I. *Scirpus validus*. *Bot. Gaz.*, **58**, 495–517.   [125]
— (1920) Diaphragms of water plants. II. Effects of certain factors upon the development of air chambers and diaphragms. *Bot. Gaz.*, **69**, 297–317.   [125]
SOL, H. H. (1958) Pretreatment and chloride uptake in *Vallisneria* leaves. *Acta bot. neerl.*, **7**, 131–73.   [135, 137]
SOLEREDER, H. (1908) *Systematic anatomy of the dicotyledons*. Rev. transln by Scott, D. H. Oxford.   [114, 123, 144–45, 149, 268]
— (1913) Systematisch-anatomische Untersuchung des Blattes der Hydrocharitaceen. *Beih. bot. Zbl.*, **30**, 24–104.   [113–14, 145, 184, 187]
SOLMS-LAUBACH, H. GRAF ZU (1883) Pontederiaceae. In: *Monographiae Phanerogamarum*, ed. Candolle, A. de and C. de, **4**, 501–35.   [20]
SOLTYS, A., UMRATH, K. & UMRATH, C. (1938) Über Erregungssubstanz, Wuchstoff und Wachstum. *Protoplasma*, **31**, 454–80.   [95, 156]
SOMSAK, L. (1963) Vegetation of the marshes between the dunes of the lowest area of the Tisa valley. (In Czech) *Acta Fac. Rerum nat. Univ. comen., Bratisl.*, **8**, 229–302.
                                                                                        [13]
SOÓ, R. (1957) Systematische Übersicht der pannonischen Pflanzengesellschaften, I. *Acta bot. hung.*, **3**, 317–73.   [13]
SOTA, E. R. DE LA (1962) Contribución al conocimiento de las Salviniaceae neotropicales. I. *Salvinia oblongifolia* Martius. II. *Salvinia auriculata* Aublet. III. *Salvinia herzogii* nov. spec. *Darwiniana*, **12**, 465–520.   [15, 16, 196, 383, 473]
— (1963) Contribución al conocimiento de las Salviniaceae neotropicales. IV. Datos morfoanatómicos sobre *Salvinia rotundifolia* Willdenow y *Salvinia herzogii* De la Sota. *Darwiniana*, **12**, 612–23.   [16, 196, 383, 473]
— (1964) Contribución al conocimiento de las Salviniaceae neotropicales. V. *Salvinia sprucei* Kuhn. *Darwiniana*, **13**, 529–36.   [16, 196, 383, 473]
SOUÈGES, R. (1952) L'albumen et l'embryon chez le *Callitriche vernalis* Kuntz. (*C. verna* L.). *C. r. hebd. Séanc. Acad. Sci.*, *Paris*, **235**, 453–56.   [17, 313]
SOUTHGATE, B. A. (1957) Synthetic detergents—a new pollution problem. *Jl R. Soc. Arts*, **55**, 485–97.   [39, 46]
SPANNER, D. C. & PREBBLE, J. N. (1962) The movement of tracers along the petiole of *Nymphoides peltatum*. I. Preliminary study with [137]Cs. *J. exp. Bot.*, **13**, 294–306.
                                                                                       [149]
SPECTOR, W. S. (ed.) (1956) *Handbook of biological data*. Saunders, Philadelphia and London.   [250]

SPEIRS, J. M. (1948) Summary of literature on aquatic weed control. *Can. Fish Cult.*, **3** (4), 20–32. [484]
SPENCE, D. H. N. (1964) The macrophytic vegetation of freshwater lochs, swamps and associated fens. In: *The vegetation of Scotland*, ed. Burnett, J. H., 306–425. Oliver and Boyd, Edinburgh and London. [9, 12, 30, 35, 37, 56–58, 154, 175, 328, 417–22, 426]
SPRUCE, R. (1908) *Notes of a botanist on the Amazon and Andes. . .during the years 1849– 1864.* ed. Wallace, A. R. London. [33, 91]
ST. JOHN, H. (1961) Monograph of the genus *Egeria* Planchon. *Darwiniana*, **12**, 293–307. [18, 305, 383, 397]
— (1962a) Note on the fruit of *Egeria Naias* Planchon. *Darwiniana*, **12**, 523. [18]
— (1962b) Monograph of the genus *Elodea* (Hydrocharitaceae). I. The species found in the Great Plains, the Rocky Mountains, and the Pacific States and Provinces of North America. *Res. Stud. Wash. St. Univ.*, **30**, 19–44. [15, 18, 304, 308– 10, 373–75, 383]
— (1963) Monograph of the genus *Elodea* (Hydrocharitaceae). III. The species found in northern and eastern South America. *Darwiniana*, **12**, 639–52. [15, 18, 304, 308, 310, 374, 383, 397]
— (1964) Monograph of the genus *Elodea* (Hydrocharitaceae). II. The species found in the Andes and western South America. *Caldasia*, **9**, 95–113. [15, 18, 304, 308, 310, 373–75, 383]
— (1965) Monograph of the genus *Elodea* (Hydrocharitaceae). IV. The species of eastern and central North America. & Summary. *Rhodora*, **67**, 1–35, 155–80. [15, 18, 304, 308–10, 375, 383]
STANKOVIĆ, S. (1960) The Balkan Lake Ohrid and its living world. *Monographiae biol.*, **9**. W. Junk, The Hague. [13]
STANT, M. Y. (1954) The shoot apex of some monocotyledons. II. Growth organisation. *Ann. Bot.*, **18**, 441–47. [94]
— (1964) Anatomy of the Alismataceae. *J. Linn. Soc. (Bot.)*, **59**, 1–42. [18, 169, 278–80]
STASON, M. (1926) The *Marsileas* of the western United States. *Bull. Torrey bot. Club*, **53**, 473–78. [16, 375]
STEARN, W. T. (1965) The self-taught botanists who saved the Kew Botanic Garden. *Taxon*, **14**, 293–98. [508]
STEEMANN NIELSEN, E. (1944) Dependence of freshwater plants on quantity of carbon dioxide and hydrogen ion concentration. *Dansk bot. Ark.*, **11** (8), 1–25. [115, 132]
— (1946) Carbon sources in the photosynthesis of aquatic plants. *Nature, Lond.*, **158**, 594–96. [115, 132]
— (1947) Photosynthesis of aquatic plants with special reference to the carbon sources. *Dansk bot. Ark.*, **12** (8), 1–71. [115, 132]
— (1951) Passive and active ion transport during photosynthesis in water plants. *Physiologia Pl.*, **4**, 189–98. [132, 136]
— (1954) On the preference of some freshwater plants in Finland for brackish water. *Bot. Tidsskr.*, **51**, 242–47. [42]
STEEMANN NIELSEN, E. & KRISTIANSEN, J. (1949) Carbonic anhydrase in submersed auto-trophic plants. *Physiologia Pl.*, **2**, 325–31. [116]
STEENIS, C. G. G. J. VAN (1948) Aponogetonaceae. *Flora Malesiana*, ser. 1, **4**, 11–12. [19, 292]
— (1949a) Ceratophyllaceae. *Flora Malesiana*, ser. 1, **4**, 41–42. [17, 33, 318]
— (1949b) Hydrocaryaceae. *Flora Malesiana*, ser. 1, **4**, 43–44. [17, 397, 516]
— (1949c) Saururaceae. *Flora Malesiana*, ser. 1, **4**, 47–48. [371, 385]
— (1949d) Podostemaceae. *Flora Malesiana*, ser. 1, **4**, 65–68. [2, 18, 284]
— (1954) Butomaceae. *Flora Malesiana*, ser. 1, **5**, 118–20. [5, 18, 254, 278, 389, 397, 401, 453, 517]
— (1957) Specific and infraspecific delimitation. *Flora Malesiana*, ser. 1, **5**, clxvii– ccxxxiv. [5, 253]
STEINBERG, R. A. (1941) Use of *Lemna* for nutrition studies on green plants. *J. agric. Res.*, **62**, 423–30. [204]
— (1946) Mineral requirements of *Lemna minor. Pl. Physiol.*, Lancaster, Pa, **21**, 42–48. [204]
STENAR, H. (1935) Embryologische Beobachtungen über *Scheuchzeria palustris* L. *Bot. Notiser*, 1935, 78–86. [323]

STERN, K. R. (1961) Chromosome numbers in nine taxa of *Potamogeton. Bull. Torrey bot. Club*, **88**, 411–14. [19]

STEUDE, H. (1935) Beiträge zur Morphologie und Anatomie von *Mourera aspera. Beih. bot. Zbl.*, **53**, 627–50. [131, 144, 149]

STEWARD, A. N., DENNIS, LA REA J. & GILKEY, H. M. (1963) *Aquatic plants of the Pacific Northwest, with vegetative keys.* edn 2. Oregon State University Press, Corvallis, Oregon. [523]

STEWART, W. N. (1947) A comparative study of stigmarian appendages and *Isoetes* roots. *Am. J. Bot.*, **34**, 315–24. [166–67]

STOKEY, A. G. (1909) The anatomy of *Isoetes. Bot. Gaz.*, **47**, 311–35. [166]

— (1951) The contribution by the gametophyte to classification of the homosporous ferns. *Phytomorphology*, **1**, 39–58. [16, 259]

STOOKEY, D. G., FORE, P. L. & MOHLENBROCK, R. H. (1964) Primary aquatic succession and floristics of Devil's Kitchen Lake, Illinois. *Castanea*, **29**, 150–55. [14, 427]

STOVER, E. L. (1928) The roots of wild rice, *Zizania aquatica* L. *Ohio J. Sci.*, **28**, 43–49. [157]

STRAŠKRABA, M. (1963) The share of the littoral region in the productivity of two ponds in southern Bohemia. *Rozpr. čsl. Akad. Věd. (mat. přírod. Věd.)*, **73** (13), 1–63. [13, 438, 442]

— (1965) Contributions to the productivity of the littoral region of pools and ponds. I. Quantitative study of the littoral zooplankton of the rich vegetation of the backwater Labíčko. *Hydrobiologia*, **26**, 421–43. [447, 452]

— (1966) Der Anteil der höheren Pflanzen an der Produktion der Gewässer. *Mitt. int. Verein. theor. angew. Limnol.*, **14**, Stoffhaushalt der Binnengewässer: Chemie und Mikrobiologie. [433]

STREITBERG, H. (1954) Über die Heterophyllie bei Wasserpflanzen mit besonderer Berücksichtigung ihrer Bedeutung für die Systematik. *Flora, Jena*, **141**, 567–97. [218, 227, 232]

SUBRAMANYAM, K. (1962) *Aquatic angiosperms: a systematic account of common Indian aquatic angiosperms.* Council of Scientific and Industrial Research, New Delhi. [33, 110, 112, 284, 289–90, 302, 305, 314, 316, 424, 516, 521, 523]

SUCKLING, E. V. (1944) *The examination of water and water supplies.* edn 5. Churchill, London. [36]

SURBER, E. W. (1949) Control of aquatic plants in ponds and lakes. *Fishery Leafl. Fish Wildl. Serv. U.S.*, **344**, 20 p. [484, 486]

— (1953) Biological effects of pollution in Michigan waters. *Sewage ind. Wastes*, **25**, 79–86. [32]

SUTCLIFFE, J. F. (1962) *Mineral salts absorption in plants.* Pergamon Press, Oxford. [133, 136–37]

SVEDELIUS, N. (1904) On the life-history of *Enhalus acoroides. Ann. R. bot. Gdns Peradeniya*, **2**, 267–97. [308]

— (1932) On the different types of pollination in *Vallisneria spiralis* L. and *Vallisneria americana* Michx. *Svensk bot. Tidskr.*, **26**, 1–12. [307]

SVENSON, H. K. (1944) The New World species of *Azolla. Am. Fern J.*, **34**, 69–84. [16, 375]

SWAMY, B. G. L. (1963) The origin of cotyledon and epicotyl in *Ottelia alismoides. Beitr. Biol. Pfl.*, **39**, 1–16. [322]

— (1966) The origin and organisation of the embryonic shoot apex in *Eichhornia crassipes. Bull. Torrey bot. Club*, **93**, 20–34. [322]

SWAMY, B. G. L. & LAKSHMANAN, K. K. (1962a) The origin of epicotylary meristem and cotyledon in *Halophila ovata* Gaudich. *Ann. Bot.*, **26**, 243–49. [322]

— & — (1962b) Contributions to the embryology of the Najadaceae. *J. Indian bot. Soc.*, **41**, 247–67. [301, 322, 324]

SWAMY, B. G. L. & PARAMESWARAN, N. (1962) On the origin of cotyledon and epicotyl in *Potamogeton indicus. Öst. bot. Z.*, **109**, 344–49. [322]

— & — (1963) The helobial endosperm. *Biol. Rev.*, **38**, 1–50. [323–24]

SWINDALE, D. N. & CURTIS, J. T. (1957) Phytosociology of the large submerged plants in Wisconsin lakes. *Ecology*, **38**, 397–407. [13, 37, 426]

SZANISZLO, P. (1961) Megjegyzések adventiv növenyeinkhez. *Bot. Közl.*, **49**, 115–21. [397]

TACKHÖLM, V. & DRAR, M. (1950) Flora of Egypt, II. *Bull. Fac. Sci. Egypt. Univ.*, **28**, 1–547. [461]

TAGEEVA, S. V. & KAZANTSEV, E. N. (1962) Movement of cytoplasm and chloroplasts in cells of detached leaves of *Elodea canadensis*. *Pl. Physiol.*, *Wash.*, **9**, 435–41. [113]

TAKHTAJAN, A. L. (1953) Phylogenetic principles of the system of higher plants. *Bot. Rev.*, **19**, 1–45. (Transln of paper in *Bot. Zh. SSSR*, **35**; 1950) [263, 266]

— (1959a) *Essays on the evolutionary morphology of plants*. Transln of 1954 Russian edn by Gankin, O. H., ed. Stebbins, G. L. American Institute of Biological Sciences, Washington, D.C. [246, 290]

— (1959b) *Die Evolution der Angiospermen*. German transln by Höppner, W. Jena. [246, 275, 279, 290]

TALLIS, J. H. & BIRKS, H. J. B. (1965) The past and present distribution of *Scheuchzeria palustris* L. in Europe. *J. Ecol.*, **53**, 287–98. [19, 412–13]

TANSLEY, A. G. (1949) *The British Islands and their vegetation*. Repr. with corrections. University Press, Cambridge. [9, 12–13, 37, 175, 417]

TAYLOR, H. J. (1927) The history and distribution of yellow *Nelumbo*, water chinquapin, or American lotus. *Proc. Iowa Acad. Sci.*, **34**, 119–24. [—]

TAYLOR, N. (1909) Zannichelliaceae, Zosteraceae, Cymodoceaceae, Naiadaceae, Lilaeaceae. *N. Am. Flora*, **17**, 13–37. [19]

TAYLOR, P. (1961) Notes on *Utricularia*. *Mitt. bot. StSamml.*, *Münch.*, **4**, 95–106. [212]

— (1964) The genus *Utricularia* L. (Lentibulariaceae) in Africa (south of the Sahara) and Madagascar. *Kew Bull.*, **18**, 1–245. [212, 349]

TAZIEFF, H. (1963) Dissolved gases in east African lakes. *Nature*, *Lond.*, **200**, 1308. [52]

TEAL, J. M. & KANWISHER, J. W. (1966) Gas transport in the marsh grass, *Spartina alterniflora*. *J. exp. Bot.*, **17**, 355–61. [64, 159, 161]

TERRAS, J. A. (1900) Notes on the germination of the winter-buds of *Hydrocharis morsusranae*. *Trans. Proc. bot. Soc. Edinb.*, **21**, 318–29. [355]

TERRELL, C. B. (1930) Wild fowl and fish attractions for South Dakota. *Rep. S. Dak. Game Fish Dep.*, 1930. [453]

THEOPHRASTUS (370–c. 285 B.C.) *Enquiry into plants*. Transln by Hort, Sir A. London, 1916. [1, 190, 516, 520]

THIENEMANN, A. (1954) *Chironomus. Binnengewässer*, **20**. [48]

THODAY, D. & SYKES, M. G. (1909) Preliminary observations on the transpiration current in submerged water-plants. *Ann. Bot.*, **23**, 635–37. [146]

THOMAS, H. H. (1958) *Lidgettonia*, a new type of fertile *Glossopteris*. *Bull. Br. Mus. nat. Hist.*, ser. A, **3**, 179–89. [267]

THOMPSON, C. H. (1896) The ligulate *Wolffias* of the United States. *Rep. Mo. bot. Gdn*, **7**, 101–11. [20]

— (1898) A revision of the American Lemnaceae occurring north of Mexico. *Rep. Mo. bot. Gdn*, **9**, 21–42. [20, 287]

THOMPSON, D'ARCY W. (1915) *On growth and form*. Cambridge. [190]

THOMSON, G. M. (1922) *The naturalisation of animals and plants in New Zealand*. University Press, Cambridge. [362–63, 397]

THUT, H. F. (1932) The movement of water through some submerged water plants. *Am. J. Bot.*, **19**, 693–709. [146, 174]

TIEGHAM, P. VAN (1866) Recherches sur la respiration des plantes submergées. *Bull. Soc. bot. Fr.*, **13**, 411–21. [121]

— (1868) Anatomie de l'*Utriculaire* commune. *Bull. Soc. bot. Fr.*, **15**, 158–62. [216]

TIMMERMANS, J. A. (1955) Essais sur le control de la végétation aquatique à l'aide d'herbicides. *Bull. Res. Stn Groenendaal*, ser. D, **17**, 38. [484, 488, 499]

TITCOMB, J. W. (1909, 1924) Aquatic plants in pond culture. *Docums Bur. Fish.*, *Wash.*, **643**, and *Rep. U.S. Commnr Fish.*, 1923–24, Appx 2, 24 p. [175, 453]

TOKURA, A. (1937) On the blooming of *Brasenia schreberi* J. F. Gmel. *J. Jap. Bot.*, **13**, 829–39. [274]

TOTH, L. (1962) On some chemical properties of *Wolffia arrhiza* (L.) Wimm. *Annls Inst. biol.*, *Tihany*, **29**, 275–82. [—]

TOURNAY, R. & LAWALRÉE, A. (1949) Les *Alisma* de la flore Belge. *Bull. Soc. r. Bot. Belg.*, **81**, 47–49. [18, 70]

TRÉBOUX, O. (1903) Einige stoffliche Einflusse auf die Kohlensäureassimilation submersen Pflanzen. *Flora*, *Jena*, **92**, 49–76. [115]

TREVIRANUS, L. C. (1848) Noch etwas über die Schläuche der Utricularien. *Bot. Ztg*, **6**, 444–48. [209, 213]

TRIMEN, H. (1871) Is *Acorus calamus* a native? *J. Bot.*, *Lond.*, **9**, 163–65. [518]

TROLL, W. (1931) Beiträge zur Morphologie des Gynaeceums. I. Über das Gynaeceum der Hydrocharitaceen. *Planta*, **14**, 1–18. [307]

TROLL, W. (1934) Beiträge zur Morphologie des Gynaeceums. IV. Über das Gynaeceum der Nymphaeaceen. *Planta*, **21**, 447–85. [271]
— (1937) *Vergleichende Morphologie der höheren Pflanzen*. Borntraeger, Berlin. [232]
TROP. AGRIC. (1959) (TROPICAL AGRICULTURIST) Chemical weed control in the tropics. (Editorial) *Trop. Agric. Mag. Ceylon agric. Soc.*, **115**, 5–6. [489]
TROUPIN, G. (1953) Plantae Africanae III. Aponogetonaceae (Nouvelle famille pour le Congo Belge). *Bull. Jard. bot. État Brux.*, **23**, 223–26. [19, 380]
TURESSON, G. (1961) Habit modifications in some widespread plant species. *Bot. Notiser*, **114**, 435–52. [6, 70, 221]
TURNER, W. (1548) *The names of herbes*. London. [518]
— (1568) *A new herball*. London. [518]
TURRILL, W. B. (1958) *British plant life*. edn 2. Collins, London. [365]
— (1959) Plant geography. In: *Vistas in botany*, **1**, ed. Turrill, W. B., 172–229. Pergamon Press, Oxford. [370]
— (1963) Some aspects of applied plant ecology. In: *Vistas in botany*, **2**, ed. Turrill, W. B., 250–99. Pergamon Press, Oxford. [43, 427]
TUTIN, T. G. (1936) New species of *Zostera* from Britain. *J. Bot., Lond.*, **74**, 227–30. [19, 102, 297]
— (1938) The autecology of *Zostera marina* in relation to its wasting disease. *New Phytol.*, **37**, 50–71. [441]
— (1942) Biological flora of the British Isles: *Zostera* L. *J. Ecol.*, **30**, 217–26. [19, 441]
— (1962) In: *Flora of the British Isles*, by Clapham, A. R., Tutin, T. G. & Warburg, E. F. edn 2. University Press, Cambridge. [228, 290, 297, 304, 366, 371, 383, 391]
— (1964) *Nymphaea* L.; *Nuphar* Sm.; *Nelumbo* Adanson. *Flora Europaea*, **1**, 204–05. [17, 275, 383, 397]
TUYAMA, T. (1940) On genus *Haloragis* and Micronesian species. *J. Jap. Bot.*, **16**, 273–85. [17, 376]
TYRON, A. F. (1964) *Platyzoma*: a Queensland fern with incipient heterospory. *Am. J. Bot.*, **51**, 939–42. [259]

UHL, N. W. (1947) *Studies in the floral morphology and anatomy of certain members of the Helobiae*. Thesis, Cornell University. [19, 294–95]
UMEMURA, K., INOKUCHI, H. & OOTA, Y. (1963) Flowering in *Lemna gibba* G3. *Pl. Cell Physiol., Tokyo*, **4**, 289–92. [252]
UNGER, F. (1862) Beiträge zur Anatomie und Physiologie der Pflanzen. XII. Neue Untersuchungen über die Transpiration der Gewächse. *Sber. Akad. Wiss. Wien*, **14**, 327–68. [145–46]
U.S.D.A. (1937) (UNITED STATES DEPARTMENT OF AGRICULTURE, BUREAU OF BIOLOGICAL SURVEY) Natural plantings for attracting waterfowl to marsh and other water areas. *Leafl. Bur. biol. Surv. U.S. Dep. Agric.*, BS 77. [452–53]
USPENSKIJ, E. E. (1913) Zur Phylogenie und Ekologie der Gattung *Potamogeton*. I. Luft-, Schwimm- und Wasserblätter von *Potamogeton perfoliatus* L. *Byull. mosk. Obshch. Ispyt. Prir.*, **27**, 253–62. [109]

VASIL'EV, V. N. (1947) Systematics and biology of the genus *Trapa* L. (In Russian) *Sov. Bot.*, **15**, 343–45. [17]
VEATCH, J. C. (1933) Some relationships between water plants and water soils in Michigan. *Pap. Mich. Acad. Sci.*, **17**, 409. [13, 175]
VEGIS, A. (1965) Bedeutung von Aussenfaktoren bei Ruhezuständen bei höheren Pflanzen. *Handb. PflPhysiol.*, **15** (2), 499–668. [356]
VERDUIN, J. (1952) The volume-based photosynthetic rates of aquatic plants. *Am. J. Bot.*, **39**, 157–59. [116]
VISCHER, W. (1915) Experimentelle Beiträge zur Kenntnis der Jugend- und Folgeformen xerophiler Pflanzen. *Flora, Jena*, **108**, 1–72. [232]
VÖCHTING, H. (1872) Zur Histologie und Entwicklungsgeschichte von *Myriophyllum*. *Nova Acta Acad. Caesar. Leop. Carol.*, **36**, 18 p. [142]
VORONICHIN, N. N. (1953) *The world of continental water plants*. (In Russian) Izdatelstvo Academii Nauk SSSR, Moscow and Leningrad. [523]
VOSE, P. B. (1962) On delayed germination in the reed canary-grass, *Phalaris arundinacea* L. *Ann. Bot.*, **26**, 197–206. [326]
VUYCK, L. (1895) Over het bloeien van *Lemna*. *Bot. Jaarb.*, **7**, 60–72. [287]

WÄCHTER, W. (1897) Beiträge zur Kenntnis einiger Wasserpflanzen. *Flora, Jena,* **83**, 367–97; **84**, 343–48. [232]

WAGER, V. A. (1928) The structure and life-history of the South African *Lagarosiphons,* and notes and descriptions of a few uncommon water plants. *Trans. R. Soc. S. Afr.,* **16**, 191–204. [18, 308]

WALKER, A. O. (1912) The distribution of *Elodea canadensis* Michaux in the British Isles in 1909. *Proc. Linn. Soc. Lond.,* **124**, 71–77. [360, 363]

WALKER, C. R. (1959) Control of certain aquatic weeds in Missouri farm ponds. *Weeds,* **7**, 310–16. [484, 486]

— (1964) Simazine and other *s*-triazine compounds as aquatic herbicides in fish habitats. *Weeds,* **12**, 134–39. [484]

WALKER, D. & LAMBERT, C. A. (1955) Boreal deposits at Kirkby Thore, Westmorland. *New Phytol.,* **54**, 209–15. [287]

WALKER, J. (1966) *Polythrinciopsis* gen. nov. (Fungi Imperfecti) on *Phragmites communis* Trin. *Aust. J. Bot.,* **14**, 195–200. [441]

WALKER, N. (1905) Pond vegetation. *Naturalist, Hull,* **585**, 305–11. [12, 331]

WALKER, T. J. & HASLER, A. D. (1949) Olfactory discrimination of aquatic plants by the bluntnose minnow *Hyborhynchus notatus* (Rafinesque). *Physiol. Zoöl.,* **22**, 45–63. [454]

WALLACE, E. C. (1963, 1964, 1966) Plant records. *Proc. bot. Soc. Br. Isl.,* **5**, 28–41, 125–43, 234–40, 345–57; **6**, 235–46. [397, 399, 413]

WALTERS, S. M. (1953) *Montia fontana* L. *Watsonia,* **3**, 1–6. [5, 223]

WANG, H.-C. (1956) A preliminary report on the morphological studies of the vegetative body and the organisation of the bud of *Nelumbo nucifera* Gaertn. (In Chinese) *Acta bot. sin.,* **5**, 425–37. [223, 254, 335, 343]

WANGERMANN, E. (1961) The effect of water supply and humidity on growth and development. *Handb. PflPhysiol.,* **16**, 618–33. [218]

WANGERMANN, E. & ASHBY, E. (1950) Morphogenesis in *Lemna minor. Proc. Linn. Soc. Lond.,* **162**, 10–13. [204]

WANGERMANN, E. & LACEY, H. J. (1953) Studies in the morphogenesis of leaves. IX. Experiments on *Lemna minor* with adenine, triiodobenzoic acid and ultra-violet radiation. *New Phytol.,* **52**, 298–311. [203, 207]

— & — (1955) Studies in the morphogenesis of leaves. X. Preliminary experiments on the relation between nitrogen nutrition, rate of respiration and rate of ageing of fronds of *Lemna minor. New Phytol.,* **54**, 182–98. [207]

WARBURG, E. F. (1962) In: *Flora of the British Isles,* by Clapham, A. R., Tutin, T. G. and Warburg, E. F. edn 2. University Press, Cambridge. [33, 341, 391]

WARD, H. B. & WHIPPLE, G. C. (1959) *Freshwater biology.* edn 2, rev. Edmondson, W. T. Wiley, New York and London. [26]

WARDLAW, C. W. (1952a) *Phylogeny and morphogenesis.* MacMillan, London. [82–83]

— (1952b) The effect of isolating the apical meristem in *Echinopsis, Nuphar, Gunnera* and *Phaseolus. Phytomorphology,* **2**, 240–42. [82–83]

— (1956) The inception of leaf primordia. In: *The growth of leaves,* ed. Milthorpe, F. L., 53–65. Butterworth, London. [82–83, 94]

— (1965) *Organisation and evolution in plants.* Longmans Green, London. [234]

WARIS, H. (1959) Neomorphosis induced in seed plants by amino acids. I. *Oenanthe aquatica. Physiologia Pl.,* **12**, 753–66. [247]

— (1962) Neomorphosis induced in seed plants by amino acids. II. *Oenanthe lachenalii. Physiologia Pl.,* **15**, 736–52. [247]

WARMING, E. (1881, 1882, 1888, 1891) Familien Podostemaceae. *K. danske Vidensk. Selsk. Skr.,* **2**, 1–34, 77–130; **4**, 443–514; **7**, 133–79. [18, 109, 113, 285]

WATT, W. D. (1966) Release of dissolved organic material from the cells of phytoplankton populations. *Proc. R. Soc.,* ser. B, **164**, 521–51. [38]

WEAVER, J. E. & CLEMENTS, F. E. (1938) *Plant ecology.* edn 2. McGraw-Hill, New York. [5]

WEAVER, J. E. & HIMMEL, W. J. (1930) The relation of increased water content and decreased aeration to root development in hydrophytes. *Pl. Physiol., Lancaster, Pa,* **5**, 69–92. [161]

WEBB, D. A. (1964) *Ceratophyllum* L. *Flora Europaea,* **1**, 206. [17, 383, 397]

WEBER, H. (1950) Morphologische und anatomische Studien über *Eichhornia crassipes* (Mart.) Solms. *Abh. math.-naturw. Kl. Akad. Wiss. Mainz,* 1950, 135–61. [183, 187]

WEBER, U. (1922) Zur Anatomie und Systematik der Gattung *Isoetes*. *Hedwigia*, **63**, 219–62. [16]

WEDDELL, H. A. (1849) Observations sur une espèce nouvelle du genre *Wolffia* (Lemnacées). *Annls Sci. nat. (bot.)*, sér. 3, **12**, 155–73. [199]

— (1872) Sur les Podostémacées en général, et leur distribution géographique en particulier. *Bull. Soc. bot. Fr.*, **19**, 50–57. [377]

WEIN, K. (1939, 1942) Die älteste Einführungs- und Ausbreitungsgeschichte von *Acorus calamus*. *Hercynia*, **1**, 367–450; **3**, 72–128, 241–91. [519]

WEINROWSKY, P. (1899) Untersuchungen über die Scheitelöffnungen bei Wasserpflanzen. *Beitr. wiss. Bot.*, **3**, 205–47. [146, 148]

WEIR, C. E. & DALE, H. M. (1960) A developmental study of wild rice, *Zizania aquatica* L. *Can. J. Bot.*, **38**, 719–39. [61, 79, 86, 113–14, 229]

WEISLO, H. (1963) Obserwacje nad klonami *Lemna trisulca* L. warnukach hodowli aseptycznej. *Acta biol. cracov.*, **6**, 171–76. [204]

WEISS, F. E. & MURRAY, H. (1909) On the occurrence and distribution of some alien aquatic plants in the Reddish Canal. *Mem. Proc. Manchr lit. phil. Soc.*, **53** (14), 8 p. [398]

WELCH, P. S. (1948) *Limnological methods*. Blakiston, Philadelphia. [26]

— (1952) *Limnology*. edn 2. McGraw-Hill, New York. [26]

WENDT, A. (1952–1958) *Die Aquarienpflanzen in Wort und Bild*. Kernen, Stuttgart. [513, 523]

WENT, F. A. F. C. (1910, 1912) Untersuchungen über Podostemonaceen, I and II. *Verh. K. Akad. Wet.*, **16**, 1–88; **17**, 1–19. [18, 109, 113]

— (1924) Sur la transformation du collenchyme en sclérenchyme chez les Podostémonacées. *Recl Trav. bot. néerl.*, **21**, 513–20. [92]

— (1926) Untersuchungen über Podostemonaceen, III. *Verh. K. Akad. Wet.*, **25**, 1–59. [18, 109, 113–14]

WEST, C. & TAKEDA, H. (1915) On *Isoetes japonica*. *Trans. Linn. Soc. Lond.*, ser. 2, **8**, 333–76. [166]

WEST, G. (1905) A comparative study of the dominant phanerogamic and higher cryptogamic flora of aquatic habit in three lake areas of Scotland. *Proc. R. Soc. Edinb.*, **25**, 967–1023. [12, 90, 267, 335, 417–18, 420–22]

— (1910) A further contribution to a comparative study of the dominant phanerogamic and higher cryptogamic flora of aquatic habit in Scottish lakes. *Proc. R. Soc. Edinb.*, **30**, 65–181. [12, 30, 229, 267, 290, 417]

WEST, R. G. (1953) The occurrence of *Azolla* in British interglacial deposits. *New Phytol.*, **52**, 267–72. [403–05]

WESTLAKE, D. F. (1959a) The effects of biological communities on conditions in polluted streams. In: *The effects of pollution on living material*, ed. Yapp, W. B., *Symp. Inst. Biol.*, **8**, 25–31. Institute of Biology, London. [25, 50]

— (1959b) The effects of organisms on pollution. *Proc. Linn. Soc. Lond.*, **170**, 171–72. [47]

— (1960) Water-weed and water management. *Instn publ. Hlth Engrs J.*, **59**, 148–60. [440, 442, 448, 484]

— (1961) Aquatic macrophytes and the oxygen balance of running water. *Verh. int. Verein. theor. angew. Limnol.*, **14**, 499–503. [437, 442]

— (1963) Comparisons of plant productivity. *Biol. Rev.*, **38**, 385–425. [429, 432, 440, 442–44]

— (1964) Light extinction, standing crop and photosynthesis within weed beds. *Verh. int. Verein. theor. angew. Limnol.*, **15**, 415–25. [32, 116, 118, 447]

— (1965a) Some basic data for investigations of the productivity of aquatic macrophytes. *Memorie Ist. ital. Idrobiol.*, **18** (Suppl.), 229–48. [149, 152, 154–55, 188, 432–33, 440–42, 452]

— (1965b) Theoretical aspects of the comparability of productivity data. *Memorie Ist. ital. Idrobiol.*, **18** (Suppl.), 313–22. [432]

— (1966a) The light climate for plants in rivers. In: *Light as an ecological factor.* ed. Rackman, O., Evans, G. C. & Bainbridge, R. *Symp. Br. ecol. Soc.*, **6**, 99–199. Blackwell, Oxford. [31–32, 116, 118]

— (1966b) A model for quantitative studies of photosynthesis by higher plants in streams. *Int. J. Air Wat. Pollut.*, **10**, 883–96. [116, 118, 447]

— (1966c) The biomass and productivity of *Glyceria maxima*. I. Seasonal changes in biomass. *J. Ecol.*, **54**, 745–53. [154, 438, 442]

WESTLAKE, D. F. (in press) Some effects of low velocity currents on the metabolism of aquatic macrophytes. *J. exp. Bot.*, **18**. [116, 118–19, 121, 130–31]
— (*in litt.*) Personal correspondence, 1964, 1965 and 1966. [152, 399, 444, 458, 487]
WETMORE, R. H. (1943) Leaf stem relationships in the vascular plants. *Torreya*, **43**, 16–28. [142]
WETTSTEIN, R. VON (1906) Die Samenbildung und Keimung von *Aponogeton* (*Ouvirandra*) *Bernierianus* (Decne) Benth. et Hooker f. *Öst. bot. Z.*, **56**, 8–13. [322]
WETZEL, R. G. (1960) Marl encrustation on hydrophytes in several Michigan lakes. *Oikos*, **11**, 223–28. [134]
— (1964) A comparative study of the primary productivity of higher aquatic plants, periphyton, and phytoplankton in a large shallow lake. *Int. Revue ges. Hydrobiol. Hydrogr.*, **49**, 1–61. [43, 442]
WHELDALE, M. (1916) *The anthocyanin pigments of plants*. Cambridge. [87, 149]
WHITE, H. L. (1937a) The interaction of factors in the growth of *Lemna*. XI. The interaction of nitrogen and light intensity in relation to growth and assimilation. *Ann. Bot.*, **1**, 623–47. [204–05]
— (1937b) The interaction of factors in the growth of *Lemna*. XII. The interaction of nitrogen and light intensity in relation to root length. *Ann. Bot.*, **1**, 649–54. [204–05]
— (1938) The interaction of factors in the growth of *Lemna*. XIII. The interaction of potassium and light intensity in relation to root length. *Ann. Bot.*, **2**, 911–17. [205]
— (1939) The interaction of factors in the growth of *Lemna*. XIV. The interaction of potassium and light intensity in relation to growth and assimilation. *Ann. Bot.*, **3**, 619–48. [205]
— (1940) The interaction of factors in the growth of *Lemna*. XV. On a rhythmic growth cycle of *Lemna* colonies associated with transference to a potassium-free nutrient solution. *Ann. Bot.*, **4**, 495–504. [200, 207]
WHITE, H. L. & TEMPLEMAN, W. G. (1937) The interaction of factors in the growth of *Lemna*. X. The interaction of nitrogen and light intensity in relation to respiration. *Ann. Bot.*, **1**, 191–204. [204–05]
WHITE, R. A. (1963) Tracheary elements of the ferns. II. Morphology of tracheary elements; conclusions. *Am. J. Bot.*, **50**, 514–22. [167]
— (1966) The morphological effects of protein synthesis inhibition in *Marsilea*. *Am. J. Bot.*, **53**, 158–65. [235]
W.H.O. (1965) (WORLD HEALTH ORGANISATION) Snail control in the prevention of bilharziasis. *Monograph Ser. Wld Hlth Org.*, **50**, 255 p. [455, 488]
WILD, H. (1961) Harmful aquatic plants in Africa and Madagascar. *Kirkia*, **2**, 1–66. Repr. as: *C.C.T.A./C.S.A. Publs*, **73**, 68 p.
[180, 197, 343, 366, 368, 375, 380, 383, 389, 397, 400, 411, 425, 453–55, 457–61, 465, 473, 477–78, 484, 486–88, 500–01, 516, 523]
WILDE, W. J. J. O. DE (1961) The morphological evaluation and taxonomic value of the spathe in *Najas*, with descriptions of three new Asiatic-Malaysian taxa. *Acta bot. neerl.*, **10**, 164–70. [19, 299–300]
— (1962) Najadaceae. *Flora Malesiana*, ser. 1, **6**, 157–71. [2, 19, 300, 372]
— (1964) Najadaceae. *Flora Neerlandica*, **1** (6), 93–96. [19]
WILKINSON, J. G. (1883) *The manners and customs of the ancient Egyptians*. ed. Birch, S. Boston. [506]
WILKINSON, R. E. (1964) Subaqueous release of herbicides from granules. *Weeds*, **12**, 69–76. [484]
WILLIAMS, R. H. (1956) *Salvinia auriculata* Aublet: the chemical eradication of a serious aquatic weed in Ceylon. *Trop. Agric.*, *Trin.*, **33**, 145–57.
[196, 433, 455, 460, 475, 478, 483, 487, 491, 493]
WILLIAMS, W. T. & BARBER, D. A. (1961) The functional significance of aerenchyma in plants. *Symp. Soc. exp. Biol.*, **15**, 132–44. [160, 163–64]
WILLIS, J. C. (1902) Studies in the morphology and ecology of the Podostemaceae of Ceylon and India. *Ann. R. bot. Gdns Peradeniya*, **1**, 267–465. [18, 111–12, 131, 284, 290, 329–30, 339, 377]
— (1914) On the lack of adaptation in the Tristichaceae and Podostemaceae. *Proc. R. Soc.*, ser. B, **87**, 532–50. [18, 109, 112, 131, 284–85, 329, 330, 377]
— (1915) The origin of the Tristichaceae and Podostemaceae. *Ann. Bot.*, **29**, 299–306. [18, 112, 284–85]
— (1917) The relative age of endemic species and other controversial points. *Ann. Bot.*, **31**, 189–208. [377]

WILLIS, J. C. (1922) *Age and area.* University Press, Cambridge.   [377]
— (1926) The evolution of the Tristichaceae and Podostemonaceae. *Ann. Bot.,* **40,** 349–67.   [18, 285, 329]
WILMOTT, A. J. (1921) Experimental researches on vegetable assimilation and respiration. XIV. Assimilation by submerged plants in dilute solutions of bicarbonates and of acids: an improved bubble-counting technique. *Proc. R. Soc.,* ser. B, **92,** 304–26.
                                                                              [115]
WILSON, K. (1947) Water movement in submerged aquatic plants, with special reference to cut shoots of *Ranunculus fluitans. Ann. Bot.,* **11,** 91–122.
                                                                     [93, 137, 145–48]
— (1957) Extension growth in primary cell walls with special reference to *Elodea canadensis. Ann. Bot.,* **21,** 1–11.   [137]
WILSON, L. R. (1935) Lake development and plant succession in Vilas County, Wisconsin. I. The medium hard water lakes. *Ecol. Monogr.,* **5,** 207–47.   [13, 30, 435]
— (1937) A quantitative and ecological study of the larger aquatic plants of Sweeney Lake, Oneida County, Wisconsin. *Bull. Torrey bot. Club,* **64,** 199–208.
                                                                      [13, 30, 175, 435]
— (1939) Rooted aquatic plants and their relation to the limnology of freshwater lakes. In: *Problems of lake biology. Publs Am. Ass. Advmt Sci.,* **10,** 107–22.
                                                                     [13, 35, 175, 434]
— (1941) The larger aquatic vegetation of Trout Lake, Vilas County, Wisconsin. *Trans. Wis. Acad. Sci. Arts Lett.,* **33,** 135–46.   [13, 30, 175, 416–17, 434–35]
WINBERG, G. G. & SIVKO, T. N. (1962) The significance of photosynthetic aeration in the oxygen balance of polluted waters. *Int. J. Air Wat. Pollut.,* **6,** 267–75.   [47]
WINTER, H. (1961) The uptake of cations by *Vallisneria* leaves. *Acta bot. neerl.,* **10,** 341–93.
                                                                         [133, 136]
WINTERRINGER, G. S. (1966) Aquatic vascular plants new for Illinois. *Rhodora,* **68,** 221–22.
                                                                              [397]
WIT, H. C. D. DE. (1958a, 1964) Aquariumplanten, I & II. *Belmontia,* ser. 3, **2,** 125 p. & 193 p. Repr. as *Het Handboek voor de Aquariumliefhebber,* **5** and **6.** Hollandia, N.V., Baarn, Netherlands. Transln as *Aquarium plants,* by Schuurman, J. A. & Higgins, V. (1964) Blandford Press, London.   [19, 102, 222, 285, 336, 372, 380, 383, 513, 523]
— (1958b) *Aponogeton stachyosporus,* sp. nov.; *Cryptocoryne wendtii,* sp. nov. *Meded. bot. Tuinen Belmonte Arbor. LandbHoogesch., Wageningen,* **2,** 91–101.
                                                              [15, 19, 102, 222, 335–36, 372, 380, 514]
— (1962) *Cryptocoryne lucens,* sp. nov.; *Cryptocoryne scurrilis,* sp. nov. *Meded. bot. Tuinen Belmonte Arbor. LandbHoogesch., Wageningen,* **6,** 92–98.   [285–86, 514]
WITHYCOMBE, C. L. (1923) On the function of the bladders in *Utricularia vulgaris. J. Linn. Soc. (Bot.),* **46,** 401–13.   [210]
WITMER, S. W. (1937) Morphology and cytology of *Vallisneria spiralis* L. *Am. Midl. Nat.,* **18,** 309–33.   [306, 323]
— (1964) *Butomus umbellatus* L. in Indiana. *Castanea,* **29,** 117–18.   [397, 401]
WODEHOUSE, R. P. (1935) *Pollen grains: their structure, identification, and significance in science and medicine.* McGraw-Hill, New York.   [278, 292]
— (1936) Pollen grains in the identification and classification of plants. VIII. The Alismataceae. *Am. J. Bot.,* **23,** 535–39.   [278]
WOHLSCHLAG, D. E. (1950) Vegetation and invertebrate life in a marl lake. *Invest. Indiana Lakes Streams,* **3,** 321–72.   [14]
WOLTERECK, I. (1928) Experimentelle Untersuchungen über die Blattbildung amphibischer Pflanzen. *Flora, Jena,* **123,** 30–61.   [243]
WOOD, C. E. (1959) The genera of the Nymphaeaceae and Ceratophyllaceae in the southeastern United States. *J. Arnold Arbor.,* **40,** 94–112.
                                              [17, 223, 269, 275, 341, 343, 372, 383, 397, 404]
WULFF, H. D. (1954) Zur Zytologie, geographischen Verbreitung und Morphologie des Kalmus. *Arch. Pharm., Berl.,* **287,** 529–41.   [319]
WUNDERLICH, W. E. (1964) Water hyacinth control in Louisiana. *Hyacinth Contr. J.,* **3,** 4–7.   [490]
WYLIE, R. B. (1904) The morphology of *Elodea canadensis. Bot. Gaz.,* **37,** 1–22.   [309]
— (1912) A long-stalked *Elodea* flower. *Bull. Labs nat. Hist. St. Univ. Iowa,* **6,** 43–52.
                                                                              [309]
— (1917a) The pollination of *Vallisneria spiralis. Bot. Gaz.,* **63,** 135–45.   [306-07]

WYLIE, R. B. (1917b) Cleistogamy in *Heteranthera dubia*. *Bull. Labs nat. Hist. St. Univ. Iowa*, **7**, 48–58. [290]
— (1920) The major vegetation of Lake Okoboji. *Proc. Iowa Acad. Sci.*, **27**, 91–97. [13]
— (1941) Some aspects of fertilisation in *Vallisneria*. *Am. J. Bot.*, **28**, 169–74. [307]

YAMAGUTI, H. (1955) Bottom deposits and higher aquatic plants of Lake Yogo, north of Lake Biwa. *Jap. J. Limnol.*, **17**, 81–90. [13, 438, 442]
YAPP, R. H. (1912) *Spiraea ulmaria*, L., and its bearing on the problem of xeromorphy in marsh plants. *Ann. Bot.*, **26**, 815–70. [70]
YASUI, K. (1911) On the life-history of *Salvinia natans*. *Ann. Bot.*, **25**, 469–83. [263, 265]
YOCOM, C. F. (1951) *Waterfowl and their food plants in Washington*. University of Washington Press, Seattle, Washington. [453]
YONGE, C. M. (1949) *The sea shore*. Collins, London. [26]
YOSHIMURA, F. (1941) On the minimum concentration of manganese necessary for the growth of Lemnaceae plants. *Bot. Mag., Tokyo*, **55**, 163–75. [206]
— (1943a) The necessity of vitamin B1 for the growth of Lemnaceae plants. *Bot. Mag., Tokyo*, **57**, 156–71. [206]
— (1943b) The significance of molybdenum for the growth of Lemnaceae plants. *Bot. Mag., Tokyo*, **57**, 371–86. [253]
— (1952) Influence of light on the consumption of nitrate and ammonia in lemnaceous plants. *Bot. Mag., Tokyo*, **65**, 176–85. [205]
YOUNT, J. L. (1963) South Atlantic states. In: *Limnology in North America*, ed. Frey, D.G., 269–86. University of Wisconsin Press, Madison, Wisconsin. [451]

ZAKHARENKOV, I. S. (1962) Effect of macrophytes on the bicarbonate system of natural waters. (In Russian) *Vopr. rybn. khozyaist. Belorusii*, 1962, 227–30. [452]
ZAKI, S. (1960) Density distribution of rooted hydrophytes in Nozha Hydrome. *Notes Mem. hydrobiol. Dep. U.A.R.*, **48**, 28 p. [13, 438, 442]
ZAWIDSKI, S. (1912) Beiträge zur Entwicklungsgeschichte von *Salvinia natans*. *Beih. bot. Zbl.*, **28**, 17–65. [263]
ZHADIN, V. I. & GERD, S. V. (1963) *Fauna and flora of the rivers, lakes and reservoirs of the U.S.S.R.* Transln by Mercado, A., ed. Finesilver, R. Israel Program for Scientific Translations Jerusalem. [13, 521, 523]
ZIMMERMAN, P. W., HITCHCOCK, A. E., KIRKPATRICK, H. & EARLE, T. T. (1950) Control of water hyacinth. *Agric. Chem.*, **5**, 45–47. Repr. as *Prof. Pap. Boyce Thompson Inst. Pl. Res.*, **2** (9), 75–86. [494, 496]
ZIMMERMANN, B. *et al.* (1956) The effects of DDD on the human adrenal; attempts to use an adrenal-destructive agent in the treatment of disseminated mammary and prostatic cancer. *Cancer, N.Y.*, **9**, 940–48. [500]
ZIMMERMANN, W. (1959) *Die Phylogenie der Pflanzen*. edn 2. Fischer, Stuttgart. [263]
ZURZYCKI, A. (1951) The influence of the wave length of light on the movements of chloroplasts in *Lemna trisulca*. *Acta Soc. Bot. Pol.*, **21**, 17–37. [204]

FURTHER REFERENCES (*added in proof*)

ABRAHAM, V. & SUBRAMANYAM, K. (1965) Studies on seeds of various taxa of *Utricularia* occurring in west Bengal. *Proc. Indian Acad. Sci.*, ser. B, **62**, 97–102.
CHADWICK, M. J. & OBEID, M. (1966) A comparative study of the growth of *Eichhornia crassipes* Solms and *Pistia stratiotes* L. in water-culture. *J. Ecol.*, **54**, 563–75.
CUTTER, E. G. (1966) Patterns of organogenesis in the shoot. In: *Trends in plant morphogenesis*, ed. Cutter, E. G., 220–34. Longmans Green, London.
FAROOQ, M. (1964) Studies in the Lentibulariaceae. I. The embryology of *Utricularia stellaris* Linn.f., var. *inflexa* Clarke. *Proc. natn. Inst. Sci. India*, ser. B, **30**, 263–99.
FUCHS, H. P. (1962) Nomenklatur, Taxonomie und Systematik der Gattung *Isoëtes* Linnaeus in geschichtlicher Entwicklung. *Beih. nova Hedwigia*, **3**, 104 p.
HILD, J. & REHNELT, K. (1966) Hydrobotanische Untersuchungen am Altrhein bei Rees (Niederrhein). *Ber. dt. bot. Ges.*, **79**, 355–72.
MCCLURE, J. W. & ALSTON, R. E. (1966) A chemotaxonomic study of Lemnaceae. *Am. J. Bot.*, **53**, 849–60.
MCNAUGHTON, S. J. (1966) Ecotype function in the *Typha* community-type. *Ecol. Monogr.*, **36**, 297–325.
NAGL, W. (1966) Über einen ungewöhnlichen Standort von *Marsilea quadrifolia* L. und ihre Vergesellschaftung. *Öst. bot. Z.*, **113**, 299–301.

ORNDUFF, R. (1966a) The origin of dioecism from heterostyly in *Nymphoides* (Meny-anthaceae). *Evolution, Lancaster, Pa*, **20**, 309–14.

— (1966b) The breeding system of *Pontederia cordata* L. *Bull. Torrey bot. Club*, **93**, 407–16.

RUDESCU, L., NICULESCU, C. & CHIVU, I. P. (1965) *Monographia Stufului din Delta Dunării*. (In Rumanian) Academiei Republicii Socialiste Romănia, Bucuresti.

STANT, M. Y. (1967) Anatomy of the Butomaceae. *J. Linn. Soc. (Bot.)*, **60**, 31–60.

TULÁĆKOVÁ, E. B. (1963) Zur Systematik der europäischen Phragmitetea. *Preslia*, **35**, 118–22.

INDEXES OF ORGANISMS AND SUBJECTS

Index of Organisms

This is essentially an index of scientific names (excluding forms, which are mostly ecological states and not distinct taxa) but it also includes the few vernacular names which are occasionally mentioned in the text. The entries include references to tables and legends to illustrations in addition to textual references. The symbol ★ denotes a monotype; † denotes a fossil taxon; × denotes a (presumed) hybrid of natural or horticultural origin. Authorities are cited for genera, subgenera, sections, species, subspecies and varieties. The names of many of the publishing authors are abbreviated or contracted. An exhaustive citation of synonymy is beyond both the aim of the index and the space available. However, certain synonyms which are quite widely used in works listed in the bibliography are cited in square brackets immediately after the name of the appropriate taxon.

Index of Subjects

CKKD